THE WORKS

OF

HUBERT HOWE BANCROFT.

THE WORKS

OF

HUBERT HOWE BANCROFT.

THE WORKS

OF

HUBERT HOWE BANCROFT.

VOLUME XXXIII.

HISTORY OF ALASKA.

1730–1885.

SAN FRANCISCO:

A. L. BANCROFT & COMPANY, PUBLISHERS,

1886.

PREFACE.

On the whole, the people of the United States have not paid an exorbitant price for the ground upon which to build a nation. Trinkets and trickery in the first instance, followed by some bluster, a little fighting, and a little money, and we have a very fair patch of earth, with a good title, in which there is plenty of equity, humanity, sacred rights, and star-spangled banner. What we did not steal ourselves we bought from those who did, and bought it cheap.

Therein we did well, have that much more to be proud of, and to confirm us in our own esteem as a great and good nation; therein lies the great merit— the price we paid. Had it been dear, as have been some meagre strips of European soil, over which France, Germany, and the rest have fought for centuries, spending millions upon millions of lives and money, all in the line of insensate folly, and for that which they could not keep and were better off without—then we would cease boasting and hold our peace. But our neighbors have been weak while we are strong; therefore it is not right for us to pay them much for their lands.

Ignoring, as we do, the birthright of aboriginal races, that have no christianity, steel, or gunpowder, we may say that the title to the Mississippi Valley was settled, and the Oregon Territory adjudged to be ours by divine right. Texas came easily; while one month's interest, at the then current rates, on the gold picked up in the Sierra Foothills during the first five years of American occupation would repay the cost of the Mexican war, and all that was given for California and the adjoining territory.

In the case of Alaska we have one instance where bluster would not win; fighting was not to be thought of; and so we could pay for the stationary icebergs or let them alone. Nor with money easy, was Alaska a bad bargain at two cents an acre. It was indeed cheaper than stealing, now that the savages receive the teachings and diseases of civilization in reservations.

In 1867 there were few who held this opinion, and not one in a hundred, even of those who were best informed, believed the territory to be worth the purchase money. If better known to-day, its resources are no better appreciated; and there are many who still deny that, apart from fish and fur-bearing animals, the country has any resources.

The area of Alaska is greater than that of the thirteen original states of the Union, its extreme length being more than two thousand miles, and its extreme breadth about fourteen hundred; while its coast-line, including bays and islands, is greater than the circumference of the earth. The island of Unalaska is almost as far west of San Francisco as San Francisco is west of the capital of the United States; while the distance from the former city to Fort St Michael, the most northerly point in America inhabited by the white man, is greater than to the city of Panamá.

With the limits of the continent at its extreme
north-west, the limit of the history of western North
America is reached. But it may be asked, what a
land is this of which to write a history? Bleak,
swampy, fog-begirt, and almost untenanted except by
savages—can a country without a people furnish material for a history? Intercourse with the aborigines
does not constitute all of history, and few except savages have ever made their abiding-place in the wintry
solitudes of Alaska; few vessels save bidarkas have
ever threaded her myriad isles; few scientists have
studied her geology, or catalogued her fauna and flora;
few surveyers have measured her snow-turbaned hills;
few miners have dug for coal and iron, or prospected
her mountains and streams for precious metals. Except on the islands, and at some of the more accessible
points on the mainland, the natives are still unsubdued.
Of settlements, there are scarce a dozen worthy the
name; of the interior, little is known; and of any correct map, at least four fifths must remain, to-day,
absolutely blank, without names or lines except those
of latitude and longitude. We may sail along the
border, or be drawn by sledge-dogs over the frozen
streams, until we arrive at the coldest, farthest west,
separated from the rudest, farthest east by a narrow
span of ocean, bridged in winter by thick-ribbed ice.
What then can be said of this region—this Ultima
Thule of the known world, whose northern point is
but three or four degrees south of the highest latitude yet reached by man?

Such is the general sentiment of Americans concerning a territory which not many years ago was
purchased from Russia, as before mentioned, at the

rate of about two cents an acre, and was considered dear at the price.

To answer these questions is the purpose of the present volume. This America of the Russians has its little century or two of history, as herein we see, and which will ever remain its only possible inchoation, interesting to the story of future life and progress on its borders, as to every nation its infancy should be.

Though it must be admitted that the greater portion of Alaska is practically worthless and uninhabitable, yet my labor has been in vain if I have not made it appear that Alaska lacks not resources but development. Scandinavia, her old-world counterpart, is possessed of far less natural wealth, and is far less grand in natural configuration. In Alaska we can count more than eleven hundred islands in a single group. We can trace the second longest watercourse in the world. We have large sections of territory where the average yearly temperature is higher than that of Stockholm or Christiania, where it is milder in winter, and where the fall of rain and snow is less than in the southern portion of Scandinavia.

It has often been stated that Alaska is incapable of supporting a white population. The truth is, that her resources, though some of them are not yet available, are abundant, and of such a nature that, if properly economized, they will never be seriously impaired. The most habitable portions of Alaska, lying as they do mainly between 55° and 60° N., are in about the same latitude as Scotland and southern Scandinavia. The area of this portion of the territory is greater than that of Scotland and southern Scandinavia combined; and yet it contains to-day but a few hundred, and has never contained more than a thousand white inhabitants; while the population of Scotland is about three millions and a half, and that of Norway and Sweden exceeds six millions.

The day is not very far distant when the coal measures and iron deposits of Scotland, and the mines and timber of Scandinavia, will be exhausted; and it is not improbable that even when that day comes the resources of Alaska will be but partially opened. The little development that has been made of late years has been accomplished entirely by the enterprise and capital of Americans, aided by a few hundred hired natives. Already with a white population of five hundred, of whom more than four fifths are non-producers, the exports of the territory exceed $3,000,000 a year, or an average of $6,000 per capita. Where else in the world do we find such results?

It may be stated in answer that the bulk of these exports comes from the fur-seal grounds of the Prybilof Islands, which are virtually a stock-farm leased by the government to a commercial company; but the present value of this industry is due mainly to the careful fostering and judicious management of that company; and there are other industries which, if properly directed, promise in time to prove equally profitable. Apart from the seal-islands, and apart from the trade in land-furs that is diverted by the Hudson's Bay Company, the production of wealth for each white person in the territory is greater than in any portion of the United States or of the world. This wealth is derived almost entirely from the land and pelagic peltry, and from the fisheries of Alaska; for at present her mines are little developed, and her forests almost intact. And yet we are told that the country is without resources!

It may be supposed that for the history of such a country as Alaska, whatever existing information there might be would be quite accessible and easily, obtained.

I have not found it specially so. Here, as elsewhere in my historic fields, there were three classes of material which might be obtained: first, public and private archives; second, printed books and documents; and third, personal experiences and knowledge taken from the mouths of living witnesses.

Of the class last named there are fewer authorities here than in any other part of my territory north of latitude 32°, though proportionately more than south of that line; and this notwithstanding three distinct journeys to that region by my agent—a man thoroughly conversant with Alaskan affairs, and a Russian by birth—for the purpose of gathering original and verbal information. All places of historical importance were visited by him, and all persons of historical note still living there were seen and questioned. Much fresh information was thus obtained; but the result was not as satisfactory as has been the case in some other quarters.

The chief authorities in print for the earlier epochs are in the Russian language, and published for the most part in Russia; covering the later periods, books have been published—at various times in Europe and America, as will be seen by my list of authorities— and have been gathered in the usual way.

The national archives, the most important of all

sources, are divided, part being in Russia and part in America, though mostly in the Russian language. Some four or five years were occupied by my assistants and stenographers in making abstracts of material in Sitka, San Francisco, and Washington. For valuable coöperation in gaining from the archives of St Petersburg such material as I required, I am specially indebted to my esteemed friend M. Pinart, and to the leading men of letters and certain officials in the Russian capital, from whom I have received every courtesy.

CONTENTS OF THIS VOLUME.

(xiii)

CHAPTER IV.

DISCOVERY OF ALASKA.

1740–1741.

CHAPTER V.

DEATH OF BERING.

1741–1742.

CHAPTER VI.

THE SWARMING OF THE PROMYSHLENIKI.

1743–1762.

CHAPTER VII.

FURTHER ADVENTURES OF THE PROMYSHLENIKI.

1760–1767.

CHAPTER VIII.

IMPERIAL EFFORTS AND FAILURES.

1764–1779.

CHAPTER IX.

EXPLORATION AND TRADE.

1770–1787.

CHAPTER XIII.
THE BILLINGS SCIENTIFIC EXPEDITION.
1785-1793.

CHAPTER XIV.
ORGANIZATION OF MONOPOLY.
1787-1795.

CHAPTER XV.
STRIFE BETWEEN RIVAL COMPANIES.
1791-1794.

CHAPTER XVI.
COLONIZATION AND MISSIONS.
1794-1796.

CHAPTER XXI.

REZANOF'S VISIT.

1804–1806.

CHAPTER XXII.

SEVEN MORE YEARS OF ALASKAN ANNALS.

1806–1812.

CHAPTER XXIII.

FOREIGN VENTURES AND THE ROSS COLONY.

1803–1841.

CHAPTER XXIV.

FURTHER ATTEMPTS AT FOREIGN COLONIZATION.
1808–1818.

CHAPTER XXV.

CLOSE OF BARANOF'S ADMINISTRATION.
1819–1821.

CHAPTER XXVI.

SECOND PERIOD OF THE RUSSIAN AMERICAN COMPANY'S OPERATIONS.
1821–1842.

CHAPTER XXVII.

THE RUSSIAN AMERICAN COMPANY'S LAST TERM.
1842–1866.

AUTHORITIES QUOTED

IN

THE HISTORY OF ALASKA.

Acta Petropolitana, 1750 et seq. In Library of Congress.
Akademie der Wissenschaften Sitzungsberichte und Abhandlungen. Berlin,
    1859 et seq.
Alaska, Archives from Unalaska and St Paul. MS.
Alaska, Army Sketches by an Officer of the U. S. Navy. In Army and
    Navy Journal, 1868–9.
Alaska, History of the Wrongs of. San Francisco, 1875.
Alaska, Report of the Icelandic Committee. Washington, 1875.
Alaska, Traders' Protective Association. San Francisco, 1869.
Alaska Commercial Company, Alaska Fur-Seal. n.pl., n.d.; By-laws. S. F.,
    1870; Extraordinary Developments in regard to the Monopoly. n.pl., n.d.
Alaska Commercial Company, Taylor vs A. C. Co. [12th Dist. Court, 1871].
    MS.
Alaska Fur-Seal Fisheries, Letter of the Secretary of the Treasury [41st
    Cong., 2d Sess., H. Ex. Doc., 129]. Washington, 1870.
Alaska Scrap Book, 1868–76, by Agapius Honcharenko. 2 vols.
Alaska Ship Building Company, Petition praying for grant of certain lands.
    [43d Cong., 2d Sess., Sen. Mis., 13.] Washington, 1875.
Albany (Or.) Register.
Alegre (Francisco Javier), Historia de la Compañia de Jesus en Nueva España.
    Mexico, 1841. 3 vols.
Alturas (Cal.), Modoc Independent.
Alvarado (Juan Bautista), Historia de California. MS. 5 vols.
American Geographical and Statistical Society. New York, 1850 et seq.
American Quarterly Review. Philadelphia, 1827 et seq.
American State Papers. Boston, 1817–19. 12 vols.; Washington, 1832–4;
    1858–61. folio. 39 vols.
Anaheim (Cal.), Gazette.
Anderson (Adam), Historical and Chronological Deduction of the Origin of
    Commerce. London, 1801. folio. 4 vols.
Anderson (Alexander C.), Northwest Coast History. MS.
Anderson (Alexander C.), Notes on Indian Tribes of British North America.
    In Historical Mag., vii. 73.
Annals of Congress. [1st to 18th Congress.] Washington, 1834–56. 42 vols.
Antioch (Cal.), Ledger.
Apostólicos Afanes de la Compañia de Jesus. Barcelona, 1754.
Arab, Log-book. 1821–5. MS.
Archivo del Arzobispado de San Francisco. MS. 5 vols.

Archivo de California. MS. 273 vols., and a great mass of loose papers.
 Documents preserved in the U. S. Surveyor-general's office at San Fran-
 cisco. Copies in my Collection. Divided as follows: Prov. St. Pap.;
 Prov. Rec.; Dept. St. Pap.; Dept. Rec.
Archivo de las Misiones. MS. 2 vols.
Archivo del Obispado de Monterey y Los Angeles. MS.
Archivo de Santa Bárbara. MS. 11 vols.
Armstrong (Alexander), Personal Narrative of the Discovery of the North-
 west Passage. London, 1857.
Arteaga (Ignacio), Tercera Exploracion, 1779. MS.
Astoria (Or.), Astorian.
Atahualpa. Journal of the Ship. MS. In Library of Department of State.
 Washington, D. C.
Atlantic Monthly. Boston, 1858 et seq.
Azanza (Virey), Ynstruccion, 1800. MS.

Baer (Karl Fr. von), See Wrangell (Contre Admiral V.), Statistische, etc.
Baird (Spencer F.), Fish and Fisheries [41st Cong., 2d Sess., Sen. Mis. Doc.,
 108; 45th Cong., 2d Sess , Sen. Mis. Doc., 49]. Washington, 1870, 1877.
Balbi (Adrien), Introduction à l'Atlas ethnographique du globe. Paris, 1826.
Bancroft (Hubert Howe), History of the Pacific States of North America.
 San Francisco, 1882 et seq. 28 vols.; Native Races of the Pacific States.
 New York, 1875. 5 vols.
Bancroft Library, MS. Scrap-books, containing classified notes used in writ-
 ing Bancroft's works.
Baranova (Alek. A.), Shizneopisanie. [Biography.] St Petersburg, 1835.
Barber (John), and Henry Howe. History of Western States and Terri-
 tories. Cincinnati, 1867.
Barrington (Daines), Miscellanies. London, 1781.
Barrow (J.), Cook's Voyages of Discovery. London, 1871.
Bashmakof (Feodor), Papers relating to Trial for Sorcery, 1829. MS.   ·
Bayly (William), The Original Astronomical Observations made by Capt.
 Cook and Lieut. Jas. King, 1770-80. London, 1782. 4to.
Beaman (C. C.), Our New Northwest. In Harper's Monthly. July, 1867.
Beardslee (L. A.), Report on condition of affairs in Alaska [46th Cong., 2d
 Sess., Sen. Ex. Doc., 105]. Washington, 1880.
Beechey (F. W.), Narrative of a Voyage to the Pacific, etc., in 1825-8.
 London, 1831, 2 vols.; Philadelphia, 1832.
Beechey (F. W.), Zoölogy of Voyage. See Richardson (J.) et al.
Belcher (Edward), Narrative of a Voyage round the World in 1836-42. Lon-
 don, 1843. 2 vols.
Bell (James), A System of Geography. Glasgow, 1836. 6 vols.
Bell (W. C.), The Quiddities of an Alaskan Trip. Portland, Or., 1873.
Belmont (Nev.), Courier.
Benton (Thomas H.), Abridgment of Debates in Congress, 1789-1856. New
 York, 1857-63. 16 vols.
Benyovski (Maurice A.), Memoirs and Travels. London, 1790.
Berens (Evgeni A.), Puteshestvie korabla R. A. Kompaniy Nikolaï. [Voyage
 of the Russian American Company's ship Nikolaï, 1837-9.] In Zapiski
 Hydr. viii.
Berg (Vassili), Khronologicheskaïa Istoria. [Chronological History of the
 Discovery of the Aleutian Islands.] St Petersburg, 1820.
Berry (M. P.), Developments in Alaska. MS.
Bidwell (John), California, 1841-8. MS.
Bigland (John), A Geographical and Historical View of the World. London,
 1810. 5 vols.
Blachke (L.), Topographia medica portus Novo-Archangelscensis. Petropoli,
 1842-8.
Blagdon (Francis William), The Modern Geographer. London, n.d. 5 vols.

Blake (Theodore A.), General Topographical and Geological Features of North-western Coast of America [40th Cong., 2d Sess., H. Ex. Doc., 177.] Washington, 1868.

Blake (William P.), Geographical Notes upon Russian America. Washington, 1868.

Blodgett (Loring), Alaska, what is it worth? In Lippincott's Mag. i. 1868.

Bloodgood (C. D.), Eight Months in Sitka. In Overland Monthly, Feb. 1869.

Bodega y Cuadra (Juan Francisco), Comento de la Navegacion, 1775. MS.

Bodega y Cuadra (Juan Francisco), Navegacion y Descubrimiento, 1779. MS.

Bodega y Cuadra (Juan Francisco), Segunda Salida, 1779. MS.

Bodega y Cuadra (Juan Francisco), Viage de 1775. MS.

Boone (J. H. A.), Russian America. In Atlantic Monthly, June, 1867.

Boston (Mass.), Daily Advertiser, Evening Transcript, Herald.

Boston in the Northwest, Solid Men of. MS.

Brockett (L. P.), Our Western Empire. Philadelphia, etc., 1881.

Brooks (Charles Wolcott), Japanese Wrecks in North Pacific Ocean. San Francisco, 1876.

Broughton (William R.), A Voyage of Discovery at the North Pacific Ocean. London, 1804.

Browne (J. Ross), Lower California. See Taylor, Alex. S.; Report upon the Mineral Resources of the States and Territories West of the Rocky Mountains. Washington, 1867; Washington, 1868; San Francisco, 1868.

Bryant (Charles), and H. H. McIntyre, Report on Alaska. [41st Cong., 2d Sess., Sen. Ex. Doc. 32.] Washington, 1869.

Burke (Edmund), An Account of the European Settlements in America. London, 1760. 2 vols.; Id., 1770. 2 vols.

Burney (James), Chronological History of North Eastern Voyages of Dis-covery. London, 1819.

Buschmann (Joh. Carl), Die Pima-Sprache und die Sprache der Koloschen, etc. [Berlin, 1856.] 4to.

Busse, Jurnal Für Russland. St Petersburg, 1794.

Bustamante (Cárlos María), Suplemento á Los Tres Siglos de Cavo. Jalapa, 1870.

Butler (William F.), The Wild North Land. Philadelphia, 1874.

California, Establecimiento y Progresos de las Misiones de la Antigua Cali-fornia. In Doc. Hist. Mex., serie iv. tom. iv.

California, Journals of Assembly and Senate, 1st to 24th sessions, 1850-81; with Appendices—103 volumes in all.

Calvo (Charles), Recueil Complet des Traités de l'Amérique Latine. Paris, 1862-9. 16 vols.

Camp (David W.), American Year Book. Hartford, 1869.

Campbell (Archibald), A Voyage round the World from 1806-12. Edinburgh, 1816; Roxbury, 1825.

Campbell (Joseph B.), Letter concerning importation of breech-loading rifles. [44th Cong., 1st Sess., H. Ex. Doc. 83.] Washington, 1876.

Cancelada (Juan Lopez), Ruina de la Nueva España. Cadiz, 1811; Telégrafo Mexicano. Cadiz, 1813 et seq.

Carr (John A.), Communications to Sec. of War in relation to illicit traffic in liquor. [43d Cong., 2d Sess. Sen Docs. 24, 27.] Washington, 1875.

Carson City (Nev.), State Register.

Cartas Edificantes, y Curiosas. Madrid, 1753-7. 16 vols.

Cartography of the Pacific States. San Francisco, 1873. MS. 3 vols.

Castañares (Manuel), Coleccion de documentos relativos al departamento de Californias. Mexico, 1845.

Castro (Manuel), Documentos para la Historia de California. MS. 2 vols.

Castroville (Cal.), Argus.

Catalá (Magin), Carta sobre Nootka, 1794. MS.

Chamisso (Louis Charles A. von), Adelbert von Chamisso's Werke. Vierte Auflage. Berlin, 1856. 6 vols.; Reise included in preceding.
Chappe d'Auteroche, Voyage en Sibérie. Paris, 1768. 3 vols.; Amsterdam, 1770. 2 vols.
Chateaubriand (F. A.), Voyages en Amérique. Paris, 1865.
Chicago (Ill.), Inter-Ocean, Tribune.
Chirikof (Alexeï), Zhurnal Puteshestvia. [Journal of Voyages.] In Imperial Naval Archives. St. Petersburg. Bundle xvi.
Chistiakof (Peter Y.), Puteshestvie korabla R. A. Kompaniy Elena. [Voyage of the Russian American Company's ship Elena 1824–6.] In Zapiski Hydr. viii.
Choris (Louis), Voyage Pittoresque autour du Monde. Paris, 1822. folio.
Clavigero (Francisco Saverio), Storia della California. Venezia, 1789. 2 vols.
Cleveland (Richard J.), Narrative of Voyages. Cambridge, 1842. 2 vols.; Boston, 1850.
Coffin (James Henry), Winds of the Globe. Washington, 1875.
Coleccion de Documentos Inéditos para la Historia de España. Madrid, 1842–80. 71 vols. [S. F. Law Library.]
Collinson (R.), Account of the Proceedings of H. M. S. Enterprise from Behring Strait to Cambridge Bay. In Lond. Geog. Soc., Jour. xxv. 194.
Columbia, Department of, General Orders. 1865 et seq.
Colyer (Vincent), Bombardment of Wrangell. Wash., 1870; Fur-seal Fisheries of Alaska [41st Cong. 2d Sess., H. Ex. Doc. 144.] Wash., 1870; Report on Indian Affairs. n.pl., n.d.
Conant (Charles T.), Letter concerning the killing of fur-bearing animals. In S. F. Bulletin, March 12, 1877.
Congressional Globe. Washington, 1836 et seq. 4to.
Congressional Record. Washington, 1874 et seq.
Cook (James), Troisième Voyage à l'Ocean Pacifique 1776–80. Paris, 1785. 4to. 4 vols.
Cook (James), Voyage to the Pacific Ocean 1776–80. London, 1784. 4to. 3 vols. plates in folio; London, 1784, 4to. 4 vols.; Philadelphia, 1818, 2 vols.
Cooley (W. D.), Maritime and inland discovery. London, 1830–1. 3 vols.
Coues (Elliott), The Fur-bearing Animals of North America. Boston, 1877; also in U. S. Geol. Surv. of the Territories. Hayden, Mis. Pub. viii.
Coxe (William), Account of the Russian Discoveries between Asia and America. London, 1787.
Crespí (Juan), Diario de la Expedicion de Mar., 1774. In Palou, Not., i. 624.
Cronise (Titus Fey), Natural Wealth of California. San Francisco, 1868; Id. with illustrations and corrections.

Dall (William Healey), Alaska and its resources. Boston, 1870; Is Alaska a paying investment. In Harper's Monthly, Jan., 1872; Letter concerning General Thomas' Alaska report. In Boston Daily Advertiser; Letter to Elliott and Maynard on condition of affairs in Alaska. Wash., 1875; On the relative value of Alaska to the United States. In Wash. Philosop. Soc. Bull., May 1871; Report upon the agricultural resources of Alaska. Wash., 1869; Report on Mt. St. Elias. In U. S. Coast Survey Rpt, 1875.
Dallas (A. G.), San Juan, Alaska and the north-west boundary. London, 1873.
Dalles (Or.), Mountaineer.
Daly (Charles P.), Annual Address Jan. 25, 1870. In American Geog. and Stat. Jour., vol. ii., pt. ii. lxxxiii.
Davidof (Gavrila I.), Dvukratnoie Puteshestvie. [Two Voyages to America.] St Petersburg, 1810. 2 vols.
Davidson (George), Coast Pilot of Alaska. Wash., 1869; Directory for Pacific Coast. Wash., 1868; Scientific Expedition to Alaska. In Lippincott's Mag., 1868, Nov. 467.

Davis (Horace), Record of Japanese vessels driven upon Northwest Coast. Worcester, 1872.

Davis (William H.), Glimpses of the Past in California. MS. 2 vols.

Dawson (George M,), Note on some of the most Recent Changes in level of the Coast. Montreal, 1877.

Dease (Peter Warren), and Thomas Simpson, Account of Recent Arctic Discoveries. In Lond. Geog. Soc., Jour. viii. 213.

Delafield (John Jr.), An Inquiry into the origin of the Antiquities of America. Cincinnati, 1839.

Departmental Records. MS. 14 vols. In Archivo de Cal.

Departmental State Papers. MS. 20 vols. In Archivo de Cal.; Id. Benicia Custom-House. 8 vols.; Id., Benicia Military. vols. 53 to 87.

De Poletica (Pierre de), Correspondence with Sec. of State, Ap. 2, 1822. In Annals of Cong. 1822, ii. 2142.

De Smet (P. J.), Missions de l'Oregon. Gand. n.d.; Oregon Missions. New York, 1847; Voyages aux Montagnes Rocheuses. Lille, 1859.

Directories, Pacific Coast Business, Langley 1871-3; Puget Sound. Murphy and Harnet.

Disturnell (J.), Influence of Climate in North and South America. New York, 1867.

Dixon (George), Remarks on the Voyages of John Meares, Esq. London, 1790; Voyage autour du Monde 1785-8. Paris, 1789. 2 vols.; Voyage round the World 1785-8. London, 1789. 4to.

Dobbs (Arthur), Account of the Countries adjoining to Hudson's Bay. London, 1744.

Dodge (Wm. Sumner), Oration at Sitka July 4, 1868. San Francisco, 1868.

Dokhturof (Pavel A.), Puteshestvie Kronshtadta do Amerikanskikh Koloniakh. [Voyage from Kronstadt to the Colonies 1820-2.] In Zapiski Hydr. viii.

Doklad Komiteta ob Ustroistvo Russkikh Amerikanskikh Koloniy. [Report of Committee on Reorganization of Russian-American Colonies.] St Petersburg, 1863-4. 2 vols.

Douglas (Sir James), Journal 1840-1. MS.

Douglas (Sir James), Private Papers, 1st and 2d series. MS. 2 vols.

Douglas (Sir James), Voyage to the Northwest Coast. In Id. Journal MS.

Douglass (William), Summary, Historical and Political, etc. of the British Settlements in North-America. Boston, 1755. 2 vols.

Downieville (Cal.), Mountain Messenger.

Du Hailly (Édouard), L'Expédition de Petropavlosk. In Revue des deux Mondes, 1858.

Duhaut-Cilly (A.), Viaggio intorno al Globo. Torino, 1841. 2 vols.

Dunn (John), The Oregon Territory and the British N. American fur-trade. Philadelphia, 1845.

Edinburgh Review. Edinburgh, 1802, et seq.

Elisa (Francisco), Salida de los tres buques para Nootka año de 1790. MS.

Elisa (Francisco), Tabla diaria de los buques para el puerto de Nootka, 1790. MS.

Elisa (Francisco), Voyage 1791, Extracts from. In Papers relating to Treaty of Wash. v., 176; also in Reply of the United States, 97.

Elliot (George H.), The Presidio of San Francisco. In Overland, iv. 336.

Elliott (Henry Wood), The History and Present Condition of the Fishery Industries. Wash., 1881; Report upon condition of affairs in Alaska. [44th Cong., 1st Sess., H. Ex. Doc. 33.] Wash., 1875; Ten Years acquaintance with Alaska. In Harper's Monthly, 1877.

Ellis (W.), Authentic Narrative of a Voyage in search of a North-west Passage in 1776-80. London, 1784. 2 vols.

Engel (Samuel), Geographische und kritische Nachrichten und Anmerkungen über die Lage der nördlichen Gegenden von Asien und Amerika. Mitau, 1772.

Erman (A.), Archiv für wissenchaftliche Kunde von Russland. Berlin, 1848.
Etholin, Extracts from letters to the Board of Managers of the Russian American Company, concerning Ross Colony. 1841. MS.
Eureka (Cal.) Northern Independent, West Coast Signal.
Evans (Elwood), History of Oregon. MS.
Extracts from Accounts of Russian American Company concerning Ross Settlement in 1847 and 1850. MS.

Falconer (Thomas), On the Discovery of the Mississippi. London, 1844; The Oregon Question. London, 1845.
Farnham (J. T. or Thos. J.), Life, Adventures and Travels in Cal. Pictorial ed. New York, 1857.
Fédix (P. A.), L'Orégon et les côtes de l'Océan Pacifique. Paris, 1846.
Fernandez (José), Cosas de California. MS.
Fernandez (José), Documentos para la Historia de California. MS.
Fidalgo (Salvador), Tabla de Descubrimientos de 1790. MS.
Fidalgo (Salvador), Viage de 1790. MS.
Filatof (Nikander I.), Puteshestvie na korabli Aiaks na Severo-zapadnom beregu Amerike. [Voyage of the Aiaks toward the north-west coast of America. 1821.] In Zapiski Hydr., viii.
Findlay (Alexander G.), Directory for the Navigation of the Pacific Ocean. London, 1851. 2 vols.
Finlayson (Roderick), Vancouver Island and the Northwest Coast. MS.
Fischer (J. Eberhard), Sibirische Geschichte. St Petersburg, 1768. 2 vols.
Flint (Timothy), History and Geography of the Mississippi Valley. Cincinnati, 1832. 2 vols.
Forbes (Alexander), California, A History of. London, 1839.
Forster (John Reinhold), History of Voyages and Discoveries made in the North. London, 1786. 4to.
Franchere (Gabriel), Narrative of a Voyage to the Northwest Coast of America, 1811–14. Redfield. 1854.
Freimann (G.), Letters. In Zapiski Russk. Geogr. Obshestvo, i.

Galaxy (The). New York, 1866 et seq.
Gmelin (Johann), Flora Siberica sive historia plantarum. St Petersburg, 1751–2. 4 vols. Voyage en Sibérie. Paris, 1767. 2 vols.
Goddard (Frederick B.), Where to Emigrate, and Why. New York, 1869.
Gold Hill (Nev.), News.
Goldschmidt (Albert), See Cartography of the Pacific Coast.
Goldstone (Louis), Memorial relative to Alaska seal fishery. [42d Cong. 1st Sess., H. Mis. Doc. 5.] Washington, 1873.
Golovnin (V. M.), Puteshestvie na shloope Kamchatka, 1815–19; [Voyage of the Kamchatka.] In Materialui, pt iv.; Review of Russian Colonies; In Russ. Am. Col., iii. 2; Zapiski. [Letters on condition of Russian American Colonies.] In Materialui, pt. i.
Gordon (James Bentley), Historical and Geographical Memoir of the N. American Continent. Dublin, 1820. 4to.
Grass Valley (Cal.), Foot Hill Tidings, National, Union.
Greenhow (Robert), History of Oregon and California. Boston, 1844; London, 1844; New York, 1845; Boston, 1845; Boston, 1847; Memoir, Historical and Political, on the Northwest Coast of North America. [26th Cong. 1st Sess., Sen. Doc. 174.] Wash. 1840.
Grewingk (C.), Beitrag zur Kenntnissder orographischen, etc., der Nordwest küste Amerikas. St Petersburg, 1850.

Habersham (A. W.), North Pacific Surveying and Exploring Expedition. Philadelphia, 1858.
Hansard (T. C.), Parliamentary Debates from 1803. London, 1812–77. [S. F. Law Library.]
Harper's New Monthly Magazine. New York, 1856 et seq.

Hartford (Conn.), Courant.
Harvey (Mrs. Daniel), Life of John McLoughlin. MS.
Haswell (Robert), Voyage of the *Columbia Rediviva*, 1787, 1701-2. MS.
Hazlitt (Wm. Carew), British Columbia and Vancouver's Island. London, 1858.
Healdsburg (Cal.), Russian River Flag.
Heceta (Bruno), Diario del Viage de 1775. MS.
Heceta (Bruno), Espedicion Marítima. In Palou, Not., ii. 229.
Heceta (Bruno), Segunda Exploracion, 1775, MS.
Heceta (Bruno), Viage de 1775. MS.
Hines (Gustavus), Oregon: Its History, Condition, etc. Buffalo. 1851.
Historical Magazine and Notes and Queries. Boston, etc., 1857-69. 15 vols.
Hittell (John S.), The Commerce and Industries of the Pacific Coast. San Francisco, 1882. 4to.
Hodgedon (D. B.), Report of Ascent of Makushin Mountain. [40th Cong., 2d Sess., H. Ex. Doc. 177.] Washington, 1869.
Holmberg (H. J.), Ethnographische Skizzen über die Völker des Russischen Amerika. Helsingfors, 1855.
Honolulu, Friend, 1843 et seq.; Polynesian, 1857 et seq.; Sandwich Island Gazette, 1836 et seq.; Sandwich Island News, 1846 et seq.
Honcharenko (Agapius), Address to the People of Alaska. In Alaska Herald 1868; Commercial Correspondence to Oppenheim & Co. of London from Oct. 1868 to Jan. 1873; Scrap Book, see Alaska.
Hooper (W. H.), Ten Months among the Tents of the Tuski. London, 1853.
Howard (O. O.), Report of Tour in Alaska, June 1875. [44th Cong. 1st Sess., Sen. Doc. 12.] Washington, 1876.
Hudson's Bay Company, Report from special committee. London, 1857.
Humboldt (Alex. de), Essai Politique sur le Royaume de la Nouvelle Espagne. Paris, 1811. folio. 2 vols. and atlas.
Hunt's Merchant's Magazine. New York, 1839 et seq.
Hutchings' Illustrated California Magazine. San Francisco, 1857-61. 5 vols.

Imperial Naval Archives. St Petersburg, 1704 et seq.
Imray (James F.), Sailing Directions for the West Coast of North America, London, 1868.
Intercolonial Correspondence of Sitka. Office of Russian American Company, in Sitka Archives. MS. vols. i.-xxiii.
International Review. New York, 1881 et seq.
Irving (Washington), Astoria. New York, 1860.
Islenief, Nouvelle carte des découvertes faites par des vaisseaux Russiens. Moscow, 1773.
Ismailof (Stepan), Zhurnal. [Journal.] MS. In Library of Department of State. Washington, D. C.
Ivashintsof (N.), Russkia krugosvetnuia puteshestvie. [Russian Voyages round the World.] In Zapiski Hydr., vii. viii.

Jackson (Sheldon), Alaska, and Missions on North Pacific Coast. New York, 1880; Alaska and its inhabitants. In American Antiq., ii. Oct., Dec. 1879. 105; Education in Alaska [47th Cong. 1st Sess., Sen. Ex. Doc. 30]. Washington, 1881.
Jacksonville (Or.), Reveille, Sentinel.
Jenkins (John S.), U. S. Exploring Expeditions. Auburn, 1850.
Jewitt (John R.), Narrative of his Adventures. Ithaca, 1849.
Journal and Proceedings of the Imperial Academy of St Petersburg from 1780 to 1867.
Juarez (Cayetano), Notas sobre Asuntos de Cal. MS.
Juvenal, Journal, 1796. MS.

Kadnikof (Nikolai K.), Puteshestvie korabla R. A. Kompaniy *Nikolai*, 1839-41. [Voyage of the Russian American Company's ship *Nikolai*, 1839-41.] In Zapiski Hydr., viii.

Kamchatka, Archives, 1792–1804. MS. and print.
Kamchatka, History of. Glocester, 176x.
Kamchatka, des Isles Kurilski et des contrees voisines, Histoire de. Lyon, 1767. 2 vols.
Kane (Thomas L.), Alaska and the Polar Regions. New York. 1868.
Karta Vkhodof K. Novo Arkhangelskomu Porty, etc., 1809, 1833, 1848.
Kelly (Walter), History of Russia. London, 1854. 2 vols.
Kerr (Robert), General History and Collection of Voyages. Edinburgh, etc., 1824. 18 vols.
Khlebnïkof (K.), Zapiski o Amerika. [Letters about America.] St Petersburg, 1861.
Khramtzof (A.), Diary. MS. In Library of Department of State. Washington, D. C.; also printed in Morskoi Sbornik.
Khromtchenko, Puteshestvie v Rossiyskom Ameriku. [Voyage to Russian America.] In St Petersburg Archives of History, 1824.
Khrushchef (Stepan), Puteshestvie Voiennago shloopa *Apollon*, 1821–24. [Voyage of the *Apollon*, 1821–24.] In Zapiski Hydr., viii.
Kirby (W. W.), Journey to the Yukon. In Smithsonian Rept., 1864, 416.
Kislakovski (Ivan M.), Puteshestvie iz Kronshtadta do Sitkhi, 1821–2. [Voyage from Kronstadt to Sitka, 1821–2.] In Zapiski Hydr., viii.
Kittlitz (F. H.), Denkwürdigkeiten einer Reise nach dem Russischen Amerika. Gotha, 1858. 2 vols.
Klochkof (Efim A.), Puteshestvie iz Khronhstadta do Sitkhi, 1821–2. [Voyage from Kronstadt to Sitka, 1821–2.] In Zapiski Hydr., viii.
Knox (Thomas W.), The Russian American Telegraph. In Excelsior Mag., i. No. 7, 1869.
Kohl (J. G.), A History of the Discovery of the East Coast of North America. Portland, 1869; Popular History of the Discovery of America. London, 1862. 2 vols.
Konny-gen (Ivan), Statement in regard to Nulato Massacre. MS.
Kostlivtzof (N.), Vuadomost o nastoiastchem polozheniy rossiysko-Amerikanskikh Koloniy. [Report of present condition of Russian American Colonies.] St Petersburg, 1860.
Kostromitin (Peter), Early Times in the Aleutian Islands. MS.
Kotzebue (Otto von), Voyage of Discovery into the South Sea and Beering's Straits. Berlin, 1819, and London, 1821. 3 vols.
Kotzebue (Otto von), New Voyage round the World. London, 1830. 2 vols.; Voyage of Discovery. London, 1831. 3 vols.
Krasheninnikof (Stepan P.), History of Kamchatka. Glocester, 1764.
Kruger (Alfred), Reminiscences. MS.
Krusenstern (A. J. von), Voyage round the World, 1803–6. London, 1813. 2 vols.; Wörter-Sammlungen. St Petersburg, 1813. 4to.

La Harpe (Jean F.), Abrégé de l'Histoire Générale des Voyages. Paris, 1816. 24 vols. and atlas.
Langsdorff (G. H. von), Voyages and Travels, 1803–7. Lond., 1813–14, 2 vols.
La Pérouse (J. G. F. de), Voyage autour du Monde. Paris, 1798, 4 vols. atlas folio; Voyage round the World, 1785–8. Lond., 1798. 3 vols.; Boston, 1801.
Laplace (C. P. T.), Campagne de Circumnavigation. Paris, 1841–54. 6 vols.
Latham (Robt. G.), The Native Races of the Russian Empire. London, 1854.
Lazaref (A.), Opis puteshestvia vokrug sveta na shloope *Ladoga*, 1822–4. [Description of a Voyage round the World in the sloop *Ladoga*, 1822–24.] In Materialui.
Ledyard (John), A Journal of Capt. Cook's last Voyage to the Pacific Ocean. Hartford, 1873.
Lesseps (Jean B. B.), Journal historique du voyage dans l'expedition de la Pérouse. Paris, 1790. 2 vols.; Travels in Kamtschatka, 1787–8. London, 1790. 2 vols.

Lettres Edifiantes et Curieuses. Lyon, 1819. 14 vols.
Lippincott's Magazine. Philadelphia, 1868 et seq.
L'Isle (J. N. de), Explication de la Carte des Nouvelles Decouvertes au Nord. Paris, 1752. 4to.
Lisiansky (Uri), A Voyage round the World, 1803-6. London, 1814. 4to.
Log Books of Vessels of Russian-American Company. In Sitka Archives. MS. 15 vols.
London, Daily Graphic, Globe, Times.
London Geographical Society Journal. London, 1831-70. 40 vols.
Los Angeles (Cal.), Express, News, Star.
Lütke (Feodor P.), Puteshestvie vokrug svieta, etc., Seniavin, 1826-9. [Journey round the World on the sloop Seniavin, 1826-9.] St Petersburg, 1835; Voyage autour du monde sur la corvette le Séniavine. Paris, 1835-6.

McCabe (James D.), A Comprehensive View of our Country and its Resources. Philadelphia, etc. n.d.
McDonald (J. L.), Hidden Treasures, etc. Gloucester, 1871.
McFarlane (James), The Coal-regions of America. New York, 1873.
McGregor (John), The Progress of America. London, 1847. 2 vols.
Mackenzie (Alexander), Voyage from Montreal to the Frozen and Pacific Oceans, 1789-93. London, 1801. 4to; New York, 1814.
McKonochie, A Summary View of the Statistics, etc., of the Pacific Ocean. London, 1818.
Macpherson (David), Annals of Commerce. London, 1801. 4to. 4 vols.
Malaspina, Disertacion sobre la legitimidad de la navegacion hecha en 1588. In Col. Doc. Inéd., xv. 228; Viaje, 1795. In Navarrete, Viages.
Maldonado (Lorencio Ferrer), Relacion del Descubrimiento del Estrecho de Anian. In Pacheco and Cárdenas, Col. Doc., v. 420; Voyage de la Mer Atlantique á l'Ocean Pacifique. Plaisance, 1812. 4to.
Malte-Brun (V. A.), Précis de la Géographie Universelle. Bruxelles, 1839. 6 vols. and atlas.
Manglave (Eugène de), Resumé de l'Histoire de Mexique. Paris, 1826.
Marchand (Étienne), Voyage autour du Monde, 1790-2. Paris, n.d. 5 vols.
Markof (Alexey), Ruskie na Vostotchnom, Okeane, etc. [The Russians on the Eastern Ocean.] St. Petersburg, 1856.
Marmier (Xavier), En Amérique et en Europe. Paris, 1860.
Martin (R. M.), The Hudson's Bay Territories, etc. London, 1849.
Martinez (Estévan José), and Gonzalo Lopez de Haro, Cuarta Exploracion, 1788. MS.
Marysville (Cal.), Appeal, California Express.
Massachusetts Historical Society. Proceedings, 1863-4. Boston, 1864.
Materialui dla Istoriy Russkikh Zasseleniy. [Material for the History of Russian Settlements.] St Petersburg, 1861. 4 parts.
Maurelle (Francisco Antonio), Compendio de Noticias, Viage de, 1774. MS.
Maurelle (Francisco Antonio), Diario del Viage de la Sonora. 1775. MS.
Maurelle (Francisco Antonio), Journal of a Voyage in 1775. London, 1780.
Maurelle (Francisco Antonio), Navegacion, 1779. MS.
Maury (M. F.), The Physical Geography of the Sea. New York, 1855; Id., 1856; Id., 1857, many other editions.
Mayer Manuscripts. A collection of 30 copies from Mex. archives.
Maynard (Washburn), Report on Alaska seal-fisheries [44th Cong., 1st Sess., H. Ex. Doc., 43]. Washington, 1875.
Meares (John), Account of Trade between North West Coast of America and China. In Meares' Voy., ed. London, 1790, lxvii.; Answer to Mr George Dixon. London, 1791; Voyages in 1788-89 from China to the N. W. Coast of America. London, 1790. 4to; Id., 1791. 2 vols.
Melanges Russes Tirés du Bulletin Historico Philologique. St Petersburg, 1858.

Mnanie Gosudarstvennavo sovieta, 1865 and 1866. [Opinion of Imperial Council.] MS. copies.
Mofras (Eugene Duflot de); Exploration de l'Orégon, des Californies, etc. Paris, 1844, 2 vols. and atlas.
Mohan (H.) et al., Pen Pictures of our Representative Men. Sac., 1880.
Morris (William G.), Report upon the resources of Alaska [45th Cong., 3d Sess., Sen. Ex. Doc., 59.] Wash., 1879.
Morskoi Sbornik. [Marine Miscellany.] St Petersburg, 1848 et seq.
Müller (Gerhard F.), Sammlung russischer Geschichten. St Petersburg, 1732–64. 9 vols.; Voyages from Asia to America. London, 1761; Voyages et découvertes faites par les Russes. Amsterdam, 1766.
Muravief (Matvei I.), Puteshestvie korabl. R. A. Kompaniy Elena iz Sitkhi. [Voyage of the Russian American Company's ship Elena from Sitka, 1820.] In Zapiski Hydr., viii.
Murphy (T. G.), History of Alaska. In Alaska Times.
Murphy and Harnet. See Directories. Puget Sound.
Murray (Hugh), Historical Account of Discoveries and Travels in N. America. London, 1829. 2 vols.

Nanaimo (B. C.), Free Press, Gazette.
Napa City (Cal.), Napa County Reporter, Register.
Narrative of Occurrences in the Indian Countries of N. America. London, 1817.
Navarrete (Martin Fernandez), Introduccion. In Sutil y Mexicana, Viage; Viages Apócrifos. In Col. Doc., Inéd., xv.
Neue Nachrichten von denen neuentdekten Insuln in der see zwischen Asien und Amerika. Hamburg, etc., 1776.
Nevada (Cal.), Journal, Transcript.
New Helvetia, Diary of Events in 1845–8. MS.
New York, Commercial Journal, Forest and Stream, Graphic, Herald, Illustrated Christian Weekly, Journal of Commerce, Post, Sun, Sunday Times, Times, Tribune.
Nicolay (C. G.), The Oregon Territory. London, 1846.
Niles' Register. Baltimore, etc., 1811–49. 76 vols.
Nordenskjöld (A. E.), The Voyage of the Vega. New York, 1882.
North American Review. Boston, 1819 et seq.
Northern Passage, Summary Observations and Facts to Show the Practicability of Success. London, 1776.
Notice sur la Calédonie Occidentale. In Nouv. An. Voy., xiv. 47.
Nouvelles Annales des Voyages. Paris, 1819–60. 168 vols.
Novosti Literatura. [Literary Novelties.] St Petersburg, 1823 et seq.

Oakland (Cal.), News, Press, Transcript.
Ogorodnikof (Ivan), Ot Niu Yorka do San Francisco. [From New York to San Francisco.] St Petersburg, 1869.
Olafsson (Jón), Alaska Lýsing a landi og Lands-Kostum, etc. Washington, 1875.
Olympia (Wash.), Commercial Age, Echo, Pacific Tribune, Puget Sound Courier, Territorial Republican, Transcript.
Overland Monthly. San Francisco, 1868–75. 15 vols.

Pacheco (Joaquin F.), and Cárdenas et al., Coleccion de Documentos Inéditos relativos al Descubrimiento, Conquista y Colonizacion de las Posesiones Españolas en America. Madrid, 1864–81. 34 vols.
Pacific Medical and Surgical Journal. San Francisco, 1858 et seq.
Pallas (Peter S.), Russiyskikh Olkrytiakh, etc. [Description of Northern Archipelago.] In Sobranie, Nordische Beiträge. St Petersburg, etc., 1781–96. 7 vols.: Reise durch verschiedene provinzen der Russischen Reichs. St Petersburg, 1771–6. 3 vols.

Palmer (A. H.), Memoir, Geographical, Political, and Commercial, on the present state, etc., of Siberia. [30th Cong., 1st Sess., Sen. Mis. Doc. 80.] Wash., 1848.
Palou (Francisco), Noticias de la California. Mexico, 1857. In Doc. Hist. Mex., ser. iv. tom. vi.–vii.; San Francisco, 1874. 4 vols.; Relacion Histórica de la Vida etc. de Junípero Serra. Mexico, 1787.
Papers relating to the Treaty of Washington. Vol. v. Berlin Arbitration. Washington, 1872.
Patterson (Samuel), Narrative of Adventures and Sufferings in Pacific Ocean. Palmer, 1817.
Payne (John), A New and Complete System of Universal Geography. New York, 1798. 4 vols.
Peirce (Henry A.), Journal of Voyages, 1839–42. MS.
Peirce (Henry A.), Rough Sketch. MS.
Pelham (Cavendish), The World. London, 1808. 4to. 2 vols.
Pena (Tomás), Diario de Viage de Perez, 1774. MS.
Pereleshin (Nikolai), Doklad. [Report.] In Morskoi, Sbornik.
Perez (Juan), Relacion del Viage, 1774. MS.
Perez (Juan), Tabla Diaria. 1774. MS.
Perry (M. C.), Narrative of the Expedition of an American Squadron to the China Sea. Washington, 1856. 4to. 3 vols.
Petaluma (Cal.), Argus, Crescent, Journal and Argus.
Petit-Thouars (Abel), Voyage autour du Monde, 1836–9. Paris, 1840–4. 5 vols.
Petrof (Ivan), Alaska as it is, In International Review. Feb. 1881; Limit of the Innuit Tribes on the Alaska Coast, In American Naturalist, July 1882; Population and Resources of Alaska. [46th Cong., 3d Sess., H. Ex. Doc. 40.] Wash., 1881.
Petrof (Ivan), The Management of the Russian American Company. MS.
Philadelphia, Inquirer,
Picolo (Francisco M.), Memorial sobre el estado de las misiones nuevamente establecidas en la California. In Cartas Edificantes, iii. 257.
Pinart (Alphonse), Les Aléoutes et leur Origine. In Revue Orientale, xii. 155; La Caverne d'Akañank Ile d'Ounga. Paris, 1875; Eskimaux et Koloches Idées Religieuses, etc. Paris, 1873; Notes sur les Koloches. Paris, 1873; Note sur les Atkahs. Paris, 1873; Voyages à la Côte Nord Ouest de l'Amérique. Paris, 1875. folio; La chasse aux animaux marins et les pêcheries chez les Indigènes de la côte N. O. Boulogne, S. M., 1875. 8vo.
Pinkerton (John), General Collection of Voyages and Travels. London, 1808–14. 4to. 17 vols.
Pioche (Nev.), Record.
Placerville (Cal.), Mountain Democrat.
Plestcheief (Sergi I.), Survey of the Russian Empire. London, 1792.
Politofsky (N.), Kratkoie Istoricheskoie Obozranie Obrazovanie y Deistvie Rossiysko-Amerik., etc. [Brief historical review of origin and transactions of Russian American Company.] St Petersburg, 1861.
Ponafidin (Zakhar I.), Puteshestvie iz Kallao do Sitkhi 1816–18. [Voyage from Callao to Sitka, 1816–18.] In Zapiski Hydr. vii.
Portland (Or.), Bee, Bulletin, Commercial, Deutche Zeitung, Herald, Oregon Herald, Oregonian, Standard, Telegram, West Shore.
Portlock (Nathaniel), Voyage round the World, 1785–8. London, 1785–8. 4to.
Port Townsend (Wash.), Argus, Democratic Press, Message.
Potechin (V.), Settlement of Ross. St Petersburg, 1859.
Poussin (G. T.), Question de l'Orégon. Paris, 1846; The United States. Philadelphia, 1851.
Prescott (Ariz.), Arizona Miner.

Quarterly Review. London, 1809 et seq.

xxxiv AUTHORITIES QUOTED.

Radlo (L.), Einige Nachrichten über die Sprache der Kaiganen. St Peters-
burg, 1858.
Randolph (Edmund), Oration before Society of Cal. Pioneers, Sept. 1860.
In Hutchings' Mag., v. 263.
Raymond (Charles W.), Report of Yukon River and island of St Paul. Jan.
1, 1870 [41st Cong., 2d Sess., H. Ex. Doc. 112]. Washington, 1870.
Raynal (G. T.), Histoire Philosophique. Paris, 1820-1. 12 vols. and atlas.
Recherches Philosophiques sur les Americains. London, 1770. 2 vols.
Red Bluff (Cal.), Independent, Sentinel.
Revilla Gigedo (Virey), Informe de 12 Abril, 1793. In Bustamante Suple-
mento, iii. 112.
Revue des Deux Mondes. Paris, 1830 et seq.
Revue Orientale et Americaine. Paris, 1859 et seq.
Richardson (Sir John), Arctic Searching Expedition. London, 1851. 2 vols.;
The Polar Regions. Edinburgh, 1861.
Richardson (J.) et al., Zoölogy of Beechey's Voyage. Lond., 1839-40.
Ridpath (John C.), A Popular History of the U. S. New York, 1877.
Rivinus (Edward F.), Atlantis, Journal des Neuesten und Wissenswürdigsten
etc. Leipzig, 1827.
Rocky Mountain Presbyterian. Denver, 1877 et seq.
Rogers (Commander John), Letters on Surveying Expedition to North Pacific
Ocean, Berings Straits, and China Seas, Aug. 1854 to June 1855. MS.
2 vols. In U. S. Navy Department. Washington, D. C.
Roquefeuil (Camille), Journal d'un Voyage autour du Monde, 1816-19. Paris,
1823. 2 vols.; Voyage round the World, 1816-19. London, 1823.
Roseburg (Or.), Western Star.
Ross (John), Narrative of a second voyage in search of a N. W. Passage.
London, 1835.
Ross Colony, Documents relating to. In Russian Amer. Col. v.
Rossi [L'Abbé], Souvenirs d'un Voyage en Orégon et en Californie. Paris,
1864.
Rotchef (Alex.), Deed of Ross to Sutter, 1841. MS.
Rothrock (Joseph T.), Flora of Alaska. In Smithsonian Report 1867. 433.
Rouhaud (Hippolyte), Les Régions Nouvelles. Paris, 1868.
Russia. Imperial Geographical Society. St Petersburg, etc., 1863 et seq.
Russia, Official Documents. Department of Foreign Affairs; Ministry of the
Interior; Ministry of War.
Russia, Treaty with, Report of Committee of Foreign Affairs, May 18, 1868.
[40th Cong., 2d Sess., H. Report 37.] Washington, 1868.
Russian America, A Collection. 7 vols. MS.
Russian America, Message of the President of the U. S. Feb. 17, 1868. [40th
Cong., 2d Sess., H. Ex. Doc. 177.] Washington, 1868.
Russian American Company, Archives. St Petersburg, 1799-1867.
Russian American Company, Charters of 1799, 1821, 1842. In Tikhmenef
Ist. Oboz. and Materialui.
Russian American Fur Company, Accounts, 1847-50. MS.
Russian American Telegraph, Statement of the Origin, Organization, etc.
Rochester, 1866.

Sacramento (Cal.), Bee, Record, Record-Union, Reporter.
Saint Amant (M. de), Voyages en Californie et dans l'Orégon. Paris, 1854.
Saint Petersburg, Archives of History.
Salem (Or.), Capital, Chronicle, Mercury, Oregon Statesman, Record.
Salt Lake City, Herald.
Salvatierra (Juan María), Cuatro Cartas sobre misiones en Californias, Nov.
1697. In Doc. Hist. Mex., serie ii., tom. i. 103; Informe al Virey, May
25, 1705. In Venegas, Noticia ii.
Sammlung aller Reisebeschreibungen. Leipzig, 1747-74. 4to. 21 vols.
San Francisco Newspapers. Alaska Appeal, Alaska Herald, Alaska Tribune,
Alta California, Argonaut, Call, Christian Advocate, Chronicle, Com-

mercial Herald and Market Review, Evening Bulletin, Examiner, Golden Era, Herald, Journal of Commerce, Mining and Scientific Press, News Letter, Occident, Pacific Churchman, Pacific Rural Press, Post, Scientific Press, Stars and Stripes, Temperance Advocate, Times, Tribune.
San José (Cal.), Argus, Mercury, Patriot, Santa Clara Argus.
Sankt Petersburger Kalender 1750, et seq.
San Luis Obispo (Cal.), Tribune.
Santa Bárbara (Cal.), Press.
Santa Clara (Cal.), News.
Santa Cruz (Cal.), County Times, Sentinel.
Sarychef (Gavrila A.), Puteshestvie i korabl *Otkrytie*. [Voyage of sloop *Otkrytie*.] St Petersburg, 1802. 4to. 2 vols.
Sauer (Martin), Account of a Geographical and Astronomical Expedition to the Northern Parts of Russia. London, 1802.
Scala (Comte de), Influence de l'Ancien Comptoir Russe en Californie. In Nouv. An. Voy., cxliv. 375.
Scammon (Charles M.), Cod-Fishery, in Overland, iv. 436; Fur Seals, in Overland, iii. 393; Whaling, Northern, in Overland, v. 548; A Russian Boat-Voyage, in Overland, xv. 554.
Scherer (Jean B.), Recherches Historiques et Geographiques sur le Nouveau Monde. Paris, 1777.
Schlözer (August L.), Allgemeine Geschichte von dem Norden. Halle, 1771.
Schmölder (Capt. B.), Neuer Praktischer Wegweiser für Nord-Amerika. Mainz, 1849.
Seattle (Wash.), Intelligencer, Pacific Tribune, Puget Sound Dispatch.
Seeman (Berthold), Narrative of the Voyage of the *Herald* 1845-51. London, 1853. 2 vols.
Seward (William H.), Communication upon the subject of an intercontinental telegraph. Wash., 1864; Our North Pacific States (Speeches), Aug. 1869. Wash., 1869.
Sgibnef (Alex. S.), Istoricheskie Ocherki. [Historical Sketches.] In Morskoi Sbornik, vol ci-ciii.
Shabelski (Achille), Voyage aux colonies russes 1821-23. St Petersburg, 1826.
Shaw (Francis A.), Brief History of Russia. Boston, 1877.
Shelikof (Grigor), Pervoie Stranstvovnie, etc. [First Voyages of the Russian Merchants, 1783 and 1787.] St Petersburg, 1790; Prodolshenie [Further Voyages 1788]. St Petersburg, 1792; Puteshestoie [Voyages]. St Petersburg, 1812.
Sibir Zolotni Dno. [Siberia's Golden Soil.] St Petersburg, 1768 et seq.
Sibirskaia Istoria. [History of Siberia.] St Petersburg, 1759 et seq.
Sibirskye Viestnik [Siberian Messenger]. St Petersburg, 1818 et seq.
Simmonds (P. L.), Sir John Franklin and the Arctic Regions. Buffalo, 1852.
Simpson (Sir George), Narrative of a Journey round the World. London, 1847. 2 vols.
Sitka, Alaska Times, MS. and print; Post, MS. and print.
Sitka Archives. In Library of Department of State, Washington, D. C. 1802-67. 182 vols. MS.
Smithsonian Institution, Annual Reports. Washington, 1853 et seq.
Sobranie Sochinenie (Literary Collections). St Petersburg, 1760 et seq.
Société de Geographie, Bulletin. Paris, 1825 et seq.
Sokolof (Alexander), Bering and Chirikof. St Petersburg, 1849; Istoria Severnyikh Puteshestviy [History of Northern expeditions 1733-43], in Zapiski Hydr. ix.; Khvostof and Davidof, in Zapiski Hydr. x.; Proiskhoshdenie Okhotska [Origin of Okhotsk], in Morskoi Sbornik; Zamechaniy o Severnikh Ekspeditziy 1738-43 [Remarks on the Account of the northern expeditions of 1733-43], in Morskoi Sbornik; Russische Entdeckungsreisen nach dem nordöstlichen Asien, etc. Berlin, 1855.
Sokolof (Vasili), Voyage of Alexander Markoff from Okhotsk to Cal., 1835. MS.
Sonora (Cal.) Herald, Union Democrat.

Southeastern Alaska, Memorial of the people to the President and Congress of the U. S. Aug. 16, 1881. n.pl., 1881.

Southern Quarterly Review. New Orleans etc., 1842 et seq.

Spanberg, Journal, in Tobolsk Archives, quoted by Sokolof. In Zapiski Hydr.

Sparks (Jared), Life of John Ledyard. Cambridge, 1828.

Staehlin (J. von), An Account of the New Northern Archipelago. London, 1774.

State Papers, Sacramento. MS., 19 vols. in Archivo de Cal.; Id., Missions and Colonization. 2 vols.

Steller (George W.), Beschreibung von dem Lande Kamtschatka. Frankfurt, etc., 1774; Reise von Kamtschatka nach Amerika. St. Petersburg, 1793.

Stevens (Isaac I.), Northwest America, address Dec. 2, 1858. Washington, 1858.

Stockton (Cal.), Gazette, Herald, Independent, San Joaquin Republican.

Sturgis (William), Northwest Fur Trade. In Hunt's Merch. Mag., xiv. 532.

Sturgis (William), Remarks on Northwest Coast. MS. [In possession of Dr Emil Bessels.] Washington, D. C.

Sumner (Charles), Speech on the Cession of Russian America to the U. S. Washington, 1867.

Sutil y Mexicana, Relacion del Viage hecho por las Goletas. Madrid, 1802. atlas. 4to.

Sutter (John A.), Examination of the Russian Grant. Sacramento, 1860.

Sutter (John A.), Personal Recollections. MS.

Syn Otechestva. [Son of the Fatherland.] St Petersburg, 1820 et seq.

Synd, see Berg (Vasili), Khronologicheskaïa Istoria, etc. St Peterburg, 1820.

Taylor (Alexander S.), Historical Summary of Lower California. In Browne's Min. Res.; Specimens of the Press. [In S. F. Mercantile Library.]

Taylor (James W.), Northwest British America. St Paul, 1860.

Tchitchinof (Zakahar), Adventures of an Employé of the Russian American Fur Company. 1802-78. MS.

Tebenkof (Mikhaïl D.), Atlas of the Northwest Coast of America. St Petersburg, 1852.

Teleskop (The Telescope). Moscow, 1825 et seq.

Thornton (J. Quinn), Oregon and California in 1848. N. Y., 1849. 2 vols.

Thomas (George H.), Report of tour in Alaska, 1869. [41st Cong., 2d Sess., H. Ex. Doc. 1.] Washington, 1869.

Tikhmenef (P.), Istoricheskoie Obozranie Obrazovanie Rossiysko Amerikanskoi Kompaniy [Historical review of the origin of the Russian American Company]. St Petersburg, 1861, 1863. 2 vols.

Tilling, Reise un die Welt. Aschaffenburg, 1854.

Tobolsk Archives. In Zapiski Hydr.

Tooke (William), View of the Russian Empire. Dublin, 1801. 3 vols.

Truman (Benjamin C.), Occidental Sketches. San Francisco, 1881.

Tulubief (Irenarkh), Puteshestvie shloopa Apollona, 1821-24. [Voyage of the Apollon, 1821-24.] In Zapiski Hydr., viii.

Tuscarora (Nev.), Times Review.

Tuthill (Franklin), History of California. San Francisco, 1866.

Twiss (Travers), The Oregon Question. London, 1846; The Oregon Territory. New York, 1846.

Tyler (Robert O.), Revised outline descriptions of the posts and stations of troops in the military division of the Pacific. San Francisco, 1872.

Tytler (Patrick Fraser), Historical View of the Progress of Discovery. Edinburgh, 1833; New York, 1855.

Ukiah (Cal.), Democratic Dispatch, Mendocino Democrat, Mendocino Herald.

Umfreville (Edward), The Present State of Hudson's Bay. London, 1790.

Unionville (Nev.), Register.

United States Coast and Geodetic Survey, C. P. Patterson Supt. Pacific Coast Pilot, Alaska. Washington, 1879.
United States Exploring Expedition [Wilkes]. Philadelphia, 1844–58. 4to, 17 vols.; folio, 8 vols.
United States Geological Surveys of the Territories, F. V. Hayden. Annual Reports, Bulletins, Miscellaneous Publications, etc. Washington, 1872 et seq.
United States Geological and Geographical Surveys, J. W. Powell. Contributions to North American Ethnology. Washington, 1876.
United States Government Documents. Agriculture, Bureau of Statistics, Census, Coast Survey, Commerce and Navigation, Commercial Relations, Education, Finance, Indian Affairs, Interior, Land Office, Navy Report of Secretary, Postmaster General, Secretary of War, Signal Service Reports, Treasury. Cited by their dates.
United States Government Documents. House Exec. Doc., House Journal, House Miscel. Doc., House Reports of Com., Message and Documents, Senate Exec. Doc., Journal, Miscel. Doc., Repts. Com. Cited by congress and session. Many of these documents have, however, separate titles, for which see author or topic.

Vallejo (Jose de Jesus), Reminiscencias Histórica. MS.
Vallejo (Mariano G.), Correspondencia Histórica. MS.
Vallejo (Mariano G.), Documentos para la Historia de California, 1769–1850. MS. 37 vols.
Vancouver (George), Voyage of Discovery to the Pacific Ocean. Lond., 1798. 3 vols. 4to. atlas in folio; Lond., 1801. 6 vols.; Voyage et Découvertes á l'Océan Pacifique, etc. Paris, An., viii. 3 vols. 4to. atlas in folio.
Vassilief (Ivan P.), Vuipiski iz Zhurnale etc. [Extract from log-book of ship Finland.] In Novosti Literatura, 1823, vi.
Vassilief (Mikhail N.), O plavanie, etc. [Voyage of Otkrnitie and Dobroie Namerenie.] In Syn Otechestva, 1820.
Venegas (Miguel), Noticia de la California y de su Conquista Temporal, etc. Madrid, 1757. 3 vols.
Veniaminof (Ioann), Schreiben aus Kamtschatka [from the Moskow Viedomost]; Zapisky ob Ostrovakh Oonalashkinskago Otdiela [Letters on Islands of Unalaska District]. St Petersburg, 1840. 2 vols.
'Veritas,' Examination of the Russian Grant. n.pl., n.d.; Is the trade of Alaska to be wrested from general competition, etc. San Francisco, 1871.
Viagero Universal (El). Madrid, 1796–1801. 43 vols.
Viages en la Costa al Norte de Californias. Copy from Spanish Archives. MS. [From Prof. Geo. Davidson.]
Victoria (B. C.), British Colonist, Chronicle, Express, Standard.
Villavicencio (Juan J.), Vida y Virtudes de el venerable P. Juan de Ugarte. Mexico, 1752.
Virginia (Nev.), Evening Chronicle, Territorial Enterprise.
Voyages, Historical Account of, round the World. Lond., 1774–81. 6 vols.; New Collection. London, 1767. 7 vols.

Wallace (D. Mackenzie), Russia. New York, 1878.
Walla Walla (Wash.), Statesman.
Ward (James C.), Three Weeks in Sitka. MS.
Washington (D. C.), Capital, Chronicle, Critic, Evening Star, Morning News, Post, Tribune.
Westdahl (Ferdinand), Alaska. MS.
White (J. W.), A Cruise in Alaska [40th Cong., 3d Sess., Sen. Ex. Doc. 8]. Washington, 1869.
Whitney (J. D.), Notice of the Mountain Heights in the U. S. San Francisco, 1862.

Whymper (Frederick), Journey from Norton Sound to Fort Yukon. In Lond. Geog. Soc. Jour., xxxviii. 219; Travel and Adventure in the Territory of Alaska. New York, 1869; Voyage et Aventures dans l'Alaska. Paris, 1871.

Wilkes (Charles), Narrative of the U. S. Exploring Expedition. Philadelphia, 1844, 4to. 3 vols.; Philadelphia, 1845, 5 vols.; London, 1845.

Woodland (Cal.), News, Yolo Democrat.

Wrangell (Ferdinand P.), The Americans of Upper California. In Teleskop, 1835, Sketch of a Journey from Sitka to St Petersburg. St Petersburg, 1836; Statistische und Ethnographische nachrichten über die Russischen Besitzungen. St Petersburg, 1839; Voyage to the northern shores of Siberia, etc., 1820-24. St Petersburg, 1841.

Wythe (W. T.), Cook's Inlet. In Overland, xiii. 64; Kodiak and Southern Alaska. In Id., viii. 505.

Yermolof (M.), Extrait d'une note sur l'Amerique russe. In Nouv. An. Voy., cxi.

Yezhcmesiechnaie Sochinenie [Monthly Magazine]. St Petersburg, 1759 et seq.

Yreka (Cal.), Journal, Union.

Yuba City (Cal.), Sutter Banner, Sutter County Sentinel.

Zabriskie (James C.), The Public Land Laws of the U. S. San Francisco, 1870; Supplement. San Francisco, 1877.

Zagoskin (A.), Pieshekhodnaia Opis Chasty Russkikh Vladeniy v Ameriku [Pedestrian Exploration of Parts of the Russian Possessions in America, 1842-4]. St Petersburg, 1847, 2 vols.

Zaikof (Stepan), Kratkoie obozranie puteshestviy na Ostrovakh, etc. [Summary of the voyages to the islands situated between Asia and America.] In Sobranie Soch.

Zapiski Admiralteistkago Departamenta. [Journal of the Admiralty Department.] St Petersburg, 1807 et seq.

Zapiski Hydrograficheskago Departamenta. [Journal of Hydrographic Department.] St Petersburg, 1842 et seq.

Zapiski Russkago Geograficheskago Obshestva. [Publications of the Russian Geographical Society.] St Petersburg, 1838 et seq.

Zapiski uchenago komiteta morskago shtaba. [Journal of Committee on Instruction of Naval Staff.] St Petersburg, 1828 et seq.

Zarembo (Dionis F.), Puteshestvie iz Khronshtadta do Sitkhi, 1840-41. [Voyage from Kronstadt to Sitka, 1840-41.] In Zapiski Hydr. viii.

Zavalishin (Dmitri I.), Dielo o Koloniy Ross (Affairs of the Ross Colony). Moskow, 1866.

Zeleniy (N.), Correspondence. In Sitka Archives, MS., vols. i.-vii.

Zhurnal departamenta narodnago prosvieshchenia. [Journal of the Department of Public Instruction.] St Petersburg, 1822 et seq.

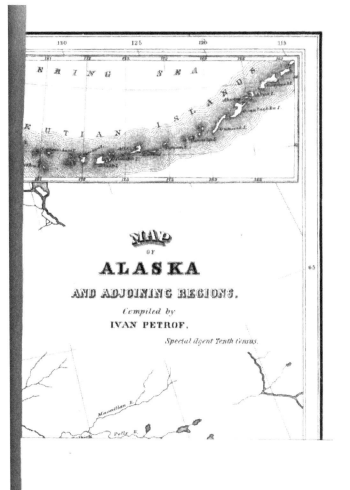

MAP
OF
ALASKA
AND ADJOINING REGIONS.
Compiled by
IVAN PETROF.

Special Agent Tenth Census.

HISTORY OF ALASKA.

CHAPTER I.

INTRODUCTORY.

In the great seizure and partition of America by European powers there was no reason why Russia should not have a share. She was mistress in the east and north as were France and Spain in the west and south; she was as grasping as Portugal and as cold and cruel as England; and because she owned so much of Europe and Asia in the Arctic, the desire was only increased thereby to extend her broad belt quite round the world. It was but a step across from one continent to the other, and intercourse between the primitive peoples of the two had been common from time immemorial. It was but natural, I say, in the gigantic robbery of half a world, that Russia should have a share; and had she been quicker about it, the belt might as well have been continued to Greenland and Iceland.

Geographically, Alaska is the northern end of the long cordillera which begins at Cape Horn, extends

through the two Americas, and is here joined by the
Nevada-Cascade range; the Coast Range from Lower
California breaking into islands before reaching this
point. It is not always and altogether that cold and
desolate region which sometimes has been pictured,
and which from its position we might expect. Its
configuration and climate are exceedingly varied.
The southern seaboard is comparatively mild and
habitable; the northern frigid and inhospitable.

Standing at Mount St Elias as the middle of a crescent, we see the shore-line stretching out in either
direction, toward the south-east and the south-west,
ending in the former at Dixon Inlet, and in the latter
sweeping off and breaking into mountainous islands as
it continues its course toward Kamchatka. It is a
most exceedingly rough and uncouth country, this
part of it; the shore-line being broken into fragments,
with small and great islands guarding the labyrinth of
channels, bays, sounds, and inlets that line the mainland. Back of these rise abruptly vast and rugged
mountains, the two great continental chains coming
together here as if in final struggle for the mastery.
The coast range along the Pacific shore of Alaska
attains an elevation in places of eight or nine thousand feet, lying for the most part under perpetual
snow, with here and there glistening white peaks fourteen or sixteen thousand feet above the sea. And the
ruggedness of this Sitkan or southern seaboard, the
thirty-miles strip as it is sometimes called, with the
Alexander archipelago, continues as we pass on, to
the Alaskan Mountains and the Aleutian archipelago.
It is in the Alaskan Range that nature assumes the
heroic, that the last battle of the mountains appears
to have been fought. The din of it has as yet hardly
passed away; the great peaks of the range stand
there proudly triumphant but still angry; grumbling,
smoking, and spitting fire, they gaze upon their fallen
foes of the archipelago, giants like themselves, though
now submerged, sunken in the sea, if not indeed

hurled thence by their victorious rivals. These great towering volcanic peaks and the quaking islands are superb beyond description, filling the breast of the beholder with awe. And the ground about, though cold enough upon the surface, steams and sweats in sympathy, manifesting its internal warmth in geysers and hot springs, while from the depths of the sea sometimes belches forth fire, if certain navigators may be believed, and the sky blazes in northern lights.

All along this sweep of southern seaboard Europeans may dwell in comfort if so inclined. Even in midwinter the cold is seldom severe or of long duration. An average temperature is 42°, though extremes have been named for certain localities of from 19° to 58°, and again from 58° below zero in January, to 95° in summer. Winter is stormy, the winds at Sitka at this season being usually easterly, those from the south bringing rain and snow. When the wind is from the north-west the sky is clear, and the cold nights are often lighted by the display of the aurora borealis. Winter breaks up in March, and during the clear cold days of April the boats go out after furs. Yet, for a good portion of the year there is an universal and dismal dampness—fogs interminable and drizzling rain; clouds thick and heavy and low-lying, giving a water fall of six or eight feet in thickness.

Much of the soil is fertile, though in places wet. Behind a low wooded seaboard often rise abruptly icy steeps, with here and there between the glacier cañons broad patches of sphagnum one or two feet thick, and well saturated with water. The perpetual snow-line of the Makushin volcano is three thousand feet above the sea, and vegetation ceases at an altitude of twenty-five hundred feet. Grain does not ripen, but grasses thrive almost everywhere on the lowlands. Berries are plentiful, particularly cranberries, though the sunlight is scarcely strong enough to flavor them well. Immense spruce forests tower over Prince William Sound and about Sitka. Kadiak is a good grazing

country, capable of sustaining large droves of cattle.
On the Aleutian Islands trees do not grow, but the
grasses are luxuriant. In a word, here in the far
north we find a vegetation rightly belonging to a much
lower latitude.

The warm Japan current which comes up along
the coast of Asia, bathing the islands of the Aleutian
archipelago as it crosses the Pacific and washing the
shores of America far to the southward, transforms
the whole region from what would otherwise be inhospitable into a habitation fit for man. Arising off the
inner and outer shores of Lower California, this stream
first crosses the Pacific as the great northern equa-
torial current, passing south of the Hawaiian Islands
and on to the coast of Asia, deflecting northward as
it goes, and after its grand and life-compelling sweep
slowly returns to its starting-point. It is this that
clothes temperate isles in tropical vegetation, makes
the silk-worm flourish far north of its rightful home,
and sends joy to the heart of the hyperborean, even
to him upon the strait of Bering, and almost to the
Arctic sea. It is this that thickly covers the steep
mountain sides to the height of a thousand feet and
more with great growths of spruce, alder, willow,
hemlock, and yellow cedar. It is the striking of this
warm current of air and water against the cold shores
of the north that causes nature to steam up in thick
fogs and dripping moisture, and compels the surcharged
clouds to drop their torrents.

Chief among the fur-bearing animals is the sea-
otter, in the taking of whose life the lives of thousands of human beings have been laid down. Of fish
there are cod, herring, halibut, and salmon, in abundance. The whale and the walrus abound in places.

Go back into the interior if you can get there, or
round by the Alaskan shore north of the islands,
along Bering sea and strait, which separate Asia and
America and indent the eastern border with great
bays into which flow rivers, one of them, the Yukon,

having its sources far back in British Columbia; ascend this stream, or traverse the country between it and the Arctic Ocean, and you will find quite a different order of things. Clearer skies are there, and drier, colder airs, and ice eternal. Along the Arctic shore runs a line of hills in marked contrast to the mountains of the southern seaboard. Between these ranges flow the Yukon with its tributaries, the Kuskokvim, Sela-wik, and other streams.

Mr Petrof, who traversed this region in 1880, says of it: "Here is an immense tract reaching from Bering strait in a succession of rolling ice-bound moors and low mountain ranges, for seven hundred miles an unbroken waste, to the boundary line between us and British America. Then, again, from the crests of Cook's Inlet and the flanks of Mount St Elias northward over that vast area of rugged mountain and lonely moor to the east, nearly eight hundred miles, is a great expanse of country ... by its position barred out from occupation and settlement by our own people. The climatic conditions are such that its immense area will remain undisturbed in the pos-session of its savage occupants, man and beast."

Before speaking of the European discovery and conquest of Alaska, let us briefly glance at the con-dition and character of those about to assume the mastery here.

It was in the middle of the sixteenth century that the Russians under Ivan Vassilievich, the Terrible, threw off the last yoke of Tartar Khans; but with the independence of the nation thus gained, the free cities, principalities, and provinces lost all trace of their former liberties. An empire had been wrung from the grasp of foreign despots, but only to be held by a despotism more cruel than ever had been the Tartar domination. Ignorance, superstition, and servitude were the normal condition of the lower classes. The nation could scarcely be placed within the category of civilization. While in Spain the ruling spirit was fanaticism, in Russia it was despotism.

Progress was chained; if any sought to improve their lot they dared not show their gains lest their master should take them. And the people thus long accustomed to abject servility and concealment acquired the habit of dissimulation to a remarkable degree. There was no recognition of the rights of man, and little of natural morality. It was a preëstablished and fundamental doctrine that the weaker were slaves of the stronger. In feudal times the main difference between the lowest class in Russia and in other parts of Europe was that the former were not bound to the soil. Their condition however was none the less abject, their slavery if possible was more complete. And what is not a little singular in following the progress of nations, Russia, about the beginning of the seventeenth century, introduced this custom of binding men to lands, just when the other states of Europe were abolishing it. Freemen were authorized by law to sell themselves. Insolvent debtors became the property of their creditors. And howsoever bound, men could obtain their liberty only by purchase.

Women, even of the better class, were held in oriental seclusion, and treated as beasts; husbands and fathers might torture and kill them, and sell the offspring, but if a wife killed her husband she was buried up to the neck and left to starve.

Pewter was unknown; only wooden dishes were in use. Each man carried a knife and wooden spoon tied to the belt or sash. Bedding was scarcely used at court; among rich and poor alike a wooden bench, the bare floor, or at the most a skin of bear or wolf, sufficed for sleeping. The domestic ties were loose; since the crimes of individuals were visited upon the whole kindred the children scattered as soon as they were able. The lower classes had but a single name, which was conferred in baptism, consequently the nearest relatives soon lost sight of each other in their wandering life. Subsequently the serfs were attached to the soil, but even to the present day an almost irresistible disposition to rove is noticeable among the Russian people.

The nobles, reared by a nation of slaves, were scarcely more intelligent than they. But few of the priests understood Greek; and reading and writing even among the nobles was almost unknown; astronomy and anatomy were classed among the diabolic arts; calculations were made by means of a string of balls, and skins of animals were the currency. Punishments were as barbarous as manners. The peculator was publicly branded with a hot iron, then sent back to his place, thus dishonoring himself and degrading his office. When a person was punished for crime, all the members of his family were doomed to suffer likewise. Every Russian who strayed beyond the frontier became a rebel and a heathen.

Nobles alone could hold land; the tillers were as slaves. True, a middle or merchant class managed amidst the general disruption to maintain some of their ancient privileges. The *gosti*, or wholesale dealers, of Moscow, Novgorod, and Pleskovo might sit at table with princes, and go on embassies; they were free from imposts and many other exactions. Even the small traders preserved some of the benefits which had originated in the free commercial cities. The priests, seeing their influence at court declining, cultivated the merchants, and married among their families.

Thus all combined to strengthen the trading class as compared with the agricultural. Taxes and salaries were paid in furs; in all old charters and other documents penalties and rewards are given in furs. The very names of the early coins of Novgorod point to their origin; we see there the *grivernik grivnui*, from the mane or long hairs along the back; the *oushka* and *poloushka*, ear and half-ear. This feature in the national economy explains to a certain extent the slow spread of civilization over the tsar's dominions.

In a country where furs are the circulating medium,
and hence the great desideratum, the people must
scatter and lead a savage life.

The same cause, however, which impeded social
and intellectual development furnished a stimulus for
the future aggrandizement of the Muscovite domain.
For more than two and a half centuries the Hanseatic
League had monopolized the foreign trade; but the
decline of Novgorod, the growing industry of the
Livonian cities, and the appearance of the ships of
other countries in the Baltic were already threatening
the downfall of Hanseatic commerce, when an unexpected discovery made the English acquainted with the
White Sea, which afforded direct intercourse with the
inland provinces of the Russian empire. The Hanse,
by its superiority in the Baltic, had excluded all other
maritime nations from Russian commerce, but it was
beyond the reach of their power to prevent the English
from sailing to the White Sea. In 1553, at the suggestion of Sebastian Cabot, England sent three vessels
under Sir Hugh Willoughby in search of a north-east
passage to China. Two of the vessels were lost, and
the third, commanded by Richard Chancellor, entered
the White Sea. No sooner did he know that the
shore was Russia than Chancellor put on a bold face
and said he had come to establish commercial relations. The tsar, informed of the arrival of the strangers, ordered them to Moscow. The insolent behavior
of the Hanse League had excited the tsar's displeasure, and he was only too glad of other intercourse
with civilized nations. Every encouragement was
offered by the Russian monarch, and trade finally
opened with England, and special privileges were
granted to the so-called Russia Company of English
merchants.

The English commercial expeditions through Russia, down the Volga, and across the Caspian to Persia,
were not financially successful, though perhaps valuable as a hint to the Portuguese that the latter did

not hold the only road to India. To Russia, also, this traffic proved by no means an unalloyed blessing. The wealthy merchants of Dantzic and other Hanse towns along the Baltic, who had enjoyed a monopoly of Russian commerce, looked on with jealousy, and it was doubtless owing to enmity in this influential quarter that Ivan failed in all his attempts to secure Esthonia and Livonia, and gain access to the Baltic seaports. On the other hand, English enterprise brought about commerce with different nations, and introduced the products of north-western Europe into the tsar's dominions. Further than this, the Muscovites copied English craft, and became more proficient in maritime affairs. An incident connected with this traffic may be considered the first link of a long chain of events which finally resulted in Russia's stride across the Ural Mountains, and the formation of a second or reserve empire, without which the original or European structure might long since have fallen. On the return of an English expedition from Persia across the Caspian, in 1573, the ship was attacked by Cossacks, who gained possession of vessel and cargo, setting the crew adrift in a boat furnished with some provisions. The Englishmen made their way to Astrakhan, and on their report of what had befallen them two armed vessels were sent out. The pirates were captured and put to death, while the cargo, worth between 30,000 and 40,000 pounds sterling, was safely landed at Astrakhan. The tsar then despatched a numerous land force to destroy the nest of robbers infesting the Lower Volga and the Caspian. His army spread dismay. The Cossacks saw that submission was death, and many leaped from the blood-stained deck of their rude barks to the saddle, being equally familiar with both. Then they banded under determined leaders and set out for countries beyond the reach of Russia's long arm. Yermak Timofeief headed one of these bands, and thus the advance of the Slav race toward the Pacific began. Rude and

spasmodic as it was, the traffic of the English laid
the foundation of Russian commerce on the Caspian.
Previous to the appearance of the English the Russians had carried on their trade with Bokhara and
Persia entirely by land; but from that time they
began to construct transport ships on the Volga and
to sail coastwise to the circumjacent harbors of the
Caspian.

Before following the tide of conquest across the
Ural Mountains, it may be well to cast a brief glance
over the contemporaneous efforts of English and Dutch
navigators to advance in the same easterly direction
by water, or rather to thread their way between the
masses of floating and solid ice besetting the navigable
channels of the Arctic, demonstrating as they do the
general impression prevalent among European nations
at the time, that the route pursued by Columbus and
his successors was not the only one leading to the inexhaustible treasures of the Indies, and to that Cathay
which the Latin maritime powers were making strenuous efforts to monopolize.

The last English expedition in search of the north-
east passage, undertaken in the sixteenth century,
consisted of two barks which sailed from England early
in 1580, and were fortunate enough to pass beyond the
straits of Vaigatz, but made no new discoveries and
brought but a moderate return to their owners.   The
Russians meanwhile kept up a vigorous coasting-
trade, their ill-shaped and ill-appointed craft generally
being found far in advance of their more pretentious
competitors.

In 1594 the states-general of Holland offered a
premium of twenty-five thousand florins to the lucky
navigator who should open the much desired high-
way.   A squadron of four small vessels commanded
by Cornelis Nay was the first to enter for the prize.
A merchant named Linschoten, possessed of considerable scientific attainments, accompanied the ex-

pedition as commercial agent, and Willem Barentz, who commanded one of the vessels, acted as pilot. They sailed from Holland on the 15th of June 1594, and arrived safely at the bay of Kilduyn, on the coast of Lapland. Here they separated, Nay heading for Vaigatz Straits and Barentz choosing a more northerly route. The latter discovered and named Ys Hoek, or Ice Cape, the northern extremity of Novaia Zemlia, while the other vessels passed through the straits, where they met with numerous Russian *lodkas*, or small craft. This southern division entered the sea of Kara, called by Linschoten the sea of Tartary, on the 1st of August. Wooden crosses were observed at various points of the coast, and the inhabitants bore evidence of intercourse with the Russians by their manner of salutation. The Samoiedes had come in contact with the advancing Muscovites in the interior as well as on the coast.

On the 11th of August, when their astronomical observations placed the vessels fifty leagues to the eastward of the straits, with land still in sight toward the east, this part of the expedition turned back, evidently apprehensive of sharing the fate of their English predecessors, who had been unfortunate in those latitudes. The two divisions fell in with each other on the homeward voyage, and arrived at Amsterdam on the 25th of September of the same year.

A second expedition sailed from Amsterdam on the same errand in 1595. It consisted of not less than seven vessels. Willem Barentz was chief in command, assisted by Heemskerk, Linschoten, and Cornelis Rijp. The departure of this squadron was for some reason delayed until July, and after weathering the North Cape a few of the vessels sailed directly for the White Sea to trade, while the others proceeded through the straits of Vaigatz. They met, as usual, with Russian lodkas, and for the first time definite information was obtained of the great river Yenissei, which the Russians had already reached by land. After prolonged battling against ice and contrary winds and currents, the expedition turned back on the 15th of September and made sail for Amsterdam.

After this second failure the states-general washed their hands of further enterprise in that direction, but the city of Amsterdam still showed some faith in ultimate success by fitting out two ships and intrusting them respectively to Barentz and Rijp. This expedition made an early start, sailing on the 22d of May 1596. Their course was shaped in accordance with Barentz' theory that more to the north there was a better chance of finding an open sea. On the 9th of June they discovered Bear Island in latitude 74° 30'. Still keeping on their first course they again encountered land in latitude 79° 30', Spitzbergen, and in July the two vessels separated in search of a clear channel to the east. On the 26th of August Barentz was forced by a gale into a bay on the east coast of Novaia Zemlia, on which occasion the ice seriously damaged his vessel. Here the venturesome Hollanders constructed a house and passed a winter full of misery, a continued struggle with famishing bears and the deadly cold. Toward spring the castaways constructed two open boats out of remnants of the wreck, fitted them out as well as they could, and put to sea on the 14th of June 1597. Six days later Barentz died. In July the unfortunates fell in with some Russian lodkas and obtained provisions. They finally reached Kilduyn Bay in Lapland, one of the rendezvous of White Sea traders. Several Dutch vessels were anchored there, and one of them was commanded by Rijp, who had returned to Amsterdam and sailed again on a private enterprise. He extended all possible aid to his former companions and obtained passage for them on several vessels. This put an end in Holland to explorations in search of a northern route to India, until the attempts of Hudson in 1608–9. The problem was partially solved by

Deshnef's obscure voyage in 1648, and after another failure by Wood in 1676, Russia made the attempt, Vitus Bering starting from Kamchatka; afterward were the efforts of Shalaürof and of Billings. Finally a Swedish expedition under Nordenskjöld accomplished the feat in 1879, after wintering on the Arctic coast.

CHAPTER II.

WHILE the maritime nations of north-western Europe were thus sending ship after ship into the Arctic
ice-fields in the hope of finding a north-eastern passage
to India, the Russians were slowly but surely forcing
their way over Siberian rivers and steppes, and even
along the Arctic coast from river-mouth to river-
mouth, and that not in search of any India, or other
grand attainment, but only after skins, and to get farther and farther from parental despotism. Their ancient homes had not been abodes of peace, and no
tender reminiscences or patriotic ties bound them to
the soil of Russia. It was rather a yearning for personal freedom, next after the consideration of the
sobol, that drew the poor Slav farther and farther
through forests and swamps away from his place of
birth; he did not care to band for general independence. Rulers were of God, the church said, and he
would not oppose them, but he would if possible escape. In view of these peculiar tendencies the open-

ing of the boundless expanse toward the east was a blessing not only to the oppressed but to the oppressors. The turbulent spirits, who might have caused trouble at home, in early times found their way to Siberia voluntarily, while later the 'paternal' government gathered strength enough to send them there.

A century sable-hunt half round the world this remarkable movement might be called. It was at once a discovery and a conquest, which was to carry Cossack and Russian across the vast continent, and across the narrowed Pacific to the fire-breathing islands. and the glistening mountains and majestic forests of Alaska. The shores of the Black and Caspian seas was the starting-point. Russia's eastern bound was then the Ural Mountains. Anika Stroganof set up salt-works there, and the people at the east brought him furs to trade. They were pretty little skins, and yielded the salt-miner a large profit; so he sent his traders as far as the great river Ob for them. And the autocrat of the empire smiled on these proceedings, and gave the salt-merchant lands, and allowed his descendants to become a power and call themselves counts.

In 1578 the grandson of the first Stroganof received a visit from a Cossack chieftain or *ataman*, named Yermak Timofeief, who with his followers had in Cossack fashion led a life of war and plunder, and was then flying from justice as administered by Ivan Vassilievich II.

Yermak's mounted followers numbered a thousand, and Stroganof was anxious they should move on; so he told them of places toward the east, fine spots for robber-knights to seize and settle on, and he sent men to guide them thither. This was in 1578. At the river Ob the Cossacks found a little Tartar sovereignty, a fragment of the great monarchy of Genghis Khan. The warlike spirit with which Tamerlane had once inspired the Tartars had long since fled. Their little kingdom, in which cattle-herding, the chase, and

traffic were the only pursuits, now remained only
because none had come to conquer them.   The Cossacks were in the full flush of national development.
They had ever been apt learners from the Tartars,
against whom they had often served the Muscovites
as advance guard.   Now Yermak was in a strait.
Behind him was the wrathful tsar, to fall into whose
hands was certain death.   Though his numbers were
small, he must fight for it.   Attacking the Tartars,
in due time he became master of their capital city,
though at the cost of half his little army.   And now
he must have more men.   Perhaps he might buy
friendship of the tsar.   A rich gift of sables, with information that he had conquered for him the kingdom
of Kutchum Khan, accomplished the purpose.   Reenforcements and confirmation of rulership were the
response.   Thus was begun the long journey of the
Russians across the continent.

Vast as is the area of Siberia its several parts are
remarkably similar.   Plants, animals, and men; climate, conditions, and customs, are more alike than on
the other side of the strait of Bering.   The country
and its contents are upon a dead level.   A net-work of
navigation is formed by the upper branches of rivers
flowing into the frozen sea through the *tundras*, or
ice-morass, of the north, so that the same kind of boats
and sledges carry the traveller across the whole country.   The fierce and cunning Cossacks of Russia were
in marked contrast to the disunited semi-nomads of
Siberia, busy as they were taming the reindeer, hunting with dogs, or fighting with the bow and arrow and
lance; and if they could conquer the Tartars of the
Ob there was no reason why they could not march
on to the Pacific.
They were a singular people, brave as Spaniards
and tough as gypsies.   Their weapons, the later European kind, of iron and gunpowder, gave them a vast
superiority over the tribes of Siberia, and their boats

and horses seem to have been made for the purpose. The latter were small and enduring, adequate to the long day's march, and like their masters accustomed to cold, hunger, thirst, and continuous fatigue. Like the chamois and reindeer they would scrape off the snow from their scanty nourishment, or if grass was wanting they were glad to get frozen fish to eat.

The invaders found it well to divide their forces, and advance in small scattered bodies, a dozen warriors sometimes subjugating a tribe; then again some hundreds were required for the occupation of a river-territory or a kingdom. There was no need of a large united army, or of any great discipline. This also suited Cossack ideas and habits, as they were republican in their way. Born equal, they everywhere met on a common footing. They chose their atamans and *sotniks*, or centurions, who, if they did not rule to suit, were quickly deposed and others elected. The highest position was open to the humblest aspirant.

It was on the Tobol that the Cossacks and Russians built their first *ostrog*, or fort, which later became Tobolsk, the head-quarters of their organized government, and the starting-point of their expeditions. Thence their conquering march was straight through the middle of Siberia, the line being equidistant from the mountains of the south and the morasses of the north, and it later became the principal line of traffic. On this line, cutting through the various river regions, the chief colonies of the country were founded. Eastward from Tobolsk, in the territory of the river Ob, the city of Tomsk; eastward from this, on the Yenissei, the city of Yenisseisk; then Irkutsk and Yakutsk in the Lena district, and finally, on the shores of the Pacific, Okhotsk, which stands upon about the same parallel as that of the starting-point. These cities grew successively one out of the other, and for every new river province the last served as a *point d'appui* for the various enterprises, military or commercial. At every important river a halt was made, during which they settled themselves more firmly, and organized their new territory. They built boats, explored up the rivers, and down them even to the frozen ocean, where they founded little settlements.

The Cossacks themselves were a light troop, but they were preceded by a still lighter, a flying advance guard, called the *promyshleniki*, a kind of Russian *coureurs des bois*. They were freebooters who hunted on their own account and at their own risk. No one could control them. They flitted everywhere in the woods and morasses, companions of wild beasts. They made the several first discoveries in Siberia, and brought home the earliest information of hitherto unknown parts.

In the spring of 1628 the Cossacks reached Lena River. The party consisted of ten men under Vassili Bugor, who had crossed over from the Yenissei on snow-shoes. Arrived at the Lena, the great central stream, lying midway between the beginning and end of their century-march, they built a boat and went down and up the river for some distance, spreading dismay and collecting their tribute of sable-skins. Ten Cossacks against the inhabitants of that great valley! I know of nothing in American history that equals it. After making the people swear submission, Bugor posted two of his men at the middle point on the river, and two each at points two hundred miles above and two hundred miles below. After three years of bluster and traffic Bugor returned to the Yenissei. In 1632 a Cossack chieftain named Beketof sailed far down the Lena and built the first ostrog on this river, among the Yakut nation. This was the Yakutski Ostrog, out of which rose later the city of Yakutsk, the capital of eastern Siberia, and which finally served as head-quarters for expeditions to the Arctic and to the Pacific. From the Lena, Siberia extends, gradually narrowing, about five or six hundred leagues further to the east. The length of the rivers decreases with the breadth of the land, and the mighty Lena is followed by the smaller Yana, Indigirka, Kolima, and at last, in the farthest corner by the Anadir which empties into the Pacific. The dis-

EASTERN SIBERIA.

covery of these more distant rivers of Siberia began in 1638. Some Cossacks, under the leadership of a certain Busa, reached the Yana by water from the mouth of the Lena, while others, under the sotnik Ivanof, penetrated on horseback to its sources from

Yakutsk. Here they heard of the Indigirka, and the year following they trotted on to the river.

In 1639 the rugged mountains on the eastern border of Siberia were crossed on horseback and on snow-shoes, and an ostrog was built on the sea-shore to which the name of Okhotsk was given. Thus the Pacific Ocean was first reached by the Russians on the shore of the Okhotsk Sea, a place destined to play an important part in the advance toward America. The discovery was achieved by Andreï Kopilof, a Cossack leader, who made his way thither from the Lena at the head of a small party, thus completing the march across the continent of Asia, in its broadest part, in about sixty years from the time of Yermak's visit to Stroganof.

The ascent of the Lena brought the Russians to Lake Baikal, and showed them another route to the Pacific, through China by way of the Amoor. The rich silver deposits in that quarter drew population from the north-western ostrogs, something after the manner of a California mining rush. The Mantchoo Tartars were most of them absent from home at the time, completing their conquest of the celestial empire, which left the Amoor region comparatively defenceless. On the return of the Tartars the Russians were obliged to relinquish some of their pretensions, though they retained their hold on the mines, and continued trade with China. In 1643 Vassili Posharkof set out from Yakutsk with one hundred and thirty-two men, and following the course of the Amoor to its mouth, and thence proceeding north and westward some distance along the coast, returned to Yakutsk in 1646 by a different route, and one direct from the Okhotsk Sea.

Sixteen Cossacks on the Indigirka took captive the ruling prince of the country. On their neighing steeds they charged his forces, armed with only bows and arrows, and vanquished them with great slaughter. In 1640 they had completed the conquest of the whole river, eight hundred miles long. Forthwith they again began to listen to tales of new streams in the east, of the Aliseia and the Kolima. Strengthened by additional troops they proceeded in 1646 to subdue this region. East of the Kolima, where Siberia approaches its termination, dwelt the warlike Chukchi, the Tschuk-tschi of German writers. Their land did not allure with sables or silver-mines, but a new attraction was found for the European. Dating existence from primeval revulsions, were found on the shores and along the banks of rivers vast deposits of fossil ivory, the tusks of the ancient mammoth elephant. Similar deposits had been found before in other parts of Siberia, but the largest were in the far north-east along the shores of the land of the Chukchi. This substance, which was called precious and a staple, exercised a powerful influence in the conquest of Siberia and in attracting emigrants to the north. Even at the present day it plays an important part in Siberian traffic, and is also found in the northern regions of America.

Isaï Ignatief, with a company of promyshleniki, set out in search of mammoth tusks toward the Chukchi country. From the mouth of the Kolima he proceeded a short distance along the Arctic seaboard in boats. The natives were shy at first, but after some traffic they told the Russians of a large mountainous land which lay westward and toward the north pole, and the outline of whose coasts could be seen from time to time from the Siberian shore. This land, they said, was rich in ivory, and there were the most beautiful tusks heaped up there in huge banks and mounds. Many believed that it was peopled and connected with Novaia Zemlia in the west and with America in the east.

With a daring which the well prepared Arctic explorer of our time can scarcely understand, the Russians committed themselves to their fragile *lodki*, or open sail-boats, of rough planks tied together with thongs, and struck out for that land of ivory toward the north pole. They sailed without compass out into that sea; they battled with the ice found there; their barks were shattered; they were frozen in at sea hundreds of versts from land. They even wintered there that they might advance a little farther the following summer. What can science or modern adventure show as a parallel? Lost on a wilderness of ice, all warmth departed, hungry, ill-clothed, with scarcely any shelter, yet still determined to achieve the land of ivory. Perhaps some of them did reach it; let us hope so, and that they obtained their fill of ivory. Nearly two centuries later the first light concerning this land came through the travels of Baron Wrangell, when it was recognized as a group of islands and named New Siberia.

Ignatief could hardly be said to have made the acquaintance of the Chukchi, so eager had he been after ivory. But better success attended the efforts of the Russians a little later. By order of the tsar Alexis, seven *kotches*, a small decked craft, were sent along the shore in search of the mouth of the river Anadir, whose head-waters had been sighted by the venturesome promyshleniki. The expedition set out from the mouth of the Kolima June 20, 1648. Of four of these vessels nothing further is mentioned; but we know that the remaining three were commanded respectively by Simeon Deshnef and Gerassim Ankudinof, Cossack chiefs, and Fedot Alexcief, *peredovchik*, that is to say, leader of promyshleniki. Deshnef, who forwarded a detailed account of his adventures to Yakutsk, speaks but incidentally of what happened before reaching Cape Chukotsk. Then he says: "This isthmus, is quite different from that which is bound by the River Tschukotschia west of the River Kolima. It lies between the north, and north-east, and turns circular towards the river Anadir. On the Russian, that is, the west side of it, there falls a brook into the sea, by which the Tschuktschi have erected a scaffold like a tower of the bones of whales. Over-against the isthmus (it is not mentioned on which side) there are two islands in the sea, upon which were seen people of the Tschuktschi nation, thro' whose lips were run pieces of the teeth of the sea-horse. One might sail from the isthmus to the river Anadir, with a fair wind, in three days and nights, and it might be travelled by land within the same time." The kotche commanded by Ankudinof was wrecked at the cape, but the inmates were saved by the other vessels. On the 20th of September Desh-nef and Alexeief made a landing and had an engage-ment with the Chukchi, during which Alexeief was wounded. After this the two kotches lost sight of each other and did not meet again. Deshnef drifted about until October, and at last he was also wrecked, as it appears, some distance to the south of the Ana-dir, in the vicinity of the river Olutorsk. He had only twenty-five men left, and with these he set out by land in search of the Anadir; but having no guide, he wandered about for ten weeks and at last reached its banks not far from the mouth. One half of his command started up the river, but hunger compelled them to return. The following summer Deshnef as-cended the Anadir in boats. He met with a tribe called the Ananli, made them tributary after con-siderable resistance, and founded the settlement of ostrog Anadirsk. Here he remained till 1650, when he was joined on the 23d of April by the Cossack Motora with a volunteer expedition from Kolimsk. Another expedition under Mikhaïl Stadukhin followed immediately after; but the latter, jealous of the suc-cesses already achieved by the others, went more to the southward for further discoveries and was never heard of again. Deshnef subsequently encountered a Yakut woman who had been with Fedot Alexeief and was told by her that Fedot and Ankudinof had been wrecked and that both had died of scurvy among the Koriaks.[1] No mention is made by any of this party of having seen the American continent, though it is not impossible that some of them did see it. They were obliged to hug the Asiatic shore, and the opposite coast can be seen from there only on a clear day.

Another account of Deshnef's voyage places it at a still earlier date, between 1580 and 1590, but the inaccuracy of this is evident.[2]

Last of all this region to be unveiled was that narrow south-eastern strip of Siberia, the Kamchatka peninsula, which, about the size and shape of Italy, projects six hundred geographical miles from the continent into Bering and Okhotsk seas. The Cossack Luka Morosko started from Anadirsk in 1669 with a roving band and penetrated far to the southward, but what he saw was not known until some time afterward. The name Kamchatka was known in Yakutsk by report from 1690. Some years later the first party of riders set out thither under the leadership of the Cossack colonel, Atlassof, who passes for the actual

---

[1] The voyage of Deshnef was almost forgotten when Muller found a record of it in Kolimsk. *Morskoi Sbornik, 1764,* 37–40; *Jefferys' Muller's Voy.,* v.–ix.

[2] An anonymous article in a literary monthly published in St Petersburg in 1769 contains the following: 'The honor of having taken the first steps toward the discovery of these new islands (which on account of their number may justly be termed an archipelago) belongs to the tsar Ivan Vassilievich II. After having conquered the whole of Siberia he desired to know its boundaries north and east, and the tribes inhabiting those far-off regions. For this purpose he sent out an expedition, which only returned during the reign of his son and successor, Tsar Feodor Ivanovich, bringing the first news of the existence of the Polar Sea on the northern shore of Siberia, and another vast ocean in the east. In some of the old Siberian archives documents have been discovered which prove that the above-mentioned expedition made some important discoveries in the Arctic Sea, and, following along its shores to the north-east, one of the smaller vessels finally rounded the extreme point, Cape Chukotsk, and arrived safely on the coast of Kamchatka. The troubled times which came over Russia after this achievement during the lawless reigns of the usurper Boris Godunof, and of the False Dmitri after him, made it impossible to think of further explorations of the Kamchatka country, and even the name was almost forgotten after the lapse of a few years.' *Yeshemiassachnaia Sochinenia, March, 1769,* 336–7.

discoveror and conqueror of Kamchatka. The Russians found in Kamchatka Japanese writings and even some Japanese sailors cast ashore there by shipwreck. From the latter they learned that the land stretched far away to the south, and were at first induced to believe that Kamchatka reached as far as Japan; as indeed it is laid down on the oldest maps.

Like the Spaniards in Mexico, the first Russians in Kamchatka were highly honored, almost deified, by the natives. That the aboriginal Americans should have ascribed divinity to the first Spaniards is not strange. They came to them from off the limitless and mysterious water in huge white-winged canoes, in martial array, with gaudy trappings and glittering armor; they landed with imposing ceremonies; their leaders were men of dignified bearing and suave manners, and held their followers in control. The first appearance of the Russians in Kamchatka, however, presents an entirely different aspect; surely the Kamchatkans of that day were satisfied with ungainly gods.

The Cossacks who came with Atlassof were rough-looking fellows, of small size, clad in furs like the Kamchatkans, most of them the offspring of unions between half Tartars and women from the native tribes of Siberia. They were filthy in their habits, and had just completed a weary ride of many months through the wilderness. They were naturally cruel and placed no restraint on their beastly propensities; nevertheless they were called gods by beings of a lower order than themselves, and it were well to propitiate them. Indeed, they did possess one attribute of the deity: they could kill. A few rusty firelocks, a few pounds of powder, and they were omnipotent. Gods are prone to quarrel as well as men, but can they die? The Kamchatkans thought not; so when they saw one of Atlassof's men struck down by another, saw the warm red blood gush from a mortal wound to stain the virgin snow, the spell

was broken. These were no gods; and thenceforth
the Russians had to fight for the supremacy. After
many expeditions and many battles, for these people
were in truth brave and lovers of liberty, the Russians, in 1706, reached the southern extremity of
the Kamchatka peninsula, where they saw the northernmost islands of the Kurile chain which points to
Japan.

Thus did the Russians, after the lapse of a century
full of toil and ravages, reach the extreme end of the
Old World. At the beginning of the eighteenth
century they found themselves on a separate strip of
coast, twelve hundred miles long, facing another
twelve hundred miles' strip, the north-west end of
America. It was hardly to be expected that they
would rest contented where they were.

The natives of Kamchatka did not appear to have
any knowledge of America, so that the Russians were
left to learn of the *bolshaia zemlia*, or 'great land'
toward the east, slowly and as they were able. Tall
trunks of fir and other trees which did not grow in
Kamchatka were thrown from time to time by currents upon the shores along the east side of that
country. Large flocks of land-birds came to the coast
occasionally from the east and disappeared again in
the same direction. Whales came from the east with
spear-heads in their backs different from any used in
Kamchatka; and now and then foreign-built boats
and other unusual objects were washed upon the
eastern coast. Even the waves carrying these tokens
did not have as long a swell as those to the south.
Hence they said this land must front a sea wholly
or partially enclosed, and that toward the north the
sides must be nearest together. Surely the Chukchi
should know something about it. Indeed, often in
their fights with these people the Russians had taken
captives with pieces of walrus ivory thrust through
their lips and cheeks, and speaking a language different from that of the Chukchi. And the story was

that the great land was no island, but had rivers and chains of mountains without end.[3]

About this time the *stolnik knias*, Vassili Ivanovich Gagarin, was present at Yakutsk, sent thither by his uncle, the governor, Prince Matveï Petrovich Gagarin, to make discoveries. He issued several orders to the *voivod*, or nobleman, Trauernicht, who commanded in that section, one of them being that he should "make diligent inquiry about the islands situated opposite the mouth of the river Kolima, and the land of Kamchatka; what people inhabited them; under whose jurisdiction they were; what was their employment;

---

[3] Matveï Strebykhin, commander of the ostrog of Anadirsk, was instructed in 1711 to collect information concerning the Chukchi and an island or continent lying to the eastward of their country. One of the results of this investigation was a deposition made and sworn to by the Yakout Cossack Peter Elianovich Popof, the promyshlenik Yegor Vassilievich Toldin, and the newly converted Yukagir Ivan Vassilievich Tereshkin, and dated Anadirsk, Sept. 2, 1711. It was to the effect that on the 13th of January 1711 Popof and the two others, who served as interpreters, were sent out by Governor Fedor Kotovskoi to visit the valley of the Anadir and receive tribute from some of the Chukchi tribes. This done they were to proceed to the cape, Chukotskoi Noss, in order to persuade the Chukchi living there to become tributary to Russia. Popof met everywhere with a peremptory refusal to pay tribute. The Chukchi said that formerly the Russians had come to their country in ships, and they paid no tribute then, and therefore they would not do it now, and Popof must expect no hostages from them. The Chukchi who dwell near the cape keep tame reindeer, and in order to find pasture for their animals they frequently change their habitation. Opposite the cape on either side, in the sea of Kolima as well as in that of Anadir, islands have been seen, which the Chukchi call a large country, and they say that the people living there have large teeth in their mouths, projecting through the cheeks. Popof found ten of these men, prisoners among the Chukchi, with their cheeks still disfigured by the projecting ivory. In summer time they sail across to the Great Land in one day, and in the winter a swift reindeer team can make it in one day over the ice. In the other land there are sables, wolves, and bears. The people are, like the Chukchi, without any government. They have the wood of cedar, larch, and fir trees, which the Chukchi sometimes obtain for their bidars, weapons, and huts. About 2,000 people live at and near the cape, but the inhabitants of the other country are said to be three times that number, which is confirmed not only by prisoners but also by one of the Chukchi, who has often been there. Another statement was essentially as follows: Opposite the cape lies an island, within sight, of no great extent, devoid of timber, and inhabited by people resembling the Chukchi, though they speak their own language. It is half a day's voyage to the island from the cape. Beyond the island there is a large continent, scarcely to be seen from it, and that only on very clear days. In calm weather one may row over the sea to the continent, which is inhabited. There are large forests, and great rivers fall into the sea. The inhabitants have fortified dwellings with ramparts of earth. Their clothes are the skins of sable and fox. The Chukchi are often at war with them. *Yeshemiassachnaia Sochinenia, 1786*, 152-6; *Muller's Voy.*, 24-6.

how large the islands were and how distant from the
continent." The commanders and Cossacks ordered
to those regions were all commissioned with such inquiries, with the promise of special rewards for such
service from the emperor, who should be informed of
any discoveries by express as soon as any authentic
report was forwarded to Yakutsk.

Orders had been issued as early as 1710 to the
commanders of Ust-Yana and Kolima to give these
discoveries their special attention. In answer, a deposition was sent in by the Cossack Yakov Permakof
of Ust-Yana, stating that he once sailed from the
Lena to the River Kolima, and that on the east side
of Sviatoi Noss he had sighted an island in the sea,
but was unable to ascertain if it was inhabited. There
was also an island situated directly opposite the river
Kolima, an island that might be seen from the continent. Mountains could be seen upon it, but it was
uncertain whether it was inhabited.

The voivod Trauernicht was further encouraged,[4]
and prepared two expeditions, one from the mouth of
the river Yana and one from the Kolima, simultaneously to search for the supposed island; for which
purpose the men were either to go in boats or travel
on the ice till it could be definitely ascertained if such
an island existed. Concerning the first-named expedition, which was begun by Merkuri Vagin, a Cossack,
Müller found several reports at Yakutsk, but in his
opinion the documents did not deserve much consideration.

Vagin departed from Yakutsk during the autumn
of 1711, with eleven other Cossacks, and in May

---

[4] Knias Matveï Gagarin wrote to the voivod, under date of January 28,
1711, as follows: 'I have heard by Cossacs and Dworanes from Jakutzk
that you intend to send a party of Cossacs and volunteers to the new country or island opposite the mouth of the river Kolima, but that you hesitated
about doing it without orders; therefore I have found it necessary to tell you
that you should by no means neglect to do it; and if other islands may be
discovered, you will be pleased to do the same with respect to them. But
above all things the expedition is to be made this present year, 1711. This
I write to you by order of his Czarish Majesty.' *Müller's Voy.*, Intr., xv.-xvi.

1712 he made a voyage from Ust-Yanskoie Simovie to the frozen sea. On this occasion the Yakov Permakof, previously mentioned, served as his guide. The party used sledges drawn by dogs, and after following the coast to Sviatoi Noss, they emerged upon the frozen ocean and travelled directly north. They came to a desert island, without wood, which Vagin estimated to be from nine to twelve days' travel in circumference. From this island they saw, farther to the north, another island or land, but as the spring was already too far advanced, Vagin dared not proceed, and his provisions running short the whole party returned to the continent, to provide themselves with a sufficient supply of fish during the summer. The point where he reached the coast was between Sviatoi Noss and the river Khroma. A Cossack had formerly erected a cross there, and after him it was named Kataief Krest. Being out of provisions, they failed in an attempt to reach the Khroma, and were compelled to eke out an existence on the sea-coast, devouring even the sledge-dogs. Vagin, however, still intended to prosecute his explorations; but his Cossacks, remembering their sufferings, to prevent a repetition, rose against their leader and murdered him, his son, the guide Permakof, and one promyshlenik. The crime was revealed by one of the accomplices and the offenders were brought to justice. During the trial it appeared that the guide Yakov Permakof did not believe the supposed large island to be really an island, but only vapor.

The other expedition, that from the Kolima, met with no better success. It consisted of a single vessel commanded by the Cossack Vassili Stadukhin, with twenty-two men. He merely observed a single promontory, extending into the sea to the east of Kolima, surrounded by ice, impenetrable by their vessels.[5]

---

[5] They used *shitiki*, or boats, the planks of which were fastened together with rawhide straps and thongs. They measured about 30 feet in length and 12 feet broad, with a flat bottom, calked with moss. The sails consisted of soft,

Another expedition was undertaken by a Cossack named Amossof. He started in 1723 with a party to search for an island reported to extend from the mouth of the Yana beyond the mouth of the Indigirka. He proceeded to the Kolima, and was prepared to sail in July 1724. According to his account he found such shoals of ice before him that he changed his course and sailed along the coast eastward to the so-called habitation of Kopaï, which he reached on the 7th of August. Here again ice drove him back, and he returned to the Kolima. The dwelling of Kopaï was about two hundred versts east of that river. Amossof also mentioned a small island situated near the continent, and during the following winter he made another journey, with sledges, of which he sent an account to the chancellery of Yakutsk. The report was to the effect that on the 3d of November 1724 he set out from Nishnoie Kolimskoie Simovie, and met with land in the frozen sea, returning to Kolima on the 23d of the same month. Upon this land he saw nothing but old huts covered with earth; it was unknown to what people they belonged, and what had become of them. Want of provisions, and especially of dog-food, had obliged him to turn back without making any further discoveries. This journey was also impeded by ridges of ice piled to a great height, which had to be crossed with the sledges. The place where Amossof left the continent to go over to the island is between the Chukotcha and the Aliscia rivers. It was an island, in circumference about a day's travel with dogs, and about the same distance from the continent, whence its high mountains can easily be seen. To the north were two other islands, likewise mountainous and separated by narrow straits. These he had not visited and did not know their extent. The first was without trees; no tracks of animals

dressed reindeer-skin, and in place of ropes, straps of elk-skin were used. The anchors were pieces of wood, to which heavy stones were fastened. *Muller's Voy.*, Introd., xviii.

were seen but those of reindeer, which live on moss.
The old huts had been constructed of drift-wood and
covered with earth. It is probable that they had
been made by Yukagirs or Chukchi, who had fled
before the first advance of the Russians, and subsequently returned to the continent.[6]

Kopaï, mentioned in Amossof's narrative, was a
chief among the Shelages, living at the mouths of the
Kolima and Aliseia rivers. He first paid tribute to
Russia at the request of Vilegin, a promyshlenik, and
in 1724 he paid tribute to Amossof. Subsequently,
however, he broke his allegiance and killed some of
Amossof's party.

The first passage by sea from Okhotsk to Kamchatka took place in 1716. One of the sailors, a
native of Hoorn in Holland, named Bush, was alive
when Müller visited Yakutsk in 1736, and he related
to him the circumstances. On the 23d of May 1714
a party of twenty Cossacks and sailors arrived at Okhotsk under command of Kosma Sokolof. These were
followed in July by some carpenters and shipwrights.
The carpenters built a vessel for sea-service, resembling the Russian lodkas in use between Arkhangel,
Pustozersk, and Novaia Zemlia. The vessel was durable—fifty-one feet long, with eighteen feet beam, and
drew when laden only three and a half feet of water.
Embarking in June 1716, they followed the coast
north-easterly till they came to the mouth of the river
Ola, where a contrary wind drove them across the sea
to Kamchatka. The land first sighted was a promontory north of the river Tigil, where they cast anchor.
Some went ashore, but found only empty huts. The
Kamchatkans had watched the approach of the vessel
and fled to the mountains. The navigators again
set sail, passed the Tigil, and arrived in one day at

---

[6] Müller does not seem to have placed much faith in Amossof's report.
He expresses the opinion that it was framed to serve private purposes and
subsequently altered to suit circumstances. *Voy.*, Introd., xx.

the mouth of the little river Kharinzobka, in the vicinity of two small islands. From Kharinzobka they went the following day to the river Itcha, keeping the sea at night and making for the land in the morning. Here, again, some men were put ashore, but they could find neither inhabitants nor houses. They soon returned and the vessel sailed down the coast till they came to the river Krutogorova. They intended to make this river, but missed its mouth, and finding a convenient bay a little to the south they anchored. On searching the country, they met with a girl who was gathering edible roots in the field, and she showed them some huts, inhabited by twelve Kamchatka Cossacks, stationed there to receive tribute. The Cossacks were sent for, and served as guides and interpreters. The vessel was then brought to the mouth of the river Kompakova, and it was resolved to winter there.[7]

Early in May 1717 they put to sea, and on the fourth day became lodged between fields of ice, and were held there for over five weeks. At last they regained the coast of Okhotsk between the river Ola and Tanisky ostrog, where they stayed several days, and then returned to Okhotsk about the middle of July. From that time there was constant navigation between Okhotsk and Kamchatka.

In 1719 the Russian government sent two navigators or surveyors, Ivan Yevreinof and Fedor Lushin, to make geographical observations, and specially to find, if possible, among the Kurile Islands the one from which the Japanese were said to obtain gold and silver. They arrived at Yakutsk in May 1720, crossed over to Kamchatka the same summer, and returned to Yakutsk in 1721.[8] Yevreinof left Lushin in Sibe-

---

[7] During the stay of Sokolof and Bush on the Kompakova, a whale was cast ashore, which had in its body a harpoon of European make, marked with Roman letters. *Muller's Voy.*, Introd., xlii.

[8] The results were kept secret and Müller could not get access to their instructions, so that nothing more is known about this voyage. *Muller's Voy.*, Introd., xliii.

ria and proceeded to Russia to report to the tsar, taking with him a map of the Kurile Islands as far as he had explored them. For the next three years, that is to say to 1724, rumors and ideas concerning the east assumed more and more definiteness in Kamchatka, and at Okhotsk, Yakutsk, and other Russian settlements, at last reaching Moscow and St Petersburg, there to find attentive listeners.[9]

Obviously the Great Land opposite, if any such there was, would present aspects quite different to the tough Cossacks and to the more susceptible Europeans from the south. The American Siberia, this farthermost north-west was once called, and if to the American it was Siberia, to the Siberian it was America. The eastern end of Asia is lashed by the keen eastern tempests and stands bleak and bare, without vegetation, and the greater part of the year wrapped in ice and snow. The western shores of America, though desolate and barren enough within the limits of Bering sea, are wonderfully different where they are washed by the Pacific and protected from the east by high chains of mountains. Here they are open to the mild westerly winds and warm ocean currents; they have a damper climate, and, in consequence, a more vigorous growth of trees and plants. In comparatively high latitudes they are covered with fine forests down to the sea-shore. This is a contrast which repeats itself in all northern countries. The ruder Sweden in the east contrasts in a like manner with the milder Norway in the west; the desolate

---

[9] Müller relates 'that in the year 1715 there lived at Kamchatka a man of a foreign nation, who, upon account of the Kamchatkan cedar-nuts and the low shrubs on which they grow, said that he came from a country to the east where there were large cedars which bore bigger nuts than those of Kamchatka; that his country was situated to the east of Kamchatka; that there were found in it great rivers where he lived which discharged themselves westward into the Kamchatkan sea; that the inhabitants called themselves Tontoli; they resembled in their manner of living the people of Kamchatka and made use of skin boats or *baidares* like those of the Kamchadales. That many years ago he went over with some more of his countrymen to Karaginskoi ostrow where his companions were slain by the inhabitants, and he alone made his escape to Kamchatka.' *Voy.*, Introd., xxviii.

eastern coast of Greenland buried in polar ice, with its western coast inhabited, and at times gay with flowers and verdure. Thus the great eastern country, the *bolshaia zemlia*, rich in harbors, shelter, woods, and sea and land animals, might well become by report among the north-eastern Asiatics a garden of paradise.

CHAPTER III.

THE KAMCHATKA EXPEDITIONS.

1725–1740.

THE excessive curiosity of Peter the Great extended
further than to ship-building, astronomy, and general
geography. Vast as was the addition of Siberia to
the Russian empire there lay something more beyond,
still indistinct and shadowy in the world's mind, and
the astute Peter determined to know what it was.
The sea of Okhotsk had been found, and it was in the
same latitude as the Baltic; the ostrog of Okhotsk
had been built, and it stood upon almost exactly the
same parallel as St Petersburg. Might not there be
for him an American Russia, as already there was a
European and an Asiatic Russia? And might not
this new Russia, occupying the same relative position
to America that the old Russia did to Europe, be
worth more to him than a dozen Siberias? He would
see. And he would know, too, and that at once,
whether the continents of Asia and America joined.

(35)

This would be a good opportunity likewise to try his new ships, his new discipline, and see what the skilled gentlemen whom he had invited from Austria, and Prussia, and Holland could do for him. There were many around him whom his enthusiasm had inspired, and who wished to try their mettle in strange adventure.

Such were the thoughts arising in the fertile brain of the great Peter which led to what may be called the two Kamchatka expeditions; that is, two principal expeditions from Kamchatka, with several subordinate and collateral voyages, the first of which was to ascertain whether Asia and America joined or were separate, and the second to thoroughly explore eastern Siberia, to discover and examine the American coast opposite, and to learn something more of the Kurile Islands and Japan. Both explorations were under the command of Vitus Bering, a Danish captain in the Russian service, who was engaged on the first about five years, the second series occupying some sixteen years, not wholly, however, under this commander.

For the guidance of his admiral, Count Apraxin, the tsar drew up instructions with his own hand. Two decked boats were to be built at Kamchatka, and, to assist Bering in the command, lieutenants Martin Spanberg and Alexeï Chirikof were appointed. Other officers as well as ship-builders and seamen were chosen, and on February 5, 1725, the expedition set out overland through Siberia. Three days thereafter the monarch died; but his instructions were faithfully carried out by his successors, Catherine the wife and Elizabeth the daughter.

Much trouble was experienced in crossing the continent, in obtaining provisions, and in making ready the ships; so that it was not until the 21st of August 1727 that Bering with Chirikof set sail in the *Fortuna*, from Okhotsk, for the southern end of the Kamchatkan peninsula, where by July of the following year they had ready another vessel, the *Gavril*, or Gabriel. Leaving the river Kamchatka the 20th of July, they coasted the eastern shore of the peninsula northward, till on the 8th of August they found themselves in latitude 64° 30', at the river Anadir. The Chukchi there told them that after rounding East Cape the coast turned toward the west. Continuing, they passed and named St Lawrence Island, and the 16th of August they were in latitude 67° 18', having passed the easternmost point of Asia, and through the strait of Bering. There the coast turned abruptly westward, as they had been told. If it continued in that direction, as was more than probable, Asia and America were not united.[1] Bering's mission was accomplished, and he therefore returned, reaching Kamchatka in September.

In connection with this first voyage of Bering, two expeditions were undertaken in the same direction under the auspices of Afanassiy Shestakof, a chief of the Yakutsk Cossacks. This bold man, whose energy was of that reckless, obstinate type that knows no defeat, went to St Petersburg and made several proposals to the senate for the subjection of the independent Chukchi and Koriaks and the unruly Kamchatkans. The eloquence with which he advanced his scheme procured him applause and success. He was appointed chief of an expedition in which to accomplish his heart's desire.

The admiralty appointed a Hollander, Jacob Hens, pilot; Ivan Fedorof, second in command, Mikhaïl Gvozdef, "geodesist," or surveyor; Herdebal, searcher of ores, and ten sailors. He was to proceed both by land and by sea. From the arsenal at Catherineburg, Siberia, he was to be provided with small cannons and mortars, and ammunition, and a captain of the Siberian regiment of dragoons at Tobolsk, Dmitri Pavlutzki,

---

[1] Müller, *Voy.* 4, is in error when he says that 'the circumstances on which the captain founded his judgment were false, he being then in a bay which, although one shore did trend to the west, the opposite shore ran again to the east.' Bering's suppositions were correct in every particular.

was ordered to join him, each receiving command over four hundred Cossacks, while at the same time all the Cossacks stationed in ostrogs and *simovies*, or winter-quarters, in the Chukchi district, were placed at their disposal. With these instructions Shestakof returned to Siberia in June 1727. At Tobolsk he remained till late in November, wintered on the upper Lena, and arrived at Yakutsk the next summer. There a dispute arose between Shestakof and Pavlutzki, which caused their separation. In 1729 Shestakof went to Okhotsk and there took possession, for the purposes of his expedition, of the vessels with which Bering had lately returned from Kamchatka. On the 1st of September he despatched his cousin, the *syn-boyarski*, or bastard noble, Ivan Shestakof, in the *Gavril* to the River Ud, whence he was to proceed to Kamchatka and begin explorations, while he himself sailed in the *Fortuna*. This vessel was wrecked near Taniski ostrog, and nearly all on board perished, Shestakof barely saving his life in a canoe. With a small remnant of his men and some friendly Tunguses and Koriaks he set out for Kamchatka on foot, but on the 14th of March 1730 he was overpowered near the gulf of Penshinsk by a numerous body of Chukchi and received a mortal wound. Only three days before this Shestakof had sent orders to Taniski ostrog that the Cossack Tryfon Krupischef should embark for Bolsheretsk in a sea-going vessel, thence make his way round the southern point of the peninsula, touch at Nishekamchatsk, and proceed to the river Anadir. The inhabitants of the "large country lying opposite to this river" he must ask to pay tribute to Russia. Gvozdef, the navigator, was to be taken on board if he desired, and shown every respect.

After battling with adverse winds and misfortunes for about two years, the explorers passed northward along the Asiatic shore, by the gulf of Anadir, noting the Diomede Islands, and perhaps catching a glimpse of the American shore. The leaders were quarrelling

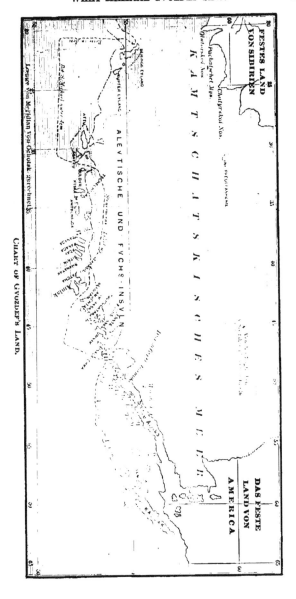

CHART OF GVOZDEF'S LAND.

continually, and Fedorof, the navigator in command, was lame and confined to his bed during nearly all the voyage. On their return to Kamchatka they made the most contradictory statements before the authorities. From Gvozdef's report we are told that at some time during the year 1730 he found himself between latitude 65° and 66°, "on a strange coast, situated opposite, at a small distance from the country of the Chukchi, and that he found people there, but could not speak with them for want of an interpreter."[2]

The land expedition was more successful. In September 1730 Jacob Hens, the pilot, received intelligence from Pavlutzki, dated at Nishnekolimsk, to the effect that Shestakof's death would not delay the expedition. Hens was to go with one of the vessels left at Okhotsk by Bering, to the river Anadir, to the head-waters of which Pavlutzki was shortly to march. Whereupon Hens proceeded in the *Gavril* to the mouth of the Kamchatka, where he arrived in July 1731, and was told that a rebellious band of Kamchatkans had come to Nishnekamchatsk ostrog, killed most of the Russians there, and set fire to the houses. The few remaining Russians took shelter in the vessel, and Hens sent men and reduced the Kamchatkans to obedience. This, however, prevented his going to the Anadir River.

[2] *Müller's Voyages*, 8-11. Of the commander of this expedition, Ivan Fedorof, we have but little information beyond the fact that he died in February 1733, and that he had been with Shestakof's expedition in 1727; that he had been ordered to join him together with the mate Hens, and the surveyor Gvozdef. His companion and assistant, and finally successor in command, Mikhaïl Spiridonovich Gvozdef, began his education in 1716, at the school of navigation, and in 1719 attended the St Petersburg Naval Academy, being in the surveying class. In 1721 he was sent on government duty to Novogorod, where he remained till 1725. In 1727 he graduated as surveyor, and was sent to Siberia to join Shestakof. After his exploration in Bering Strait, he was arrested in 1735 by the governor of Siberia at Tobolsk, upon an erroneous accusation, and sent back to Okhotsk in 1736. In 1741 he explored and surveyed the Okhotsk coast for 200 versts southward, and in 1742 he accompanied midshipman Schelting to the Shantar Islands, at the mouth of the Amoor. After the disbandment of the Kamchatka expedition he remained in Siberia till 1754, when he was appointed teacher in the naval corps of cadets. The date of his death is not known. *Zapiski, Hydrografi-cheskago Departamenta*, ix. 78-87.

It is possible that Gvozdef's voyage was of greater importance than the

Meanwhile Pavlutzki had arrived at Anadirskoi ostrog in September 1730, and the following year he undertook a campaign against the obstinate Chukchi. On the 12th of March 1731 he put in motion his column, composed of 215 Russians, 160 Koriaks, and 60 Yukagirs, moving along the head-waters of some of the northern tributaries of the Anadir, and then turning northward to the coast of the Arctic. After marching two months at the rate of about ten versts a day, stopping frequently to rest, Pavlutzki arrived at the frozen sea, near the mouth of a river. For two weeks he travelled eastward along the coast, mostly upon the ice and far from the shore. This was done, probably, for the purpose of avoiding an encounter with the natives, but at last, on the 7th of June, a large body of Chukchi was seen advancing,

writers of that period ascribed to it. In the year 1743 Captain Spanberg of Bering's expedition was commissioned by the imperial government to investigate the results of this voyage. In case of a failure to obtain satisfactory information, Spanberg was to take command of another expedition to review and correct the work of Gvozdef and Fedorof. Spanberg evidently entered upon this duty with his usual energy, and as upon his report the order for a new expedition was countermanded from St Petersburg, we may suppose that Spanberg at least was satisfied that the information obtained by Gvozdef and Fedorof was satisfactory. Spanberg found in addition to two depositions made to Gvozdef on the subject an original journal kept by Fedorof alone, 'for his own personal remembrance.' With the help of this document a chart was compiled by Spanberg under Gvozdef's supervision, illustrative of the voyage in question. The chart was finally transmitted to the admiralty college, where copies were executed, but the original can no longer be found. In his journal we find, after a detailed accurate description of the Diomede Islands, leaving no room for doubt as to their identity, an entry to the effect that after sailing from the mouth of the Anadir River they steered in an easterly direction, and after sailing five days with favorable wind, they saw land on their left side (northerly side), and hoped to find it an island. They made directly for this land, but when they had approached within half a verst, they saw that it was not an island, but a continent. The coast was sand and there were dwellings on the shore, and a number of people. There was also timber on this land, spruce and larch. They coasted along this land, keeping it on the left side for five days, and then, not seeing the end of it, they did not dare to go any farther in that direction because the water became too shallow for their small craft. The same statement was confirmed in the deposition of Shurikhin, a member of the expedition, also examined by Spanberg. Gvozdef, Fedorof, and Shurikhin agree in the statement that the natives of the 'continent' used skin boats covered on top or the Eskimo's kiak, which is found only on the American side of the strait. The description of the land would fit well the country about Norton Sound, the only point on all that coast where the timber approaches the shore. The shallow water found going to the southward, would also indicate that they approached the remarkable shoals lying off the mouths of the Yukon River. *Sokolof, Istoria; Morskoi Sbornik*, passim.

and as they would not listen to Pavlutzki's summons
to obedience, he attacked and put them to flight.
About the last of June another battle was fought
and with the same result. After a rest of three days
the march toward Chukotskoi Noss was resumed, but
another larger body of natives was met with there and
a third battle ensued, during which some articles were
recovered which had been in possession of Shestakof.
Pavlutzki claimed this engagement, also, as a victory
and declared his total loss in the three battles to have
been but three Russians, one Yukagir, and five Koriaks killed. But the Chukchi were by no means
subdued. After reaching the cape the expedition returned across the country in a south-easterly direction
and in October reached ostrog Anadirskoi.[3] Pavlutzki finally died at Yakutsk with the rank of voivod.
His explorations were carried on with indomitable
courage and rare ability, and altogether his achievements furnish a worthy prelude to those of Bering
and Chirikof a few years later. The feat of marching
across the country of the warlike Chukchi was not
repeated till half a century later, when a party under
Billings, not as an army defying interference, but as
an humble expedition, were suffered to pass by the
insolent natives, who robbed them at every step with
impunity.

The second Kamchatka expedition, under the
auspices of the empress Elizabeth, was the most
brilliant effort toward scientific discovery which up
to this time had been made by any government.[4] It

[3] *Muller's Voy.*, 11–15; *Coxe's Russian Discoveries*, 237; *Burney's Chron.
Hist.*, 128–37, 196 et seq.
[4] The sources of information concerning this expedition are numerous, but
not altogether satisfactory. The first account, brief and wholly unreliable,
was published by the Parisian geographer De L'Isle, in 1752, in a pamphlet
entitled *Explication de la Carte des Nouvelles Decouvertes au Nord de la Mer
du Sud.* In 1753 there was printed at Berlin, also in French, and immediately translated into English and German, though never published in Russian,
a *Letter of a Russian Naval Officer*, which was ascribed to Müller, who con-
tradicted the statements of De L'Isle, and gave his own version. Engel, in
his *Geographische und Kritische Nachrichten*, ii. 44, 47, endeavors to prove

must be borne in mind that Siberia, discovered and named by the Cossacks in the sixteenth century, was in the earlier part of the eighteenth but little known to European Russia, and the region round

Müller to be the author of the letter. In 1758 Müller published a volume entitled *Voyages and Discoveries of the Russians in the Arctic Sea, and the Eastern Ocean*, in both German and Russian, which was translated into English in 1771, and into French in 1776. The volume is accompanied by maps, and covers the entire ground, without, however, going into minor details, and without doing justice to the vast work performed by the attendant scientists. This was the chief authority until Sokolof took up the subject in a lengthy communication to the Zapiski Hydrograficheskago Departamenta in 1851.

In 1820 another brief description of the expedition was furnished by Sarychef, under the title of *Voyages of Russian Naval Officers in the Arctic Seas, from 1734 to 1742*, printed in vol. iv. of the publications of the Russian admiralty department. In the mean time other publications connected with or resulting from the expedition, though not treating of it, appeared at various times, such as the *Flora Siberica*, by Gmelin, published serially between 1749 and 1769; *A Voyage through Siberia*, also by Gmelin, in 1752; A history of Siberia, under the title of *Sammlung russischer geschichten*, by Müller, in 1732–6; *Description of the Kamchatka Country*, by Krashennikof, in 1755; *History of Siberia*, by Fisher, in 1768 (this was in German, the Russian translation appearing only in 1774); *Description of the Kamchatka Country*, by Steller, in 1774; *Journal of a Voyage from Kamchatka to America*, also by Steller, published in 1793, in *Pallas, Neue Nord. Beitr.; A Detailed Description of the Voyages from the White Sea to the Gulf of Obi* appeared in the *Four Voyages of Lutke*, in 1826; in 1841 Wrangell published a *Voyage in Siberia*, with frequent allusions to the second Kamchatka expedition. A few articles on the results of the expedition in the fields of natural history, astronomy, and history appeared in papers of the Imperial Academy of Sciences, and the documents collected by Müller from the Siberian archives for his history of Siberia have been published from time to time in the proceedings of the imperial Russian historical and archæological commission. The most reliable source of information upon this subject has been found in the archives of the Russian naval department. The documents concerning the doings of the Bering expedition comprise 25 large bundles of over 30,000 pages; these documents extend over a period of 17 years, between 1730 and 1747. The archives of the hydrographic department of the Russian navy contain the journals of navigation of nearly all the vessels engaged, all in copies only. The original journals and maps were sent in 1754 to Irkutsk and placed in the hands of Miatlef, governor of Siberia, with a view to a resumption of the labors of the expedition; thence the papers were transferred in 1759 to Governor Saimonof at Tobolsk, and they were finally given to Sokolof. above mentioned, by N. N. Muravief, governor general of eastern Siberia, for the purpose of writing an account of the expedition. The greater part of these documents were copies made by pupils of the naval corps of cadets and of the nautical academy, and though written clearly and carefully, they are full of egregious errors. The collection comprises over 60 manuscript volumes. The copies of the original maps accompanying the journals were also carelessly made. In the archives and library of the imperial academy there exists the so-called 'Müller Portfolio,' containing a large number of reports, letters, and journals of members of the academy accompanying the expedition, written in Russian, French, German, and Latin. The only naval journal found in this collection was kept by Master Khitrof, and is the most valuable thing in the portfolio. Sokolof's account of the second Kamchatka expedition begins with the following dedication of his work to Peter the Great: 'To thee I dedicate this work, to thee without

Kamchatka scarcely at all. The maps of the day were problematical. The semi-geographical mission of the surveyors Lushin and Yevreinof to the Kurile Islands in 1719–21 had been barren of results. The first expedition of Bering from 1725 to 1730 had advanced along the river routes to Okhotsk, thence by sea to Kamchatka, and northward to the straits subsequently named after him, but made few discoveries of importance, determining the astronomical positions of points and places only by latitude without longitude, but revealing the trend of the Kamchatka coast to the northward. The expedition of Shestakof from 1727 to 1732 was more of a military nature, and resulted in little scientific information. The exploration of Hens, Fedorof, and Gvozdef, made about the same time, was scarcely more satisfactory in its results, though it served to confirm some things reported by Bering during his first voyage.

Russia wished to know more of this vast uncovered region, wished to map its boundaries, and mark off her claim. The California coast had been explored as far as Cape Mendocino, but over the broad area thence to the Arctic there still hung the great Northern Mystery,[5] with its Anian Strait, and silver mountains, and divers other fabulous tales. The northern provinces of Japan were likewise unknown to the enlightened world; and now the Muscovite, who had sat so long in deep darkness, would teach even the Celt and Saxon a thing or two.

Soon after the return of Bering from his first expedition, namely, on the 30th of April 1730, the commander presented to the empress two letters called by him, "Proposals for the Organization of the

whom it would not exist, since the discoveries described in the same are the fruit of the great ideas conceived by thee, the benefactor, father, and organizer of this vast empire; to thee are thy subjects indebted for law, good order, and influence within and without, as well as for morality, knowledge, and everything else that makes a nation fortunate and important.' *Zapiski Hydrografi-cheskago Departamenta*, ix. 199.

[5] For a full exposition of which see *Hist. Northwest Coast*, i., and *Hist. Cal.*, i., passim, this series.

Okhotsk and Kamchatka country," and advised an immediate discovery of routes to America and Japan for the purpose of establishing commercial relations with these countries. He also recommended that the northern coast of the empire between the rivers Ob and Lena be thoroughly explored.[6] The organization of the country already known, commanded the first attention of the empress, to which end she issued, on the 10th of May 1731, an oukaz ordering the former chief *prokuror*, or sergeant-at-arms of the senate, Skorniakof Pisaref, then in exile, to assume control of the extreme eastern country, and be furnished with the necessary means to advance its interests. The residence of the new official was to be Okhotsk, to which point laborers and settlers were to be sent from Yakutsk, together with a boat-builder, three mates, and a few mechanics.[7] The exile-governor did not however long hold his position. Scarcely had he assumed office when the second Kamchatka expedition was decided upon and Vitus Bering received the supreme command of all the territory included in his explorations.

At that time several circumstances combined to carry forward the plans of Bering to their highest consummation. The empire was at peace and the imperial cabinet was presided over by Count Oster-mann, who had formerly been secretary of Admiral Cruce, and had devoted considerable attention to naval affairs. In the senate the expedition was earnestly supported by the chief secretary Kirílof; in the ad-miralty college Count Golovin presided as the ruling

[6] Appendix to Sokolof's Second Expedition. *Zapiski Hydrograficheskago Departamenta*, ix. 434.

[7] Grigor Skorniakof Pisaref was appointed to command Okhotsk as an in-dependent district. His annual salary was fixed at 300 rubles, 100 bushels of rye meal, and 100 buckets of brandy. This individual had a checkered career. In 1715 he was a captain in the Preobrashenski lifeguards, and attached to the academy of naval artillery; in 1719, he was made comman-der of the naval academy; in 1720 he published a book, *Practical Manual of Statistics and Mechanics;* in 1722 he was made 'chief prokuror' of the senate; in 1723 he was relieved from the academy by Captain Narishkin; in 1727, he was punished with the knout and sent to Siberia as an exile. *Morskoi Sbor-nik,* i. 11, 17.

spirit, while the prokuror was Saimonof, the rival of Kirilof. The foreign members of the Academy of Sciences, in order to preserve their prestige, were looking about for fields of activity, anxious to serve their new fatherland. The spirit of Peter the Great was yet alive among the leading subjects of the empire; his plans were still fresh in the memory of men, and all were eager to execute his progressive purposes. And soon all Siberia was flooded with men of science searching out things both larger and smaller than sables, and throwing Cossack and promyshlenik completely into the shade. By toilsome processes the necessary means of subsistence and materials were collected at the central stations throughout Siberia, and along the thirteen hundred leagues of Arctic sea-coast were placed at various points magazines of supplies for explorers. From six to seven months were sometimes occupied in transporting from the forest to the seaports trees for ship-building. And many and wide-spread as were the purposes, every man had his place. To every scientist was given his work and his field, to every captain the river he was to reconnoitre, or the coast he was to explore. And when the appointed time came there set forth simultaneously, from all the chief river-mouths in Siberia, like birds of passage, little exploring expeditions, to begin their battle with the ice and the morass. Some brought their work to a quick and successful issue; others encountered the sternest difficulties.

But the adventures which chiefly concern us are those pointing toward the American continent, which were indeed the central idea of all these undertakings, and by far the most important outcome from this Siberian invasion by the scientists. Before embarking on the first great eastern voyage of discovery, let us glance at the personnel of the expedition.

Captain-commander Ivan Ivanovich Bering, so the Russians called him, notwithstanding his baptismal name of Vitus, was a Dane by birth, as I have said, who had been in the Russian naval service about thirty years, advancing gradually from the rank of sub-lieutenant since 1704. He was strong in body and clear of 'mind even when nearly sixty; an acknowledged man of intelligence, honesty, and irreproachable conduct, though in his later years he displayed excessive carefulness and indecision of character, governed too much by temper and caprice, and submitting too easily to the influence of subordinates. This may have been the effect of age, or of disease; but whatever the cause, he was rendered thereby less fit to command, especially so important and hazardous an adventure in so inhospitable a region as Siberia at the beginning of the eighteenth century. He had been selected by Peter the Great to command the first expedition upon the representations of admirals Seniavin and Sievers, because " he had been to India and knew all the approaches to that country." [8] After his return he had advanced gradu-

[8] In the archives of the admiralty council in St Petersburg there is still preserved a manuscript copy of the original instructions indited by Peter the Great for the first Bering expedition. The instructions were finally promulgated by the admiralty college, or perhaps by Count Apraxin, and had been corrected in the great tsar's own handwriting, to read as follows:

'1. To select such surveyors as have been in Siberia and have returned thence; upon which, at request of the senate, the following surveyors were ordered to the province of Siberia: Ivan Evreinof (died), Feodor Lushin, Peter Skobeltzin, Ivan Svostunof, Dmitri Baskakof, Vassili Shetilof, and Grigor Putilof.

'2. To select from naval lieutenants or second lieutenants, such as are fit to be sent to Siberia and Kamchatka. In the opinion of Vice-admiral Sievers and Contre-admiral Seniavin, the most desirable individuals of that class were lieutenants Stanberg (Spanberg?), Zveref or Kessenkof, and the sub-lieutenants Chirikof and Laptief. It would not be bad to place over these as commander either Captain Bering or Von Verd; Bering has been to East India and knows the routes, and Von Verd was his mate.

'3. To select from the master-mechanics or apprentices such as are able to build a decked boat according to our model used with big ships; and for the same purpose to select four carpenters with their instruments, as young as possible, and one quartermaster and eight sailors. The boat-builder apprentice, Feodor Kozlof, has all the required qualifications, being able to draught plans of decked boats and to build them. (In Peter the Great's own handwriting: It is absolutely necessary to have some mate or second mate who has been to North America.)

'4. The usual complement of sails, blocks, ropes etc., and four falconets, with the necessary ammunition, should be increased by half—doubled, in Peter's own handwriting.

'5. If such a mate cannot be found in the fleet it is necessary to write immediately to Holland for two men, experienced navigators in the Northern or Japan seas, and to forward them at once by way of Anadirsk. Vice-admiral

ally to the rank of captain-commander, and had received a cash reward of a thousand rubles, an amount commonly granted at that time to envoys returning from distant countries. He was now anxious to obtain the rank of contre-admiral for his long services and discoveries. The admiralty college made representations to that effect to the imperial cabinet, but no reply was received.[9]

Next in command, appointed with Bering, and who had served as junior officer on the first expedition, and now a captain, was Alexeï Ilich Chirikof, one of the best officers of his day, the pride and hope of the fleet. Russian historians are perhaps a little inclined to

Sievers promises to forward these men immediately if they can be found in the imperial fleet Another addition in Peter's own handwriting: The rigging may be omitted, the rest is all right. Signed on the 23d of December, 1724.'

[9] Berg in his researches into Siberian history found several documents giving biographical details concerning Bering and his family, which may be of some interest to the reader. He had with him in Siberia his wife and children, two sons named Thomas and Unos, who were still alive in the city of Revel when Sokolof wrote his history of the expedition. The wife, Anna Matveievna, was a young and lively woman and apparently not without influence; possibly a little unscrupulous. At all events it is known that in consequence of certain rumors the senate issued an order in September 1738 to keep an eye on the wife of Captain-commander Bering, then on her way from Siberia, as well as on other members of the expedition about to return, and to detail for the purpose an 'able man.' This supervision was proved to be necessary on the Siberian frontier, as it appeared that the lady carried in her baggage a large quantity of furs and government property. However, on her arrival at Moscow she surrendered everything, made a few presents to the customs officials, and hurried to St Petersburg, where she informed the inspectors that she did not belong to Siberia but to St Petersburg. In 1744, when she asked for a widow's pension, or the award of her husband's salary for one year, she declared that she was 39 years of age; and in 1750, when she again petitioned for a pension, her age was given as 40—not an uncommon mistake made by ladies. As characteristic of Bering's mind, Sokolof produces a letter written by him to Lieutenant Plunting, who at that time, 1738, was quarrelling with the commander of the port of Okhotsk, Pisaref. 'You know yourself better than I what kind of a man Pisaref is,' he writes. 'It is always better when a rabid dog is about, to get out of his way in order not to be bitten when it is none of our business. You are yourself somewhat to blame, and perhaps you think that as an officer you are exempt from punishment, but if Captain-commander Villebois was your commander, you would have been punished though you are an officer. I know not under what weak commanders you have served to cause you to act as you do; remember this and take care of yourself in the future, if you would avoid a sore head. Nobody knows his fate, perhaps you will be an admiral yet, as has happened to Nikolaï Fedorovich Golovin, president of the admiralty college, but formerly he was only a sub-lieutenant under my command; and look at Shafirof, what honors have been bestowed upon him, according to our latest letters. Pisaref's fate is fortunately hidden from him. That may be your consolation.' Zap. Hydr., ix. 209–10.

magnify the faults of Bering the Dane as well as the merits of Chirikof the Russian. The latter they say was well educated, courageous, and straightforward, bright of intellect as well as thoughtful, and whose kind heart the exigencies of the cruel naval service had never been able wholly to debase. He had graduated from the naval academy in 1721, and had been at once promoted to a sub-lieutenancy, skipping the rank of midshipman. He was at first attached to the fleet, but subsequently received an appointment at the naval academy as instructor of the marines of the guard. While in that position he was presented to Peter the Great by Sievers and Seniavin as one of the officers selected to join the first Bering expedition. He was placed under the immediate command of Bering, together with Spanberg, in 1725. Before setting out he was promoted to lieutenant, and gave evidence throughout the expedition of great courage and common-sense. On his return in 1730 he was made a captain-lieutenant; two years later, in 1732, he was again promoted and made full captain, "not by seniority but on account of superior knowledge and worth," as they said. At the time of his appointment he was on special duty at Kazan, and he returned to St Petersburg only a few days before the departure of the expedition in February 1733; but he still found time to give most valuable assistance in framing the final instructions.[10]

The third in command was Captain Martin Petrovich Spanberg, a countryman of Bering, a native of Den-

[10] It is remarkable that in all the accounts of quarrels between the heads of the various detachments of scientists and naval officers serving under Bering's command, the name of Chirikof is never found. He seems to have had the good-will of every one and escaped all complaints from superiors; he had with him in Siberia a wife and daughter. On his return from the American coast he lived in the town of Yenisseisk, suffering from consumption until 1746; in that year he was ordered to St Petersburg, and upon his arrival was again appointed to the naval academy. In the same year he was transferred to Moscow to look after some naval affairs of importance, and on that occasion he made several propositions for the organization of further exploring expeditions. He died in 1747 with rank of captain-commander. *Morskoi Sbornik*, iv. 213–14.

mark. It is not known when he entered the Russian
service, but he accompanied the first expedition as
senior officer. He was illiterate, with a reckless au-
dacity, rough, and exceedingly cruel, avaricious and
selfish, but strong in mind, body, and purpose, of great
energy, and a good seaman. His bad reputation extended over all Siberia, and was long preserved in the
memory of the people. Sibiriaks feared him and his
wanton oppression. Some of them thought him a
great general, while others called him an escaped ex-
ecutioner. He was always accompanied by a dog of
huge dimensions, which it was said would tear people
to pieces at his master's command. Chirikof thought
him possessed of some sparks of a noble ambition, but
all was put down by his subordinates to a love of
tyranny. His knowledge of the Russian language was
exceedingly limited. Having been made a captain-
lieutenant during the first expedition, he was now a
captain, like Chirikof, but higher on the list   Little
is said of his share in the work performed by the expedition, but his name occurs in hundreds of complaints
and petitions from victims of his licentiousness, cruelty,
and avarice. He was just the man to become rich.
On his return from Siberia he brought with him a
thousand yards of army cloth, a thousand bales of fur,
and whole herds of horses. He carried to Siberia
his wife and son, and they accompanied him at sea.[11]
Such is the character of the man as presented by
Russian authorities, which are all we have on the
subject. Again it will be noticed that while Chirikof,
the Russian, is highly praised, Spanberg, the Dane,
is roundly rated, and we may make allowance accordingly.

[11] He returned to St Petersburg from Siberia without orders in 1745, and
was promptly placed under arrest and remanded for trial. His sentence was
death, but in the mean time other charges had been preferred, based upon complaints of the people of Siberia, and the sentence was postponed. After many
delays he was released at the request of the Danish ambassador. In 1749 he
was given the command of a newly constructed man-of-war, which foundered
on leaving the harbor of Arkhangelsk; for this he was again tried by court-
martial and again acquitted. He died at last in 1761, with the rank of captain of the first class. Sokolof, in *Zap. Hydr.*, ix. 215-26.

Of the other officers of the expedition there is not
much to be said, as they were not prominently connected with the discovery of the American coast.
Lieutenant Walton, the companion of Spanberg, was
an Englishman who had entered the Russian service
only two years before. Midshipman Schelting was an
illegitimate son of Contre-admiral Petrovski, a Hollander. He was twenty-five years of age and had
been attached to the fleet only two years. Lieutenant
Lassenius, the senior officer of the Arctic detachments, who was instructed to explore the coast beyond
the Lena river, was a Dane. He had also but recently
entered the Russian service. According to Gmelin
he was a skilful and experienced officer; later he was
relieved by Lieutenant Laptief, also an old lieutenant
who had been recommended to Peter the Great for
the first expedition as a considerate and courageous
man. The less said of the morals of any of these
mariners the better. Neither the age nor the nation
was conspicuous for justice or refinement. Drinking
and gambling were among the more innocent amuse-
ments, at least in the eyes of the sailors, among whom
were the most hardened villains that could be picked
out from the black sheep of the naval service. There
can be no doubt that an almost brutal discipline was
sometimes necessary, but the practice of it was common. In regard to honesty, we must not suppose that
the appropriation of public property by officers of the
government was then regarded as a greater crime than
now.

Upon the request of the senate the imperial academy had instructed its member, Joseph de L'Isle,
to compile a map of Kamchatka and adjoining countries; but not satisfied with this, the senate demanded
the appointment of an astronomer to join the expedition accompanied by some students advanced in astronomy, and two or three versed in mineralogy. Two
volunteers for this service were found among the

academicians, Johann Gmelin, professor of chemistry
and natural history, and Louis de L'Isle de la Croyère,
a brother of the map-maker and professor of astronomy. These were joined by a third, Gerhard Müller,
professor of history and geography. The senate
accepted these, but ordered further twelve students
from the Slavo-Latin school at Moscow to be trained
in the academy for the proposed expedition. The
admiralty college urged the necessity of extending
the exploration over the whole northern coast of
Siberia, and it was then that were appointed as commanders subordinate to Bering, Spanberg, and Chirikof, one lieutenant, three sub-lieutenants, and a
command of servants and soldiers numbering one hundred and fifty-seven in all. A few members of the
college proposed to send the whole expedition to the
coast of Kamchatka round the world by sea, the
earliest plan toward circumnavigation conceived by a
Russian; but their counsel did not prevail.[12]

The command of the proposed expedition to Japan
was given to Captain Spanberg, assisted by Lieutenant Walton and Midshipman Schelting. The exploration of the northern coast was intrusted to lieutenants
Muravief and Pavlof; lieutenants Meygin, Skuratof,
and Ovtzin were also appointed but subsequently relieved by Masters Minnin, Pronchishchef, and Lassenius. The two latter died and were replaced by two
brothers, the lieutenants Hariton and Dmitri Laptief.
Another detail consisted of three lieutenants, Waxel,
Plunting, and Endogarof, four masters, twelve master's
mates, ship and boat builders, three surgeons, nine
assistant surgeons, a chaplain, six monks, commissaries,
navigators, a number of cadets and sailors, all numbering five hundred and seventy men. From the
academy the final appointments were the naturalist
Gmelin and the historian Müller, who were subsequently relieved by Steller and Fisher; the astronomer

---

[12] Both Berg, in his *Lives of Admirals*, ii. 238, and Gmelin, in his *Voyage
in Siberia*, make mention of these proposals.

De L'Isle de la Croyère, with five students, four surveyors, who were increased in Siberia by four more,
an interpreter, an instrument-maker, two artists, and
a special escort of fourteen men. An engineer and
architect named Frederick Staël was also attached to
the expedition for the construction of roads and harbors, but he died on his way to Siberia.

Müller and Gmelin were both young men, the first
being twenty-eight and the other twenty-four. They
were learned and enthusiastic German scientists who
had come to Russia several years before, one as a
doctor of medicine and professor of chemistry and
natural history, the other as professor of history and
geography. Both attained distinction in the scientific
world. De L'Isle de la Croyère was also well educated, though conspicuous rather as a lover of good
eating and drinking, than as a learned man.[13]

Another scientific member of the expedition, who
joined it somewhat later, was George Wilhelm Steller.
He was born in Winsheim, Franconia, on the 10th
of March 1709. He studied theology and natural
science in the universities of Wittenberg, Leipsic, and
Jena, and settled in Halle, devoting himself chiefly
to anatomy, botany, and medicine. He proceeded to
Berlin and passed a brilliant examination, and in 1734
he joined the Russian army before Dantzic, doing
duty as staff-surgeon. In December he was sent to
St Petersburg with a ship-load of wounded soldiers.
Here he accepted the position of *leib medicus*, or body-
surgeon to the famous bishop of Novgorod, Theo-
phanos Prokopovich, a favorite of Peter the Great,
and with him he remained till his death, except when
serving in Siberia.

When Bering left St Petersburg to enter upon his

---

[13] According to Berg and Sokolof, Gmelin returned to his own country
shortly after returning from this expedition in the year 1749, having obtained
his final discharge from the Russian service. He died in 1755. Müller was
appointed historian in the Academy of Science in 1747; from 1754 to 1765 he
was conference secretary of the academy; in 1765 he was appointed director
of the Foundling House of Moscow, and in 1766 he was placed in charge of
the Moscow archives of the foreign office. He died in 1783.

second expedition, Steller, then of the imperial academy, was ordered to join the expedition specially to examine the natural history of Kamchatka. He reached his new field in 1738. In 1740, after giving ample proof of his ability and energy by making frequent and valuable shipments of specimens for the museum of the academy, he forwarded a petition to the senate for permission to accompany Lieutenant Spanberg on his voyage to Japan. While awaiting an answer he was importuned by Bering to join his expedition. Steller replied that in the absence of orders he would draw upon himself the displeasure of the authorities, but the commander said he would assume all responsibility and provide him with an official memorandum to that effect, and a regular appointment to take charge of the department of natural science in his expedition. Steller finally consented, and we are indebted to him for some of the most reliable information concerning the Russian discoveries on the American coast.[14]

In consideration of distance and privations the empress doubled every salary. The departure of the expedition began in February 1733. Bering and Chirikof were instructed to build at Okhotsk or in Kamchatka, wherever it was most convenient, two vessels of the class then called packet-boats, and then to proceed, in accordance with the plans of Professor De la Croyère, without separating, to the exploration of the American coast, which was supposed to lie but a short distance from Kamchatka. After reaching that shore they were to coast southward to the forty-fifth parallel, and then return to the north, crossing

[14] These scientists had a way of marrying, with the view of throwing some part of their infelicities upon their wives. Steller tried it, as Müller and Fisher had done, and as the rough old sea-captains used to do, but he found his wife one too many for him. She was the widow of a certain Doctor Messerchmidt, and daughter of a Colonel Von Böchler, and did not at all object to become the wife of the rising young scientist, but to go to Siberia, Kamchatka, perhaps to the north pole, was quite a different matter. True, she promised him, but that was before marriage, which of course did not count. And the sorrowful Steller was at last obliged to go wifeless to his ice-fields, leaving his spouse to flirt the weary hours away at the gay capital. *Morskoi Sbornik*, c. 145.

back to Asia at Bering Strait. If the season proved
too short they were authorized to go into winter-quarters, and conclude the work the following season.
Captain Spanberg was to proceed from Okhotsk in
the direction of Japan with one ship and two sloops,
beginning his explorations at the Kurile Islands. In
order to facilitate the progress of the expedition the
local Siberian authorities were instructed to erect on
the banks of the principal rivers, and on the Arctic,
beacons to indicate the location of the magazines of
provisions and stores for the various detachments, and
also to inform all the nomadic natives of Siberia and
the promyshleniki, that they must assist the members
of the expedition as far as lay in their power.

One important purpose of the expedition was to
discover a new route to the Okhotsk Sea without
passing Yakutsk, by going through the southern districts of Siberia, and striking the head-waters of the
Yuda, which had been reported navigable. A warning was attached to the instructions against crossing
the Amoor, "in order not to awaken the suspicions of
the Chinese government." The academicians Gmelin
and Müller were intrusted with the exploration of
the interior of Siberia and Kamchatka, assisting each
other in their researches, and making a general geographical survey with the assistance of the cadet engineers attached to their detachment. Croyère, with
some of the students who had been in training at
the observatory of the academy for several years, was
to make astronomical observations along the route
of progress, and accompany Bering to the coast of
America. He was granted great liberty of action, and
furnished with ample means, the best instruments to
be obtained at that time, and a numerous escort of
soldiers and laborers.

It was an unknown country to which they were
all going, and for an unknown time. The admiralty
college had thought six years sufficient, but most
were going for sixteen years, and many forever. Be-

sides nearly all the officers, a number of the rank and
file were taking with them their wives and children.
Lieutenant Ovtzin and one naval officer were the first
to leave for Kazan in order to begin their preparations.   Captain Spanberg with ten mechanics set out
next to erect temporary buildings along the road and
in the towns of Siberia, for the accommodation of the
expedition.   In March 1733 other members took their
departure, followed by lengthy caravans loaded with
supplies from the storehouses of the admiralty.   The
scientists from the academy tarried in St Petersburg
till August, and then proceeded to Kazan to join their
companions.   At the beginning of winter the whole
force had advanced as far as Tobolsk, where they went
into winter-quarters.   In the spring of 1734 the expedition embarked on small vessels built during the
winter on the rivers Ob, Irtish, and Yenissei.   The
main body arrived at Yakutsk in the summer of 1735,
after having wintered at some point beyond Irkutsk.
Bering himself had proceeded by land from Tobolsk
and reached Yakutsk in October 1734, in advance of
nearly all his assistants.   Here the winter was again
utilized for the construction of boats, and in the spring
of 1735 the lieutenants Pronchishchef and Lassenius
proceeded northward down the Lena River, with the
intention of sailing eastward along the Arctic coast.
The transportation of men and stores to Okhotsk
was accomplished partly in boats, and partly on horseback over a rugged chain of mountains.   This proved
to be the most laborious part of the journey.   Captain
Spanberg had been the first to arrive at Okhotsk,
having travelled in advance of the expedition; but
on arrival he discovered, to his dismay, that nothing
had been done by the local commander to prepare for
the reception of so large a body.   Not a building had
been erected, not a keel laid, and the only available
logs were still standing in the forest.   Spanberg went
to work at once with his force of mechanics, but lack
of provisions caused frequent interruptions as the men

were obliged to go fishing and hunting. After a while the commander of the Okhotsk country, Skorniakof Pisaref, made his appearance. He offered no excuse and his presence did not mend matters. Pisaref and Spanberg had both been invested with extraordinary powers, independent of each other, and both were stubborn and inclined to quarrel. The former lived in a fort a short distance up the river, while the latter had built a house for himself at the mouth of the river, where he intended to establish the port. Each had his separate command, and each called himself the senior officer, threatening his opponent with swift annihilation. Each lorded it over his dependants and exacted abject obedience, and we may well imagine that the subordinates led a wretched life.

Bering at Yakutsk encountered much the same difficulties as Spanberg, but on a larger scale. His supplies were scattered along the road from the frontier of Asia to Yakutsk awaiting transportation, and the most urgent appeals to the Siberian authorities failed to secure the requisite means.[15] It had been the captain-commander's intention to facilitate his intercourse with the natives of Kamchatka by means of missionary labor. Immediately after his return from the first expedition, he had petitioned the holy

[15] Sgibnef, in his *History of Kamchatka*, gives the reasons for the delay. It would seem after all that government was none too rigorous in Siberia. It appears that the quarrels between Spanberg and Pisaref were preceded by petty altercations between the latter and the voivod in command at Yakutsk. As early as 1732 Pisaref had been instructed to draw all necessary supplies from Yakutsk, but the voivod Shadovski refused to give him anything. Pisaref complained to the governor at Irkutsk and received an oukaz empowering him to confine Shadovski in irons until he issued what was needed for the prosecution of work at Okhotsk. Subsequently another oukaz came to Tobolsk ordering Shadovski to arrest Pisaref, which was no sooner done than the order was revoked. Meanwhile working parties were forwarded to Okhotsk every year, but want of provisions forced them to desert before anything had been accomplished. Numbers of these workmen died of starvation on the road. *Morskoi Sbornik*, cv. 25-7. Under date of October 7, 1738, an order was issued from the chancellery of Irkutsk providing for the preparation of 'sea-stores' for the Bering expedition in Kamchatka. The quantity was determined to the pound, as well as the quality, and special instructions were given for the manufacture of liquor from *sarana*, a kind of fern, and for its preservation in casks. If necessary, the whole population of Kamchatka was to be employed in gathering this plant, and to be paid for their labor in tobacco. Sgibnef, in *Morskoi Sbornik*, ci. 137-40.

synod for missionaries to undertake the conversion of
the Kamchatkans. The senate promulgated a law
exempting all baptized natives of that country for ten
years from the payment of tribute to the government.
The first missionary selected for the new field was the
monk Filevski, a great preacher and pillar of the
church, but before reaching Kamchatka he was
arrested on the river Aldan, for assaulting and half
killing one of the monks of his suite, and for refusing
to hold divine services or to read the prayers for the
imperial family. Religion in Siberia had seemingly
run mad. After his arrival in Kamchatka he added
much to the general confusion by acts of violence and
a meddlesome spirit, which stirred up strife alike
among clergy and laity, Russians and natives.

The position of Bering was exceedingly trying; on
him must fall the odium attending the faults and
misfortunes of them all. Throughout the journey,
and afterward to the end, complaints were forwarded
to Irkutsk, Tobolsk, and St Petersburg. That he
was a foreigner made it none the less a pleasure for
the Russians to curse him. The senate and admiralty
college were exasperated by reason of the slow movement, being ignorant of the insurmountable obstacles.
First among the accusers was the infamous Pisaref,
who charged both Bering and Spanberg with licentiousness and "excessive use of tobacco and brandy."
He reported that up to that time, 1737, nothing had
been accomplished for the objects of the expedition,
and nothing could be expected beyond loss to the
imperial treasury; that the leaders of the expedition
had come to Siberia only to fill their pockets, not
only Bering, but his wife, who was about to return to
Moscow; and that Bering had received valuable presents at Irkutsk from contractors for supplies. Another officer in exile, a captain-lieutenant of the navy,
named Kozantzof, represented that Bering's force was
in a state of anarchy, that all its operations were
carried on at a wasteful expenditure, and that in his

opinion nothing would come of it all.   Spanberg himself began to refuse obedience to Bering, complaining
bitterly of the delay in obtaining stores for his voyage to Japan.   Bering's immediate assistant, Chirikof,
received instructions from St Petersburg to inquire
into some of these complaints.   Another of the officers
of the expedition, Plunting, being dissatisfied with
Bering's non-interference in his quarrel with Pisaref,
insulted the former and was tried by court-martial
and sentenced to the ranks for two months.   To revenge himself, the young lieutenant sent charges
to St Petersburg, reflecting on Bering's conduct, one
of which was illicit manufacture of brandy and the
expenditure of powder in making fireworks, as well as
the "employment of the drum corps for his own amusement, though there was nothing to rejoice over."

The members of the academy also became dissatisfied and complained of abuse and ill-treatment on the
part of Bering, asking to be relieved from obedience
to him as commander.   In 1738 the expense of the
expedition, which had not then left the sea-coast, was
over three hundred thousand rubles in cash paid from
the imperial treasury, without counting the great
quantities of supplies furnished by the various districts in kind.   At this rate Alaska would cost more
than it could be sold for a hundred years hence.   The
empress issued an oukaz on the 15th of September
1738, instructing the senate and the admiralty college to review the accounts of the Kamchatka expedition, and ascertain if it could not be carried on
without such a drain on the treasury.   The senate
reported that the cost thus far made it necessary to
continue the work or all would be lost.   Much time
was wasted in correspondence on these matters, and
only at the beginning of 1739 did the main body reach
Okhotsk.   In July an officer named Tolbukhin arrived
with orders from the empress to investigate the "doings
of Bering."   He was followed in September by Larionof, another officer who had been ordered to assist

him. The supply of provisions at Okhotsk was altogether inadequate to the large number of men stationed
there. During the winter following the suffering
became so great that Bering was obliged to send large
detachments away to regions where they could support
themselves by hunting. At that time the whole force
consisted of 141 men at Okhotsk, 192 employed in the
magazines and in the transportation of stores, 70 at
Irkutsk, 39 in attendance upon the various officers

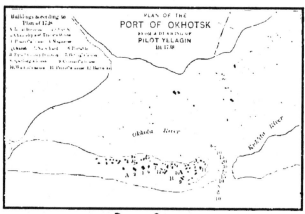

PLAN OF OKHOTSK.

and scientists, and 141 on the three vessels already
built, in all 583 men. Under Spanberg's active supervision two vessels had been built, the brigantine, *Arkhangel Mikhaïl*, and the double sloop, *Nadeshda*, or
Hope; and two old craft, the *Fortuna*, reconstructed
in some degree from the first of that name, and the
Gavril, had been repaired. Spanberg was ready to
go to sea in September, but lack of provisions detained
him.[16] In October the sloop *Fortuna* was sent to Kam-

[16] According to Bering's report of November 29, 1737, the quantity of
provisions on hand in all his magazines in Okhotsk and Kamchatka consisted
of 10,499 pounds of flour; 1,784 lbs. grits; 249 lbs. hard bread; 650 lbs. salt;
182 lbs. dried fish; 211 lbs. butter; 48 lbs. oil; and 683 buckets of brandy. At
the same time he forwarded a requisition for 1738 for: 1,912 lbs. flour; 2,566

chatka for a cargo of pitch for the ship-building at Okhotsk. The mate Kodichef, and the surveyor Svitunof, in charge, were instructed to carry the provisions that had accumulated in the Kamchatkan magazines to Bolsheretsk, as the most convenient port from which to transfer them to the vessels of Bering's expedition. The student Krashennikof also went to Kamchatka in the *Fortuna*. On the 13th of October, when about to enter the river at Bolsheretsk, the wretched craft was overtaken by a gale and thrown upon the shore. The future historian of Kamchatka, Krashennikof, reached the land "clad in one garment only."

Despite the apparently insurmountable difficulties resulting from want of transportation and lack of supplies, Bering and Chirikof found themselves in readiness to go to sea in the month of August 1740. At that time the number of men at Okhotsk belonging to the expedition was 166, with 80 engaged in the transportation of stores over the mountain trails. During the summer the astronomer Croyère with his suite had arrived at Okhotsk, accompanied by the naturalist Steller. Toward the end of August an event occurred that filled Bering and his officers with joy. The great stumbling-block of the expedition and its most persistent enemy, Pisaref, was relieved from his official position by another exile, Antoine Devière, a former favorite of Peter the Great, and chief of police of St Petersburg.[17] According to Sgibnef, Devière was the first honorable and efficient com-

lbs. meal; 2,369 lbs. hard bread; 1,026 lbs meat; 410 lbs. fish; 554 lbs. butter; 75 lbs. oil; and 320 buckets of brandy. For the year 1739 his requisition for his own and for Spanberg's expedition was: 930 lbs. flour; 2,565 lbs. meal; 4,617 lbs. hard bread; 1,025 lbs. meat; 410 lbs. fish; 546 lbs. butter; 103 lbs. salt, and 660 buckets of brandy. With the flour it was not only necessary to make kvass, but to bake hard bread; the meal was oatmeal, which was issued because pease and barley could not be obtained. *Zap. Hydr.*, ix. 337.

[17] It was in 1738 that Antoine Devière was chief of police of the Russian capital, but falling into disgrace he was sent to Siberia. In 1741 he was made commander of Okhotsk, and in 1742 recalled to St Petersburg by Elizabeth, made a count, and restored to his former position. He died in 1745. *Morskoi Sbornik*, cv. 31, 33.

mander of Okhotsk.   He sold the property which his predecessors had dishonestly obtained, and with the proceeds paid the arrears of salaries.   Under his active supervision buildings were erected, a school established, and everything arranged for a quick despatch of the American expedition.[18]

[18] It was at the suggestion of Bering that Devière opened this the first school in Kamchatka in 1741; it was located at Bolsheretsk and began its operations with 20 pupils. *Morskoi Sbornik*, ci. 142.

CHAPTER IV.

DISCOVERY OF ALASKA.

1740-1741.

SIX years the grand expedition had occupied in
crossing Siberia; no wonder subordinates swore and
the imperial treasurer groaned. But now the de-
voutly wished for hour had come, the happy consummation was at hand. New islands and new seas should
pay the reckoning, while the natives of a new continent should be made to bleed for all this toil and
trouble.

The 15th of August 1740 had been fixed as the day
of departure, but just as they were about to embark
Captain Spanberg arrived from Yakutsk with the intelligence that an imperial courier was at hand with
despatches requiring answers. This delayed the expedition till the 1st of September, when the double
sloop with stores was despatched in advance. At the
mouth of the river she ran aground, and the transfer

of cargo became necessary, after which she was again made ready.   On the 8th of September the expedition finally embarked.   Bering commanded the *Sv Petr*, and Chirikof the *Sv Pavel*, the two companion vessels having been named the St Peter and the St Paul. Bering's second was Lieutenant Waxel, while with Chirikof were lieutenants Chikhachef and Plunting.[1] The double sloop was commanded by Master Khitrof and the galiot by second mate Rtishchef.   Passengers on the double sloop were Croyère, Steller, the surveyor Krassilnikof, and the student Gorlanof.   The vessels were all fitted out with provisions for a year and eight months, but the grounding of the double sloop caused considerable loss in both provisions and spare rigging.

In crossing the Okhotsk Sea the vessels parted company, but they all reached the harbor of Bolsheretsk in safety about the middle of September.   Here they landed the two members of the academy for the purpose of exploring the Kamchatka peninsula, and took on board the mate Yelagin.   The little fleet then passed round the southern end of the peninsula to the gulf of Avatcha, where the *Sv Pavel* arrived the 27th of September, and the *Sv Petr* the 6th of October. The sloop met with a series of disasters and was compelled to return to Bolsheretsk on the 8th of October, and to remain there for the winter.   The galiot also returned for the winter, unable to weather Cape Lopatka so late in the season, and this rendered it necessary to transport supplies overland from Bolsheretsk

---

[1] With Waxel was a young son. The other officers of the *Sv Petr* were Eselberg, mate; Yushin, second mate; Lagunof, commissary; Khotiaintzof, master; Jansen, boatswain; Ivanof, boatswain's mate; Rossilius, ship's constable; Feich, surgeon; Betge, assistant surgeon; Plenisner, artist and corporal of Cossacks; and among the sailors the former Lieut. Ovtzin, who had been reduced to the ranks. In Kamchatka the force was increased by Khitrof, the marine, and Johann Synd, a son of Feich, the father returning to St Petersburg on account of ill-health. On the *Sv Pavel* were: Dementief, master; Shiganof and Yurlof, second mates; Chaglokof, commissary; Korostlef, master; Savelief, boatswain; Kachikof, ship's constable; the monk Lau, who also served as assistant surgeon; the force being further increased in Kamchatka by Yelagin, mate, and the marine Yurlof. The second mate Shiganof, and Yurlof, were subsequently promoted in Kamchatka.

to Avatcha during the winter, an operation attended with great difficulties and loss.[2] Bering approved of the selection of Avatcha Bay as a harbor, by Yelagin, it being the best on the coast. A few buildings had been erected, and to these the commander proceeded at once to add a church. The place was named Petropavlovsk.[3]

Beaching his vessels for the winter, Bering secured the services of the natives for the transportation of supplies from Bolsheretsk, and then distributed his command in small detachments, requiring them to live for the most part on such game and fish as they could catch. Removed from the interference of local authorities, which had been troublesome at Okhotsk, Bering passed a quiet winter and concluded the final preparations for sea in accordance with his plans. Croyère and Steller joined him in the spring; and with the opening of navigation, in accordance with instructions, on the 4th of May 1741 the commander assembled his officers, including the astronomer, for general consultation. Each present was to give his views, and a majority was to decide. All were of opinion that the unknown shore lay either due east or north-east; but this sensible decision, the adoption of which would have saved them much suffering and disaster, was not permitted to prevail. Science in Russia was as despotic as government. The renowned astronomer De L'Isle de la Croyère had made a map presented by the imperial academy to the senate.

---

[2] The sloop finally reached Avatcha the following summer but only after two exploring vessels had gone to sea. According to Steller a supply-ship met the vessels of the expedition in the outer harbor, and the greater portion of the cargo was transferred to the *Sv Petr. Steller, Beschreibung von Kamtschatka*, i. 112. The galiot returned to Okhotsk during the summer in charge of second mate Shigonof, and carrying as passengers Krashennikof, with a valuable collection of notes as the result of his investigations. *Zap. Hydr.*, ix. 371.

[3] According to Müller the church was dedicated to the apostles Peter and Paul, and the harbor derived its name therefrom; but subsequent investigations of the local archives by Sokolof and Polonski seemed to indicate that the church, a small wooden structure, was erected in memory of the birth of the virgin, and that the harbor was named after the two ships. Its name occurs on the earliest pages of the journals of the expedition. *Muller, Sammlung russischer geschichten.* i. 22; *Sokolof*, in *Zap. Hydr.*, ix. 372.

That august body had forwarded it to Bering, and
the author's brother, present at the council, also had
with him a copy. No land was set down upon this
chart toward the east, but some distance south-east
of Avatcha Bay, between latitudes 46° and 47°, there
was a coast extending about 15° of longitude from west
to east. The land was drawn in such a manner as to
indicate that it had been sighted on the south side,
and the words *Terres vues par dom Jean de Gama*
were inscribed upon it. The absurdity of sending out
an expedition for discovery, requiring it to follow
mapped imagination, seems never to have occurred to
the Solons of St Petersburg, and this when they
knew well enough that the continents were not far
asunder toward the north.

The mariners thought it safer to go by the chart,
which after all must have some influence on the land,
the drawing having passed through such imperial
processes, and hence arrived at the fatal determination
to steer first south-east by east in search of the Land
of Gama, and after discovering it to take its northern
coast as a guide to the north-east or east; but if no
land was found in latitude 46°, then the course should
be altered to north-east by east till land was made.
The coast once found, it was to be followed to latitude
65°. The action of the several officers under every
conceivable emergency was determined by the council.
All were to return to Avatcha Bay by the end of
September.[4] Yet with all the care, when put into
practice, their plans were found to be exceedingly defective. Steller went on the *Sv Petr*, while Croyère
was attached to Chirikof's vessel. The crew of the

---

[4] It is not known who Juan de Gama was, nor when the pretended discovery was made by him. In 1649 Texeira, cosmographer to the king of Portugal, published a map on which 10 or 12 degrees north-east from Japan, in
latitude 44° and 45°, were represented a multitude of islands and a coast extending toward the east, labelled: 'Terre vue par Jean de Gama, Indien, en
allant de la Chine à la Nouvelle Espagne.' The situation of the 'Land of
Gama,' on Texeira's maps, seems to be the same as the 'Company's Land'
discovered by the *Kastrikom* under Martin Geritzin de Vries, in 1643, or
perhaps earlier. *Muller's Voy.*, i. 37-8; *Burney's Chronol. Hist.*, 162-3.

Sv Petr numbered seventy-seven, and that of the *Sv Pavel* seventy-five. Both ships had still provisions left for five and a half months, with one hundred barrels of water, sixteen cords of wood, and two boats each.

On the morning of the 4th of June 1741, after solemn prayer, the two ships sailed from Avatcha Bay with a light southerly wind.[5] Noon of the second day saw them thirty miles from Light House Point. Chirikof, who was about five miles to windward of Bering, noticed that the latter steered southward of the course proposed. Signalling Bering that he would speak with him, Chirikof proposed that they should keep as near together as possible to avoid final separation in a fog. He also spoke of the manifest change from the agreed course, whereat Bering appeared annoyed, and when later Chirikof signalled to speak with him a second time the commander paid no attention to it. As we proceed we shall find serious defects in the character of both of these men. For a commander-in-chief, Bering was becoming timid, and perhaps too much bound to instructions; for a subordinate, Chirikof was dogmatic and obstinate. About noon of the 6th of June Bering ordered Chirikof to proceed in advance, trusting apparently more to his skill and judgment than to his own. On the 7th of June the wind changed to the north and increased. In the course of the next few days the two ships approached each other occasionally and exchanged signals, but Chirikof remained in the lead. In the afternoon of the 12th they found themselves in latitude 46,° and came to the conclusion that there was no Gama Land such as given in the chart, and at 3 o'clock they changed their course to east by north. On the 14th the wind drew ahead, blowing strong

---

[5] Details of Bering's voyage in the archives of St Petersburg consist of reports and journals by Waxel, Yuskin, and Khitrof, the first two in copies, the latter in the original. Of Chirikof's voyage there are copies of journals by himself and by Yelagin his mate. A few other details have been obtained from Steller and Müller. *Zap. Hydr.*, passim.

from the eastward, and compelling to a more northerly course for nearly two days, till they found themselves in latitude 48°, Bering keeping to the windward
of Chirikof on account of the better sailing qualities
of his vessel. Chirikof finally signalled for instructions, and asked how long the northerly course was
to be pursued. Bering's answer was to follow him
and he would see.

A few hours later the course was changed to the
southward. On the 15th the wind was a little more
to the south and the northerly course was resumed.
On the 18th, in the morning, Bering informed Chirikof that as they were in latitude 49° they must turn
south, but Chirikof said that with the prevailing wind a
change was impracticable, and it would be best to continue the course east by north. The following day in
latitude 49° 30' the wind increased, blowing violently
from the east, and sails were shortened during the night.
Next morning Chirikof sighted the *Sv Petr* about
three leagues to the north, but Bering did not see
him, and thinking himself to the windward shaped his
course to the north-west. This manœuvre completed
the separation of the vessels forever. Bering made
every effort to find the consort; he spent three days
between latitudes 50° and 51°, and finally sailed south-
east as far as 45°, but all in vain. Chirikof had taken
an easterly course and his subsequent movements were
entirely distinct from those of his commander.

First let us follow the fortunes of Chirikof, who
must ever be regarded as the hero of this expedition.

After losing sight of the *Sv Petr*, which he thought
was to the northward, Chirikof allowed the *Sv Pavel*
to drift a while, so that his commander might find
him. Then he steered south-east in search of him,
and after making two degrees of longitude to the
eastward, on the morning of the 23d of June he found
himself in latitude 48°. A council of officers decided
that it was folly to waste time in search of Bering,

and that they would prosecute the object of the voyage, which was to find land toward the east. Hence with light, favorable winds, the *Sv Pavel* went forward, occasionally shaping her course a little more to the north, until on the 11th of July signs of land were seen in drift-wood, seals, and gulls. Without slacking his speed, but casting the lead constantly, Chirikof proceeded, and during the night of the 15th he sighted land in latitude 55° 21.' Thus was the great discovery achieved. The high wooded mountains looming before the enraptured gaze of eyes long accustomed to the tamer glories of Siberia, were at once pronounced to belong to the continent of America.[6]

Day broke calm and clear; the coast was visible in distinct outlines at a distance of three or four miles; the lead indicated sixty fathoms, and the ship was surrounded by myriads of ducks and gulls. At noon it was still calm, and an observation gave the latitude as 55° 41'. A boat was lowered but failed to find a landing-place. In the evening a light wind arose, and the vessel stood north-westward along the shore under short sails. Toward morning the wind increased from the eastward with rain and fog, and the bright green land which they had found was lost to them again. At last, some time after daylight, high mountains once more appeared above the clouds, and at noon of the 17th the entrance to a great bay was observed in latitude 57° 15'. The mate, Dementief, was ordered to explore the entrance in the long-boat manned with ten armed sailors.[7]

The party was furnished with provisions for several days, with muskets, and other arms, including a small

[6] Sokolof declares emphatically that the point of land made was a slight projection of the coast between capes Addington and Bartholomew of Vancouver's map. *Zap. Hydr.*, ix. 399.

[7] The mate, Abram Mikhaïlovich Dementief, is spoken of by Müller in his *Letter of a Russian Naval Officer*, as a man of good family, young, good-looking, kind-hearted, skilled in his profession, and anxious to serve his country. Sokolof in his history of the expedition hints at a love affair at Okhotsk, which had ended unhappily. *Morskoi Sbornik*, cv. 113; *Zap. Hydr.*, iv. 400-1.

brass cannon. Chirikof issued instructions to meet probable emergencies, and explained how they were to communicate with the ship by signals. The boat was seen to reach the shore and disappear behind a small projection of land; a few minutes later the preconcerted signals were observed, and it was concluded that the boat had landed in safety.[8] The day passed without further information from the shore. During the next and for several successive days, signals were observed from time to time, which were interpreted to mean that all was well with Dementief. At last, as the party did not return, Chirikof began to fear that the boat had suffered damage in landing, and on the 23d Sidor Savelief, with some sailors, a carpenter and a calker, was sent ashore to assist Dementief, and repair his boat if necessary.[9] The strictest injunctions were issued that either one or both of the boats should return immediately. Their movements were anxiously watched from the ship. The small boat was seen to land, but no preparation for a return could be observed. A great smoke was seen rising from the point round which the first crew had disappeared.

The night was passed in great anxiety; but every heart was gladdened when next morning two boats were seen to leave the coast. One was larger than the other, and no one doubted that Dementief and Savelief were at last returning. The captain ordered all made ready for instant departure. During the bustle which followed little attention was paid to the approaching boats, but presently they were discovered to be canoes filled with savages, who seemed to be as much astonished as the Russians, and after a rapid survey of the apparition they turned shoreward, shouting Agaï! Agaï! Then dread fell on all, and

[8] Sokolof omits in his account the mention of Dementief's signal after reaching the land, but the fact is confirmed by Chirikof's own journal in both the original, and the translation in *Sammlung aller Reisbeschr.*, xx. 372.

[9] This date is differently given by different authors; in the *Sammlung* the date is the 21st; the number of Savelief's companions is also variously placed at from three to six. *Muller's Voyage*, 41; *Zap. Hydr.*, ix. 401.

Chirikof cursed himself for permitting the sailors to appear on deck in such numbers as to frighten away the savages, and thus prevent their seizure and an exchange of prisoners. Gradually the full force of the calamity fell upon him. His men had all been seized and murdered on the spot, or were still held for a worse fate.

He was on an unknown and dangerous coast, without boats, and his numbers greatly reduced. A strong west wind just then sprang up and compelled him to weigh anchor and run for the open sea. His heart was very sore, for he was a humane man and warmly attached to his comrades. He cruised about the neighborhood for several days, loath to leave it, though he had given up the shore parties all as lost, and as soon as the wind permitted he again approached the point which had proved so fatal to his undertaking. But no trace of the lost sailors could be discovered. A council of officers was then called to determine what next to do.[10]

All agreed that further attempts at discovery were out of the question, and that they should at once make for Kamchatka. With his own hand Chirikof added to the minutes of the council, "Were it not for our extraordinary misfortunes there would be ample time to prosecute the work." The *Sv Parel* was then headed for the north-west, keeping the coast in sight. The want of boats prevented a landing for water, which was now dealt out in rations; they tried to catch rain and also to distil sea-water, in both of which efforts, to a certain extent, they were successful.

On the 31st of July, at a distance of about eighteen miles to the north, huge mountains covered with snow were seen extending apparently to the westward. The

[10] Sokolof gives the date of this council as the 26th, 11 days after the discovery of land. Chirikof and Müller, as well as the *Sammlung*, make it the 27th. All accounts agree that the latitude observed on the day of the council was 58° 21'. The quantity of water on hand was then 45 casks. *Müller's Voyage*, 42; *Zap. Hydr.*, ix. 402.

wind increased and veered to the westward, with rain
and fog. The course was changed more to the southward, and on the 2d of August they again sighted
land to the westward,[11] but it soon disappeared in
the fog.

On the 4th of September in latitude 52° 30′ they
discovered high land in a northerly direction, probably the island of Unalaska. Two days later, after
considerable westing with a favorable wind, land was
again sighted in latitude 51° 30′; and on the evening
of the 8th, while becalmed in a fog, they were alarmed
by the roar of breakers, while soundings showed
twenty-eight fathoms. Chirikof anchored with difficulty owing to the hard rocky bottom, and the following morning when the fog lifted he found himself in
a small shallow bay less than a mile in width and
surrounded by tremendous cliffs, probably Adakh
Island. The mountains were barren, with here and
there small patches of grass or moss. While awaiting a favorable wind, they saw seven savages come
out in seven canoes, chanting invocations, and taking
no notice of the presents flung to them by the Russians.[12] A few canoes finally approached the ship,
bringing fresh water in bladders, but the bearers refused to mount to the deck. Chirikof in his journal
describes them as well built men resembling the Tartars in features; not corpulent but healthy, with
scarcely any beard. On their heads they wore shades
made of thin boards ornamented with colors, and
feathers of aquatic birds. A few also had bone carvings attached to their head-dress.[13] Later in the day
the natives came in greater numbers, fourteen *kyaks*,
or small closed skin boats, surrounding the vessel,

[11] Sokolof in *Zap. Hydr.*, ix. 403, insists that this land was the point discovered by Bering 10 days before; but there can be but little doubt that it
was the island of Kadiak.

[12] Sokolof on the authority of Chikhachef asserts that these natives refused
beads, tobacco, pipes, and other trifles, asking only for knives, but how the
savages expressed this desire he does not explain, nor does he show how they
knew anything about iron implements. *Zap. Hydr.*, ix. 404.

[13] *Chirikof's Journal*, in *Imperial Naval Archives*, xvi.

which they examined with great curiosity, but they refused to go on board. Toward evening by slipping an anchor they got to sea, and on the 21st high land was sighted again in latitude 52° 36′,[14] probably the island of Attoo, the westernmost of all the Aleutian chain. Chirikof supposed that all the land he saw hereabout was part of the American continent; for when he pressed northward, indications of land were everywhere present, but when he turned southward, such indications ceased. The presence of sea-otters was frequently remarked, though they could not realize the important part this animal was to play in shaping the destinies of man in this region. The 21st of August orders were issued to cook the usual quantity of rye meal once a day instead of twice, and to decrease the allowance of water. As an offset an extra drink of rum was allowed.[15]

Despite the scurvy and general despondency discipline was rigidly enforced, and finally, when the water for cooking the rye meal could be spared but once a week, no complaints were heard. Yet cold, excessive moisture and hunger and thirst were making constant and sure inroads. By the 16th Chirikof and Chikhachef were both down with the scurvy, and one man died the same day. Five days later the captain was unable to leave his berth, but his mind remained clear and he issued his orders with regularity and precision. Midshipman Plunting was also unable to appear on deck. The ship's constable, Kachikof, died the 26th, and from that time one death followed another in quick succession. On the 6th of October Lieutenant Chikhachef and one sailor died, and on the 8th Plunting's sufferings were ended. The sails were

[14] In his description of the expedition the astronomer, Croyère, becomes confused, saying that after losing sight of land on the 4th, no more was seen till the 20th, when the ship came to anchor 200 fathoms from a mountainous coast in latitude 51° 12′, where 21 canoes appeared. *Sammlung*, xx. 395.

[15] From the journal of the mate Yelagin we learn that on the 14th there remained only 12 casks of water, and that the rye mush was furnished once a day, the other meals consisting of hard bread and butter. Salt beef was boiled in sea-water. *Naval Archives*, xvi.

falling in pieces owing to constant exposure to rain
and snow, and the enfeebled crew was unable to repair them. Slowly the ship moved westward with
little attempt at navigation. The last observation had
been made the 2d of October, but only the longitude
was found, indicating a distance of eleven degrees from
the Kamchatka shore. Fortune helping them, on the
morning of the 8th land appeared in the west, which
proved to be the coast of Kamchatka in the vicinity
of Avatcha Bay. A light contrary wind detained
them for two days, and having no boats they discharged a cannon to bring help from the shore.

Of those who had left this harbor in the *Sv Pavel*
less than five months before, twenty-one were lost.
The pilot, Yelagin, alone of all the officers could appear
on deck, and he finally brought the ship into the harbor of Petropavlovsk, established by him the preceding winter. The astronomer, Croyère, who had for
weeks been confined to his berth, apparently keeping
alive by the constant use of strong liquor, asked to be
taken ashore at once, but as soon as he was exposed to
the air on deck he fell and presently expired. Chirikof, very ill, was landed at noon the same day.[16]

[16] Sokolof with much national pride exults in the achievements of Chirikof,
a true Russian, as against Bering the Dane. 'And thus having discovered
the American coast 36 hours earlier than Bering,' he writes, 'eleven degrees
of longitude farther to the east; having followed this coast three degrees
farther to the north; and after having left the coast five days later than
Bering, Chirikof returned to Kamchatka, eight degrees farther west than
Bering's landing-place, a whole month earlier; having made on his route the
same discoveries of the Aleutian Islands. During this whole time the sails
were never taken in, and no supply of fresh water was obtained; they suffered
equally from storms, privations, disease, and mortality—the officers as well
as the men. How different were the results, and what proof do they not
furnish of the superiority of the Russians in scientific navigation!' So the
learner is often apt to grow bold and impudent and despise the teacher. The
great Peter was not above learning navigation from Bering the Dane. *Zap.
Hydr.*, ix. 407-8.

CHAPTER V.

DEATH OF BERING.

1741-1742.

WE will now return to the commander. Possibly we might imagine Chirikof easily reconciled to a separation from his superior, who, instead of striking out intelligently for the achievement of a purpose, allowed himself to be carried hither and thither by omnipotent winds and imperial instructions. But not so Bering. With the loss of Chirikof and the *Sv Pavel* his right arm was gone. For a whole day he drifted in a strong gale under reefed sails before he would leave the spot to take the direction in which he supposed Chirikof to be. Then he was obliged to lie to again, and on the morning of the 22d, finding himself twelve leagues south of the point of separation, it was concluded in a council of officers to abandon further search and resume their course, not the last course of east by north as it should have been, but to the southward till latitude 46° was reached, where they had already been and seen nothing. It

(75)

was now evident that Bering was becoming incompetent; that, deprived of the assistance of Chirikof's
stronger mind and sounder judgment, he intended to
follow strictly the resolutions of the Avatcha council.
He would steer south-east by east to latitude 46°,
then change the course to east by north, and thus
waste in mid-ocean the brief days of the short
northern summer. The 24th saw Bering at the
southernmost point named, where numbers of birds
seemed to indicate land ahead, and tempted him to
continue to latitude 45° 16', when finding nothing,
and convinced for a second time of the inaccuracy of
Croyère's chart, he again bent his course east by
north, which was changed the third day to north-
north-east to compensate for having gone below
latitude 46°. The wind changed repeatedly from
south-west to south-east, being always light and accompanied with clouds and fogs; but nothing special
occurred until the 9th of July, when a strong easterly wind compelled them to head more to the north
until they reached latitude 51° 30'. The wind then
changed, allowing them to steer north-east by east.
From time to time they were misled by land-floating
drift, and weeds, and marine mammals, but the lead
indicated a depth of between one hundred and ninety
and two hundred fathoms.

The second month was now at hand, and Bering
ordered a reduced allowance of water. From the 12th
of July he was so firmly convinced of the close proximity of land that he hove to at night lest he should run
aground. Five weeks had elapsed since the *Sv Petr*
had left Avatcha Bay and the ship's log showed that
forty-six degrees of longitude separated them from
their point of departure, and still the land remained
invisible. The wind became more favorable, blowing
from the west, and Bering concluded to change his
course to the northward in order to fall in the sooner
with the land.

On the 13th, in latitude 54° 30', in a council of

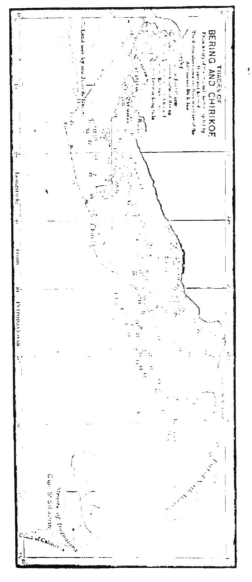

TRACES OF CHIRIKOF AND BERING.

officers, another change to north-north-east was determined on.   These frequent changes and the general
indecision in the management of the expedition proved
almost fatal; but about noon of the 16th, in latitude
58° 14′, the lookout reported a towering peak and a
high chain of snow-covered mountains, without doubt
Mount St Elias, and the extending range.   A north

KYAK ISLAND.

wind held them off from the point first seen, but on the
evening of the 20th they came upon an island in 59°
40′,[1] which was Kyak, but which they called St Elias
from the day.

---

[1] In his calculation of latitude Bering was seven minutes in error, while
in longitude he was eight degrees out of the way. Such a difference may be
accounted for on the ground that Bering's observations were based upon dead

It will be remembered that Chirikof found land on the night of the 15th while Bering saw Mount St Elias at noon of the 16th, which would give the former priority in the honor of discovery by say thirty-six hours.[2] But even Chirikof, who amongst Russians was the noblest and most chivalrous of them all, if we may believe the story of Gvozdef, may not justly set up the claim as first discoverer of north-western-most America. True, Gvozdef saw only what any one might see in sailing through the strait of Bering— he says he saw or found himself on the land opposite to Asia. Other Europeans had passed that way before Gvozdef, and the savages had crossed and re-crossed before ever Europeans were there; so we may well enough leave out these two sides of the northern strait, and call Chirikof the first discoverer of land opposite Kamchatka, which it was the object of this imperial expedition to find, and which he certainly was the first to achieve.

After these years of preparation and weeks of tempest-tossing we should expect to see the Dane de-lighted on reaching the grand consummation of the united ambitions of monarchs and mariners. But if

reckoning, without allowing for the ocean and tidal currents which in those waters often cause a gain or loss of seven leagues a day. The identity of Kyak is established by comparing Bering's with Cook's observations which would be enough even if the chart appended to Khitrof's journal had not been preserved. At first both Cook and Vancouver thought it Yakutat Bay, which they named after Bering, but both changed their minds. As late as 1787 the Russian admiralty college declared that the island of Tzukli (Mon-tague of Vancouver) was the point of Bering's discovery, but Admiral Sary-chef, who examined the journals of the expedition, pointed at once to Kyak Island as the only point to which the description of Bering and Steller could apply. Sarychef made one mistake in applying the name of Cape St Elias to the nearest point of the mainland called Cape Suckling by Cook. *Zap. Hydr.*, ix. 383–4.

[2] The date of Bering's discovery, or the day when land was first sighted by his lookout, has been variously stated. Müller makes it the 20th of July, and Steller the 18th; the 16th is in accordance with Bering's journal, and according to Bering's observation the latitude was 58° 28'. This date is con-firmed by a manuscript chart compiled by Petrof and Waxel with the help of the original log-books of both vessels. The claim set up by certain Spanish writers in favor of Francisco Gali as first discoverer of this region is based on a misprint in an early account of his voyage. For particulars see *Hist. Cal.*, i., this series.

we may believe Steller, when his officers gathered
round with their congratulations Bering shrugged his
shoulders as he glanced at the rugged shore and said,
"A great discovery no doubt, and the accomplishment
of all our desires; but who knows where we are, when
we shall see Russia, and what we shall have to eat in
the mean time?"[3]

Beating up with a light wind Bering succeeded in
gaining anchorage on a clay bottom under the lee
of the island in twenty-two fathoms. Two boats
were sent ashore, one under Khitrof to reconnoitre,
and another in which was Steller in search of water.
Khitrof found among the small islands in the gulf a
good harbor. He saw some rude deserted huts whose
owners had probably retreated on the approach of the
Russians. The habitations were constructed of logs
and rough planks, and were roofed with bark and dried
grass. A few semi-subterranean structures of sods
evidently served as storehouses. On entering, the
Russians picked up some rough cordage, a whetstone
on which copper implements had been sharpened, a
small box of poplar wood, a rattle made of baked clay,
several broken arrows, and articles of household furniture.[4] In another place the men came upon a cellar
in which was a quantity of dried salmon. Of this
Khitrof took two bundles. There were several red
foxes which seemed not at all frightened at the sight
of the Russians. To compensate the natives for the
fish taken, some trifles of Russian manufacture, tobacco
and clay pipes, were left.

Steller's party landed on another island and found
a cellar or subterranean storehouse with some red
salmon, and herbs dressed in a manner customary
with the Kamchatkans. He also found ropes made
of sea-weed, and various household utensils. Going
inland he came to a place where some savages had
been eating, and had left there an arrow and an in-

[3] *Steller's Diary*, 190.
[4] For full description of these people see *Native Races*, i., this series.

strument for lighting fire by friction. Steller also gathered plants to analyze on shipboard. He regretted that no more time was granted him in which to examine the American coast, his whole stay covering only six hours, while the sailors were filling the water-casks.[5] The latter reported having found two fire-places lately in use. They saw pieces of hewn wood, and the tracks of a man in the grass; some smoked fish was also brought on board and was found quite palatable.

Early next morning, the 21st of July, contrary to his custom Bering came on deck and ordered anchor up. It was no use for the officers to call attention to the yet unfilled water-casks, or beg to see something of the country they had found. The Dane was deaf alike to argument and entreaty. For once during the voyage he was firm. He and a hundred others had been working for the past eight years to the one end of seeing that land; and now having seen it, that was the end of it; he desired to go home. It would have been as well for him had he tarried long enough at least to fill his water-casks.

Dense clouds obscured the sky as Bering began his return voyage, and rain fell incessantly. Dismal forces were closing in round the Dane, to whom Russia was very far away indeed. By soundings a westerly course was shaped along a depth of from forty to fifty fathoms, by which means he was enabled to avoid the coast he could not see. On the 25th the general opinion in council was that by steering to the south-

[5] Steller in vain begged the commander to let him have a small boat and a few men with which to examine the place. Perched upon a steep rock the enthusiastic scientist was taking in as much as possible of America when the crusty Dane ordered him aboard if he would not be left. In his journal, edited by Pallas, Steller describes the situation as follows: 'On descending the mountain, covered with a vast forest without any trace of road or trail, I found it impossible to make my way through the thicket and consequently reascended; looking mournfully at the limits of my observation I turned my eyes toward the continent which it was not in my power to explore, and observed at the distance of a few versts a smoke ascending from a wooded eminence. Again receiving a positive order to join the ship I returned mournfully with my collection.' *Pallas, Steller's Journal,* passim.

west the coast of Kamchatka must be finally reached.
Easterly winds drove the vessel to within a short
distance of some shore invisible through the fog, and
the greatest caution had to be observed in keeping
away from the banks and shoals indicated by the
soundings. On the 26th land was made once more,
probably the coast of Kadiak, but an easterly wind
and shallow water prevented a landing. Too much
land now, to avoid which a more direct course south
was taken; but progress was impeded by the numerous islands which skirted the continent, hidden in impenetrable fog.

On the 30th an island was discovered which Bering
named Tumannoi, or Foggy Island, but no landing
was made.[6] Little progress was made among the
islands in August, owing to the thick mist and contrary winds. As the water gave out and scurvy came
the ship once more found itself among a labyrinth of
islands with high peaks looming in the distance. The
largest then in view was named Eudokia. A small
supply of water, consisting of a few casks only, was
obtained there, the heavy surf making the landing
dangerous. At a new council held the 10th, in latitude 53°, to which petty officers were admitted, it was
determined that as it had been decided to return to
Kamchatka at the end of September, and it was then
already near the middle of August, and the harbor of
Petropavlovsk was at least 1,600 miles distant, while
twenty-six of the company were ill, a further exploration of the American coast had become impracticable,
and it was necessary to proceed to the parallel of
Petropavlovsk, and then sail westward to Kamchatka.

Now, it is very plain to one having a knowledge of
the currents that it was much easier to make such a
resolution than to carry it out. Further than this, all

[6] The charts of the imperial academy at St Petersburg, in the last quarter
of the eighteenth century, located this point variously as a portion of Kadiak
and as the island of Trinidad, of the Spanish discoverers. It is now known
that Foggy Island was Ukamok, named Chirikof Island by Vancouver, in
latitude 55° 48'.

attempts to proceed to the westward were baffled by the barrier of land. Then they must have water, and so they anchored on the 30th, at a group of islands in latitude 54° 48'. Here the first death occurred—a sailor named Shumagin succumbed to scurvy. His name was given to the island, and a supply of brackish water was obtained.[7]

The commander now fell ill, and was soon confined to his cabin. The *Sv Petr* was at this place six days. One night a fire had been observed on a small island toward the north-east, and while the larger boats were engaged in watering, Khitrof went there with five men, but only, after a long pull, to find the people gone. In attempting to return, a strong head-wind threw them upon the beach of another island, and kept them there till the 2d of September, when they were relieved by the larger boat. During the next two days several unsuccessful attempts were made to proceed, for the ship's position was perilous. After a violent storm, which lasted all night, loud voices were heard on the nearest island on the morning of the 5th. A fire was plainly visible, and to the great joy of the discoverers two canoes, each containing a native, advanced toward the ship. They stopped, however, at a considerable distance displaying sticks adorned with eagles' feathers; and with gestures invited the Russians to come ashore. The latter, on the other hand, threw presents to the savages, and endeavored to induce them to approach the vessel, but in vain. After gazing with mingled wonder and dread for a time at the strange craft, the natives paddled for the shore.

Lieutenant Waxel, accompanied by nine men well armed, went to pay them a visit. They beckoned them to come to the boat; the savages in return beckoned the strangers to disembark. At last Waxel

[7] Müller states that the name was applied to the group, while an officer of the navy, with the expedition, in a letter published anonymously, says that only the island which furnished the water was named after the deceased sailor.

ordered three men to land, among them the interpreter, while he moored the boat to a rock.[8]

Expressions of good-will were profuse on both
sides, the natives offering a repast of whale-meat.
Their presence on the island was evidently temporary,
as no women or children or habitation could be seen,
and for every man there was just one *bidarka*, or skin
canoe having two or three seats—the Russian term
for an improved kyak. No bows, arrows, spears, or
any other weapons which might have alarmed the
strangers, were visible, and the Russians went about
freely among the natives, taking care, in accordance
with strict injunctions of Waxel, not to lose sight of
the boat. Meanwhile one of the natives summoned
courage to visit Waxel in the boat. He seemed to
be an elder and a chief, and the lieutenant gave him
the most precious thing he had—brandy; the savage
began to drink, but immediately spat it out, crying to
his people that he was poisoned. All Waxel's efforts
to quiet him were unavailing; needles, glass beads, an
iron kettle, tobacco, and pipes were offered in vain.
He would accept nothing. He was allowed to go,
and at the same time Waxel recalled his men. The
natives made an attempt to detain them, but finally
allowed the two Russians to go, keeping hold of the
interpreter. Others ran to the rock to which the
boat was moored and seized the rope, which Waxel
thereupon ordered cut. The interpreter in the mean
time pleaded with the Russians not to abandon him,
but they could afford no aid. As a final effort to save
the interpreter two muskets were discharged, and as
the report echoed from the surrounding cliffs, the savages fell to the ground while the interpreter sprang
into the boat. As the ship was making ready to sail
next day seven of these savages came and exchanged
gifts. This was on the 6th of September. After a

[8] The interpreters accompanying the expedition belonged to the Koriak
and Chukchi tribes, and were of no use in conversing with the natives, but
they were bold and inspired the islanders with confidence, being in outward
appearance like themselves.

very stormy passage land was sighted again on the 24th, in latitude 51° 27'.[9] There was a coast with islands and mountains, to the highest of which Bering gave the name of St John, from the day.

The position of the ship was critical. Finally they escaped the dangerous shore, only to be driven by a storm of seventeen days' duration down to latitude 48°. Disease spread. Every day one or more died, until there were scarcely enough left to manage the ship. "The most eloquent pen," said Steller, "would fail to describe the misery of our condition." Opinion was divided whether they should seek a harbor on the American coast or sail directly to Kamchatka. Bering was profuse in his promises to celestial powers, slighting none, Catholic or Protestant, Greek or German. He vowed to make ample donations to the Russian church at Petropavlovsk and to the Lutheran church at Viborg, Finland, where some of his relatives resided.

A northerly course was kept until the 22d of October, when an easterly breeze made it possible to head the unfortunate craft for Kamchatka. Only fifteen casks of water remained, and the commander was so reduced by sickness and despondency that the burden of affairs fell almost wholly on Waxel. On the 25th land was sighted in latitude 51° and named St Makarius. This was the island of Amchitka. On the 28th another island in latitude 52° was named St Stephen (Kishka). On the 29th in latitude 52° 30' still another island was discovered and named St Abram (Semichi Island). On the 30th two other islands were sighted and mistaken by the bewildered navigators as the first of the Kuriles. On the 1st of November in latitude 54° they found themselves within about sixteen miles of a high line of coast.

[9] The latitude of the land was variously reported by Waxel, and subsequently by Chirikof from his examination of journals, at 51° 27', 52° 30', and 51° 12'. It is safe to presume that the St John's mountain of Bering was situated either on the island of Umnak or on one of the Four Peaks Islands. Sokolof was of the opinion that it was Atkha Island. *Zap. Hydr.*, ix. 393.

The condition of the explorers still continued critical.
Notwithstanding sickness and misery the decimated
crew was obliged to work night and day, in rain, snow,
and cold; the sails and rigging were so rotten that
it was dangerous to set much canvas, even if the crew
had been able.[10] At last, on the 4th, the lookout sighted
land.   It was distant; only the mountain tops appearing above the horizon; and though the *Sv Petr* was
headed directly for the land all day, they could not
reach it.   An observation at noon made the latitude
56°.

"It would be impossible to describe," says Steller,
"the joy created by the sight of land; the dying
crawled upon deck to see with their own eyes what
they would not believe; even the feeble commander
was carried out of his cabin.   To the astonishment
of all a small keg of brandy was taken from some
hiding-place and dealt out in celebration of the supposed approach to the coast of Kamchatka."

On the morning of the 5th another misfortune was
discovered.   All the shrouds on the starboard side
were broken, owing to contraction caused by frost.
Lieutenant Waxel at once reported to the commander,
who was confined in his berth, and from him received
orders convoking a council of officers to deliberate
upon the situation.   It was well known that the fresh
water was almost exhausted, and that the ravages of
scorbutic disease were becoming more alarming every
day.   The continuous wetting with spray and rain
became more dangerous and insupportable as the cold
increased, covering with a coat of ice the surface of
every object exposed to its action, animate or inani-

---

[10] Müller writes: 'The sickness was so dreadful that the two sailors who
used to be at the rudder were obliged to be led to it by two others who could
hardly walk, and when one could sit and steer no longer another in but little
better condition supplied his place.' *Müller's Sammlung*, 51.   The commander
was still confined to his cabin; the officers though scarcely able to walk, were
quarrelling among themselves; the crew were dying at the rate of one or two
every day; no hard bread, no spirits, and but very little water; dampness and
cold; and to all this was added the almost certainty of impending disaster.
Sokolof, in *Zap. Hydr.*, ix. 393.

mate. Soon the council came to the conclusion that it was necessary to seek relief at the nearest point of land, be it island or continent.[11] The wind was from the north, and the soundings indicated between thirty and forty fathoms over sandy bottom. After steering south-west for some time the soundings decreased to twelve fathoms, and the vessel was found to be only a short distance from the shore. Then at the command of Waxel, over the bows of the doomed ship, down went the anchors of the *Sv Petr* for the last time. It was 5 o'clock in the afternoon. The sea began to rise, and in less than an hour a cable broke. Then other cables were lost; and just as the despairing mariners were about to bend the last one on board, a huge wave lifted the vessel over a ledge of rocks into smooth water of about four fathoms, but not before seriously injuring the hull. This action of the elements settled the fate of the expedition; there was no alternative but to remain for the winter on that coast, ignorant of its extent and location as they were. It was on a calm moonlit night that the stormy voyage of over four months was thus suddenly terminated.[12]

All able to work were landed to prepare for disembarking the sick. A preliminary shelter was constructed by digging niches into the sandy banks of a small stream and covering them with sails. Driftwood was found along the shore, but there was no sign of any timber which might be made useful. No trace of human occupation was visible. On the morn-

[11] Steller maintains that Bering refused to give the necessary orders, supposing that it would still be possible to reach Avatcha, and that he was supported in his opinion by Ovtzin; but the contrary opinion of Waxel and Khitrof prevailed. *Sokolof,* in *Zap. Hydr.,* ix. 397.

[12] A letter of one of the officers says: 'In endeavoring to go to the west we were cast on a desert isle where we had the prospect of remaining the greater part of our days. Our vessel was broken up on one of the banks with which the isle is surrounded. We failed not to save ourselves on shore, with all such things as we thought we had need of; for by a marked kindness of providence the wind and waves threw after us upon the shore the wreck and the remains of our vessel, which we gathered together to put us in a state, with the blessing of God, to quit this desolate abode.' *Burney's Chronol. Hist.,* 172–3. See also *Sokolof,* in *Zap. Hydr.,* ix. 399.

ing of the 8th preparations for landing the sick
were completed and the work began. Many of the
unfortunates drew their last breath as soon as they
come in contact with the fresh air, while others expired during the process of removal. During the day
following Commander Bering was carried ashore. He
had been daily growing weaker, and had evidently
made up his mind that he must die. Four men carried him in a hand-barrow well secured against the
air. Shortly afterward the last remnant of the unfortunate ship was torn from its single cable and came
upon the shore. Steller searched in vain for anti-
scorbutic herbs and plants under the deep snow, and
there was no game or wild-fowl at hand. The only
animals visible on land were the *pestsi* or Arctic foxes,
exceedingly bold and rapacious. They fell upon the
corpses and devoured them almost before the survivors
could make preparations for their burial. It seemed
to be impossible to frighten them away. The stock
of powder was small, and it would not do to waste
it on beasts; it must be kept for killing men. The
sea-otter was already known to the Russians from a
few specimens captured on the coast of Kamchatka,
and among the Kurile Islands. Soon the castaways
discovered the presence of these animals in the surrounding waters. The flesh seemed to them most palatable, and Steller even considered it as anti-scorbutic.
The skins were preserved by the survivors and subsequently led to the discovery of a wealth that Bering
and Chirikof had failed to see in their voyages of
observation.[13]

Some relief in the way of provisions was afforded
by the carcass of a whale cast upon the beach. It

[13] At that time the Chinese merchants at Kiakhta paid from 80 to
100 rubles for sea-otter skins; 900 sea-otters were killed on the island by
the crew of the *Sv Petr;* the skins were divided equally among all, but
Steller was most fortunate. In his capacity of physician he received many
presents, and he bought many skins, the property of persons who in the uncertainty of living held them in light esteem. His share alone is said to have
amounted to 300 choice skins, which he carried with him to Kamchatka. *Steller's Journal*, 172, 175, passim; *Müller, Sammlung*, 54–5.

was not very delicate food, but proved of great service when nothing better could be had. It afforded also the material for feeding lamps during the long dreary nights of winter. No distinction was made in the division of food between officers and men; every one had a fair and equal portion. Lieutenant Waxel was now recognized as general manager, the commander being beyond duty. Misfortune and misery had toned down the rough aggressiveness of the lieutenant, and nearly all of the wise regulations thereafter adopted must be credited to him, though he frequently acted upon Steller's advice. Both did their utmost to give occupation to all who were able as the only remedy against their mortal enemy, the scurvy.

Toward the end of November Khitrof and Waxel also were prostrated by disease, and the prospect before the castaways was indeed a gloomy one. The excursions to different parts of the island in search of food and fuel became more and more contracted, and dull despair settled upon the whole community.

As for the commander, no wonder he had longed to return; for it was now apparent to all, as it may have been to him these many days, that he must die. And we can pardon him the infirmities of age, disease, and temper; the labors of his life had been severe and his death was honorable, though the conditions were by no means pleasing. Toward the last he became if possible more timid, and exceedingly suspicious. He could hardly endure even the presence of Steller, his friend and confidant, yet this faithful companion praises his firm spirit and dignified demeanor.

It was under such circumstances that Vitus Bering died—on this cold forbidding isle, under the sky of an Arctic winter, the 8th of December 1741, in a miserable hut half covered by the sand which came trickling down upon him through the boards that had been placed to bar its progress. Thus passed from earth, as nameless tens of thousands have done, the illustrious commander of the expeditions which had disclosed the separation of the two worlds and discovered north-westernmost America.

On the 10th of December the second mate, Khotiaintzof, died, and a few days later three of the sailors. On the 8th of January death demanded another victim, the commissary Lagunof, making thirty-one up to this time.[14]

At length the survivors began slowly to improve in health. The ship's constable, Rossilius, with two men, was despatched northward to explore; but they learned only that they were on an island. Later the sailor, Anchugof, was ordered southward, and after an absence of nearly four weeks he returned half-starved, without information of any kind. Another was sent west, but with the same result. It was only then that many would believe they were not on the shore of Kamchatka, and that it depended upon their own exertions whether they ever left their present dwellings, certainly not very attractive ones, these excavations in the earth roofed over with sails.[15] The foreigners formed a separate colony in one large cavity. There were five of these, Steller, Rossilius, Plenisner, Assistant Surgeon Betge, and a soldier named Zand. Waxel occupied a dwelling by himself and another private domicile had been constructed by the two boatswains, Ivanof and Alexeïef. All the others lived together in one large excavation.

The provisions were by no means abundant, but

[14] A list of the effects of Bering and the petty officers, preserved in the naval archives, contains: 3 quadrants, 1 chronometer, 1 compass, 1 spy-glass, 1 gold watch, 1 pair of pistols, 8 copper drinking-cups, a few pipes, 11 books on navigation, a bundle of charts, 2 bundles of calculations, 7 maps, and 8 dozen packs of playing-cards. With the exception of the playing-cards, all were sold at auction in Kamchatka, and brought 1,000 rubles. *Sokolof*, in *Zap. Hydr.*, ix 10, 11.

[15] Nagaïef, an assistant of Sokolof in the collection and digestion of documents concerning the expedition, states that he found original entries of Waxel and Khitrof in the journal, to the effect that after Bering's death the only two remaining officers declared their willingness to temporarily resign their rank and put themselves on an equality with the men, but that the latter refused, and continued to obey their superiors. *Morskoi Sbornik*, cvi. 215.

great care was exercised in distributing them, keeping always in view the possibility of a further sea-voyage in search of Kamchatka. The principal food was the meat of marine mammals killed about the shore, sea-otters, seals, and sea-lions. Carcasses of whales were cast ashore twice during the winter, and though in an advanced state of putrefaction they yielded an abundant supply to the unfortunates, who had ceased to be very particular as to the quality of their diet. In the spring the sea-cows made their appearance and furnished the mariners with an abundance of more palatable meat. The only fuel was drift-wood, for which they had to mine the deep snow for eight or ten miles round. The winter was cold and stormy throughout, and the approach of spring was heralded by dense fogs hanging about the island for weeks without lifting sufficiently to afford a glance at the surrounding sea.

A council was now held and some proposed sending the single remaining ship's boat for assistance; others were of the opinion that the ship itself, though half broken up, might still be repaired; but finally it was determined to take the wreck entirely to pieces and out of them construct a new craft of a size sufficient to hold the entire company. A singular question here presented itself to these navigators, accustomed as they were to the iron discipline of the imperial service, Would they not be punished for taking to pieces a government vessel? After some discussion it dawned on their dim visions that perhaps after all the punishment of their dread ruler might be no worse than death on that island. Hence it was solemnly resolved to begin at once; the wreck was dismantled, and in May the keel was laid for the new vessel.

The three ship's carpenters were dead, but a Cossack who had once worked in the ship-yard at Okhotsk was chosen to superintend the construction, and he proved quite successful in drawing the plans and

moulding the frames.[16] The lack of material and
tools naturally delayed the work, and it was the 10th
of August before the vessel could be launched. She
was constructed almost wholly without iron, and measured thirty-six feet in length at the keel, and forty-
one feet on deck, with a beam of twelve feet and a
depth of hold of only five and a half feet. She was
still called the *Sv Petr*. The vessel had to be provisioned wholly from the meat of sea-animals.[17]

On the 16th of August,[18] after a stay of over
nine months on this island, to which they gave the
name of Bering, at the suggestion of Khitrof, and
after protracted prayers and devotions, this remnant
of the commander's crew set sail from the scene of
suffering and disaster. On the third day out, as might
be expected from such construction, the vessel was
found to be leaking badly, and within half an hour
there were two feet of water in the hold. Some lead
and ammunition were thrown out, and the leak was
stopped. On the ninth day the hearts of the unhappy
crew were gladdened by a full view of the Kamchatka
shore, and on the following day, the 26th of August,
the juvenile *Sv Petr* was safely anchored in the bay
of Avatcha. The survivors were received by the few
inhabitants of Petropavlovsk with great rejoicing;
they had long since been given up as dead. They
remained at the landing-place to recuperate for
nearly a year, and finally proceeded to Okhotsk in
1743.[19]

[16] He succeeded so well in his undertaking that he received as reward from
the grateful empress the patent of nobility. *Sammlung*, xx. 394.

[17] *Zap. Hydr.*, ix. 413. The author of the *Sammlungen* states that when
the sea-otters disappeared in March the Russians had recourse to dogs, bears,
and lions, meaning of course seals (*seehund*), fur-seal (*seebär*), and sea-lions.
Sammlung, xx. 393.

[18] Sokolof makes the date of departure the 12th. *Zap. Hydr.*, ix. 413;
obviously an error on the part of some one.

[19] In the church of Petropavlovsk there is still preserved a memorial of
this event; a silver mounted image of the apostles Peter and Paul with the
inscription, 'An offering in memory of our miraculous rescue from a barren
island, and our return to the coast of Kamchatka, by lieutenant Dimitri
Ovtzin, and the whole company, August 1741.' *Polonski, Kamchatka Archives,
MS.*, vol. xiii.

Before he had fairly recovered from the effects of his last voyage, Chirikof made another effort to see something more of the American coast which he had found. He commanded the *Sv Pavel* again, but the only officer of the former voyage now with him was the pilot Yelagin.[20] Sailing from Avatcha Bay the 25th of May 1742, he shaped his course due east. His progress was slow, and on the 8th of June he sighted the first land in latitude 52°. Only the snow-covered tops of high mountains were visible above the fog and clouds which enveloped the island called by Chirikof, St Theodore, but which we know to-day as Attoo. A series of southerly gales then set in which carried the ship northward to latitude 54° 30'. On the 16th of June, owing to the wretched condition of the vessel, it was deemed best to return to Kamchatka. On the way back the *Sv Pavel* passed within a short distance of the island where at that moment Bering's companions were still suffering. Chirikof sighted the southern point of the island and named it St Julian. The expedition reached Petropavlovsk the 1st of July.[21]

[20] Müller, *Voyage*, 112, maintains that Chirikof intended to search for Bering; but Sokolof scouts the idea upon the ground that he could not have had the faintest suspicion of his whereabouts; it was then believed that Bering and all his crew had perished. *Sokolof*, in *Zap. Hydr.*, ix. 414.

[21] As this last attempt of Chirikof ends the operations of the expedition which accomplished the discovery of the American coast, the official list of all those engaged in the enterprise in its various branches, taken from Bering's private journal, will not be out of place. The names are arranged according to rank as follows: Captain-commander, Vitus Bering; captains, Martin Spanberg and Alexeï Chirikof; lieutenants, Dmitri Laptief, Yegor Endogurof, William Walton, Peter Lassenius, Dmitri Ovtzin, Stepan Muravief, Mikhaïl Pavlof, Stepan Malygin, Alexeï Skuratof, Ivan Sukhotin, Hariton Laptief, Ivan Chikhachef; midshipman, Alexeï Schelting; mates, Sven Waxel, Vassili Promchishchef, Mikhaïl Plunting, Andreïan Eselberg, Lev Kazimerof, Ivan Kashelef, Fedor Minin, Sofron Khitrof, Abram Dementief; second mates, Ivan Vereshchagin, Ivan Yelagin, Matveï Petrof, Dmitri Sterlegof, Semen Cheliuskin, Vassili Rtishchef, Vassili Andreïef, Gavril Rudnef, Peter Pazniakof, Marko Golovin, Ivan Biref, Kharlam Yushin, Moïssei Yurlof, Andreï Shiganof; marines, Vassili Perenago, Joann Synd, Andreïan Yurlof; naval cadets, Mikhaïl Scherbinin, Vassili Khmetevski, Ossip Glazof, Emilian Rodichef, Andreï Velikopolski, Fedor Kanishchef, Sergeï Spiridof, Sergeï Sunkof; commissaries, Agafon Choglokof, Fedor Kolychef, Stepan Ivashenin, Ivan Lagunof; navigators, Ivan Beluï, Mikhaïl Vosikof; assistant navigators, Dmitri Korostlef, Nikita Khotiaïntzof; boatswains, Niels Jansen, Sidor Savelief; boatswain's mate, Fedor Kozlof; boat-builders, Andreï Kozmin, William Butzovski, Henrich Hovins, Caspar Feich; assistant surgeons, Ivan Stupin, William Berensen, Peter Brauner, Sim Gren, Thomas Vinzen-

In the August following, and before the survivors of Bering's party could reach that port, Chirikof sailed for Okhotsk.

dorf, Henrich Schaffer, Elias Günther, Kiril Shemchushuykof, Moritz Armenus, Andreas Heer, Ivan Paxin, Henrich Hebel, Mikhaïl Brant, Matthias Betge, Johann Lau; academicians, Gerhard Müller, Johann Gmelin, Louis Croyère; Professor Johann Fischer; adjunct, George Wilhelm Steller; students, Stepan Krashennikof, Fedor Popof, Luka Ivanof, Alexeï Tretiakof, Alexeï Gorlonof; instrument-maker, Stepan Ovsiannikof; painter, Johann Berkhan; draughtsman, Johann Lursenino; translator, Ilia Yakhoutof; surveyors, Andreï Krassilnikof, Nikifor Chekin, Moïsseï Oushakof, Alexander Ivanof, Peter Skobeltzin, Dmitri Baskakof, Ivan Svistunof, Vassili Shetilof, Vassili Selifontof, Ivan Kindiarof, Vassili Somof, Mikhaïl Gvozdef; assistant surveyors, Mikhaïl Vuikhodzef, Fedor Prianishnikof, Alexeï Maksheïef, Ivan Shavrigin; assayer, Simon Gardebol; mineralogists, Dmitri Odintzof, Friedrich Weidel, Elias Schehl, Zakar Medvedef, Agapius Leskin, Ivan Samoilof. There was also one parish priest, with six subordinate members of the clergy. The following is the naval roster of Bering's command as distributed among the various divisions of the expedition.

ROSTER OF BERING'S COMMAND IN 1740.

RANK.	On the Ships of			On the Double Sloops			Total.
	Bering.	Chiri-kof.	Span-berg.	of Span-berg.	with Arctic Exped.	In the White Sea.	
Captain Commander......	1	..	..	..	..	..	1
Captains...............	..	1	1	..	..	..	2
Lieutenants.............	1	1	..	1	3	2	8
Midshipmen	..	..	..	1	..	..	1
Mates..................	1	1	2	..	..	..	4
Second Mates	2	2	..	2	3	2	12
Naval Cadets............	..	..	2	..	3	2	7
Surgeons...............	1	1	1	..	..	..	3
Ass't Surgeons	1	1	..	2	3	2	9
Medical Cadets..........	2	2	..	..	..	..	4
Boatswains.............	1	1	..	..	..	..	2
Boatswain's Mates.......	2	2	1	2	3	2	12
Quartermasters..........	2	2	1	2	3	2	12
Commissaries...........	1	1	1	..	..	..	3
Buglers................	2	..	2	..	..	..	4
Constables.............	1	1	1	2	3	2	10
Cannoneers.............	6	6	2	4	6	4	28
Writers................	1	1	2	..	3	..	7
Navigators.............	1	1	..	..	..	..	2
Sailors................	12	12	12	4	6	4	50
Rope-makers	3	3	4	4	9	4	27
Sail-makers	3	3	2	4	9	4	25
Carpenters.............	3	3	3	6	9	6	30
Coopers...............	3	3	2	4	6	4	22
Sergeants..............	1	1	1	2	..	2	6
Corporals	1	1	..	..	..	..	2
Privates...............	24	24	20	52	78	52	250
Drummers	1	1	1	..	..	..	3
Total...............	77	75	61	92	147	94	546

Call it science, or patriotism, or progress, there is this to be said about the first Russian discoveries in America—little would have been heard of them for some time to come if ever, had it not been for the beautiful furs brought back from Bering Island and

According to the ledgers of the admiralty college the expenditure in behalf of the expedition up to the end of the year 1742 has been as follows:

		Rubles.	K.
At St Petersburg	For pay and uniform	30,383	5½
	For provisions	684	76
	For transportation	3,103	67¼
	For scientific instruments......	73	52
	For various stores.............	5,206	54¾
	Total	39,451	55½
At Kazan...............	Cash...........................	4,754	.....
	Rigging, lumber, and provisions.	1,107	25¼
At Arkhangelsk.........	....	10,801	47½
	Total	56,114	82¾
At Ilinsk		2,178	73
In the Province of Siberia.	Cash, provisions, and stores....	229,525	33
	Sundry expenditure..........	72,840	79½
	Grand total................	360,659	13¾

Sokolof, in *Zap. Hydr.*, ix. 446–52.

Spanberg made a reconnoissance in the sea of Okhotsk in 1740. In September 1741 he crossed from Okhotsk to Kamchatka with the packet-boat *Sv Ioann*, the brigantine *Arkhangel Mikhaïl*, the double sloop *Nadeshda*, and the sloop *Bolsheretsk*, this being the beginning of an official expedition to Japan. Although the squadron was so pretentious, and had on board many learned men who were to expound the mysteries of those parts, nothing of importance came from it. This was one branch of the explorations included in Bering's scheme. Another was a survey of the coast of Okhotsk Sea by Lieutenant Walton in 1741.

Explorations were also carried on along the Kamchatka coast. In 1742 Surveyor Oushakof explored the coast from Bolsheretsk northward to Figil, and from the Bay of Avatcha to Cape Kronotzkoi. A portion of this work had previously been attempted by the pilot Yelagin in 1739, and maps prepared by him are still preserved in the naval archives at St Petersburg, but for some reason the later survey was adopted as authority. Steller and Gorlanof continued their investigations in Kamchatka until 1744. In accordance with instructions they also experimented in agricultural pursuits, meeting with no success in their attempts. When the combined commands of Chirikof, Waxel, and Spalding arrived at Okhotsk, they found orders awaiting them to proceed to Yakutsk and remain there for further instructions. This order virtually ended the expedition. The leaders claimed that all its objects had been attained as far as possible. Many of the officers and scientists

elsewhere. Siberia was still sufficient to satisfy the
tsar for purposes of expatriation, and the Russians
were not such zealots as to undertake conquest for
the sake of conversion, and to make religion a cloak

had already returned before accomplishing their task; others were still
detained by sickness and other circumstances; others again had died and the
force still fit for duty of any kind was very much reduced. The provisions
amassed with such immense labor and trouble had been expended, the rigging
and sails of ships were completely worn out, the ships themselves were unseaworthy, and the resources of all Siberia had been nearly exhausted. The
native tribes and convict settlers had been crushed by the most oppressive requisitions in labor and stores, and even the forests in the immediate vicinity
of settlements had been thinned out to an alarming extent for the requirements of the expedition. In 1743 a famine raged in eastern Siberia to such
an extent that in the month of September an imperial oukaz ordained the
immediate suspension of other operations. The force was divided into small
detachments and scattered here and there in the more fertile districts of
Siberia. The temporary suspension of the labors of the expedition was followed by an entire abandonment of the work. The Siberian contingents
returned to their proper stations, the sailors and mechanics belonging to the
navy were ordered to Tomsk and Yenisseisk. Through intrigues at the
imperial court the commanders were long detained in the wilds of Siberia;
Chirikof and Spanberg until 1746, Waxel until 1749, and Rtishchef until
1754, when a new expedition was already on the *tapis*. The original charts
and journals of the expedition were forwarded to Irkutsk only in 1754, though
official copies had certainly been taken previous to that time. From Irkutsk
they were removed in 1759 to the city of Tobolsk, and again copied. No
reason was given for retaining the originals, but it is certain that they were
destroyed during a fire in Tobolsk in 1788. *Zap. Hydr.*, v. 265. Records of
promotions conferred upon a few members of the expedition have been preserved. Ovtzin and Laptief were made lieutenants on Waxel's recommendation in 1743; Alexeï Ivanof and Yelagin were promoted to the same rank on
Chirikof's recommendation in 1744. On the 20th of November 1749 an imperial oukaz bestowed a money reward upon all the survivors of Bering's
command on the *Sv Petr*, 'for having suffered many unheard of hardships.'
Khitrof was made a lieutenant and finally captain of the first rank. Waxel
was promoted to a captain of the second rank in 1744, while all his command
obtained a reward in money from the admiralty college. In 1754 the force
of Lieutenant Rtishchef at Tomsk consisted of 42 men, and that of Lieutenant
Khenetevski at Okhotsk, of 46 men; the last two officers evidently remained
in Siberia, as they are mentioned again in the archives of Okhotsk as captains
in 1773.

The marine Synd, who undertook the unfortunate expedition to Bering
Straits, also remained in Siberia, promoted to the rank of lieutenant, and
died at Okhotsk in 1770. *Siberian Archives; Müller*, 9th ser.; *Zap. Hydr.*, v.
268. The young widow of the astronomer De la Croyère in 1774 married
Captain Lebedef, who was assigned to the command of Kamchatka. *Sgibnef*,
in *Morskoi Sbornik*, cii. 5, 55. The town of Okhotsk had received a great
impetus during the operations of the Bering expedition, for which it served
as the maritime base. A few rude vessels were constructed at Okhotsk
during the first decade of the eighteenth century, and official records are still
in existence of all the shipping constructed at that port from the year 1714
to modern times. Up to the time when Bering's expedition left Okhotsk for
the interior of Siberia 19 vessels were enumerated in this list. The first of
these vessels was a *lodka*, a craft with one mast, half-decked over, 27 feet in
length, with 18 (!) feet beam, drawing with a full cargo only three feet and
a half of water. The keel was laid at Okhotsk in May 1714, and she was

for their atrocities; hence, but for these costly skins,
each of which proclaimed in loudest strains the glories
of Alaska, the Great Land might long have rested

launched in May 1716. The builder was carpenter Kiril Plotnitzki(?). The
vessel had a brief existence, for she stranded in 1721, and was finally burned
for the iron in 1727. The second vessel was of the same class. The keel was
laid in 1718 for the first Kamchatka expedition, but she was never finished,
and rotted on the stocks. The third was also a lodka, 54 feet in length by 18
in width; she was constructed at Oudsk, near Okhotsk, in 1719, by one Teta-
rinof. This craft also was never launched, and finally fell to pieces. The
fourth vessel, also a lodka, was begun by a carpenter named Kargopoltzof,
in 1720, and launched in 1723. Bering caused her to be retimbered in 1727,
and in 1734 the vessel was beached as unseaworthy, but she was finally
repaired in 1741 and wrecked on the Kurile Islands in the same year. The
fifth, a lodka, was built near Okhotsk in 1724, but was never finished 'for
want of material.' The sixth vessel constructed at Okhotsk was the shitika
Fortuna, built in one year by a marine, Chaplin, probably an Englishman,
and launched in June 1727. In 1730 the *Fortuna* was hauled up as unseaworthy, but in 1731 she was repaired once more and finally retimbered in
1737, and wrecked in the same year near Bolsheretsk. The seventh on the
list, the *Sv Gavril*, was constructed under Bering's immediate supervision at
Nishekamchatsk in the year 1728. In 1737 she was retimbered by Lieutenant Spanberg at Okhotsk. In 1738 she was wrecked on the coast of Kamchatka, but again repaired in the following year, 1739. She was finally broken
up as unseaworthy in 1755. The eighth vessel constructed at Okhotsk was
the *Vostochnui Gavril*, or Eastern Gabriel, built in 1729 by Sphanef for Shestakof's expedition. After Gvozdef's voyage to Bering Strait the *Eastern
Gabriel* was wrecked in October 1739 by Fedoref near Bolsheretsk. The *Lev*
(Lion) was also built by Sphanef at Okhotsk in 1729, but was burned by the
hostile Koriaks in September of the same year. A lodka built by Churekaief
in 1729 is the tenth on the list. The navigator Moshkof used this craft for
an exploration of the Shantar Islands, but she proved unseaworthy and was
abandoned. Next on the list is the brigantine *Arkhangel Mikhail*, begun at
Okhotsk in 1735 and launched in 1737 for Bering's second expedition. The
builders were Rogachef and Kozmin, superintended by Spanberg himself.
The brigantine did good service, but was finally wrecked in 1753. The 12th
on the list is the double sloop *Nadeshda*, with three masts (?) and gaff-top-
sails. She was begun by the same builders at Okhotsk in 1735 and launched in
1737. This also proved a useful craft, but she was finally wrecked in 1753
by one Naoumof on the Kurile Islands. The sloop *Bolsheretsk* was built by
Spanberg in 1739 of birch timber, and provided with 18 oars. She was
declared to be unseaworthy in 1745. The galiot *Okhotsk*, the 14th on the
list, was built by Rogachef at Okhotsk in 1737. Ten years later she was
repaired, and wrecked the year after. The packet-boat *Sv Petr*, the vessel
in which Bering sailed, was also built by Rogachef and Kozmin in 1741.
She was wrecked and rebuilt on Bering Island in the same year, as we have
seen. The vessel of Chirikof, the big *Sv Pavel*, was built by the same persons in Okhotsk and launched in 1740, and only four years later she was
abandoned as unseaworthy. The next on the list is the packet-boat *Ioan
Krestitel*, or St John the Baptist, built in Okhotsk by Kozmin 1741, for Spanberg's expedition, and wrecked near Bolsheretsk in October 1743, under command of Lieutenant Khmetevski. The sloop *Elizaveta*, the 18th on the list,
was built at Okhotsk by Kozmin, wrecked on the Kamchatka coast in 1745,
repaired, and wrecked again in 1755. The small *Sv Petr*, built on Bering
Island out of the remains of the larger vessel, was sunk on the coast of Kamchatka in 1753, but raised and beached in 1754. *Okhotsk Archives; Sgibnef,
Moiskoi Sbornik, 1855*, 12–210.

undisturbed. Be that as it may, it was chiefly on the
voyages of Bering and Chirikof that Russia ever after
based her claim to the ownership of north-westernmost America.[22]

[22] The voyages of Vitus Bering have furnished material for much learned
discussion. The French astronomer De L'Isle de la Croyère advanced the
claim of having been largely instrumental in their accomplishment, more so perhaps than he was justly entitled to, though it cannot be denied that he had
much to say in the organization of the second expedition under Bering. With
the honor of having planned the expedition, he should not attempt to escape
the odium of having furnished it with such villainous charts, to which may be
attributed most of that suffering and loss of life which followed. Nor is he by
any means just to Bering, seeking as he does in his account to deprive him of
any part in the discovery, claiming that Chirikof's party made the only discovery worthy of mention. He does not even state that Bering touched upon
the American coast at all; according to his narrative Bering 'sailed from Kamchatka, but did not go far, having been compelled by a storm to anchor at a
desert island where he and most of his companions perished.' An author
makes nothing by such trickery. His attempted deceit is sure sooner or
later to fall back upon his own head. Nor will it do to pretend ignorance.
Professor Müller, of the imperial academy of science, accompanied Bering
on his last voyage. At the time De L'Isle was writing his treatise Müller
was living in the same street in St Petersburg, and meeting as they must
have done daily, it would have been easy to ascertain the truth if he had
wished to know it. That such wretched maps as Croyère's should have been
given to the world by Russia, or in her name, is all the more to be deplored,
because the Russians, though they had then scarcely gained a place among
seafaring nations, had made the most strenuous efforts at discovery in waters
so inhospitable that people less inured to the rigors of climate, and less de-
spotically governed, would never have thought of navigating them. Others
may have furnished the idea which the Russians alone, who to be sure would
reap the first benefits from such discoveries, were possessed of power and
endurance to carry out.

CHAPTER VI.

THE SWARMING OF THE PROMYSHLENIKI.

1743-1762.

ONE would think that, with full knowledge of the sufferings and dangers encountered by Bering's and Chirikof's expeditions, men would hesitate before risking their lives for otter-skins. But such was not the case. When a small vessel was made ready to follow the course of the *Sv Petr* and the *Sv Pavel* there was no lack of men to join it, though some of them were still scarcely able to crawl, from the effects of former disaster. As the little sable had enticed the Cossack from the Black Sea and the Volga across the Ural Mountains and the vast plains of Siberia to the shores of the Okhotsk Sea and the Pacific, so now the sea-otter lures the same venturesome race out among the islands, and ice, and fog-banks of ocean.

The first to engage in hunting sea-otters and other fur-bearing animals, east of Kamchatka, was Emilian Bassof, who embarked as early as 1743, if we may believe Vassili Berg, our best authority on the subject.[1] Bassof was sergeant of the military company

[1] *Berg, Khronologicheskaïa Istoria Otkrytiy Aleutskikh Ostrovakh*, 2, 3, pas-

of lower Kamchatka, whose imagination had become excited by the wealth brought home by Bering's crew. Forming a partnership with a merchant from Moscow, Andreï Serebrennikof, he built a small *shitika*[2] which he called the *Kapiton*, sailed to Bering Island, passed the winter there, and returned to Kamchatka in the following year.[3] A second voyage was made the following July,[4] with Nikofor Trapeznikof as partner, the same vessel being employed. Besides Bering Island, Bassof also visited Copper Island, and collected 1,600 sea-otters, 2,000 fur-seals, and 2,000 blue Arctic foxes. From this trip Bassof returned on the 31st of July 1746. A third voyage was undertaken by Bassof in 1747, from which he returned in the following year, and embarked for a last voyage in 1749.[5]

sim. Most authorities are silent concerning this expedition, but Sgibnef, *Morskoi Sbornik*, cii. 74, states that Bassof sailed on his first voyage in 1743.

[2] The shitikas, from the Russian *shi-it*, to sew, were vessels made almost without iron bolts, the planks being 'sewed' together or fastened with leather or seal-skin thongs.

[3] From papers preserved in the chancellery of Bolsheretsk. See also *Berg, Khronologicheskaïa Istoria*, 3, 4.

[4] The author of *Neue Nachrichten* doubts the authenticity of these statements. But, as Berg had access to all the archives, we may safely accept his statement, though in the chronological table appended to his work the expedition of the *Kapiton* is omitted. *Berg, Khronol. Istoria, Appendix.* Sgibnef states that Bassof formed a partnership with Trapeznikof in 1747 to undertake 'the second voyage,' from which they realized a return of 112,220 rubles. *Morskoi Sbornik*, cii.-v. 74.

[5] A report to the commander of Okhotsk with reference to the third voyage was discovered by Prince Shakhovskoi in the archives of Okhotsk. From this document Berg gives the following extracts: 'Most respectful report of Sergeant Emilian Bassof to the councillor of the port of Okhotsk:—After having set out with some Cossacks upon a sea-voyage last year (1747), in search of unknown islands, in the shitika *Sv Petr*, at our own expense, we arrived at a previously discovered small island,' Copper Island. 'On the beach about 50 pounds of native copper was gathered. On the south-eastern side of the same island we found some unknown material, some ore or mineral, of which we took a pound or two. Our men picked up 205 pebbles on the beach great and small, and among them were two yellow ones and one pink. We also found a new kind of fish...We brought with us to the port of Nishekamchatsk sea-otters male and female 970 skins, and the same number of tails, and 1,520 blue foxes. These furs were all divided in shares among those who were with me on the above-mentioned voyage...Sergeant Emilian Bassof.' *Berg, Khronol. Istoria*, 4. The ship *Sv Petr*, Captain Emilian Bassof, is likewise mentioned in Berg's tabular list of voyages under date of 1750. 'A fortunate event which occurred while I was engaged in collecting information with regard to these voyages,' says Berg, 'placed me in possession of papers containing the names of owners of vessels and the furs shipped on those occa-

All was still dark regarding lands and navigation eastward. But when Bassof's reports reached the imperial senate an oukaz was forwarded at once to the admiralty college ordaining that any charts compiled from Bering's and Chirikof's journals, together with their log-books and other papers, should be sent to the senate for transmittal to the governor general of Siberia. The admiralty college intrusted the execution of this order to the eminent hydrographer Admiral Nagaïef, who finally compiled a chart for the guidance of hunters and traders navigating along the Aleutian Islands.[6]

Bassof was scarcely back from his first voyage and it was noised abroad that he had been successful, when there were others ready to follow his example. A larger venture was set on foot early in 1745, while Bassof was still absent on his second voyage, under the auspices of Lieutenant Lebedef, he who had married Croyère's widow. While in command at Bolsheretsk he issued a permit for a voyage to the newly discovered islands, on the 25th of February, to the merchants Afanassi Chebaievskoi of Lalsk and Arkhip Trapeznikof of Irkutsk. Their avowed purpose was to hunt sea-otters and make discoveries eastward of Kamchatka. Associated with them were Yakof Chu-

sions: 1st, papers obtained from Court Counsellor Ivan Ossipovich Zelonski; 2d, some incomplete data compiled by myself while living at Kadiak from verbal tradition and private letters; 3d, letters I found in Mr Shelikof's archives; and 4th, letters I received between the years 1760 and 1785 from the merchant Ivan Savich Lapin, of Solikamsk.' The dates given of Bassof's four voyages are 1743, 1745, 1747, and 1749. *Berg, Khronol. Istoria*, 6.

[6] *Morskoi Sbornik*, cii. 11, 55. The editor of the *Sibirsky Viestnik* (Siberian Messenger), G. I. Spasski, in 1822, devoted four numbers of his publication to a minute description of Copper Island, accompanied by a chart indicating Bassof's occupation of the place, as on its northern side two bays are named Bassofskaya and Petrofskaya respectively, after Bassof and one of his vessels. From the description in the *Viestnik* it is evident that Bassof wintered on Copper Island in 1749, and obtained most of his furs there. A cross which was preserved on the island for many years, bore an inscription to the effect that Yefim Kuznetzof, a new convert (probably a Kamchatka native), was added to Bassof's command on the 7th of April 1750. It is probable that the baptism of this convert took place on the island, and that the name of the man was added to Bassof's list only when he became a Christian.' *Sib. Viestnik, 1822*, numbers 2 to 6, passim. Bassof died in 1754, leaving a daughter with whom the merchant, Lapin, one of Berg's authorities, was personally acquainted. *Khronol. Istoria*, passim.

prof, Radion Yatof, Ivan Kholchevnikof, Pavel Kar-
abelnikof, Larion Beliaief, Nikolai Chuprof, Lazar
Karmanof, and Kiril Kozlof.[7] They built a large
shitika and named it the *Yevdokia*. As *morekhod*, or
navigator, they engaged a Tobolsk peasant named
Mikhaïl Nevodchikof, who had been with Bering, and
who was even credited by various authors with the
discovery of the Aleutian Islands.[8] In these expeditions the bold promyshleniki were ever the main-stay.
Nevodchikof was doubtless aware that Bassof had collected his furs at Bering and Copper islands, but trusting to his memory, or perhaps following the advice of
other companions of Bering, he passed by these islands, shaping his course south-east in search of the land
named by Bering Obmannui, or Delusive Islands. The
Yevdokia had sailed from the mouth of the Kamchatka on the 19th of September 1745,[9] and after a voyage of six days the adventurous promyshleniki sighted
the first of the Blishni group of the Aleutian isles.
Passing by the first, Attoo, Nevodchikof anchored near
the second, Agatoo, about noon of the 24th. Next
morning over a hundred armed natives assembled on
the beach and beckoned the Russians to land, but it
was not deemed safe in view of their number; so they
threw into the water a few trifling presents, and in
return the natives threw back some birds just killed.
On the 26th Chuprof landed with a few men armed
with muskets for water. They met some natives, to

---

[7] *Bolsheretsk Archives; Neue Nachr.*, 9, 10.
[8] From the fact that Nevodchikof was called a peasant we must not infer
that he was an agricultural laborer, but simply of the peasant class, one of
the numerous castes into which Russian society was divided. The so-called
'civil classes' of society outside of government officials were merchants,
kuptzui, again divided into first, second, and third guild; tradesmen, *mesh-
chaninui*, and peasants, *krestianinui;* but many of the latter class were
engaged in trade and commerce. Ivan Lapin told Berg that he knew Nevodchikof personally, and that he had served with Bering on his voyage to
America in 1741. Nevodchikof was a silversmith from Oustioug, and came
to Siberia in search of fortune. Meeting with no success he went on to Kamchatka, and there finding himself without a passport he was taken into the
government service. Lapin was in possession of a silver snuffbox, the work
of Nevodchikof. *Khronol. Istoria*, 7.
[9] *Neue Nachr.*, 10; *Khronol. Ist.*, 7.

whom they gave tobacco and pipes, and received a stick ornamented with the head of a seal carved in bone. Then the savages wanted one of the muskets, and when refused they became angry and attempted to capture the party by seizing their boat. Finally Chuprof ordered his men to fire, and for the first time the thundering echoes of musketry resounded from the hills of Agatoo. One bullet took effect in the hand of a native; the crimson fluid gushed forth over the white sand, and the long era of bloodshed, violence, and rapine for the poor Aleuts was begun.[10] As the natives had no arms except bone-pointed spears, which they vainly endeavored to thrust through the sides of the boat, shedding of blood might easily have been avoided. At all events the Russians could not now winter there, so they worked the ship back to the first island, and anchored for the night.

The following morning Chuprof, who seems to have come to the front as leader, and one Shevyrin, landed with several men. They saw tracks but encountered no one. The ship then moved slowly along the coast, and on the following day the Cossack Shekhurdin, with six men, was sent ashore for water and to reconnoitre. Toward night they came upon a party of five natives with their wives and children, who immediately abandoned their huts and ran for the mountains. In the morning Shekhurdin boarded the ship, which was still moving along the shore in search of a suitable place for wintering, and returned again with a larger force. On a bluff facing the sea they saw fifteen savages, one of whom they captured, together with an old woman who insisted on following the prisoner.[11] The two natives, with a quantity of scal-

[10] When the natives perceived the wound of their comrade they threw off their garments, carried him into the sea, and endeavored to wash off the blood. *Khronol. Ist.*, 8; *Neue Nachr.*, 13. See *Native Races*, vol. i., this series.

[11] 'Es gelang ihren auch, ungeachtet der Gegenwehr, welche die Insulaner mit ihren Knöchernen Spiessen leisteten, selbige herunter zu jagen und einen davon gefangen zu nehmen, der sogleich aufs Schiff gebracht ward. Sie ergriffen auch ein altes Weile, welche sie bis zur Hütte verfolgt hatten, und brachten auch diese, mit dem zugleich erbeuteten Seehundsfett und Fellen, zum Schiff.' *Neue Nachrichten*, 14, 15.

blubber found in the hut, were taken on board the *Yevdokia.* A storm arose shortly after, during which the ship was driven out to sea with the loss of an anchor and a yawl.

From the 2d to the 9th of October the gale continued; then they approached the island and selected a wintering-place for the ship. The natives were less timid than at first, though they found in the hut the bodies of two men who had evidently died from wounds received during the scuffle on the bluff. The old woman, who had been released, returned with thirty-four of her people; they danced and sang to the sound of bladder-drums, and made presents of colored clay, receiving in return handkerchiefs, needles, and thimbles. After the first ceremonial visit both parties separated on the most friendly terms. Before the end of the month the same party came again accompanied by the old woman and several children, and bringing gifts of sea-fowl, seal-meat, and fish. Dancing and singing were again indulged in.

On the 26th of October Shevyrin, Chuprof, and Nevodchikof, with seven men, set out in search of their new friends and found them encamped under a cliff. On this occasion they purchased a *bidar,*[12] with an extra covering of skin, for two cotton shirts. They found stone axes and bone needles in use among the natives, who seemed to subsist altogether upon the flesh of sea-otters, seals, and sea-lions, and upon fish.

The reign of violence and bloodshed already inaugurated on the island of Agatoo was quickly established on Attoo. Two days prior to his visit to the friendly natives, Chuprof, anxious to acquire a more minute knowledge of the island, sent out one of his subordinates, Alexeï Beliaief, with ten men to explore. This man discovered several habitations with whose in-

[12] 'Und fanden sie unter einem Felsen (*Utess*), Kauften von ihnen ein *Baidar* (ledernen Kahn) und eine Baidarenhaut, wovor sie ihnen zwey Hemden gaben und zurükkehrten, ohne die geringste Feindseligkeit erfahren zu haben.' *Neue Nachr.*, 15. The bidar was an open skin boat, and the largest of the class.

mates he managed to pick a quarrel, in the course of which fifteen of the islanders were killed.[13] Even the Cossack Shekhurdin, who had accompanied Beliaief, was shocked at such proceedings and went and told Chuprof, who said nothing, but merely sent the butchering party more powder and lead.[14]

These and like outrages of the promyshleniki were not known in Russia until after several years, and if they had been it would have made little difference.[15] Their efforts were successful; but we may easily believe that the interval between December 1745 and the day when the *Yevdokia* departed, which was the 14th of September 1746, was not a time of rejoicing to the people of Attoo. To this day the cruelties committed by the first Russians are recited by the poverty-stricken remnants of a once prosperous and happy people.

The return voyage was not a fortunate one; for six weeks the heavily laden craft battled with the waves, and at last, on the 30th of October, she was cast upon a rocky coast with the loss of nearly all her valuable cargo. Ignorant as to their situation the men made their way into the interior, suffering from cold and hunger, but finally they succeeded in finding some

[13] There is little doubt that this encounter was wilfully provoked, and the male natives slaughtered for a purpose. Berg merely hints that women were at the bottom of it, but in the *Neue Nachr.* it is distinctly charged that Beliaief caused the men to be shot in order to secure the women. Some dispute about an iron bolt that had disappeared, and which the natives could or would not return, was seized upon as an excuse. *Berg, Khronol. Ist.*, 8, 9; *Neue Nachr.*, 16.

[14] In the *Neue Nachr.*, 16, Chuprof is accused of a plan for the destruction of a number of natives, by means of a porridge seasoned with corrosive sublimate.

[15] An islander, Temnak, was carried away to Kamchatka on the *Yevdokia*. He claimed to be a native of At (Attoo?). In 1750 he was sent to Okhotsk with Nevodchikof, after having been baptized at Nishckamchatsk by the missionary Osoip Khotumzevskoi. He was fitted out with clothing at the expense of the government and named Pavel Nevodchikof, the pilot having acted as his godfather, and finally adopting him. 'Schon am 24sten October hatte *Czjuprow* zehn Mann, unter Anführung des *Larion Beajew* zu kundschaften ausgeschikt. Dieser fand verschiedene *Iurten* (Wohnungen), der Insulaner und weil er ihnen feindselig begegnete und die wenigen Insulaner sich daher mit ihren Knöchernen Lanzen zwi Wehre setzten, so nahm er daher Gelegenheit alle Männer funfzehn an der Zahl zu erschiessen, un die zwrükgebliebenen Weiber zur Unzucht gebrauchen zu Können.' *Neue Nachr.*, 11.

human habitations.   On questioning the natives they learned to their consternation that they were not on the mainland, but on the island of Karaghinski off the coast of Kamchatka.   The Koriaks were already tributary to the Russians, and treated their visitors kindly until Beliaief made advances to the wife of the *yessaul*, or chief, whose wrath was with difficulty assuaged.   Finally in May 1747 a descent was made on the island by an armed party of Olutorski, a warlike tribe living near the mouth of the Olutorsk river on the mainland.[16]

In a bloody fight during which many natives and

[16] The origin of the word *aleut* may perhaps be referred to these people. The first mention of the Olutorski tribe was in a report of the Cossack Atlassof, the conqueror of Kamchatka, in 1700. He states that on the coast of Kamchatka the Liutortzi are called strangers by the surrounding Koriaks, whom they much resembled. *Morskoi Sbornik*, ci. 4–73.   In 1714 Afanassi Petrof, a nobleman, built on the Olutorsk river an ostrog of the same name; he was freely assisted by the natives. In the following year Petrof forwarded all the tribute he had collected, consisting of 141 bundles of sables, of 40 skins each, 5,640 red foxes, 10 cross foxes, 137 sea-otters, two land-otters, and 22 ounces of gold taken from a wrecked Japanese junk. Subsequently the natives revolted and killed Petrof and nearly all his followers. *Morskoi Sbornik*, ci. 4–82, 296.   It is probable that when the Russians first encountered the natives of the Aleutian Islands, being already acquainted with the Olutorski, they applied that name, pronounced by them Aliutorski, to a race that certainly resembles the latter.   On the whole coast of Kamchatka these Olutorski were the only whale-hunters, a pursuit followed also by Aleuts. Russian authors generally derive the name from the Aleut word *allik*, What dost thou want? If this phrase ever was in general use it has entirely disappeared, and it certainly is no nearer the word Aleut, or Aleutski, as the Russians pronounce it, than is Olutorski. *Choris*, pt. vii. 12.   Engel, in *Geographische und Kritische Nachrichten*, i. v. 6, 7; vi.-vii., refers to an article in the *Leydener Zeitung*, Feb. 26, 1765, where it is said that 'the traders from the Kovima (Kolima), sailed out of that river and were fortunate enough to double the cape of the Chukchi in latitude 74°; they then sailed southward and discovered some islands in latitude 64°, where they traded with the natives and obtained some fine black foxes of which some specimens were sent to the empress as a present. They named these islands Aleyut, and I think that some of them adjoined America.' Engel then goes on to say: 'These sailors called these islands "Aleyut;" the word seems to me to be somewhat mutilated. Müller says that the island situated half a day's journey from Chukchi land, is inhabited by people named Akhyukh-Alial, and it appears that these traders actually come to this island, or perhaps to another one also situated in that neighborhood, the people of which Müller calls Peckale; he also speaks of a great country lying farther to the east named Kitchin Aliat. I believe, therefore, that the said Aleyut is nothing but the Aliat or Aeliat which forms the ending of both of the above-mentioned names.' It is evident that Engel confounds the voyages of the promyshleniki to the Aleutian Islands with the discovery of the Diomede Islands in Bering Straits. The Kitchin Aliat may bear some relation to either the Kutchin tribes of the American coast or more probably to the Innuit or Eskimos.

several Russians were killed, the invaders were defeated, and as they left the island the Olutorski declared their intention to return with reënforcements and to exterminate the Russians and all who paid tribute to them.   The promyshleniki were anxious to be off, and the islanders freely assisted them in constructing two large bidars.   On the 27th of June they departed, and arrived at the ostrog of Nishekamchatsk on the 21st of July with a little over three hundred sea-otter skins, the remnant of the valuable cargo of the *Yevdokia*.[17]

Immediately upon receiving information of the discovery of the Aleutian isles, Elizabeth issued as pecial oukaz appointing Nevodchikof to their oversight with the rank of a master in the imperial navy, in which capacity he was retained in the government service at Okhotsk.   In accordance with the old laws which exacted tribute from all savage tribes, Cossacks were to be detailed to make collections during the expedition that might be sent forth.

Meanwhile the several reports, and the rich cargoes brought back by Bassof's vessels, had roused the merchants of Siberia.[18]   In 1746 the Moscow merchant Andreï Rybenskoi, through his agent, Andreï

[17] Some discrepancy exists in our authorities with regard to dates and details of the latter part of this expedition.   Berg briefly states that Nevodchikof sailed from Attoo Sept. 14, 1746, and that his vessel was wrecked the 30th of Oct. on an island, where he was obliged to pass the winter. *Khronol. Ist.*, 10, 11.   A few lines farther on we are told that the party returned to Kamchatka in July 1746, with 300 sea-otters and with but a small portion of the original crew, having lost 52 men on the voyage.   The same author states that on the strength of a report of the outrages committed upon natives, presented by the Cossack Shekhurdin, all the survivors were subjected to legal process.   To add to the confusion of dates and data, Berg subsequently tells us that the value of the cargo brought back to Kamchatka by Nevodchikof was 19,200 rubles (much more than 300 sea-otters would bring at that time), and that the *Yevdokia* was wrecked in 1754! *Khronol. Ist.*, 11, 12.   In the *Neue Nachr.*, 17, 18, the dates are less conflicting, and we are informed that Nevodchikof's party returned in two bidars with 320 sea-otters, of which they paid one tenth into the imperial treasury.   The number of lives lost during the voyage is here placed at only 12 Russians and natives of Kamchatka.

[18] Making due allowance for the low prices of furs at that time, and the comparatively high value of money, Bassof's importations cannot be considered over-estimated at half a million dollars. *Berg, Khronol. Ist.*, 11.

Vsevidof, also Feodor Kholodilof of Totemsk, Nikofor Trapeznikof, and Vassili Balin of Irkutsk, Kosma Nerstof of Totma, Mikhaïl Nikilinich of Novo Yansk, and Feodor Shukof of Yaroslavl,[19] petitioned the commander of Bolsheretsk for permission to hunt, and two vessels were fitted out. The navigator selected for Kholodilof's vessel was Andreï Tolstykh, a merchant of the town of Selengisk, who was destined to play a prominent part in the gradual discovery of the Aleutian chain. The two vessels sailed from the Kamchatka River within a few days of each other. One, the *Sv Ioann*, commanded by Tolstykh, sailed the 20th of August manned by forty-six promyshleniki and six Cossacks. They reached Bering, or Commander, Island, and wintered there in accordance with the wishes of Shukof, Nerstof, and other shareholders in the enterprise. After a moderately successful hunting season Tolstykh put to sea once more on the 31st of May 1747. He shaped his course to the south in search of the island reported by Steller on June 21, 1741.[20] Failing in this he changed his course to the northward, and finally came to anchor in the roadstead of Nishekamchatsk on the 14th of August. During the voyage he had collected 683 sea-otters and 1,481 blue foxes, and all from Bering Island. Vsevidof sailed from Kamchatka the 26th of August 1746, and returned the 25th of July 1749, with a cargo of over a thousand sea-otters and more than two thousand blue foxes.[21]

[19] *Neue Nachr.*, 18, 19; *Berg, Khronol. Ist.*, 11, 12. These merchants desired to build two vessels at their own expense 'to go in pursuit of marine animals during the following year;' they also asked for permission to employ native Kamchatkans and Russian mariners and hunters, and to make temporary use of some nautical instruments saved from a wreck. *Neue Nachr.*, 20. This Trapeznikof was evidently the same who was in partnership with Bassof the preceding year.

[20] *Steller's Journal*, i. 47.

[21] *Berg, Khronol. Ist.*, app. It is probable that Vsevidof passed the winter following his departure on Copper Island, as on the earliest charts a bay on the north-eastern side of that island is named Vsevidof's Harbor. In a description of Copper Island, published in the *Sibirski Viestnik*, it is stated that on the 2d of March 1747 two promyshleniki named Yurlof and Vtoruikh fell from a cliff and died of their injuries. These men could only have be-

About this time a voyage was accomplished over an entirely new route. Three traders in the north, Ivan Shilkin of Solvichegodsk, Afanassi Bakof of Oustioug, and one Novikof of Irkutsk, built a vessel on the banks of the Anadir River and called it *Prokop i Zand*.[22] They succeeded in making their way down the river and through the Onemenskoi mouth into the gulf of Anadir. From the 10th of July 1747 to the 15th of September these daring navigators battled with contrary winds and currents along the coast, and finally came to anchor on the coast of Bering Island. On the 30th of October, when nearly the whole crew was scattered over the island hunting and trapping and gathering fuel, a storm arose and threw the vessel upon a rocky reef, where she was soon demolished. Bethinking themselves of Bering's ship, with remnants of that and of their own, and some large sticks of drift-wood, the castaways built a boat about fifty feet long. In this cockle-shell, which was named the *Kapiton*, they put to sea the following summer. Despite their misfortune the spirit of adventure was not quenched, and the promyshleniki boldly steered north-eastward in search of new discoveries. They obtained a distant view of land in that direction, and almost reached the continent of America, but the land disappeared in the fog, and they returned to Commander Islands. After a brief trip to Copper Island they reached the coast of Kamchatka in August 1749.[23]

longed to Vsevidof's vessel. Berg says that Ivan Rybinskoi of Moscow and Stephen Tyrin of Yaroslaf in 1747 despatched a vessel named *Ioann*, which sailed for the nearest Aleutian Islands and returned in 1749 with 1,000 sea-otters and 2,000 blue foxes, the cargo being sold for 52,590 rubles, which is but another account of Vsevidof's voyage. *Khronol. Ist.*, 14.

[22] *Berg, Khronol. Ist.*, 16. This name is given in the Russian edition of Berg, *Perkup i Zant*. The latter will be remembered as one of the sailors with Bering's expedition, and the former is a common Russian name. The men of that name were probably employed to build the vessel.

[23] The cargo of the *Kapiton* was valued only at 4,780 rubles, and it is difficult to understand how they could carry furs representing even this small value in a vessel of that size. On account of the rigging, artillery, and ship's stores of various kinds left by Bering's companions on the island named after him, an order had been issued from Okhotsk prohibiting traders from landing

The first effort to obtain a monopoly of traffic with
the newly discovered islands was made in February
1748, by an Irkutsk merchant named Emilian Yugof,
who obtained from the senate for himself and partners[24]
an oukaz granting permission to fit out four vessels
for voyages to the islands "in the sea of Kamchatka,"
with the privilege that during their absence no other
parties should be allowed to equip vessels in pursuit
of sea-otters. In consideration of this privilege Yugof's
company agreed to pay into the imperial treasury one
third of the furs collected. A special order to this
effect was issued to Captain Lebedef, the commander
of Kamchatka, from the provincial chancellery at Irkutsk under date of July 1748. Yugof himself, however, did not arrive at Bolsheretsk till November 1749,
and instead of four ships he had but one small vessel
ready to sail by the 6th of October 1750. This boat,
named the *Sv Ioann*, with a crew of twenty-five men
and two Cossacks, was wrecked before leaving the coast
of Kamchatka. Over a year passed by before Yugof
was ready to sail again. He had received permission
to employ naval officers, but his associates were unwilling to furnish money enough for an expedition on
a large scale. The second ship, also named the *Sv
Ioann*, sailed in October 1751. For three years nothing was heard of this expedition, and upon the statement of the commander of Okhotsk that the instructions
of the government had been disregarded by the firm,
an order was issued from Irkutsk, in 1753, for the con-
fiscation of Yugof's property on his return.[25] Captain

there until the government property could be disposed of. The craft constructed by Bassof and Serebrennikof was consequently seized by the government authorities immediately after entering port. The confiscated vessel was
subsequently delivered to the merchant Ivan Shilkin, with permission to
make hunting and exploring voyages to the eastern islands. *Neue Nachr.*, 30.
The prohibitory order concerning Bering Island was disregarded altogether
by the promyshleniki, who made a constant practice of landing and wintering
there. *Berg, Khronol. Ist.*, 16.

[24] These were Ignatiy Ivanof and Matvei Shchorbakof of St Petersburg,
and Petr Maltzof, Arkhip Trapeznikof, Feodor Solovief, and Dmitri Yagof
of Irkutsk. *Neue Nachr.*, 20.

[25] *Kamchatka Archives*, 1754.

Cheredof, who had succeeded Captain Lebedef in the command of Kamchatka, was at the same time authorized to accept similar proposals from other firms, but none were made. On the 22d of July 1754, the *Sv Ioann* unexpectedly sailed into the harbor of Nishekamchatsk with a rich cargo which was at once placed under seal by the government officials. The leader of the expedition did not return, but the mate Grigor Nizovtzof presented a written report to the effect that the whole cargo had been obtained from Bering and Copper islands, and that Yugof had died at the latter place. The cargo consisted of 790 sea-otters, 7,044 blue foxes, 2,212 fur-seals.[26]

It is evident that the authorities of Bolsheretsk did not consider this first monopoly to extend beyond Bering and Copper islands, as even before Yugof sailed other companies were granted permission to fit out sea-otter hunting expeditions to "such islands as had not yet been made tributary." Andreï Tolstykh, who had served as navigator under Kholodilof, obtained permission from the chancellery of Bolsheretsk to fit out a vessel, and sailed on the 19th of August 1749, arriving at Bering Island the 6th of September. Here he wintered, securing, however, only 47 sea-otters, and in May of the following year he proceeded to the Aleutian Islands, first visited by Nevodchikof. Here he met with better luck, and finally returned to Kamchatka the 3d of July 1752, with a cargo of 1,772 sea-otters, 750 blue foxes, and 840 fur-seals.[27]

The enterprising merchant Nikofor Trapeznikof of

---

[26] The furs were subsequently released on the payment of the stipulated one third. *Neue Nachr.*, 33.

[27] Tolstykh reported that he came to an island the inhabitants of which had not previously paid tribute; they seemed to be of Chukchi extraction, as they tattooed their faces in a similar manner and also wore labrets or ornaments of walrus ivory in their cheeks. According to his statement these 'Aleuts' had killed two natives of Kamchatka without the least provocation. On another island the natives voluntarily paid tribute in sea-otter skins. *Neue Nachr.*, 26. It is difficult to determine from this report which island Tolstykh visited; the description of the natives would point to St Lawrence Island, but the tribute paid in sea-otter-skins can only have come from the Aleutian chain. Probably he had sailed to the northward first and then changed his course to the Aleutian Islands. See *Native Races*, vol. i. this series.

Irkutsk also received permission to sail for the Aleutian Islands in 1749 under promise of delivering to the government not only the tribute collected from the natives, but one tenth of the furs obtained. Trapeznikof built a ship, named it the *Boris i Gleb*, and sailed in August. He passed four winters on various islands, returning in 1753 with a cargo valued at 105,736 rubles. The Cossack Sila Shevyrin acted as tribute-gatherer on this adventure.[28] During the same year, 1749, the merchants Rybinskoi and Tyrin sent out the shitika *Sv Ioann* to the Near Islands, the vessel returning in August 1752 with 700 sea-otters and 700 blue foxes.[29]

Late in 1749 Shilkin built the *Sv Simeon i Anna* and manned her with fourteen Russians and twenty natives of Kamchatka. The Cossack Alexeï Vorobief, or Morolief, served as navigator; Cossacks Ivan Minukhin and Alexeï Baginef accompanied the ship as tribute-gatherers. They left the coast of Kamchatka the 5th of August 1750, but after sailing eastward two weeks the vessel was wrecked on a small unknown island. Here the party remained till the following autumn, during which time Vorobief succeeded in constructing a small craft out of the wreck and drift-wood. This vessel was named the *Yeremy* and carried the castaways to Kamchatka in the autumn of 1752, with a cargo of 820 sea-otters, 1,900 blue foxes, and 7,000 fur-seals, all collected on the island upon which they were wrecked.[30]

[28] It seems that the island of Atkha was first discovered during the voyage of Trapeznikof. Cook and La Pérouse call it *Atghka*, and Holmberg *I Acha. Cartog. Pac. Coast*, MS., iii. 470. Shevyrin acknowledged that he had received tribute to the amount of one sea-otter each from the following natives: Igja, Oeknu, Ogogoetakh, Shalukiankh, Alak, Tukun, Ononushau, Kotogsiogn, Oonashayupu, Lak, Yoreshugilaik, Ungalikan, Shati, and Chyipaks. *Bolsheretsk Archives, 1754; Neue Nachr.* 24–5; *Berg, Khronol. Ist.*, 18.

[29] She was a lucky craft, making continuous voyages till 1763, and bringing over 5,000 sea-otters from the islands. *Berg, Khronol. Ist.*, 18, 19.

[30] *Neue Nachr.*, 19. Berg states that the *Simeon i Anna* carried a crew of 14 Russian and 30 natives of Kamchatka, and that the party returned with 1,980 sea-otters, collected on one of the small islands adjoining Bering Island. *Khronol. Ist.*, 24. The fact that fur-seals formed a part of the cargo would confirm the assumption that the locality of the wreck was one of the group of the Commander Islands.

By this time the merchants of Siberia and Kamchatka had gathered confidence regarding the traffic, and ship-building became the order of the day. Unfortunately, even the first principles of naval architecture were ill understood at Kamchatka, and so late as 1760 the promyshleniki made exceeding dangerous voyages in most ridiculous vessels—flatboats, shitikas, and similar craft, usually built without iron and often so weak as to fall to pieces in the first gale that struck them. As long as the weather was calm or nearly so, they might live, but let a storm catch them any distance from land and they must sink. We should naturally suppose that even in these reckless, thoughtless promyshleniki, common instinct would prompt greater care of life, but they seemed to flock like sheep to the slaughter. We must say for them that in this folly their courage was undaunted, and their patience under privations and suffering marvellous. Despotism has its uses.

He who would adventure here in those days must first collect the men. Then from the poor resources at hand he would select the material for his vessel, which was usually built of green timber just from the forest, and with no tool but the axe, the constant companion of every Russian laborer or hunter. Rope for the rigging and cables it was necessary to transport on pack-horses from Irkutsk, whence they generally arrived in a damaged condition, the long hawsers being cut into many pieces on account of their weight. Flour, meat, and other provisions were purchased at Kirensk and Yakutsk at exorbitant prices. In such crazy craft the promyshleniki were obliged to brave the stormy waters of the Okhotsk Sea and navigate along the chain of sunken rocks that lined the coast of Kamchatka.[31]

[31] Müller says the price of iron in Okhotsk in 1746 was half a ruble, or about 40 cents. a pound. *Voy.*, i. 82. The crews were obtained in the following manner: The merchant would notify his agent, or correspondent, living at Irkutsk, Yakutsk, or Kirensk, who would engage hunters and laborers; each agent hiring a few men, providing them with clothing, and sending them to

Nikofor Trapeznikof had been very fortunate in his first venture with the *Boris i Gleb*, and therefore concluded to continue. In 1752 he sent out the same vessel in command of Alexeï Drushinnin, a merchant of Kursk. This navigator shaped his course for Bering Island, but wrecked his vessel on a sunken rock when approaching his destination. No lives were lost and enough of the wreck was saved to construct another craft of somewhat smaller dimensions, which they named the *Abram*. In this vessel they set out once more in 1754, but after a few days' cruising in the immediate vicinity another shipwreck confined them again to the same island in a worse predicament than before.

Meanwhile Trapeznikof had fitted out another shitika, the *Sv Nikolaï*, with the Cossack Radion Durnef as commander, and the Cossack Shevyrin as tribute-gatherer. Durnef called at Bering Island and took from there the greater part of the crew of the *Boris i Gleb*, leaving four men in charge of surplus stores and the wreck of the *Abram*. The *Sv Nikolaï* proceeded eastward and made several new discoveries. Durnef's party passed two winters on some island not previously known to the promyshleniki, and finally they returned to Kamchatka in 1757 with a cargo valued at 187,268 rubles. This

---

Okhotsk. There they were first employed in building and equipping the ship; and we may imagine what kind of ship-carpenters and sailors they made. There was one benefit attending this method, however; as these men had never seen a ship or the ocean they could not realize the danger of committing their lives to such vessels, though the navigators could not have been ignorant of the risk to their own lives. Before sailing, an agreement with the list of shares was drawn up and duly entered in the book. This each signed or affixed his mark thereto. For example: If the vessel carried a crew of 40 men, including the navigator and the *peredovchik*, or leader of hunters, acting also as ship's clerk, the whole cargo, on the return of the vessel, was divided into two equal shares, one half going to the owners, and the other half being again divided into 45, 46, or perhaps 48 shares, of which each member of the ship's company received one, while of the additional five or six shares three went to the navigator, two to the peredovchick, and one or two to the church. It sometimes happened that at the end of a fortunate voyage the share of each hunter amounted to between 2,000 and 3,000 rubles; but when the voyages were unsuccessful the unfortunate fellows were kept in perpetual indebtedness to their employer.

was the most successful venture of the kind undertaken since the first discovery of the island.[32]

In 1753 three vessels were despatched from
Okhotsk, the respective owners of which were An-
dreï Serebrennikof of Moscow, Feodor Kholodilof of
Tomsk, and Simeon Krassilnikof of Tula.   They ex-
pressed their intention to search for the Great Land,
as the American continent was then called by these
people.   Serebrennikof's vessel was commanded by
Petr Bashnakof, assisted by the Cossack Maxim
Lazaref, as tribute-collector, and carried a crew of
thirty-four promyshleniki.   Serebrennikof sailed in
July 1753, shaping his course directly east from
Kamchatka, and arrived at some unknown islands
without touching any of those already discovered.
The ship was anchored in an open bight not far from
shore, when an easterly gale carried it out to sea.
During the storm four other islands were sighted, but
as no one on board was able to make astronomical
observations the land could not be located definitely
on the chart.[33]   For some time the heavy sea prevented the navigators from landing, and the wind carried them still farther to the east.   At last three
islands suddenly appeared through the fog, and before
the sails could be lowered the ship was thrown upon
one of them.   When the mariners reached the shore
they were met by armed natives, who threw spears
and arrows at them.   A few discharges of fire-arms,
however, soon scattered the savages.[34]

The wrecked hunters remained on the island till

[32] *Neue Nachr.*, 31.   The cargo was itemized as follows: 2,205 sea-otters
killed by the ship's company, and 732 sea-otters purchased of the natives for
articles of trifling value, making a formidable total of 3,027 sea-otters.   The
immense quantity of these animals killed by the promyshleniki themselves,
is proof that the islands upon which they wintered had not been visited before.
[33] *Neue Nachr.*, 35–6.
[34] According to Bashnakof this island was 70 versts in length and surrounded by 12 smaller islands.   This description is applicable to the island
of Tanaga, and on the strength of this circumstance Count Benyovski, the
Kamchatkan conspirator, ascribes the discovery of the eastern Aleutian or
Fox Islands to Serebrennikof, one of the owners of the ship.   *Benyovski's
Memoirs and Travels*, i. 83.

June 1754, and then sailed for Kamchatka in a small boat built out of the remains of the other. The cargo landed at Nishekamchatsk was of too little value to be registered in the official lists of shipments.[35]

Kholodilof's vessel sailed from Kamchatka in August 1753, and according to the custom generally adopted by the promyshleniki was hauled up on Bering Island for the winter, in order to lay in a supply of sea-cow meat. Nine men were lost here by the upsetting of the bidar, and in June of the following year the voyage was continued. A serious leak was discovered when running before a westerly gale, but an island was reached just in time to save the crew. There they remained till July 1755.[36] This expedition returned to Kamchatka late in 1755 with a cargo of sixteen hundred sea-otter skins.

The vessel fitted out by Krassilnikof did not sail until the summer of 1754, immediately after Captain Nilof assumed command of the military force at Okhotsk, and temporary command of the district.[37] Bering Island was reached in October, and after laying in a stock of sea-cow meat and preparing the vessel, Krassilnikof set out once more in August of the following year. A stormy passage brought him to an island that seemed densely populated, but he did not deem it safe to land there; so he faced the sea again, was tossed about by storms for weeks and carried to the westward until at last Copper Island came in sight again, on which a few days later the ship was totally wrecked.[38] The crew was saved and

---

[35] Bashnakof was wrecked again in 1764, when Tolstykh picked him up on Attoo Island. *Attoo*, the westernmost of the Aleutian Islands. Holmberg, 1854, writes *Attu*, and near it another *I Agattu*. *Cartog. Pac. Coast*, MS., iii. 482; *Berg, Khronol. Ist.*, 25–7; *Neue Nachr.*, 35–6.

[36] This was the island previously visited by Trapeznikof. In the spring, before Kholodilof's party sailed, they were joined by a Koriak and a native of Kamchatka, who stated that they had deserted from Trapeznikof's ship, intending to live among the natives. There had been six deserters originally, but four had been killed by the natives for trying to force their wives. The other two had been more cautious, and were provided with wives by their hosts, and well treated. *Neue Nachr.*, 54; *Berg, Khronol. Ist.*, 21.

[37] *Morskoi Sbornik*, cv. 11, 40.

[38] *Neue Nachr.*, 37–8.

a small quantity of provisions stored in a rudely constructed magazine. The ship's company was then
divided into several small hunting parties, five men
remaining near the scene of the wreck to guard the
provisions. Three of the men were drowned on the
15th of October.[39] And as a crowning disaster a
tidal wave destroyed their storehouse, carrying all
that remained of their provisions into the sea. After
a winter passed in misery they packed up their furs
in the spring, a poor lot, consisting of 150 sea-otters
and 1,300 blue foxes, and managed to make the crossing to Bering Island in two bidars, which they had
constructed of sea-lion skins. From Bering Island a
portion of the company returned to Kamchatka in
the small boat *Abram,* built by Trapeznikof's men.[40]

In 1756 the merchants Trapeznikof, Shukof, and
Balin fitted out a vessel and engaged as its commander the most famous navigator of the time,
Andreï Tolstykh. The ship was named after the commander and his wife, who accompanied him, *Andreian i
Natalia,* almost the first departure from the established custom of bestowing saint's names upon ships.
Tolstykh sailed from the Kamchatka River in September, with a crew of thirty-eight Russians and
natives of Kamchatka, and the Cossack Venedict
Obiukhof as tribute-collector. The usual halt for the
winter was made on Bering Island, but though an
ample supply of meat was obtained not a single sea-
otter could be found. Fifteen years from the first
discovery of the island had sufficed to exterminate
the animal. Nine men of the Krassilnikof expedition were here added to the crew, and in June 1757
Tolstykh continued his voyage, reaching the nearest
Aleutian island in eleven days. They arrived at a

---

[39] *Berg, Khronol. Ist.,* 29.
[40] Finding that the *Abram* could not carry the whole cargo of furs and
crew, 12 men were selected from the ship's company to return on that small
vessel, while 11 others were taken away by the ships of Serebrennikof and
Tolstykh. Two were engaged by the trader Shilkin for another voyage of
discovery. *Neue Nachr.,* 39–40.

favorable moment; Trapeznikof's ship, the *Sv Nikolai*, was on the point of sailing for Kamchatka and several chiefs had assembled to bid their visitors farewell. Satisfactory arrangements were at once entered into for the collection of tribute and a continuation of peaceful intercourse. The most influential chief, named Tunulgasan, was received with due solemnity and presented with a copper kettle and a full suit of clothes of Russian pattern. This magnificent gift induced him to leave several boys in charge of the Russians, for the avowed purpose of learning their language, but really to serve as hostages.

In accordance with instructions from the Okhotsk authorities Tolstykh endeavored to persuade the chief of Attoo to visit Kamchatka in his vessel, but in this he failed. After living on this island in peace with the natives for over a year, Tolstykh departed with 5,360 sea-otters and 1,190 blue foxes, and reached Kamchatka in the autumn of 1758.[41]

An unfortunate voyage was made about this time by a vessel belonging to the merchant Ivan Shilkin, the *Kapiton*, which it will be remembered was built out of a wreck by Bakof and Novikof.[42] Ignaty Studentzof was the Cossack accompanying this expedition, and upon his report rests all the information concerning it extant. They sailed from Okhotsk in September 1757, but were forced by stress of weather to make for the Kamchatka shore and pass the winter there, to repair a damage. Setting sail again in 1758 they touched at Bering Island, passed by Attoo

[41] *Neue Nachr.*, 43; *Berg, Khronol. Ist.*, app.
[42] The *Kapiton* had been confiscated by the government, but was finally delivered to Shilkin to reimburse him for losses incurred. Berg mentions especially that iron bolts were freely used in repairing this vessel. As early as 1752 a trader named Glazachef established iron-works at Nishekamchatsk, and being enabled to sell such iron as he could manufacture cheaper than it could be imported, he made a fortune. Subsequently Behm, commander of Kamchatka, persuaded him to transfer the works to the government, and remain in charge at a fixed salary. Glazachef finally left the service, and his successors not understanding the business, failed. The whole annual yield of the works never exceeded one thousand pounds of metal, and under Behm's successor the enterprise was abandoned altogether. *Morskoi Sbornik*, ciii. 13, 14.

where Tolstykh was then trading, and went on to the eastward, finally bringing up near an unknown island. A party sent ashore by Studentzof to reconnoitre were beaten off by a band of natives, and immediately afterward a sudden gale drove the ship from her anchorage to sea.[43] The mariners were cast upon a rocky island in the neighborhood, saving nothing but their lives, a small quantity of provisions, and their fire-arms. While still exhausted from battling with the icy waves they beheld approaching a large bidar with natives. There were only fifteen able to defend themselves, but they put on what show of strength and courage they could command and went to meet the enemy. One of the men, Nikolaï Chuprof, who had "been to the islands" before and spoke the Aleut language, implored the natives for assistance in their distressed condition, but the answer was a shower of spears and arrows.[44] A volley from the guns, however, killing two, put them to flight as usual. Starvation followed, and there were seven long months of it. Sea-weed and the water-soaked skins of sea-otters washed ashore from the sunken vessel were their only food. Seventeen died, and the remainder were saved only by the putrid carcass of a whale cast ashore by the sea. Rousing themselves they built a boat out of driftwood and the remains of their wreck, killed 230 sea-otters within a few days prior to their departure, and succeeded in reaching the island where Serebrennikof's vessel was then moored, and near which they anchored. But a gale arising, their cables snapped, and the boat went down with everything on board save the crew. Only thirteen of this unfortunate company of thirty-nine finally returned to Kamchatka on Serebrennikof's vessel.[45] After an absence of four years in search of a fortune they landed destitute even of clothing.

[43] *Berg, Khronol. Ist.*, 35–6.
[44] This was the brother of the notorious Yakof Chuprof who committed the infamous outrages upon the natives during Nevodchikof's first voyage to the islands; Nikolaï accompanied his brother then. *Berg, Khronol. Ist.*, 37.
[45] *Neue Nachr.*, 37–8; *Berg, Khronol. Ist.*, 45–6.

Thus from year to year the promyshleniki pushed eastward step by step. A merchant of Turinsk, Stepan Glottof, was the first to visit and carry on peaceful traffic with the inhabitants of Umnak and Unalaska. He commanded the small craft *Yulian*, built at Nishe-kamchatsk by Nikoforof, in which he sailed on the 2d of September 1758, accompanied by the Cossack Savs Ponomaref, who was instructed to persuade the Aleuta to become Russian subjects and pay tribute. Niko-forof intended the vessel to go at once in search of new islands without stopping at any of those already known to the promyshleniki; but long-continued con-trary gales compelled Glottof to winter at Bering Island, where he remained till the following August. Thence he sailed eastward for thirty days and landed on an unknown island.[46] There the hunters con-cluded to spend the winter; but they found the na-tives so friendly that three seasons passed before Glottof thought of returning to Kamchatka. The *Yulian* arrived at Bolsheretsk on the 31st of August 1762, with a large and valuable cargo containing be-sides cross and red foxes the first black foxes from the Aleutian Islands.[47]

Two other vessels are said to have been despatched to the islands in 1758, by the merchant Simeon Krassilnikof, and Nikofor Trapeznikof, but only of one of them, the *Vladimir*, have we any information. The leaders of this expedition were the peredovchik, Dmitri Païkof, and the Cossack Sava Shevyrin. They put to sea from Nishekamchatsk on the 28th of Sep-

[46] Umnak, according to *Berg, Khronol. Ist.*, 36.

[47] In Berg's summary of fur shipments the cargo of the *Yulian* is itemized as follows: Tribute to the government, 11 sea-otters and 26 black foxes; cargo, 1,465 sea-otters, 280 sea-otter tails, 1,002 black foxes, 1,100 cross foxes, 400 red foxes, 22 walrus-tusks, and 58 blue foxes; the whole valued at 130,450 rubles. *Khronol. Ist., App.* In the *Neue Nachr.*, no mention of this voyage is made; Coxe also is silent on the subject. The fact of the presence of walrus-tusks shows that there was traffic in the article between the Una-laskans and the natives of the Alaska peninsula, where the huge pennipeds still abound. The Cossack Ponomaref sent to the authorities at Okhotsk quite a correct map of the Aleutian archipelago, indicating eight large islands north-east of Unalaska. He says that the merchant Peter Shishkin assisted him in compiling a chart. *Berg, Khronol. Ist.* 37.

tember, with a crew of forty-five men, made the passage to Bering Island in twenty-four hours, and there hauled up their vessel for the winter. On the 16th of July 1759 Païkof set sail once more, taking at first a southerly course.[48]

It is not known how far Païkof pursued his southerly course, but he discovered no land and returned to the north, arriving in the vicinity of Atkha Island the 1st of September. Finding no convenient harbor he went on to Umnak Island and made preparations to pass the winter. The ship's company was divided into three *artels*, or parties, the first of which was commanded by Alexeï Drushinnin and stationed on the island of Sitkhin.[49] The Cossack, Shevyrin, took ten men to Atkha and the remainder of the crew established their winter-quarters in the immediate vicinity of the vessel under command of Simeon Polevoi. Païkof was evidently only navigator and had no command on shore. The first season passed in apparently peaceful intercourse with the natives.[50]

[48] A general impression prevailed among the promyshleniki of the time that there was land to the southward of the Aleutian Isles. Ivan Savich Lapin, from whom Berg obtained much information, stated that Gavril Pushkaref, a companion of Bering, who had survived the terrible winter on Bering Island, always asserted positively that there must be land to the southward. The sea-otters and fur-seals, he said, though found about Bering Island and its vicinity during the summer, invariably disappeared in a southerly direction. It was known that they did not go to Kamchatka or to the Kurile Islands, and though ignorant as to the actual whereabouts of the otters and seals, Pushkaref frequently assured Lapin and Trapeznikof that they could make their fortune by discovering the winter haunts of these animals in the south. *Berg, Khronol. Ist.*, 38.

[49] According to Cook, *Seetien*; and La Pérouse, and Holmberg, *Sitchin. Cartog. Pac. Coast*, MS., iii. 474. In *Neue Nachr.* it is spelled Sitkin, while Berg has Sigdak. *Khronol. Ist.*, 39; *Umnak Island*, south-west of Unalaska. On Cook's *Atlas*, 1778, written *Umanak;* La Pérouse, 1786, *Oumnak;* Holmberg, 1854, *I Umnak. Cartog. Pac. Coast*, MS., iii. 458; *Neue Nachr.*, 49.

[50] The custom of the promyshleniki after establishing themselves on an island, was to divide the command into small parties, each of which was stationed in the immediate vicinity of a native village, whose chief was induced by presents to assist in compelling his people to hunt, on the pretext perhaps that the empress, who, although a woman, was the greatest and most benignant being on earth, required such service of them. When they returned their catch was taken and a few trifling presents made them, such as beads and tobacco-leaf. Two objects were at once accomplished by the cunning promyshleniki. While all the able-bodied men were thus away gathering skins for them, they were having their own way with the women of the villages. Actual trade or exchange of Russian manufactures for skins was carried on

their stock of wood and water. They then proceeded to what they considered to be the island of "Alaksha," but whether this party actually wintered on the peninsula of Alaska is not quite clear. As soon as a suitable harbor had been found the ship was beached, and the crew proceeded to erect winter-quarters on shore. The inhabitants of the vicinity received the Russians in a friendly manner; they traded honestly, and gave their children as hostages.[56] However, this peace and good-will were not of long duration. The lawless promyshleniki of Bechevin's soon gave the natives much trouble, fully justifying them in any retaliation.

In January 1762 Golodof and Pushkaref, with a party of twenty hunters, coasted in bidars in search of food, and landed upon an adjoining island.[57] While indulging in their customary outrages they were surprised by a body of natives who killed Golodof and another Russian, and wounded three more. Shortly afterward the Russian camp was attacked, four men killed, as many wounded, and the huts reduced to ashes. In May the Cossack Lobashkof and one of the promyshleniki went to bathe in a hot spring situated about five versts from the harbor, and were killed by the natives.[58] In return the Russians put seven of the hostages to death. The islanders again attacked the Russian camp, but were repulsed.

As it was evident that the natives had determined

[56] The Russians received nine children as hostages, and in addition they engaged two men and three women to work for them. *Neue Nachr.*, 53–4.

[57] It is impossible to determine which island this was. In *Neue Nachr.* it is called Uniunga, a name not to be found on any chart. Berg calls it Ounga, but there is no evidence to indicate that the men of Bechevin's expedition proceeded around the peninsula and north-eastward as far as the Shumagin Islands. *Neue Nachr.*, 54; *Berg, Khronol. Ist.*, 43. The name of Ounungun, applied to the Unalaska people by their western neighbors, according to Pinart, may throw some light upon this question; it is probable that the locality of Golodof's and Pushkaref's exploits was not the peninsula at all, but Agunalaksh, the Aleut name of Unalaska, which was subsequently abbreviated by the Russians.

[58] *Neue Nachr.*, 55. This is another point in support of the theory that the *Gavril* landed on Unalaska. Five versts (three and a half miles) from the principal settlement on Unalaska Island are hot springs, aboriginally resorted to for curing rheumatic and skin diseases. Hot springs exist also near the settlement of Morshevoi on the south point of the peninsula, but they are within less than half a mile from the shore.

upon the destruction of the entire company, the outlying detachments were recalled. The ship was then
repaired and the whole command returned to Umnak
Island.   There they took on board two natives with
their families, who had promised to pilot them to other
islands; but as soon as the vessel had gained the open
sea a violent gale from the eastward drove her before
it until on the 23d of September the mariners found
themselves near an unknown coast, without masts,
sails, or rudder, and with but little rigging. The land,
however, proved to be Kamchatka, and on the 25th
the helpless craft drifted into the bay of Kalatcheva,
seventy versts from Avatcha Bay. Bechevin landed
his cargo, consisting of 900 sea-otters and 350 foxes,
valued at 52,570 rubles.[59] The cove where the landing
was effected subsequently received the name of Beche-
vinskaia.

Charges of gross brutalities, committed during this
voyage, have been made against Sergeant Pushkaref.
On leaving the Aleutian Isles the crew of the *Gavril*,
with Pushkaref's consent, took with them twenty-five
young women under the pretext that they were to be
employed in picking berries and gathering roots for
the ship's company.   When the coast of Kamchatka
was first sighted a boat was sent ashore with six men
and fourteen of these girls. The latter were then
ordered to pick berries. Two of them ran away and
were lost in the hills, and during the return of the
boat to the ship one of them was killed by a man
named Korelin.[60] In a fit of despair the remaining
girls threw themselves into the sea and were drowned.
In order to rid himself of troublesome witnesses to
this outrage, Pushkaref had all the remaining islanders
thrown overboard, with the exception of one boy,
Moise, and Ivan, an interpreter who had been in
the service of Andreï Serebrennikof. Three of the

---

[59] *Berg, Khronol. Ist.*, app.
[60] *Neue Nachr.*, 56. Berg states that it was Pushkaref himself who had
accompanied the women to the shore. *Khronol. Ist.*, 45.

women had died before leaving the islands.[61]   An imperial oukaz issued from the chancellery at Okhotsk to a company consisting of Orekhof, Lapin, and Shilof, who asked permission to despatch an expedition to the islands, enjoins on the promyshleniki the greatest care and kindness in their intercourse with the natives.   The eleventh paragraph of the oukaz reads as follows: "As it appears from reports forwarded by Colonel Plenisner, who was charged with the investigation and final settlement of the affairs of the Bechevin company, that that company during their voyage to and from the Aleutian Islands on a hunting and trading expedition committed indescribable outrages and abuses on the inhabitants, and even were guilty of murder, inciting the natives to bloody reprisals, it is hereby enjoined upon the company about to sail, and especially upon the master, Ismaïlof, and the peredovchik, Lukanin, to see that no such barbarities, plunder, and ravaging of women are committed under any circumstances."   The whole document is of a similar tenor and goes far to prove that the authorities were convinced that the outrages reported to them had in truth been committed.[62]

From this time forward the authorities of Siberia evidently favored the formation of privileged companies, and the Bechevin investigation may be considered as the beginning of the end of free traffic in the American possessions of the Russian empire.

[61] *Neue Nachr.*, 57; *Berg, Khronol. Ist.*, 45.
[62] *Berg, Khronol. Ist.*, 45-52.   The oukaz is signed by Captain-lieutenant Sava Zubof, and dated August 29, 1770.   Berg found in some letters written by the collegiate chancellor Anton Ivanovich Lassef, a civil engineer of the government at Irkutsk, a notice to the effect that Bechevin suffered much during a penal inquisition with torture, conducted against him in 1764 by K*A*K*, probably Knias (Prince) Alexander Korzakof, who is mentioned as having been detailed on a government mission to Irkutsk about that time.

CHAPTER VII.

· THE first vessel which sailed to the Aleutian Islands under protection of a special imperial oukaz was the *Andreian i Natalia,* owned and commanded by Andreï Tolstykh, a man of courage and perseverance, who during his three previous voyages had amassed some fortune, and concluded to adventure it on this turn.[1]

The *Andreian i Natalia* left Kamchatka the 27th of September 1760. In two days Bering Island was reached, when in accordance with custom the ship was hauled up for the winter. In the June following Tolstykh again put to sea, steering at first southerly, then northward, arriving at Attoo Island the 5th of August.[2]

[1] Tolstykh began his official report as follows: 'By virtue of an oukaz of her Imperial Majesty, the Empress Elizabeth Petrovna, issued through the Chancellery of Bolsheretsk in Kamchatka, on the 4th day of August 1760, and in pursuance of an order deposited with Lieutenant Vassili Shmalef, I was permitted to put to sea with the Cossacks Petr Vassiutinski and Maxim Lazaref, detailed for this service.' *Berg, Khronol. Ist.,* 53; *Neue Nachr.,* 59; *Shelikof, Puteshestvie,* 134; *Grewingk, Beitrag zur Kenntniss der nordwest-küste Amerikas,* 315.

[2] He met a vessel returning to Kamchatka, probably the *Sv Peter i Sv*

jects of Russia and to pay tribute, the voyage was
duly reported to the empress, who subsequently rewarded Tolstykh and the two Cossacks.[5]

One vessel was despatched to the islands in 1760,
but our information concerning it is meagre. It was
built and fitted out under the auspices of the merchant Terentiy Chebaievski, and under the immediate
superintendence of his clerk Vassili Popof. Berg
claims to have found a notice in the papers of Zelonski to the effect that Chebaievski's vessel returned
in 1763 with a cargo valued at 104,218 rubles.[6]

A plan had been formed by this combination of
wealthy merchants for making a thorough examination of the Aleutian chain and the adjoining continent, and then to decide upon the most favorable
locality for opening operations on a larger scale. The
object of the expedition was well conceived and deserving of success, but a chain of unfortunate circumstances combined to frustrate their designs. Three of
the ships fitted out by the partners were destroyed
with all on board, and the fourth returned without
even paying expenses.[7] We have the names of only two
of the three vessels destroyed, the *Zakhar i Elizareta*

[5] Berg states that among the papers of the former governor of eastern
Siberia, Dennis Ivanovich Checherin, he found a rescript of the empress
Catherine of which he gives the following copy: 'Dennis Ivanovich: Your
communication concerning the subjection into allegiance to Me of six hitherto
unknown islands, as well as the copies of reports of Cossack Vassiutkinski and
his companions, I have read with satisfaction. Such enterprise pleases Us
very much. It is to be deplored that the papers giving a more detailed
description of the islands and their inhabitants have been lost during the
wreck of the vessel. The promise of reward from Me to the merchant Tolstykh, returning to him the tenth part of proceeds accruing to Our treasury
from each sea-voyage, I fully approve, and hereby order you to carry out
this design. You will also promote the Cossacks Vassiutkinski and Lazarof for
their services to the rank of Nobles in your district. May God grant them
good success in their projected voyage next spring and a safe return at its
conclusion. You will impress upon the hunters that they must treat their
new brethren and countrymen, the inhabitants of Our newly acquired islands,
with the greatest kindness and without any oppression or abuse. March 2,
1766. Catherine.' *Berg, Khronol. Ist.*, 66-7; *Grewingk, Beitrag.*, 315.

[6] *Khronol. Ist.*, app.; *Grewingk, Beitrag*, 315. It was evident that Popof
did not sail with this expedition, for we see him mentioned as an active partner
in the more extensive enterprises undertaken in 1762 by Trapeznikof, Protassof,
and Lapin, Berg's best and most frequently quoted authority of the history
of that period. See also *L'Auteroche, Voyage en Siberie*, ii. 113; *Antidote*, i.

[7] *Veniaminof*, i. 118-131.

commanded by Drushinnin, owned by Kulkof, and the *Sv Troïtska*, or Holy Trinity, commanded by Ivan Korovin. The third is known to have been commanded by Medvedef, a master in the navy. The fourth vessel was the property of Trapeznikof, but who commanded her is not known.[8]

The *Zakhar i Elizareta* sailed from Okhotsk the 6th of September 1762, wintered at Avatcha Bay, and proceeding the following July reached Attoo, where seven of the shipwrecked crew of the *Sv Petr i Sv Pavel* were taken on board. One of these was Korelin, who alone survived this expedition and furnished a report of it. From Attoo Drushinnin proceeded to Adakh, where another vessel, the *Andreian i Natalia* was then anchored, but as the natives all produced receipts for tribute signed by Tolstykh, Drushinnin contented himself with filling his water-casks and moved on.[9]

From Adakh the *Zakhar i Elizareta* proceeded to Umnak where a party of Glottof's men were then

---

[8] *Veniaminof*, i. 118. The ship of Medvedef was lost at Umnak; the ship commanded by Drushinnin was manned with 34 Russians of whom three only returned. Among them was Bragin who is mentioned in *Sarychef*, ii. 37, as having wintered on Kadiak Island in 1763. Berg claims that Drushinnin's crew consisted of 8 natives of Kamchatka and 34 Russians, including the peredovchik Miasnikh. *Khronol. Ist.*, 58.

[9] *Neue Nachr.*, 72–3. The *Neue Nachrichten* is a small octavo printed in German black letter and published in Hamburg and Leipsic in 1776. It bears no authorship on the title-page but the initials J. L. S. Most bibliographers have pronounced it anonymous, as the authorship is involved in some uncertainty. The library of congress has the work catalogued under Stählin or Strahlin. M. J. Von Stæhlin published an account of the new northern archipelago in the *Petersburger Geographischer Kalender* in 1774. This was translated into English in London, during the same year, in a small octavo volume. There is, however, no reason to believe that Stæhlin was the J. L. S. of *Neue Nachrichten*, as many of his statements in the other work do not agree with the text of the latter. A man named A. L. Schlözer published in the year 1771, at Halle, Germany, a quarto volume of over 400 pages entitled *Allgemeine Geschichte, Von dem Norden*, treating on kindred subjects. It is probable that in Mr Schlözer we find the original J. L. S., as the first of the initials might easily have been inadvertently changed. It is a significant fact that in Shelikof's voyage we find whole passages and pages almost the verbal translation from the *Nachrichten*. Explanations and corrections of this volume were subsequently published under the auspices of Buffon in the *Sept Epoques de la Nature, Grewingk., Beitrag* and *Pallas Nordische Beiträge*, i. 273. Further than this, in *Acta Petropolitana*, vi. 126, J. A. L. Von Schlözer is mentioned as author of *Neue Nachrichten*, and corresponding member of the Imperial Academy of Sciences.

hunting. The peredovchik Miasnikh was sent out
with thirty-five men to explore the coast. They went
to the north-eastern end of the island, and after meeting everywhere with indications of the recent presence
of Russians, they returned to the ship about the middle of September. On the day of their return letters
were also received through native messengers from
the vessels commanded by Korovin and Medvedef,
who had lately located themselves on the islands of
Umnak and Unalaska. Drushinnin at once sent out
a reconnoitring party to the latter island, and in due
time a favorable report was received inducing the
commander to move his craft to Unalaska, where he
anchored the 22d near the northern end of the island.
When the cargo had been landed and a foundation
had been laid for a winter habitation, two of the chiefs
of neighboring villages voluntarily opened friendly
intercourse by offering hostages. Others from more
distant settlements soon followed their example.

This friendly reception encouraged Drushinnin to
adhere to the old practice of dividing his force into
small parties for the winter in order to secure better
results both in hunting and in procuring subsistence.
The peredovchik accordingly sent out Petr Shekalef
with eleven men; another party of eleven men under
Mikhaïl Khudiakof, and a third of nine men under
Yefim Koshigin. The last named remained at the
harbor; Khudiakof located his party at Kalekhtak;
while Shekalef went to the little island of Inaluk,
about thirty versts distant from the ship. Drushinnin
accompanied the latter party. Stepan Korelin, who
subsequently alone survived to relate the occurrences
of that disastrous winter, was also a member of the
Inaluk party who had constructed a cabin in close
proximity to the native habitation, containing some
twenty inmates. The relations between the promyshleniki and the natives appeared to be altogether
friendly, and no trouble was apprehended until the
beginning of December. On the 4th a party of five

men set out in the morning to look after the fox-traps.[10] Drushinnin, Shekalef, and Shevyrin then paid a visit to the native dwelling. They had just entered the low aperture when they were set upon by a number of armed men, who knocked down Shekalef and Drushinin with clubs and then finished them with the knives they bought of them the day before. Shevyrin had taken with him from the house an axe, and when the excited savages turned their attention to him he made such good use of his weapon that he succeeded in regaining the Russian winter-quarters alive, though severely wounded. Bragin and Korelin at once began to fire upon the Aleuts with their muskets from within, but Kokovin, who happened to be outside, was quickly surrounded, thrown down, and assaulted with knives and spears until Korelin, armed with a huge bear-knife, made a gallant sortie, wounded two of the islanders, put the others to flight, and rescued his half-dead comrade.[11]

A close siege of four days followed this sanguinary onslaught. The fire-arms of the Russians prevented a charge by the enemy, but it was unsafe to show themselves outside the hut even for a moment, in search of water or food. To add to their apprehensions, the savages displayed in plain view the garments and arms of their comrades who had gone to visit the fox-traps, a sure indication that they were no longer among the living. Under the shelter of night the Russians launched a bidar and pulled away out of the harbor, the natives watching their movements, but making no attempt to pursue. Once out of sight of their enemies Korelin and the other fugitives landed, pulled

[10] Berg states that Drushinnin sent out these men and then resolved to visit the dwelling of the natives with the remainder of his men, Korelin, Bragin, Shevyrin, Kokovin, and one other. In the *Neue Nachrichten* we find an account of the occurrence differing considerably in its details. Drushinnin's name is not mentioned, while the number remaining at home is given as five, Shekalef, Korelin, Bragin, Shevyrin, and Kokovin. There is every reason to believe, however, that Berg was correct, as Drushinnin was with the party and does not appear in any account of subsequent events. *Khronol. Ist.*, 59; *Neue Nachr.*, 75–6.

[11] *Neue Nachr.*, 77; *Coxe's Russian Discoveries*, i. 38; *Veniaminof*, i. 22.

their boat upon the beach, and set out across the hills to Kalekhtak, where they expected to find Khudiakof and his detachment. It was after dark when they reached the neighborhood. They fired signal-guns, but receiving no reply they wisely kept at a distance. Before long, however, they found themselves pursued by a horde of savages, and discovering an isolated, precipitous rock near the beach which could be defended for a time, they concluded to make a stand there. With their fire-arms they finally beat off the pursuers and resumed their retreat, this time with but little hope of finding those alive who had remained with the ship. Presently an object caught their eyes which confirmed their worst apprehensions. It was the main-hatch lying on the beach, having been washed up by the waves. Without waiting further confirmation of their fears the four men took to the mountains, hiding in the ravines until nightfall. Under cover of darkness they approached the anchorage, only to find the ship broken up, and some stores with the dead bodies of their comrades scattered on the beach. Gathering a few packages of dried fish and some empty leather provision-bags they stole away into the hills, where a temporary shelter was hastily constructed. Thence they made occasional excursions at night to the scene of disaster, which must have occurred simultaneously with those of Inaluk and Kalekhtak, in search of such needed articles as had been left by the savages.[12] The leather provision-bags, though cut open, were very acceptable as material for the construction of a small bidar.

From the 9th of December 1763 until the 2d of

[12] Davidof tells a story of the manner in which the Aleuts secured a simultaneous onslaught upon all three of the Russian detachments. According to him, they resorted to the old device of distributing among the chiefs of villages bundles of sticks, equal in number, one of which was to be burned each day till the last designated the day. *Drukratnoie Puteshestoie*, ii. 107. Veniaminof ridicules the story and declares it to be an invention of Davidof, as the Aleuts had numbers up to a thousand and could easily have appointed any day without the help of sticks. *Veniaminof, Zapiski*, i. 118. No mention of it is made in *Neue Nachrichten*. Berg also quotes Davidof. *Shelikof's Voyage*, 97.

February 1764 these unfortunates remained in hiding, but on the latter date their bidar was successfully launched, and before morning the party had emerged from Kapiton Bay, coasting to the westward in search of one of Trapeznikof's vessels commanded by Korovin.[13] Though travelling only at night and hiding among the cliffs by day, they were soon discovered by the natives, and in the vicinity of Makushin village they were compelled to sustain a siege of five weeks in a cave, exposed to constant attacks.[14] During this whole time they suffered intensely from hunger and thirst, and would certainly have succumbed had it not been for an ample supply of powder and lead which prevented their enemies from engaging them at close quarters. At last on the 30th of March the fugitives succeeded in joining their countrymen under Korovin, who were then stationed on the southern shore of Makushin Bay. Shevyrin died at Unalaska during the same year; the other three, Korelin, Kokovin, and Bragin, recovered their strength, but only the former finally reached Kamchatka with Solovief's vessel, after passing through additional vicissitudes.

The ship *Sv Troïtska*, which Korovin commanded, was fitted out in 1762 by Nikofor Trapeznikof,[15] and

[13] Veniaminof in relating this occurrence adds that a charitable native found the fugitives during the winter, and not only failed to betray them, but supplied them with provisions, paying them occasional stealthy visits at night. *Veniaminof, Zap.*, i. 99.

[14] *Berg, Khronol. Ist.*, 72; *Dvulr. Put.*, ii. 113.

[15] Berg succeeded in collecting the following data concerning the transactions of this enterprising citizen of Irkutsk. In the course of 25 years he despatched 10 vessels upon voyages of discovery to the eastward of Kamchatka. His shitika *Nikolaï* made three voyages between 1762 and 1766. A small boat named the *Fish* returned in 1757 with an exceedingly rich cargo, valued at 254,900 rubles. The *Sv Troïtska*, the *Sv Petr i Sv Parel*, and one other vessel which returned in 1763 with a cargo valued at 105,730 rubles, also belonged to Trapeznikof. The sea-otter-skins alone brought by these expeditions numbered over 10,000. Berg concludes as follows: 'It would be of interest to know how much wealth Trapeznikof realized out of all these enterprises. Ivan Savich Lapin told me that through losses sustained in some of his undertakings, and through the bankruptcy of some of his debtors, Trapeznikof suddenly found himself reduced from wealth to poverty.' His old age was passed in straitened circumstances, and he left barely enough to defray the expenses of his burial. *Khronol. Ist.*, 62-3, *App.*

sailed from the mouth of the Kamchatka River on
the 15th of September, with a crew of thirty-eight
Russians and six Kamchatkans. They passed the
winter on Bering Island, remaining until the 1st of
August of the following year. The ship fitted out
by Protassof and commanded by Medvedef had also
wintered there, and before sailing the two commanders
made some exchanges in their crews. After sustaining some loss by death, Korovin had at the time of
his departure from Bering Island thirty-seven men
and Medvedef forty-nine. Both vessels made a short
run to the Aleutian Islands, reaching the straits between Umnak and Unalaska on the 15th of August.
Medvedef concluded to remain on Umnak Island
while Korovin selected an anchorage on the Unalaska
shore. The native villages on the coast appeared to
be deserted, but a short distance inland some inhabited
dwellings were found. The chief of the settlement
offered several small boys as hostages, and produced
tribute receipts signed by the Cossack Ponomaref.
Korovin evidently was satisfied with his reception, as
he returned immediately to the ship, landed his whole
cargo, erected a large hut of drift-wood, and built
several bidars for his hunting parties.[16]

In a few weeks all the arrangements for the winter
were made, and Korovin set out with two boats
manned by nine men each, one of them commanded
by Barnashef, who had visited the island previously
with Glottof. They visited three villages in succession, meeting everywhere with a friendly reception on
the part of the chiefs, but nearly all the adult males
appeared to be absent from home. After the safe
return of this party another expedition was sent out
to the east side of the island whence they also returned unmolested accompanied by some hostages,
having met during their journey with some men of
Drushinnin's party. Feeling now safe, Korovin sent
out a hunting party of twenty-three under Barnashef,

[16] *Pallas, Nordische Beitrage,* i. 274.

in two bidars, to the west end of the island. Each boat carried eight muskets and every man had a pistol and a lance; provisions had been prepared for the winter.

At various times during the season letters were received from the detached parties reporting their safety, but about the middle of December Korovin received warning that a large force of natives was marching toward the ship with hostile designs. The Russian commander at once called his men under arms

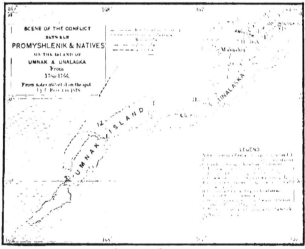

SCENE OF CONFLICT.

and kept a strict watch. The following day about seventy savages made their appearance carrying bundles of sea-otter skins in order to throw the promyshleniki off their guard; but Korovin would allow only ten of them to approach his house at the same time. The savages perceiving that their design was known, and that surprise had become impossible, disposed of their furs quietly and retreated. On the same evening, however, three natives of Kamchatka came to the house in a great fright, reporting that they belonged to Kulkof's ship, that is to say Drushinnin's party, and that the vessel had been destroyed and all their comrades killed.

The promyshleniki, now thoroughly alarmed, prepared for defence. After remaining unmolested for two days, a large force attacked and besieged them closely for four days, during which time two Russians were killed with arrows, and five natives were counted dead on the field. On the fifth day the enemy retreated to a cave near by, keeping up, however, a vigilant blockade, and making it dangerous to proceed any distance from the house. Worn out with constant watching and firing, Korovin at last concluded to bury his iron, the article most coveted by the savages, and his stores of blubber and oil under the house, and to retreat to the ship. His plan was carried out, and the ship anchored within a short distance of the shore. The danger of sudden attack was thus lessened, but hunger and the scurvy were there as relentless as the savages. At length, on the 26th of April, reënforced by the three fugitives from Drushinnin's command, Korovin put to sea, but so reduced was his crew that the ship could scarcely be worked. During a gale on the 28th the unfortunate promyshleniki were wrecked in a cove on Umnak Island. Several of the sick died or were drowned, and eight of the hostages made their escape. The arms, ammunition, some sails, and a few sea-lion skins were all that could be saved. A temporary shelter and fortification was constructed of empty casks, sails, and skins, where the remaining sixteen, including three disabled by scurvy, the three hostages, and the faithful interpreter, Kashmak, hoped to secure some rest before beginning a new struggle. Their hope was in vain. During the first night a large party of savages approached stealthily from the sea and when within a few yards of the miserable encampment discharged their spears and arrows with terrible effect, piercing the tent and the barricade of sea-lion skins in many places. Two of the Russians and the three hostages were killed, and all the other Russians severely wounded.[17]

The onslaught was so sudden that there was no time to get ready the fire-arms, but Korovin with four of the least disabled seized their lances and made a sortie, killing two of the savages and driving away the remainder. Covered with wounds, the five brave men returned to their comrades, now thoroughly disheartened. In the mean time the gale had continued unabated, breaking up the stranded vessel and scattering the cargo upon the beach. Soon after daylight the natives returned to resume the work of plunder, the Russians being too feeble to interfere. They carried off what booty they could and remained away two days, during which time such of the wounded promyshleniki as were still able to move about picked up what fragments of provisions and furs the savages had left, also a small quantity of iron.[18] On the 29th died one of the wounded men, who was also suffering from scurvy. Three days afterward one hundred and fifty islanders approached from the east and fired at the Russians with muskets, but the bullets fell wide of the mark.[19] They then set fire to the dry grass in order to burn out the fugitives. A constant firing of the Russians, however, foiled their efforts, and at last the savages retired. The victors found themselves in such a state of prostration that they remained on the same spot until the 21st of July, when the few survivors, twelve in number, six of whom were natives of Kamchatka, embarked in a roughly constructed bidar in search of Medvedef's party. After ten days of coasting the sufferers arrived at a place where the charred remains of a burned vessel, of torn garments, sails and rigging, gave evidence of another disaster.

[17] *Veniamiof, Zap.*, i. 132–4; *Sarychef, Putesh.*, ii. 30.
[18] A portion of this iron was set aside as an offering to the shrine of the saint whose assistance they implored in their distress. *Neue Nachr.*, 93–4.
[19] This is the first instance recorded of the use of fire-arms by the native Aleutians. *Neue Nachr.*, 95; *Sgibnef*, in *Morskoi Sbornik*, c. 46.

Filled with alarm the fugitives landed and hastened up to a house which had escaped destruction. It was empty, but in an adjoining bath-house twenty dead bodies were found, among them that of the commander Medvedef. There was some indication of the corpses having been dragged to the spot with straps and belts tied around their necks, but no further details of the catastrophe could be obtained, and not a soul survived to tell the tale.[20] Necessity compelled Korovin to remain at this ghastly spot, and preparations were made to repair the house for the approaching winter, when Stepan Glottof, who in the mean time had arrived on the other side of Umnak Island, made his appearance with eight men. The so lately despairing promyshleniki were wild with joy, and forgetting on the instant their hunger and diseases, they planned further ventures, agreeing with Glottof to hunt and trade on joint account.

The voyage of Glottof, covering the four years from 1762 to 1765 inclusive, was by far the most important of the earlier expeditions to the islands, and constitutes an epoch in the swarming of the promyshleniki.

A new vessel to which was given the old name of *Andreian i Natalia*[21] was built in the Kamchatka River by Terentiy Chebaievski, Vassili and Ivan Popof, and Ivan Lapin, and sailed on the 1st of October 1762, under command of Glottof, wintering at Copper Island.[22]

---

[20] *Neue Nachr.*, 105; *Veniaminof, Zap.*, i. 98; *Berg, Khronol. Ist.*, 70.

[21] Ship nomenclature in Alaskan waters at this time is confusing. St Peter and St Paul were the favorites, but there were other names continued from one ship to another, and the same name was even given to two ships afloat at the same time.

[22] *Sarychef, Putesh.*, ii. 37. During the winter Yakof Malevinskoi, with 13 men, was sent to Bering Island in a bidar with instructions to gather up what useful material still remained of Bering's vessel, which seems to have been a magazine of naval stores for the promyshleniki for nearly a quarter of a century. Malevinskoi, who died shortly after his voyage to Bering Island, was very successful in his mission. He secured between eight and nine hundred pounds of old iron, 400 pounds of rigging and cable, some lead, several thousand strings of beads, and some copper. *Neue Nachr.*, 105. For a time the

On the 26th of July 1763 Glottof again put to sea,
and after a tedious and stormy voyage sighted Umnak on the 24th of August. Having previously
visited this island and Unalaska, whence he brought
the first black foxes to Kamchatka, the commander
concluded not to loiter there, but to sail on in search
of new discoveries. Passing eight large islands and
a multitude of smaller ones, Glottof finally anchored
on the 8th of September off the coast of a large and
mountainous island, called Kikhtak by the natives,
but now known as Kadiak. The first meeting of the
Russians with the inhabitants of this isle was not
promising. A few of the savages approached the
ship in their kyaks, but the Aleut interpreter, Ivan
Glottof, a godchild of the commander, could not converse with them, and when on landing some habitations were discovered, they were found to be deserted.
A few days later a party came to the Russian camp
with an Aleutian boy who had been captured several
years before during a hostile descent of the Kadiak
people upon the island of Sannakh, and through him
intercourse was held. Glottof endeavored to persuade the savages to pay tribute to the imperial government and to furnish hostages, but they refused.
The natives here were of fiercer aspect, more intelligent and manly, and of finer physique than those of

authorities at Kamchatka had forbidden the promyshleniki to visit Copper
Island, under the impression that valuable deposits of copper were located
there. In 1755 Peter Yakovlef, a mining engineer, was ordered to the island
to investigate the matter. On the north-west point, where the native copper
had been reported to exist, was a narrow reef of rocks some 20 or 30 fathoms
in width, partially covered at flood tide, but Yakovlef stated that he could
not discover any indication of copper there. On another reef, running still
farther out into the sea, he noticed two veins of reddish and greenish appearance, but the metal had long since been removed with the aid of picks and
adzes. At the foot of this reef, however, he found pieces of copper evidently
smoothed by the action of the sea. Captain Krenitzin in 1768 reported that
much copper was found on the island, that it was washed up by the sea in
such quantities that ships could be loaded with it. *Pallas, Nord. Beitr.*, i. 253.
The author, however, remarks that at the time of his writing, 1780, the copper
had greatly diminished in quantity and but few pieces larger than a bean
could be found. Zaïkof, another navigator, reported about the same time
that copper was washed upon the beach, but that one of the promontories
presented every appearance of a copper-mine.

the more western isles. At first they would not even
allow the interpreter to remain temporarily with the
Russians, but a few days later the boy made his
appearance in the Russian camp, and subsequently
proved of great service to his new patrons.[23] Under
such circumstances Glottof deemed it best not to discharge the cargo, but to keep the ship moored in a
bay near the mouth of a creek, where she floated at
every high tide. A strict watch was kept night and
day. Early one morning a large body of armed
islanders crept up to the anchorage unobserved, and
sent a shower of arrows upon the Russian sentinels
hidden behind the bulwarks on the deck. The guards
discharged their muskets, and the deafening sound
sent the savages scattering. In their wild alarm they
left on the ground rude ladders, packages of sulphur,
dried moss, and birch bark, a proof of their intention
to fire the ship, and also of the fact that the Kadiak
people were a race more warlike and more dangerous
to deal with than the Aleuts. They were certainly
fertile in both offensive and defensive devices; for
only four days after the first attack, previous to which
they had been unacquainted with fire-arms, they
again made their appearance in large force, and provided with ingeniously contrived shields of wood and
wicker-work intended to ward off the Russian's bullets.
The islanders, however, had not had an opportunity
of estimating the force of missiles propelled by powder,
for the Russians had purposely fired high during their
attack, and another rout was the result of a second
charge.

The defeated enemy allowed three weeks to pass by
without molesting the intruders, but on the 26th of
October there was yet another attack. The elaborate
preparations now made showed wonderful ability for
savages. Seven large portable breastworks, conceal-

---

[23] This boy was subsequently taken to Kamchatka and baptized under
the name of Alexander Popof. *Neue Nachr.*, 100; *Veniaminof, Zap.*, i. 102.
For manners and customs of the aborigines see *Native Races*, vols. i. and iii.,
this series.

ing from thirty to forty warriors each, were seen approaching the vessel early one morning, and when near enough spears and arrows began to drop like hail upon the deck. The promyshleniki replied with volley after volley of musketry, but this time the shields appeared to be bullet-proof and the enemy kept on advancing until, as a last resort, Glottof landed a body of men and made a furious charge upon the islanders, who were growing more bold and defiant every moment. This unexpected attack had the desired effect, and after a brief struggle the savages dropped their shields and sought safety in flight. The result of this third battle caused the natives to despair of driving off the Russians, and to withdraw from the neighborhood.[24]

Deeming it dangerous to send out hunting parties, Glottof employed his men in constructing a house of drift-wood and in securing a good supply of such fish as could be obtained from a creek and a lagoon in the immediate vicinity of the anchorage. Late in December two natives made their appearance at the Russian camp. They held a long parley with the interpreter from a safe distance, and finally came up to the house. Kind treatment and persuasion seemed to have no effect; nor did presents even; instinctively these most intellectual of savages felt that they had met their fate. They went away with some trifling gifts, and not another native was seen by the disappointed Glottof till April of the following year. Four men then came to the encampment and were persuaded to sell some fox-skins, taking glass beads in payment. Ah, the vanity of humanity! Cotton and woollen goods had no attractions. Ornament before dress. They appeared at last to believe in Glottof's professions of friendship, and went away promising to persuade their people to come and trade with the Russians. Shortly

[24] *Neue Nachr.*, 109-10; *Berg, Khronol. Ist.*, 66. The point at which Glottof made his first landing was near the southern end of the island, probably near the present village of Aiakhtalik.

afterward a party brought fox and sea-otter skins, accepting glass beads; and friendly intercourse ensued until Glottof was ready to sail from the locality, where his party had suffered greatly from disease without deriving much commercial advantage.[25]

Glottof felt satisfied, however, that he was near to the American continent, because he noticed that the natives made use of deer-skins for dress. In the immediate vicinity of the Russian encampment there was no timber, but the natives said that large forests grew in the northern part of the island.[26]

Through Holmberg's researches in Kadiak we possess the deposition of a native of the island, which evidently refers to Glottof's sojourn on Kadiak. Holmberg states that he passed two days in a hut on the south side of the island, and that he there listened to the tales of an old man named Arsenti Aminak, whom he designates as the "only speaking monument of pagan times on Kadiak." A creole named Panfilof served as interpreter, and Holmberg took down his translation, word for word, as follows: "I was a boy of nine or ten years, for I was already set to paddle in a bidarka, when the first Russian ship with two masts appeared near Cape Aliulik. Before that time we had never seen a ship; we had intercourse with the Aglegnutes of Aliaska peninsula, with the Tnaianas of the Kenai peninsula, and with the Koloshes; and some wise men even knew something of the Californias; but ships and white men we did not know at all. When we espied the ship at a distance we thought it was an immense whale, and were curious to have a better look at it. We went out to sea in our bidarkas, but soon discovered that it was no whale, but another unknown monster of which we were

<hr>

[25] During the winter the scurvy broke out among the crew and nine Russians died. *Neue Nachr.*, 111; *Berg, Khronol. Ist.*, 66; *Sarychef, Putesh.*, ii. 38.

[26] On the 25th of April Glottof sent Luka Vtorushin, with 11 men, in search of material to make hoops for water-casks; he returned the following day with a supply, and reported groves of alder and willow at a distance of about 30 miles. *Neue Nachr.*, 115.

afraid, and the smell of which (tar probably) made us sick. The people on the ship had buttons on their clothes, and at first we thought they must be cuttle-fish, but when we saw them put fire into their mouth and blow out smoke we knew they must be devils, as we did not know tobacco then. The ship sailed by the island of Aiakhtalik, one of the Goose Islands at the south end of Kadiak, where then a large village was situated, and then passed by the Cape Aliulik (Cape Trinidad) into Kaniat (Alitak) Bay, where it anch-ored and lowered the boats. We followed full of fear, and at the same time curious to see what would become of the strange apparition, but we did not dare to approach the ship. Among our people there was a brave warrior named Ishinik, who was so bold that he feared nothing in the world; he undertook to visit the ship and came back with presents in his hand, a red shirt, an Aleut hood, and some glass beads. He said there was nothing to fear, 'they only wish to buy our sea-otter skins and to give us glass beads and other riches for them.' We did not fully believe his statement. The old and wise people held a council in the *kashima*,[27] and some said: 'Who knows what sick-ness they may bring us; let us await them on the shore, then if they give us a good price for our skins we can do business afterward.'

"Our people formerly were at war with the Fox Island people, whom we called Tayaoot. My father once made a raid upon Unalaska and brought back among other booty a little girl left by her fleeing parents. As a prisoner taken in war she was our slave, but my father treated her like a daughter, and brought her up with his other children. We called her Plioo, which means ashes, because she had been taken from the ashes of her house. On the Russian ship which came from Unalaska there were many

[27] A large building where the men work in the winter, and also used for councils and festivities. For a full description of these people see *Native Races*, vol. i., this series.

Aleuts and among them the father of our slave. He came to my father's house, and when he saw that his daughter was not kept like a slave but was well cared for, he told him confidentially, out of gratitude, that the Russians would take the sea-otter skins without payment if they could. This warning saved my father, who, though not fully believing the Aleut, acted cautiously. The Russians came ashore together with the Aleuts and the latter persuaded our people to trade, saying: 'Why are you afraid of the Russians? Look at us, we live with them and they do us no harm.' Our people, dazzled by the sight of such quantities of goods, left their weapons in the bidar and went to the Russians with their sea-otter skins. While they were busy trading, the Aleuts, who carried arms concealed about them, at a signal from the Russians fell upon our people, killing about thirty and taking away their sea-otter skins. A few men had cautiously watched the result of the first intercourse from a distance, among them my father. These attempted to escape in their bidarkas, but they were overtaken by the Aleuts and killed. My father alone was saved by the father of his slave, who gave him his bidarka when my father's own had been pierced with arrows and was sinking. In this bidarka he fled to Akhiok. My father's name was Penashigak. The time of the arrival of this ship was the month of August, as the whales were coming into the bays and the berries were ripe. The Russians remained for the winter, but could not find sufficient food in Kaniat Bay. They were compelled to leave the ship in charge of a few watchmen and moved into a bay opposite Aiakhtalik Island. Here was a lake full of herrings and a kind of smelt. They lived in tents here through the winter. The brave Ishinik, who first dared to visit the ship, was liked by the Russians and acted as a mediator. When the fish decreased in the lake during the winter the Russians moved about from village to village. Whenever we saw a boat coming at a distance we fled to the hills, and when we returned no *yukala* (dried fish) could be found in the houses. In the lake near the Russian camp there was a poisonous kind of starfish; we knew it very well, but said nothing about it to the Russians. We never ate them, and even the gulls would not touch them; many Russians died from eating them. But we injured them also in other ways. They put up foxtraps and we removed them for the sake of obtaining the iron material. When the Russians had examined our coast they left our island during the following year."[28]

On the 24th of May Glottof finally left Kadiak, and passing through the numerous islands lining the south coast of the Alaska peninsula made a landing on Umnak with the intention to hunt and trade in the same locality which he had previously visited. When the ship entered the well known bay the houses erected by the promyshleniki were still standing, but no sign of life was visible. The commander hastened to the shore and soon found signs of death and destruction. The body of an unknown Russian was there; Glottof's own house had been destroyed, and another building erected near by.[29]

On the 5th of July an exploring party of sixteen discovered the remains of Medvedef's ship, and the still unburied bodies of its crew. Upon consultation it was decided to take steps at once to ascertain whether any survivors of the disaster were to be found on the island. On the 7th of July some natives

[28] This narrative of which we have given above only the portion relating to Glottof's visit, coming as it does from the mouth of an eye-witness, is interesting, but it is somewhat difficult to determine its historical value, as it is impossible to locate or identify all the various incidents. The first part evidently refers to the landing of Glottof, though there is a wide discrepancy between the latter's account and that of Arsenti Aminak; in his estimate of time the latter is certainly mistaken and he does not mention the hostile encounters between natives and Russians related by Glottof. He also ascribes the mortality among the invaders to the consumption of poisonous fish instead of to the actual cause, the ravages of scorbutic disease. *Holmberg, Ethnographische Skizzen; Sarychef, Putesh.*, ii. 42-3; *Grewingk Beitr.*, 316.

[29] *Berg, Khronol. Ist.*, 70; *Pallas, Nord. Beitr.*, i. 276.

approached the vessel and endeavored to persuade
Glottof to land with only two men, for the purpose
of trading, displaying at the same time a large number
of sea-otter skins on the beach. When they found
that their devices did not succeed, they retreated to
a distance and began to fire with muskets at the ship,
without, however, doing any damage. Later in the
day a few natives came off in their canoes and paddled round the ship. As Glottof was desirous of obtaining information concerning the recent occurrences
on the island, the bold natives were not molested, and
finally one of them ventured on board the ship, par-
taking of food, and told freely all that had happened
since Glottof's visit, hinting also at the existence of
Korovin's small party in some part of the island.
He acknowledged that it had been the intention of
the natives to kill Glottof after enticing him to land,
imagining that they would have no difficulty in dealing with the crew after the leader was despatched.
After a vain attempt to find Korovin's camp, some
natives advised the Russians to cross the island to
the opposite side, where they would find their countrymen engaged in building a house beside a brook. The
information proved correct, and the hearts of Korovin
and his men were soon gladdened by the appearance
of their countrymen.

Glottof evidently did not intend to feed the additional members in idleness. In a few days he sent
out Korovin with twenty men in a bidar to reconnoitre the coast of Umnak and search for fugitive Russians who might have survived the various massacres.
For a long time he could find no living soul, Russian
or native; but at last, in September, he fell in with
some parties of the latter. They greeted the Russians with musket-shots, and would not listen to
overtures. At various places where Korovin attempted to stop to hunt the natives opposed his
landing, and engagements ensued. At the place of
the massacre of Barnashef and his crew, his bidar

and the remains of his cargo were found, and a few
women and boys who lingered about the place were
taken prisoners and questioned as to the details of
the bloody episode.

Later in the winter Korovin was sent out again
with a party of men and the Aleut interpreter, Ivan
Glottof. They proceeded to the western end of Unalaska and there learned from the natives that a Russian vessel commanded by Solovief was anchored in
one of the harbors of that island. Korovin at once
shaped his course for the point, but reached it only
after several sharp engagements with the natives,
inflicting severe loss upon them. He remained with
Solofief three days and then returned to the scene of
his last encounter with the natives, who seemed to
have benefited by the lesson administered by Korovin,
being quite tractable and willing to trade and assist
in hunting. Before the end of the year the deep-
rooted hatred of the Russian intruders again came to
the surface, and the hunters concluded to return to
the ship. On the passage from Unalaska to Umnak
they had two engagements and were finally wrecked
upon the latter island. As it was midwinter they
were forced to remain there till the 6th of April following, subject to the greatest privations. After
another tedious voyage along the coast the party at
last rejoined Glottof with a small quantity of furs
as the result of the season's work. On account of
Korovin's failures in hunting, Glottof and his partners declared the agreement with them void. The
brave leader, whose indomitable courage alone had carried his companions through an appalling succession of
disasters, certainly deserved better treatment. The
Kamchatkans belonging to his former crew entered
Glottof's service; but five Russians concluded to cast
their lots with him. In June they found Solovief,
who willingly received them into his company, and in
his vessel they finally reached Kamchatka.[30]

<hr/>

[30] The vessel commanded by Solovief was owned by Ouledovski, a mer-

Solovief had been fortunate in his voyage from Kamchatka to Umnak, passing along the Aleutian isles with as much safety and despatch as a trained sea-captain could have done, provided with all the instruments of modern nautical science. In less than a month, a remarkably quick passage for those days, he sighted the island of Umnak, but finding no convenient anchorage he went to Unalaska.

A few natives who still remembered Solovief from his former visit, came to greet the new arrivals and informed them of the cruel fate that had befallen Medvedef and his companions. The Cossack Korenef was ordered to reconnoitre the northern coast of the island with a detachment of twenty men. He reported on his return that he had found only three vacant habitations of the natives, but some fragments of Russian arms and clothing led him to suspect that some of his countrymen had suffered at the hands of the savages in that vicinity. In the course of time Solovief managed to obtain from the natives detailed accounts of the various massacres. The recital of cruelties committed inflamed his passions, and he resolved to avenge the murder of his countrymen. His first care, however, was to establish himself firmly on the island and to introduce order and discipline among his men. He adhered to his designs with great persistency and unnecessary cruelty.[31]

chant of Irkutsk. It was the *Sv Petr i Sv Pavel* which we have so often met; it had sailed from the mouth of the Kamchatka river on the 24th of August 1764. *Berg, Khronol. Ist.*, 73.

[31] Berg, while faithfully relating the cruelties perpetrated by Solovief, seems to have been inclined to palliate his crimes. He says: 'A quiet citizen and friend of mankind reading of these doings will perhaps execrate the terrible Solovief and call him a barbarous destroyer of men, but he would change his opinion on learning that after this period of terrible punishment the inhabitants of the Aleutian Islands never again dared to make another attack upon the Russians. Would he not acknowledge that such measures were necessary for the safety of future voyagers? Curious to know how Solovief succeeded in his enterprise, and how he was situated subsequently, I questioned Ivan Savich Lapin concerning his fate, and received the following answer: His many fortunate voyages brought him great profits, but as he was a shiftless man and rather dissipated in his habits, he expended during every winter passed at Okhotsk or in Kamchatka the earnings of three years of hardships, setting out upon every new voyage with nothing but debts

Solovief had not quite finished his preparations when the savage islanders, made bold by frequent victories, attempted the first attack, an unfortunate one for the Aleuts. The promyshleniki, who were ready for the fray at any moment, on this occasion destroyed a hundred of their assailants on the spot, and broke up their bidars and temporary habitations. With this victory Solovief contented himself until he was reënforced by Korovin, Kokovin, and a few others, when he divided his force, leaving half to guard the ship while with the others he set out in search of the "blood-thirsty natives," who had destroyed Drushinnin and Medvedef.

The bloodshed perpetrated by this band of avengers was appalling. A majority of all the natives connected with the previous attacks on the Russians paid with their lives for presuming to defend their homes against invaders. Being informed that three hundred of the natives had assembled in a fortified village, Solovief marched his force to the spot. At first the Russians were greeted with showers of arrows from every aperture, but when the natives discovered that bullets came flying in as fast as arrows went out, they closed the openings, took down the notched posts serving as ladders, and sat down to await their fate. Unwilling to charge upon the dwellings, and seeing that he could not do much injury to the enemy as long as they remained within, Solovief managed to place bladders filled with powder under the log foundation of the structure, which was soon blown into the air. Many of the inmates survived the explosion only to be despatched by the promyshleniki with muskets and sabres.[32]

behind him. He lost his life in the most miserable manner at Okhotsk.' *Berg, Khronol. Ist.*, 75–6. Among his companions Solovief acquired the nickname of 'Oushasnui Soloviy,' the 'terrible nightingale,' a play upon his name, Solovey being the Russian for nightingale. *Baer* and *Wrangell, Russische Besitzungen*, 192.

[32] Davidof states that Solovief put to death 3,000 Aleuts (?) during this campaign. *Dvukr. Purtesh.*, ii. 108. Berg writes on the authority of Lapin that 'only' 200 were killed. *Khronol. Ist.*, 75. Veniaminof discusses the deeds of Solovief and his companions in a dispassionate way, relying mainly on

At the end of his crusade, Solovief, having succeeded in subjugating the natives, established 'friendly intercourse' with them. A few of the chiefs of Unalaska tendered their submission. During the winter his men suffered from scurvy, and many died.[33] Observing which the savages regained courage and began to revolt. The people of Makushin village were the most determined, but Solovief managed to entrap the chief, who confessed that he had intended to overpower the Russians and burn their ship. In June two more of the scurvy-stricken crew died, and Solovief was only too glad to accept of the offer of Korovin and his companions, who had only just arrived, to join his expedition. The Cossack Shevyrin died on the third of August and another Russian in September.[34]

Late in the autumn Solovief again despatched Korenef with a detachment of promyshleniki to the northern part of the island. He did not return until the 30th of January 1766, and was immediately ordered out again to explore the west coast. During the first days of February a young Aleut named Kyginik, a son of the chief, came voluntarily into the Russian camp and requested to be baptized, and to be permitted to remain with the promyshleniki. His wish was willingly complied with, and if the promyshleniki claimed a miracle as the cause of the action, I should acquiesce. Nothing but the mighty power of

what he heard by word of mouth from Aleut eye-witnesses of the various transactions. He accused Berg of attempting to make Solovief's career appear less criminal and repulsive, and declares that 'nearly a century has elapsed since that period of terror, and there is no reason for concealing what was done by the first promyshleniki, or for palliating or glorifying their cruel outrages upon the Aleuts.' He had no desire to enlarge upon the great crimes committed by ignorant and unrestrained men, especially when they were his countrymen; but his work would not be done if he failed to tell what people had seen of the doings of Solovief and his companions. Veniaminof stated on what he calls good authority, that Solovief experimented on the penetrative power of musket-balls by tying 12 Aleutians together and discharging his rifle at them at short range; report has it that the bullets lodged in the ninth man. *Zap.*, ii. 101.

[33] One died in February, five in March and April, and six in May; all these were Russians with the exception of one, a Kamchatkan. *Neue Nachr.*, 141.

[34] *Neue Nachr.*, 143.

God could have sanctified the heart of this benighted one under these bright examples of Christianity. In May Solovief began his preparations for departure, collecting and packing his furs for the voyage and repairing his vessel. He sailed the 1st of June and reached Kamchatka the 5th of July.[35]

At Okhotsk there was great disorder, amounting almost to anarchy, under the administration of Captain Zybin, up to 1754, when the latter was relieved by Captain Nilof, who subsequently became known and lost his life during the famous convict revolt of Kamchatka under the leadership of Benyovski.[36] In 1761 Major Plenisner was appointed to the command of Kamchatka for five years; he held this position until relieved by Nilof.[37]

In 1765 a new company was formed by Lapin, Shilof, and Orekhof, the latter a gunsmith from Tula. They built two vessels at Okhotsk, naming them after those excessively honored apostles the *Sv Petr* and the *Sv Pavel*, and crossed over to Bolsheretsk, where they remained till August.[38] The *Sv Petr* was commanded by Tolstykh and carried a crew of forty-nine Russians, twelve natives of Kamchatka, and two Aleuts. Acting under the old delusion that there must be land somewhere to the southward, Tolstykh steered in that direction, but after a fruitless cruise of two months he concluded to make the port of Petropavlovsk to winter; but on the 2d of October in attempting to anchor near Cape Skipunskoi, in a gale, the vessel was cast upon the rocks and broken in pieces.[39]

[35] The cargo collected during this murderous expedition consisted of 500 black foxes and 500 sea-otters, a portion of the latter having been brought into the joint company by Korovin and his companions. *Neue Nachr.*, 146.

[36] *Morskoi Sbornik*, cv. 40; *Sgibnef*, in *Id.*, cii. 76.

[37] Plenisner was to receive double pay while in command, and he was instructed to send out the naval lieutenant Synd with two ships to explore the American coast, and also to send another expedition to explore the Kurile Islands. *Sgibnef*, in *Morskoi Sbornik*, cii. 37–8.

[38] The authorities of Bolsheretsk asserted that the party sailed only after all the liquor obtained for the voyage had been drank. *Berg, Khronol. Ist.*, 76–7.

[39] *Neue Nachr.*, 49. Berg mentions that in this wreck only three out of a crew of 63 were saved, but he does not state whether Tolstykh was among the survivors.

The *Sv Pavel* was commanded by Master Afanassiy Ocheredin, and carried a crew of sixty men. Sailing from Bolsheretsk the 1st of August they steered for the farther Aleutian Isles, and went into winter-quarters the 1st of September in a bay of Umnak. At first the natives were friendly, but as soon as tribute was demanded intercourse ceased for the winter, and the Russians suffered greatly from hunger and disease. Scarcely had the promyshleniki begun to overcome the dread disease in the spring, with the help of anti-scorbutic plants, when Ocheredin sent out detachments to demand tribute of the natives. In August 1767 a peredovchik named Poloskof, was despatched with twenty-eight men in two boats to hunt. Having heard of the massacre of Medvedef and Korovin, he passed by Unalaska and established himself at Akutan, distributing small detachments of hunters over the neighboring islands. In the following January he was attacked and four of his men killed. Onslaughts were made by the natives at the same time upon Ocheredin's vessel and another craft commanded by Popof, who was then trading at Unalaska. In August Poloskof rejoined Ocheredin, and their operations were continued until 1770.[40]

Ocheredin's share of the proceeds was 600 sea-otters, 756 black foxes, 1,230 red foxes; and with this rich cargo he arrived at Okhotsk on the 24th of July 1770.[41] The partners in this enterprise received in addition to a large return on their investment gracious acknowledgments from the imperial government. In 1764, when the first black fox-skins had

[40] In the month of September 1768 Ocheredin was notified by Captain Levashef, of the Krenitzin expedition, to transfer to him (Levashef) all the tribute collected. With an armed vessel anchored in Kapiton Bay, Popof and Ocheredin met with no further opposition from the natives. *Unalaska* to the south-west of the Alaska peninsula. On Cook's *atlas*, 1778, written *Oonalaska;* La Pérouse, 1736, *Ounalaska; Sutil y Mex., Viage, I. Unalaska;* Holmberg, *I. Unalaschka. Cartog. Pac. Coast,* MS., iii. 454.

[41] *Berg, Khronol. Ist.,* app. Two natives of the island, Alexeï Solovief and Boris Ocheredin, were taken to Okhotsk on the *Sv Pavel* with the intention of sending them to St Petersburg, but both died of consumption on their journey through Siberia. *Neue Nachr.,* 162-3.

been forwarded to the empress, gold medals were awarded to the merchants Orekhof, Kulkof, Shapkin, Panof, and Nikoforof. Desirous of obtaining a more detailed account of the doings of her subjects in the far east, Catherine ordered to be sent to St Petersburg one of the traders, promising to pay his expenses. When this order reached Okhotsk only one merchant engaged in the island trade could be found, Vassili Shilof. He was duly despatched to the imperial court, and on arriving at St Petersburg was at once granted an interview by the empress, who questioned him closely upon the locality of the new discoveries, and the mode of conducting the traffic. The empress was much pleased with the intelligent answers of Shilof, who exhibited a map of his own making, representing the Aleutian Islands from Bering to Amlia. This the empress ordered to be deposited in the admiralty college.[42]

Three other vessels were despatched in 1766–7, but of their movements we have but indefinite records. The *Vladimir*, owned by Krassilnikof and commanded by Soposhnikof, sailed in 1766, and returned from the Near Islands with 1,400 sea-otters, 2,000 fur-seals, and 1,050 blue foxes. In the following year the *Sv*

[42] In the *Shurnal Admiralttiestv Kollegiy*, under date of Feb. 5, 1767, the following entry can be found: 'The Oustioushk merchant, Shilof, laid before the college, in illustration of his voyages to the Kamchatka Islands, a chart on which their location as far as known is laid down. He also gave satisfactory verbal explanations concerning their inhabitants and resources. The college having inspected and examined this chart and compared it with the one compiled by Captain Chirikof, at the wish and will expressed by Her Imperial Majesty, and upon careful consideration, present most respectfully the following report: The college deems the report of Shilof concerning navigation and trade insufficient for official consideration, and in many respects contradictory; especially the chart, which does not agree in many important points with other charts in the hands of the college; and moreover it could not be expected to be correct, being compiled by a person knowing nothing of the science and rules of navigation. On the other hand, as far as this document is concerned we must commend the spirit which instigated its conception and induced the author to undergo hardships and dangers in extending the navigation and trade of Russia. And we find in it the base upon which to build further investigation and discoveries of unknown countries, which well deserves the approbation of our most Gracious Imperial Majesty.' Two imperial oukazes were issued, dated respectively April 19 and April 20, 1767, granting Shilof and Lapin exemption from military duty and conferring upon each a gold medal for services rendered. *Berg, Khronol. Ist.*, 70–2.

multitude of imaginary islands extending up to latitude 64° 59', and reported a mountainous coast not far
from the land of the Chukchi," between latitude 64°
and 66°, which he conjectured to be the American
continent. On the 2d of September he began his
return voyage, following the coast down to Nishekamchatsk, but not until 1768 did his expedition
return to Okhotsk.[2]

Another and far more important expedition under
the immediate auspices of the imperial government
was organized by Chicherin, governor of Siberia,
under instructions of the admiralty college. As early
as 1763 Chicherin had reported to the imperial government the latest discoveries among the Aleutian
Isles by Siberian traders, pointing at the same time
to the necessity of having these discoveries verified
by officers of the navy, who might be appointed as

[2] Stæhlin in his *Account of the New Northern Archipelago*, 12–15, gives a
strangely garbled report of this expedition, as follows: 'The empress...erect-
ing a commercial company composed of Russian merchants for trading with
the new islands, and to further promote this end, the admiralty office at
Okhotskoi, on the sea of Penshinsk, had orders from her Majesty to assist this
trading company of Kamchatka in the prosecution of their undertaking; to
provide them with convoys, and to endeavor to procure all possible information relative to the islands and coast they intended to visit to the north and
north-east beyond Kamchatka. In the year 1764 these traders accordingly
sailed from the harbor of Ochotskoi with some two-masted galiots, and single-
masted vessels of the kind in Siberia called *dostchennikof* (covered barges),
under a convoy from the aforesaid admiralty office, commanded by Lieutenant
Syndo. They passed the sea of Ochotskoi, went round the southern cape of
Kamchatka into the Pacific Ocean, steering along the eastern coast, keeping
northward, and at last came to an anchor in the harbor of Peter-Paul, and
wintered in the ostrog or palisaded village. The next year they pursued their
voyage farther northward, and in that and the following year, 1765 and 1766,
they discovered by degrees the whole archipelago of islands of different sizes,
which increased upon them the farther they went between the 56th and 67th
degrees of north latitude, and they returned safely in the same year. The
reports they made to the government chancellery at Irkutsk, and from thence
sent to the directing senate, together with the maps and charts thereto
annexed, made a considerable alteration in the regions of the sea of Anadir
and in the situation of the opposite coast of America, and gave them quite a
different appearance from that in the above-mentioned map engraved in the
year 1758. This difference is made apparent by comparing it with the amended
map published last year, 1773, by the academy of sciences, and is made still
more visible by the accurate little map of the newly discovered northern
archipelago, hereto annexed, which is drawn up from original accounts.' The
'accurate little map' referred to is perhaps the most preposterous piece of imaginary geography in existence, a worthy companion of the charts of Croyère.

commanders of the trading vessels and instructed to keep correct journals of their exploring voyages. This report was duly considered by the empress and resulted in the organization of the Krenitzin expedition.[3]

The empress issued a special oukaz instructing the admiralty college to detail a number of officers of the navy, intrusting the command to the most experienced among them versed in the science of navigation and kindred branches of knowledge.[4]

The expedition, having been recommended to the special attention of the admiralty college with instructions to keep its destination secret, was at once set on foot. The command was given to Captain-lieutenant Petr Kumich Krenitzin, who was to select his companions.[5] All were placed under the immediate command of the governor of Siberia, and were to proceed to the newly discovered islands on the vessels of traders, one on each, without assuming any command, turning their attention solely to taking astronomical observations and to noting all they saw. At the same

---

[3] The results of this expedition were published by Coxe in 1780. He obtained his information principally from the historian Robertson, who had been granted access to the archives of the navy department by the empress. Pallas translated Coxe's account into his *Nordische Beitrage*, published in 1781; and in the same year a Russian translation appeared in the *Academic Monthly* and was republished in the selections from the monthly. Robertson, however, had no opportunity to look into the details of the organization and management of the expedition, and confined himself to results; consequently the actual details of the enterprise remained unknown until Sokolof investigated the subject, having access to the original journals and charts. *Zap. Hydr.*, x. 17-71.

[4] A portion of the oukaz reads as follows: ' We promise our imperial goodwill not only to the commander of the expedition but to all his subordinates, and assure them that upon their safe return from their voyage every participant shall be advanced one step in rank and be entitled to a life pension in proportion to the salary received during the voyage. On account of the distance to be traversed and the hardships to be encountered, I grant to each member of the expedition double pay and allowance of subsistence from the time of departure to the day of return; this extra allowance to continue for a period of two years.' *Sokolof, Irkutsk Archives.* With the final instructions the gracious sovereign forwarded to Governor Chicherin a gold watch for each of the officers in command.

[5] In order to mislead the public with regard to the objects of the expedition the admiralty college gave it the official name of 'An Expedition for the Exploration of the Forests on the rivers Kama and Brela.' *Sokolof, Zap. Hydr.*, 75.

time the governor was informed that if he deemed it better to employ government vessels, he might engage ships of the promyshleniki, or build new crafts, and despatch Krenitzin and his chief assistant on two of the latter, independent of the trader's fleet.[6]

Krenitzin was promoted to captain of the second rank, and Lieutenant Mikhaïl Levashef, whom the commander had chosen for his chief assistant, to be captain-lieutenant. All the subalterns were advanced one step in rank, as had been promised them. The command took its departure from St Petersburg the 1st of July 1764, arriving in Tobolsk the 17th of September.[7] At this place the expedition was reënforced by ten cadets from the local school of navigation, and also provided with additional supplies and stores. They left Tobolsk at the beginning of March 1765, arriving at Yakutsk in July and at Okhotsk in October, after a difficult journey over the tundra and mountains intervening between Yakutsk and the sea.[8]

[6] The instructions of the governor began with these words: 'Fully aware of your knowledge and your zeal for the glory of her Imperial Majesty, and the benefit of your country, the admiralty college expects you to employ all your ardor and perseverance in the prosecution of this enterprise.' There was also a 'secret addition' to these instructions. Believing that the expedition about to be despatched along the Arctic coast of Siberia under command of Chichagof, to search for the north-east passage, would finally reach Kamchatka and meet there the vessels of the Krenitzin expedition, the admiralty college thought it necessary to establish a code of signals known to the commanders of both squadrons. These signals consisted of an extraordinary arrangement of the sails, frequent lowering and hoisting of flags, and discharges of cannon. In their endeavors to provide for all contingencies the framers of these instructions also suggested that in times of fog, and in the absence of fire-arms or ammunition, the vessels should approach each other as nearly as possible, when the command was to shout three times 'agaï!' in a manner similar to the shout of 'hurrah!' by troops, and if the other vessel should answer with the same cry, three times reʾ eated, the crew of the first was again to shout, 'Boshe pomogi!' God help you, also three times, and await from the other vessel the reply, 'Da, pomoshet i nam!' yes, he will help us. Then when all these signals had been correctly answered the crew of the first vessel was to shout, 'Umnak Island!' three times, and await an answer from the other crew of 'Onnekotan Island!' three times repeated. *Irkutsk Archives; Sokolof, Zap. Hydr.*, x. 76–7. Sokolof also mentions that the expedition was fitted out with 12 quadrants and the charts of Bering, of the merchant Shishkin, and of Vertlugof; those of the last two covering respectively the Aleutian Islands and north-eastern Siberia and Japan.

[7] The subaltern officers consisted of seven mates, Dudin 1st, Dudin 2d, Shebanof, Krasheninnikof, Chinenoi, Stepanof, and Sralef; one corporal, and four quartermasters. *Zap. Hydr.*, x. 77–8.

[8] At Yakutsk Krenitzin received another batch of instructions from the

Upon the receipt of full reports of the expedition, the thrice gracious and benignant Catherine expressed her thanks to Governor Chicherin for all his arrangements in a special rescript, hoping for complete success of the undertaking. The empress also thanked the governor for "framing such wise instructions." In alluding to the departure of Krenitzin for the coast from Yakutsk she wrote: "May the Almighty bless his journey. I am sure that you will not slacken your zeal in promoting the enterprise, and whatever occurs during the journey worthy of note you will report to me at once. I am now waiting with impatience news of his farther progress."[9]

When Krenitzin arrived at Okhotsk he found to his great disappointment that the vessels intended for his use were not ready, the keels only having been laid and a few timbers selected for the frames. All labor had been suspended for lack of timber. When Chicherin was informed of this he instructed Krenitzin to temporarily supersede Captain Rtishchef, second in command of Okhotsk, and to superintend in person the construction of his vessels. If he should find it impossible to complete the ships, he was authorized to engage others from the traders. Through Colonel Plenisner, Krentzin also encountered obstacles to his progress.[10]

prolific pen of Chicherin, advising the commander to obtain from the merchants who had already visited the Aleutian Isles, a detailed description of their discoveries, and to locate them on his charts; to turn his special attention to the large and populous island of Kadiak, which should be circumnavigated if possible and thoroughly explored in order to ascertain whether it was an island or mainland. *Irkutsk Archives; Sokolof*, x. 78–9; *Sarychef*, ii. 37; *Pallas, Nord. Beitr.*, i. 282.

[9] The imperial rescripts are in *Irkutsk Archives; Zapiski Hydr.*, dated Oct. 11, 1764; April 11, July 11, and Oct. 12, 1765.

[10] Col. Plenisner, who commanded the military station at Okhotsk, quarrelled with Krenitzin and sent complaints to Irkutsk. The governor wrote to Krenitzin, instead of replying to the accuser, as follows: 'Perhaps Plenisner will cause you trouble. From my knowledge of you, and I had the honor of knowing you for some time at Tobolsk, I conclude that you will give him no provocation; but I do not know Plenisner personally. It seems to me that there is something in the air of Okhotsk that causes all officers stationed there to quarrel.' After assuring Krenitzin of his sincere friendship, the governor advised him to avoid all petty quarrels in order not to displease the empress, and concluded as follows: 'If Plenisner seriously interferes with your arrange-

At last, in August 1766, the ships were completed
and launched, a brigantine called the *Sv Ekaterina*
and a hooker, the *Sv Pavel;* two others, old vessels,
had also been fitted out, the galiot *Sv Pavel* and the
Gavril.[11] The squadron sailed from Okhotsk the 10th
of October. The third day out, at a distance of only
ten leagues from Okhotsk, all the vessels became separated from each other. On the 17th Krenitzin first
sighted land in latitude 53° 45', and the following day
the brigantine was discovered to be leaking badly,
rendering it necessary to run for the land. A gale
arose, and the result was a total wreck twenty-five
versts north of Bolsheretsk, near the small river Ontok,
the crew reaching the shore in safety the 24th. Levashef, on the hooker *Sv Pavel*, sighted the coast of
Kamchatka on the 18th, and on the 22d approached
the harbor of Bolsheretsk, but waited to take advantage of a spring tide to cross the bar. On the following day a storm came up, causing the vessel to break
from her cables. Levashef attempted to put to sea,
but failing he finally ran the ship ashore on the 24th,
about seven versts from Bolsheretsk River. The
crew and the greater part of the cargo were landed.
The *Sv Gavril* succeeded in entering Bolsheretsk
harbor, but was overtaken by the same storm and cast
upon the beach. The galiot *Sv Pavel* drifted out of
her course into the Pacific, and after more than two
months of agony the thirteen survivors, among whom
was the commander, found themselves on one of the

---

ments, I give you permission to report directly to her Imperial Majesty, and
to the admiralty college, but I hope that God will not let it come to that,
and that He will give you peace and good-will. Such is my sincere wish.'
Irkutsk Archives; Zap. Hydr., x. 80; *Morskoi Sbornik*, cv. 49–50.

[11] The expeditionary force was distributed as follows: the *Sv Ekaterina*,
commanded by Krenitzin, carried 72 men; the hooker *Sv Pavel*, commanded
by Levashef, 52; the galiot *Sv Pavel*, commanded by Dudin 2d, 43; and the
Sv Gavril, commanded by Dudin 1st, 21. The cost of fitting out the expedition reached the sum of 100,837 rubles, then a large amount of money. The
empress wrote Chicherin on the subject of expense under date of May 28,
1764: ' Perhaps the execution of my plans will involve some expenditure of
money, and therefore I authorize you to employ for the purpose the first funds
coming into your treasury, sending a strict account of expenditure to the
admiralty college.' *Zap. Hydr.*, x. 81.

Kurile Islands with their vessel a wreck. Such was
the beginning, and might as well have been the end,
of the empress' grand scientific expedition.

The shipwrecked crews passed the winter at Bolsheretsk, where they were joined during the following
summer by mate Dudin 2d, and the survivors of the
crew of the wrecked galiot. The hooker *Sv Pavel* and
the *Sv Gavril* were repaired, Levashef taking command of the former with a crew of fifty-eight, while
Krenitzin sailed in the latter with a crew of sixty-
six. Each vessel was provided with a large bidar.
Sailing from Bolsheretsk the 17th of August 1767,
the expedition arrived at Nishekamchatsk on the 6th
of September. Here another winter must be passed.
The *Sv Gavril* was unfit for navigation, and Krenitzin concluded to take the galiot *Sv Ekaterina*, Synd,
commander, just returned.[12] Chichagof, about the
meeting with whom the admiralty college had been

[12] For a description of bidars and bidarkas see *Native Races*, vol. i., this
series. The galiot *Sv Ekaterina* had 3 mates, 1 second mate, 3 cadets, 1
boatswain, 1 boatswain's mate, 2 quartermasters, 1 clerk, 1 surgeon, 1 ship's
corporal, 1 blacksmith, 1 carpenter, 1 boat-builder, 1 sail-maker, 1 infantry
soldier, 41 Cossacks, 9 sailors, and 2 Aleuts—a total of 72. The hooker *Sv
Pavel*, carried 4 mates, 4 cadets, 4 quartermasters, 1 surgeon, 1 ship's corporal,
1 locksmith, 1 carpenter, 1 turner, 1 soldier, 38 Cossacks, 5 promyshleniki,
2 Aleuts, and 1 volunteer, a Siberian nobleman. The provisions were distributed as follows:

Galiot, *St Ekaterina.*	Pounds.	Hooker, *Sv Pavel.*	Pounds.
Hard bread	51		...
Flour	476	Flour	504
Groats	47	Groats	168
Salt	52	Salt	53
Butter	134	Butter	103
Meat	13	Meat	100
Dried fish, bundles of	286	Dried fish, bundles of	201
Salt fish, barrels	20	Salt fish, barrels	13
Brandy, buckets	27	Brandy, buckets	45
Casks of water	47	Casks of water	34
Wood, fathoms	8	Wood, fathoms	6
Powder	20	Powder	17

The armament consisted of 2 copper half-pound falconets, 2 small iron
falconets and 1 large iron cannon, 39 muskets, 6 musketoons, and 13 rifles.
Irkutsk Archives; Zap. Hydr., ix. 68-9.

so anxious, had in the mean time already accomplished
two journeys, 1765–6, also attended by misfortune.
The winter was passed by the men in boiling sea-
water for salt, and in making tar out of spruce. They
also constructed two large bidars and some water-
casks, and in the spring all hands were busy fishing.
By the first of April the ice began to disappear from
the river, and on the 1st of July both vessels were
ready for sea. The Krenitzin expedition was not
only unlucky, but it seemed to carry a curse with it.
One of the crew of the *Sv Pavel*, a Cossack named
Taborukin, landed in Kamchatka not quite cured of
an attack of small-pox and infected the whole neighborhood. In two years the population was more than
decimated.[13]

On the 21st of June the ships were towed out of
the mouth of the Kamchatka River, and on the 22d
they spread their sails, steering an easterly course and
stopping at Bering Island for water. Owing to contrary winds their progress was slow, and on the 11th
of August, in latitude 54° 33', the two ships became
separated during a strong south-south-west gale and
thick weather. On the 14th of August Krenitzin
sighted the islands of Signam and Amukhta; on the
20th of the same month he reached the strait between
Umnak and Unalaska, called by him Oonalaksha.
Here he met with the first Aleuts, whom he was to
know only too well in the future. These natives were
evidently acquainted with Russians, for on approaching the vessel they cried "zdorovo!" good health;
they also asked, "Why do you come? Will you live
quietly and peacefully with our people?" They were
assured that the new arrivals would not only live in
peace but make many presents. This was the 1st
of November, and the Aleuts returned to Unalaska.
On the 22d Levashef's craft also appeared and both
vessels proceeded together to a bay on the north side
of Unalaska, Captain Harbor. Here they laid in a

---

[13] *Sgibnef*, in *Morskoi Sbornik*, cii. 40–7.

supply of fresh water with the assistance of the natives. On the following day an Aleut reported that
the inhabitants of Akutan and Unalga had killed
fifteen of Lapin's crew who had wintered on Unga.
Without investigating the report both commanders
hoisted their anchors and proceeded northward. On
the 30th of August they entered the strait between
Unimak and the peninsula. The hooker grounded,
but was released next day without damage, and the
search for a wintering harbor was continued.[14]

On the 5th of September the two ships separated
not to meet again until the following spring. On the
18th of September Krenitzin succeeded in finding a
beach adapted to haul up his vessel for the winter on
the island of Unimak, while Levashef proceeded to
Unalaska and anchored on the 16th of September in
the innermost cove of Captain Harbor, still known by
his name.[15]

About the middle of October, before Krenitzin had
succeeded in erecting winter-quarters of drift-wood,
the only material at hand, two large bidars appeared
filled with natives who demanded presents. They
received some trifles with a promise of additional gifts
if they would come to the ship. In the mean time
the strangers had questioned the interpreter, anxious
to discover the strength of Krenitzin's crew, when
suddenly one of the natives threw his spear at the
Russians. Nobody was injured and the savages
retreated under a severe fire of muskets and cannon
from ship and shore. Fortunately the cannonade

[14] Krenitzin's instructions contained a statement that a good harbor had
been discovered in that locality by Bechevin's vessel commanded by Golodof
and Pushkaref in 1762. *Neue Nachr.*, 52. It has already been intimated
above that Bechevin did not actually reach the peninsula, then called Alaksha
Island, but wintered on Unalaska, which abounds in good harbors. According to Cook, *Oonemak;* La Pérouse, *Ouinnak; Sutil y Mex., Viage, Isla Unimak;* Holmberg, *I. Unimak. Cartog. Pac. Coast*, MS., iii. 450.

[15] Levashef chose for his wintering place an anchorage at the head of the
inner bay of Illiuliuk, sheltered by two little islands from the north wind,
and near the mouth of two excellent trout-streams. The location of his camp
can still be traced, the ground-plan of four great subterranean winter-huts
being still plainly visible, though now covered with a luxuriant growth of
grasses and shrubs.

proved as harmless as the spear-throwing. Insignificant as was this encounter, it proved the beginning of bitter strife. All the subsequent meetings with the natives were of a hostile character. While exploring the peninsula shore two Cossacks were wounded by spears thrown by hidden savages, and one night a native crawled up stealthily to within a few yards of the Russian huts, but was discovered, and fled.[16]

In the month of December scurvy appeared, the first victim being a Cossack who had been wounded by the savages. In January 1769 the number of sick had reached twenty-two, and in April only twelve of the company were free from disease, and those were much weakened by hunger. The whole number of deaths during the winter was thirty-six. During December and January the savages kept away, but in February they once more made their appearance, and a few traded furs, whale-meat, and seal-blubber for beads.[17] On the 10th of May some natives brought letters from Levashef, and the messengers received a liberal compensation. On the 24th the galiot was launched once more, and on the 6th of June Levashef joined Krenitzin's party.

Levashef had also met with misfortune during the winter. It is true that the natives did not attack him because the promyshleniki who had passed the preceding winter at Unalaska had left in his hands thirty-three hostages, the children of chiefs, but rumors were constantly afloat of intended attacks, making it

---

[16] Krenitzin's journal states that during the night numerous voices were heard on the strait, and guns were twice discharged in the direction of the camp, while signals could be distinguished imitating the cry of the sea-lion. On account of the impending danger five sentries were posted. *Irkutsk Archives; Zap. Hydr.*, ix. 91.

[17] The daily journal of Krenitzin contains an entry to the effect that on the night of the 11th of April several bidars were discovered in the strait, and that they were fired upon twice by the Russians with canister. Such treatment certainly did not serve to pacify the natives. It seems that during the whole winter it had been the practice to fire from time to time during the night in order to 'prevent any savages skulking about from attempting an attack.' Three times during the winter severe shocks of earthquake were felt—on January 15th, February 20th, and March 16th. *Krenitzin's Journal; Irkutsk Archives; Zap. Hydr.*, x. 91-2.

necessary to exercise vigilance. Lack of food and fuel caused great suffering among the crew; it was impossible to live comfortably on board the ship, and the huts constructed of drift-wood were frequently thrown down by the furious gales of winter. The weather was very boisterous throughout the season, and in May the number of sick had reached twenty-seven.[18] Obviously they must return; so on the 23d of June both vessels left their anchorage. During the voyage they became separated, Krenitzin arriving at Kamchatka the 29th of July, and Levashef on the 24th of August.[19]

The winter was passed by the expedition at Nishekamchatsk, but as there were little provisions and no money the suffering was great. The only available source of supply was the dried fish of the natives, which had to be purchased at exorbitant prices.[20] On the 4th of July both vessels were ready for sea, when Captain Krenitzin attempting to cross the river in a dug-out, the frail craft capsized and he was drowned. Levashef assumed command, and having assigned Dudin 2d to the galiot he sailed from Kamchatka the 8th, arriving at Okhotsk the 3d of August. Levashef returned to St Petersburg, arriving there the 22d of October 1771; seven years and four months from his departure. The expedition was a praiseworthy effort, but miserably carried out.

Meanwhile, fresh information had reached St Petersburg of the successes of the Russian promyshleniki on the Aleutian Islands, telling the empress and her

---

[18] Levashef's journal under date of December 16th contains the following: 'Nearly all the men say that we are doomed to perish, that we have been abandoned by God; we have bad food, and but little of that, and we can find no shelter from the snow-storms and rain.' *Levashef's Journal; Irkutsk Archives; Zap. Hydr.*, x. 93.

[19] *Zap. Hydr.*, x. 94; *Coxe's Russian Dis.*, 300; *Pallas, Nord. Beitr.*, i. 279.

[20] An entry in Krenitzin's journal states that 200 pounds of flour were sent from Bolsheretsk to his relief, but it spoiled in transmittal. Nineteen barrels of salt fish were also transported overland across the peninsula. On the 28th of September 1769, and on the 4th of May 1770, heavy earthquakes occurred, and on the latter date the Kluchevskaia volcano was in eruption. *Krenitzin's Journal; Zap. Hydr.*, x. 94.

learned society a hundredfold more of Alaska than
they were ever to learn from their special messengers.
Tolstykh reported that during a cruise among the
islands in his ship *Andreian i Natalia,* 1760 to 1764,
he subjugated six islands and named them the
Andreienof group, as we have seen. Another report stated that four vessels of one company had
been despatched in 1762 to Unalaska and Umnak.
Glottof reported that he had wintered at Kadiak in
1763. In 1766, as already stated, the merchant Shilof
arrived at St Petersburg and was presented to the
empress.[21]

An important change of government policy now took
place in the treatment of the Aleuts. Upon Krenitzin's representations the collection of tribute by the
promyshleniki and Cossacks was prohibited by an

[21] The information furnished by Levashef's journal was divided into four
heads: A description of the island of Unalaska; the inhabitants; tribute;
traffic. The description was superficial, adding scarcely anything to previous
accounts. In regard to tribute Levashef stated that it was paid only by those
who had given their children as hostages. The promyshleniki's mode of carrying on trade is described as follows: 'The Russians have for some years
past been accustomed to repair to these islands in quest of furs of which they
have imposed a tax upon the inhabitants. They go in the autumn to Bering
and Copper islands, and there pass the winter employing themselves in killing
fur-seals and sea-lions. The flesh of the latter is prepared for food, and is
esteemed a great delicacy. The skins of the sea-lions are carried to the eastern
islands. The following summer they sail eastward to the Fox Islands and
again haul up their ships for the winter. They then endeavor to procure by
force, or by persuasion, children as hostages, generally the sons of chiefs;
this accomplished they deliver fox-traps to the inhabitants and also sea-lion
skins for the manufacture of bidarkas, for which they expect in return furs
and provisions during the winter. After obtaining from the savages a certain
quantity of furs as tribute or tax, for which they give receipts, the promyshleniki pay for the remainder in beads, corals, woollen cloth, copper kettles,
hatchets, etc. In the spring they get back their traps and deliver the hostages.
They dare not hunt alone or in small numbers. These people could not com-
prehend for some time for what purpose the Russians imposed a tribute of
skins which they did not keep themselves, for their own chiefs had no revenue;
nor could they be made to believe that there were any more Russians in
existence than those who came among them, for in their own country all the
men of an island go out together.' The most important part of Levashef's
report is the description of the inhabitants, which furnishes some valuable
ethnological information. See *Native Races,* passim, this series. The hydrographic results of the expedition were meagre. The navigators of this costly
enterprise had no means of ascertaining the longitude, and consequently their
observations were very unsatisfactory. They located Unimak, Unalaska, and
Umnak between latitudes 53° 29' and 54° 38'. Special charts were made of
Unimak, the northern coast of Unalaska, and the harbor of St Paul, now
known as Captain Harbor. *Levashef's Journal; Irkutsk Archives; Zap. Hydr.,*
x. 97-203; *Coxe's Russian Dis.,* 220-2.

imperial oukaz.[22]   The business of fitting-out trading expeditions for the Aleutian Isles continued about as usual, notwithstanding the terrible risks and misfortunes.   Of hunting expeditions to discovered islands it is not necessary to give full details.

In the year 1768 a company of three merchants, Zassypkin, Orekhof, and Moukhin, despatched the ship *Sv Nikolai* to the islands, meeting with great success; the vessel returned in 1773 with a cargo consisting of 2,450 sea-otters and 1,127 blue foxes.[23]   The *Sv Andrei—Sv Adrian* according to Berg—belonging to Poloponissof and Popof, sailed from Kamchatka in 1769.   In 1773 she was wrecked on the return voyage in the vicinity of Ouda River.   The cargo, consisting of 1,200 sea-otters, 996 black foxes, 1,419 cross foxes, and 593 red foxes, was saved.[24]   The same year sailed from Okhotsk the *Sv Prokop*, owned by the merchants Okoshinikof and Protodiakonof.   She returned after four years with an insignificant cargo of 250 sea-otters, 20 black and 40 cross foxes.[25]   In 1770 the ship *Sv Alexandr Nevski*, the property of the merchant Serebrennikof, sailed for the islands and returned after a four years' voyage with 2,340 sea-otters and 1,130 blue foxes.[26] 'Shilof, Orekhof, and Lapin, in July of the same year, fitted out once more the old ship *Sv Pavel* at Okhotsk, and despatched her to the islands under command of the notorious Solovief.   By this time the Aleuts were evidently thoroughly subjugated,

[21] Berg claims that this oukaz was not issued until 1779, 10 years after Krenitzin returned. *Khronol. Ist.*, 80. Berg's statements concerning the Krenitzin expedition are brief and vague.   The best authority on the subject now extant is Sokolof, who had access to the archives of Irkutsk, and who published the results of his investigation in volume x. of *Zap. Hydr.*   The description of Krenitzin's voyage in *Coxe's Russian Dis.*, 221 et seq., is based to a certain extent on questionable authority, but it was translated verbally by Pallas in his *Nord. Beitr.*, i. 249–72.   The same account was copied in German in *Büsching's Magazine*, vol. xvi., and strangely enough retranslated into Russian by Sarychef.

[22] *Berg, Khronol. Ist.*, app.; *Grewingk, Beitr.*, 317.

[23] *Berg, Khronol. Ist.*, 64–6, app.   The nature of the cargo proves that the voyage extended at least to Unalaska.

[24] *Berg, Khronol. Ist.*, 67.   No reason for the ill-success of this venture has been transmitted.

[25] *Berg, Khronol. Ist.*, 86.

as the man who had slaughtered their brethren by
hundreds during his former visit passed four additional years in safety among them, and then returned
with an exceedingly valuable cargo of 1,900 sea-otters,
1,493 black, 2,115 cross, and 1,275 red foxes.   He
claims to have reached the Alaska peninsula, and describes Unimak and adjoining islands.[27]

The next voyage on record is that of Potap Zaïkof,
a master in the navy, who entered the service of the
Shilof and Lapin company, and sailed from Okhotsk
on the 22d of September 1772, in the ship *Sv Vladimir*.   Zaïkof had with him a peredovchik named Sho-
shin and a crew of sixty-nine men.[28]   At the outset
this expedition was attended with misfortune.   Driven
north, the mariners were obliged to winter there,
then after tempest-tossings south they finally reached
Copper Island, where they spent the second winter.

Zaïkof made a careful survey of the island, the first
on record, though promyshleniki had visited the spot
annually for over twenty-five years.   Almost a year
elapsed before Zaïkof set sail again on the 2d of July
1774, and for some unexplained reason twenty-three
days were consumed in reaching Attoo, only seventy
leagues distant.   Having achieved this remarkable
feat he remained there till the 4th of July following.   The progress of Zaïkof on his eastward course
was so slow that it becomes necessary to look after a
few other expeditions which had set out since his departure.

The ship *Arkhangel Sv Mikhaïl*, the property of
Kholodilof, was fitted out in 1772, and sailed from Bol-
sheretsk on the 8th of September with Master Dmitri
Polutof as commander, and a crew of sixty-three men.
This vessel also was beached by a storm on the coast

---

[27] *Pallas, Nord. Beitr.*, viii. 326–34; *St Petersburger Zeiting*, 1782—an extract from Solovief's journal.   Another *Sv Pavl*, despatched in 1774 by a
Tobolsk trader named Ossokin, was wrecked immediately after setting sail
from Okhotsk.   *Grewingk, Beitr.*, 319.

[28] *Berg, Khronol. Ist.*, 87; *Pallas, Nord. Beitr.*, iii. 274–88; *Grewingk,
Beitr.*, iii. 18.

of Kamchatka; after which, passing the tardy Zaïkof, Polutof went to Unalaska, where he remained two years, trading peaceably, and then proceeded to Kadiak. On this last trip he set out on the 15th of June 1776, taking with him some Aleutian hunters and interpreters. After a voyage of nine days the *Sv Mikhaïl* anchored in a capacious bay on the east coast of the island, probably the bay of Oojak on the shores of which the Orlova settlement was subsequently founded. The natives kept away from the vicinity of the harbor for some time, and a month elapsed before they ventured to approach the Russians. They were heavily armed, extremely cautious in their movements, and evidently but little inclined to listen to friendly overtures. Polutof perceived that it was useless to remain under such circumstances. He finally wintered at Atkha, and the following year returned, landing at Nishekamchatsk. The total yield of this adventure was 3,720 sea-otters, 488 black, 431 cross, 204 red, 901 blue foxes, and 143 fur-seals.[29]

Thus Polutof accomplished an extended and profitable voyage, while the trained navigator Zaïkof was yet taking preparatory steps, moving from island to island, at the rate of one hundred miles per annum.[30] The latter had on the 4th of July 1775 sailed from Attoo, leaving ten men behind to hunt during his absence. On the 19th the *Sv Vladimir* reached Umnak, where another vessel, the *Sv Yevpl*, or St Jewell, owned by the merchant Burenin, and despatched in 1773 from Nishekamshatsk, was already anchored. Aware of the bloody scenes but lately acted thereabout, Zaïkof induced the commander of the *Sv Yepvl*

---

[29] *Berg, Khronol. Ist.,* app.

[30] From papers furnished him by Timofeïf Shmalef, Berg heard of another vessel belonging to the merchants Grigor and Petr Panof, which sailed for the islands in 1772. *Khronol. Ist.,* 96–7; *Grewingk, Beitr.,* 319. Another voyage undertaken in 1772 is described by Pallas in *Nord. Beitr.,* ii. 308–24, under the following title: 'Des Peredofschik's Dimitry Bragin Bericht von einer im Jahre 1772 angetretenen einjährigen Seereise zu den zwischen Kamtschatka und Amerika gelegenen Inseln.' Since Grewingk describes this voyage as occupying the four years from 1772 to 1776, it is rather doubtful whether the description applies to the one year voyage of Bragin.

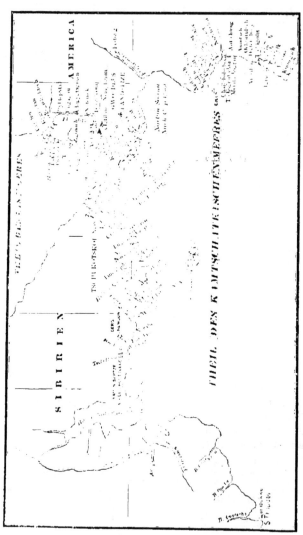

BRAGIN'S MAP.

to hunt on joint account.[31] The agreement was that the *Sv Yevpl* should remain at Umnak with thirty-five men, while the *Sv Vladimir*, with sixty men and fully provisioned, was to set out in search of new discoveries. On rejoining, the furs obtained by the two parties were to be divided. Zaïkof sailed eastward on the 3d of August, and in three weeks reached the harbor where Krenitzin wintered with the *Sv Ekaterina*. Here the commander of the expedition considered himself entitled to a prolonged rest, and consequently he remained stationary for three years, making surveys of the neighborhood while his crew attended to the business of hunting and trapping.[32]

On the 27th of May 1778 the *Sv Vladimir* put to sea once more, steering for the bay where the companion ship was anchored. Upon this brief passage, which at that time of the year can easily be accomplished in three days, Zaïkof managed to spend fifty-three days. At last, however, the juncture of the two ships was effected and the furs were duly divided, but after attending to these arduous duties the captain concluded to wait another year before taking his final departure for Okhotsk. Not until the 9th of May 1779 did Zaïkof sail from Umnak, and after brief stoppages at Attoo and Bering islands the *Sv Vladimir* found herself safely anchored in the harbor of Okhotsk on the 6th of September.[33]

---

[31] The *Sv Yevpl* sailed for the islands in 1773, and returned in 1779. In the cargo were 63 land-otters, the first shipped by the promyshleniki, and proving that this vessel must have reached the continent. *Berg, Khronol. Ist.*, 97, app. A comparison of this cargo with the furs carried back by the *Sv Vladimir* would indicate that Zaïkof must have taken the lion's share on closing the partnership.

[32] Berg thought it improbable that Zaïkof should have known anything of astronomical observations (he was a master in the navy!), but he acknowledged that Zaïkof did discover an error committed by Captain Krenitzin in placing his anchorage five degrees too far to the westward. *Khronol. Ist.*, 98.

[33] With all his apparently unnecessary delays, Zaïkof in his report to the owners of the vessel made a very good showing compared with the results of other voyages. During an absence of more than 7 years he lost but 12 out of his numerous crew, and his cargo consisted of 4,372 sea-otters, 3,949 foxes of different kinds, 92 land-otters, 1 wolverene and 3 wolves—the first brought from America—18 minks, 1,725 fur-seals, and 350 pounds of walrus ivory, the

Two of the owners of the *Sv Vladimir*, Orekhof and Lapin, proceeded to St Petersburg with a present of three hundred choice black foxes for the empress. The gift was graciously received; the donors were entertained at the imperial palace, decorated with gold medals, and admitted to an interview with Catherine, who made the most minute inquiries into the operations of her subjects in the easternmost confines of her territory. The indebtedness of the firm to the government for nautical instruments and supplies, timber, and taxes, was also remitted.[34]

It has been elsewhere mentioned that the promyshleniki and traders occasionally ventured upon voyages from the coast of Kamchatka to the eastward islands in open boats or bidars. Two of these expeditions took place in 1772, under the auspices of a merchant named Ivan Novikof. The voyage of over a thousand miles from Bolsheretsk around the southern extremity of Kamchatka to the islands was twice safely performed, the whole enterprise netting the owners 15,600 rubles. Considering the higher value of money in those times and the insignificant outlay required in this instance, the enterprise met with encouraging success.

From this time to the visit of Captain Cook, single traders and small companies continued the traffic with the islands in much the same manner as before, though a general tendency to consolidation was perceptible.[35]

whole valued at 300,416 rubles. Berg declares that at the prices established by the Russian-American Company at the time of his writing, 1812, the same furs would have been worth 1,603,588 rubles. *Khronol. Ist.*, 91–3.

[34] Berg also states that this present was made after the return of the *Sv Vladimir* from the islands, but he speaks of the journey of Orekhof and Lapin as having taken place in 1776. The discrepancy may be owing to a typographical error. *Khronol. Ist.*, 93–4.

[35] In 1774 the merchants Protodiakonof and Okoshinikof fitted out the ship *Sv Prokop* for the second time, but on her return from a fourth cruise the owners refused to engage again in such enterprises, having barely covered expenses during a period of eight years.

CHAPTER IX.

EXPLORATION AND TRADE.

1770-1787.

IT was a time of rapid and sweeping political changes
at the imperial court. All along the road to Siberia,
to Yakutsk, and even to Okhotsk and Kamchatka, one
batch of exiles followed another, political castaways,
prisoners of war, or victims of too deep diplomacy,
as much out of place in this broad, bleak penitentiary
as would be promyshleniki and otters in St Petersburg. In one of these illustrious bands was a Polish
count, Augustine Benyovski by name,[1] who had
played somewhat too recklessly at conspiracy. Nor
was Siberia to deprive him of this pastime. Long
before he reached Yakutsk he had plotted and organized a secret society of exiles with himself as chief.
The more prominent of the other members were a
Doctor Hoffman, a resident of Yakutsk, Major Windblath, Captain Panof, Captain Hipolite Stepanof,
Colonel Baturin, and Sopronof, the secretary of the

---

[1] Sgibnef states that Benyovski did not call himself count or baron in
Kamchatka, but simply beinosk or beinak. *Morskoi Sbornik*, cii. 51.

society.[2] 'The object of this association very naturally
was to get its members out of limbo; or in other words
mutual assistance on the part of the members in
making their escape from Siberia. The chief exacted
from each his signature to a written agreement, done
in the vicinity of Yakutsk, and dated the 27th of
August 1770. After a month of tedious progress
through the wastes of eastern Siberia, the count's
party was overtaken by a courier from Yakutsk who
claimed to have important despatches for the commander of Okhotsk; at the same time he reported
that Dr Hoffman was dead. The suspicions of Benyovski and his companions were aroused. Persuading the tired courier that he needed a little rest, they
feasted him well, and after nightfall while he slept
they ransacked his satchel, and took therefrom a
formidable-looking document which proved to contain
an exposé of their plans, obtained from Hoffman's
papers. Benyovski was equal to the emergency. He
wrote another letter upon official paper, with which
he had provided himself at Yakutsk, full of the most
sober recommendations of the exiles to the commander
of Okhotsk. This document was inserted into the
pilfered envelope, and carried forward to its destination by the unsuspecting messenger.[3]

The forged letter did its work. When Benyovski
and his companions arrived at Okhotsk they were
received with the greatest kindness by Colonel Plenisner,[4] the commandant, who regarded them as unfortunate gentlemen, like himself, not for a moment to
be placed in the category of criminals. Hence he
granted them every privilege, and supplied them freely
with food, clothing, and even arms. Being a man of
little education and of dissipated habits, Plenisner was

---

[2] *Benyovski's Memoirs and Travels*, i. 67.
[3] *Benyovski's Memoirs and Travels*, i. 72; *Morskoi Sbornik*, cii. 97.
[4] This man was probably the same mentioned in connection with the second
expedition of Bering and Shestakof's campaign in the Chukchi country, and
who was appointed to the command of Kamchatka in January 1761, for a
term of five years. *Syibnef*, in *Morskoi Sbornik*, cii. 37–8.

easily deceived by the plausible tongue of the courtly Pole, who quickly perceived that he had made an egregious mistake in framing his forged letter. He saw that residence at Okhotsk promised favorable opportunity for escape in view of the confidence reposed in him by the commander, though he had thought that Kamchatka offered the best facilities, and had urged in the letter early transportation of the exiles to that locality. Though willing to oblige his new friends, in every possible manner, Colonel Plenisner did not dare to act in direct opposition to his orders, and in October a detachment of exiles, embracing all the conspirators, was sent by the ship *Sv Petr i Sv Pavel* to Bolsheretsk, Kamchatka,[5] where they were transferred to the charge of Captain Nilof, commandant of the district.[6]

[5] Benyovski describes this craft as of 200 tons burden, armed with 8 cannons, and manned with a crew of 43, commanded by Yesurin and Korostilof. The vessel was laden with flour and brandy. *Benyovski's Memoirs and Travels*, i. 79-80.

[6] Benyovski claims that the passage was an exceedingly stormy one, and that the ship was on the verge of destruction, owing to the incapacity and drunkenness of both officers and men, when he, a prisoner in irons, took command and by his 'superior knowledge of navigation succeeded in shortening sail and bringing the vessel into its proper course, thus saving the lives of all on board.' As the passage was a short one we may doubt the statement of the boastful Benyovski. The count also claimed that the privileges subsequently granted him by Nilof were based upon his heroic action on this occasion. Nilof had formerly been the commandant of the Cossack ostrog of Ishiga, but Zubritski when recalled to St Petersburg summoned him as his successor in 1769. He was given to drink, and easily deceived, and had already been victimized by an exiled official named Ryshkof. The latter having failed in various attempts to trade with the natives, prevailed upon Nilof to advance sums from the public funds for the purpose of engaging in agricultural experiments. Of course the money was lost and the experiments resulted in failure. *Sgibnef*, in *Morskoi Sbornik*, cii. 51-69. Shortly after their arrival the following regulations concerning the exiles were promulgated at Bolsheretsk: 1st. The captives were to be liberated from close restriction and furnished with food for three days; after which they were to provide their own subsistence. 2d. The chancellery was to furnish each exile with a gun and lance, one pound of powder, four pounds of lead, an axe, some knives, and other utensils with which to build themselves a house. They were at liberty to select a location within half a league of the town; each man was to pay to the government 100 rubles during the first year in consideration of the advance, payments to be made in money or skins at the option of the exiles. 3d. Each exile was bound to labor one day of each week for the government, and they were not allowed to absent themselves from their location over 24 hours without permission of the commandant. Each was also to furnish the treasury of Bolsheretsk with 6 sables, 2 foxes, 50 gray squirrels, and 24 ermines annually.

We may as well take it for granted before proceeding further that three fourths of all that Benyovski says of himself are lies; with this understanding I will continue his story, building it for the most part on what others say of him.

In Kamchatka as in Okhotsk through his superior social qualifications the count was enabled to gain the confidence and good-will of the commander, so that the hardships of his position were greatly alleviated. He was not obliged to join his companions in the toilsome and dangerous chase of fur-bearing animals, finding more congenial employment in Captain Nilof's office and residence.[7] The count accompanied his patron on various official tours of inspection, in which he came in contact with his numerous fellow-exiles scattered through the interior in small settlements. His original plan of escape from the Russian domains was ever present in his mind and he neglected no opportunity to enlarge the membership of his secret society. In order to ingratiate himself still more with Nilof he resorted to his old trick of forgery, and revealed to the credulous commander an imaginary plot to poison him and the officers of his staff. He claimed in his memoirs that in consideration of this service Nilof formally revoked his sentence of exile.[8]

While still travelling with Nilof in the beginning of 1771, Benyovski intercepted a letter directed to the former by one of the conspirators betraying the plot.[9]

[7] Benyovski goes out of the way to prove himself a great rascal. He explains how he ingratiated himself with Nilof and his family, claiming that he was employed as tutor to several young girls and boys, and that in his capacity of clerk to the father he forged reports to the imperial government, praising the conduct of the exiles. He also states that he made use of his fascinations to work upon the feelings of one of the young daughters, and to gain control of her heart and mind. Sgibnef, however, a careful and industrious investigator, says, first, that the count did not play upon the affections of Nilof's daughter, and secondly that Nilof never had a daughter. *Benyovski's Memoirs and Travels*, i. 150-2; *Morskoi Sbornik*, cii. 51-69.

[8] *Benyovski's Memoirs and Travels*, i. 135-7. Sgibnef, however, states that no amnesty or special privileges were granted to Benyovski. *Morskoi Sbornik*, cii. 69.

[9] Benyovski gives the following list of members of the secret society of exiles: Benyovski, Panof, Baturin, Stepanof Solmanof, Windblath, Krustief, and Vassili, Benyovski's servant. Later a large number was added, among them

The traitor, whose name was Leontief, was killed by order of the court. The plan settled upon for final action was to overcome the garrison of Bolsheretsk, imprison the commander, plunder the public treasury and storehouses, and sail for Japan or some of the islands of the Pacific with as many of the conspirators as desired to go.[10]

Benyovski's statement of his exploits at Kamchatka, for unblushing impudence in the telling, borders the sublime. Arriving at Bolsheretsk on the 1st of December a half-starved prisoner clothed in rags, he was advanced to the position of confidant of the acting governor before two weeks had elapsed, being also the accepted suitor for the hand of his daughter. During the same time he had succeeded in rousing the spirit of revolt not only in the breasts of his fellow-exiles, but among the free merchants and government officials, who he claimed were ready to rise at a moment's warning and overthrow their rulers. Within a few days, or weeks at the most, this grand conspiracy had not only been called into existence but had survived spasms of internal dissensions and attempted treason, all suppressed by the strength and presence of mind of one man—Benyovski. Then he tells how he cheated the commander and others in games and sold his influence for presents of furs and costly garments. On the 1st of January 1771 a fête took place at the house of Captain Nilof. Benyovski claims that it

many who were not exiles: Dumitri Kuznetzof, a free merchant, Afanassiy Kumen, a Cossack captain; Ivan Sibaïef, captain of infantry; Alexeï Protopop, archdeacon of the church, free; Leonti Popof, captain of infantry, free; Ivan Churin, merchant, free; Magnus Meder, surgeon-general of the admiralty, exiled for 20 years; Ivan Volkof, hunter, free; Kasimir Bielski, Polish exile; Grigor Lobchof, colonel of infantry, exile; Prince Heraclius Zadskoi, exiled; Julien Brandorp, exiled Swede; Nikolaï Serebrennikof, captain of the guards, exile; Andreï Biatzinin, exile. All the members of the Russian church joining the conspiracy were obliged first to confess and receive the sacrament in order to make their oath more binding. *Benyovski's Memoirs and Travels*, i. 108–9.

[10] At that time the province was estimated to contain over 15,000 inhabitants classified in the official returns as follows: 22 infantry officers; 422 Russian riflemen; 1,500 Cossacks and officers; 26 civil officers; 82 Russian merchants; 700 descendants of exiles (200 females), free; 1,600 exiles: 8,000 males and 3,000 female natives of Kamchatka; 40 Russian men. *Benyovski's Memoirs and Travels*, i. 301; *Morskoi Sbornik*, ciii. 81.

had been arranged to celebrate his betrothal to Afanassia Nilof, to whom he had promised marriage,
though already possessed of a wife in Poland. In
his diary he states at length how he suppressed
another counter-conspiracy a few moments before proceeding to the festive scene, and sentenced two of his
former companions to death. Meanwhile Benyovski's
cruel and arbitrary treatment of his associates had
made him many enemies, and reports of his designs
reached the authorities. He succeeded repeatedly in
dispersing the growing suspicion, but finally the danger became so threatening that he concluded to precipitate the execution of his plot.

On the 26th of April Captain Nilof sent an officer
with two Cossacks to Benyovski's residence with
orders to summon him to the chancellery, there to
give an account of his intentions. The summons of
the chief conspirator brought to the spot about a
dozen of his associates, who bound and gagged the
captain's messengers. Then hoisting the signal of
general revolt, which called all the members of the
society together, he proceeded to Nilof's quarters,
where the feeble show of resistance made by the
trembling drunkard and his family furnished sufficient
excuse for a general charge upon the premises. During
the mêlée the commander was killed. The murder was
premeditated, as the best means of preventing partici-
pants from turning back.

Before resolving upon the final attack, Benyovski
had secured the services of the commander of the
only vessel then in port, the *Sv Petr i Sv Pavel*,
and as soon as the momentary success of the enterprise was assured his whole force was set to work to
repair and fit out this craft. The magazines and
storehouses were ransacked, and not satisfied with
the quantity of powder on hand, he shipped a supply
of sulphur, saltpetre, and charcoal necessary for the
manufacture of that article.[11]

[11] Benyovski's own inventory of the 'armament' of the *Sv Petr i Sv*

The interval between Benyovski's accession to power and his departure to Bolsheretsk was filled with brief trials and severe punishments of recreant members of his band who endeavored to open the way for their own pardon by the old authorities by betraying the new. The knout was freely used, and the sentence of death imposed almost daily. At last on the 12th of May the *Sv Petr i Sv Pavel* sailed out of the harbor of Bolsheretsk midst the firing of salvos, the ringing of bells, and the solemn te deum on the quarter-deck. The voyage is involved in mystery, caused chiefly by the contradictory reports of Benyovski himself. He says he anchored in a bay of Bering Island on the 19th of May, after a passage of seven days, took on board twenty-six barrels of water, and sailed again, after a brief sojourn on the island, during which he claimed to have fallen in with a Captain Okhotin of the ship *Elizaveta*, whom Benyovski describes as an exiled Saxon nobleman.

On the 7th of June he claims to have communicated with the Chukchi in latitude 64°, and only three days later, on the 10th of June, he landed on the island of Kadiak, over 1,000 miles away. Another entry in the count's diary describes his arrival on the island of Amchitka, one of the Andrïanovski group, on the 21st of June, and two days later the arrival of the ship at Ourumusir, one of the Kurile Islands, is noted. In explanation of this remarkable feat he gives the speed of his vessel at ten and a half knots an hour, which might be true, driven by a gale. The only part of this journey susceptible

Pavel was as follows: '96 men, 9 of them females; 8 cannon; 2 howitzers; 2 mortars; 120 muskets with bayonets; 80 sabres; 60 pistols; 1,600 pounds of powder; 2,000 pounds of lead; 800 pounds of salt meat; 1,200 pounds of salt fish; 3,000 pounds of dried fish; 1,400 pounds of whale-oil; 200 pounds of sugar; 500 pounds of tea; 4,000 pounds of spoiled flour; 40 pounds of butter; 113 pounds of cheese; 6,000 pounds of iron; 120 hand-grenades; 900 cannon-balls; 50 pounds of sulphur; 200 pounds of saltpetre; several barrels of charcoal; 36 barrels of water; 138 barrels of brandy; 126 cases of furs; 14 anchors; sails and cordage; one boat and one skiff.' *Memoirs and Travels*, i. 271.

of proof is the arrival of the survivors in the harbor
of Macao on the Chinese coast.[12]

The successor of the murdered Nilof was Major
Magnus Carl von Behm, who was appointed to the
full command of Kamchatka by an imperial oukaz
dated April 30, 1772, but he did not assume charge
of his district until the 15th of October of the following year, having met with detention in his progress
through Siberia.[13]

In 1776 the name of Grigor Ivanovich Shelikof
is first mentioned among the merchants engaged in
operations on the islands and coast of north-west
America. This man, who has justly been called the
founder of the Russian colonies on this continent, first
came to Okhotsk from Kiakhta on the Chinese frontier and formed a partnership with Lebedef-Lash-
tochkin for the purpose of hunting and trading on
the Kurile Islands. This field, however, was not
large enough for Shelikof's ambition, and forming
another partnership with one Luka Alin, he built a

---

[12] Sgibnef states that Benyovski was informed after his departure from
Bering Island that a party of his associates had laid plans to detain the vessel
and return to Kamchatka. Several of the accused were punished by flogging,
while Ismaïlof and Paranchin, with the latter's wife, were put ashore on an
island of the Kurile group, whence they were brought back by Protodiakonof,
a trader, in 1772. This would explain the circumstance that Cook could not
obtain any definite information concerning Benyovski's voyage from Ismaïlof
when he met the latter at Unalaska in 1778. *Sgibnef*, in *Morskoi Sbornik*, c.
ii. 62-3. From Macao Benyovski managed to reach the French colony on
Madagascar Island, and finally he proceeded to Paris with the object of obtaining the assistance of the French government in subjugating the natives
of Madagascar. Here he met with only partial success, but definite information is extant to the effect that on the 14th of April 1774 Benyovski embarked
for Maryland on the ship *Robert and Anne*. He was accompanied by his
family and arrived at Baltimore on July 8th the same year, with a cargo of
merchandise for Madagascar valued at £4,000. In Baltimore he succeeded
in obtaining assistance from resident merchants, who chartered for him a
vessel of about 450 tons, the *Intrepid*, armed with 20 guns, and with this craft
he sailed from Baltimore on October 25, 1784. The last letter received from
the count was dated from the coast of Brazil. A few months later he reached
his destination and at once organized a conspiracy for the purpose of setting
up an independent government on the island of Madagascar, but in an action
with French colonial troops he was killed on the 23d of May 1786.

[13] Major Behm's salary was fixed at 600 rubles per annum, and his jurisdiction was subsequently extended over the Aleutian Islands by an oukaz of the
governor general of Irkutsk. *Sgibnef*, in *Morskoi Sbornik*, iii. 7.

vessel at Nishekamchatsk, named it of course the *Sv Pavel*, and despatched it to the islands.[14] Another vessel of the same name was fitted out by the most fortunate of all the Siberian adventurers, Orekhof, Lapin, and Shilof. The command was given to Master Gerassim Grigorovich Ismaïlof, a man who subsequently figures prominently in explorations of Alaska, and of whom Cook speaks in terms of high commendation.[15]

Leaving the discussion of the voyages of English and French explorers, which took place about this time, to another chapter, we shall follow the movements of Siberian traders and promyshleniki up to the point of final amalgamation into a few powerful companies. In 1777 Shelikof, Solovief, and the Panof brothers fitted out a vessel named the *Barfolomeï i Varnabas*, which sailed from Nishekamchatsk and returned after an absence of four years with a small cargo valued at 58,000 rubles.[16] In the same year another trader, who was to play a prominent part in the development of the Russian colonies in the Pacific, first appears upon the scene. Ivan Lari-

[14] It was commanded by Sapochnikof, of whom Cook speaks in terms of praise. This vessel returned in 1780 with a cargo valued at 75,240 rubles. *Berg, Khronol. Ist.*, 101, app.

[15] Cook spells his name Erasim Gregorieoff Sin Ismyloff. *Cook's Voy.*, ii. 497. Gregorief Sin is an obsolete form of Grigorovich, both signifying 'son of Grigor.' Ismaïlof was considered one of the most successful navigators among the Russian pioneers. Much of this reputation he doubtless owed to the information received from Cook, who speaks of his intelligence and acuteness of observation. Concerning his escape from Benyovski, see note 12. The name of Ismaïlof's vessel, the *Sv Pavel*, led Corporal Ledyard, of Cook's marine guard, and subsequently a self-styled American colonel, into the mistake of reporting that he saw at Unalaska the very vessel in which Bering made his voyage of discovery, the corporal being unaware that that craft had been destroyed. *Life of Ledyard*, 86; *Pinkerton's Voy.*, xvi. 781–2; *Cook's Third Voy.*, ii. 494, 523. Berg states that he could find no accounts of the present voyage beyond a brief notice of Ismaïlof's return in 1781 with a very rich cargo valued at 172,000 rubles. *Khronol. Ist.*, 101. His peredovchik was Ivan Lukanin. He commanded the *Trekh Sviatiteli* in 1783, the vessel on which Shelikof himself embarked, the *Simeon* in 1793, on which occasion he met Vancouver's officers, without telling them of his intercourse with Cook, and the *Alexandr* in 1795. *Berg, Kronol. Ist.*, Table ii., app.

[16] Berg, *Khronol Ist.*, mentions the despatch of the ship *Alexand Nevski* by the brothers Panof in 1776, and its return in 1779, but gives no details of the voyage. This is probably an error. See p. 169.

novich Golikof, a merchant of the town of Kursk, who held the office of collector of the spirits tax in the province of Irkutsk,[17] formed a partnership with Shelikof. At joint expense they built a ship named *Sv Andreï Pervosvannuï*, that is to say St Andrew the First-called, which sailed from Petropavlovsk for the Aleutian Islands. This vessel was subsequently wrecked, but the whole cargo, valued at 133,450 rubles, was saved.[18] Another ship, the *Zossima i Savatia*, was despatched in the same year by Yakof Protassof, but after remaining four years on the nearest Aleutian isles, the expedition returned with a small cargo valued at less than 50,000 rubles. In 1778 the two Panof brothers associated themselves with Arsenius Kuznetzof, also one of the former companions of Benyovski,[19] and constructed a vessel named the *Sv Nikolaï*, which sailed from Petropavlovsk. This craft was absent seven years and finally rewarded the patience of the owners with a rich cargo consisting of 2,521 sea-otters, 230 land-otters, and 3,300 foxes of various kinds.[20] The same firm despatched another vessel in the same year, the *Kliment*, which returned in 1785 with a cargo of 1,118 sea-otters, 500 land-otters, and 830 foxes. The commander of this expedition was Ocheredin.[21]

---

[17] *Berg. Khronol. Ist.*, 102.

[18] *Berg, Khronol. Ist.*, app.; *Grewingk, Beitr.*, 321.

[19] *Berg, Khronol. Ist.*, 103; *Syn Otechestra, 1821*, No. 27.

[20] *Berg, Khronol. Ist.*, 105. The nature of the cargo would indicate that at least a portion of the cruise was spent in the vicinity of the mainland of Alaska.

[21] Though Polutof appears to have brought it home. Berg during his sojourn at Kadiak had an opportunity to converse with a hunter named Tuyurskoi, who had been one of Ocheredin's crew. This man stated that the expedition had passed the winter of 1779 at Kadiak, and that they had with them 60 Aleuts for the purpose of hunting sea-otters. The Kadiaks, however, would not allow these men to hunt, scarcely permitting them to land even. During the whole winter, which was passed under constant apprehension of attacks, only 100 sea-otters were secured, and 20 of the crew died of scurvy. In the spring the promyshleniki made all haste to proceed to Unalaska. *Berg, Khronol. Ist.*, 104-7. Berg also states that another craft of the same name, *Sv Nikolaï*, the property of Shelikof and Kozitzin, sailed for the islands in 1778, but he could find no details concerning the voyage in the archives beyond the statement that the same vessel made three successive voyages in the same direction. *Kadiak*, east of the Alaska peninsula. On

The ship *Sv Ioann Predtecha*, or St John the Fore-
runner, belonging to Shelikof and Golikof, sailed
from Petropavlovsk in 1779, and remained absent six
years without proceeding beyond the nearest Aleutian
Islands, finally returning to Okhotsk with a cargo of
little value. In the following year the brothers Panof
fitted out once more the *Sv Yevpl*. This old craft was
wrecked on her return voyage not far from Kamchatka, but the cargo, valued at 70,000 rubles, was
saved and brought into port by another vessel.[22]

With the funds realized from the sale of the cargo
of the *Sv Pavel* Shelikof had constructed another craft,
with the intention of extending his operations among
the islands. The vessel was named the *Sv Ioann Ryl-·*
skoi, St John of Rylsk, and sailed from Petropavlovsk
in 1780.[23]

The *Sv Prokop*, fitted out by the merchants Shu-
ralef and Krivorotof, also sailed in 1780, but was
wrecked on the coast of Kamchatka soon after leaving Okhotsk. Four vessels sailed for the islands in
1781, the *Sv Pavel*, despatched for the second time by
Shelikof and Alin; the *Sv Alexeï*, despatched by the
merchant Popof; the *Alexandr Nevski*, belonging to
the firm of Orekhof, Lapin, and Shilof;[24] and *Sv
Georgiy*, fitted out by Lebedef-Lastochkin and Shelikof, wherein Pribylof made the all-important discovery
of the Fur Seal Islands in 1786,[25] which will be duly

Cook's *Atlas*, 1778, *P⁴ Kadjac*; La Pérouse, 1786, *J. Kichtak*; Dixon, 1789,
Kodiac; Vancouver, 1790-95, *Kodiak*; *Sutil y Mex.*, *Viage, Isla Kadiac*;
Holmberg, *Kadjak. Cartog. Pac. Coast*, MS., iii. 434.

[22] *Berg, Khronol. Ist.*, 107; *Grewingk, Beitr.*, 323.

[23] After an absence of six years this vessel returned, but was wrecked on
the coast of Kamchatka. The cargo, however, comprising 900 sea-otters and
over 18,000 fur-seals, was saved. Shelikof seems to have been the first among
the traders to deal more extensively in fur-seals. Up to 1780 he had imported
70,000 of these skins. *Berg, Khronol. Ist.*, 106-7.

[24] The *Sv Pavel* returned after a five years' cruise with a cargo valued at
35,000 rubles; the *Sv Alexeï* also returned after an absence of five years and
met with great success; the *Alexandr Nevski*, which had just made a cruise
to the Kurile Islands under the command of the Greek, Eustrate Delarof, was
placed under the command of Stepan Zaïkof for this expedition, and returned
in five years with a rich assortment of furs, valued at 283,000 rubles, *Berg,
Khronol. Ist.*, 807-9. See note 19.

[25] After an eight years' cruise Pribylof returned to Okhotsk with a cargo of
2,720 sea-otters, 31,100 fur-seals, nearly 8,000 foxes, and a large quantity

discussed in its chronological order. For 1782 only
one departure of a trading-vessel for the islands has
been recorded. This vessel was fitted out by Yakov
Protassof at Nishekamchatsk.[26] Lebedef-Lastochkin
organized a special company in 1783 for the purpose
of extending his operations on the islands. The capital
of this enterprise was divided into sixty-five shares,
most of them being in Lebedef's hands.[27]

In 1783 the first direct attempt was made by the
Russian traders to extend their operations to the mainland of America, to the northward and eastward of
Kadiak. The fur-bearing animals had for some years
been rapidly disappearing from the Aleutian Islands
and the lower peninsula, and despairing of further
success on the old hunting-grounds the commanders
of three vessels then anchored at Unalaska came to
the conclusion that it was best to embark on new discoveries. They met and agreed to submit themselves
to the leadership of Potap Zaïkof, a navigator of some

of walrus ivory and whalebone. *Berg, Khronol. Ist.*, 107; *Veniaminof*, i. 131–2;
Sauer's Astron. and Geog. Exped., 246; *Grewingk, Beitr.*, 323.

[26] Protassof's vessel returned in 1786, and according to Berg his cargo con-
sisted chiefly of fur-seals. *Berg, Khronol. Ist.*, 111. As the discovery of the
Seal Islands occurred in that year the skins must have been obtained at the
Commander Islands.

[27] Berg furnishes a full list of the share-holders, which may serve to demon-
strate how such affairs were managed in those early times. The 65 shares
were divided as follows: The merchant Lebedef-Lastochkin, 34 shares; Yefim Popof, 1 share; Grigor Deshurinskoi, 1 share; Elias Zavialof, 1 share;
Ivan Korotaief, 1 share; Vassili Neviashin, 1 share; Mikhaïl Issaief, 1 share;
Vassili Shapkin, 2 shares; Vassili Kulof, 1 share; Mikhaïl Tubinskoi, 1 share;
Feodor Nikulinskoi, 2 shares; Arseni Kuznetzof, 1 share; Vassili Krivishin,
1 share; Mikhaïl Dushakof, 2 shares; Ivan Lapin, 2 shares; Alexeï Polevoi,
1 share; Ivan Bolsheretak, 2 shares; Dmitri Lorokin, 1 share; the manu-
facturer, Ivan Savelief, 5 shares; the citizen, Ssava Chebykin, 1 share; the
citizen, Spiridon Burakof, 1 share; and Court Counsellor Peter Budishchef,
2 shares: total, 65.

In the division of profits there were to be added to this number 1 share
for the church, and the orphans in the school of Okhotsk; 1 share to the
peredovchik, Petr Kolomin, 1 share to the boatswain, Durygin, 1 share to
the navigator, Potap Zaïkof, and 2 shares to such of the crew as distinguished
themselves during the voyage by industry, bravery, or otherwise, making the
value of 1 share at the division of profits one seventy-first of the whole proceeds. *Berg, Khronol, Ist.*, 109, 211; *Grewingk, Beitr.*, 324; *Pallas, Nord.
Beitr.*, vi. 165, 175. At the end of the cruise the first vessel sent by this
company was wrecked on the island of St Paul. The cargo was saved, but
proved barely sufficient to cover expenses.

reputation, and leave to him the selection of new hunt-ing-grounds. These vessels were the *Sv Alexeï*, com-manded by Eustrate Delarof; the *Sv Mikhaïl*, under Polutof, and the *Alexandr Nevski*, commanded by Zaïkof. The latter had learned from Captain Cook and his companions during their sojourn in Kam-chatka that they had discovered a vast gulf on the coast of America and named it Prince William Sound.[23] To this point he concluded to shape his course.

On the 27th of July the three ships were towed to anchorage in a small cove, probably on the north side of Kaye Island, which, as they subsequently discov-ered, was named Kyak by the natives. Boats and bidarkas were sent out at once in various directions in search of game and of inhabitants—the few natives observed on entering the bay having fled to the hills at sight of the Russians. On the third day one of the detached parties succeeded in bringing to the ships a girl and two small children, but it was not until the middle of August that anything like friendly intercourse could be established, and the natives in-duced to trade peltries.[29]

On the 18th the bidarchik Nagaief returned to the anchorage with quite a number of sea-otter skins, all made into garments, and reported the discovery of a large river—the Atnah, or Copper—which he had ascended for some distance. He had met with a large body of natives in a bidar and traded with them, both parties landing on the beach at a distance of six hundred fathoms from each other and then meeting half-way. These people informed him that at their home was a safe harbor for ships, referring of course

[23] Zaïkof had obtained rough tracings of some of the charts compiled by Cook in exchange for favors extended to the English discoverer. *Tikhmenef*, i. 113. It is supposed that the *Sv Yerpl*, 1773–79, reached the continent, and probably the *Sv Nikolaï* and others, but this was accidental.

[29] Two natives who were kept as hostages on Zaïkof's vessel stated that Kyak was not a permanent place of residence, but was visited only in search of game by the people seen by the Russians, their homes being to the west-ward, at the distance of 'two days' paddling,' from which statement we may conclude that they were from Nuchek or Hinchinbrook Island. *Zaïkof's Jour-nal*, in *Sitka Archives*, MS., iv.; *Tikhmenef*, *Ist. Obos.*, ii., app. 3.

to Nuchek, where both English and Spanish ships had already called. Many days were spent by Zaïkof in futile attempts to secure a native guide to the safe harbor mentioned as having already been visited by ships, but bribes and promises proved of no avail, and at last he set out in the direction of the island of Khta-aluk (Nuchek), plainly visible to the westward. The commanders of the two other ships must have sailed before him and cruised about Prince William Sound—named gulf of Chugach by the Russians—in search of hunting-grounds, and this scattering of forces beyond the bounds of proper control proved dangerous, for the Chugatsches were not only fiercer than the Aleuts, but they seemed to entertain positive ideas of proprietary rights.

The combined crews of the three vessels, numbering over three hundred, including Aleut hunters, would surely have been able to withstand any attack of the poorly armed Chugatsches and to protect their hunting parties, but they wandered about in small detachments, committing outrages whenever they came upon a village with unprotected women and children. The Russians, who had for some time been accustomed to overcome all opposition on the part of the natives with comparative ease, imagined that their superior arms would give them the same advantage here. They soon discovered their mistake. The Chugatsches, as well as their allies from Cook Inlet, and even from Kadiak, summoned by fleet messengers for the occasion, showed little fear of Russian guns, and used their own spears and arrows to such advantage that the invaders were themselves beaten in several engagements.

In the harbor of Nuchek Nagaief met twenty-eight men from the Panof company's ship, the *Alexei*, fourteen of whom had been wounded by the Chugatsches during a night attack. They had left their ships on the 15th of August, a month previous, in search of this bay, numbering thirty-seven men, besides peredovchik Lazaref, who was in command, but had searched in vain. One dark night, while encamped on an island, their sentries had been surprised, nine men killed, and half of the remainder wounded. With the greatest difficulty only had they succeeded at last in beating off with their fire-arms their assailants armed merely with spears, bows and arrows, and clubs. Other encounters took place. On the 18th of September one of the parties of Russians surprised a native village on a small island; the men fled to the mountains, leaving women, children, and stores of provisions. The considerate promyshleniki seized "only half" the females—probably not the oldest—and some of the food. During the next night, however, the men of the village, with reënforcements from the neighborhood, attacked the Russian camp, killing three Russians and a female interpreter from Unalaska, and wounding nine men. During the struggle all the hostages thus far obtained by capture escaped, with the exception of four women and two small boys. The Russians now proceeded to the harbor selected as winter-quarters,[30] and active operations ceased for the time.

The favorable season had been so foolishly wasted in roaming about and quarrelling with the natives, who took good care not to reveal to their unwelcome visitors the best fishing and hunting grounds, that food became scarce early in the winter. Besides this it was found necessary to keep one third of the force continually under arms to guard against sudden assaults; and this hostility naturally interfered with the search for the necessary supplies of fish, game, fuel, and water. The result was that scurvy of a very malignant type broke out among the crews, and nearly one half of the men died before spring released them and enabled Zaïkof to refit his vessel and

[30] The description of this harbor is not very clear, but the probability is that it was one of the bays on the north end of Montagu, or Sukluk, Island, which is named Zaïkof Harbor on Russian maps. This is also confirmed by traditions of the natives collected on the spot by Mr Petrof in 1881.

sail for the Aleutian isles, after an experience fully as
dismal as that encountered a few years later, in nearly
the same locality, by Captain Meares, who might have
saved himself much misfortune had he known of Zaïkof's attempt and its disastrous result.

Thus unfortunately ended the attempt of the Russians to gain a foothold upon the continental coast of
America.[31]

The only subordinate commander of this expedition
who seems to have actually explored and intelligently

[31] Eustrate Delarof subsequently gave Captain Billings the following account of this expedition: 'On arriving at Prince William Sound a number of
canoes surrounded the vessel and on one of them they displayed some kind of
a flag. I hoisted ours, when the natives paddled three times around the ship,
one man standing up waving his hands and chanting. They came on board
and I obtained fourteen sea-otter skins in exchange for some glass beads; they
would accept no shirts or any kind of clothing; they conducted themselves
in a friendly manner, and we ate, drank, and slept together in the greatest
harmony. They said that two ships had been there some years previously,
and that they had obtained beads and other articles from them. According to
their description these vessels must have been English (they referred of course
to Cook's expedition); the natives had knives and copper kettles which they
said they obtained by making a 14 days' journey up a large river and trading
with other natives who brought these goods from some locality still farther
inland (a Hudson's Bay Company post?)—Suddenly, on the 8th of September,
the natives changed their attitude, making a furious attack on my people.
I knew of no cause for this change until one of my boats returned, when I
learned that there had been quarrelling and fighting between the boat's crew
and the natives. I have no doubt that my people were the aggressors.
Polutof's vessel was at that time in the vicinity and I left him there.' Sauer's
Geog. and Astron. Exped., 197. Martin Sauer, the secretary of Captain Joseph
Billings, states that while at Prince William Sound in 1790 he fell in with a
woman who had been forcibly detained by Polutof and had subsequently
become acquainted with Zaïkof. She praised the latter as a just man and
related how her people revenged themselves on Polutof for his ill-treatment.
A wood-cutting party had been sent ashore from each vessel and had pitched
their tents a short distance from each other. It was very dark and only one
man was on the watch near a fire on the beach. The natives crawled up
unnoticed by the sentry, killed him, and then stealing into Polutof's tent
massacred him and his companions without molesting Zaïkof's tent or any of
his people. Bitter complaints were made by the Chugatsche people of the doings of Polutof who had seized their furs without paying for them and had
carried off by force many of the women. Sauer's Geog. and Astron. Exped., i.
187, 190; Grewingk, Beitr., 323; Pallas, Nord. Beitr., i. 212. In the historical
review attached by Mr Dall to his Alaska and its Resources, the author has
committed blunders which can be ascribed only to his inability to understand
the Russian authorities. Under date of 1781 he remarks that 'Zaïkof explored in detail Chugách Gulf and wintered on Bering Island...A vessel,
called the St Aezius, commanded by Alexeïef Popof, was attacked by natives
in Prince William Sound. Zaïkof explored Captain's Harbor, Unalaska, July
1-13, 1783.' Id., 307. Mr Dall's Zaïkof expedition of 1781 is, of course, the
same with that of 1783, when he wintered on Montagu (not Bering) Island, in
a bay still bearing his name. The Alexeï, as we have seen above, was commanded by Delarof.

described these unknown regions, was Nagaief, the discoverer of Copper River. Nearly all the valuable information contained in Zaïkof's journal came from this man.[32]

This failure to extend their field of operations seriously checked the spirit of enterprise which had hitherto manifested itself among the Siberian merchants, and for some time only one small vessel was despatched from Siberia for the Aleutian Islands.[33]

The year 1786, as already mentioned, witnessed the discovery of the Fur Seal Islands, the breeding-ground of the seals, and therefore of the highest importance. The Russian promyshleniki who first visited the Fox Islands soon began to surmise the existence of some islands in the north by observing the annual migration of the fur-seals through the passes between certain of the islands—northward in the spring and southward in the autumn, when they were accompanied by their young. This surmise was confirmed by an Aleut tradition to the effect that a young chieftain of Unimak had once been cast away on a group of islands in the north, which they called Amik.[34] The

[32] Nagaief told Zaïkof that the natives he had encountered called themselves Chugatches, and that they met in war and trade five other tribes: 1st, the Koniagas, or people of Kadiak; 2d, a tribe living on a gulf of the main land between Kadiak and the Chugatsche country, named the Kinaias; 3d, the Yullits, living on the large river discovered by Nagaief; 4th, a tribe living on the coast of the mainland from Kyak Island eastward, called Lakhamit; and 5th, beyond these again the Kaljush, a warlike tribe with large wooden boats. This description of the tribes and their location was doubtless correct at the time, though the 'Lakhamite' (the Aglegmutes) have since been pushed eastward of Kyak Island by the Kaljushes, or Thlinkeets. Nagaief also correctly stated that the Yullits, or Copper River natives, lived only on the upper river, but traded copper and land-furs with the coast people for sealskins, dried fish, and oil. *Zaïkof's Journal*, MS.; *Sitka Archives*, iv.; *Tikmenef, Ist., Oboer.*, ii., app., 7, 8. Zaïkof's own description of the country, its resources, its people, and the manners and customs, is both minute and correct. His manuscript journal is still in existence, and it furnishes proof positive that his visit to Prince William Sound in 1783 was the first made by him or any other Russian in a sea-going vessel.

[33] The *Sv Georgiy* left Nishekamchatak on Panof's account, and returned in two years with a little over 1,000 fur-seals and less than 200 blue foxes, having evidently confined its operations to the Commander Islands. The same vessel made another voyage in 1787, remaining absent six years, but with an equally unsatisfactory result. *Berg, Khronol. Ist.*, 114-15.

[34] A term and incident commemorated in a native song. *Veniaminof, Zapiski*, ii. 269; i. 17; *Sarychef, Putesh.*, i. 28.

high peaks of his native place had guided him back after a short stay. While furs remained abundant on the groups already known, none chose to expose himself in frail boats to seek new lands; but in and after 1781 the rapid depletion of the hunting-grounds led to many a search for Amik; yet while it lay within two days' sail from the southern isles, a friendly mist long hid the home of the fur-seals from the hunters.

In 1786 this search was joined by Master Gerassim Pribylof,[25] who for five years had been hunting and trading with little profit on the islands, in the *Sv Georgiy*, fitted out by Lebedef-Lastochkin and his partners. Although reputed a skillful navigator, he cruised for over three weeks around the Amik group without finding them, though constantly meeting with unmistakable evidence of the close proximity of land. At last, in the first days of June, fate favored the persistent explorer; the mantle of fog was lifted and before him loomed the high coast of the eastern end of the most southern island. The discovery was named St George, after Pribylof's vessel; but finding no anchorage the commander ordered the peredovchik Popof and all the hunters to land, with a supply of provisions for the winter, while he stood away again for the Aleutian Islands, there to spread such reports as to keep others from following his path.

The shores of St George literally swarmed with sea-otters, which undisturbed so far by human beings could be killed as easily as those of Bering Island during the first winter after its discovery. Large numbers of walrus were secured on the ice and upon the adjoining small islands; arctic foxes could be caught by hand, and with the approach of summer the fur-seals made their appearance by thousands.[36]

<hr/>

[25] His name was Gerassim Gavrilovich Pribylof. Veniaminof gives his name as Gavrilo on one occasion. *Zapiski*, ii. 271. He was a master in the navy, connected with the port of Okhotsk, but entered the employ of Lebedef-Lastochkin and his partners in 1778. *Id.*

[36] Shelikof in a letter to Delarof, dated Okhotsk, 1789, stated that during

On the 29th of June, 1787, an unusually clear atmosphere enabled the promyshleniki to see for the first time the island of St Paul, thirty miles to the northward; and the sea being smooth a bidar was at once despatched to examine the new discovery. The party landed upon the other island the same day, and named it St Peter and St Paul, the saints of the day.[37] The first half of the name, however, was soon lost in popular usage and only St Paul retained. The group was known as the Pribylof.[38]

While Shelikof was one of the partners who had fitted out the *Sv Georgiy*, he does not appear to have held a large interest and looked with no little envy on the success achieved by what must be regarded as rivals to his own company. He did not waste much time, however, in unpleasant sentiments, but set about at once to secretly buy up more shares in the Lebedef company. In this undertaking he succeeded so well that he could look with equanimity upon the fierce rivalry growing up between the two large firms; no matter which side gained an advantage, he felt secure. He was certainly the first who fully understood the actual and prospective value of Pribylof's discovery.

the first year the hunters obtained on the newly discovered islands 40,000 fur-seal skins, 2,000 sea-otters, 400 pounds (14,400 lbs.) of walrus ivory, and more whalebone than the ship could carry. Shelikof upbraided Delarof for not having anticipated this discovery, with two good ships at his command. *Tikhmenef, Ist. Obozr.*, ii. app. 21.

[37] Owing to the constant fog and murky atmosphere that envelop the islands, the less elevated St Paul is rarely seen from St George, while the hills of the latter are frequently visible from St Paul.

[38] The claim of Pribylof to their first European discovery was thrown into doubt by the report that the Russians on reaching the island of St Paul found the brass hilt and trimming of a sword, a clay pipe, and the remains of a fire. The statement was confirmed by all who effected the first landing on St Paul. *Veniaminof, Zapiski*, ii. 268. Berg, who has traced the course of nearly every other vessel in these waters, states that nothing was known of Pribylof's present voyage beyond his return with a rich cargo. *Khronol, Ist.*, 104. One reason for this was the secrecy observed for some time. La Pérouse met Pribylof shortly after his return, but learned nothing.

CHAPTER X.

OFFICIAL EXPLORATIONS.

1773-1779.

Russian Supremacy in the Farthest North-west—The Other European Powers would Know what it Means—Perez Looks at Alaska for Spain—The 'Santiago' at Dixon Entrance—Cuadra Advances to Cross Sound—Cook for England Examines the Coast as far as Icy Cape—Names Given to Prince William Sound and Cook Inlet—Revelations and Mistakes—Ledyard's Journey—Again Spain Sends to the North Arteaga, who Takes Possession at Latitude 59° 8'—Bay of La Santísima Cruz—Results Attained.

The gradual establishment of Russian supremacy in north-westernmost America upon a permanent basis had not escaped the attention of Spanish statesmen. Within a few years after the disastrous failure of the Russian exploring expeditions under Krenitzin and Levashef, a succinct account of all that had been accomplished by the joint efforts of the promyshleniki and the naval officers, under the auspices of the imperial government, had been transmitted to the court of Spain by its accredited and secret agents at St Petersburg.[1]

Alarmed by tidings of numerous and important discoveries along the extension of her own South Sea coast line, Spain ordered an expedition for exploring

---

[1] The communications concerning Russia's plans of conquest in Asia and America, forwarded to the court of Spain from St Petersburg, make mention of an expedition organized in 1764. Two captains, named Cwelincow and Ponobasew in the document, were to sail from Arkhangel in the White Sea, and meet Captain Krenitzin, who was to sail from Kamchatka. This is a somewhat mixed account of the Krenitzin and Levashef expedition, which did not finally sail till 1768, but was expected to fall in with lieutenants Chichagof and Ponomaref, who were instructed to coast eastward along Siberia and to pass through Bering Strait.

and seizing the coast to the northward of California. In 1773 accordingly the viceroy of Mexico, Revilla Gigedo, assigned for this purpose the new transport *Santiago*, commanded by Juan Perez, who was asked to prepare a plan of operations. In this he expressed his intention to reach the Northwest Coast in latitude 45° or 50°; but his orders to attain a higher latitude were peremptory, and it is solely owing to this that the voyage falls within the scope of the present volume. Minute directions were furnished for the ceremonies of claiming and taking possession. The wording of the written declaration, to be deposited in convenient and prominent places, was prescribed. The commander was instructed to keep the object of his voyage secret, but to strike the coast well to north, in latitude 60° if possible, and to take possession above any settlements he might find, without, however, disturbing the Russians. Appended to his instructions was a full translation of Stæhlin's *Account of the New Northern Archipelago*, together with the fanciful map accompanying that volume. Each island of the Aleutian group was described in detail, besides many others, the product of the fertile imagination of such men as Stæhlin and De l'Isle de la Croyère. Even the island of Kadiak, which had then only been twice visited by promyshleniki, was included in the list.

The *Santiago* sailed from San Blas January 24, 1774, with eighty-eight men, including two missionaries and a surgeon. The incidents of nearly the whole of this voyage occurred south of the territory embraced by this volume; but between the 15th and 17th of July Perez and his companions sighted two capes, the southernmost of which he thought was in latitude 55°, and the other about eight leagues to the north. These points were named Santa Margarita and Santa Magdalena, respectively.[2]

---

[2] The latitude given by Perez, if correct, would make it difficult to locate these capes so as to agree with the minute and circumstantial description of the contours of the coast; but allowing for an error which might easily arise

These capes, the southernmost point of Prince of
Wales Island, and the north point of Queen Charlotte
Island, lie on both sides of the present boundary of
Alaska, but Perez and his men had intercourse with
the inhabitants of the latter cape only. The mere
sighting of one of the southern capes of Alaska, and
its location by rough estimate, would scarcely justify
a discussion of the voyage of Juan Perez in the annals
of Alaska, were it not for an apparently trifling incident
mentioned in the various *diarios* of this expedition. In
the hands of the natives were seen an old bayonet and
pieces of other iron implements, which the pilot conjectured must have belonged to the boats' crews lost
from Chirikof's vessel somewhere in these latitudes in
1741.[3]   In the absence of all knowledge of any civilized visitor to that section during the interval between Chirikof's and Perez' voyages we cannot well
criticise the conclusion arrived at. It could scarcely
be presumed that at that early date a Russian bayonet should have passed from hand to hand or from
tribe to tribe, around the coast from the Aleutian
Islands, or perhaps Kadiak, a distance of from eight
hundred to one thousand miles. It appears highly
probable that Chirikof's mishap occurred in this vicinity, the Prince of Wales or Queen Charlotte Islands,
and in that case the present boundary of Alaska
would be very nearly identical with the northern
limit of the territorial claims of Spain as based upon
the right of discovery. The avowed objects of this
voyage had not been obtained by Perez; he did not
ascend to the latitude of 60°; he did not ascertain the
existence of permanent Russian establishments, and
he made no discoveries of available sea-ports. His
intercourse with the Alaskan natives, if such they

from the imperfect instruments of the times, we must come to the conclusion
that Perez discovered Dixon Sound. The allusion to an island situated to
the west of the northernmost cape, the Santa Christina or Catalina of the re-
corders of the voyage, can scarcely refer to any point but the Forrester Island
of our modern maps.
   [3] *Maurelle, Compendio de Noticias*, MS., 169.

were, was carried on without anchoring. The details of the expedition of Perez, so far as they relate to incidents that occurred south of the line of 54° 40', are discussed in my *History of the Northwest Coast*.[4]

The second Spanish expedition which extended its operations to Alaskan waters was organized in the following year, 1775. The command was intrusted to Bruno Heceta, a lieutenant and acting captain, who selected the *Santiago* as his flag-ship. Juan Perez sailed with Heceta as pilot and second in command. The small schooner *Sonora*, or *Felicidad*, accompanied the larger craft as consort, commanded by Lieutenant Juan Francisco de Bodega y Cuadra, with Antonio Maurelle as pilot.[5]

The expedition sailed from San Blas March 16th. After going far out to sea and returning to the coast again in latitude 48° on the 14th of July, taking possession of the country, and after a disastrous encounter with the savages of that region, the two vessels became separated during a northerly gale on the 30th of July.[6]

The *Sonora* alone made discoveries within the present boundaries of Alaska. After the separation the little craft, only 36 feet in length, was boldly headed

[4] Not less than four journals or diaries of the voyage are extant. Two of these were kept by the missionaries or chaplains of the expedition, Crespi and Peña; the first has been printed in *Palou, Noticias*, i. 624–88, and the other was copied from the manuscript *Viages al Norte de California*, etc., in the Spanish Archives. The third journal, entitled *Perez, Relacion del Viage*, etc., *1774*, is contained in the Mayer manuscripts and also in *Maurelle, Compendio de Noticias*, MS., 159–75. The fourth journal is also a manuscript under the title, *Perez, Tabla Diaria*, etc., contained in *Maurelle, Compendio*, 179–85. Brief mention of this voyage can also be found in *Navarrete, Sutil y Mex., Viage*, 92–3; *Humboldt, Essai Pol.*, 331–2; *Mofras, Explor.*, i.; *Navarrete, Viages Apóc.*, 53–4; *Greenhow's Mem.*, 69; *Id., Or. and Cal.*, 114–17; *Twiss' Hist. Or.*, 55–6; *Id., Or. Question*, 66–7; *Falconer's Or. Question*, 19; *Id., Discov. Miss.*, 62; *Bustamante*, in *Cavo, Tres Siglos*, iii. 119; *Palou, Vida*, 160–2; *Forbes' Hist. Cal.*, 114–16; *Calvo, Col. Trat.*, i. 338; *Nicolay's Oregon Ter.*, 30–2; *Findlay's Directory*, i. 349–50; *Poussin, Question de l'Oregon*, 38–9; *MacGregor's Prog. Amer.*, i. 535; *Tikhmenef, Istor. Obosr.*, i. preface; *Baranof*, in *Sitka Archives*, MS., i. Nos. 5 and 6.

[5] See *Hist. Northwest Coast*, i. 158, this series.

[6] The outward and homeward voyage of the *Santiago* has been fully related in *Hist. Northwest Coast*, i., this series.

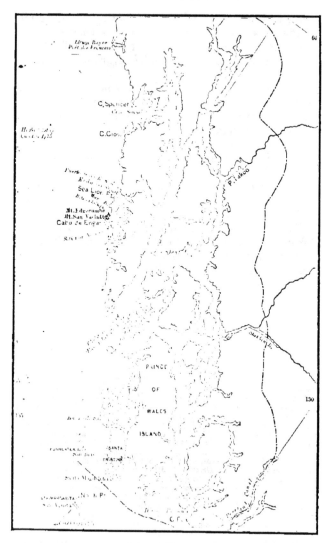

CUADRA'S VOYAGE.

seaward and kept upon a general north-westerly course. On the 13th of August indications of land were observed, though the only chart in their possession, that of Bellin, based upon Russian discoveries and to a great extent upon imagination, placed them at a distance of one hundred and sixty leagues from the continental coast. Cuadra's latitude, by observation, on that day was 55° 40′. During the next two days the signs of land became stronger and more frequent, and the navigators, in the belief that they were approaching the Tumannoi or Foggy Islands of Chirikof, observed the greatest caution.

At last, on the 16th, came in view a mountainous coast among whose many peaks was one they called San Jacinto, and the prominent cape jutting from it the Cabo de Engaño. Their description of both cape and mountain is so clear as to leave no doubt of their identity with the Mount Edgecumbe of Cook and the cape of the same name. That the original nomenclature has not been preserved is owing to Spain's neglect in not publishing the achievements of her explorers.

On the following day the goleta put to sea again, weathering Cape Engaño and following the coast in a north-westerly direction until another wide estuary was discovered and named the bay of Guadalupe, subsequently known as Shelikof Bay or Port Mary. Here Cuadra anchored for the day, observing the wooded shores rising at an acute angle from the sea. In the morning of the 18th two canoes, containing two men and two women, emerged from the head of the bay, but at the sight of the vessel they hurriedly landed and fled. The explorers then put to sea again and proceeded in a northerly direction until a good anchorage was found in latitude 57° 20′, with a good sandy beach and convenient watering-places.

A landing was effected at the mouth of a stream, near a deserted hut and a stockaded enclosure, probably used for defence by the natives. The instructions of the viceroy, concerning the forms of taking possession, were carried out so far as circumstances would permit.[7]

During the ceremonies no natives were in sight, but after returning to their vessel the Spaniards saw the savages take up the cross which they had planted and place it before their hut, as if to say "this is the better place."

On the 19th another landing was made, when the natives emerged from the forest waving a white cloth attached to a pole in token of peaceful intentions. The signal was answered by the Spaniards and the savages advanced slowly to the opposite bank of the stream. They were unarmed and accompanied by women and children. A few trifling presents were offered and received by one of the natives who waded into the middle of the stream. This friendly intercourse was, however, suddenly interrupted when the Spaniards began to fill their water-casks. The women and children were at once sent away and the men assumed a threatening attitude. The Spaniards prepared for defence while preserving an unconcerned air, and finally the savages retreated.

The place of this first landing of Spanish explorers upon Alaskan soil was called the anchorage "de los Remedios" and can be nothing else than the entrance to Klokachef Sound between Kruzof and Chichagof islands.[8]

[7] The entry in the journal referring to this event was as follows: 'El mismo dia bajaron á tierra con los preparativos que ofrecia su poco tripulacion y arreglados á la instruccion tomaron posesion, dejando los documentos y la cruz colocados con la seguridad posible, habiendo arbolado en aquel puesto las banderas del Rey nuestro Señor.' *Viajes al Norte*, MS., 25.

[8] In the journal of this voyage contained in the *Viajes al Norte*, the country is described as full of mountains, their base covered with pines like those at Trinidad, but barren or covered with snow toward the summit. The 'Yndios,' said to resemble those met with in latitude 41°, were clothed chiefly in furs. The latitudes as observed by Cuadra at Cape Engaño, Guadalupe Bay, and the Entrada de los Remedios, agrees with our positions for Cape Edgecumbe, Shelikof Bay, and the southern shore of Klokachef Sound, but the Spanish explorer places the longitude of the last anchorage some twelve miles to the westward of Cabo de Engaño. This would lead to the conclusion that the ceremony of taking possession took place just inside of Sea-lion Point, a very exposed position, while the description of the country coincides better with Kalinin cove, a few miles to the eastward. See *Karta Vkhodov Novo Arkhangelskomu Porta*, etc., 1809, 1833, and 1848.

The weather was cold and threatening during the sojourn of the *Sonora* in this bay, and both officers and the poorly clothed and sheltered crew began to suffer from scurvy. They took a west-north-westerly direction on the 21st, in order to ascertain whether their discovery was located on the west or east shore of the Pacific, a doubt engendered by the great difference in longitude between the Russian discoveries as indicated on Bellin's chart and their own; and having by that time reached a latitude of 57° 58', or the vicinity of Cross Sound, they changed their course to the southward to examine carefully all the inlets of the coast.

On the 24th of August, in latitude 55° 14', the explorers entered a magnificent sound extending far to the northward and abounding in sheltered anchorages. Cuadra was ill, but he ordered the *piloto* to take possession in the name of Spain, and for the second time the royal banner of Castile waved over Alaska. The sound was called Bucareli, a name still preserved on many maps. It is located on the west coast of the island subsequently named after the prince of Wales.[9]

After a careful inspection of the bay, during which not an aboriginal was to be seen, the *Sonora* once more stood out to sea, sighting six leagues from the harbor an island which was named San Blas, the same seen in 1774 by Juan Perez from Cape Santa Margarita, and named by him Santa Cristina. It is now known as Forrester Island. A landing was effected and water obtained, while the south point of Prince of Wales Island, named Santa Magdalena by Perez, was plainly in view.[10] Contrary winds kept the little craft beating about until the navigators succeeded in again making the coast in latitude 55° 50',

[9] The piloto expressed the opinion that this bay was the scene of Chirikof's 'landfall,' and the place where his boat's crew perished was one of the northern arms of the bay in the latitude named by the Russian discoverer. The Spaniard did not seem to take longitude into the account at all. *Viajes al Norte*, MS., 30.

[10] *Viajes al Norte*, MS., 31. Cuadra named it Cabo de San Agustin.

where a deep indentation was observed, with its western
point in latitude 56° 3'.   Thence a high mountainous
coast was seen extending north-westerly to a point
marking the southern limit of the broad estuary
bounded by Cabo de Engaño in the north.[11]

From the 28th of August to the 1st of September
the winds compelled the navigators to hug the shore
in the vicinity of latitude 56° 30'.   The crew, weakened by scurvy, were unable to combat the adverse
winds.   The vessel was swept by tremendous seas;
spars and portions of the rigging were carried away;
and when at last a steady strong north-wester began
to blow, both commander and pilots concluded that
further efforts to gain the desired latitude were useless.   The prow of the *Sonora* was turned southward
and the swelling sails soon carried her far away from
Alaska.[12]

Orders for another Spanish expedition to the north
coast were issued in 1776, but preparations were not
completed till 1779, or until after Cook's important
English explorations in this quarter.

The voyage of Captain Cook with the ships *Resolution* and *Discovery* has been discussed at length in
an earlier volume, with reference to discoveries on the
Northwest Coast south of the present boundary of
Alaska.   It is only necessary here to repeat briefly a few
paragraphs from Cook's secret instructions from the admiralty and to take up the thread of narrative where
I dropped it in the historic precincts of Nootka.[13]

[11] The description furnished by the journal of these discoveries is not clear,
but the *ensenada* may probably be identified with Christian Sound, or Clarence
Sound, on our modern maps.
[12] The log of the *Sonora* as copied in the *Viajes al Norte* places the expedition in latitude 55° 4' on the 14th of August, and from that date till the 8th
of September Cuadra's operations were confined to present Alaskan waters.
The highest latitude, 57° 57', was reached the 22d, in the vicinity of Cape
Cross, or the south point of Yacobi Island. *Viajes al Norte*, MS., 56–8. Accounts of this voyage can also be found in *Heceta, Segunda Exploracion;
Maurelle, Diario del Viaje de la Sonora, 1775*, No. 3 of *Viages al Norte;
Maurelle's Journal of a Voyage in 1775*, London, 1781, in *Barrington's Miscel-
lanies*. See also *Hist. Northwest Coast*, vol. i., this series. Juan Perez
Cuadra's pilot died before reaching San Blas.
[13] The instructions were signed by the 'Commissioners for executing the

After ordering the commander to go from New Zealand to New Albion and avoid touching Spanish territory, the document goes on to say: "And if, in your farther progress to the northward, as hereafter directed, you find any subjects of any European prince or state upon any part of the coast you may think proper to visit, you are not to disturb them, or to give them any just cause of offence, but on the contrary to treat them with civility and friendship. Upon your arrival on the coast of New Albion you are to put into the first convenient port to recruit your wood and water, and procure refreshments, and then to proceed northward along the coast, as far as the latitude of 65,° or farther, if you are not obstructed by lands or ice; taking care not to lose any time in exploring rivers or inlets, or upon any other account, until you get into the before-mentioned latitude of 65°." After being enjoined at length to make a thorough search for a navigable passage into Hudson or Baffin bays, Cook is further instructed as follows: "You are also, with the consent of the natives, to take possession, in the name of the King of Great Britain, of convenient situations in such countries as you may discover, that have not already been discovered or visited by any other European power...but if you find the countries so discovered are uninhabited, you are to take possession of them for his Majesty, by setting up proper marks and inscriptions, as first discoverers and possessors." During the discussion of Cook's progress in viewing the coasts of Alaska I shall have occasion to refer to these instructions.[14]

On the 26th of April 1778 the expedition sailed out of Nootka Bay on its northward course, but violent gales drove it from the land which was not made again until the evening of May 1st in latitude 55°

Office of Lord High Admiral of Great Britian and Ireland, etc., Sandwich, C. Spencer, and H. Palliser, through their secretary, Ph. Stephens, on the 6th of July 1776.' *Cook's Voy.*, i. introd. xxxiv.-xxxv.

[14] *Cook's Voy.*, i. introd. xxxii.-xxxv.

20', in the vicinity of Port Bucareli, discovered by
Cuadra three years before.

On the 2d and 3d of May Cook passed along the
coast included in Cuadra's discoveries of 1775, giving
to Mount San Jacinto and the Cabo de Engaño the
name of Edgecumbe. Puerto de los Remedios was
named bay of Islands, and Cook correctly surmised
its connection with the bay lying eastward of Cape
Edgecumbe. In the morning of the 3d the two sloops
had reached the highest latitude attained by Cuadra;
a high mountain in the north and a wide inlet were
called Mount Fairweather and Cross Sound respectively, by which names both are known to this day.[15]
Cape Fairweather has since been named Cape Spencer.
On the 5th Mount St Elias was sighted above the
northern horizon, one hundred and twenty miles away,
and the following day the broad opening of Yakutat,
or Bering, Bay was observed.[16]

Proceeding slowly along the coast with baffling
winds, he on the 10th gave the name of Cape Suckling to the cape forming the southern extremity of
Comptroller Bay, but owing to 'thick' weather Kyak
Island, named Kaye by Cook, was not discovered until
two days later.[17] At the foot of a tree on the south
point of Kaye Island a bottle was deposited containing
a paper with the names of the ships and date of 'discovery,' and a few coins. For some reason the ceremony of taking possession was omitted, though Cook
must have believed in the existence of all the conditions mentioned in his instructions and relating to
'uninhabited' discoveries.[18]

The name of Comptroller Bay was also applied to
the indentation bearing that designation to-day. The

[15] The 3d of May is marked in the calendars as 'Finding of the Cross;'
hence the name applied to the sound.

[16] Cook discusses at length the identity of this with Bering's landing. He
does not, however, advance any very cogent reasons for his belief.

[17] In another chapter of this volume I have stated my reasons for believing
this to have been the scene of Bering's discovery and Steller's brief exploration of the country in 1741.

[18] Cook's Voy., ii. 351-3.

sight of the south point of Nuchek Island, named by him Cape Hinchinbrook, led Cook to indulge in hopes of finding a passage to the north beyond it, the towering heights that border Prince William Sound not being visible at the time. A leak in the *Resolution* induced the commander to seek shelter, and the ships were anchored in one of the coves of Nuchek Bay, the Port Etches of later maps. A boat's crew sent out to hunt met with a number of natives in two skin canoes, who followed them to the immediate vicinity of the ships, but would not go on board.[19] On the following day, the 13th, Cook sailed again in search of a safer anchorage, without discovering the landlocked cove on the north side of the bay subsequently selected by the Russians for their first permanent establishment in this region. The next anchorage was found some eight leagues to the northward at Snug Corner Cove, still known by that name. Here considerable intercourse with the natives took place. They were bold, inclined to thievery, and apparently unacquainted with fire-arms.[20]

After several vain attempts to find a northern passage the two ships turned southward, and the largest island in the sound was discovered and named Mon-

[19] The natives made the same sign of friendship described by the Spanish explorers in connection with the Alexander Archipelago, displaying a white garment or skin, and extending their arms. The people were evidently of Innuit extraction, but had adopted some of the practices of their Thlinkeet neighbors in the east, such as powdering the hair with down, etc. *Comptroller Bay*, at the mouth of the Atnah or Copper River, so called by Cook in his *Atlas*, 1778, and also by Dixon and Vancouver; La Pérouse, 1786, B⁴ du *Controle;* *Sutil y Mex., Viage, B. Controlleur. Cartog. Pac. Coast,* MS., iii. 394.

[20] These natives not only attempted to take away a boat from the ship's side, but upon the report of one of their number, who had examined the *Discovery*, that only a man or two were visible on her decks, the whole band of visitors hastily paddled over to the other vessel with the evident intention of taking possession of her. The appearance of the crew, who had been engaged on some duty in the hold, caused the savages to change their mind. *Cook's Voy.*, ii. 359. Cook here also noticed for the first time that these natives had a few glass beads of light blue, a circumstance he wrongly considered as an indication of intercourse with other tribes visiting the Hudson's Bay Company's posts in the far north-west. Blue glass beads were among the few articles of trade in the hands of the Russian promyshleniki, and doubtless found their way to Prince William Sound from Kadiak by way of Cook Inlet.

tagu, the Sukluk of the natives. The name of Prince William Sound was then applied to the whole inlet.

On the 21st Cape Elizabeth, the south-eastern point of Cook Inlet, was first sighted and named; and as the western shore of that great estuary was not visible, the hopes of finding an open passage to the northward were once more revived. A gale, however, prevented the explorers from rounding the cape, and necessitated a southerly course, which brought into view the point of land named Cape St Hermogenes by Bering—the eastern cape of Marmot Island. Thence the course was northward, which opened before the eyes of the explorer the broad estuary still bearing the name of the commander. Believing that Kadiak and Afognak islands, with Point Banks, formed but a part of the mountainous coast to the westward, with Cape Douglas in the foreground, Cook entered the inlet full of hope. Was not the Aliaska of Russian maps represented as an island? And must not this wide passage lead the navigator into the Arctic Ocean between this island and the continent? The discovery of an extension of the high mountains to the north of Cape Douglas did not discourage him.[21] On the same day, however, the 27th of May, these high hopes were crushed, as far as Cook himself was concerned. The haze hanging over the land in the west suddenly disappeared, and what had been taken for a chain of islands stood revealed as the summits of a mountain range, connected everywhere and showing every characteristic of a continent..

Though fully convinced of the futility of the attempt Cook continued to beat his vessels up the inlet.[22] The strong ebb-tides, running at a velocity of four or five knots, greatly retarded their progress, and as

---

[21] 'As it was supposed to be wholly unconnected with the land of Cape Elizabeth,' says Cook; 'for, in a N. N. E. direction, the sight was unlimited by everything but the horizon.' *Cook's Voy.*, ii. 386; *Juvenal, Jour.*, MS., 31-2.

[22] 'I was now fully persuaded that I should find no passage by this inlet; and my persevering in the search of it here, was more to satisfy other people, than to confirm my own opinion.' *Cook's Voy.*, ii. 386.

the winds were either light or unfavorable, it became necessary to anchor the vessels every time the tide turned against them. The muddy water and the large quantities of floating trees led Cook to believe himself within the mouth of a large river, and without fully ascertaining the fact, he sailed away from his new discovery unchanged in his opinion.[23]

The first natives were encountered on the 30th, and a larger party, including women and children, visited the ships the following day. The scene of this meeting was in the vicinity of West Foreland, or the present village of Kustatan. These savages were described by Cook as resembling the natives of Prince William Sound, speaking the same language and using the same kind of skin-covered canoes. From this fact we must infer that the Innuit in those days occupied more of the coast of Cook Inlet than they do to-day. It is probable, however, that these people were not permanent residents, but engaged in a hunting expedition away from their home.[24] Blue beads and long iron knives were found in the possession of all these peoples. We know that these articles came from the Russians, but Cook was loath to acknowledge the presence of another European power.[25]

On the first of June the boats sent out to explore returned after having entered the Turn-again arm of the inlet and the mouth of the Kinik River, and in

[23] The coast of Cook Inlet rests upon a base of blue clay washed by the tides, and this fact contributed more to the discoloration of the water than the few rivers emptying into the inlet.

[24] Still higher up the inlet Cook saw a native propel his kyak with a double-bladed paddle, and as this implement is used only by the natives of the Aleutian Islands, and occasionally by those of the northern shores of Bering Sea, it becomes all the more probable that the advance of the Russians to Kadiak, and their presence among the Shumagin Islands, had already instigated the sea-otter hunters to undertake long journeys in search of their quarry. *Cook's Voy.*, ii. 389-92. On the other hand, the natives encountered on the Kenai Peninsula, on the occasion of taking possession of the country, were evidently Tinnehs, or Kenai proper, to judge from the description of their ornaments, clothes, and weapons, and from the fact that they had dogs and were apparently without canoes.

[25] Cook mentions that the natives called iron *goone*. Now *chugun*, or rather *chugoon*, is Russian for cast-iron, though also used for all iron articles by the ignorant classes. *Cook's Voy.*, ii, 392.

the afternoon Lieutenant King was despatched to take possession of the point at which the above-mentioned arm branches off to the eastward. Some lords aboriginal were present, but it is nowhere written that King asked their permission to take possession of the country, as the admiralty had ordered.

On the 4th of June the latitude of the Iliamna volcano was ascertained, but the mountain was not named.[26] On the 5th of June the two ships emerged from the inlet that had been entered with such flattering hopes, and proceeded southward along the coast of the continent in search of an opening to the westward and northward. The season was fast advancing and much remained to be done, so they hastened forward. Shuiak Island, Afognak, and Kadiak were placed on their chart as one continuous coast and part of the continent, while names were given only to the prominent headlands.[27] On the 16th Foggy Island, the Tumannoi of Bering, was made, and on the 19th the two ships were passing through the Shumagin group, the largest island of which Cook erroneously put down as Kadiak on his chart. In this vicinity the *Discovery* was approached by several canoes and a letter enclosed in a case was delivered by one of the natives, who bowed and took off his cap in good European fashion. The document was written in Russian and dated 1778.[28] Unable to understand

---

[26] The only local names about the inlet which we can trace to Cook are: Cape Douglas, Mt St Augustine (Chernobira Island), Turn-again River, Point Possession, Anchor Point, Point Bede, Cape Elizabeth, Barren Islands. The inlet was named Cook River by order of Lord Sandwich, the explorer having left a blank in his journal. *Cook's Voy.*, ii. 396.

[27] The north point of Shuiak was named Point Banks; the easterly point of Afognak, Cape Whitsunday, and the entrance to the strait between the latter island and Kadiak, Whitsuntide Bay. The description of this locality does not, however, agree with the published sketch. *Cook's Voy.*, ii. 404, and *Chart of Cook River*, 353. Cape Chiniatsk was named Cape Greville and is still thus indicated on English and American sailing-charts. Cape Barnabas and Two-headed Cape correspond with the east point of Sitkhalidak Island and Nazigak Island at the entrance of Kaguiak Bay. The island Sitkhinak was named Trinity on the 14th of June, and subsequently the south point of Kadiak obtained the same designation. *Cook's Voy.*, ii. 407-9.

[28] In the body of the note there was also a reference to the year 1776, the date of a Russian expedition to Kadiak. *Cook's Voy.*, ii. 414.

its contents, Cook paid no attention to it. These
natives as well as those subsequently met with at
Halibut (Sannakh) Island used the double-bladed
paddle, a certain indication that they were Aleuts,
hunting for the Russians.[29]

Passing Unimak with its smoking volcanoes and
failing to notice the best pass into Bering Sea, between Unimak and Akun, the explorers at last managed to cross into the narrowest and most dangerous
of all these passes, between Unalga and Unalaska.
After a long search for an anchorage the vessels were
safely moored in Samghanooda Bay, opening into
Unalga Strait. Intercourse with the natives was at
once opened, and one of them delivered another Russian note. The principal object in seeking this anchorage was water, and hence the stay there was brief;
but from the manners of the people and articles in
their possession, Cook felt assured at last that he was
on ground occupied by the Russians. The necessary
business was quickly despatched, and on the 2d of
July the two ships stood out to sea again with every
prospect of an open field of exploration in the north.
The north coast of the Alaska peninsula was followed
till the north shore of Bristol Bay loomed before
them, and made another change of course necessary.
Cook's disappointment was great. Not until the 16th
of July was hope again revived by the sight of Cape
Newenham, the southern point of the estuary of the
Kuskokvim.[30]

Without imagining himself in the mouth of a river,
Cook pushed forward until stopped by shoals, which
to his dismay extended in every direction but that
from which he had come. After a brief interview

[29] Cook also mentions that they did not understand the language of the
natives of Prince William Sound, and that one of them wore a black cloth
jacket and green breeches. *Cook's Voy.*, ii. 417.

[30] Here Lieutenant Williamson was sent ashore to ascend a mountain and
obtain a view. He saw no land, except in the north, and after taking formal
possession returned to the ship. Cook gave the name Bristol Bay to the
whole bend of the coast betwen Unimak Island and the cape just discovered.
Voy., ii. 430-4.

with some natives, who also were found in possession of iron knives, all haste was made to extricate the vessel from the network of shoals. At last, on the 28th, the soundings made a westerly course possible, which was on the following day changed to the northward, and on the 3d of August land was made again, and the ships anchored between an island and the main. The former was named Sledge Island, from a wooden sledge with bone runners found upon it. The next discovery, named King Island, was made on the 7th, and at last, on the 9th, the western extremity of the American continent lay clearly before them, the coast beyond receding so far to the eastward as to leave no room for doubt.[31]

After a brisk run across to the coast of Asia the ships returned to the Alaskan shore and located Icy Cape, the eastern limit of the arctic cruise, Cape Mulgrave, and Cape Lisburne, but ice barred further progress on the American coast as well as on that of Asia. On the 29th Cook named Cape North and concluded to return southward, postponing a further examination of the Polar Sea for another season— which never came for him. On the evening of the 2d of September the ships passed East Cape. The following day St Lawrence Bay was revisited and examined,[32] and on the 5th the ships were again headed for the American coast. During the following day Norton Sound was entered and names were applied to Cape Derby, at the entrance of Goloni Bay, and Cape Denbigh.

Cook remained in this sound until the 17th of September in order to fully ascertain the fact of his being then on the coast of the American continent and not on the fabulous island of "Alaschka" represented

---

[31] *Cook's Voy.*, ii. 444.

[32] The editor of *Cook's Voyage*, in vol. ii. 473, comments upon the curious coincidence that Bering passed between St Lawrence Bay and St Lawrence Island on August 10, 1728, and 50 years later, on August 10, 1778, Cook passed the same spot, naming the bay after the patron saint of that day in the calendar. Due allowance for the difference between dates in the Julian and Gregorian calendars, however, spoils this nice little 'coincidence.'

upon Stæhlin's map of the *New Northern Archipelago.*
Captain King had been intrusted with the examination of Norton Bay, the only point where the existence
of a channel was at all probable.[33]

On leaving Norton Sound it was Cook's intention
to steer directly south in order to survey the coast intervening between his last discovery and the point he had
named Shoalness on the Kuskokvim; but the shallow-
ness of that part of Bering Sea compelled him to run
far to the westward, and prevented him from seeing
anything of the Yukon mouth, and the low country
between that river and the Kuskokvim, and the island
of Nunivak.[34]　After obtaining another sight of St
Lawrence Island, which he named Clark, Cook steered
south-south-west and on the 23d sighted St Matthew
Island, which he named Gore.[35]

On the 2d of October Unalaska was sighted, and
passing Kalekhtah Bay, called Egoochshac by Cook,
the two ships anchored in Samghanooda Bay on the
3d of October.　Both vessels were at once overhauled
by the carpenters for necessary repairs, and a portion
of the cargo was landed for the purpose of restowing.[36]

[33] *Cook's Voy.*, ii. 482–3. I find that Captain Cook makes mention of the
fact that one of the natives inquired for him by the title of 'capitane,' which
he considers a case of misunderstanding. It is, however, not at all improbable
that the Russian word *kapitan* had been preserved among the natives of the
vicinity of Bering Strait since Bering's and Gvozdef's time.

[34] Cook supposed, however, the existence of a large river in that vicinity,
as the water was comparatively fresh and very muddy. *Cook's Voy.*, ii. 491.

[35] Cook claims to have seen sea-otters here, but was probably mistaken,
for this animal was never found there by subsequent visitors, and the place
being uninhabited, there was nothing to drive them away.　The Pribylof group
were the northernmost point from which sea-otters were ever procured, and
there they became quickly exterminated.

[36] During a visit of Mr Ivan Petrof to Samghanooda Bay on the 3d of
October 1878, the 100th anniversary of Cook's landing, he obtained from the
natives a few traditions relative to Cook's visit.　One old chief stated that
his father had told him of two English ships that had anchored in Samghanooda, which is now known as 'English Bukhta.'　The time of their stay had
been somewhat lengthened in transmittal from father to son, for it was
claimed that the ships wintered there, that the people caught fish and killed
seals for the visitors, and that several of them 'kept native women with them.'
See *Cook's Voy.*, ii. 521.　The old chief also stated that the 'English' had
built houses and pointed out a spot where an excavation had evidently been
made long years ago.　This last report referred of course only to some temporary shelter for protecting the landed cargo.　The same man pointed out
to Mr Petrof the position in which the ships had been moored, according

While the ship's companies were engaged in watering, repairing, fishing, and gathering berries as an
anti-scorbutic, a messenger arrived on the 8th with a
note written in Russian for the commander of each
vessel, and a gift, consisting of a salmon pie, baked of
rye-meal. There was no one able to read the notes,
but, being now sure that some Russians resided in the
immediate vicinity, Cook caused a suitable return to
be made in the shape of sundry bottles of liquor. Corporal John Ledyard was sent with the returning
messenger to find the Russians, invite them to the
anchorage, and obtain all available information concerning their discoveries in American waters.[37]

Ledyard's experience on this occasion has been described by himself and transmitted to posterity by his
biographer. He succeeded in his mission, passed a
few days at the settlement of Illiuliuk, and brought
back three Russian hunters, who were well received,
and who freely imparted such information as could be
conveyed by signs and numerals.[38] They promised to

to the recollection of his father, a position which agreed exactly with that
indicated on Cook's chart of Samghanooda, which the chief certainly never
had seen.

[37] Cook's Voy., ii. 495. Cook merely says that he sent Ledyard, but in
Sparks' Life of Ledyard, 79–80, it is claimed that he volunteered and thereby
relieved Cook from the dilemma of selecting an officer for such a 'dangerous'
expedition. The present of bread was in accordance with an ancient Russian
custom, still observed, of presenting bread and salt to new arrivals in a town,
dwelling, or neighborhood, emblematic of the wish that the recipient might
never want for the necessaries of life. Among the wealthy the most elaborate confectionery and silver or gold receptacles take the place of bread and
salt on such occasions.

[38] Ledyard's narrative of this excursion seems to me somewhat highly colored, though evidently written in good faith. The man was 'sensational' by
nature. His native guides evidently did not take him to his destination by
the shortest route. There is and was at that time an easy path only 12 miles
in length from the head of Samghanooda Bay to Captain Harbor, where lay the
Russian settlement. Ledyard was made to walk '15 miles into the interior' on
the first day, to a native village, where he passed the night, and where 'a young
woman seemed very busy to please' him, and on the following day he again
walked until three hours before dark ere reaching Captain Harbor, which he
called 'four leagues over.' It is about five miles. The distance he claims to
have walked after this was measured by 'tired and swollen feet,' but finally he
was carried across to the settlement, squeezed into the 'hole' of a two-hatch
bidarka. He was hospitably entertained after due exchange of civilities and
delivery of Cook's presents. The next morning the repellent odors of a
matutinal meal composed of 'whale, sea-horse, and bear' upset Ledyard's
stomach, though bears and walruses are unknown in Unalaska. The weather

bring a map showing all the Russian discoveries. On
the 14th the commander of the Russian expedition in
this quarter arrived from a journey and landed near
Samghanooda. His name was Gerassim Grigorovich
Ismailof.[39]

The usual civilities were exchanged and Cook had
every opportunity of questioning his visitor, but it is
evident that the advantage was with the Russian, who
learned from the Englishman what was of the utmost
importance to the Siberian merchants, while he told
what he chose, holding back much information in his
possession, for instance the visit of Polutof to Kadiak
in 1776 and the long residence at Unimak Strait of

being bad he remained another day and examined the settlement, counting
thirty Russians and seventy Kamchatkans. He also visited a small sloop of
30 tons, lying near the village, and thus describes his feelings on that occasion: 'It is natural to an ingenuous mind, when it enters a town, a house, or
ship, that has been rendered famous by any particular event, to feel the
full force of that pleasure, which results from gratifying a noble curiosity. I
was no sooner informed that this sloop was the same in which the famous
Bering had performed those discoveries which did him so much honor, and his
country so much service, than I was determined to go on board of her and
indulge in the generous feelings the occasion inspired.' He remained an hour,
enjoying himself, I trust, without the slightest suspicion of the fact that
the craft he had in his mind had been broken up on Bering Island, and
that the sloop constructed from the remains was at that time lying fathoms
deep under the surface on the Asiatic shore. The sentimental Yankee
returned to the ships in less than one day. *Sparks' Life of Ledyard*, 85–90.

[39] The report given by Ismailof of Cook's visit was received by Major
Behm, commander of Kamchatka in April 1779. The document simply stated
that two English ships had anchored on the north side of Unalaska; that he
(Ismailof) had rendered the visitors every assistance in obtaining food and
water, and that they had communicated by signs only, owing to his ignorance
of the English language. *Sgibnef*, in *Morskoi Sbornik*, ciii. 7, 21. Ismailof
evidently took a more sensible view of Cook's expedition than did the authorities in Kamchatka. At the time of the presence of the two ships in Avatcha
Bay, Behm was on the point of leaving for Irkutsk, but in view of the 'critical
condition of the country' he consented to remain at the head of affairs. The
general impression was, that the vessels had come at the instigation of Benyovski with hostile intent. A deputation of men not connected with the
public service was first sent to meet the strangers, probably to 'draw fire,'
consisting of Behm's servant, a merchant, and a clerk. At the same time
runners and messengers were despatched to all the forts and ostrogs to put
the garrisons upon their guard. The subsequent friendly intercourse with
the strangers was carried on under constant apprehension. The desired supplies were furnished free of charge, because, as Shmalef wrote, 'the high
price we must have asked would have incensed them.' Shmalef never believed in the scientific objects of the expedition and urged the forwarding of
reënforcements. The presents of curiosities made to Behm were all by him
transmitted to the imperial academy, in order to purge himself of all suspicion
of having been bribed by the enemy. *Sgibnef*, in *Morskoi Sbornik*, ciii. 7, 22–6.

be sought north of Bering Strait, beyond Icy Cape, leading probably to Baffin Bay; yet it would be madness to attempt the passage during the short time the route might be free from ice. Hardly less hopeful appeared the prospect for sailing westward along the northern coast of Siberia. The sea nearer the pole would probably be less obstructed by ice. Clarke

COOK'S VOYAGE NORTHERN SECTION.

died August 22d, as the vessels approached Petropavlovsk, and here he was buried. Captain Gore took the expedition home by way of Japan, China, and Cape of Good Hope. While in China several small lots of sea-otter skins were disposed of by men and officers at prices which seemed fabulous, and the

excitement created by this success resulted in quite a
rush of vessels to the Northwest Coast, and a brisk
competition sprang up with Russians in the purchase
of furs there and in their sale in China.[42]

In 1776 orders were issued in Spain to fit out
another expedition to the north, to continue and complete the discoveries of Cuadra made the previous
year; but the execution of the plan was delayed, and
not until February 11, 1779, did two vessels, the
Princesa and the *Favorita*, sail from San Blas, with
Lieutenant Ignacio Arteaga in command, and Cuadra
as second.[43]

On the 28th of April the expedition, which had
orders to attain a latitude of 70°, found itself in latitude 54° 45', and on the 2d of May the vessels entered
Bucareli Sound, Arteaga anchoring in a sheltered
bay on the south side, which he named Santa Cruz,
and Cuadra exploring the north side of the sound,
but finally joining his commander in the Puerto de
Santa Cruz on the 5th. As soon as Cuadra had reported to Arteaga for orders, it was resolved to fit
out an expedition of two boats for a thorough exploration of the interior of the sound. The crews of both
vessels were constantly employed in preparing the
boats, supplying wood and water, and assisting the
officers in their astronomical observations. On the
13th a solemn mass was celebrated on shore, with
accompaniment of music and artillery, a cross was

[42] Captain King, who wrote the last volume of *Cook's Voyage*, pointed out
the advantages of this trade, and suggested methods to be observed therein.
Cook's Voy., iii. 430–8.

[43] See *Hist. Northwest Coast*, passim, this series. Also, *Arteaga, Tercera
exploracion hecha el año 1779 con las Fragatas del rey, 'la Princesa,' mandada
por el teniente de navío don Ignacio Arteaga, y la 'Favorita' por el de la misma
clase don Juan Francisco de la Bodega y Cuadra, desde el puerto de San Blas
hasta los sesenta y un grados de latitud*, in *Viages al Norte de Cal.*, MS., No. 4;
*Maurelle, Navegacion hecha por el Alférez de Fragata de la Real Armada Don
Francisco Antonio Maurelle destinado de segundo capitan de la Fragata 'Favorita,' Id.*, MS., No. 5. *Bodega y Cuadra, Segunda salida hasta los 61 grados
en la Fragata 'Nuestra Señora de los Remedios,' alias la 'Favorita,' Año de
1779*, MS., id., No. 6½; *Bodega y Cuadra, Navegacion y descubrimientos hechos
de orden de S. M. en la Costa septentrional de California, 1779*, in *Mayer,
MSS.*, No. 13.

erected in a prominent place, and under waving of
flags and salvos of musketry the country was taken
possession of in the name of the king, the savages
gazing stolidly at this insanity of civilization.

On the 18th the two boats sailed from the bahía
de la Santísima Cruz, with a complement of five officers, four soldiers, and twenty-four sailors. They
were provisioned for eighteen days. The result of
the expedition was the earliest and best survey ever
made of the most important harbor of Prince of Wales
Island.[44]

During the absence of the boats on this errand
the natives gathered in numbers about the ships in
the bahía de la Santísima Cruz. The strict orders of
the commander to avoid a conflict, and to ignore small
thefts, soon worked its evil effect upon these children
of nature, who could not understand leniency or un-
willingness to punish robbery and to recover losses,
unless it was based upon weakness or lack of courage.
Working parties on the shore were molested to such
an extent that it became necessary to surround them
with a cordon of sentries only five paces apart, and
sailors were robbed of their clothes while washing
them. Under these circumstances the return of the
lanchas with their crews was hailed with joy; but by
by this time over eighty canoes manned by a thousand
savages were in the bay and great caution was necessary to avoid hostilities. Even the firing of cannon
did not seem to frighten the Indians, and when a ·

[44] The officers were Francisco Maurelle, José Camacho, Juan Bautista
Aguirre, Juan Pantoja, and Juan García. The armament consisted of 8 falconets and 20 muskets, with 25 rounds of ammunition for each. They proceeded first to the south-western point, San Bartolomé, of the entrance to the
sound, and then around the western shore, carefully sounding and locating
bays, islets, and points. The names applied were very numerous. the most
important being as follows: puerto de San Antonio, puerto de la Asuncion;
the islands San Ignacio and Santa Rita; puerto de la Real Marina; canal de
Portillo; bahía de Esquivel; canal de San Cristóbal; the islands of San Fernando and San Juan Bautista; boca del Almirante; bahía de San Alberto;
puerto del Bagial; puerto de San Nicolás; the caños del Trocadero; the
island of Madre de Dios; puerto de la Caldera; puerto de la Estrella; puerto
del Refugio—which was subsequently found to be a passage—and the puerto
de los Dolores.

canoe was struck by a ball and the inmates fell, the effect was only temporary. Arteaga seized a chief in order to obtain the return of two sailors who had been reported as held captive in the native village, but it was found that the Spaniards had voluntarily joined the savages with the intention to desert.[45]

During the last days of June the two ships were moved across the sound to the bay of San Antonio, and thence they finally sailed the 1st of July, taking a north-westerly course along the coast. Mount St Elias was sighted on the 9th,[46] and a few days later Kaye, or Kyak, Island was named Cármen. The next anchorage, probably Nuchek Bay, was named Puerto de Santiago, and a boat expedition went to ascertain whether the land was connected with the continent. The officer in charge reported that he had convinced himself that it was an island.[47] The usual forms of taking possession were observed, being the third ceremony of the kind performed upon nearly the same ground within a year—by Cook in 1778, by a party of Zaïkof's men, who had been despatched in a bidar from Cook Inlet, in June 1779, and again by Arteaga. Cuadra, in his journal, expressed the conviction that a large river must enter the sea between Cármen Island and the harbor of Santiago, thus correctly locating Copper River, which both Cook and Vancouver failed to observe.[48]

[45] With the avowed object of 'gaining a better knowledge of the people and their customs,' Arteaga sanctioned the purchase of five children. Two girls, aged respectively seven and eight years, were taken on board the *Princesa*, and the boys, between five and ten, on the *Favorita*. *Tercera Exploracion*, in *Viages al Norte*, MS., etc., 111.

[46] Alluded to as Cape St Elias in the journal, 'Ygualmente tenian á la vista el elevado promontorio de San Elias sobre las nubes, presentándose en forma de un pan de azúcar;' but it is doubtful what point or mountain this was, for the ships were at a great distance from the shore. *Tercera Expl.*, in *Viages al Norte*, MS., etc. 113.

[47] If this was really Nuchek, or Hinchinbrook Island, the Spaniards anticipated Vancouver's discovery of the fact by 14 years. *Tercera Expl.*, in *Viages al Norte*, MS., 116–17. During this boat expedition many canoes of the natives were seen, and on one of them a flag was displayed showing the colors red, white, and blue.

[48] Arteaga, while at this anchorage, convened a junta of officers for the purpose of considering the advisability of returning at once to San Blas. His

On the 28th the ships put to sea once more, taking a south-westerly course, without attempting to find a passage at the head of Prince William Sound as Cook had done in the preceding year, and on the 1st of August they found an anchorage formed by several islands in latitude 59° 8'. Formal possession was again taken and the largest island of the group named Isla de la Regla. This was the Cape Elizabeth of Cook, who had failed to notice its separation from the continent. The Iliamna volcano on the west shore of Cook Inlet was sighted from this point and named Miranda.[49]

After a short stay at this anchorage, Arteaga concluded to give up further explorations and to sail direct for Cape Mendocino. The departure took place on the 7th of August, and thus ended, so far as relates to Alaska, an expedition which would have been of the greatest importance had it not been for the English explorations of the year preceding. Arteaga and his officers could know nothing of Cook's investigations and believed themselves the first to explore the region already visited by the *Resolution* and *Discovery* between Cross Sound and Cape Elizabeth, but even after deducting from the result of their work

own timidity could not prevail against the ambitious courage of Maurelle and Cuadra, who insisted that some further discoveries must be attempted before relinquishing so costly an expedition. *Tercera Expl.*, in *Viages al Norte*, MS., 117.

[49] In the journals this mountain was described as bearing a striking resemblance to the Orizaba of Mexico and the peak of Teneriffe. *Viages al Norte*, MS., 120. A map of the anchorage is still in existence, pasted in at the end of the manuscript entitled *Azanza, Ynstruccion*, etc. This map represents the islands of the Cape Elizabeth group—Tzukli of the Russians—and the adjoining coast of the Kenai peninsula, but, though correct in its contours, with the exception of representing the mainland as islands—Ysla de Maurello in the north and Ysla de San Bruno in the east—it does not correspond in its details with the narrative contained in *Viages al Norte*. There is a discrepancy even between the map and the legend, the latter stating that 'haviendose tomado seg.do posesion en la Ysla de San Antonio,' but no such island is on the chart. The projecting points of the mainland are named as stated above; the island containing Cape Elizabeth was named Ysla de San Aniceto, and the smaller islands and rocks el Sombrero, de Ayala, de San Angel, de Arriaga, la Monja, los Frailes. The point where possession was taken is marked with a cross on the N. w. point of San Aniceto. The opening between the latter and the mainland is named ensenada de Nuestra Señora de la Regla. The latitude is correctly given as 59° 8', the long. 49° 11' w. of San Blas. *Azanza, Ynstruccion*, etc.

all that may be affected by Cook's prior discovery, the careful survey of Bucareli Sound, in connection with Heceta's and Cuadra's prior explorations, presents a basis for Spain's claims to the coast region to latitude 58° so far as relative right of discovery is concerned, attended by the ceremony of taking possession. A little more energy or ambition on Arteaga's part would have led to a meeting with the Russians and made the subsequent expedition of Martinez and Haro unnecessary.[50]

The viceroy of Mexico declared himself highly pleased with the results of the voyage, and advanced one step the rank of all the officers on both vessels. At the same time he stated that no further discoveries in a northerly direction would be undertaken for the present.[51]

[50] The sloop *Kliment*, belonging to the Panof Company, was cruising about Kadiak at the very time of Arteaga's presence at La Regla. *Berg, Khronol. Ist.*, 104.

[51] *Cartas de los Excelentisimos Sres Vireyes don Antonio Bucareli, don Martin de Mayorga,* etc., in *Viages al Norte,* MS., etc., 126-7.

CHAPTER XI.

COLONIZATION AND THE FUR-TRADE.

1783-1787.

FIRST ATTEMPTED SETTLEMENT OF THE RUSSIANS IN AMERICA—VOYAGE OF
GRIGOR SHELIKOF—PERMANENT ESTABLISHMENT OF THE RUSSIANS AT
KADIAK—RETURN OF SHELIKOF—HIS INSTRUCTIONS TO SAMOILOF, COL-
ONIAL COMMANDER—THE HISTORIC SABLE AND OTTER—SKINS AS CUR-
RENCY—TRAPPING AND TRIBUTE-COLLECTING—METHOD OF CONDUCTING
THE HUNT—REGULATIONS OF THE PEREDOVCHIKI—GOD'S SABLES AND
MAN'S—REVIEW OF THE FUR-TRADE ON THE COASTS OF ASIA AND AMER-
ICA—PERNICIOUS SYSTEM INTRODUCED BY THE PROMYSHLENIKI—THE
CHINA MARKET—FOREIGN RIVALS AND THEIR METHOD—ABUSE OF
NATIVES—COOK'S AND VANCOUVER'S OPINIONS OF COMPETITION WITH
THE RUSSIANS—EXTIRPATION OF ANIMALS.

WE enter here a new epoch of Alaska history.
Hitherto all has been discovery, exploration, and the
hunting of fur-bearing animals, with little thought of
permanent settlement. But now Grigor Ivanovich
Shelikof comes to the front as the father and founder
of Russian colonies in America.[1]

[1] One of the chief authorities for this period of Alaska history, and indeed
the only full account of Shelikof's visit to America, is a work written by himself and published after his death. It is entitled *Grigoria Shelikhova Stran-
stvovanie*, etc., or *Grigor Shelikof's Journeys from 1783 to 1787, from Okhotsk
to the Eastern Ocean and the Coast of America*, with a *prodolshenie*, or continuation. Printed at St Petersburg in 1792-3, 12mo, with maps. In 1793
both of these books were translated by one J. J. Logan into English and published in one 8vo volume at St Petersburg. Pallas printed a German translation, chiefly remarkable for inaccuracies, in his *Nord. Beitr.*, vi. 165-249.
And still another German translation appeared in *Busse's Journal für Russland, 1794*, i. Shelikof's first volume contains voluminous descriptions of the
Aleutian Islands, with whole passages, and even pages, identical in every
respect with corresponding passages in the anonymous German *Neue Nachrichten*, the authorship of which I ascribe to J. L. Schlözer. It is safe to
assume that Shelikof had access to this work published some 20 years before
his own, and used it in writing his own volume. Shelikof's book was republished in one volume, without maps, in 1812, under title of *Puteshestvie G.
Shelikhova 1783-1790*. It seems that the directors of the Russian American

In 1783 the company of Siberian merchants of which Shelikof and Ivan Golikof were the principal share-holders, finished three ships at Okhotsk for operating on a larger scale in the region then designated as the *ostrova*, or the islands. The ships were the *Trekh Sviatiteli*, Three Saints, the *Sv Simeon*, and the *Sv Mikhaïl*. On the 16th of August they sailed with one hundred and ninety-two men in all, the largest force which had hitherto left the Siberian coast at one time. Shelikof and his wife,[2] who accompanied her husband in all his travels, were on the *Trekh Sviatiteli*, commanded by Ismaïlof. The first part of the voyage was stormy, the wind contrary, and the ships were unable to leave the sea of Okhotsk, but on the 2d of September the squadron anchored near the second Kurile island, for the purpose of watering, and then passed safely into the Pacific. On the 12th a gale separated the vessels, and after prolonged and futile efforts to find the *Sv Mikhaïl*, Shelikof concluded to pass the winter on Bering Island with the two other vessels. Thanks to the enforcement of wise regulations framed by Shelikof, the crews suffered but little from scurvy, and in June of the following year the expedition steered once more to the eastward. A few stoppages were made on Copper, Atkha, and other islands, with a longer stay at Unalaska, where the two ships were repaired, and refitted with water and pro-

Company resented the publication of the book. In the 'Secret Instructions' forwarded to Baranof in 1802 occurs the following reference to this subject: 'You must send your communications to the chief administration direct, and not to Okhotsk, since the company has very little to do with provincial authorities, and also because the government at present has many views concerning America that must be kept a profound secret, being confided only to you as chief manager. Therefore it is not proper to forward such information through the government authorities at Irkutsk, where no secret could be preserved. As a proof of this may serve you the endorsed book of *Grigor Shelikof's Travels*. It is nothing but his journals transmitted to governor general Jacobi, on whose retirement it was stolen from the chancellery by Mr Piel, and printed against the will of the deceased. Consequently secrets of state were exposed. I refer to the location of tablets claiming possession of the country for Russia.' *Sitka Archives*, MS., Con. I., 1-21.

[2] *Shelikof, Putesh.*, i. 2. Natalia Shelikof was possessed of great energy and business capacity. After her husband's death she managed for many years not only her own but the company's business. *Tikhmenef, Istor. Obos.*, ii., app. 108-13.

visions. The *Simeon* had been separated from her
consort during the voyage along the Aleutian chain,
but she made her appearance in the harbor a few days
after the arrival of the *Sviatiteli*. Shelikof obtained
two interpreters and ten Aleutian hunters, and leaving
instructions for the guidance of the *Sv Mikhail* he
shaped his course for the island of Kikhtak, subsequently named Kadiak.[3] The voyage was devoid of
incident, and on the 3d of August 1784 the two ships
entered a capacious bay on the south-east coast of the
island, between cape Barnabas and the two-headed
cape of Cook, and anchored in its westernmost branch,
naming it after the ship *Trekh Sviatiteli*, Three Saints.[4]
Armed parties of promyshleniki were sent out in
boats and bidars to search for natives, but only one
succeeded, and brought news that a large body of
aboriginals had been found. They had avoided a
meeting, however, and it was not until the following
day that another exploring party returned with one
of the natives. Shelikof treated the captive kindly,
loaded him with presents, and allowed him to return
to his people. On the 5th there was an eclipse of the
sun which lasted an hour and a half, and caused much
uneasiness among the natives, who naturally connected the phenomenon with the appearance of the
Russians.[5]

[3] *Shelikof, Putesh.*, i. 36. *Kikhtak*, or *Kikhtowik*, is the Innuit word for
island. At the present day the natives of the peninsula speak of the Kadiak
people simply as *Kikhtagamutes*, islanders. The tribal name appears to have
been Kaniag and the Russian appellation now in use was probably derived
from both. Glottof first landed and wintered on the island in 1763, after
which it was several times visited.

[4] The shores of Three Saints Harbor are generally steep and rocky, but
about a mile from its entrance a gravelly bar or spit from the southern side
forms a horseshoe, opening into the interior of the bay. Such locations
were peculiarly adapted to the requirements of the Russians at that time.
The small land-locked basin formed by the spit was deep enough for such
vessels as they had; the shelving shore enabled them to beach their vessels
during winter and to utilize them as dwellings or fortifications, while the
level sandbar afforded convenient building sites. The adjoining hills and
mountains being devoid of timber, there was no danger of surprise from the
land, and water enclosed three sides of the settlement.

[5] *Shelikof, Putesh.*, i. 51. It has been hinted that Shelikof used this little
incident in imitation of the Spanish discoverer of America, to impress the
savages with his occult powers. The one who had been so kindly received

Another exploring party was sent out on the 7th with instructions to select hunting-grounds, and if possible to circumnavigate the island and observe its coasts. After two days, when about ten leagues from the anchorage, this expedition fell in with a large party of savages who had taken up a position on a *kekour*,[6] or detached cliff, near the shore, surrounded by water. An interpreter was at once sent forward to open friendly intercourse, but the islanders told the messenger to inform the Russians that if they wished to escape with their lives they should leave the island at once. The natives could not be persuaded to abandon this hostile attitude, and the exploring party returned to the harbor to report.

Shelikof at once proceeded to the spot with all the men that could be spared from the encampment, but when he reached the scene he found the savages in formidable numbers and full of courage. Peaceful overtures were still continued,[7] but were wholly lost on the savages. Arrows began to fly, and the Russians retired to the ships to prepare for defence. Not long afterward the Koniagas stole upon the Russian camp one dark night, and began a desperate fight which lasted till daylight, when the savages took to flight.[8] But this was by no means the end of it. From his Koniaga friend Shelikof learned that his people were only awaiting reënforcements to renew the attack. He accordingly determined to anticipate them by possessing himself at once of their strong-

returned voluntarily in a few days and did not leave Shelikof again as long as the latter remained on the island.

[6] Such places, to which the Russians applied the Kamchatka name of *kekour*, were often used by the natives as natural fortifications and places of refuge. War parties or hunting expeditions would leave their women and children upon such cliffs for safe-keeping till their return.

[7] In Shelikof's journal, which was published after his death, the number of natives was given at 4,000, but one tenth would be nearer the truth. In his official report to the governor of eastern Siberia no figures are given. *Tikhmenef, Istor. Obos.*, i. 8; *Shelikof, Putesh.*, i. 10, 11. Lissianski was informed in 1804 by a native eye-witness that only 400 men, women, and children were on the *kekour*. *Liss. Voy.*, 180.

[8] *Tikhmenef, Istor. Obos.*, i. 9; *Shelikof, Putesh.*, i. 113-16. Shelikof reports this affair as having occurred on the 12th of August.

hold on the rocky islet. A small force of picked promyshleniki approached the enemy in boats. A heavy
shower of spears fell on them; but the havoc made
by a few discharges of grape from the falconet aimed
at the huts caused great consternation, and a general
stampede followed, during which many were killed,
while a large number lost their lives by jumping over
the precipice, and as Shelikof claims, over one thousand were taken prisoners.[9] The casualties on the
side of the Russians were confined to a few severe
and many trifling wounds. Shelikof claims that he
retained four hundred of the prisoners, allowing the
remainder to go to their homes, and they were held
not as regular captives, but in a kind of temporary
subjection. "At their own desire," as Shelikof puts
it, "they were located fifty versts away from the harbor without any Russian guards, simply furnishing
hostages as a guarantee of good faith and good behavior." The hostages consisted of children who were
to be educated by the Russians.[10]

Nor was this second battle the end of native efforts
for life and liberty. Attacks still occurred from time
to time, generally upon detached hunting or exploration parties, but in each case the savages were repulsed with loss. The promptness with which they
were met evidently destroyed their confidence in
themselves, arising from their easy victory over the
first Russian visitors.

Meanwhile no time was lost in pushing prepara-

---

[9] *Shelikof, Putesh.*, i. 18. Says Shelikof in his journal: 'I do not boast
of the shedding of blood, but I am sure that we killed some of our assailants.
I endeavored to find out the number, but failed because they carried their
dead with them and threw them into the sea.' Compare *Tchitchinof's Adventures*, MS., 36–7; *Sokolof's Markof's Voy.*, MS., 7–9.

[10] *Tikhmenef, Istor. Obos.*, i. 10. Shelikof writes: 'I retained 400 prisoners, furnished them with provisions and all necessary appliances for trapping and hunting, and placed them in charge of a native named Kaskak.'
Putesh., i. 18, 19. The same name of Kaskak occurs in the narrative of a
native of Kadiak collected by Holmberg, relating to the first landing of Russians on Kadiak Island, 20 years prior to Shelikof's arrival. Sauer writes
eight years later that 200 young females were then kept as hostages. A
party of women had once been captured and retained, though wives were
exchanged for daughters. He places the population of the island at 3,500.
Billings' Voy., 171.

tions for permanent occupancy of the island. In a few weeks dwelling-houses and fortifications were erected by the expert Russian axemen, and Shelikof took care to furnish his own residence with all the comforts and a few of the luxuries of civilization, such as he could collect from the two vessels, in order to inspire the savage breast with respect for superior culture. And, indeed, as time passed by, the chasm dividing savage and civilized was filled, the Koniagas ascending in some respects and the Russians descending. The natives watched with the greatest curiosity the construction of houses and fortifications after the Russian fashion, until they voluntarily offered to assist. A school was conducted by Shelikof in person; he endeavored to teach both children and adults the Russian language and arithmetic, and to sow the seeds of Christianity. According to his account he turned forty heathens into Christians during his sojourn on Kadiak; but we may presume that their knowledge of the faith did not extend beyond the sign of the cross, and perhaps repeating a few words of the creed without the slightest understanding of its meaning. So that when the pious colonist asserts that the converts began at once to spread the new religion among their countrymen we may conclude that he is exaggerating.[11]

As soon as possible Shelikof turned his attention once more to the exploration of the island. A party of fifty-two promyshleniki and eleven Aleuts from the Fox Islands went to the north and north-east in four large bidars, accompanied by one hundred and ten Koniagas in their own bidarkas. This was in May 1785. The object of the expedition was to make the acquaintance of the inhabitants of the adjoining

[11] Shelikof dwells at length upon his efforts to induce the Koniagas to become subjects of Russia, and claims to have met with success. He also planted vegetables, but could not prevail upon the Kadiak people to eat or cultivate them. Train-oil and fish pleased them better. *Putesh*, i. 30–2; *Tikhmenef, Istor. Obos.*, i. 11; *Grewingk, Beitr.*, 323; *Pallas, Nord. Beitr.*, i. 170.

islands and the mainland. After a cruise in Prince
William Sound and Cook Inlet, the party returned
in August with a small quantity of furs, yet reporting a not unfriendly reception, and bringing twenty
hostages from the latter place. If we consider the
hostile attitude assumed by the same people two years
before toward Zaïkof, we must credit Shelikof with
good management. On their return all proceeded
for the winter to Karluk, where salmon abounded.[12]
From this point and from the original encampment
on Three Saints Bay, detachments of promyshleniki
explored the coast in all directions during the winter,
notably along the Alaska peninsula, learning of Iliamna Lake and of the different portage routes to the
west side.

Despite all precautions the scurvy broke out in the
Russian camps and carried off numbers, but instead
of taking advantage of the weakened condition of the
Russians, the natives willingly assisted in obtaining
fresh provisions. One exception to this good understanding occurred on the island of Shuiak, situated
north of Afognak. A quantity of goods had been intrusted by one of Shelikof's agents to the chief of
Shuiak, to purchase furs during the winter. When
asked for a settlement he not only refused but killed
the messengers. An expedition was sent in the spring
which succeeded in bringing the recreant chief to
terms, and in establishing fortified stations on Cook
Inlet and Afognak.[13]

On the 25th of February 1786 Shelikof received a
letter from Eustrate Delarof, who was then at Unalaska, stating that the ship *Sv Mikhaïl*, which had
been separated from Shelikof's squadron in a gale,
had arrived at that place the previous May. She

---

[12] Karluk, situated on the west coast of Kadiak, is a settlement upon the
river of the same name, which furnishes a larger quantity of salmon than any
other stream of its size in Alaska. See *Cartog. Pac. States*, MS., iii. passim.

[13] A war party of 1,000 men of the Chugatsches and Kenais which had been
summoned by the Shuiak chief, to attempt the destruction of Shelikof's settlement, also dispersed before it was fully organized. *Tikhmenef, Istor. Obos.*,
i. 12, 13; *Shel.kof, Putesh.*, i. 51–3; *Pallas, Nord. Beitr.*, vi. 185–6.

reached the port minus one mast and otherwise damaged, and repairs to the vessel occupied nearly the
whole summer. When at last ready for sea she was
cast upon the rocks and injured to such an extent as
to require additional repairs. Despairing of getting
off the *Sv Mikhaïl* that season, Delarof despatched
thirteen men divided into several detachments as
messengers to Kadiak in search of assistance. Six of
them succumbed to cold and hunger during a detention of many weeks on the Alaska peninsula, and five
more died after reaching Kadiak. Soon after this
the craft arrived at Three Saints, and the commander,
Assistant Master Olessof, who had been three years
making the voyage from Okhotsk to Kadiak, was deposed and the peredovchik Samoilof invested with the
control of both vessels, one of which was to cruise
northward and eastward from Kadiak and the other
westward and northward, if possible as far as Bering
Strait.

Early in March Shelikof despatched an exploring
party eastward with orders to proceed to Bering's
Cape St Elias, and to erect a fort as the beginning
of a settlement. He resolved to abandon the fort on
Cook Inlet as too far removed from his base of operation, and to enlarge the fortified station on Afognak
Island, besides establishing several others.[14] These
and other arrangements made, Shelikof prepared to
return to Okhotsk, and the peredovchik, Samoilof,
formerly a merchant in Siberia, was appointed to the
command of the infant colony. His instructions demanded above all the extension of Russian control
and establishments eastward and south, and the exclusion of rival traders.[15]

[14] *Shelikof, Putesh.*, i. 57; *Pallas, Nord. Beitr.*, vi. 186. See *Juvenal's Jour.*, MS., 27–8.
    [15] These instructions dated May 4, 1786, were printed in the original crude form, in the appendix to *Tikhmenef, Istoricheskaia Obosranie*, ii. The docu-ment contains much that is highly interesting. The small number of Russians assigned to each isolated station makes it evident that Shelikof was not appre-hensive of renewed hostilities on the part of the natives, and confirms the suspi-cion that his previous reports of their number, bravery, and fierce disposition

Shelikof took his departure in May, accompanied by a number of native adults and children, some to be retained and educated, others to be merely impressed with a view of Russian life and power. He landed at Bolsheretsk on the 8th of August, and thence proceeded to Petropavlovsk,[16] and overland to

were exaggerated. Of 113 Russians then in the new colony, and 50 others expected from Unalaska, he ordered the following disposition to be made: 40 men at the harbor of Three Saints; 11 at the bay of Ugak (Orlova); 30 on the islands of Shuiak and Afognak; 10 or 11 at either Uganak, Chiniak, or Aiakhtalsk; 30 at Karluk; 20 at Katmak (Katmai), and 11 at a station between Katmala and Kamuishak Bay. These trading-posts were separated from each other by long distances of land and water, and extended over hundreds of miles. The instructions further specify that 'immediately upon the arrival of reënforcements from Okhotsk, stations should be established in the Kenai and Chugatsch countries,' and 'with all possible despatch farther and farther along the coast of the American continent, and in a southerly direction to California, establishing everywhere marks of Russian possession.' If expected reenforcements failed to arrive, only three stations were to be maintained—at the harbor, Afognak, and Karluk. Paragraph 7 of the instructions announced that Shelikof would take with him to Okhotsk forty natives—adults and children of both sexes—'some in satisfaction of their own desire,' and others, 'prisoners from various settlements.' One third of these natives were to be returned by the same ship, after 'seeing the fatherland and observing our domestic life;' another third were to be forwarded to the court of her imperial Majesty; while the remainder, consisting chiefly of children, were to be educated in Okhotsk or Irkutsk 'to enable them in the future to exercise a civilizing influence among their countrymen.' Other paragraphs relate to the maintenance of the strictest discipline among the Russians; the employment of spies among the natives; to explorations and voyages of discovery southward to latitude 40°; the construction of buildings and fortified block-houses; the purchase of articles of native manufacture—garments, utensils, etc.; the collection of minerals, ores, and shells for transmission to St Petersburg; sanitary regulations to prevent scurvy; the collection of boys from 'latitude 50° in California, northward to Aliaska,' to be educated in the Russian language; the exclusion of other trading firms in this the country then occupied, 'by peaceable means, if possible;' the expulsion of worthless and vicious men from the company; the maintenance of a school at Three Saints, and other business details. The document furnishes strong evidence of Shelikof's far-sightedness, energy, ambition, and executive ability. After holding Samoilof responsible for the strict observance of these instructions, the writer signed himself: 'Grigor Shelikof, member of the company of Sea-voyagers in the Northern Ocean.' Three supplementary paragraphs contain directions for a 'minute survey' by Bocharof of the island Kuiktak, the American coast from Katmak to the gulfs of Kenaï and Chugachuik, and 'if possible' around Kadiek [probably Kyak, or Kayes, Island]. This is the first mention of the term Kadiek or Kadiak, subsequently applied to the island Kuiktak, and to this mistake of Shelikof the origin of the present name may be traced.

[16] When Shelikof was on the point of leaving Bolsheretsk for Okhotsk he was informed that an English vessel had arrived at Petropavlovsk. The vessel proved to be the Lark, and belonged to the East India Company. From Peters, the captain, Shelikof purchased a large amount of goods, reselling them to merchants of Totma and to agents of the Panof company at a profit of 50 per cent. Capt. Peters brought a letter from the directors of his company to the commander of Kamchatka asking permission to exchange the products of their respective territories. A Baron Stungel or Stangel, prob-

Okhotsk and Irkutsk, where he arrived in April 1787, after suffering great hardships on his journey. There he lost no time in taking initiatory steps with the view of obtaining for his company the exclusive right to trade in the new colony and other privileges, the results of which belong to another chapter.

We have seen how the Cossacks were enticed from the Caspian and Black seas, drawn over the Ural Mountains, and lured onward in their century-march through Siberia to Kamchatka, and all for the skin of the little sable. And when they had reached the Pacific they were ready as ever to brave new dangers on the treacherous northern waters, for the coveted Siberian quadruped was here supplanted by the still more valuable amphibious otter. As furs were the currency of the empire, the occupation of the trapper, in the national economy, was equivalent to that in other quarters of the gold-miner, assayer, and coiner combined. In those times all the valuable skins obtained by the advancing Cossacks were immediately transported to Russia over the routes just opened.

The custom was to exact tribute from all natives who were conquered *en passant* by the Cossacks, as a diversion from the tamer pursuit of sable-hunting. As early as 1598 the tribute collected in the district of Pelymsk, just east of the Ural Mountains, amounted to sixty-eight bundles of sables of forty skins each.[17] In 1609 this tribute was reduced from ten to seven

ably an exile, who was in command at that time, consented under certain conditions. Shelikof, who was well received on board of the *Lark* and 'treated to various liquors,' describes the vessel as two-masted, with 12 cannon, and carrying a large crew consisting of Englishmen, Hindoos, Arabs, and Chinamen. Of the four officers one was a Portuguese. *Putesh.*, i. 60-4. The *Lark* was subsequently wrecked on Copper Island with the loss of all on board but two. The survivors were forwarded to St Petersburg overland. *Viages al Norte*, MS., 316. Upon finishing his business with Capt. Peters, Shelikof at once set out for Irkutak.

[17] *Istoria Sib.*, vi. 23. In the same year Botcha Murza, a Tunguse chief who had been made a prince by the Russians, presented forty sables to the government, and forty additional skins on the occasion of his marriage, promising to repeat the gift every year. An oukaz issued the same year exempted the aged, the feeble, and the sick from paying tribute.

sables per adult male, but there seemed to be no decrease in the number collected.[18]   Nine years later,
however, the animal seems to have been nearly exterminated, as the *boyar* Ivan Semenovich Kurakin
was instructed to settle free peasant families in the
district.   After this the principal Cossack advance
was into the Tunguse country.   In the tribute-books
of 1620–1 the latter tribe is entered as tributary at
the rate of forty-five sables for every six adult males.
In 1622 nine Tunguse paid as high as ninety-four
sables.[19]   Whenever a breach occurred in the flow of
sable-skins into Moscow the Cossacks were instructed
to move on, though the deficiency was not always
owing to exhaustion of the supply.[20]

Thus the authorized fur-gatherers advanced from
one region to another across the whole north of Asia,
followed, and in some instances even preceded, by
the promyshleniki or professional hunters.   The latter formed themselves into organized companies, hunting on shares, like the sea-faring promyshleniki of
later times, and like them they allowed the business
to fall gradually into the hands of a few wealthy merchants.   The customs adopted by these hunters go far
toward elucidating much that seems strange in the
proceedings of the promyshleniki on gaining a foothold upon the islands of the Pacific.   A brief description will therefore not be amiss.

The hunting-grounds were generally about the head-
waters and tributaries of the large rivers, and the
journey thence was made in boats.   Three or four
hunters combined in building the boat, which was
covered, and so served as shelter.   Provisions, arms,

---

[18] In that year the total tribute amounted to 66 bundles, of 40 skins each,
and 39 sables.   In 1610 it increased to 75 bundles and 12 sables. *Ist. Sib.*, vi.
26-7.

[19] *Ist. Sib.*, vi. 218.   A force of 40 Cossacks was sufficient to collect tribute
and preserve order among the Tunguse.

[20] In 1607 complaints reached the tsar that traders from Pustozersk would
go among the natives of the Berezof district before tribute had been collected,
making it difficult to obtain the government's quota. *Ist. Sib.*, vi. 35.

bedding, and a few articles of winter clothing made up
the cargo. A jar of yeast or sour dough for the
manufacture of *kvass*, to keep down the scurvy, was
considered of the highest importance. Material for
the construction of sleds and a few dogs were also
essential, and when all these had been collected and
duly stowed, each party of three or four set out upon
their journey to a place previously appointed. As
soon as the whole force had assembled at the rendezvous election was made of a *peredovchik*, or foreman,
a man of experience, and commanding respect, to
whom all promised implicit obedience. The peredovchik then divided his men into *chunitzi*, or parties,
appointing a leader for each, and assigning them their
respective hunting-grounds. This division was always
made; even if the *artel*, or station, consisted of only
six men they must not all hunt together on the same
ground.[21] Until settled in winter-quarters all their
belongings were carried in leather bags. Before the
first snow fell a general hunt was ordered by the peredovchik to kill deer, elks, and bears for a winter's
supply of meat, after which the first traps were set
for foxes, wolves, and lynx. With the first snow fall,
before the rivers were frozen, the whole party hunted
sables in the immediate vicinity of the general winter-
quarters, with dogs and nets. The peredovchik and
the leaders were in the mean time engaged in making
sleds and snow-shoes for their respective chunitzis.
When the snow was on the ground the whole artel
was assembled at the winter-quarters and prayers were
held, after which the peredovchik despatched the
small parties to the sable grounds with final instructions to the leaders. The latter preceded their men
by a day in order to prepare the station selected; the
same practice prevailed in moving stations during the
winter. The first station was named after some church
in Russia, and subsequent stations after patron saints
of individual hunters. The first sables caught were

[21] *O Sobolnuie Promyssla*, 29–42.

always donated to some church or saint, and were called God's sables. The instructions of leaders were mainly to the effect that they should look well after their men, watch carefully their method of setting traps, and see that they did not gorge themselves in secret from the common store of provisions.[22]

During the height of the season stations were frequently changed every day, for it was thought that prolonged camping at any one place would drive away the sables. When the season closed the small parties returned to head-quarters, where the leaders rendered their accounts to the peredovchik, and at the same time reported all infractions of rules by the men. The accused were then heard, and punished by the peredovchik if found guilty.[23] When all arrangements for returning to the settlement were completed the peredovchik would make the rounds of all the stations to see that every trap was closed or removed, so that no sable could get into them during the summer.

In Alaska the methods of the hunters underwent many changes, owing to the different physical features of the field and the peculiarities of the natives. The men engaged for these expeditions were of a very mixed class; few had ever seen the ocean, and many were wholly untrained for their vocation. They were engaged for a certain time and paid in shares taken from one half of the proceeds of the hunt, the other

[22] The instructions contained also an admonition to observe certain superstitious customs, traces of which could be found nearly a century later among the servants of the Russian American Company. For instance, certain animals must not be spoken of by their right names at the stations, for fear of frightening the sables away. The raven, the snake, and the wild-cat were tabooed. They were called respectively the 'upper,' or 'high one,' the 'bad one,' and the 'jumper.' In the early times this rule extended to quite a number of persons, animals, and even inanimate objects, but the three I have mentioned survived till modern times. *O Sobolnuie Promysla*, 29–42.

[23] The promyshleniki were treated much like children by their leaders. Some offenders were made to stand on stumps for a time, and fast while their comrades were feasting, while others were fined for the benefit of the church. Thieves were cruelly beaten, and forfeited a portion of their *ushina*, or dividend (literally supper), as it was held that their crime must have brought bad luck and decreased the total catch. *O Sobolnuie Promysla*, 56–7.

half of the cargo going to the outfitter or owner. If the crew consisted of forty men, including navigator and peredovchik, their share of the cargo was usually divided into about forty-six shares, of which each member received one, the navigator three, the foreman two, and the church one or two. In case of success the hunters realized quite a small fortune, as we have seen, but often the yield was so small as to keep the men in servitude from indebtedness to their employer. The vessel[24] was provided with but a small stock of provisions, consisting of a few hams, a little rancid butter, a few bags of rye and wheat flour for holidays, and a quantity of dried and salted salmon. The main stock had to be obtained by fishing and hunting, and to this end were provided fire-arms and other implements serving also for defence. Since furs in this new region were obtained chiefly through the natives, articles of trade formed the important part of the cargo, such as tobacco, glass beads, hatchets and knives of very bad quality, tin and copper vessels, and cloth. A large number of *kleptsi*, or traps, were also carried. Thus provided the vessel sets sail with *bozhe pomoshtch*—God's help.

Mere trade soon gave way to a more effective method of obtaining furs. Natives were impressed to hunt for the Russians, who, as a rule, found it both needless and dangerous for themselves to disperse in small parties to catch furs. Either by force or by agreement with chiefs the Aleuts and others were obliged to give hostages, generally women and children, to ensure the safety of their visitors, or performance of contract. They were thereupon given traps and sent forth to hunt for the season, while the Russians lived in indolent repose at the village, basking in the

[24] 'Their galliots are constructed at Okhotsk or Nishnekamchatsk, and government, with a view of encouraging trade, has ordered the commandants of those places to afford as much assistance as possible to the adventurers, besides which, the materials of the very frequently wrecked transport vessels, though lost to government, are found the chief means of fitting out such an enterprise, and greatly lessen the expense.' *Sauer's Geog. and Astron. Exped.*, 275.

smiles of the wives and daughters, and using them also as purveyors and servants. When the hunters returned they surrendered traps and furs in exchange for goods, and the task-masters departed for another island to repeat their operation.

The custom of interchanging hostages while engaged in traffic was carried eastward by the Russians and forced upon the English, Americans, and Spaniards long after the entire submission of Aleuts, Kenaï, and Chugatsches had obviated the necessity of such a course in the west. Portlock was compelled to conform to the custom at various places before he could obtain any trade, but as a rule four or five natives were demanded for one or two sailors from the ship.[25] On Cross Sound, Sitka Bay, and Prince of Wales Island the hostages were not always given in good faith; they would suddenly disappear and hostilities begin. As soon as they ascertained, however, that their visitors were watchful and strong enough to resist, they would resume business.

Meares observes, among other things relating to Russian management, that wherever the latter settled the natives were forbidden to keep canoes of a larger size than would carry two persons. This applied, of course, only to the bidarka region, Kadiak, Cook Inlet, and portions of Prince William Sound. The bidars, or large canoes, were then as now very scarce, being made of the largest sea-lion skins, and used only for war or the removal of whole families or villages. The Russians found them superior to their own clumsy boats for trading purposes, and acquired them, by purchase and probably often by seizure under some pretext, as fast as the natives could build them. In their opinion the savages had no business to devote themselves to anything but hunting.

A portion of the catch was claimed as tribute, although the crown received a very small share, often none. Tribute-gathering was a convenient mantle to

[25] *Portlock's Voy.*, 269.

cover all kinds of demands on the natives, and there can be no doubt that in early times at least half the trade was collected in the form of tribute, by means of force or threats, while at the same time the authorities at home were being petitioned to relinquish its collection, "because it created discontent" among the natives.

The tribute collected by the earlier traders was never correctly recorded. The merchants frequently obtained permission from the Kamchatka authorities to dispense with the services of Cossack tribute-gatherers, and gradually, as the abuses perpetrated under pretext of its collection came to the ears of the home government, the custom was abandoned altogether. Subsequently the Russian American Company obtained a right to the services of the Aleuts on the plea that it should be in lieu of tribute formerly paid to the government. At the same time it was ordained that those natives who rendered no regular services to the company should pay a tribute. The latter portion of the programme was, however, never carried out. The Chugatsches and the more northerly villages of Kenaï never furnished any hunters for the company unless with some private end in view, and no tribute paid by them ever reached the imperial treasury.

Another method of obtaining furs, outside of the regular channels of trade, was in furnishing supplies in times of periodical famine caused by the improvidence of the simple Aleuts. A little assistance of this kind was always considered as a lien upon whatever furs the person might collect during the following season. This pernicious system, unauthorized as it was by the management, survived all through the regime of the Russian American Company, and one encounters traces of it here and there to the present day.

At the time of the first advance of Russians along the coast in a south-easterly direction native auxiliaries, usually Aleuts, were taken for protection as well as for the purpose of killing sea-otters. Soon the plan was extended to taking Aleut hunters to regions where trade had been made unprofitable by unlimited competition. This was first adopted on a larger scale by Shelikof and brought to perfection under the management of Delarof and Baranof. From a business point of view alone it was a wise measure, since it obviated the ruinous raising of prices by savages made impudent by sudden prosperity, and at the same time placed a partial check on the indiscriminate slaughter of fur-bearing animals. Yet it opened the door to abuse and oppression of the natives at the hands of unscrupulous individuals, and in the case of the docile and long since thoroughly subdued Aleuts it led to something akin to slavery. It was also attended with much loss of life, owing to ignorance, carelessness, and foolhardiness of the leaders of parties. It certainly must have been exceedingly annoying to the natives of the coast thus visited to see the animals exterminated which brought to them the ships of foreigners loaded with untold treasures. The Kaljush hunters could not fail to perceive that the unwelcome rivals from the west, though inferior in strength, stature, and courage, were infinitely superior in skill, and indefatigable in pursuit of the much coveted sea-otter.

It was but natural that in a brief period the very name of Aleut became hateful to the Kaljush and Chugatsches, who allowed no opportunity to escape them for revenge on the despised race, not thinking that the poor fellows were but helpless tools of the Russians. Numerous massacres attested the strong feeling, but this by no means prevented the Russians from pursuing a policy which, to a certain extent, has been justified by the result. As the minds at the head of affairs became more enlightened, measures for the protection of valuable animals were adopted, the execution of which was possible with the docile Aleut hunters, while it would have been out of the question with the stubborn and ungovernable Kaljush.

As long as operations were confined to Prince William Sound, with the inhabitants of which the Aleuts, and especially the Kadiak people, had previously measured their strength in hostile encounters, the plan worked well enough. Subsequently, however, contact with the fierce Thlinkeets of Comptroller Bay, Yakutat, and Ltua inspired the western intruders with dismay, rendering them unfit even to follow their peaceful pursuits without an escort of four or five armed Russians to several hundred hunters. On several occasions a panic occurred in hunting parties, caused merely by fright, but seriously interfering with trading operations. Vancouver mentions instances of that kind, when Lieutenant Puget and Captain Brown at Yakutat Bay successively assisted Purtof, who commanded a large party of Aleuts sent out by Baranof.[26]

The reports of these occurrences by Purtof and his companions corroborate the statements of Puget and Brown, but naturally the former do not dwell as much upon the assistance received as upon services rendered. With regard to Captain Brown's action, however, the Russian report differs somewhat.[27]

Previous to the arrival of the Russians a considerable interchange of products was carried on by certain of the more enterprising tribes; the furs of one section being sold to the inhabitants of another. The long-haired skins of the wolverene were valued highly for trimming by tribes of the north who hunted the reindeer; and the parkas or shirts made from the skins of the diminutive speckled ground-squirrel (*Spermophilus*) of Alaska, which occurs only on a few islands of the coast, were much sought by the inhabitants of nearly all regions where the little animal does not exist. The newcomers were not slow to recognize the advantages to

[26] *Vancouver's Voy.*, iii. 233–5.
[27] For Purtof's report, see *Tikhmenef, Istor. Obos.*, ii. app. 66–7.

be gained by absorbing the traffic. Within a few years it was taken from the natives along the coast as far north as Cook Inlet and Prince William Sound, but beyond that and in the interior a far-reaching commerce, including the coasts of Arctic Asia in its ramifications, has existed for ages and has never been greatly interfered with by the Russians, who frequently found articles of home manufacture, originally sold by traders in Siberia, in the hands of the tribes who had the least intercourse with themselves.

Captain Cook indulged in profound speculations with regard to the channels through which some of the natives he met with on the Northwest Coast had acquired their evident acquaintance with iron knives and other implements, but this, the most probable source, was unknown to him. Later navigators found evidence of the coast tribes assuming the rôle of middlemen between the inhabitants of the interior and the visitors from unknown parts. In August 1786 Dixon was informed by natives on Cook Inlet that they had sold out every marketable skin, but that they would soon obtain additional supplies from tribes living away from the sea-shore.

A century of intercourse with the Caucasian races has failed to eradicate the custom of roaming from one continent to another for the sake of exchanging a few articles of trifling value. The astuteness displayed by these natives in trade and barter was certainly one of the reasons which caused the Russians to devise means of getting at the furs without being obliged to cope with their equals in bartering.

As far as the region contained within the present boundaries of Alaska is concerned, the fur-trade toward the end of the last century was beginning .to fall into regular grooves, which have never been essentially departed from except in the case of the Kaljush, who, relying on their constant intercourse with English and American traders, persistently refused to be reduced to routine and system, and maintained an independent and frequently a defiant attitude toward the Russians. Under the rule of the Russian American Company the prices paid to natives for furs were equal in all parts of the colonies with the exception of Sitka and the so-called Kaljush sounds, where a special and much higher tariff was in force.[28]

A more gradual change began also to affect the share system of the Russians, embracing two kinds of share-holders, those who with invested capital had a voice in the management and their half of the gross receipts, and another class, laboring in various capacities for such compensation as fell to their lot when the settlements were made at stated times and after every other claim had been satisfied. The disadvantages of this system were obvious. On one hand the laborer was entirely dependent upon the agents or managers of his immediate station or district, who were sometimes honest, but far oftener rascals, while on the other hand the hunters and trappers and those in charge of native hunting-parties had every inducement to indulge in indiscriminate slaughter of fur-bearing animals without regard to consequences.

By the time Kamchatka was discovered and conquered the number of private traders had greatly increased, and another market for costly furs had been opened on the borders of China, a market of such im-

[28] The introduction of a well-defined business system as well as regulations to check the threatened extermination of fur-bearing animals came only with the establishment of a monopoly, and this involved both time and intrigue. The founder of the so-called colonies as well as his successors in the management had but one object in view, to control the fur-trade of Russia in Europe and Asia. Shelikof was shrewd enough to understand that in order to obtain special privileges or protection from the government, it was necessary to make a display of some more permanent business than the fur-trade; and with the sole view of furthering this end projects of colonization and ship-building were launched in rapid succession, but there can be no doubt that Shelikof himself had no faith in these undertakings, for with his sanction the convicts, mechanics, and farmers sent from Siberia by the authorities were at once distributed among the trading posts and vessels of the Shelikof and Golikof Company. *Petrof, Russ. Am. Co.*, MS., 2-4.

portance that not only the carrying of skins to Russia
was curtailed, but large shipments of furs were made
from Russia to the Chinese frontier, principally beavers
and land-otters from Canada, these skins being carried
almost around the world at a profit.[29]

No attempt was made by Russians during the
eighteenth century to send furs to China by water.
That route was opened by English traders to the
Northwest Coast as soon as it became generally known
that furs had been disposed of in China to great advantage by the ships of Captain Cook's last two expeditions. The sea-otter and sable shipments from the
Aleutian Isles and Kamchatka were still consigned
to Irkutsk, where a careful assortment was made.
The inferior and light-colored sables, the foxes of the
Aleutian Isles, the second grade of sea and land
otter, etc., were set aside for the Chinese market.
Defective skins were sent to the annual fair at Irbit,
for sale among the Tartars, and only the very best
quality was forwarded to Moscow and Makaria, where
Armenians and Greeks figured among the ready purchasers.[30]

The first large shipment of sea-otters was brought
to China by Captain Hanna, who with a brig of sixty
tons collected in six weeks, on King George Sound,
five hundred whole sea-otter skins, and a number of
pieces amounting to about sixty more. He sailed
from China in April 1785 and returned in December,
making the voyage exceedingly profitable.[31]   Hanna

[29] The following shipments of this kind are recorded by Coxe, from the
Hudson Bay territory to London and St Petersburg and thence overland to
Kiakhta: in 1775, 46,460 beavers and 7,143 otters; in 1776, 27,700 beavers
and 12,080 otters; in 1777, 27,316 beavers and 10,703 otters. The skins
brought at St Petersburg from 7 to 9 rubles for beavers, and from 6 to 10
rubles for otters; while at Kiakhta the beaver sold at from 7 to 20 rubles, and
the otter from 6 to 35 rubles. *Coxe's Russ. Disc.*, 337–8.
[30] The Chinese at that time understood the art of coloring sables and other
furs so perfectly that the deception was not observable. Consequently they
preferred to purchase a low-priced and inferior article. *Sauer's Geog. and
Astron. Exped.*, 15.
[31] Skins of the first grade brought $60 each. Hanna had 140 of these, 175
of the second grade, worth $40; 80 of the third, worth $30; 55 of the fourth
at $15, and 50 of the fifth at $10. The pieces were also sold at the rate of $10

sailed again on the same venture in 1786, but though he remained absent until the following year, his cargo did not bring over $8,000. Two other vessels, the *Captain Cook* and the *Experiment*, left Bombay in January 1786, and after visiting in both King George and Prince William sounds returned with 604 sea-otters, which sold for $24,000, an average of $40 a skin.

La Pérouse, who visited the coast in the same year, forwarded an extensive report to his government concerning the fur-trade of the Northwest Coast. He states that during a period not exceeding ten days he purchased a thousand skins of sea-otters at Port des Français, or Ltua Bay; but only few of them were entire, the greater part consisting of made-up garments, robes, and pieces more or less ragged and filthy. He thought, however, that perfect skins could easily be obtained if the French government should conclude to favor a regular traffic of its subjects with that region. La Pérouse entertained some doubts as to whether the French would be able to compete profitably with the Russians and Spaniards already in the field, though he declared that there was an interval of coast between the southern limits of the Russian and the northern line of Spanish operations which would not be closed for several centuries, and was consequently open to the enterprise of any nation.[32] Among other suggestions he recommended that only vessels of 500 or 600 tons should be employed, and that the principal article of trade should be bar-iron, cut into lengths of three or four inches. The value of the 3,231 pieces of sea-otter skin collected at Port des Français is estimated in the report at 41,063 Spanish piastres.[33]

per whole skin. Hanna realized $20,000 out of this short cruise. *Dixon's Voy.*, 315–22.

[32] *La Pérouse, Voy.*, iv. 162–72.

[33] A peculiarly French idea is advanced by La Pérouse in a note to his report on the fur-trade of the north-west. He and his officers refused to derive any profit from the experimental mercantile transactions during the expedition. It was settled that such sums as were realized from the sale of

After duly weighing the question in all its aspects the French commander came to the conclusion that it would not be advisable to establish at once a French factory at Port des Français, but to encourage and subsidize three private expeditions from some French seaport, to sail at intervals of two years.

From Dixon we learn that La Pérouse's expectations, as far as the value of his skins was concerned, were not realized. He reports that the French ships *Astrolabe* and *Boussole* brought to Canton about 600 sea-otters of poor quality, which they disposed of for $10,000.[34]

In January 1788 the furs collected by Dixon and Portlock in the *King George* and *Queen Charlotte* were sold as follows: The bulk of the cargo, consisting of 2,552 sea-otters, 434 pups, and 34 foxes, sold for $50,000, and at private sale 1,080 sea-otter tails brought $2,160, and 110 fur-seals $550. According to Berg the number of sea-otters shipped from the Northwest Coast to Canton previous to January 1, 1788, was 6,643, which sold at something over $200,000 in the aggregate.

After this shipments increased rapidly with the larger number of vessels engaging in this trade, as I have shown in my *History of the Northwest Coast*.[35] A large proportion of them were English, though they labored under many disadvantages, and as the English captains who came to Canton were not allowed

the skins in China should be distributed among the crew. The commander ingeniously reasons that the share of each sailor will be sufficient to enable the whole crew to get married on their return and to raise families in comfortable circumstances, who, 'in course of time, will be of the greatest benefit to the navy.' *La Pérouse, Voy.*, iv. 167.

[34] *Dixon's Voy.*, 315–22. In the same place the result of the Bengal Fur Society's experiment with the *Nootka*, Capt. Meares, is given as follows: 267 sea-otters, 97 pieces and tails, 48 land-otters, and 41 beavers and martens were sold at Macao for $9,692. Fifty prime sea-otters sold at Canton for $91 each, bringing $4,550. Nearly the whole cargo had been obtained at Prince William Sound. About the same time the cargo of the *Imperial Eagle*, Capt. Barclay, obtained chiefly from Vancouver Island, sold for $30,000. See *Hist. Northwest Coast*, vol. i. 353, this series.

[35] In 1792 there were at least 28 vessels on the coast, more than half of them engaged in fur-trade. *Hist. Northwest Coast*, i. 238 et seq., this series.

to trade in their own or their owners' name, but were obliged to transact their business through the agents of the English East India Company, they did not take very kindly to the trade. The merchants of other nations held the advantage to the extent that, even if forced to dispose of their furs at low prices, they could realize one hundred per cent profit on the Chinese goods they brought home, while the English, on account of the privileges granted the East India Company, could not carry such goods to England. The British merchants, however, knew how to evade these regulations by sending to Canton, where the ships of all nations were free to come, vessels under the flags of Austria, Hamburg, Bremen, and others. Thus Captain Barclay, or Berkeley, who sailed from Ostend in the *Imperial Eagle* under the Austrian flag, was an Englishman.

On the other hand, Russian influence was continually at work on the Chinese frontier and even at Peking, to counteract the influx of furs by water into the Celestial empire. When Marchand arrived at Macao from the Northwest Coast he found a temporary interdict on the traffic.[36] This benefited the Russian only to a certain extent, for new hunting-grounds were discovered by the now roused traders, and the immense influx of fur-seal skins from the Falkland Islands, Terra del Fuego, New Georgia, South Shetland, and the coast of Chile to China caused a general depreciation in this article toward the end of the last century.[37]

The jealousy of foreign visitors on the part of Russians was but natural in view of the mischief they created. Along the whole coast from Cook Inlet

---

[36] When the *Solide* arrived at Macao, Marchand was much disappointed on learning that strict orders had been issued from Peking to purchase no more furs from the north-west coast of America. This compelled him to take what furs he had to Europe. *Marchand, Voy.*, ii. 368-9.

[37] Three and a half millions of skins were taken from Masa Fuero to Canton between 1793 and 1807. *Dall's Alaska*, 492.

down to Sitka and Queen Charlotte Sound, whenever English and subsequently American competition
entered the field, the prices of sea-otter skins experienced a steady rise till the temptation to kill the animal indiscriminately became so great as to overcome
what little idea the natives had of husbanding their
resources.   On the other hand the most prolific sea-
otter grounds, the southern end of the Alaska peninsula and the Aleutian Islands, exempt from the visits
of mercantile rovers, have continued to yield their
precious furs to the present day.

These foreigners had an additional variety of goods
with which to tempt the untutored son of the wilderness, and were not scrupulous about selling even destructive weapons.   The demand for certain articles
of trade by the natives, especially among the Thlinkeets, was subject to continuous changes.   When
Marchand arrived in Norfolk Sound he found the
savages disposed to drive hard bargains, and skins
could not be obtained for trifles.   Tin and copper vessels and cooking utensils were in request, as well as
lances and sabres, but prime sea-otters could be purchased only with European clothing of good quality,
and Marchand was obliged to sacrifice all his extra
supplies of clothing for the crew.   The natives seemed
at that time, 1791, to have plenty of European goods,
mostly of English manufacture.   Favorite articles
were toes of iron, three or four inches in length, and
light-blue beads.   Two Massachusetts coins were
worn by a young Indian as ear-rings.   They were
nearly all dressed in European clothing and familiar
with fire-arms.   Hammers, saws, and axes they valued
but little.[38]

The rules with regard to traffic on individual account
on board of these independent traders were quite as

<hr>

[38] In 10 days Marchand obtained in trade 100 sea-otters of prime quality,
mostly fresh; 250 young sea-otters, l'ght colored; 36 whole bear-skins, and
13 half skins; 37 fur-seals; 60 beavers; a sack of squirrel-skins and sea-otter
tails; a marmot robe, and a robe of marmot and bear. *Marchand, Voy.*, ii.
3-12.

stringent as those subsequently enforced by the Russian American company. Among the instructions furnished Captain Meares by the merchant proprietors we find the following: "As every person on board you is bound by the articles of agreement not to trade even for the most trifling articles, we expect the fullest compliance with this condition, and we shall most assuredly avail ourselves of the penalty a breach of it will incur. But as notwithstanding, the seamen may have laid in iron and other articles for trade, thinking to escape your notice and vigilance, we direct that, at a proper time, before you make the land of America, you search the vessel carefully, and take into your possession every article that can serve for trade, allowing the owner its full value." [39]

A few years sufficed to transform the naturally shrewd and overbearing Thlinkleets into the most exacting and unscrupulous traders. Prices rose to such an extent that no profit could be made except by deceiving them as to the value of the goods given in barter. Some of the less scrupulous captains engaged in this traffic even resorted to violence and downright robbery in order to make a showing. Guns, of course, brought high prices, but in many instances, where the trader intended to make but a brief stay, a worthless article was palmed off upon the native, who, in his turn, sought to retaliate by imposing upon or stealing from the next trader. [40]

Nor did the foreigners hesitate to commit brutalities when it suited their interest or passion, notwithstanding Meares' prating about "humane British commerce." The English captain certainly had nothing to boast of so far as his own conduct was concerned in the way of morality, honesty, and humanity. Certain subjects of Spain and Russia were exceedingly

[39] *Meares, Voy.*, app.
[40] One of the natives of Tchinkitané (Sitka) complained to Marchand of a gun he had purchased of an English captain and broken in anger because it would 'only go crick, but never poohoo!' *Marchand's Voy.*, ii. 69. Marchand and Rocquefeuille both claim that the natives of the Northwest Coast prefer French guns to any other.

cruel to the natives of America, but for innate wickedness and cold-blooded barbarities in the treatment of savage or half-civilized nations no people on earth during the past century have excelled men of Anglo-Saxon origin. Such was the conduct of the critical Meares toward the Chugatsches that they would probably have killed him but for the timely warning of a young woman whom he had "purchased for the winter."

Instances of difficulties arising between English traders and natives of Prince William Sound are too numerous to mention in detail in this place, but it is certain that as soon as the former withdrew and the Russians were enabled to manage affairs in their own way, a peaceful and regular traffic was carried on. These captains were too ready to attribute cruelty to their rivals, and at times on mistaken grounds.

Captain Douglas, who visited Cook Inlet in the *Iphigenia*, observed what he called "tickets or passports for good usage" in the hands of the natives. Meares offers an explanation of this incident, saying that "these tickets are purchased by the Indians from the Russian traders at very dear rates, under a pretence that they will secure them from ill-treatment of any strangers who may visit the coast; and as they take care to exercise great cruelty upon such of the natives as are not provided with these instruments of safety, the poor people are only too happy to purchase them on any terms." Meares then adds with charming self-complacency: "Such is the degrading system of the Russian trade in these parts; and forms a striking contrast to the liberal and humane spirit of British commerce."[41] It is scarcely necessary to say that these papers were receipts for tribute paid by these natives, who had for several years been considered and declared subjects of the ruler of all the Russias.[42]

[41] *Meares' Voy.*, ii. 129, ed. 1791.
[42] An explanation of the bitterness displayed in Captain Meares' utterance

The cause for these insinuations must be looked for in the greater success of the Muscovites, who could be met with everywhere, and as they did not purchase the skins, but had the animals killed by natives in their service, competition was out of the question. At Prince William Sound Portlock discovered that the natives did not like the goods he had to offer; only when he obtained others from Captain Meares did trade improve. The English traders frequently complained in their journals of the Russians as having absorbed the whole traffic, yet Portlock himself acknowledges that during the summer of 1787 he sent his long-boat repeatedly to Cook Inlet, and that each time the party met with moderate success and friendly treatment on the part of Russians and natives in their service.[43]

Vancouver, who as far as the Russians are concerned may be accepted as an impartial observer, expresses the opinion that "the Russians were more likely than any other nation to succeed in procuring furs and other valuable commodities from those shores." He based his opinion partly upon information received from Ismaïlof at Unalaska, but principally upon his own observations on the general conduct of the Russians toward the natives in the several localities where he found the latter under Russian control and direction. The English explorer reasons as follows: " Had the natives about the Russian establishments in Cook's Inlet and Prince William's sound been oppressed, dealt hardly by, or treated by the Russians as a conquered people, some uneasiness among them would have been perceived, some desire for emancipation would have been discovered; but no such disposition appeared—they seemed to be

on the subject of Russian traders can be found in a passage of his journal in which he complains that wherever he went in the *Nootka*, from Unalaska to the head of Cook Inlet, he found that the Russians already monopolized the trade, and the natives had nothing left to offer in exchange for English goods. A boat sent up the Inlet was constantly watched by two Russian bidars. *Meares' Voy.*, xi.

[43] *Portlock's Voy.*, 242-3.

held in no restraint, nor did they seem to wish, on
any occasion whatever, to elude the vigilance of their
directors." The Indians beyond Cross Sound were
less tractable and the Russians evidently became satisfied to remain to the westward of that region.[44]

Notwithstanding all the abuses to which the Aleuts
had to submit at the hands of the early traders and
the Russian company, it is safe to assume that a people which has absolutely no other resource to fall back
upon would have long since been blotted out of existence with the extermination of the sea-otter, had they
been exposed to the effects of reckless and unscrupulous competition like their more savage and powerful
brethren in the east. As it is, they are indebted to
former oppression for their very existence at the present day.

There can be no doubt that in their hands alone
would the wealth of the coast region be husbanded,
for their interests now began to demand an economic
management, and their influence by far exceeded that
of any other nation with whom the natives had come
in contact. Long before the universal sway of the
Russian American Company had been introduced we
find unmistakable signs of this predilection in favor of
those among all their visitors who apparently treated
them with the greatest harshness while driving the
hardest bargains. The explanation lies in the fact
that the Russians were not in reality as cruel as
the others, and, above all, that they assimilated more
closely with the aborigines than did other traders.
At all outlying stations they lived together with and
in the manner of the natives, taking quite naturally
to filth, privations, and hardships, and on the other
hand dividing with their savage friends all the little

[44] *Vancouver's Voy.*, iii. 500. Portlock, some years earlier, claimed that
the natives informed him they had recently had a fight with the Russians in
which the latter were beaten; and also that he was requested to assist the
natives against the Russians, but refused. *Portlock's Voy.*, 115–22. *Juvenal's
Jour.*, MS., 30 et seq.

comforts of rude civilization which by chance fell to
their lot.

Cook and Vancouver expressed their astonishment
at the miserable circumstances in which they found
the Russian promyshleniki, and both navigators agree
as to the amicable and even affectionate relations existing between the natives of the far north-west of this
continent and their first Caucasian visitors from the
eastern north. Captains Portlock and Dixon even
complained of this good understanding as an injury
to the interests of others with equal rights to the
advantages of traffic with the savages. The traffic
then carried on throughout that region is scarcely
worthy of the name of trade; it was a struggle to
seize upon the largest quantity of the most valuable
furs in the shortest time and at the least expense,
without regard for consequences.

When Portlock and Dixon visited Cook Inlet and
Prince William Sound in 1786 the trade in those
localities seemed to be already on the decline. In the
former place a few days were sufficient to drain the
country of marketable furs.

How much the fur-trade had deteriorated on Cook
Inlet at the beginning of the last decade of the eighteenth century is made evident by such reports of
managers as have been preserved. The total catch
for several years, during which time two ships well
manned and hundreds of natives were employed, did
not exceed 500 sea-otters and a comparatively small
number of other furs. This was certainly a great
falling-off, but it may be partly ascribed to the wran-
gling of rival companies whose retainers used every
means to interfere with each other. Large quantities
of furs were destroyed, houses and boats were broken
up, and blood was sometimes shed. The decline of
trade during this period was not arrested till the
country had been for years subjected to the arbitrary
rule of the Russian American Company, though of

course the fur business never recovered its former
prosperity.

Traces of populous settlements abound on the shores
of the inlet, and it is evident that the numerous villages were abandoned to desolation at about the same
time. The age of trees now growing over former
dwellings enables the observer to fix the date of de-
population within a few years, long before any of the
epidemics which subsequently swept the country.

With the unrestrained introduction of fire-arms
along the coast southward from Prince William Sound
the sea-otters were doomed to gradual extermination
throughout that region, though the country suffered·
no less from imported Aleuts, who far surpassed the
native sea-otter hunters in skill, and had no interest
in husbanding production. Long before American
traders took a prominent part in these operations the
golden days of the sea-otter traffic had passed away.

In 1792 Martin Sauer predicted that in fifteen
years from that time the sea-otter would no longer
exist in the waters of north-western America, and he
had not seen the devastation on the coast south of
Yakutat. The organization of the Russian American
Company alone prevented the fulfilment of his prophecy as far as concerns the section which came under
his observation.

This state of affairs the traders had not failed to
reveal to the government long before this, coupled
with no little complaint and exaggeration. Officials
in Siberia aided in the outcry, and the empress was
actually moved to order war vessels to the coast,
but various circumstances interfered with their departure.[45] Nevertheless, from the rivalry of English

[45] Shelikof complained that 'the advantages which rightfully belong to
the subjects of Russia alone are converted to the benefit of other nations who
have no claim upon the country and no right to the products of its waters.'
Lieutenant-general Ivan Bartholomeievich Jacobi, who then filled the office
of governor general of Irkutsk and Kolivansk, reported to the empress
that it was necessary to protect without delay the Russian possessions on the
coast of America with armed vessels, in order to prevent foreigners from
interfering with the Russian fur-trade. In reply Catherine ordered five war-

and American traders, the Shelikof and Golikof Company does not appear to have suffered to any great extent, if we may judge from a list of cargoes imported by that firm during a term of nine years. Their vessels during the time numbered six; one, the *Trekh Sviatiteli*, making two trips. The total value of these shipments between the years 1788 and 1797 was 1,500,000 roubles—equal then to three times the amount at the present day.[46]

This result was due partly to more wide-spread and thorough operations than hitherto practised, and partly to the compensation offered by a varied assortment of furs. Thus, while the most valuable fur-bearing animal, the sea-otters, were becoming scarce in the gulf of Kenaï, large quantities of beavers, martens, and foxes were obtained there.

The distribution of fur-bearing animals during the last century was of course very much the same as now, with the exception that foxes of all kinds came almost exclusively from the islands. The stone foxes —blue, white, and gray—were most numerous on the western islands of the Aleutian chain and on the Pribylof group. Black and silver-gray foxes, then very valuable, were first obtained from Unalaska by the Shilof and Lapin Company and at once brought into fashion at St Petersburg by means of a judicious presentation to the empress. Shipments of martens and minks from a few localities on the mainland were insignificant, and the same may be said of bears and wolverenes. The sea-otter's range was not much more extended than at present; but on the southeastern coast they were ten times more numerous than now. They were never found north of the

vessels to be fitted out to sail in 1788, under command of Captain Mulovskoi, with the rank of brigadier. The war with Sweden probably interfered with this expedition. *Berg, Khronol. Ist.*, 158. It must be remembered, however, that the Billings expedition was under way at that time.

[46] The details are given by Bergh as follows: In 1786 the *Sviatiteli* brought furs valued at 56,000 rubles; in 1789 the *Sviatiteli*, 300,000; in 1792 the *Mikhail*, 376,000; in 1793 the *Sv Simeon*, 128,000; in 1795 the *Phœnix*, 321,138; in 1795 the *Alexandr*, 276,550; in 1796 the *Orel*, 21,912; total rbls., 1,479,600. *Khronol. Ist.*, 169.

Aleutian isles and the southern extremity of the Alaska peninsula.

The fur-seal frequented the same breeding-grounds as now and many were killed on the Aleutian and Commander islands while on their annual migration to and from the rookeries. The value of the skins was small and the market easily overstocked, often necessitating the destruction of those on hand. Beavers and land-otters were obtained only in Cook Inlet, as the vast basin of the Yukon had not then been tapped. The skins of this class for the overland trade with China, as has been stated, were purchased in England of the Hudson's Bay Company, and carried nearly around the globe. Black bears were occasionally purchased, but rarely appeared in the market, being considered as most suitable presents to officials and persons of high rank whose good-will might serve the interest of individual traders or companies. Lynx and marmot skins found only a local demand in the form of garments and trimmings.

CHAPTER XII.

FOREIGN VISITORS.

1786-1794.

FRENCH INTEREST IN THE NORTH-WEST—LA PÉROUSE'S EXAMINATION—
DISCOVERY OF PORT DES FRANÇAIS—A DISASTROUS SURVEY—ENGLISH
VISITORS—MEARES IS CAUGHT IN PRINCE WILLIAM SOUND—TERRIBLE
STRUGGLES WITH THE SCURVY—PORTLOCK AND DIXON COME TO THE
RESCUE—THEIR TWO YEARS OF TRADING AND EXPLORING—ISMAÏLOF
AND BOCHAROF SET FORTH TO SECURE THE CLAIMS OF RUSSIA—A TREACH-
OROUS CHIEF—YAKUTAT BAY EXPLORED—TRACES OF FOREIGN VISITORS
JEALOUSLY SUPPRESSED—SPAIN RESOLVES TO ASSERT HERSELF—MAR-
TINEZ AND HARO'S TOUR OF INVESTIGATION—FIDALGO, MARCHAND, AND
CAAMAÑO—VANCOUVER'S EXPEDITION.

THE activity displayed by different nationalities in
the exploration of the Northwest Coast, together
with allurements of trade and of the interoceanic
problem, called to this region also the attention of the
French government; and when in August 1785 La
Pérouse was despatched from Brest with two frigates,
the *Astrolabe* and *Boussole*, the latter commanded by
De Langle, on a scientific exploring tour round the
world, he received instructions to extend it to the
farthest north-west, and report also on trade prospects. After a tedious voyage round Cape Horn, the
coast of Alaska was sighted on the 23d of June 1786
near latitude 60°, where the gigantic outline of Mount
St Elias rose above the clouds. The impression made
upon the natives of sunny France by the gloomy
aspect of this coast was not more favorable than that
conceived by the earlier Spanish and English visitors.
The contrast was too great between the palm-groves
and taro-fields of Hawaii so lately witnessed, and

these snowy mountains of this northern mainland
with their thin blackish fringe of sombre spruce-
forest. At any rate, contrary to his instructions,
which were to explore the Aleutian Islands, La Pérouse with wisdom shaped his course south-eastward
along the coast.[1]

For some time no landing could be effected, the
vessels not approaching near enough to the shore
to distinguish bays and headlands. In two instances
boats were lowered to reconnoitre, but the reports of
officers in charge were not favorable. The wide opening of Yakutat or Bering Bay was thus passed unawares, but a little to the southward La Pérouse
observed what he considered certain indications of the
discharge of a large river into the sea.[2]

On the 2d of August an inlet was sighted a short
distance below Cape Fairweather, and on the following
day the two frigates succeeded in gaining an anchorage. The navigator felt exultant over this discovery
of a new harbor, and expressed himself in his journal
to the effect "that if the French government had entertained ideas of establishing factories in this part
of the American coast, no other nation could pretend
to the smallest right of opposing the project."[3] The

[1] Indeed the illustrious French navigator had deviated from his instructions ever since leaving Madeira. He made the northern coast in the month
designated, but a year earlier than had been contemplated, having deferred
his explorations in the south Pacific. The instructions prescribed, that he
should 'particularly endeavor to explore those parts which have not been
examined by Captain Cook, and of which the relations of Russian and Spanish
navigators have given no idea. He will observe whether in those parts not
yet known some river may not be found, some confined gulf, which may, by
means of the interior lakes, open a communication with some part of Hudson
Bay. He will push his inquiries to Behring's Bay and to Mount St Elias
and will inspect the ports Bucarelli and Los Remedios. Prince William Land
and Cook river having been sufficiently explored, he will, after making Mount
St Elias, steer a course for the Shumagin Islands, near the peninsula of Alaska.
He will afterward examine the Aleutian Islands,' etc. *La Pérouse, Voy.*, i.
70-75.

[2] One indentation of the coast was named De Monti Bay; and La Pérouse's
French edition asserts that this was Bering Bay with the anchorage of Port
Mulgrave named by Dixon in the following year. Dixon's position of Port
Mulgrave was lat. 59° 33' and long. 140° w. of Greenwich, while La Pérouze
located the bay De Monti at 59° 43' and 140° 20'. Both longitudes were in-
correct in regard to Port Mulgrave.

[3] The editor of the journal of La Pérouse, in his effort to establish the

newly discovered port, called Ltua by the natives, was
named rightly and modestly Port des Français, which
gave no undue personal prominence to any one. Exploring and surveying parties in boats were sent out
at once, while the remainder of the crews were employed in watering the ships and re-stowing cargo in
order to mount six cannons that had thus far been
carried in the hold.[4]

The bay of Ltua represents in its contours the letter T, the foot forming its outlet into the sea. The
cross-bar consists of a deep basin terminating in
glaciers. La Pérouse alludes to it as "perhaps the
most extraordinary place in the world," and describes
the upper part as "a basin of water of a depth in the
middle that could not be fathomed, bordered by peaked
mountains of an excessive height covered with snow . . .
I never saw a breath of air ruffle the surface of this
water; it is never troubled but by the fall of immense
blocks of ice, which continually detach themselves from
fine glaciers, and which in falling make a noise that
resounds far through the mountains. The air is so
calm that the voice may be heard half a league away,
as well as the noise of the sea birds that lay their eggs
in the cavities of these rocks." Though charmed with
the weird grandeur of the scenery, the explorers were
disappointed in their expectation of finding a river or
channel offering a passage to the Canadian lakes or
Hudson Bay.

Intercourse with the natives began with the first

French discoverer's claim to priority on this part of the coast, ignores Cook
as having been 'too far from the shore,' but carefully traces the movements
of Dixon whom he seems to have looked upon as the commander of the expedition, consisting of the *King George* and *Queen Charlotte*, and shows that
La Pérouse sighted Mount St Elias and other points far earlier. The editor
seems to make a fine distinction between Prince William Sound and the
'northwest coast' of America. La Pérouse himself gives so careful and un-
biassed a description of what he saw on the Alaskan coast as to impress the
reader with a feeling of confidence not generally derived from a perusal of
the narratives of his English and other predecessors and successors in the
field of exploration.

[4] This was done, according to the editor of the journal, not from fear of
Indians on the spot, but with a view of defence against pirates in the China
seas they were so soon to visit.

day, and soon they came in large numbers, allured
from a distance it was supposed. Contrary to his
expectations La Pérouse found the savages in possession of knives, hatchets, iron, and beads, from which,
with clearer discrimination than Cook, he concluded
these natives to have indirect communication with the
Russians, while the latter navigator ascribed such
indications to inter-tribal traffic originating with Hudson Bay posts.[5] It was convenient for the Englishman thus to ignore the presence of any rival in these
parts.   Traffic was carried on with moderate success,
the chief article of barter being iron, and some six
hundred sea-otter skins and a number of other furs
were obtained. To so inexperienced a trader the
business transacted appeared immense, leading the
commander to the opinion that a trading-post could
easily collect twenty thousand skins per annum, yet
he leaned rather to occasional private trading expeditions than to the fixed establishment.   The thieving
propensities of the natives annoyed the French very
much, and in the hope of keeping the robbers away
La Pérouse purchased of the chief an island in the
bay, where he had established his astronomical station; but though a high price was paid for the worthless ground there was no abatement of thefts.   The
savages would glide through the dense spruce thicket
at night and steal articles from under the very heads
of sleepers without alarming the guards.

On July 13th a terrible misfortune befell the expedition. Three boats had been sent out to make
final soundings for a chart, including the passage leading out to sea. As the undertaking was looked upon
in the light of a pleasure excursion, affording an opportunity for hunting, the number of officers accompanying the party was larger than the duty required, seven

[5] We have no evidence of the advance of Ismaïlof's boats to the point previous to the arrival of the French frigates. The seal-skin covering of a large
canoe or bidar discovered here would point to visits of Aglegmutes or Chugatsches. The natives stated that of seven similar boats, six had been lost
in the attempt to stem the fearful tide-rip at the entrance to the bay.

in all, while the crews consisted of eighteen of the best men from both vessels. On approaching the narrow channel at the entrance of the bay, two of the boats were drawn into the resistless current and engulfed in the breakers almost before their inmates were aware of their danger. The third boat, the smallest, narrowly escaped a like fate. Not a man of the first two was saved, not even a single body was washed ashore.[6] A monument to the drowned party was erected on the point of island purchased of the chief, and it was named L'Isle du Cénotaphe.[7] Weighing anchor July 30th the squadron sailed along the coast without making any observations, but on the 6th of August the weather cleared, enabling La Pérouse to determine his position in the vicinity of Norfolk Sound.[8] Puerto de Bucareli and Cape Kaigan were passed by, and unfavorable weather foiled the attempt to run into Dixon Entrance, whereupon the expedition passed beyond Alaska limits.[9] Superficial as were his observations, La Pérouse came to the conclusion that the whole coast from Cross Sound to Cape Hector, the south point of Queen Charlotte Island, was one archipelago.[10]

During the year 1786 much progress was made in the exploration of the Alaskan coast between Dixon

[6] The victims were: from the *Boussole*, d'Escures, de Pierrevert, de Montarnal (officers), and 8 men; from the *Astrolabe*, de la Borde Marchainville, de la Borde Boutervilliers, Flassan (officers), and 7 men. The two de la Borde were brothers.

[7] The monument bore an inscription, and at its foot a bottle was buried containing a brief narrative of the melancholy occurrence.

[8] He recognized the Cabo de Engaño and Mount San Jacinto of the Spaniards without alluding to Cook's nomenclature of Mount and Cape Edgecombe. He looked into Norfolk Sound from the group of islands at its southern entrance, and named two bays to the southward, of which he saw only the mouths, Port Neiker and Port Guibert (probably Port Banks and Whale Bay). On the following day he named Cape Ommaney (Cape Chirikof) and Christian Sound (Chirikof Bay). The Hazy Islands he renamed Isles de la Croyère. *La Pérouse, Voy.*, ii. 165-7.

[9] The details of La Pérouse's explorations and observations south of this point can be found in *Hist. Northwest Coast*, i., and *Hist. Cal.*, i., this series.

[10] In the following year the *Astrolabe* and *Boussole* reached the coast of Kamchatka; but though the French officers met a number of individuals identified with the history of Alaska, the circumstances of their sojourn in the harbor of Petropavlovsk have no immediate connection with this narrative.

Entrance and the Alaska Peninsula. The *Captain
Cook* and the *Experiment*, under captains Lowry and
Guise, sailed in June from Nootka for Prince William Land, where they obtained a small lot of furs.
More extensive are the experiences recorded of John
Meares.[11] He sailed from Malacca in the *Nootka* May
29, 1786. A companion ship, the *Sea Otter*, also
fitted out in Bengal, had sailed before him with the
intention of meeting in Prince William Sound, but
was never heard of. Amlia and Atkha, of the Aleutian group, were sighted the 1st of August, and after
passing unawares to the northward of the islands
during a fog he was on the 5th piloted into Beaver
Bay by a Russian. While taking in water, Meares
and his officers were hospitably entertained by the
Russians on Unalaska under Delarof, yet the Englishman delights none the less to sneer at their poverty
while extolling the 'generous' and 'magnanimous' conduct of the British trader, as represented in himself.

On arriving at the mouth of Cook Inlet soon after,
he heard that two vessels had already visited that
part of the coast that summer, and seeing indications
of Russians everywhere he passed on to Prince William Sound, imagining himself first on the ground.
On his way he gave the name of Petrie to Shelikof
Strait. In his eagerness to gather all the sea-otter
skins possible, Meares allowed the season to slip by
till too late for a passage to China and no choice
remained but to winter in the sound. He first tried
the anchorage of Snug Corner Cove, discovered by
Cook, but subsequently moved his vessel to a sheltered
nook nearer the mainland, in the vicinity of the present village of Tatikhlek.

---

[11] *Voyages made in the years 1788 and 1789 from China to the North-west
Coast of America, to which is prefixed an Introductory Narrative of a Voyage
performed in 1786, from Bengal in the ship Nootka*, by John Meares, Esq.,
London, 1790. Of this work several editions have been published. The impression created by a perusal of Meares' narrative, especially in the light of
his later transactions at Nootka, is that he was an insincere and unscrupulous
man, and that he was so regarded by Portlock is evident from the manner in
which the latter bound him to the fulfilment of his promises.

The vessel was but ill-supplied with the provisions necessary for a long winter in the far north, but the best arrangements possible under the circumstances were made. The ship was covered. Spruce beer was brewed; but the crew preferring the spirituous liquor which was served out too freely for men on short allowance of food, and the supply of fresh fish meanwhile being stopped, scurvy broke out. Among the first victims was the surgeon. Funerals became frequent. At first, attempts were made to dig a shallow grave under the snow; but as the survivors became few and lost their strength, the bodies were dropped through cracks in the ice, to become food for fishes long before returning spring opened their crystal vault. At last the strength of the decimated crew was barely sufficient to drag the daily supply of fuel from the forest a few hundred yards away. The savages, who kept themselves well informed, grew insolent as they waited impatiently for the last man to die.

In April some natives from a distant part of the sound visited the vessel. A girl purchased by Meares at the beginning of the winter for an axe and some beads, and who had served as interpreter, declared them to be her own people and went away with them— a rat leaving a doomed ship.

The depth of despondency had been reached when Meares heard of the arrival of two ships in the sound. Without a seaworthy boat or a crew he was obliged to await a chance visit from the new-comers. A letter intrusted to some natives failed to reach its destination. In the evening of the 8th of May, however, Captain Dixon of the *Queen Charlotte* arrived in a whaleboat and boarded the *Nootka*, which was still fast in the ice. Learning of Meares' distress he promised all necessary assistance.[12]

[12] Meares complained that Dixon would make no promise until the matter had been submitted to Portlock, and that he would hold out no hope for supplies; but Dixon writes: 'I had...satisfaction in assuring him that he should be furnished with every necessary we could possibly spare. As Captain

Meares now had one of his boats repaired, and proceeded to Portlock's vessels, on the north side of Montague Island, where relief was obtained. Portlock insisted, however, that Meares should cease at once to trade with the natives and leave the field to him, and the latter yielded, though he complained bitterly.[13] A month after the departure of the *Queen Charlotte* in search of furs the *Nootka* left the scene of so much misery and disaster, her commander bidding a reluctant farewell to the coast of Alaska in conformance with his promise to Captain Portlock.

This was the second visit to Alaska of Portlock and Dixon. They had sailed from England in August 1785 in the ship *King George* and *Queen Charlotte*, and first approached the vicinity of Cook Inlet on the 16th of July 1786. Less dismayed than Meares at the presence of Russians, they moved past them up to the head of Cook Inlet, and there met with considerable success in trading.[14]

After a sojourn of nearly a month the *King George*

Meares' people were now getting better, he desired me not to take the trouble of sending any refreshments to him, as he would come on board of us very shortly in his own boat.' *Dixon's Voy.*, 155.

[13] Meares gives his readers the impression of a strong bias in this matter, and one inclines to credit the two naval officers, whose narratives bear the stamp of truth. Further than this the wild statements, if not deliberate falsehoods, of Meares in connection with the Nootka controversy are well known. Dixon states the case as follows: ' In the forenoon of the 11th Captain Meares and Mr Ross left us. They were supplied with what flour, sugar, molasses, brandy, etc., we could possibly spare; and in order to render them every assistance in our power, Captain Portlock spared Captain Meares two seamen to assist in carrying his vessel to the Sandwich Islands, where he proposed going as soon as the weather permitted.' *Id.*, 158.

[14] On the 10th of July the ships had stood into a capacious opening on the east side near the entrance of the inlet. The place was named Graham Bay, and a cove on the north side near the entrance was called Coal Harbor, several scams of that mineral being visible along the bluffs. A party of Russians with a number of native hunters were encamped near a lagoon, the site of the later trading-post of Alexandrovsk. Seeing no prospect of trade here, Portlock concluded to proceed up the inlet or river as he presumed it to be. The highest point reached by him was Trading Bay, in the vicinity of the present village of Toyonok, just east of North Foreland. Here some trading was done, evidently with Kadiak or Chugatsch hunting parties; for they all used the kyak, or skin canoe, and had no permanent villages on the shore. Portlock assumed from the signs of these natives that they asked his assistance against the Russians, but in this he was probably mistaken. *Dixon's Voy.*, 60–69; *Portlock's Voy.*, 102–17

and *Queen Charlotte* left the inlet on the 13th of August, with the intention to examine Prince William Sound. A succession of contrary winds and thick weather interfered with this plan. For over a month the vessels kept near the coast, sighting many points previously determined by Spanish and English explorers, but finding it impossible to make a landing, until finally, on the 28th of September, when in the vicinity of Nootka Sound, Captain Portlock gave up all hopes of further trade that season and headed for the Hawaiian Islands.

After wintering there Portlock sailed once more for the Alaskan coast, and sighted Montague Island on the 23d of April. Natives who visited the ships on the west side of the island were without furs, but pointed to the head of the sound, repeating the word 'Nootka,' which puzzled Captains Portlock and Dixon not a little, until the latter finally fell in with Meares as before stated. The *Queen Charlotte* stood down the coast, while Portlock moved to Nuchek Harbor to await the long-boat of the *King George* which had been despatched for Cook Inlet on the 12th of May, with orders to return by the 20th of June.[15] The boat returned on the 11th, reporting such success that she was fitted out anew and despatched upon a second trip with positive orders to return by the 20th of July.

Portlock's prolonged stay at Nuchek enabled him to form a very good chart of the bay, which he named Port Etches, while a cove on the west side was called Brook Cove.[16] Trade was not very active, and boats sent to various parts of the sound did not

[15] The boat was commanded by Hayward, third mate.
[16] A smoke-house was erected for the purpose of curing salmon; an abundance of spruce beer was brewed and a number of spars were secured from the virgin forest lining the shores of the bay. At the head of one of the coves an inscription was discovered upon a tree, which Portlock believed to be Greek, made by a man living among the natives, but which of course was Russian. Portlock left a wooden vane and inscription on Garden Island to the south side of Nuchek Harbor. Garden strawberries are now found on this and other points of Nuchek Island—probably the result of Portlock's experiment. *Voy.*, 232, 243.

meet with much success, some of them being robbed
not only of trading goods and provisions, but of
clothes and arms belonging to the men.   The whaleboat and yawl were left high ashore by the ebb-tide
to the eastward of Nuchek Island, and in that helpless condition the crews were surrounded by two hundred natives and completely stripped, the only result
of the expedition being the discovery that Nuchek
was an island, a fact already ascertained by the
Spaniards.

On the 22d of July the long-boat returned from
her second and less remunerative voyage to Cook
Inlet, and three days later the *King George* sailed out
of Port Etches, passing round the west side of Montague Island.   Portlock sighted Mount Fairweather,
but failed to find Cross Sound, which he had looked
for in vain the preceding season.   On the 5th of
August he found a harbor, which was named after
himself, about twelve leagues to the southward of
Cape Cross as located by Cook.[17]   Here the *King
George* anchored once more and the boats were sent
out in search of inhabitants and trade.   Only a few
natives visited the ships, for no permanent settlement
existed thereabout.   The long-boat, however, under
Hayward, made a quite successful trip to Norfolk
Sound, passing on the return voyage through Klokat-
chef Sound Cook Bay of Islands.[18]   On the 23d of
August the *King George* set sail; left the coast of
Alaska for the Hawaiian Islands, the next rendezvous
appointed with Dixon.

[17] The latitude of the ship's position in this harbor is given as 57° 46', but
while Portlock's sketch seems plain enough, no later navigator has confirmed
the contours of the bay.   On the latest chart issued by the United States
Hydrographic Office a simple break in the coast line under the latitude given
is indicated as Portlock Harbor.   It must exist somewhere on the west coast
of Chichagof Island.

[18] The inhabitants of Norfolk Sound had shown some disposition to hostility toward the crew of the long-boat, but about the ship they confined
themselves merely to stealing.   Dixon, in his narrative, spoke of having seen
here a white linen shirt worn by an Indian, which he believed to be of Spanish make, but it is much more probable that the garment had found its way
there from some point of the coast where the *Astrolabe* and *Boussole* had
touched.

Dixon had in the mean time sailed eastward along the coast, and more fortunate than Portlock he did not overlook the wide entrance of Yakutat Bay, which he entered the 23d of May. He discovered and surveyed a fine harbor on the south side, which he named Port Mulgrave. Here the *Queen Charlotte* remained nearly two weeks, meeting at first with some success in trading, though the natives were in possession of Russian beads and ironware. An exploration of the neighborhood in boats convinced Dixon that the shores of the bay were thinly peopled.[19]

On the 4th of June he proceeded eastward in search of some port where better trade might be found. Owing to his distance from the coast he failed to observe Cross Sound, but on the 11th he sighted Mount Edgecombe, and the following day entered and named Norfolk Sound.[20] A survey was made which resulted in a very fair chart. Natives made their appearance as the ship was passing into the bay and for three days trade was brisk.

On the 24th of June the *Queen Charlotte* left Norfolk Sound, and on the following day another harbor was observed and named Port Banks, probably the present Whale Bay, in latitude 56° 35'. The wind not being favorable no attempt was made to enter, and about the 1st of July Dixon left the coast of Alaska to meet with his first marked success in trading at Clark Bay on the north-western extremity of Queen Charlotte Islands. The events of his voyage below this point are told in another volume.[21]

[19] Dixon estimated a population of only 70, including women and children, which is much too low. His description of the natives is not very accurate. See *Native Races*, i. passim, this series.

[20] The natives seemed to Dixon more easy to deal with than those at Port Mulgrave. During an exploration of the bay in boats some inconvenience was experienced from their thieving propensities. The astronomical position of his anchorage on the east shore of Kruzof Island was lat. 70° 3', long. 135° 58'. He applied the name of White Point to the Beach Cape of the Russians. The whole estuary was named after the duke of Norfolk.

[21] *Hist. Northwest Coast*, i., this series. All our information concerning the visits of the *King George* and *Queen Charlotte* to the Alaskan coast is derived from the narratives of Dixon and Portlock, and to a limited extent from that of Meares. Portlock's narrative was published in London in 1799 under the

The next exploration of Prince William Sound and
the coast east of it took place during the second voyage of the *Trekh Sviatiteli*, in connection with Shelikof's plans for the development and extension of his
colony. This vessel had arrived at Kadiak from
Okhotsk in April 1788 and was at once despatched
upon a trading and exploring voyage to the eastward,
under Ismaïlof and Bocharof, both holding the rank of
masters in the imperial navy with special instructions
furnished by Jacobi, then governor general of Siberia,
and supplemented by orders of Eustrate Delarof who
had succeeded Samoilof in the command of the colony.
The crew consisted of forty Russians and four natives
of Kadiak who were to serve as interpreters.   In addition to as full an armament and equipment as circumstances would allow the expedition was supplied
with a number of painted posts and boards, copper

title of *A Voyage round the World, but more particularly to the North-West Coast
of America: performed in 1785, 1786, 1787, and 1788*, 4to.   The volume bears
evidence of the honest and careful investigations by a strict disciplinarian
who left the commercial part of his enterprise to others.   It is profusely
illustrated with maps and sketches of scenery, etc.   The latter, made chiefly
by an apprentice named Woodcock, have evidently suffered at the hand of
the engraver, for it is scarcely probable that the young man should have
originally represented Alaska with groves of palms and other tropical trees,
to say nothing of three-story houses.   Another remarkable feature is that,
though the special charts and sketches are generally correct, the general chart
of the coast from Norfolk Sound to Kadiak is full of glaring inaccuracies.
Beginning in the east, Portlock Harbor in dimensions is represented out of
all proportion to those of the special chart and the text.   The next discrepancy occurs at Nuchek Island, called Rose Island on the chart, which is drawn
at least four times too large, and its contours as well as those of Port Etches
are not in conformity with the special chart and the text.   Montague Island
is also represented too large, three very deep and conspicuous bays on its
north-eastern end are omitted, though the vessel's track is laid down within
a mile of the shore, and the harbors on the west coast are not laid in to agree
with special charts and text.   In Cook Inlet, Graham Harbor is made at
least six times too large, but Cape Elizabeth is depicted for the first time
correctly as an island.   Shelikof Strait, though known to the Russians for
several years, and named Petrie by Meares, is still closed on this chart and
its upper portion, just south of Cape Douglas, retains the name of Smoky Bay,
given by Cook.   The strait between Kadiak and Afognak is duly indicated,
but the former island is represented as part of the continent, while Afognak
and Shuiak are made one island and named Kodiac.   The coast of the Kenaï
peninsula between Cape Elizabeth and Prince William Sound was evidently
laid down from Vancouver's chart, but its corrections in Prince William
Sound have been entirely ignored.   The compilation of the general chart must
have been entrusted to incompetent hands, without being revised by any one
familiar with Portlock's notes and surveys.

plates and medals, "to mark the extent of Russia's domain." [22]

On the 2d of May the ship put to sea, and three days later made Cape Clear, the southernmost point of Montague Island.[23] No safe anchorage was found until the 10th, when the *Trekh Sviatiteli* entered the capacious harbor of Nuchek or Hinchinbrook Island. On the same day an exploring party was sent out in boats, and on the northern side of the island a wooden cross was erected with an inscription claiming the country as Russian territory.[24]

The events of 1787–8 must have been puzzling to the natives of Prince William Sound. Englishmen under the English flag, Englishmen under the Portuguese flag, Spaniards and Russians, were cruising about, often within a few miles of each other, taking possession, for one nation or the other, of all the land in sight. The *Princesa* from Mexico appears to have left Nuchek two days before the Russians arrived there; the *Prince of Wales*, Captain Hutchins, must have been at anchor in Spring Corner Cove about the same time, and shortly after the *Iphigenia*, Captain Douglas, entered the same cove,[25] while Portlock left traces near by two months later. Douglas touched the southern part of Alaska also in the following year, and sought to acquire fame by renaming Dixon Entrance after himself.

Bocharof carefully surveyed the inner harbor, the Brook Cove of Portlock, and named it St Constantine and St Helena, after the day of arrival. On the 27th of May the *Trekh Sviatiteli* returned to the coast of Montague Island. Some trading was done here de-

---

[22] *Shelikof, Putesh.*, ii. 2, 3.

[23] The two navigators declared that this was the Cape St Elias of Bering, without any apparent basis for their opinion and without considering that in such a case the Russian discoverer could never have been within thirty miles of the American continent.

[24] At its fort a copper plate was buried, proclaiming the same. *Id.*, ii. 7.

[25] The latter found the following inscriptions cut into the bark of two trees: 'Z. Etches of the *Prince of Wales*, May 9, 1788,' and 'John Hutchins.' *Meares' Voy.*, 316.

spite the presence of the English who paid such prices
as the Russians never dreamed of.[26]

By advice of a native Ismaïlof proceeded to Achakoo
Island,[27] some distance to the southward, which was
described as abounding in sea-otters. Not finding a
harbor he landed in a boat with seventeen men and a
Chugatsch pilot. After trading amicably for some
time the commander sent off a party of eight men to
gather eggs on the cliffs, but they soon came back
reporting that several bidars filled with Chugatsches
were approaching. This aroused suspicion among the
promyshleniki, and their alarm was increased by the
discovery that the Chugatsch guide had disappeared.
The chief in command of the native hunting party
professed to have no knowledge of the deserter, and
offered to go in search of him with five Russians in a
bidar. Four of these men the cunning savage sent
into the interior upon a false trail, and then drawing
a spear from under his parka he attacked the remaining Russian with great fury. One of the other men
returned to assist his comrade, but both had a severe
struggle with the savage, who was at last despatched
with a musket ball.[28] As soon as the others returned
the party hurried on board, the anchor was raised,
and all speed was made to depart.

On the 1st of June the *Trekh Sviatiteli* arrived at
the island of Kyak,[29] which was uninhabited, though
the natives from the mainland came at times to hunt
sea-otters and foxes. The adjoining coast was thoroughly explored, but the inhabitants fled in alarm,
abandoning their huts and canoes whenever the clumsy
boats of the Russians came in sight. After a slow
advance easterly, the large bay of Yakutat was reached
on the 11th of June. Here the chief of the Thlin-

[26] They found the chiefs rather diffident in accepting one of the Russian
medals sent out by Governor Jacobi. The presence of a Spanish *fragata* on
the other side of the Island may have had something to do with it.
[27] Ochek of Russian charts and Middleton Island of Vancouver.
[28] *Shelikof, Putesh.,* ii. 29–31.
[29] Koniak in *Ismailof's Journal;* Kaye of Cook. *Pallas, Neue Nordische
Beiträge,* v. 211.

keet nation made his appearance, having travelled up
the coast from his winter residence at Chilkaht with a
retinue of over two hundred warriors including two
of his sons. Intercourse was carried on with great
caution, but in trading Ismaïlof was much more successful than Dixon. In addition to his purchases he
obtained a large number of skins from his Kadiak
hunters, who in their bidarkas could go far out to sea,
where the open wooden canoes of the Thlinkeets did
not dare to follow. In order to draw attention from
this rivalry ceremonious visits and exchange of presents were kept up. The Russian commander could
not have failed to hear of Dixon's visit, but not a
word about it can be found in his journal. In this
he probably obeyed instructions, for even business
letters from the islands to Siberia were in those
days frequently tampered with by the authorities of
Okhotsk and Kamchatka, and it was the interest of
Shelikof and his partners to have English claims to
prior occupation ignored.

Ismaïlof dwells much upon his efforts to induce the
Thlinkeet chiefs to place themselves under the protection of Russia, and before leaving he presented to
Chief Ilkhak the portrait of Tsarovich Paul " at his
earnest request," and decorated him with one of the
medals sent out by the governor general of Siberia.
Copper plates inscribed "Possession of the Russian
Empire" were also buried on two points on the bay.[30]
Two enslaved boys of the Chugatsch and Chilkaht
tribes were purchased, who proved of great service
as interpreters, and in giving information concerning
the coast southward and eastward.

From Yakutat the *Trekh Sviatiteli* proceeded eastward in search of another harbor. The Chugatsch boy
acted as pilot and pointed out the mouths of several
rivers, but no landing-place was discovered until the

---

[30] Two years later not a trace could be found of portraits, medal, or copper plates, which makes it appear that Ilkhak's respect for the Russian imperial family was not as great as represented. *Ismaïlof's Journal*, 14–15.

third day, when the vessel entered Ltua Bay or Port des Français. Trade was quite active here for some days, and in the mean time Ismaïlof carried out his secret instructions by establishing marks of Russian occupation at various points, and perhaps destroying the monument left by La Pérouse.[31]

The results of Ismaïlof's explorations during the summer of 1788 were of sufficient importance to stimulate Delarof to further attempts in the same direction, but before following these it is necessary to turn our attention to a visit of the Spaniards in the same year.

Roused by the reports of La Pérouse and others concerning the spread of Russian settlements in the far north, and the influx of English and other trading vessels, the Spanish government in 1787 ordered the viceroy of Mexico to despatch at once an expedition to verify these accounts and examine the north-western coast for places that might be desirable of occupation in anticipation of foreign designs. On March 8, 1788, accordingly the fragata *Princesa* and the paquebot *San Cárlos*, under Alférez Estévan José Martinez and the pilot Gonzalo Lopez de Haro, set sail from San Blas, with the additional instructions to ascend to latitude 61° and examine the coast down to Monterey; to avoid all trouble with the Russians, and to conciliate native chiefs with gifts and promises.[32]

[31] No reference is made in his journal to the tablets and monument placed by the French, though he was informed by the natives of the visit of two large ships to the harbor and saw many tools and implements marked with the royal *fleur de lis*. A small anchor similarly marked was secured. The reports of Ismaïlof and Bocharof have been preserved in their original bad spelling and grammar, not easy to imitate, and we must therefore presume that they were written in the unsatisfactory and fragmentary shape in which we find them.

[32] A man should, if possible, be obtained from each tribe speaking a distinct tongue, as interpreter; frequent landings must be made for exploration and taking possession; Russian establishments must be closely inspected to ascertain their strength, object, etc. 'No deberán empeñar lance alguno con los buques rusos ó de otra nacion.' Provisions were taken for 15 months. It was at first proposed to send the fragatas *Concepcion* and *Favorita*, under Teniente Camacho and Alférez Maurelle, but sickness and delays caused the change to be made. For details of instructions, etc., see *Cuarta exploracion de*

Without touching any intermediate point they arrived before Prince William Sound May 17th, anchoring eleven days later on the north side of Montague Island in a good harbor, which was named Puerto de Flores. Here they took possession and remained till the 15th of June in friendly intercourse with the natives, while the boats were sent out to explore in the vicinity.[33] Without further effort to examine the sound, Martinez turned south-eastward, sighting the Miranda volcano on the 24th of June, and anchoring at the east point of Trinity Island three days later. Shelikof Strait was named Canal de Flores.[34] Meanwhile Haro, who had lost sight of the consort vessel, sailed close along the east coast of Kadiak, and notified by a native of the Russian colony at Three Saints he visited it, and entertained the officers in return.

Delarof, the chief of the colony, understood the object of the Spaniards, and took the opportunity to impress upon them that the tsar had firmly established his domain in this quarter as far as latitude 52° by means of six settlements with over four hundred men, who controlled six coast vessels and were regularly supplied and visited by three others. It was also proposed to found a station at Nootka in the following year.[35] In the interest of ruler and employers this

descubrimientos de la costa setentrional de California hasta los 61 grados... por...José Martinez...1788, in Viages al Norte, MS., No. vii.

[33] No Russians were met; yet a log-house was found in a bay near the north end of the island, probably a relic of Zaïkof's wintering four years before. Martinez long persisted in declaring that the entrance here did not lead to Prince William Sound.

[34] The east point of Trinity was called Florida Blanca. A taciturn Russian who had lived there for nine years, came on board and offered to care for the cross erected by the Spaniards.

[35] Delarof had 60 Russians and 2 galeotas at his place; at Cabo de Rada were 37 men; at Cape Elizabeth, 40 men; on a small island in Canal de Flores, latitude 58°, 40 men; a reënforcement of 70 men had sailed for Cook Inlet to sustain the establishment there; in latitude 52° 20' on the continent were 55 men and one galeota; at Unalaska, 120 men with two galeotas. Total, six establishments with six galeotas and 422 men, besides a galeota with 40 men, which annually sailed on the coast as far as Nootka, gathering furs and storing them in two magazines at Prince William Sound. Every other year two fragatas came from Siberia with men and supplies, going as far as Nootka and replacing the men whose term of service had expired. Cuarta Explor., in Viajes al Norte, MS., pt. vii. 309–10. Delarof's stories were readily believed

exaggeration of facts seemed perfectly proper, and it assisted no doubt to reconcile.the Spanish government to Russian occupation in the extreme north, but the hint about a projected establishment at Nootka assisted greatly to precipitate active measures by Spain, which resulted only in a humiliating withdrawal on her part in favor of a stronger and more determined power, which effectually checked the advance of Russia. The wily Greek overreached himself.

Haro now rejoined his leader, and both vessels left on July 5th for Unalaska.[36] While anchoring off its northern point, Martinez on July 21st took possession in the name of Spain, and was shortly after visited by Russians from the station on the eastern side of the island, to which the vessels now proceeded.[37] Here they remained till August 18th, caring for the sick and taking in supplies, with the kind assistance of Potap Zaïkof, the commandant. Martinez considered the season too far advanced to explore the coast eastward, or even to seek Nootka, and all speed was thereupon made for the south, the *Princesa* stopping at Monterey, in California, to recruit, while Haro lingered for a time round the islands with half an intention to do something more toward the fulfilment of the orders from Mexico, and then hurried straight to San Blas to cover faintheartedness and neglect under the plea probably that the knowledge obtained from Russians of their doings and intentions, and of the frequency of foreign visits, made coast exploration less needful under the circumstances, while it was above all urgent to impart the news to the governor.[38]

by Haro, whose liking for the commandant was greatly influenced by the similarity of his name, in its original Greek form, to his own.

[36] Lighting a group called del Fuegos, the Shumagin Islands, and 'el cabo donde dijeron los rusos de Kodiac que habia vn establecimiento de 55 indivi- duos y una galeota sobre la costa firme en 52° 20'.' *Id.*, 312; but this must be a misunderstanding. On the 11th they anchored off an island recorded as Kodiac, and on the 16th they sight the active volcano on Unimak.

[37] The *Princesa* entered on July 28th; the *San Cárlos*, again separated, rejoined her a week later. There were 120 men at this place.

[38] On reporting the despatch of the present expedition, Viceroy Flores expressed himself to the king as if he expected that Russians would have to

The indiscreet hint of Delarof was not lost at Mexico, for Viceroy Flores resolved at once to send back Martinez and Haro to secure Nootka, at least, from Russian and other intruders, and thence to extend Spanish settlement if the king should so direct. This expedition, and the momentous question to which it gave rise, have been fully considered in my *History of the Northwest Coast.*

While in occupation of Nootka the Spaniards made several exploring tours, and one of these, under Lieutenant Salvador Fidalgo, was directed to complete what Martinez had left undone by examining the coast from latitude 60° southward. He was provided with Russian and English interpreters. He set sail from Nootka on May 4, 1790, in the paquebot *Filipino*, and entered Prince William Sound on the 23d, taking the vessel into the nearest large bay on the eastern side, which was named Menendez. After exploring its shores till June 9th he proceeded northward, naming successively the bays of Gravina, Rivella Gigedo,[39] Mazarredo, and Valdés. After more than one detention from fogs and gales Fidalgo passed round to Cook Inlet in the begining of July, and was piloted into Coal Harbor which he chose to name Puerto de Revilla Gigedo.[40]

Learning of the arrival of Billings' expedition at Kadiak the Spanish commander hastened forth on August 8th to meet it, but came too late. After a short interview with Delarof he turned eastward with a view to reach the continental coast and explore it as

be ousted by force. *Id.*, 291. Bustamante assumes that the strength of the Russians alone kept the Spaniards back. *Cavo, Tres Siglos*, iii. 148–9.

[39] At the head of this bay the movements of glaciers was attributed to an active volcano which received the name of Fidalgo; the isle at the entrance to the bay was called del Conde. On the western side Port Santiago was entered. The north end of the sound is placed in 61° 10'. The Indians proved very friendly, assisting both with provisions and labor.

[40] Without paying attention to the reports of previous Spanish explorers Fidalgo caused the Cape Elizabeth of Cook to be explored anew, and finding it an isle, with a harbor to the northeast, he applied fresh names. Two points to the west and north in the inlet were called Gaston and Cuadra. Below Cape Elizabeth was observed Camacho Island.

HIST. ALASKA. 18

Charlotte Island, where his most valuable explorations were made during a vain effort to find better trade.[47] Several other traders visited the southern shores of Alaska during these and following years, but the few records left of their movements concern chiefly my *History of the Northwest Coast*, to which I refer the reader for text as well as maps.

The result of the Nootka controversy, brought about by hasty action of the Spaniards, as well as the belief in an interoceanic passage, revived by Buache and others, and supported by the revelation of numerous channels all along the Northwest Coast, determined the English government to send an expedition to this region. The explorations of Cook west and north of latitude 60° were deemed conclusive, but below this point they required to be completed and verified. This commission was entrusted to George Vancouver, who departed from England in April 1791 in the sloop *Discovery* of twenty guns, accompanied by the tender *Chatham* of ten guns, under Lieutenant W. R. Broughton. The year 1792 was spent in explorations south of the Alaska line, but in July 1793 the expedition reached the entrance of Portland Inlet and sent boats to examine its two branches. The dawning hope of here finding Fonte's passage was quickly dissipated, and the boats proceeded northward through Behm Canal. On descending its southwestern turn along Revilla Gigedo Island, as it was now shown to be, Vancouver had a narrow escape from a party of natives who attacked his boat with muskets and other weapons. The prompt appearance of the second boat changed the turn of affairs. The party now passed into Duke of Clarence Strait—named by Caamaño after Admiral Fonte—and returned to the ships.[48]

[47] As related in *Hist. Northwest Coast*, i., this series. *Marchand, Voyage autour du Monde*, i. 288–92; ii. 1 et seq. The natives of Norfolk Sound are spoken of as extremely immoral.

[48] The names applied on the map along this tour are Portland Inlet and its

These proceeded August 17th up the last named strait to Port Protection on the north end of Prince of Wales Island, which was reached September 8th, after an intermediate stay at Port Stewart. The boats meanwhile explored past Cape Caamaño, the highest point reached by the Spanish explorer of this name, and up Prince Ernest Sound round Duke of York Island, which later discoveries dissolved into a group. The mouth of the Stikeen was observed, but not as the outlet of a large stream.[40] The season now well advanced, it was resolved to terminate the extensive surveys for the season and seek a well earned rest in sunnier latitudes.

Vancouver congratulated himself that " there would no longer remain a doubt as to the extent or the fallacy of the pretended discoveries said to have been made by De Fuca and De Fonte." He had demonstrated that the continent, with a range of mountains broken by rivers alone, extended from Columbia River to beyond the northern extreme of Prince of Wales Island. To the part of the main below Pitt Archipelago he applied the names of New Hanover and New Georgia; thence to the northern line of the present survey, New Cornwall.

On the 21st of September the vessels left Port Protection, and passed Port Bucareli, southward by way of Nootka and California to the Hawaiian Islands, there to winter. On March 15, 1794, sails were again

two branches, Portland Canal and Observatory Inlet, the latter examined shortly before by Mr Brown of the *Butterworth;* Bocas de Quadra; Behm Canal, in honor of the Kamchatkan governor who showed attention to Cook's expedition in 1779; the points at its entrance were called Sykes and Álava, the latter after the commandant at Nootka. Along this canal: New Eddystone rock—resembling a lighthouse—Walker Cove, Burrough Bay, Traitor Cove—to commemorate the attack by natives—Port Stewart and Beaton Island; Point Vallenar, the north end of Gravina Island, and Cape Northumberland, its south point, besides a number of intermediate promontories.

⁴⁹ Along the east side of Prince of Wales Island and its adjoining parts are marked Moira Sound, Wedge Island, Cholmondeley Sound, Port Grindall. The entrance to Prince Ernest Sound is marked by points Onslow and Le Mesurier, and along its course are Bradfield Canal, and Duncan Canal. Along the western extension of Duke of Clarence Strait, Point Baker forming the north end of Prince of Wales Island, Conclusion Island, and Affleck Canal; below lie Coronation and Warren Islands, the latter facing Cape Pole.

set for the north, and on April 5th Trinity Island was sighted.[50] Seven days later the *Discovery* entered Cook Inlet and proceeded northward to its very head. Finding that it was not the mouth of a large river as Cook had supposed, a fact well known to the Russians, Vancouver changed the name to its present form. The *Chatham* having arrived, both vessels visited the factory half way up the inlet in charge of Zaïkof,[51] and rounded Cape Elizabeth May 14th, en route for Prince William Sound, where anchor was cast in Port Chalmers on the west side of Montague Island. Boats were now sent out to examine the sound and adjoining lands, and the *Chatham* proceeded to survey the main coast to Yakutat Bay, there to await the *Discovery*.

The survey of the sound resulted in a number of corrections, notably on the maps of Cook, yet Spanish and other existing nomenclature was as a rule maintained. Aid was also obtained from Russian material from which source the configuration of Kadiak Island and the region westward had to be adopted.[52] The Russians under Baranof, who resided on Kadiak and controlled chiefly establishments along the sea border, observed greater reticence, as noticed in connection with Ismaïlof's exploration; but those of the other company, occupying Cook Inlet and Hinchinbrook Island, were more communicative. They admitted that the easternmost factory was on this island, though trading expeditions roamed beyond toward Nootka. The total force employed was about four hundred, independent of native employés. The abo-

[50] On the 3d Akamok Island was sighted and named after Chirikof.

[51] A smaller factory existed higher up on the opposite western side. Alexandrovsk escaped observation. Names were applied to several points along the coasts and at the head, and the harbor at Cape Elizabeth was renamed Port Chatham. The portage from Turn-again Arm to Prince William Sound was noticed.

[52] Among the names added to the Sound chart, were Port Bainbridge, Passage Canal, and Port Wells, where the supposed volcano of the Spanish expedition is referred to merely as a moving glacier. One of the inlets received the name of Fidalgo, to commemorate his exploration. The island north-east of Hinchinbrook was called Hawkins. Copper River received no place on the chart. The waters of the sound were found to have encroached rapidly on the shore line during the past decade.

riginal population appeared exceedingly scanty, especially on the sound. Vancouver "clearly understood
that the Russian government had little to do with
these settlements; that they were solely under the
direction and support of independent mercantile companies," whose members appeared to live highly contented among the natives, exercising over them an
influence due not to fear but to affection, and fostered
by training the children in the Russian language and
customs.[53]

The *Discovery* left the sound June 20th to join the
consort vessel,[54] which was observed in Yakutat Bay
and instructed to follow. This bay was named after
Bering "from a conviction of its being the place that
Beering had visited."[55] A Russian party under Purtof, with nearly a thousand natives from Kadiak and
Cook Inlet, hunted here at the time, though amidst
many apprehensions, owing to the rather unfriendly
attitude of the inhabitants. Near by appeared the
Jackall, Captain Brown, cruising along this coast for
the third consecutive season.[56]

Cross Sound was entered on July 7th, and anchor
cast in Port Althorp, on the north end of Chichagof
Island, called after King George by Vancouver. From
here a boat explored Lynn Canal[57] which almost
touches the headwaters of the mighty Yukon, and

[53] *Vancouver's Voy.*, iii. 199–201. The natives of the sound were not so
docile, yet hardly less trusted by the Russians. This assimilation of the two
peoples must give the Russians a decided 'advantage over all other civilized
nations' for controlling trade.

[54] Cape St Elias of Kyak Island was renamed Cape Hamond; and lower
on the coast names were applied to several points.

[55] The Bering Bay as located by Cook was voted a mistake. While applying this name to Yakutat, Mulgrave was retained for the harbor on its south
shore. The points at the entrance to the bay received the names Manby and
Phipps. Port des Français was missed. As the *Chatham* was leaving Kyak
Island a letter came from Shields, the English shipbuilder employed by Shelikof, offering his services. It was too late to turn back for an interview with
him.

[56] Brown had sent the *Butterworth*, his leading vessel, to England in 1793,
coming to this coast in the tenders *Jackall* and *Prince le Boo*. He now turned
for Cross Sound, with whose inlets he was well acquainted. *Id.*, 207.

[57] So named after Vancouver's birth-place in Norfolk. Berners Bay, Hood
Bay, Port Frederick, and a number of capes were named, notably capes Spencer and Cross at the entrance of Cross Sound.

CHAPTER XIII.

THE BILLINGS SCIENTIFIC EXPEDITION.

1785-1793.

FLATTERING PROSPECTS—COSTLY OUTFIT—THE USUAL YEARS OF PREPARA-
TION—AN EXPECTANT WORLD TO BE ENLIGHTENED—GATHERING OF
THE EXPEDITION AT KAMCHATKA—DIVERS WINTERINGS AND SHIP-BUILD-
ING—PRELIMINARY SURVEYS NORTH AND SOUTH—AT UNALASKA AND
KADIAK—RUSSIAN REWARDS—PERIODIC PROMOTION OF BILLINGS—AT
ST LAWRENCE ISLAND—BILLINGS' LAND JOURNEY—WRETCHED CONDI-
TION OF RUSSIAN HUNTERS—END OF THE TRIBUTE SYSTEM—RESULT
OF THE EXPEDITION—SARYCHEF'S SURVEYS—SHELIKOF'S DUPLICITY—
PRIESTLY PERFORMANCE.

THE most promising of all scientific exploring expeditions undertaken by the Russian government for
the acquisition of a more perfect knowledge of its
new possessions in Asia and America was that commanded by Captain Joseph Billings, an Englishman
who had served under Cook. The enterprise was
stimulated by the report of La Pérouse's departure
upon a similar errand. The empress issued an oukaz
on the 8th of August 1785, appointing Billings to
the command of "A Secret Astronomical and Geographical Expedition for navigating the Frozen Sea,
describing its Coasts, and ascertaining the Situation
of the Islands in the Seas between the two Continents
of Asia and America."[1]

The senate and admiralty college confirmed and
supplemented the appointments, and in September
Lieutenant Sarychef of the navy was despatched to
the port of Okhotsk with a party of ship-builders,
under orders to construct two vessels in accordance

---

[1] *Sauer's Geog. and Astron. Exped.*, 1.

with plans furnished by another Englishman, Mr Lamb Yeames. The governor general of Irkutsk and Kolivansk had received instructions to furnish the necessary material.

Captain Billings set out upon his journey a few weeks later, accompanied by Lieutenant Hall, Surgeon Robeck, Master Batakof of the navy, and Martin Sauer, secretary of the expedition.[2]

The party did not leave Irkutsk until the 9th of May 1786. Two medical officers and naturalists were added at the last moment—a German, Dr. Merck, with an English assistant, John Main.

On the 29th the expedition arrived at Yakutsk, where the necessary arrangements had been made for supplies of provisions and stores and the required means of transportation for the different divisions to the mouth of the Kovima or Kolima river and to Okhotsk. Lieutenant Hall was in command of the latter and Lieutenant Bering of the former. Lieutenant Hall's division arrived at Okhotsk soon after Billings and a few attendants had reached that seaport on the 3d of July. As it was found that more time would be consumed in building the ships than had been expected, Billings took some steps with a view of visiting the Chukchi country first, and to that end placed himself in communication with Captain Shmalef who was much respected by both Kamchatkans and Chukchi. On the 3d of August all the officers, with the exception of Lieutenant Hall, set

[2] Sauer gives the personnel of the expedition, as it departed from St Petersburg, as follows: Joseph Billings, commander; lieutenants, Robert Hall, Gavril Sarychef, and Christian Bering, a nephew of Vitus Bering; Master Afanassia Bakof, rigger and store-keeper; masters Anton Batkhof and Sergeï Bronnikof; surgeons, Michael Robeck and Peter Allegretti; draughtsman, Luka Voronin; one mechanician, two ship-builders, two surgeon's mates, one master's mate; one boatswain; three 'court hunters' for stuffing birds, etc.; eight petty officers, seven soldiers, riflemen, and Martin Sauer as private secretary and journalist. At Irkutsk the following additions were made: two Russian book-keepers and accountants, Vassily Diakonof and Feodor Karpof; Lieutenant Polossof of the army, who was acquainted with the Chukchi language; six petty officers from the school of navigation at Irkutsk; three men who understood the construction of skin boats; one turner, one locksmith; fifty Cossacks commanded by a sotnik; two drummers—in all 69 men in addition to the 36 from St Petersburg. *Id.*, 12, 13.

out for the Kovima River, the last named taking the place of Lieutenant Sarychef in superintending the construction of the ships.   Toward the end of September Billings and his party arrived at Verkhnoi Kovima, but only to find that winter had already set in with great severity, and to meet with almost insurmountable difficulties in obtaining shelter and supplies.   The sufferings during the winter were very great on account of the extreme cold as well as the scarcity of provisions; but better times came with spring.

The work of preparing for the northward trip was never relaxed, and on the 25th of May 1787 the main body of the expedition set out on two vessels which had been constructed during the winter, the *Pallas* and the *Yasatchnoi.*   Near the mouth of the river Captain Shmalef was found awaiting them with some guides and interpreters and a large quantity of dried reindeer meat.   The ostrog Nishnekovima was reached on the 17th of June.   There more deer-meat was procured and then the expedition passed on into the Arctic.[3]

They steered eastward and on the 21st of June reached the place where Shalanrof had perished in 1762.   A cross marked the spot, and another was found near the remains of huts erected by Laptief and his party in 1739.   Their progress was continued with many interruptions until the 25th of July, when an observation showed latitude 69° 35′ 56″, longitude, 168° 54′, and Billings concluded to give up all further attempts and return to Nishnekovima.[4]

When the party arrived at Yakutsk it was found

[3] In accordance with the imperial oukaz Billings here assumed the rank of a fleet captain of the second class, the necessary oath being administered by a priest brought for that purpose. *Id.,* 69–70.

[4] Sauer and many of the officers were of the opinion that everything looked favorable for a passage into the Pacific.   Captain Sarychef even offered to undertake the enterprise in an open bidar, with six men, intending to camp on the beach every night, but Billings was deaf to all entreaties and contented himself with inducing a majority of his officers to sign a statement that it would be wiser to return to the Kovima. *Id.,* 77–8.

that a large quantity of the most important stores was still awaiting transportation at Irkutsk, necessitating a journey to that city on the part of Billings and several of his officers. This little excursion delayed the expedition till September 1788, when the greater part of the command was once more assembled at Okhotsk. The first and largest of the two vessels destined for the voyage was not launched until the following July. She was named the *Slava Rossie*, Glory of Russia. The second ship, the *Dobraia Namerenia*, Good Intent, was launched in August, but was wrecked while attempting to cross the bar at Okhotsk. In order to get quickly at the iron work with which to build a new vessel the hull of the *Namerenia* was burned.[5] On the 19th of September the *Slava Rossie* sailed at last and arrived at Petropavlovsk on the 1st of October. Here the ship was unrigged and the whole party went into winter-quarters to await the arrival of a store-ship with supplies in the spring.

Early in March 1790 additional news arrived, warning Billings of the presence of a Swedish cruiser, the *Mercury*, Captain Coxe, with sixteen guns, in the waters he was about to navigate.[6] The *Slava Rossie* mounted sixteen brass guns, but they were only three-pounders. Despite the apprehension created, no change was made in the plans.

On the 1st of May the whole expedition embarked and stood out to sea on an easterly course. The voyage was tedious, no land being sighted till the 22d, when the island of Amchitka appeared in the north. On the 1st of June the island of Unalaska was

[5] On the 14th of September a courier arrived from Russia with intelligence which almost put an end to further progress of the expedition. War had broken out with Sweden, and the Russian government was much in want of money and naval officers. *Id.*, 143.

[6] Pribylof reported that the Swedish cruiser mentioned in Billings' instructions had actually visited the Aleutian Islands during the summer, but in view of the abject misery and privations in which he found the Russian traders living, the humane Captain Coxe abstained from hostilities and even made Pribylof, whom he had questioned concerning the Russian establishments, very acceptable presents of bread, brandy, some clothing, and a quadrant. *Id.*, 212.

made, and on the 3d some natives came on board, followed in the afternoon by a Russian in an eight-oar bidar. The latter conducted the vessel into Bob-rovoi (Beaver) Bay. Here a supply of water and ballast was procured and on the 13th of June the expedition sailed again to the north-east and north.[7]

In a few days Sannakh and the Shumagin Island were reached,[8] where the *Slava Rossie* was visited by a large party of Aleuts who were hunting for the Panof company under superintendence of a Russian. On the 26th of June a Russian boarded the ship; he was accompanied by two hundred natives and came from Shelikof's establishment on Kadiak Island. On the 29th the expedition arrived in Trekh Sviatiteli, or Three Saints Harbor, the site of the first permanent settlement on the island. Eustrate Ivanovich Delarof was then in command of the colony. He told Sauer that he had despatched that year six hundred double bidarkas, each manned by two or three natives, to hunt sea-otters, sea-lions, and fur-seal; they were divided into six parties, each in charge of a Russian peredovchik.[9]

The establishment at that time consisted of about fifty Russians, including officers of the company and Master Ismaïlof, the same whom Cook met at Una-laska in 1778. He was stationed at Three Saints to look after the interests of the government. The buildings numbered five of Russian construction, the barracks, offices, and counting-house, besides store-houses, blacksmith, carpenter, and cooper shops, and a ropewalk. Two vessels of about eighty tons each

---

[7] Sauer states that the Russians then on that part of the island belonged to Cherepanof's company, who had resided there eight years and expected to be relieved that season by a party from Okhotsk. The author dwells upon the cruel treatment of the Aleuts at the hands of the ignorant and overbearing promyshleniki. *Id.*, 150-61.

[8] Though writing soon after Bering's and Steller's reports were published, Sauer states that these islands received their name from the 'discoverer, a Russian sailor of Bering's expedition.' The poor fellow did nothing beyond dying of scurvy in that neighborhood.

[9] *Juvenal's Jour.*, MS., 1 et seq. Sauer bestows the highest praise upon the strict justice and humanity with which Delarof managed the affairs of the colony. *Sauer's Geog. and Astron. Exped.*, 170-1.

stood upon the beach, armed and well guarded, serving as a place of refuge in case of attack. Several gardens planted with cabbage and potatoes, and some cows and goats, added to the comfort of the settlers.[10]

In the report of Billings' visit to Kadiak mention is made of the water-route across the Alaska peninsula by way of Iliamna Lake. The natives persisted in calling the peninsula an island, *kikhtak*, because they could pass in their canoes, without portage, from Shelikof Strait into Bristol Bay, their main source for supplies of walrus ivory for spear-heads, fish-hooks, and various implements.

The astronomical tent, and another constituting a portable church, had been pitched as soon as the expedition arrived, and remained standing till the 6th of July, when the *Slava Rossie* once more set sail. Delarof accompanied Billings for the purpose of visiting a Spanish frigate reported by the natives to be cruising at the mouth of Cook Inlet.[11] The commander of the expedition also intended to visit the Spanish ship, but the wind was unfavorable, and by the 8th of July they had only reached the island of Afognak where a settlement had already existed. On the 12th of July, in the neighborhood of Barren Islands, Delarof left the *Slava Rossie* in a canoe, giving up all hope of reaching Cook's Inlet with the ship. He was intrusted with messages for the Spaniards and the vessel was headed for Prince William Sound.

On the 19th of July the *Slava Rossie* was anchored

[10] During the stay of the *Slava Rossie* at Three Saints Bay one of the officers of the company applied to the priest accompanying the expedition to baptize a native woman with whom he had been living several years and had children; they were then formally married, and Sauer speaks with much satisfaction of the excellent manner in which their household affairs were managed. From the promyshleniki and sailors in employ of the company much complaint was heard of the high prices they were obliged to pay the company for the very necessaries of life, making it almost impossible to live without becoming indebted to their employers. *Id.*, 173.

[11] On this occasion Sauer makes an evidently erroneous statement to the effect that he was informed the Spaniards were in the habit of visiting the Russian settlements annually, exchanging provisions and sea-otter skins for hardware and linen. *Id.*, 184; *Jurenal's Jour.*, MS., 50 et seq.

in the same bay of Montague or Tzaklie Island where Cook passed some time in 1778. The astronomical tent was at once erected on shore under a sufficient guard, while boat parties set out to explore. The natives were quite peaceable in view of the formidable armament of the *Slava Rossie*, but they made bitter complaints against Russian traders who had formerly visited them, especially the party under Polutof in 1783. They were assured that they need not apprehend any ill-treatment from government vessels carrying the same flag as the *Slava Rossie*. It was found necessary, however, to exercise the greatest vigilance to prevent them from stealing.[12]

While at this anchorage, Captain Billings, who thought he had reached the Cape St Elias discovered by Bering, assumed, in accordance with his instructions, an additional rank, the customary oath being administered by the priest attached to the expedition. Sauer ridiculed this theory and located Cape St Elias to his own satisfaction on Kaye Island.

Lieutenant Sarychef went out with a boat's crew, and during an absence of three days he met several parties of natives and saw the cross erected by Zaïkof under Shelikof's order. On one occasion the crafty natives endeavored to entice him into a shallow channel where his boat would be left grounded by the tide and his party exposed to attack. The device did not succeed, however, and Sarychef heard of the danger he had escaped only after his return to Okhotsk, from the Aleut interpreter. After Sarychef's return to the ship a very old native came on board and stated that his home was on Kaye Island which he plainly described. With regard to the number and nation-

---

[12] Sauer states that on one occasion, when Billings entertained some of the natives in his tent on shore, the servant set down a tray in such a manner that a corner of it, containing some spoons, protruded from under the canvas. One of the natives attempted to appropriate the spoons, but a water-spaniel lying in the tent sprang at him, seized the hand holding the plunder, and held the thief until ordered to relinquish his hold—a circumstance which, in Sauer's opinion, thereafter 'kept them (the natives) honest afterwards in the dog's presence.' *Sauer's Geog. and Astron. Exped.*, 188.

ality of ships that had visited his people, he was not positive, but remembered well that when he was a boy a ship had approached Kaye Island for the first time. When a boat was sent ashore the natives fled into the interior, returning only after their visitors had departed. They found their domiciles despoiled of many articles and some provisions, while some beads, tobacco, and iron kettles had been deposited in their place. As this account corresponds altogether with Steller's report of Khitrof's landing in 1741, Sauer and Sarychef came at once to the conclusion that Kaye Island must be the locality of Bering's discovery.

Sauer conceived a wild plan of remaining alone among the natives of Prince William Sound to carry on explorations, with a faint hope of discovering the long sought for passage into the northern Atlantic. Billings very properly refused to sanction the plan, much to the chagrin of his Quixotic secretary.

A few good spars were secured for the ship and a small supply of fresh fish, and on the 1st of August a council of officers came to the conclusion that it was best to return to Kamchatka. The stock of provisions was not sufficient to maintain the whole company during the winter in a country apparently without any reliable natural resources; the season was far advanced and it appeared scarcely safe to continue the work of surveying in an almost unknown region with a single vessel. A south-westerly course was adopted, but the winds were adverse, and by the beginning of September the *Slava Rossie* was still tossing about in unknown seas, unable to obtain any correct observations. A squall carried away the foremast and other spars and it was found impossible to touch at Unalaska to replenish the water-casks and land the Aleut interpreters. On the 24th of September one of the latter attempted suicide by cutting his throat, despairing of ever seeing his country again. The supply of water and provisions was almost exhausted and they had reasons to believe themselves still many hundred miles from the coast of Kamchatka; but in spite of the many evils threatening him on every side Billings continued upon his course, and at last, on the 14th of October, the *Slava Rossie* entered the Bay of Avatcha, with a large part of her crew suffering from scurvy.

The remainder of the expedition had arrived from Okhotsk during the summer, bringing the iron and other material saved from the wrecked *Dobraia Namerenia*, and the first thing to be done was to build another ship. The ship-carpenters and a force of men were at once despatched to Nishnekamchatsk, where suitable timber was more abundant, and the work progressed vigorously under superintendence of Captain Hall. The other officers passed most of their time at Bolsheretsk in the enjoyment of social intercourse with the families of government officers and merchants.

One of the navigators attached to the expedition, named Bronnikof, having died during the summer, Billings engaged in his stead Gerassim Pribylof, who in the service of the Lebedef-Lastochkin company had recently discovered the islands of St George and St Paul, the annual retreat of the fur-seals.

Early in April 1791 the members of the expedition once more assembled at Petropavlovsk, and orders were forwarded to Captain Hall, who was to command the new vessel, to meet the *Slava Rossie* at Bering Island between the 25th and 30th of May. In case of failure to meet, a second rendezvous was appointed at Unalaska.

On the 19th of May the ships sailed out of Avatcha Bay after a long detention by baffling winds. On the 28th Bering Island was made, but the weather being boisterous it was concluded not to wait for the consort, but to go on to Unalaska. The first landing was made on the island of Tanaga, where they found a village inhabited by women and a few old men, who explained that all the able-bodied hunters had been carried off to the east ward by Lukanin and his company. The people complained that this party had also taken with them many women. The Aleuts carried to Kamchatka against their will, during the last voyage, were here set ashore with no other compensation than a few articles of clothing, a little tobacco, and a brief document exempting them from compulsory services with the trading companies.

On the 25th of June the harbor of Illiuliuk on Unalaska Island was reached, but nothing had been heard of Hall and his vessel. Billings at once declared that he would give up his former intention to make a thorough exploration of Cook Inlet and vicinity, and proceed at once to St Lawrence Bay, in the Chukchi country, after depositing at Unalaska some provisions for Captain Hall with a few men to guard them.[13] Instructions were also left for the consort to immediately follow the *Slava Rossie* to St Lawrence Bay. The officers, especially Sarychef and Sauer, were greatly disappointed at this change of plans, and the latter in his journal expressed the opinion that too rapid promotion had an evil effect on Captain Billings, who seemed to have lost all ambition to make discoveries, and haughtily refused advice from the most experienced of his companions.[14]

After landing the men and provisions for Hall, the

---

[13] The men left there were Surgeon Allegretti, Ensign Ivan Alexeïef and one sailor. *Id.*, 229. Juvenal, *Jour.*, MS., 27 et seq., refers to the doings of the Lebedef-Lastochkin Company.

[14] Sauer uses the following strong language: 'Nothing in the world could have afforded me less satisfaction than this resolution, which I regarded as the conclusion of an expedition that was set on foot with unbounded liberality by the most magnanimous sovereign in the world; which had raised the expectation of all nations to the highest pitch, and induced mankind to anticipate the satisfaction of obtaining the most complete knowledge of the geography of this unknown part of the globe, together with a conviction of the existence or non-existence of a north-west passage. But, alas! after so many years of danger and fatigue; after putting the government to such an extraordinary expense; after having advanced so far in the attempt, even at the very time when we were in hourly expectation of our comfort, and, as appeared to me, being just entering upon the grand part of the undertaking, thus to abandon it was the most unaccountable and unjustifiable of actions.' *Sauer's Geog. and Astron. Exped.*, 230.

Slava Rossie put to sea on the 8th of July. Passing through the Pribylof and St Matthew islands, they made land on the 20th of July, which turned out to be Clerke Island (St Lawrence). Billings landed in person; the natives who had been discerned walking on the beach disappeared as soon as the boat approached the shore. The party returned in the evening, having visited some abandoned habitations and met some domesticated dogs. A party of natives crossing a lake in the direction of the ocean beach was frightened back by a musket-shot fired to warn Billings, who had strayed some distance by himself.

On the 27th of July the explorers at last caught sight of the American continent, in the vicinity of Cape Rodney. Billings, with the naturalist, draughtsman, and two other officers were landed in boats. The party made a fire of drift-wood on the beach and then dispersed in search of inhabitants. A few were found, and friendly intercourse was established by means of an Anadir Cossack who spoke the Chukchi language. The natives conducted their visitors to a temporary dwelling and treated them hospitably. The following day some trading was carried on and the explorers returned to the ship with considerable difficulty owing to stormy weather.[15]

On the 2d of August the expedition reached its highest latitude, 65° 23′ 50″, sighting the islands in mid-channel of Bering Strait, and the following day the *Slava Rossie* anchored in St Lawrence Bay. From this point Billings proposed to set out overland, with a small party, in the direction of the Kovima, while Sarychef was to take the vessel back to Unalaska. Two guides and interpreters, Kobelef and Dauerkin, had been on the coast ever since 1787, awaiting the

---

[15] A bidar, purchased from the natives, with four sailors, did not reach the ship till the 31st. The men reported that they had been cast ashore, and at daylight found themselves surrounded by a number of natives, with whom they traded, though giving them a bad character. Sauer remarks on this occasion: 'I cannot guess what articles of trade they had; but they obtained several skins of black and red foxes, martens, etc. I hope that the natives had not the greater reason to complain.' *Id.*, 247.

expedition, and Billings lost no time in perfecting preparations for his dangerous journey, taking his final departure on the 13th of August.[16]

The commander appeared confident of his purpose, but those he left on the ship by no means shared that feeling. They considered the large quantity of goods carried as presents an additional danger, which proved true according to the report of the journey. As soon as they left the coast they found themselves completely in the power of the Chukchi who were to accompany them across the country. They were led over a roundabout route and systematically robbed at every opportunity. As their store of goods decreased the insolence of the natives increased and on more than one occasion they narrowly escaped slaughter.

On the day after Billings' departure Sarychef sailed for Unalaska. The *Slava Rossie* was now but ill provided with food, water, and firewood, but anxiety on account of Hall with the consort made it necessary to steer for the Aleutian isles instead of proceeding to Petropavlovsk for supplies. The passage was comparatively short, however, and on the 28th of August they anchored once more in Illiuliuk harbor. Captain Hall had arrived there a few days after Billings' departure and sailed for St Lawrence Bay in accordance with instructions; thence he returned, arriving three days later.

The anchorage chosen for the two vessels during the winter was a longitudinal cove on the west side of Illiuliuk Bay, protected by a low island, now connected with the adjoining shore by a narrow neck. Some shops and huts for officers were erected, but the greater part of the crews remained on board of the *Slava Rossie* and the *Chernui Orel*, or Black Eagle, as Captain Hall's vessel had been named. Sauer intimates that the principal reason of the sailors for

---

[16] The company numbered 12—Capt. Billings, Dr Merck the naturalist and his assistant Mr Main, Masters Batakof and Gileïef of the navy; Varonin, the draughtsman, and Leman, surgeon's mate; the two interpreters, Kobel f and Dauerkin, and two soldiers and a boy attending on the captain. *Id.*, 255.

remaining on board was, that while on the ships they were entitled to a daily allowance of brandy which could not have been issued to them on shore. The officers doomed to pass a wretched winter in this desolate place were captains Robert Hall and Gavril Sarychef, Lieutenant Christian Bering, Surgeon-major Robeck, Surgeon Allegretti, and Bakof, Bakulin, Erling, Pribylof, and Sauer. Billings' orders had been to collect tribute from the Aleutian isles, and Hall took the necessary steps to notify the natives of his purpose. The Aleuts came voluntarily with contributions of fox and sea-otter skins, especially after it became known that the government officers generally returned the full value of the skins in trinkets. In the expectation that at least one of his ships would winter at Unalaska, Billings had given orders that stores of dried fish should be prepared, and this order had been generally obeyed by the natives; but with all that the crews of the two vessels were but poorly provided for the long, cold winter. The knowledge of the dreadful sufferings of their predecessors in that harbor, Captain Levashef and his crew, of the Krenitzin expedition, in 1768, may have hastened the coming of the scurvy; at all events, a month had not passed before several men were attacked with it, and before the end of the year one victim was buried. With the new year the disease became more violent, and toward the end of February 1792 they buried as many as three in one day. In March a change for the better set in, after seventeen of the best men had found their graves. With the greatest difficulty the two ships were brought into condition to undertake the return voyage to Petropavlovsk, but the task was at last accomplished on the 16th of May.

During the winter tribute had been collected from about five hundred natives, amounting to a dozen sea-otter skins and six hundred foxes of different kinds, and in return for these all the trinkets and tobacco, quite a large quantity, had been distributed. A party consisting of some Russians from Shelikof's establishment at Kadiak and some natives had paid a visit to the winter-quarters of the expedition in search of syphilitic remedies, brandy, and tobacco. The former they obtained from the surgeons together with proper directions for using them. The natives with this party made many complaints of ill-treatment at the hands of Russian promyshleniki, which Sauer considered well founded.[17]

The return from Unalaska was accomplished with better despatch than might have been expected from the miserable condition of the vessels. On the 7th of June the *Slava Rossie* lost sight of the *Chernui Orel*, and on the 16th the former vessel entered Avatcha Bay. An English ship, the *Halcyon*, Captain Barclay, was in the harbor, with a cargo of ironware and ship-chandlery much needed on the coast, but the stupid port authorities would not allow the captain to dispose of any of his goods.

The explorers were anxious to proceed to Okhotsk, but deeming it impracticable to enter that port with the *Slava Rossie* it was concluded to despatch the *Chernui Orel*, with as many members of the expedition as she could carry, while the remainder awaited the arrival of the annual transport vessel from Okhotsk. Shortly after the sailing of the first detachment news was received from Captain Billings and his party. They had undergone the greatest sufferings, but were then, in February 1792, on the river Angarka within a few days' march of the Kovima. The object of the dangerous journey had to a great extent been frustrated by the restrictions imposed upon the helpless explorers by the impudent Chukchi.

[17] He also says: 'Shelikof has formed a project to obtain the sole privilege of carrying on this trade without a rival, and he will probably, one day or other, succeed; but not before the scarcity of furs lessens the value of this trade and renders fresh capital necessary for making new excursions to discover other sources of commerce, or rather of wealth; then the directors of the present concern will explore the regions of Amercia, and if nothing advantageous occurs, they will doubtless retire from the concern, secure in their possessions, and leave the new members to pursue the undertaking.' *Id.*, 275-6.

They had destroyed the surveying outfit and would not allow any notes to be taken or calculations to be made. Captain Billings communicated his intention of proceeding to Yakutsk with all possible speed and desired Sauer to join him there as soon as practicable.[18]

Letters from St Petersburg were received about the same time, announcing that a French vessel, under the flag of the republic, had sailed for Petropavlovsk, and ordering that every facility of trade should be afforded to the supercargo, a M. Torckler. A few days later the ship arrived and was found to be the *La Flavia*—also heard of on the American coast—with a crew of sixty men besides the officers. Her cargo consisted chiefly of brandy. One cannot but note the difference in official action with regard to the useful cargo of iron-ware brought by Barclay the same year, and that of the *La Flavia*, consisting of the chief element of destruction and ruin among the half-savage inhabitants of that region. The French ship remained during the whole winter, retailing the cargo, for nobody in Petropavlovsk had the means to buy it in bulk. She sailed June 1, 1793, for Canton.

Thus came to an end, as far as concerns the Russian possessions in America, an expedition inaugurated on a truly magnificent scale after long years of preparation. The geographical results may be set down at next to nothing, with the exception of the thorough surveys of Captain Bay in Illiuliuk Harbor on Unalaska Island. Every other part of the work had already been done by Cook. The knowledge obtained by Billings during his march from St Lawrence Bay to the Kovima proved of no great importance, based as it was to a great extent on hearsay from the treacherous Chukchi, who would not allow any mem-

---

[18] The members of the expedition still at Petropavlovsk were Capt. Bering, Masters Bakof and Bakulin, Mr Sauer, and Surgeon-general Robeck. Major Shmalef was in command of the province. *Id.*, 285.

ber of the band to make personal observations. An important feature, however, was the preliminary experience gained by Sarychef, who subsequently published the most complete and reliable charts of the Aleutian Islands, a work upon which, as far as the territory included in Sarychef's own observations is concerned, even Tebenkof could make few if any improvements. Their reliability stands acknowledged to the present day. But few corrections have been made in his special charts of harbors by modern surveys. As far as it is possible to judge now, it seems that Martin Sauer's estimate of his commander was nearly correct, and we may concur in his opinion that the failure of the expedition in its chief objects was due to the leader's incapacity and false pride, which prevented him from accepting the advice of others well qualified and willing to give it; but there were also other reasons, as we shall see. It was almost a miracle that he did not furnish a tragic finale to a series of blunders by losing his life during his foolhardy journey through the country of the Chukchi.

The principal benefit derived from this costly undertaking was the ventilation of abuses practised by unscrupulous traders upon helpless natives. The authorities in Siberia and St Petersburg became at last convinced that an end must be put to the barbarous rule of the promyshleniki. The cheapest and easiest way to accomplish this was to grant control of the whole business with American coasts and islands to one strong company that might be held responsible to the government for its conduct. Those members of the Billings expedition who revealed the unsatisfactory state of affairs in these outlying possessions of Russia did not intend to aid Shelikof and his partners in their ambitious schemes, but such was the effect of their reports. Another result was to abolish the custom of collecting tribute from the Aleuts; the method introduced by Sarychef—to return the full value in tobacco and trinkets for skins tendered as tribute—would have effectually prevented the government from deriving any benefit from that source.

If the expedition revealed abuses it also gave rise to others. Many private individuals enriched themselves by contracts for supplying the expedition at the different stages of its progress, especially at Irkutsk, Yakutsk, and Okhotsk. Sauer mentions in his journal that on his return voyage he found the officials at Yakutsk, whom he had left in comparative poverty, in much improved circumstances, bordering upon affluence, and he ascribes the change to the fact that these people had been engaged in furnishing horses for the transportation of stores to the Kovima and to Okhotsk.

The experience gained in the way of navigation and management of similar expeditions was of some value; and in this connection it is rather a significant fact that during the first voyage of the *Slava Rossie*, under the immediate command of Billings, the scurvy was successfully combated,[19] yet in the following year the two ships had been anchored in Illiuliuk harbor but a few weeks when the dreaded disease broke out with such violence that the combined efforts of Sarychef and Hall, two medical men, and Martin Sauer failed to arrest its ravages.

With regard to the supplementary instructions relative to the Swedish cruiser *Mercury*, nothing was done by Billings, though the vessel did visit the Aleutian Islands according to the report of Pribylof. The apprehensions on this account seem to have been great. A set of minute instructions was furnished to traders on the islands, to regulate their conduct in case the privateer appeared, but in Pribylof's intercourse with

---

[19] Billings, formerly of Cook's expedition, had evidently learned something of that navigator's effective method of combating the scurvy. The surgeon's journal contains the following remarks: 'It was only toward the end of the voyage, when our bread was out and we were reduced to a short allowance of water, that the scurvy made its appearance. At this time pease and grits, boiled to a thick consistency in a small quantity of water, and buttered, were substituted for salted provisions. The primary symptoms of scurvy then appeared, but on arriving at Petropavlovsk a treatment of bleeding, thin drink, and fresh fish restored all hands in a very short time.' *Id.*, 208–9.

Captain Coxe, the former did not use any of the precautions enjoined.[20]

The hand of the future monopolists can be discerned, shaping events, from a period preceding that of Billings' expedition, though perhaps Martin Sauer was not able to see it. Notwithstanding his belief to the contrary, the members of the Shelikof Company, already in virtual possession of their exclusive privileges of trade, were then making strenuous efforts to extend operations instead of drawing out of the business. Shelikof, Baranof, and Delarof knew far better than Billings' sanguine secretary what wealth was in the country. Where he saw nothing but indications of quick decline, energetic preparations were in progress for a healthy revival of business. For many years after the period set by Sauer even the vessels of small opposition companies continued to visit the islands and portions of the mainland.

One proof of the confidence of Shelikof in the stability of the business for many years to come is furnished by his efforts to establish a settlement in

[20] The instructions issued in 1790 to the Shelikof-Golikof Company contained the following: 'Necessary measures will be taken in accordance with secret instructions, by order of the empress, to protect the establishments of the company and its stores of goods and furs against the attacks of pirates, which have been sent out for that purpose by the Swedish government, under the command of English captains, and all possible means will be employed to avert this danger, threatening the hunters as well as the company's property. If, in spite of all precautions, these privateers enter any Russian harbor or land parties of men, efforts must be made to repulse them, and, if possible, to capture and detain them.   In such a case a party of natives will be formed, in bidarkas, decorated with beads and paint; they will approach the vessel with signs of admiration and friendship, beckoning to the people on board to land, displaying sea-otter skins, and presenting them with a few. Having in this way induced as many as possible of the crew to land, the natives will meet them with their customary dances and all signs of satisfaction, in the mean time endeavoring to decoy the vessel into some dangerous place. During all this time not one Russian must show himself, but they must all be hidden in convenient places prepared for that purpose, and when the deluded party approaches some defile or ambush, the hidden Russians will emerge at a given signal to attack both the vessel and the men on shore, endeavoring to capture the leaders, etc.' In case of fortune favoring the hostile visitors the instructions direct that, 'if possible, the most important among the Russians or natives must endeavor to escape in bidars or bidarkas by passages where the ship cannot follow, while others may approach the vessel at night and attempt to scuttle it or cause it to leak.' *Tikhmenef, Istor. Obosr.*, i. 33-4.

the vicinity of Cape St Elias and to begin ship-building there. "I have made representations to the
government," he wrote to Baranof, "with regard to
ship-building and agriculture at Cape St Elias. During my sojourn at Kadiak it was known to me that
the mainland of America from Unga Island to the
regions inhabited by the Kenaï enjoys better climatic
conditions than the island of Kadiak. The soil is fit
for cultivation, timber is plentiful," etc. Baranof
wrote in reply that he entertained no hope of succeeding in agricultural experiments at Yakutat, especially near the coast, as the place was situated between
59° and 60° north latitude. He also stated that the
shores of the gulf of Chugachuik and portions round
Kenaï were composed of very high and rugged mountains.

The peculiar search for agricultural lands outside of
Kadiak shows plainly that the wily traders were not
in earnest in their search. Kadiak is the spot most
favored by nature as far as climate and soil are concerned. No other place in all that vast region can
furnish feed for cattle or boast of rich fisheries, useful
timber, and fertile vegetable-gardens in close proximity to each other. But all this was carefully hidden
from the knowledge of the government and attention
was drawn toward a region where failure was a certainty, in order to obtain the services of such laborers
and mechanics as might be forwarded from Siberia
in conformity with Shelikof's representations to the
imperial court. It was a wily scheme and proved
successful with regard to the introduction of skilled
labor into the colonies without much expense to the
company, who obtained the privilege of selecting useful
men among Siberian exiles and convicts. The best of
these picked men, as we shall see in a succeeding chapter, never reached the proposed settlement at Yakutat,
and the few who did perished or were captured during
the sacking of the place by the Thlinkeets.

It is safe to presume, also, that Billings had reasons

for not doing anything against the men who were
preparing to assume supreme control over the Russian
possessions in America, despite a little episode with
his Russian secretary at Petropavlovsk, who was sent
back to Okhotsk in irons, because he had revealed
some of the secret instructions of his commander to
members of the Shelikof Company.[21]   His strange
apathy in the matter of making new discoveries or
surveys in the vicinity of Cook Inlet and Prince William Sound may have been due to influence brought
to bear from that direction, and not, as Sauer intimates, to mere superciliousness and pride engendered
by rapid promotion.

In the case of subsequent government expeditions
and inspectors visiting the colonies the same influence
became more perceptible and undeniable, a circumstance which justifies us, to a certain extent, in viewing in a similar light the results of this expedition
and the events recorded in this chapter.

An enterprise that objected to general competition,
and especially one with unscrupulous men at its head,
was sure to bring about the employment of questionable means in its furtherance.   Bribery was the easiest
and perhaps the most innocent means employed to
secure immunity from interference by either government or rival traders, and there is ground for suspicion
that it was brought into play during the cruise of the
Slava Rossie.

The subordinate members of the expedition, captains Sarychef and Hall, the medical men and Sauer,
appear to have taken the side of the suffering natives
against the grasping traders, but in the official reports
to the government these men had no voice.   Billings'
report has never been published, and we can only
conjecture its tenor.   The journal and notes of Martin
Sauer were published nearly ten years later, and could
in no way have influenced the Russian government.

[21] *Id.*, 213.

That the traders did not like the presence of government officers among them was but natural. The officers belonged to a class far above any of the traders in social standing as well as rank, and they took no pains to conceal their contempt for the semi-barbarous plebeians. Individuals of some education, like Delarof, met with a certain degree of consideration, but all others were treated like dogs. Even Baranof, after he had been in supreme command of the colonies for many years, was snubbed by lieutenants and midshipmen of the navy, and it was found necessary to obtain for him a civil rank in order to insure even common respect from government officials. Under such circumstances the merchants considered themselves justified in resorting to any means by which officers might be disgusted with the country and exploring expeditions made to appear unnecessary to the government.

In the case of Sarychef, Hall, and Sauer, who passed a winter on Unalaska Island, this plan seems to have worked satisfactorily, as not one of them had anything good to say of a country where they suffered intensely from scurvy and lack of provisions. The fact that a party of Russians and natives from Kadiak visited the expedition in its winter-quarters demonstrates the possibility of carrying on the work of exploration and surveying on Unalaska and neighboring islands during the winter, but no such attempt was made, though the whole company suffered from the effects of inactivity. With the example before them of the Kadiak party, already referred to in the earlier pages of this chapter, strengthened by that of Martin Sauer, who almost alone retained comparatively good health by constantly moving about, it is difficult to find any valid reason for the apathy shown by the officials in command. The work actually accomplished by Sarychef must have been completed before the appearance of the scurvy. Sauer's original ambition, which caused him to make the foolhardy proposition of remaining alone among the Chugatsches, seems to have cooled, and after returning to Kamtchatka he confined his visionary plans to the exploration of the Kurile Islands and perhaps Japan or China. We have no record, however, that any of his plans reached the stage of execution.

In support of his schemes Shelikof had been the prime mover in the request to have a missionary establishment appointed for the colonies, and in his reports he claimed to have converted large numbers of natives to Christianity. It is safe to presume, however, that his success as a religious teacher was not sufficient to prepare the field for the priest attached to Billings' expeditions, who evidently considered that his whole duty consisted in holding services for his companions once a week, and in administering the customary oath to Captain Billings whenever the latter assumed an additional rank in accordance with the imperial oukaz containing his instructions. On the second voyage from Petropavlovsk the commander did not expect further promotion, and we find no mention of the priest. He was probably left behind as one whose earthly work was done. Sauer gave him a bad character and called him half-savage.

The stay of the *Slava Rossie* was besides too short at any one place during the first voyage to allow of missionary work on the part of the priest, though a portable church—a large tent—was set up at every anchorage. Shelikof had not hesitated to perform a primitive rite of baptism, but he could not legally marry people, and the ceremony performed on Kadiak Island, as before mentioned, was consequently the first that ever took place in the country. The wife of Shelikof had accompanied him on his visit to America, but from that solitary example the natives could not have acquired much knowledge of the institution of Christian marriage.

Shelikof's application for missionaries had great

weight with the commission intrusted to consider the demand of his company for exclusive privileges, but the first members of the clergy who landed upon the islands of the American coast in response to the call did not meet with the hearty coöperation they may have expected at the hands of the traders. Taking time and circumstances into consideration, this was but natural. All the Russians, from the chief trader down, were laboring 'on shares,' and shared alike in the scanty provisions furnished at very irregular intervals, while every man was expected to eke out additional supplies by hunting and fishing whenever he could obtain a few days from other pursuits. The clergymen, who had certainly every reason to look for supplies of food to the traders who had desired their presence, were, therefore, considered as an undesirable element by lawless individuals, long removed from all association with even the forms of civilization. Idlers were not wanted in the camps of the promyshleniki, where scant fare was the rule, and for some years after their arrival among the race with whose language they were unacquainted, the missionaries could do little. Complaints of shortcomings and even ill-treatment were at first quite numerous, and by some priests it was alleged that the commanders of stations, where they had taken up their residence, made them work for their living. This may well have been the case in instances where agents were compelled to give way to popular demand; the semi-barbarous hunters perhaps had another ground for harboring ill-feeling toward their clerical guests—the latter interfered to a certain extent with the more than free use made of native women by the promyshleniki. Still, the *arkhemandrit*, or prior, Ioassaf, sent out to superintend the missions, was treated with respect, as the managers of the companies recognized the necessity of restraining their subordinates in his case. A man in his position could and did do good service in settling difficulties between rival firms and individuals.

CHAPTER XIV.

ORGANIZATION OF MONOPOLY.

1787-1795.

SHELIKOF'S GRAND CONCEPTION—GOVERNOR-GENERAL JACOBI WON TO THE
SCHEME—SHELIKOF'S MODEST REQUEST—ALASKA LAID UNDER MONOP-
OLY—STIPULATIONS OF THE EMPRESS—HUMANE ORDERS OF KOZLOF-
UGRENIN—PUBLIC INSTRUCTIONS AND SECRET INJUNCTIONS—DELAROF'S
ADMINISTRATION—SHELIKOF INDUCES BARANOF TO ENTER THE SER-
VICE OF HIS COMPANY—CAREER AND TRAITS OF THE NEW MANAGER—
SHIPWRECK OF BARANOF ON UNALASKA—CONDITION OF THE COLONY—
RIVALRY AND OTHER TROUBLES—PLANS AND RECOMMENDATIONS—EN-
GAGEMENT WITH THE KALJUSHES—SHIP-BUILDING—THE ENGLISHMAN
SHIELDS—LAUNCH AND TRIBULATIONS OF THE 'PHŒNIX.'

THE idea of a subsidized monopoly of trade and
industry, to embrace all Russian discoveries and colonies on the shores of the north Pacific, first arose in
the fertile brain of Grigor Shelikof, whose original
establishment on Kadiak Island has been the subject
of a preceding chapter. Once seized with this conception, Shelikof hastened forward the execution of
it with all the ardor of his nature. He hurried from
Kamchatka to Okhotsk and Irkutsk, travelling without intermission in the dead of winter until he reached
the capital of eastern Siberia and delivered to General Jacobi, the governor general, a detailed account,
with maps, of the countries he had visited, and plans
of the fortifications erected. He then asked of the
governor general instructions for the management of
the people thus added to the Russian empire, and
aid toward obtaining from the empress a recognition
of his labors.[1]

[1] I will quote here a few concluding lines of the lengthy document presented to Jacobi by Shelikof: 'Without the approval of our monarch my

Unlike his predecessors, Shelikof was not satisfied
with a single hunting season on the island of Kadiak,
but, as we have seen, proceeded at once to the establishment of permanent settlements. After the presentation of his report to General Jacobi, the clever
trader asked permission to send a few ships to Chinese
ports, in case of an interruption to the overland trade
with Kiakhta. The permission was not granted at
that time. Meanwhile Golikof, Shelikof's partner,
had profited by a temporary sojourn of the empress

labors would be altogether unsatisfactory to me and of but little account to
the world, since the principal object of all my undertakings has been to incorporate the newly discovered seas, countries, and islands into our empire
before other powers could occupy and claim them, and to inaugurate enterprises which will add to the glory of our wise empress and secure profits to
her and to our countrymen. I trust that my hopes of seeing wise measures
adopted for the government and protection of the distant regions discovered
by me are not without foundation, and that we shall be enabled to establish
these discoveries to the best possible general advantage.' *Tikhmenef, Istor.
Obos.*, i. 15. Captain Golovnin, who inspected the colonies in 1818, in a letter
to the imperial navy differs from Shelikof as to the merits of the colo-
nizer. He states that '*Shelikof's Voyage* was printed at St Petersburg in
1791. Aside from the barbarous style of the book and the stupidity exhibited
on every page, we cannot fail to notice some intentional falsehoods, showing
how crafty and far-seeing this man was. In the first place he appropriates to
himself without any conscientious scruples the discovery of Kadiak and
Afognak, when it is well known that Bering sighted those islands and named
a point Cape Hermogen, and Cook, five years before Shelikof's voyage, ascertained that the cape was only a small island. Cape Goviatskoi on Kadiak
Island was named Cape Greville by Cook, and furthermore, a Russian galiot
wintered at Kadiak as early as 1763, its commander being a certain Glottof,
while Shelikof arrived there only in 1784, but what is more stupid than anything else is, that on the title-page of his book he claims to be the discoverer
of the island he calls Kuikhtak, forgetting that on page 20 of his book he
acknowledges that in 1761 a Russian vessel stopped at that island. Where
was the discovery? What place did he find that Cook did not see? Later
Shelikof asserts that he found 50,000 inhabitants on the island, and that in
a fight he with a force of 130 attacked 4,000 men, fortified upon a high rock,
taking 1,000 prisoners. According to Captain Lissianski's inquiries Shelikof
fell upon 400 people, including women and children; but 50,000 inhabitants
never existed upon the island—the number now being 3,000, and even if we
suppose that the company succeeded in destroying four fifths, the original
population could have been only 15,000. Now, the question is, What induced
Shelikof to lie thus boldly and impudently? He answers this question himself, in his book, when he asserts that, without knowing the language of the
inhabitants, he succeeded in one winter in converting a large number of them
to the sacred doctrines of our religion, and that by simply telling them of the
wisdom, humanity, and kindness of the empress of Russia, he made such an
impression upon their minds that the natives were filled with love and
admiration for her Majesty, and at once voluntarily submitted to her sceptre.
Now, it is clear that Shelikof wished to make the government believe that he
had discovered a new country and added 50,000 bona fide subjects to Russia.'
He did not fail in his calculations, as he received very flattering rewards.'
Golovnin, Zapiski, in *Materialui*, i. 52–3.

at Kursk, and had presented to her a chart of Shelikof's voyage. Her Majesty inquired into the company's achievements, and finally granted Shelikof
permission to come to St Petersburg and present
himself at court with Golikof.

Shortly after this the empress asked Jacobi his
opinion as to the best means of establishing the Russian dominion on the islands of the eastern ocean, and
on the coast of America, and also as to the best mode
of governing the savage tribes and ameliorating their
·condition. In answer Jacobi forwarded a lengthy
report in which he approved the proposed despatch
of a fleet from the Baltic[2] to protect navigation in
the Pacific, and mentioned that he had forwarded to
the regions in question thirty copper shields, bearing
the imperial coat of arms and the inscription, "Country
in possession of Russia," intended, as he says, "for
the better assertion of Russia's rights, founded upon
discovery." The shields were intrusted to navigators
of the Shelikof and Golikof Company. Jacobi also
recommended that the collection of tribute from the
natives should be abolished and replaced by a voluntary tax. He pointed out the disadvantages to both
traders and natives resulting from the tribute system,
and suggested that by impressing the savages with a
sense of the power of the empress and her tender care
for all, even her most distant subjects, and by allowing them to deliver to government agents a voluntary
contribution or tax, much good might be accomplished.
According to Jacobi's opinion, the collection of tribute
hastened the extermination of fur-bearing animals.

With regard to the proposed amelioration Jacobi
said that there could be no doubt of the truth of

---

[2] The empress intended to afford safer navigation and traffic by sending
war-vessels from the Baltic under command of Captain Mulovski. Mulovski's
vessels were to separate upon arrival in the northern Pacific, one division to
go to the American coast, under his own command, and the other to proceed
to the Kurile Islands, but on account of the war with Sweden the squadron
did not sail. Lieutenant Trevenen, who had sailed under Cook, was engaged
to join for discovery purposes. *Tikhmenef, Istor. Obos.*, i. 16; *Burney's Chron.
Hist. Voy.*

Shelikof's report, and that it would be but a just
recognition of what the Shelikof Company had done
for the commerce of Russia, and for the country at
large, to grant them the exclusive right of hunting
and trading in the islands and territories discovered
by their vessels.[3] He even added that it would be
unfair to allow new-comers to enjoy the present peace
to which Shelikof had reduced Kadiak. Without
regard for the claims of any who had preceded them,
they alone should be rewarded, because they had a
larger force and conquered without exterminating.[4]

He further argued that unless the Shelikof Company was afforded special privileges the successes
gained by the founders of the first settlement on the
islands would be neutralized by the unrestrained actions of lawless adventurers. Cruelty would increase,
and the natives would submit to no such infliction after
the enjoyment of peaceful intercourse with Shelikof.
In conclusion Jacobi implored his imperial mistress
to intrust the management of the latest additions to
her domain to a man who "was known to have many
times set aside his love of gain in the interest of
humanity." What Jacobi himself was to receive in
case of Shelikof's success the governor general does
not say. The hundreds who had done more and suffered more than these who would now have it all to
themselves, to them he denied every right or reward.

The empress ordered the imperial college of commerce, through its president, Count Chernyshef, to
examine in detail all questions connected with the
fur-trade in those parts, and the means of advancing
the interests of Russia in the eastern ocean. The

[3] The limits of these 'discoveries' Jacobi, with reckless liberality, placed
at from latitude 49° to 60° and from eastern longitude 53° to 63° from Okhotsk.
Tikhmenef, Istor. Obos., i. 20.

[4] Jacobi advanced the idea that so far 'as known nobody else was then
engaged in business where Shelikof had succeeded in establishing the dominion of Russia, though some vessels had been in the neighborhood in
1761, 1767, and 1780, but they reached only a promontory of Kadiak named
Aiekhtatik, and the hunters of those vessels were held in check by the natives
and prevented from hunting, though their number was large enough to resist
attack.' *Tikhmenef, Istor. Obos.*, i. 22.

committee appointed in pursuance of this order presented a long report in March 1788,[5] which seemed to have been wholly impressed with the ideas of Jacobi. After reviewing the apparent merits of the case and the policy of the proposed measure, the committee finally recommended that the request of Shelikof and Golikof for exclusive privileges be granted, and that the enterprise be subsidized with a loan of two hundred thousand rubles from the public treasury, without interest, for a period of twenty years, the capital to be returned in instalments. The outlay, it was added, would likewise be repaid tenfold in the form of taxes and import and export duties.

In pursuance of this report an imperial oukaz was issued September 28, 1788, granting the company exclusive control over the region actually occupied by them, but no further, thus leaving rival traders free sway in adjoining parts. Assistance from the public treasury was refused because of foreign wars. The empress was made to say: "As a reward for services rendered to the country by the merchants Shelikof and Golikof by discovering unknown countries and nations, and establishing commerce and industries there, we most graciously confer upon them both swords and gold medals, the latter to be worn around the neck, with our portrait on one side, and on the reverse an explanatory inscription that they have been conferred by order of the governing senate for services rendered to humanity by their noble and bold deeds."[6] By the same oukaz all former laws for the collection of tribute from the Aleuts were revoked.

[5] Report of committee on commerce, March 1788. *Tikhmenef, Istor. Obos.*, i. 237. It dwelt at length upon the sacrifices of Shelikof, and pointed to the fact that owing to the failure of a regular supply of valuable furs from Siberia and the islands the overland trade with China was interrupted, to the great loss of Russian merchants who had large sums invested in goods salable only in the Chinese market; while the articles previously imported from China directly into Russia and Poland, such as teas, silks, and nankeens, could be obtained only through foreign maritime nations at a great increase of cost.

[6] A special letter of acknowledgement was issued by the sovereign on October 11th, which is printed in *Tikhmenef, Istor. Obos.*, i., app., 1.

While this was but a half-way measure toward his ambitious schemes Shelikof had to content himself for a time. He returned to Irtkutsk, there to fit out two vessels, one for the Aleutian isles, and one for the Kuriles, and to plan for a more complete victory, by which to become master of all Alaska.

Two important documents were issued in 1787 by the commander of Okhotsk, which indicate that the authorities by no means placed implicit faith in the humanity of the Shelikof Company or its servants. Both papers bear the same date, June 15th; and one is directed to navigators and traders, while the other is intended as a reassuring proclamation to the native chiefs as representatives of their people. The first sets forth that in view of many complaints of ill-treatment of Aleuts having reached Okhotsk, traders and navigators are enjoined to treat with the utmost kindness all Aleuts who have acknowledged themselves Russian subjects, and not to carry them away from home without their free consent. The document concludes as follows: "The highest authorities have already been informed of all your former outrages committed upon the islanders, but they must cease henceforth, and you must endeavor to act in conformity with the wishes of our most gracious empress, who is anxious to give protection to every inhabitant of her dominions. Do not believe or flatter yourselves that your former deeds will escape punishment, but be convinced that sooner or later every transgression of the laws of God or our monarch will meet with its due reward. I trust that these prescriptions will be observed at once, and you must not forget that it is the first duty of every faithful Russian subject to report any transgression of the laws which comes under his observation. To this I append my own signature and the seals of the province of Okhotsk and of the district of Nishekamchatsk, this 15th day of June 1787. Grigor Kozlof-Ugrenin, colonel and commander of the province of Okhotsk."

The second document is at once characteristic of the empress and important in itself.   I reproduce it in full in a note.[7]

[7] ' To the Chiefs and People inhabiting the Aleutian Islands in the North-eastern Ocean, subjects of the Russian Empire: The Mother of her country, the great and wise Empress of the Imperial throne of All the Russias, Eka-terina Alexeïevna, having always at heart the welfare of her faithful subjects, extends her especial protection and attention to those nations who have but lately become subjects of the Russian Empire, and has deigned to instruct the present Governor-general of Irkutsk, Major-general and Cavalier Klichke, to send to our islands, by way of Kamchatka, and to the Kurile Islands, Russian medals, which have been forwarded to you.   They were sent to you as proof of the motherly care of the Empress; and it was ordered that these medals should be given to those islanders who are already under control of the Russian crown, while at the same time it was intended to issue them also to such as wished to enter the Russian Empire hereafter.   These medals will be distributed at every place where the Russian trading-vessels can land in safety, and thus they will protect you against ill-treatment not only by Rus-sian hunters, but at the hand of our allied powers who may visit your shores. From the latter you may feel entirely safe, for even if any foreign vessel should attempt to appropriate your islands to its own country, the sight of these medals of the Russian Empire would disperse all such thoughts, and if any disputes should arise they will be settled by friendly negotiations with these powers.   As far as the Russian vessels are concerned that visit your islands for the purpose of trade and hunting the fur-bearing animals, I have already received through the hands of my officials at Kamchatka and Okhotsk several complaints, the first through Sergeant Alexeï Buynof, the second from the son of the chief of the Andreianof Islands, Izossim Polutof, and the third from the Aleut of the Lissievski Islands, Toukoutan Ayougnin; from which complaints I have learned to my sorrow of the inhumanities inflicted upon you by our Russian trading-ships, of which the government up to this time had received no information; it was thought that no actual violation of the laws had taken place in those distant regions.   But now your peti-tions have been forwarded by me to the highest authorities and I trust that you will before long receive full satisfaction.   In the mean time I ask you to be content and not to doubt the kindness and justice of the great Empress of All the Russias who is sure to defend and protect you, knowing your sin-cere submission to her sceptre.   You must show this order to all Russian ves-sels that visit you and it will protect you in so far that every inhabitant of your islands may remain in his village, and cannot be compelled to go to any other island unknown to him.   But if one of you goes abroad with his free consent, he will be provided with food and clothing until the time of his re-turn, and the food shall be such as he has been accustomed to.   If you believe that you have been ill-treated by our people belonging to the Russian Em-pire, or if you have suffered compulsion or injury at their hands, I advise you to take notice of their name and that of their ship, and what company of merchants they belong to, and in due time you can forward your complaints upon the matter, and upon satisfactory proof such men will be punished according to their offences and you will get satisfaction.   Information has also reached me to the effect that the hunters receive from you furs of good qual-ity as tribute, but change them and forward poor skins to the Empress; therefore I advise you to mark such skins with special signs and tokens, mak-ing cuts or brands which cannot be easily changed, and if it is done in spite of these precautions the offenders will be punished very severely.   Further-more I assure you of the continued protection and care of all the inhabitants of your islands by her most gracious Imperial Majesty and her supreme gov-ernment, as well as of the best wishes of the Commander of the Province of

The new order of things established by Kozlof did not cause any immediate change in the demeanor of the Russian promyshleniki, and it is doubtful whether the humane document addressed to the natives was ever read or translated to one of them. According to the testimony of Sarychef and Sauer, matters had not improved much when they visited the country several years later. Yet upon the few individuals who were then planning for a monopoly of the fur-trade in the Russian possessions on the American coast, the hints contained in the documents quoted were not lost. They recognized the fact that such boons as they craved from the government could be obtained only by the adoption of a policy of humanity and obedience to the laws, wholly different from the ruthless transactions of private traders. Shelikof, the shrewdest of all the plotters, had, as we have shown, originated this policy, and he lived long enough to see that so far as his plans were concerned it worked to perfection. His instructions to Samoilof, to whom he left the command of his colony on returning to Okhotsk, were admirably calculated to impress the reader with a sense of the wisdom, humanity, and

Okhotsk and the district and township of Nishnekamtchatsk. Signed the 15th day of June 1787, by Grigor Kozlof-Ugrenin.'
Three copies still extant of the original document bear the following signatures: 'Have read the original. Master Gavril Pribylof.' 'Have read the copy. Master Potap Zaikof.' 'Have read the copy. Foreman Leontiy Nagaief.'
When Kozlof-Ugrenin issued his two manifestoes he had not met La Pérouse and the other officers of the French north-western expedition, for the *Boussole* and *Astrolabe* did not reach the bay of Avatcha until September, 1787. La Pérouse and M. de Lesseps, his Russian interpreter, testify to the excellent character of Ugrenin, who appears to have been actuated by a sincere desire to improve the condition of all the inhabitants, Russians and savages, of the vast province under his command. At that time the government of that region was organized as follows: Since Cook's visit to Kamchatka the country had been attached to the province of Okhotsk, under one governor, Colonel Kozlof-Ugrenin; under him Captain Shmalef was superintendent of the native Kamchatkans; Lieutenant Kaborof commanded at Petropavlovsk, with one sergeant and 40 Cossacks; at Nishnekamtchatsk there was a Major Elconof, while at Bolsheretzk and Verkhneïkamchatsk only sergeants were in command. The income derived from Kamchatka by the government was out of all proportion to the expenditure involved. In 1787 the tribute collected from the natives amounted to 300 sable-skins, 200 gray and red foxes, and a few sea-otters, while nearly 400 soldiers and many officers were maintained in the country. *La Pérouse, Voy.*, iii. 167-9, 202.

disinterestedness of the writer,[8] ordering as they did
the good treatment of the natives, their instruction
in Russian laws, customs, and religion, the establishment of schools for the young, and the promotion
of discipline and morality among the Russians as an
example to the aborigines. Much of this was intended chiefly for the sake of effect, since the company by no means intended to expend any particular
efforts for the advancement of the natives. The
secret instructions to the same agent, though mainly
verbal, contained clauses which indicated how far
philanthropy was supposed to further the predomi-
nant aim, the advancement of the company. For a

[8] This remarkable document, of which I have given specimens, was dated
the 14th of May 1786, and has been printed in full by Tikhmenef in the
appendix to his second volume. Speaking of the natives of Kadiak and the
Chugatsches, Shelikof says: 'In pacifying the inhabitants you should explain
to them the benefits resulting from our laws and institutions, and tell them
that people who become faithful and permanent subjects of the empress will be
protected, while evil-disposed people shall feel the strength of her arm. When
visiting the different stations you must investigate complaints against your
subordinates by first hearing each party separately and then together...You
will instruct them in building good houses, and in habits of economy and
industry...The school I have established for the instruction of native children
in reading and writing Russian must be enlarged...As soon as possible the
sacred books and doctrines of our church should be translated into their
language by capable translators...I take with me to Siberia 40 natives, males
and females, old and young. Some of these I will send back on the same
ship, after showing them some of our villages, and the way we live at home,
while a small number will be forwarded to the court of her imperial Majesty;
the remaining children I will take with me to be instructed in the schools of
Okhotsk and Irkutsk, and through them their families and tribes will acquire
a better knowledge of our country and the laws and good order reigning
there...With regard to the officers and men connected with the three vessels
left in your care you will maintain good order and discipline among all classes,
and strictly enforce obedience, as we cannot expect the natives to accept rules
which we do not obey ourselves...Traffic with the Aleuts must be carried on
in an honest manner, and cheating must be punished. Quarrels and disputes
must be settled by arbitration...Hostages and native employés must be well
treated, but should not be taken into our houses without your special permission; serving-women must not be taken into our houses, unless for the purpose
of sewing and similar work...Stores of provisions for at least two years must
be kept at every station to enable you to assist the natives in times of famine.
...At all the forts warm and comfortable quarters must be erected for the
Aleuts, and also stables for the cattle I have ordered to be shipped from
Okhotsk...My godson Nikolaï, who has always faithfully served the company and whom I have fed and clothed at my own expense, I recommend to
your special care, and hope that he will have no cause to complain of the
company's treatment in return for his faithful services, and also that this godson of mine may receive further instruction and be taught to respect God and
the emperor, and the laws of God and of the country.' *Tikhmenef, Istor. Obos.*,
ii., app., 8–19.

time rival traders must be tolerated, but as soon as sufficient strength was acquired they should be excluded from the districts occupied by the Shelikof men.[9]

Limited as were the plans with regard to actual execution, Samoilof lacked the qualifications to carry them out, or to grasp the real object of their framer, and Shelikof knew it. As soon as he returned from Kadiak, therefore, he began to look about for a proper person, and his choice fell on Alexander Baranof, a merchant then engaged in trade on the Anadir River. Shelikof's first proposals to Baranof were declined principally because his own business was moderately prosperous and he preferred independence. One of the partners of the company, Eustrate Delarof, a Greek,[10] was then selected to manage affairs in the colony, but his powers were more local and confined

[9] Article 24. 'If any other company sends out one or two ships and people to engage in the same trade with us, you must treat them in a friendly manner and assist them to do their business quickly and to leave again, giving them to understand at the same time at what an immense sacrifice we have established our stations and what risks we have run in pacifying the Americans, cautioning them not excite the natives by ill-treatment or cheating, which would cause little danger to them who are here only temporarily, but might easily cause the destruction of our establishments, extended all over this region at great risk and expense and to the greatest benefit of the country in general. But when I have sent out two more vessels well manned, in addition to the three now at your disposal, you must take a more resolute stand, drive off all intruders, and declare the Russian sovereignty over all the country on the American continent and California, down to the 40th degree of north latitude.' *Tikhmenef, Istor. Obos.*, ii., app., 16. Shelikof himself acted up to his ideas on the subject. In 1786 the ship *Sv Pavel*, belonging to the Lebedef-Lastochkin Company, came to Kadiak with 35 men, commanded by Peredovchik Kolomin. They were advised to move on, and told that there was an abundance of sea-otters in Cook Inlet. Kolomin followed the advice, and established the first permanent station on the mainland, a fact to which Shelikof took good care never to give any prominence before the government or the public. *Tikhmenef, Istor. Obos.*, i. 30. Sauer writes in reference to this policy: 'Ever since Shelikof formed his establishment at Kadiak no other companies have dared to venture to the eastward of the Shumagin Islands. I am inclined to think that Lukhanin's vessel will be the last that will attempt to visit these islands for furs, and probably he will obtain hardly any other than foxes.' *Geog. and Astron. Exped.*, 276.

[10] Eustrate Ivanovich Delarof, a native of the Peloponese, established himself as a merchant in Moscow and subsequently became a partner in firms trading with America. He was in command of many vessels, stations, and expeditions. He finally became a director of the Russian American company, and was honored by the government with the rank of commercial councillor. *Khlebnikof, Shizn. Baranova*, 14.

than those Shelikof had intended to confer upon
Baranof. Delarof's administration at Kadiak won
him the good-will of all under his command, both
Russians and natives, and he received well merited
praise from all visitors, Spanish, English, and Russian. In all reports concerning Delarof, prominence
is given to his justice to all, and his kindness to the
natives; but just and amiable men are not usually
of the kind chosen to manage a monopoly. In this
instance Delarof was too lenient to suit his avaricious
and unscrupulous partners. Shelikof never lost sight
of Baranof, and when the treacherous Chukchi with
whom he was trading robbed him of his goods and
reduced him to poverty, it did not require much persuasion to induce him to enter the service of the
Shelikof Company at a compensation of ten shares,
equivalent to about one sixth of the net proceeds.
A mutual agreement was drawn up between the company and Baranof on the 18th of August 1790,[11] and
the instructions already issued to Samoilof and Delarof were in the main confirmed. Operations must
be extended also along the coast southward, and steps
might be taken to obtain supplies from other quarters
besides Siberia

Alexandr Andreïevich Baranof was born in Kargopol, eastern Russia, in 1747. At an early age he
went to Moscow, and was engaged as clerk in retail
shops until he established himself in business in 1771.

---

[11] The contract, in addition to instructions with regard to the treatment of
natives, contained some outlines of what the company expected to accomplish
under Baranof's management. He was to seek a harbor on the left (north)
side of the Alaska peninsula and thence a communication with Cook Inlet
by means of a short portage, reported by the natives. Of this he was to
make use in case of attack by hostile cruisers. In addition he was furnished
with ample instructions how to act in case of such attacks upon the different
stations. A ship accompanied by a fleet of canoes was to go to Cape St Elias
and thence to Nootka, to ascertain whether any foreign nations had established themselves on the coast between the Russians and Spaniards. Baranof
was also to enter into communication with the English merchant McIntosh,
engaged in the East India and China trade, in order to make arrangements
for supplying the Russian settlements with goods and provisions. *Tikhmenef,
Istor. Obos.*, i. 32-4.

Not meeting with success he emigrated to Siberia in 1780, and undertook the management of a glass factory at Irkutsk. He also interested himself in other industries, and on account of several communications to the Civil Economical Society on the subject of manufactures he was in 1789 elected a member of the society. It was a humdrum life of which he soon tired, and after acquainting himself with the resources and possibilities of the country, he set out eastward with an assortment of goods and liquors which he sold to the savages of Kamchatka and the adjoining country. At first his operations were successful,[12] but when in 1789 two of his caravans were captured by Chukchi he found himself bankrupt, and yielded to Shelikof's importunate offers to go to America. He had a wife and children at his home in Kargopol, Russia, but during his subsequent residence of almost thirty years in the colonies he never saw his family again though he provided amply for them.

Alexander Baranof was no ordinary man, and never throughout his whole career did Shelikof display clearer discrimination and foresight than in the selection of this agent. He was a man of broad experience, liberal-minded and energetic, politic enough to please at once the government and the company, not sufficiently just or humane to interfere with the interests of the company, yet having care enough, at what he decreed the proper time, for the conventionalities of the world to avoid bringing discredit on himself or his office. Notwithstanding what certain Russian priests and English navigators have said, he was not the lazy, licentious sot they would have us believe. That he was not burdened with religion, was loose in morals, sometimes drunk, and would lie officially without scruple, there is no doubt; yet in all this he was conspicuous over his accusers in that his indul-

<hr>

[12] He established trading posts in Kamchatka and on the Anadir. *Khleb-nikof, Shizn. Baranova,* 3–5. See also *Golovnin,* in *Materialui,* i. 9–10; *Petrof, Russ. Am. Co.,* MS., 10; *Irving's Astoria,* 465; *Hist. Northwest Coast,* ii. 222, this series; and the rather inimical version of *Juvenal, Jour.,* MS., 18–19.

gences were periodical rather than continuous, and not carried on under veil of that conventional grace and gravity which cover a multitude of sins.

He was frequently seized with fits of melancholy, due partly to uncongenial surroundings,[13] and would at other times break out in passionate rage, during which even women were not safe from his blows. This exhibition, however, was invariably followed by contrite generosity, displayed in presents to the sufferers and in a banquet or convivial drinking bout with singing and merriment, so that his fits came to be welcomed as forerunners to good things. His hospitality was also extended to foreigners, though with them he observed prudent reticence. The poor could always rely upon his aid, and this benevolence was coupled with an integrity and disinterestedness at least far above the usual standard among his associates.[14]

Compare him with Grigor Shelikof, who certainly did not lack broad vision and activity, and Baranof was the abler man. Both belonged to the shrewd yet uncultured and somewhat coarse class which then formed the main element even among the rich men in Siberia. In vital deeds Baranof the agent rises superior to Shelikof the principal, belongs more to history, as one who in executing difficult plans shows himself often a greater man than he who conceived them. Indeed, if for the next two or three decades Baranof, his acts and his influence, were absent, Russian American history for that period would be but a blank. Among all those who came from Russia, he alone was able to stem the tide of encroachment by roving traders from the United States and Great Britain. He was any day, drunk or sober, a match for the navigator who came to spy out his secrets.

[13] To disgust at his low companions, says Davidof, but he was not much more refined himself. *Dvukr. Putesh.*, i. 192.
[14] Of this Davidof has no doubt, for 'he is not accumulating wealth though having every opportunity to do so.' *Id., Juvenal, Jour.*, MS., 19-20.

As for the natives his influence over them was unbounded, chiefly through the respect with which his
indomitable courage and constant presence of mind
impressed them.[15] And yet the savage who came
perhaps from afar expressly to behold the famed
leader, was not a little disappointed in his insignificant appearance as compared with his fierce and bushy
bearded associates. Below the medium height, thin
and sallow of complexion, with scanty red-tinged
flaxen hair fringing a bald crown, he seemed but an
imp among giants. The later habit of wearing a short
black wig tied to his head with a black handkerchief,
added to his grotesque appearance.[16]

On the 10th of August 1790, Baranof sailed from
Okhotsk on the ship *Trekh Sviatiteli*, commanded by
Master Bocharof, who was then considered the most
skilful navigator in those waters.[17] When only a few
days from port it was discovered that the water-casks
were leaking. The ship's company was placed on short
allowance, but disease made its appearance, and it was
thought impossible to sail direct to the settlement at
Kadiak as had been the intention. On the 28th of
September the vessel was turned into the bay of Koshigin, Unalaska, to obtain a supply of fresh water, but
on the 30th, when about to leave again, a storm threw
the ship upon the rocky shore. The men escaped
with belongings, but only a small part of the cargo
was saved. Within five days the wreck broke in
pieces, and a messenger was sent to Kadiak to report
the loss, but failed to reach that place.[18]

[15] Davidof was deeply impressed with this leader of men who controlled not
only the hostile savage but the vicious and unruly Russian, and rose supreme
to every hardship and danger in advancing affairs in this remote corner.
[16] *Id.*, 194; *Tchitchinof, Adv.*, 2-4; *Markof, Ruskie no Vostotchnom*, 52.
[17] Bocharof was at Okhotsk in 1771, at the time of the insurrection headed
by the Polish exile, Count Benyovski. The latter compelled Bocharof to go
with him, and finally took him to France. Thence he was returned to St
Petersburg by the Russian embassador at Paris, and the empress ordered him
to resume his duties at Okhotsk. To this involuntary circumnavigation of the
world Bocharof was indebted for much of his proficiency in nautical science.
Khlebnikof, Shizn. Baranova, 5.
[18] A man named Alexander Molef was sent upon this errand with a num-

Thrown upon his own resources, Baranof distributed his men, fifty-two in number, over the island to shoot seals and sea-lions and dig edible roots, the only food the island afforded during the winter. The leader labored with the men and lived with them in the underground huts which they constructed. The dried salmon and halibut obtained occasionally from the Aleuts were a luxury, and on holidays a soup was made of rye flour of which a small quantity had been saved. The winter was not wholly lost to Baranof, who seized this opportunity to study the people, both Russians and natives, with whom he had thrown his lot for so many years to come, and whom he was to rule without a shadow of actual or apparent support from the government. It was here that he formed plans which were afterward of great service to the company.[19]

Spring coming, three large bidars were made in which to push on to Kadiak, with two of which Bocharof was to explore and hunt along the northern coast of the Alaska peninsula. Twenty-six men were assigned to this expedition while Baranof took a crew of sixteen in the third boat, leaving five at Unalaska to guard what had been saved from the cargo and rigging of the wrecked ship. Toward the end of April 1791 the three bidars put to sea, and on the

ber of Aleuts. When only a hundred miles from Kadiak the party was attacked by the natives of the Alaska peninsula, on which occasion five of the Aleuts were killed. Molef, though severely wounded, managed to launch his bidarka and make his way to Unga, where he remained until picked up by Baranof the following year. *Id.*, 7.

[19] Baranof's letter written at this time presents a vivid picture of life there. 'I passed the winter in great hardships,' he says, 'especially when the weather was bad. Sometimes two months passed by without a possibility of going any distance, but I made use of every clear day to go out with my gun in search of some addition to our larder. On one of these excursions I fell into one of the traps set for foxes and was slightly wounded...I boiled salt of very good quality, as white as snow, and used it for salting fish, and seal, and sea-lion meat. As far as cooking with oil is concerned we were fasting all the time, and the week before Easter we were compelled to fast altogether, but on Easter Monday a dead whale was cast ashore and furnished us a feast. In the same week we killed three sea-lions, and the famine was at an end. I had become accustomed to think no more of flour or bread.' *Khlebnikof, Shizn. Baranova*, 8. Only three men died of scurvy.

10th of May they separated in Issanakh Strait, at the southern end of the peninsula. After an absence of five months Bocharof rejoined his comrades at Kadiak by a portage route across the peninsula, bringing not only furs but a number of good charts.[20] During his whole journey Baranof was prostrate with fever; nevertheless he insisted that the party should not only advance but explore, being unwilling to lose the calm weather so essential for a safe passage from island to island or from cape to cape along the coast of the mainland. He arrived at Three Saints, Kadiak, the 27th of June.

Baranof at once assumed command of all the establishments of the Shelikof-Golikof Company, relieving Eustrate Delarof.[21] At this time the company was in actual possession of Kadiak and a few of the smaller adjacent isles; the principal settlement being still at the bay of Three Saints. The superficial pacification of the natives by Shelikof had been completed by Delarof so far as Kadiak and vicinity were concerned, though they remained in their primitive condition. The opinion of all but Delarof was that they could be held in subjection only by force of arms or fear, and that upon the first sign of weakness or relaxation of vigilance on the part of the Russians they would rise and destroy them. As much system had been secured as lay in the power of one right-minded, intelligent man, surrounded by an unruly band of individuals but little if any above the criminal class. I have said of Delarof that he was strict in his sense of justice and of fair administrative ability. The contemplation of this amiable Greek's

---

[20] Bocharof intended to extend his explorations to the coast of the Aglegmutes, but his skin boats were found to be waterlogged from incessant use, and it was concluded to make a portage across a narrow part of the peninsula. This was accomplished in three days. The bidars were then repaired and the party crossed to Kadiak, reaching Three Saints on the 12th of September.

[21] Delarof remained manager of the company until July 1791. *Tikhmenef, Istor. Obos.*, i. 27, 28.

character affords a pleasant relief from the ordinary conduct of the Russians in America. Had there been more such men, I should have less to record of outrage, cruelty, and criminal neglect; had Delarof been bad enough to please his directors Baranof might have remained at home.

From his head-quarters at Kadiak, Delarof had despatched expeditions to the mainland, at the entrance of Cook Inlet, or the gulf of Kenaï, as the Russians always persisted in calling it, and there he had established a permanent station which he named Alexandrovsk. Otherwise the whole of this inlet was occupied by Lebedef-Lastochkin, who also held the islands discovered by Pribylof. The people of the Alaska peninsula had not yet permitted any Russians to settle among them, and were held to be hostile. The adjoining Prince William Sound was also occupied, and on the Aleutian isles three private trading companies were still doing business, under the management of Orekof, Panof, and Kisselef respectively.

Thus on every side rival establishments and traders were draining the country of the valuable staple upon which rested the very existence of the scheme of colonization. To the east and north there were Russains, but to the south-east the ships of Englishmen, Americans, and Frenchmen were already traversing the tortuous channels of the Alexander archipelago, reaping rich harvests of sea-otter skins, in the very region where Baranof had decided to extend Russian dominion in connection with company sway. Although they could not expect to succeed so well further north, here these traders had every advantage. They enjoyed comparatively easy communication with home points; they were skilled navigators, and came in large well equipped vessels laden with goods far superior to anything the Russians could afford to bring by sled or on the backs of horses across Siberia. They could also be more lavish with their low-priced articles since they were under no expense in main-

taining permanent forts or establishments or a large
retinue of servants. As occasional visitors only, without permanent interests in the land, they could deal
out fire-water, risk occasional cheatings and open acts
of violence, while Baranof, with his few men of permanent residence, among warlike tribes, must be constantly on his guard against acts provocative of
hostilities.

It was necessary that he should bestir himself to
widen the operations of the company ere the field
was exhausted, and this had been his determination,
but he did not as yet possess the necessary vessels,
men, and supplies to do much. The loss of the *Trekh
Sviatiteli* was indeed a formidable hindrance; skin
boats alone could well be used, and to these the men
had more than one objection, the risks of sea voyages,
and the disadvantages in point of defence, carrying
capacity, and convenience. These objections were
the more serious in view of the greater stubbornness
and hostility of the mainland tribes as compared
with the docile Aleuts. Another trouble was that
for several years no supply-ships had arrived from
Siberia, and the Russian hunters and laborers were
reduced to the necessity of sharing the scanty subsistence of the natives. Dissatisfaction was therefore general among the employés, including the natives, and this together with the sight of want among
the conquering race served to rouse the insolence and
hostility of tribes around.

Some of these troubles Baranof managed to overcome by his own energy and strength of will; for
others he must obtain the coöperation of the company. Among other measures he urged Shelikof
most eloquently to labor for a consolidation of the
various trading companies, and thereby to secure to
the new corporation the large number of valuable sea-
otter skins then scattered throughout the small rival
establishments of the mainland. At the same time
he approved of a suggestion made before his departure

to build ships in America, and urged that no delay be allowed in forwarding material to him from Kamchatka. He saw the advantage to the company of exhibiting vessels built in their colony and the necessity of making himself independent of the vessels forwarded at long and irregular intervals from the Asiatic ports. This would ensure not only supplies but the means of cruising down the coast.

Without having seen or met any of the English or American traders then operating in the Sitka region he conceived the plan of obtaining from them not only provisions but trading goods, and asked Shelikof for authority to do so; he knew that in the Pribylof Islands, then recently discovered, he had a treasury from which he might draw the means to purchase whatever he wanted of the foreign traders, and that he would thus be enabled to buy from them with one class of furs the means of battling with them on their own ground for the purchase of sea-otter skins, then the most valuable fur in the market. This plan of operation, though temporarily delayed, was finally adopted and successfully carried out under Baranof's supervision.

Knowing that his letters in some form would fall under the eye of the government, Baranof worded his communications with great care, and with respect to the well seeming plan to introduce missionaries he wrote to the directors of the company: "Send me a well informed priest, one who is of a peaceable disposition, not superstitious, and no hypocrite." With the same view of impressing upon the authorities the humane disposition of the company's traders, he requested Shelikof to send him numerous articles not included in the invoices of the firm, but suitable as gifts to the natives, at the same time explaining that he wished to conquer the savages with kindness. He asked to have the articles purchased and forwarded at his own expense so that "should he give them all away, the company would suffer no loss, while, on the other hand, any profit made on the consignment should be transferred to the firm." [22]

During the autumn and winter of 1791 Baranof made himself thoroughly acquainted with the wants and capabilities of his new domain under the intelligent guidance and instruction of Delarof, who returned to Okhotsk in 1792, and at the same time severed his connection with colonial matters. The latter took passage in the ship *Sv Mikhaïl*, which had been in the colonies ever since Shelikof's first arrival, taking with him Bocharof as navigator, many of the promyshleniki whose term of contract had expired, and all the furs collected by him during his administration.

The new manager soon recognized the desirability of removing the principal settlement of the company from Three Saints to Pavlovsk harbor, on the north side of Kadiak, in latitude 57° 36' according to Captain Lissianski's observations. The reasons lay partly in the better harbor, and chiefly in the abundance of forests at the latter place, facilitating the erection of necessary buildings and fortifications. [23]

In the spring of 1792, however, Baranof was gratified by the appearance of a chief from the northern side of the peninsula, whom Bocharof, during his voyage of exploration the preceding year, had presented with a medal bearing the Russian coat of arms. The savage dignitary, who was at the head of one of the most populous tribes of the peninsula, brought with him quite a large following, including six host-

[22] 'Such are my plans,' he wrote, 'but their execution depends upon providence. My first steps into these regions were attended with misfortune, but perhaps I shall be permitted to conquer in the end. I will either vanquish a cruel fate or fall under its repeated blows. Want and hardships I can bear with patience and trust in providence, especially when the sacrifice is made for the sake of true friendship.' *Khlebnikof, Shizn. Baranova*, 10.

[23] In 1880 only one dilapidated log-house and one native semi-subterranean hut marked the site of the earliest permanent location of the Russians, and these buildings are perched upon the hillside, overlooking the sand spit, from which floods and tidal waves have long since eradicated all traces of former occupancy. A representation of the settlement as it appeared in 1790 has been preserved in *Sauer's Geog. and Astron. Exped.*, and in Sarychef's description of the same expedition.

ages. He assured Baranof that his people desired to
live in friendship with the Russians. In return he
asked the latter to protect him against certain tribes
living farther north in the interior of the country.
As a proof of his sincerity, the chief offered to locate
himself and all his family in the immediate vicinity
of one of the company's establishments. The proposition was evidently the result of fear of his neighbors
rather than good feeling toward the Russians, nevertheless it was cheerfully accepted as the first indication of the possibility of a better understanding with
the independent natives of the peninsula. An alliance of this kind was especially desirable on account
of the importance at that time placed on the possession of the portage across the narrow neck of land
separating the waters of Iliamna Lake from the
Koiychak River, and with Russians so few in number and scattered over so broad a region, peaceable
relations were essential.

Advantage was at once taken of the proposal to
extend operations in this quarter, and other expeditions were also despatched, one under Ismaïlof in the
only large vessel left to them, the *Sv Simeon*, chiefly for
seeking new fields.[24] Baranof himself proceeded to the
gulf of Chugatschuik, Prince William Sound, with
two well manned bidars in order to become acquainted
with the inhabitants of that region. Dreading the
Russians and a possible state of dependence, the forbidding Chugatsches concealed themselves from Baranof at every point. At last he succeeded in meeting
a few of the tribes and obtained from them seven
hostages. Hereabout he fell in with the ship *Phœnix*,
Captain Moore, from the East Indies, and obtained
information on foreign traffic in the Alexander archipelago, which served him greatly in forming plans for
future operations. He conceived quite a friendship

[24] Baranof wrote concerning Ismaïlof's achievements that 'he went out to
make discoveries, but discovered nothing beyond doubtful indications of land.'
Tikhmenef, Istor. Obozr., ii. app., 36.

for the commander, from whom he received as a 'present' a native of Bengal.[25]

Soon after his meeting with Moore, Baranof proceeded to Nuchek Island, near the mouth of Copper River, and encamped within a short distance of the cove where subsequently the Konstantinovsk redoubt was built. Finding the supply of fish limited, he concluded to send a bidar manned by Russians and a part of the Aleut hunters to Sukli (Montagu) Island in search of better fishing-grounds, capable of furnishing a winter's supply for his party. On the 20th of June this expedition set out, and Baranof remained on Nuchek Island with only sixteen Russians. He had heard rumors of hostile intentions on the part of the savages, but placed little faith in them. To avoid unnecessary risks, however, he intended to remove his little force to a small island in the bay, on the day following the departure of his exploring party. In the middle of the night, which was very dark and stormy, the sentries gave the alarm. Five of the sixteen men had been placed on guard, but the darkness was so dense that a numerous body of armed natives had advanced to within ten paces of the encampment without being seen. In a moment the Russians had seized

[25] Baranof gives an interesting account of this meeting in one of his letters to Shelikof: 'Being about to establish a station for the winter, I fell in with an English vessel, which had come from the East Indies, by way of Canton and Manila to America in the vicinity of Nootka, and from there he had followed the coast to Chugatsch, trading with many tribes and collecting a large quantity of furs. He had lost a mast in a gale and replaced it at Chugatsch and for that reason he had concluded to return direct to Canton. The ship, named the *Phœnix*, was 75 feet long and had two masts. The captain is an Englishman, of Irish extraction, named Moore. He met first with my bidarka fleet, and then came to my anchorage, where he lay five days during stress of weather. I was on board nearly all the time and was entertained at the captain's table. We conversed a great deal on various subjects, and though we did not understand each other very well, we managed to make use of the German language which I had imperfectly learned as a boy, but almost forgotten since. The captain made me a present of one [East] Indian, who is my private attendant during the winter, but in the summer he serves in the capacity of an able seaman. He understands English well and I have taught him considerable Russian. I did not make any present in return beyond a few fox-skins and some *kamtakas* of Aleut workmanship and some other trifles. I also heard news of Capt. Coxe from him. He died at Canton. We were on very friendly terms and Capt. Moore visited me several times on shore in my tent.' *Tikhmenef, Ist. Obosr.*, ii., app., 36.

their arms and were firing on the savages. According to Baranof their fire was for a long time without any visible effect, owing to the wooden armor and shields and helmets of the savages, which were of sufficient thickness to stop a bullet fired at some distance. The movements of the enemy seemed to be guided by one commander, and by shouting to each other they preserved unity of action in the darkness. Their flint and copper-headed arrows and spears fell thick and fast, wounding several of the Russians and many of the Aleuts, several of them fatally. The latter did not even make a show of resistance, but seemed possessed of the one idea of escaping by water in their bidarkas. As the assailants had several large war-canoes not many of these attempts were successful. One small cannon, a one-and-a-half-pounder falconet, was at last brought into position, and did some execution, at the same time encouraging the Aleuts to rally around the Russians in their encampment. Fortunately Ismaïlof's vessel happened to be at anchor not far off, and a few of those who fled in their canoes at the beginning of the affray, had in the mean time reached it, and obtained a bidar full of armed men for the relief of Baranof. The appearance of this boat caused six large wooden war-canoes to beat a hasty retreat. One explanation, though not very plausible, of this unexpected attack was that the Yakutat tribe of Kaljushes had combined with the Aglegmutes to avenge themselves for injuries received at the hands of the Chugatsches during the preceding year. Knowing that the *Sv Simeon* was anchored four versts away, and ignorant of Baranof's presence, they had mistaken the Russian encampment for a Chugatsch village and attacked it in the dark. When the mistake was discovered, the savages were induced to persevere in their efforts by hopes of rich booty, only to pay dearly for the attempt and to retreat deeply demoralized.[26]

[26] Baranof wrote to Shelikof as follows: 'We found 12 killed on the spot; the wounded had been carried off, but a wake of blood was visible a verst

This affair caused Baranof to change his plans. Instead of wintering in Prince William Sound as had been his intention, he turned to the gulf of Kenaï by the shortest route. He strengthened his outlying stations there and hastened the work of fortification and then proceeded to Kadiak. On his arrival at Pavlovsk harbor, he found that the ship *Orel*, that is Eagle, had arrived from Okhotsk, commanded by the Englishman Shields, and laden partly with material for new ships, though by no means of the description most essential for opening operations. Although despatched in the autumn of 1791, vessels had been compelled to winter in Kamchatka. Shields had learned the art of ship-building in England, but had subsequently entered the Russian military service and obtained the rank of sub-lieutenant.[27]

At the same time came orders to proceed at once with ship-building. This placed Baranof in an em-

---

or two behind their canoes. At the very first onset they killed on our side a man named Kotovchikof from Barnaül, and Paspelof from Tumensk died two weeks later. Of the heathen—the Aleuts—9 were killed and 15 wounded. As for myself, God protected me, though my shirt was torn by a spear and the arrows fell thickly around me. Being aroused from a deep sleep I had no time to dress, but rushed out as I was to encourage the men and to see that our only cannon was moved to wherever the danger was greatest. Great praise is due to the fearless demeanor of my men, many of whom were new recruits. I mention among them Feodor Ostrogin and Zakhmilin. One of the Chugatsch hostages brought us four men who had been captured by the Chugatsch people. From these we learned that our assailants had expected 10 canoes full of warriors from the Copper River and that they intended to proceed to the gulf of Kenaï after annihilating the Chugatsch tribe.' *Tikhmenef, Istor. Obosr.*, ii. app. 37–8. Khlebnikof, in his life of Baranof, relates this incident in a somewhat different manner as to details, and, strange to say, he quotes as his authority a letter from Baranof to Shelikof. They retreated in 5 canoes while they had arrived in 6. *Shizn. Baranova*, 16–17. Yet they carried off 4 captives. *Tikhmenef, Istor. Obos.*, i. 38–9, 64–5.

[27] Shelikof wrote to Baranof on this occasion: 'We send you now iron, rope, and sail-cloth for one ship which, with the assistance of Shields, you will be able to fit out, and if you succeed you may lay the keel for two or three other vessels of various dimensions. You should endeavor to push their construction far enough ahead to enable you to complete them without further assistance of a shipwright. Everything you need for this shall be sent by the next opportunity. You should teach the Americans to pick oakum, make ropes, sew at the sails, and help the blacksmiths.' *Id.*, i. 39–40. The iron appears to have been forgotten. Shields had formerly served as lieutenant in a Yekaterinburg regiment, but as he was both ship-builder and navigator by profession, Shelikof engaged him for service in the new colonies. The first proof of his proficiency in his business was the packet-boat *Orel*, which he constructed at Okhotsk. *Khlebnikof, Shizn. Baranova*, 18.

barrassing position, for he had not yet completed the
transfer of the principal settlement from Three Saints
to Pavlovsk harbor and there was urgent necessity to
erect at once a number of buildings at the latter place,
to shelter both men and stores during the winter. He
was, however, determined to obey, and while pushing
the work at Pavlovsk as much as possible, he lost no
time in selecting a suitable place for ship-building.
On Kadiak and Afognak islands the trees were neither
abundant nor large enough, and it was found necessary to look to some more distant region. During his
recent stay in Prince William Sound he had observed
to the west of it a well protected bay, which seemed
in every way suitable for his undertaking. The place
was called Voskressenski, or Sunday harbor, also
known as Blying Sound, and not only furnished excellent timber, but a considerable rise and fall of the
tide afforded exceptional facilities for building, launching, and repairing vessels. Shelikof's orders had been
to send Shields back to Okhotsk after consulting him
concerning the work on hand, but Baranof found it
necessary to detain him in order to obtain serviceable
plans for his vessel. He wrote to Shelikof that his
complement of men capable of doing any work on the
vessel was so exceedingly small that he could not
afford to send away his most valuable assistant, but
would retain him during that and the following season,
hoping in the mean time to receive further shipments
of stores and material.[28]

The necessary buildings, quarters for the men, and
storehouses were at once erected at Voskressenski
harbor, and all that winter the mountains of Kenaï
peninsula echoed the vigorous blows of axemen and
the crash of falling trees. Nearly all the planks were
hewn out of the whole log, a waste of time and ma-

[28] 'We have,' wrote Baranof, 'only half a keg of tar, three kegs of pitch,
not a pound of oakum, not a single nail, and very little iron for so large a
vessel. What little canvas you sent us we have been compelled to use for
bidarka sails and tents, for those we had were entirely worn out by long
usage.' *Tikhmenef, Istor. Obos.*, ii., app. 39.

terial made necessary by the absence of large saws.
The iron needed in the construction had been collected
from pieces of wreck in all parts of the colonies, and
though rust-eaten and of poor quality, it was made to
serve.   Steel for axes had to be prepared from the
same material.   In his anxiety to push the work Baranof even attempted to extract iron from some ore
his men had picked up.   He had seen iron-furnaces
during his life in Siberia, but found himself unable to
obtain the coveted metal by any such rude processes
as he could devise.[29] For tar he devised a poor mixture of spruce gum and oil.   The English ship-builder
regarded with wonder and contempt the primitive
dock-yard, and without a purveyor possessed of the
indomitable determination and activity of Baranof, he
could never have earned the reputation of constructing the first ship on the north-westernmost coast of
America.

To obtain provisions was difficult.   The men could
not be allowed to hunt or fish, and no other station
was prepared to furnish supplies.   Heavy requisitions
were made upon the *yukola*, or dried fish, of the natives, entailing want and hardships upon them, while
the ship-builders were reduced to the scantiest allowance to sustain them in their arduous task.

The lack of canvas was another serious inconvenience.   Without a proper suit of sails the first
American ship could never reach the coast of Siberia
or Kamchatka and impress the authorities with the
reality of all the Shelikof Company claimed to have
done in the way of improvements and industrial enterprise in the colonies.   It is astonishing to what
expense and infinite trouble the company was willing
to go for the sole purpose of effect.   A far better
ship could have been built without any serious difficulty and at much less cost either in Kamchatka or at
Okhotsk.   The problem of supplying the necessary

---

[29] Madame Shelikof indicates that the smelting of iron ore promised well
enough to warrant the engagement of an experienced man. *Letter*, in *Id.*

canvas was made more difficult by the circumstance
that the native hunters, who had until then been paid
for their season's work with a few beads and glass
corals, refused to accept that currency any longer, and
almost unanimously demanded to be paid in garments
made of canvas.

April 1793 saw the new craft far enough advanced
to make Shields' constant superintendence unnecessary. Baranof, who had no great liking for the foreigner, seized the opportunity of giving him additional
work by ordering him upon a voyage of discovery in
the *Orel.* Rumors of the existence of unknown islands, rich in seals and sea-otters, in various parts of
the new possessions had been afloat for some time.
Baranof never expressed any belief in these reports, but
in order to get Shields and his four English sailors out
of the way for the summer, he promised the former two
shares of the furs obtained from any island discovered
by him, for two years, and to the sailors twenty sea-
otters each. With grim satisfaction the crafty old
manager noted the fact that the premiums offered
were never earned, and that the *Orel* was tossed
about by storms and finally reached Voskressenski
harbor in a much damaged condition. In the mean
time the *Sv Simeon* had arrived with more laborers,
provisions, and tools, and work was resumed with
renewed vigor.

At last in August 1794 the great work was achieved
as the first vessel built in north-western America glided
from the stocks into the waters of the Pacific, under
the name of *Phœnix.*[20] While not so important or difficult a performance as those of Vasco Nuñez and
Cortés, it was one of which Baranof might justly feel
proud. He had made the first practical use of the
timber of what was then termed "the vast deserts of

[20] No explanation is given by my authorities why Baranof selected this
name, but we may conclude that it was suggested to him by the English
vessel which visited those waters in 1792.

America," and had used it for a purpose that might be expected to benefit not only his employers, but his country.

Most of the men who assisted Shields had seen only the nondescript vessels of Siberian traders, many of them half decked, and built usually without an iron bolt or brace, the planks being lashed together with raw-hide thongs. The present result was therefore all the more gratifying, crude as it was. The vessel was built of spruce timber, and measured 73 feet in length, the upper deck being 79 feet, with a beam of 23 feet and a depth of 13½ feet. Notwithstanding the size, the capacity being only about one hundred tons, it was provided with two decks and three masts, in order to present an imposing appearance and do credit to its projectors.[31] The calking above the water-line was done with moss; and for paint, tar and whale-oil were used.[32] The sails consisted of pieces and scraps of canvas for which the warehouses and magazines of the company in Kamchatka and in the colonies had been ransacked. The result was a number of sheets of different qualities and color, presenting the most grotesque appearance.[33]

By the 4th of September the *Phœnix* was despatched upon her first voyage to Kadiak, where Baranof hoped to improve upon the outfit. On the way the flimsy rigging snapped before the first breeze, and the vessel entered Pavlovsk not with swelling sails, but towed by boats. She was also badly ballasted, and presented on the whole an appearance far from imposing. Nev-

---

[31] Tikhmenef calls it 180 tons. *Istor. Obos.*, i. 57-8.

[32] Boiled at various times in small quantities the paint was unequal in color, giving the hull a strange, spotted appearance. This, however, extended only a little above the water-line, as they did not have enough even of such paint to color the whole.

[33] These sails, some spars, and a quantity of iron work for the new vessel prepared by mechanics in Kadiak were transported to the ship-yard early in April, before the sea-going vessels had completed their necessary repairs, so that the conveyance had to be made in large skin boats or bidars, which crept cautiously to Cook Inlet. From here the material was carried over dangerous glaciers and mountains to Voskressenski harbor. *Baranof, Shizn.*, 152.

ertheless joy reigned in the settlement, and the event was celebrated by solemn mass and merry feasting.[34]

A few weeks were spent in refitting and rigging the *Phœnix*, and on the 20th day of April this first-born of the Alaskan forests set out upon the voyage to the shores of Asia, commanded by Shields, the builder. The voyage was made in about a month, a speed unprecedented in the annals of Russian navigation in the north Pacific. At Okhotsk the *Phœnix* was received with volleys of artillery, the ringing of bells, and the celebration of mass. The ghost of the great Peter is gratified; for in the flesh the monarch never dreamed of so early and so significant an achievement resulting from the royal pupilage.

All the servants of the Shelikof Company then awaiting transportation from this port, and the soldiers stationed at the ostrog were at once called into requisition to assist in finishing Baranof's wonderful three-master. She had made her first voyage without cabin or deck houses, and these were now added, together with the necessary polishing and painting, and new sails and rigging. From this time forth until her loss during a dark stormy November night, in the gulf of Alaska, the *Phœnix* made regular trips between Okhotsk and the colonies. Shelikof and his partners did not fail to dwell forcibly and pointedly in their petitions and reports upon the fact that their company maintained communication between the colonies and the mother country by means of a "frigate" of their own construction, built with American timber and launched in American waters.

This success Baranof followed up by laying the keels of two other vessels, of smaller size, forty and thirty-five feet in length respectively, which were launched in 1795, and named *Delphin* and *Olga*.[35]

[34] The leaders tried their teeth on the only ram left of the sheep consignment, and then sought relief from the struggle in copious draughts of cheering liquor. *Baranof, Shizn.*, 155–6. Baranof attended the launching, but came back in a bidarka, as if distrusting Shields and his work.

[35] *Tikhmenef, Istor. Obos.*, i. 40.

CHAPTER XV.

LIKE the Spaniards in Central America and Mexico, no sooner had the Russians possession of their
part of America than they fell to fighting among
themselves. In 1786 the *Sv Pavl*, of the Lebedef-
Lastochkin Company, had come to Kadiak with
thirty-eight men, commanded by Peredovchik Kolomin. Jealous of intrusion on their recently acquired
hunting-ground, the Shelikof party gave the new-
comers a hint to move on, and incautiously pointed to
Cook Inlet or the gulf of Kenaï as a profitable region.
The result was a permanent establishment in Alaska,
on Kassilof River in that inlet. It consisted of two
log buildings protected by a stockade, and bore the
name of St George.[1]

The Shelikof Company already possessed, near the
entrance of the inlet, a fort named Alexandrovsk,
which had a more pretentious appearance. It formed

---

[1] It was situated on a bluff, and presented to the wondering savages quite
a formidable aspect. *Juvenal, Jour.*, MS., 36.

a square with poorly built bastions at two corners, and displayed the imperial arms over the entrance, which was protected by two guns. Within were dwelling and store houses, one of them provided with a sentry-box on the roof.[2] The situation of the other fort higher up the inlet, near the richer fur region, gave it the advantage in hunting; yet, for a time, friendly relations continued to exist between the rivals as well as with the natives.

In August 1791 the ship *St George*, also belonging to the Lebedef-Lastochkin Company, arrived in the inlet. The commander of this second expedition was one Grigor Konovalof, and his advent seems to have been the signal for strife and disorder. His proceedings were strange from the beginning; he did not land at the mouth of the Kassilof River, where Kolomin was already established, but went about twenty miles farther, to the Kaknu, landed his crew of sixty-two Russians, discharged his cargo, beached his vessel, and began to erect winter quarters and fortifications surrounded with a stockade and defended by guns. This fort was named St Nicholas.[3] All this time he neglected to communicate in any manner with the other party of the same company. Kolomin at last

[2] Smithy, room for boiling oil, and other conveniences existed. *Fidalgo*, in *Viajes al Norte*, MS., 358-9. See also *Humboldt, Essai Pol.*, ii. 348.

[3] Tikhmenef, in speaking of this episode, commits some errors from insufficient acquaintance with the various localities. He writes of Kassilof and St Nicholas as the same place, while in reality the latter is thirty miles to the northward of the former. In claiming that Konovalof, by erecting fortifications at Kassilof, or St Nicholas, seized upon settlements founded by Shelikof in 1785, Tikhmenef makes another mistake. The only lodgment made by Shelikof on Cook Inlet was near its mouth, and was subsequently named Alexandrovsk. Furthermore, Shelikof was a partner in Lebedef-Lastochkin's enterprise, as as well as in the company formed under special protection of the government. *Tikhmenef, Istor. Obos.*, i. 30; *Juvenal, Jour.*, MS., 6 et seq. When Vancouver anchored off the mouth of the Kenaï or Kaknu river in 1794 he was saluted by two guns from a building on the high bank, from which also floated the Russian flag. A miserable path led up the steep ascent through masses of filth and offal. The establishment occupied a space of about 120 yards square, enclosed with a stout paling of pine logs, 12 feet high. The largest building, 35 yards long, served as barracks, consisting of one large room with sleeping-benches on the sides, divided into stalls. The commander, at that time Stepan Zaïkof, lived in a smaller house by himself. There were over twenty other small buildings. The 70-ton sloop belonging to the station, armed with two guns, was in a dilapidated condition. *Vancouver's Voy.*, iii. 140-1.

ventured to inquire to what company they belonged. The answer was brief and insolent, Konovalof claiming that he had been invested with supreme command, and instructed to seize everything in the hands of Kolomin, who must henceforth report to him. While ready to believe that such authority had been conferred,[4] the latter did not choose to surrender either his men or his furs; but as his term was about ended, he prepared to close his affairs and transfer the company's business to his successor after the winter, in the expectation of sailing for Okhotsk in the spring. While thus engaged, Kolomin's party was surprised by the arrival of a large bidar sent by Konovalof, and commanded by Amos Balushin. Without making any excuse or explanation, Balushin proceeded a short distance up the Kassilof River, to where Kolomin's winter supply of dried fish was stored, and carried all away.[5]

Shortly afterward a party of natives, en route to St George, were intercepted on the Kaknu by Konovalof's men and robbed of all their effects. This outrage was repeated on a party from Toyunok, a village on the upper part of the inlet, no compensation whatever being tendered for the furs taken. Being anxious to come to some understanding, Kolomin went out to meet his rival, but the interview was brought to an end by Konovalof firing off his pistol, without injury, however, to any one. After this Kolomin considered the country in a state of war, kept constant watch, and posted sentries. Moreover, there was fear that the savages, who could not fail to notice the quarrels between the Russians, might attack the weaker with a view to capturing the furs gathered by Kolomin during his residence of

---

[4] 'I had only twenty-seven men left of my crew, and as we were waiting to be called back we thought that Konovalof spoke the truth, and congratulated ourselves on having a new commander.' *Tikhmenef, Istor. Obos.,* ii. app. part ii. 51. The *Sv Pavl* had been sent home in 1789 with a cargo of his furs, and since then nearly 2,000 more skins had been collected.

[5] A demand for explanation elicited only threats. *Id.*

four years among them. Konovalof aggravated the situation by sending men to press some of Kolomin's *kayurs*, or native servants, into his own service, and the former on meeting with objections threatened to fire on the other party.[6] The ease with which this outrage was perpetrated encouraged another attack with a larger force, during which the remaining servants and the hostages were carried off, so that Kolomin had to send both for fresh recruits and for provisions. Even in this effort he met with trouble, for Lossef, the faithful lieutenant of Konovalof, dogged his footsteps, intercepted most of the levy, and maltreated the messengers.[7]

Kolomin had already complained to the Shelikof Company of this persecution, and as soon as the ice broke up on the inlet he proceeded to Kadiak, to confirm his previous report and urge Baranof to occupy the whole gulf. He advanced the opinion that, unless some responsible power interfered at once, all which he and his men had accomplished toward pacifying the natives and building up a profitable trade would be lost. Baranof by no means felt inclined to interfere between rival agents, particularly since the aggressive party would evidently not hesitate at shedding the blood even of their own countrymen; not that he lacked the courage, but he feared to risk his company's interests and men in fratricidal war, which might also arouse the natives. Moreover, his patron Shelikof possessed shares in the other company, and he preferred to report to him so that the matter might be settled by the principals. At the same time, however, he sent a warning to the St Nicholas people that

[6] The men were actually ordered to fire, but hesitated. Lossef, their leader, upbraided them, saying: 'It is not your business; we have already killed four Russians.' 'Wait until spring,' he exclaimed to Kolomin's party, 'and we will come to your station with fifty men and take away all the hostages you have.' *Tikhmenef, Istor. Obos.*, ii. app. part ii. 52–3. A converted native of Kadiak was robbed of his young wife and unmercifully beaten.

[7] Three men were deprived of their weapons and placed in the stocks for two days. Drushinin, an elder among the hunters, who came to expostulate, was put in irons.

he, as representative of one of the partners in the Lebedef Company, could not allow any aggressive measures that might be prejudicial to trade. This had the effect of greatly tempering the feeling of the St Nicholas party against Kolomin's men as of their own company, but directed their hostility against the rival company. They declared that the whole territory bordering upon the gulf of Kenaï belonged exclusively to the Lebedef Company, ignoring all previous arrangements between their acknowledged head and Shelikof. They certainly controlled nearly all the trade, and to this end they had erected another station higher up the inlet, on the western shore, and placed there a score of Russians.[3]

Robbery and brutal outrages continued to be the order of the day, though now committed chiefly for the purpose of obtaining sole control of the inlet, to the neglect of legitimate pursuits. Meanwhile Kolomin's men managed to hold their own, and, as the persecution of the Konovalof party gradually relaxed, their sympathies actually turned toward the latter in their effort to oust the Shelikof men from the field.

Thus the history of Cook Inlet during the last decade of the eighteenth century is replete with romantic incidents—midnight raids, ambuscades, and open warfare—resembling the doings of mediæval *raubritters*, rather than the exploits of peaceable traders. The leaders lived in rude comfort at the fortified stations, surrounded by a dusky harem containing contributions from the various native villages within the peredovtchik's jurisdiction. Offences against the dignity of the latter were punished quickly and effectually with the lash or confinement in irons or the stocks, if the offender had not too many friends among the Russian promyshleniki, and with extreme severity, verging upon cruelty, in cases where the culprit belonged to the

---

[3] It consisted of one large house about 50 feet long and 24 feet wide. *Vancouver's Voy.*, iii. 122.

unfortunate class of kayurs. The Russians did little work beyond the regular guard duty, and even that was sometimes left to trusted individuals among the native workmen and hangers-on of the station.

All manual labor was performed by natives, especially by the female 'hostages,' and children of chiefs from distant villages left at the stations by their parents to be instructed in Russian life and manners. The training which they were forced to undergo, far from exercising any civilizing influence, resulted only in making them deceitful, cunning, and more vicious than they had been before. Every Russian there was a monarch, who if he wanted ease took it, or if spoils, the word was given to prepare for an expedition. Then food was prepared by the servants, and the boats made ready, while the masters attended to their arms and equipments. The women and children were intrusted to the care of a few superannuated hunters left to guard the station, and the brave little band would set out upon its depredations, caring little whether they were Indians or Russians who should become their victims. The strangest part of it all was, that the booty secured was duly accounted for among the earnings of the company.[9]

Affairs were assuming a serious aspect. Not only were the Shelikof men excluded from the greater part of the inlet, but they were opposed in their advance round Prince William Sound, which was also claimed by the Lebedef faction, though the Orekhof and other companies were hunting there. The station which the Lebedef men made their base of operations was situated on Nuchek Island, at Port Etches, and consisted of the usual stockade, enclosing dwelling and store houses.[10] In support of his claims, Konovalof

[9] Shelikof, who held shares in both his own and the Lebedef Company, had the advantage of not only recovering what he lost by these plundering enterprises, but receiving his proportionate share of the losses in the Shelikof Company.

[10] Vancouver, *Voy.*, iii. 172, found one side of it formed by an armed vessel of 70 tons, hauled on shore.

declared that he possessed government credentials granting to his company exclusive right to all the mainland region. Yet he refused to exhibit even copies of such documents. Finding the Shelikof men disposed to yield, the others began to encroach also on the limited district round the Shelikof settlement, near the entrance to Cook Inlet, by erecting a post on Kuchekmak Bay, and the natives were forbidden, under pain of death, from trading with their rivals. From this post they watched the movements of the Shelikof men with a view to circumvent them. Forty bidarkas under Kotelnikof were intercepted, and although a number escaped, a portion of the crew, including the leader, was captured. Another party under Galaktianof, on the way from Prince William Sound, was chased by a large force, and efforts were made to attack Baranof himself. It was not proposed to keep the Russians prisoners, but merely to seize the furs and enslave all natives employed by Shelikof in the interdicted region. Fortunately Baranof had left the sound before the raiders arrived, and they passed on to the eastern shore, there to encroach on the trade established with the Yakutat Kaljushes by the Shelikof men, who held hostages from three of the villages. Not long after came Balushin with a stronger force; and one day, when the chief of one of the villages had set out upon a hunt with nearly all the grown males, the Russians entered it and carried off the women and children to a neighboring island.[11] They also made inroads on the northern part of the Alaskan peninsula which had been brought into friendly relations through Bocharof. Out of four friendly villages in Ilyamna and Nushagak, they plundered two and carried the people into captivity.

Their success was due partly to the personal bravery

---

[11] Balushin had destroyed the coat-of-arms bestowed upon the chief by order of the governor-general of Irkutsk, telling him that it was but a child's toy. *Tikhmenef, Istor. Obos.*, ii. app. part ii. 43.

and superior dash of the men. Baranof freely acknowledged in later years that, individually, the promyshleniki of the Lebedef Company were superior to those under his command at the beginning of his administration; and according to Berg, he ventured to assert that, had he commanded such men as Lebedef's vessels brought to the shores of Cook Inlet and Prince William Sound, he would have conquered the whole north-western coast of America.

Toward the end of 1793 Baranof had received a small reënforcement with the *Orel*, so that after deducting the loss by drowning and other casualties, one hundred and fifty-two men were left to him. The number of the Lebedef men is not recorded, but it cannot have been much inferior, for reënforcements had come in the *Sv Ivan*. The latter occupied an admirable strategic position, with control of two great navigable estuaries and other places offering easy communication and access to supplies. They were also better provided with goods and ship-stores than Shelikof's company.[12]

It was not so much these advantages of his assailants, however, that kept Baranof from energetic measures against them, but rather a consideration for the different interests of his patron, and for the lives of his countrymen. He was awaiting an answer to his reports from Siberia. This forbearance served only to encourage the other party, as we have seen, till at last Baranof's patience was exhausted. With the report of a fray between the rival posts on the inlet came the rumor that the ship-yard at Voskressenski Harbor was to be taken, and this appeared probable from the special animosity shown to the Englishmen there engaged. When not absolutely needed at the yard, they were sent to explore; and on several of

[12] Baranof reported, late in 1793, that he owed many bales of rope and four pouds of tobacco to the Lebedef Company, but, in view of the depredations committed by men belonging to the latter, he 'did not intend to return the goods until some action was taken upon his complaints to the authorities at Okhotsk.'

these occasions they had been set upon, robbed, and ill-treated, sometimes narrowly escaping with their lives.[13]

Baranof now hastened to the spot, and observing the need for interference, assumed the peremptory tone of one invested with authority. He sent a letter to Konovalof, then at his stockade at St Nicholas on the Kaknu River, with a summons to appear at once before him, stating that he had been authorized by the governor of Siberia to settle all disputes between rival traders. He expected soon to be invested with such powers, in answer to the urgent petitions of Shelikof and his partners, and thought that he might exercise the privilege in advance. This had its effect. Without suspecting that the order had no more foundation than his own boasted rights to possession, the conscience-stricken man hastened to obey what was supposed to be an official summons. He appeared before Baranof and offered apologies for his conduct, but the latter would listen to no explanation; he placed him in irons, and kept him under close guard until Ismailof arrived with his vessels, when not only the ringleader but seven of his companions who had also tendered their submission were taken to Kadiak and placed in confinement.

Finally Konovalof was made to answer at Okhotsk, but before a lenient committee, so that he readily managed to clear himself, and was restored to a command in Alaska. Meanwhile Stepan Zaïkof had succeeded him as chief at St Nicholas. Kolomin still held his command and Balushin controlled the establishment on Nuchek.[14]

---

[13] The prevailing starvation at the ship-yard was chiefly due to the interference of the Lebedef men with supplies.

[14] One reason for this clemency appears in a letter addressed by Lebedef and Shelikof jointly, to the archimandrite Ioassof, requesting him to investigate the charges against Konovalof and others, yet expressing the hope that the accused will not be found 'too guilty to be allowed to work off, in one company or the other, their indebtedness to their employers, and thus save the shareholders from loss.' If, however, Konovalof should be found too deeply involved to admit of his further employment, he was 'to be set at

While Baranof's firmness served to check the perpetration of extreme abuses, a certain hostility continued to be exhibited for some time. The evil was too deeply rooted to be eradicated all at once, but harmony was gradually restored, partly through the influential mediation of Archimandrite Ioassof, who arrived soon after as leader of a missionary party. At the same time came a large reënforcement for Baranof, with authority to form settlements in any part of Alaska, and right to claim the country for five hundred versts round such settlements, within which limits no other company could set foot. Against such power the Lebedef faction could not possibly prevail, particularly since Shelikof positively instructed Baranof to use both force and cunning to remove the rivals. Reverses also overtook them, and a few years later they abandoned the field.[15]

It was indeed time that Baranof should assert himself, for the insolence and outrages of the aggressors had created general discontent among the tribes. Those of Lake Skilakh were actually plotting the destruction of all Russians on the Kénaï peninsula, and to this end they endeavored to bridge over the old feud between them and the Chugatsches of Prince William Sound; receiving also encouragement from the treacherous tribes on the other side of the inlet, from Katmaï northward, who had successfully opposed all attempts to form Russian settlements in their midst. The measures now taken by Baranof to maintain better order and reassure the natives, as well as the *coup de main* with Konovalof, which added

liberty to shift for himself.' *Id.*, ii. app. part ii. 57–8. Ioassof, indeed, did not report him to be so bad as Baranof desired. Among the accused was Stepan Kosmovich Zaïkof, a brother of Potap Zaïkof, a man of considerable ability and knowledge. Ivan Koch, commander of Okhotsk, in a letter upbraids his dear friend Stepan Kuzmitch, and threatens him with the severest punishment if found guilty.

[15] 'You must declare in your reports,' wrote Shelikof, 'that the outrages upon the Kenaïtze were of the most disgraceful character, but that it is in your power to plant your settlements wherever you please, even on the gulf of Kenaï.' *Id.*, 69.

not a little to advance his influence, served to check
the threatened uprising. His assertion of authority
was equally necessary among his own subordinates,
whose loyalty had been corrupted by the insinuations
of emissaries from the other camp, and whose respect for their chief had begun to wane under his
forbearance toward the rivals, whereby numerous
hardships were entailed upon them through loss of
trade and curtailment of rations.[16] He assembled
the men, represented to them the obligations to
which they had voluntarily subscribed when engaged,
and showed the evil they were inflicting also on themselves by discontent, want of harmony, and refusal to
do the required work. He had full power to arrest
those who refused implicit obedience, and he would
use that power. Those who had complaints should
present them, and he would seek to redress their
wrongs.[17] This firm speech, together with a liberal
distribution of liquor, had a wonderful effect, and thus
by means of a little determined self-assertion Baranof
established for himself an undisputed authority, with
a reputation as a leader of men.[18]

The party war ended, Baranof breathed freely once
more, and 1794 witnessed a decided impulse to his different enterprises. The most notable of these was the
one intrusted to Purtof and Kulikatof for operating
in Yakutat Bay, of which a preceding visit had brought
most encouraging reports.[19] Preparations were made

[16] They appear to have received less compensation than the other company employees. Of the latter, Fidalgo reports: 'Sus sueldos llegaban los
mayores á cuatro pesos: que los jefes subalternos gozaban 500 al año.' But
he evidently ignores the share system. For each employee the company paid
a tribute of two dollars a year. *Salida*, etc., in *Viajes al Norte*, MS., 369.

[17] This characteristic address is given in full in *Tikhmenef, Istor. Obos.*, ii.
app. part ii. 47–9. It contains several allusions to historic anecdotes on
the value of unity, and dwells on the absurd pretensions to better comforts
by men who at home in Siberia were content to live as pigs.

[18] Some time before this he had interfered between rival traders of the
companies Orekhof, Panof, and Kisselef, located on Prince William Sound,
and after patching up a temporary peace between them he had seized the
greater part of their furs, under the pretext of taking them to Kadiak for safe
keeping.

[19] Tikhmenef refers confusedly to an expedition in 1793 of 170 bidarkas,

on a large scale. The station on Cook Inlet had been appointed as a rendezvous, and on the 7th of May a fleet of five hundred bidarkas assembled there, bringing natives from Kadiak, Kenaï, the Alaskan peninsula, and the nearest Chugatsch villages. More boats and men were to be collected at Prince William Sound, where Baranof had gone in person to levy forces. All these were arranged in subdivisions, each in charge of a Russian.

At Voskressenski Bay the Yakutat expedition was furnished with additional trading goods and some guns and ammunition. After being delayed at Grekof Island till the 22d of May, Purtof set out with his whole fleet for the mouth of Copper River, intending to pass by Nuchek Island, where the Lebedef Company was then established. At the eastern point of Montague Island they were intercepted by some Lebedef hunters in bidarkas, who presented a letter from Balushin and Kolomin. This document warned Purtof not to encroach upon any territory already occupied by the other company. The messengers were instructed to add, that they had established an artel of twenty Russians at Tatitliatzk village on the gulf of Chugatsch, and also at the mouth of Copper River, and that the Shelikof hunters must not advance in that direction. Without allowing himself to be intimidated, Purtof informed the messengers that he was on his way to the American continent in pursuance of secret orders from the government. In hunting sea-otters he would not touch upon any ground occupied by others.

The following evening, while preparing to camp for the night on a small island adjoining Nuchek, he discovered a party of eight Lebedef hunters near by and invited them to supper, after which the time passed in friendly exchange of news. Early in the morning, however, before the Lebedef men were stirring, Pur-

escorted by Shields, which brought back 2,000 sea-otter skins. *Istor. Obos.*, i. 40-1.

tof moved silently away with his force and made a
quick passage to the second mouth of Copper River,
and there fell in with Chugatsches who had been trading with the Lebedef men at Nuchek.   Finding that
no station or regular hunting party of the Lebedef
Company existed here, he took his party to Kaniak
Island, near the river, purposing to lay in a supply of
halibut as provisions, and to hunt sea-otters.   Over a
hundred skins were obtained the first day, but the
second day's hunt proved entirely futile and the expedition moved northward along the coast of the mainland.[20]

On the 31st of May the whole party encamped on
the beach, and within a short distance of a large Aglegmute village, though without being aware of the fact.
During the night some of the hunters became alarmed
at the sound of numerous voices proceeding from the
woods.   An armed detachment composed of the most
courageous ventured to penetrate into the forest, and,
guided by the smell of smoke and the cries of children,
made their way to the village, which was situated on
the opposite side of a river.   During the confusion
occasioned by their unexpected arrival, they succeeded
in capturing the chief and his brother, and then made
good their retreat to the camp.   One of their number,
however, a Kadiak interpreter, was intercepted and
killed by the natives.   The chief and his brother were
taken to the camp, treated to food and drink, and piled
with presents, until they promised to call together
their people the following day to negotiate with the
Russians.   The brother was commissioned to arrange
the matter, and by the 3d of June all of the Aglegmute
tribe dwelling in that vicinity came to the camp.
With the help of a judicious distribution of presents,
Purtof succeeded in prevailing upon the savages to
give seven hostages, including two natives of Yakutat
Bay.[21]

[20] During a brief halt on the beach a native hut was discovered, but the
inhabitants had fled, leaving all their effects.   A little food was taken by the
Aleuts, in return for which Purtof deposited some coral beads.

[21] In accordance with orders from the government, the savages were ques-

As soon as the weather permitted, Purtof proceeded to Icy Bay, called Natchik by the natives, and by the 10th of June his hunters had secured four hundred sea-otter skins, all that could be obtained. The party then moved on to Yakutat Bay, accompanied by the Aglegmute chief of the tribe, and a Kadiak native who spoke the Kaljush language. These two were sent in advance to assure the people of the peaceful character of the expedition.[22] The chief soon returned from the Yakutat village with the son of the Kaljush chieftain and three others as hostages, profusely ornamented with beads, furs, and feathers. The interpreter had been detained as hostage on the other side, but it was found necessary to surrender also a Russian ere confidence could be established. Accompanied by fifteen of his best warriors, the Kaljush chief then proceeded in state to the camp, and after the usual ceremonies negotiations began in earnest. Purtof declared that the Russians desired to live in friendship with them, and the chief, who probably had been plied with strong drink, made a formal present to his new allies of the southern portion of the bay and the small islands situated therein. The feelings of the latter underwent a change, however, when he came to reflect on the advantage gained by his visitors, and found that they also hunted on their own account, venturing far out to sea where the clumsier canoes of the Kaljush dared not follow. He and his followers were ready to trade, but they objected to see their stock of fur seals exhausted by strangers without any benefit to themselves.[23]

tioned whether they or any of the neighboring tribes held in their possession any European prisoners, but this they positively denied. It was thought that some of La Pérouse's men might have escaped drowning only to fall into the hands of the savage inhabitants of the vicinity.

[22] At the southern point of Yakutat Bay a hunt was organized, but only ten sea-otters could be found. In making a landing through the surf, two natives of Kadiak were drowned.

[23] The chief made a long speech before Lieutenant Puget, which he understood to convey this meaning. *Vancouver's Voy.*, ii. 234.

Trouble appeared, indeed, to be brewing, but the arrival of the *Chatham* of Vancouver's expedition, under Lieutenant Puget, served to prevent any disturbance. Purtof maintained a most friendly intercourse with the English, to whom he also tendered provisions, and received in acknowledgment letters of commendation. Through some of the sailors it was understood that English war-vessels might appear within two years to take possession of Cook Inlet and other places, and, unworthy of credit as this report was, it failed not to be transmitted to the government by the somewhat agitated fur traders. Vancouver himself held a much higher opinion, both of their territorial rights and control of trade, than a clearer view of affairs might have conveyed, for he was ignorant of their dissensions, and regarded all as united in one common interest; while the sight of the large native fleets controlled by Purtof must have exalted the idea of their influence and of their ability to distance competitors. The departure of Vancouver's expedition was no doubt a great relief to Baranof at least, who appears to have been afraid of his coming across the English shipwrights, and luring them away[24] ere he could dispense with their services.[25]

While the *Chatham* remained, Purtof's command occupied a position near the anchorage. Other parties of natives arrived from the interior of the bay and from Ltua, giving occasion for further feasting, presents, and exchange of hostages. The large number of guns, and the abundance of lead and powder in the possession of these new arrivals, pointed to visits from European trading vessels, and at this very time the *Jackall*, Captain Brown, entered the bay in quest of furs, to the deep chagrin of Purtof.

[24] The letters given to Purtof were even suspected for a while to be documents intended to support English claims. See letter of Mme Shelikof, in *Tikhmenef, Istor. Obos.*, ii. app. part ii. 108 et seq.

[25] Of this fear Vancouver knew nothing, for the Russians leaders were profuse in offers of services, even to the use of the ship-yard.

As soon as the war-vessel departed, the treacherous Kaljushes assumed a threatening attitude, and delayed from day to day the promised delivery of additional hostages under various pretexts. At the same time the interpreters left with the savages at the beginning of the negotiations were held under strict surveillance, and not allowed to communicate with their countrymen. At last Purtof decided upon a display of force to support his demands for the surrender of his own men at least, and approached the village in bidarkas with all the armed men at his command. The squadron was reënforced by a boat with six armed men from the *Jackall*.[26]

The presence of the Englishmen had no doubt an effect, for the interview resulted in the surrender of a chief from Afognak Island, with a promise to deliver up the remaining hostages.

On the following day came eight men in a large bidar, bringing three more natives of Kadiak, but two were still detained. Fearing that foul play was intended, Purtof detained some relatives of the Yakutat chief, and carried the hostages whom he held from the Aglegmutes on board the *Jackall* for safe keeping. This reprisal proved effectual; the necessary exchange of hostages was made, and, after expressing his thanks to Captain Brown, Purtof took his party out of the bay of Yakutat with five hundred and fifteen sea-otter skins obtained in a little over two weeks.

On the return voyage, while the expeditionary force was encamped on an island near Nuchek,[27] Purtof despatched a letter to Repin, of the Lebedef Company, informing him that he had explored the coast of the continent and pacified the natives of several villages by exchanging hostages. He offered to verify

[26] Captain Brown's statement, as given by Vancouver, would make it appear that Purtof asked for assistance, but the latter states that the English joined of their own accord, 'though we tried to dissuade them from doing this, and did not require their assistance.' This was on July 1st.

[27] Purtof persisted in calling this island Aglitzkoi, that is to say, English.

this statement, and on the appearance of Samoïlof, the navigator of the Lebedef Company, allowed him to talk freely with the interpreters, and to copy a list of the villages and chiefs from whom he had obtained hostages. This would seem to be a strange proceeding in view of the hostility between the two parties, but it was of the greatest importance for the Shelikof Company, at that juncture, to make good their claim of precedence on the continent, in view of the impending grant of exclusive imperial privileges.

The success of Purtof, who brought with him a promise from the Thlinkeet chief of a large supply of sea-otter skins for the next visit, resulted in the despatch of another expedition the following year, under Zaïkof, who commanded a sea-going vessel.[28] The chief failed to fulfil his promise, and the Russians had to content themselves with the sea-otters captured by their native hunters on the bay. Four hundred skins were secured, and the hunters prepared to follow up their success, regardless of the manifest ill-feeling of the bay people, which threatened to become more bitter than during the former visit. What the result may have been is difficult to say, for just then two Aleuts were seized with small-pox, and panic-stricken the party hastened away.[29] Zaïkof now steered in search of islands reported to exist between Kadiak and the continent to the east. He ranged for over a month to the southward and again to the north, until, sighting the snow-clad peaks of the Chugatsch alps and the Kenaï mountains, he was forced to admit the futility of his quest.

[28] Seventeen Russians, besides natives, accompanied him.
[29] La Pérouse noticed signs of the disease among the coast tribes, and Portlock assumes that they must have caught it from some vessel which had touched near Cape Edgecumbe. No person younger than 14 years bore the marks. *Portlock's Voy.*, 272; *Marchand, Voy.*, ii. 52-3.

CHAPTER XVI.

COLONIZATION AND MISSIONS.

1794-1796.

NOTWITHSTANDING the quarrels between rival trad-ing companies and occasional emeutes among the na-tives, caused in almost every instance by the greed of the Russians, colonization in Alaska had thus far been attended with fair success. The Russian seal-hunters had suffered no such hardships as did the Spanish settlers in Central America, the early colonists of New England, or the convict band that ten years after Captain Cook sailed from Nootka in quest of a north-east passage to Hudson's Bay founded on Port Jack-son the first city in Australasia. Apart from the seal fisheries, however, the resources of the country were as yet undeveloped. On the island of Kadiak was raised a scant crop of vegetables; at Voskressenski, as we have seen, was built the first vessel ever launched into the waters of the North Pacific; but throughout the settlements was felt a sore need of skilled labor, and in some of them, as Shelikof would have us believe, of missionaries to educate the natives and instruct

(351)

them in the true faith. Application was therefore
made for clergymen and for exiles trained to handi-
craft.[1] The request was granted, and in August 1794
the *Irekh Sviatiteli* and the *Ekaterina*, two of the
Shelikof Company's vessels,[2] arrived at Pavlovsk with
provisions, stores, implements, seeds, cattle, and a hundred and ninety-two persons on board, among whom
were fifty-two craftsmen and agriculturists, and eighteen clergymen and lay servitors in charge of the
archimandrite Ioassaf.[3] "I present you," writes Shelikof to Baranof, "with some guests who have been selected by order of the empress to spread the word
of God in America. I know that you will feel as
great a satisfaction as I do that the country where I
labored before you, and where you are laboring now
for the glory of our country, sees in the arrival of
these guests a hopeful prophecy of future prosperity."
Shelikof's merits as teacher and pastor have already
been related;[4] the treatment which the missionaries
received from his dram-drinking colleague will be
mentioned later. Priests were not wanted among the
promyshleniki, and if they sojourned in their midst
must earn their daily bread as did the rest of the
community. They might serve, however, to bring
into more thorough subjection the docile Aleuts.

By the *Ekaterina*, Baranof received a lengthy communication from Shelikof and from Polevoi Golikof's
representative, relating to the establishment of an agricultural colony near Cape St Elias on Yakutat Bay.
The instructions on this matter were to take the place

---

[1] Shelikof and Golikof requested that clergymen be appointed for missionary work in the Aleutian Islands and offered to defray all expenses.
By oukaz of June 30, 1793, Catherine II. ordered the petition granted. At
the same time Shelikof asked the governor of Irkutsk to use his influence
with the crown to procure the despatch of a certain number of exiles, skilled
as blacksmiths, locksmiths, and foundrymen, and of ten families trained to
agriculture. The request was granted by oukaz of December 31, 1793.
Tikhmenef, Istor. Obos., i. 42-3.
[2] Both built at Okhotsk. The former, though only 63 feet in length, had
on board 260 tons of cargo, besides 120 casks of water.
[3] There were also 121 hunters, 4 clerks, and 5 Aleuts.
[4] This vol., p. 227.

of all that had previously been sent.[5]   Accompanying them was a document touching only on the private affairs of the company.   Thanking Baranof for his exhaustive reports, Shelikof concludes: "And now it only remains for us to hope that, having selected on the mainland a suitable place, you will lay out the settlement with some taste, and with due regard for beauty of construction, in order that when visits are made by foreign ships, as can not fail to happen, it may appear more like a town than a village, and that the Russians in America may live in a neat and orderly way, and not, as in Okhotsk, in squalor and misery caused by the absence of nearly everything necessary to civilization.   Use taste as well as practical judgment in locating the settlement.   Look to beauty as well as to convenience of material and supplies.   On the plans as well as in reality leave room for spacious squares for public assemblies.   Make the streets not too long, but wide, and let them radiate from the squares.   If the site is wooded, let trees enough stand to line the streets and to fill the gardens, in order to beautify the place and preserve a healthy atmosphere.   Build the houses along the streets, but at some distance from each other, in order to increase the extent of the town.   The roofs should be of equal height, and the architecture as uniform as possible. The gardens should be of equal size, and provided with good fences along the streets.   Thanks be to God that you will at least have no lack of timber.   Make the plan as full as possible, and add views of the sur-

[5] The letter was dated from Okhotsk on the 9th of August, 1794.   Orders had been received from the governor of Irkutsk that the agriculturists, including ten families, should be forwarded to the spot near Cape St Elias where Shelikof had promised to establish the first agricultural settlement on the north-west coast of America; but it was claimed that a clause in the instructions permitted the site of this colony to be changed, if a more suitable location could be found, and finally the exiled agriculturists were scattered throughout the settlement and employed in various kinds of labor.   Most of the exiles of whatever occupation arrived in the *Catherine* after much delay, caused by a stay at Unalaska, and by a violent gale in Akutan Pass, during which several head of cattle were lost.   Khlebnikof, *Shizn. Baranova*, 24–5, states that the remainder of the live-stock reached Kadiak in safety.

HIST. ALASKA. 23

roundings. Your work will be viewed and discussed at the imperial court." In another part of this letter Baranof is reproached for exchanging visits with captains of English vessels, and warned that he might be carried off to Nootka or California, or some other desolate place.

The latter portion of this epistle appears to have been written for the purpose of deceiving the empress, to whom the plans of the proposed settlement were to be shown, though we cannot but admire the comprehensive scope of Shelikof's imagination when he thus conceives the idea of building a well ordered city in the American wilderness. Although such an undertaking would require all the means and men at the disposal of the Shelikof-Golikof Company, he was engaged, besides other ventures, in forming a second association under the name of the North American Company, for the purpose of making permanent settlements on the mainland, and in building ships for yet a third enterprise of which he was the leading man—the Predtecha Company, then holding temporary possession of the Pribylof Islands, but left without means of carrying away their seal-skins by the loss of their only vessel. The estimated complement for the North American Company was a hundred and twenty men, of whom seventy were despatched in July 1794, and about thirty in 1795. Its main object was to aid in supplanting foreigners in the trade with the natives, to extend this traffic from Unalaska to the Arctic Ocean, and to enter into commercial intercourse with the people living on the American coast, opposite Cape Tehcukotsk. Moreover, Shelikof cherished in secret the hope of making some new discovery on the American continent, leading to the long-sought-for passage into Baffin's Bay.

As soon as Shelikof had despatched his vessels from Okhotsk, he returned in 1794 to Irkutsk for the purpose of organizing there a central office for the management of his many enterprises, thus preparing for the future consolidation of all the Russian companies in America. This was the inception of the great Russian American Company, which was to be fully organized only after its originator's death. Meanwhile Baranof could do, and knew that he was expected to do, but little toward carrying out his superior's brilliant schemes of colonization. On all the principal islands of the Aleutian group, and at some points on the mainland, the best locations for agriculture and cattle-raising had been selected and fortified several years before; additional hunting grounds and a few harbors had also been chosen, and sites marked out at the mouths of rivers for trading posts with the natives. But the time was not yet ripe for establishing new settlements, and meanwhile in accordance with private instructions Shelikof kept the exiles busily employed, some of them at Kadiak, and the mechanics probably at Voskressenski, where, it will be remembered, the *Delphin* and *Olga* were launched in 1795.[6]

The *Trekh Sviatitelei* had arrived a few weeks before these vessels were completed, after a two years' voyage from Kamchatka, with her cargo of stores and provisions in good order and intact—a rare occurrence in the early history of the Russian colonies. Several days were now devoted to feasting and rejoicing, in which traders, priests, and servants alike participated. The colonists were, however, no longer in fear of want, for experiments made in the planting of several kinds of vegetables and occasionally of cereals had been fairly successful, and, though they possessed few implements, they had seed in abundance for either purpose.[7] Thus, with a never failing supply of fish, an abundance of food was, as they thought, assured.

---

[6] Four of the exiled families selected for the company were detained by Shelikof at Okhotsk, to serve as a nucleus for a proposed settlement on one of the Kurile Islands.

[7] Father Simeon and one of the lay brothers of the mission, named Philip, made some experiments in sowing turnips and potatoes which succeeded well. The archimandrite mentions a man named Saposhnikof, who planted a pound of barley in a sheltered nook and harvested 60 pounds. *Tikhmenef, Istor. Obos.*, ii. app. part ii. 102. With this exception, nothing appears to have

In December of this year Baranof set forth on a
journey round Kadiak, his purpose being to make
arrangements for the hunting season, and to ascertain
the population of the island, which was found to consist of 6,206 persons, the sexes being about equally
divided.[8] About seven hundred bidarkas, each holding two men, could be assembled at the different stations.

Though the archimandrite had previously described
Baranof as a man who "continually sat in his house
hatching mischief," and, in a letter to Shelikof, had
declared that he could see no sign that any of his
schemes of colonization were likely to be carried out,
the chief manager certainly took some steps toward
establishing the much-talked-of settlement near Cape
St Elias. Intrusting the management of affairs at
Kadiak to his assistant Kuskof,[9] he sailed for Yakutat
in the transport *Olga*,[10] and arrived at the village near
Cape St Elias on the 15th of July, 1796, finding there
the *Trekh Sviatitelei*, which had reached the new settlement on the 25th of June. The few men left at the
place the previous autumn were found in good health,
but complained of having been frequently in want of
food during the winter. Baranof himself remained
here two months, superintending the erection of buildings; and after taking hostages from the natives and
leaving a garrison of fifty men, returned to Kadiak.

Meanwhile the *Ekaterina*, with a portion of the
exiles on board, and the transport *Orel*, under command of Shields, had sailed for Cape St Elias, the latter
convoying four hundred and fifty bidarkas bound for

been done with the imported seed of rye and oats, as the only implements for
breaking up the ground were forked sticks.
    [8] There were 3,221 males and 2,985 females.
    [9] Ivan Alexandrovich Kuskof, a merchant of Totma, came to America
with Baranof, in the capacity of clerk. He was soon appointed assistant, and
as we shall see intrusted with important commands. He left the service of
the company in 1821, returned to Russia by way of Okhotsk in 1822, and
died at Totna in 1823. *Khlebnikof, Shizn. Baranova*, passim.
    [10] It was intended that Pribylof, the discoverer of the fur-seal islands,
should take command, but his decease occurred before the departure of the
expedition.

Ltua Bay,[11] where in a few days 1,800 sea otter skins were secured.

Thus, at length, the settlement on Yakutat Bay was fairly started with every prospect of success; but this, the first convict colony established in the far north, like the one sent forth two years later to people the desert wastes of Australia, was doomed to suffer many disasters. During the very first winter news reached Kadiak that the village was in danger of being abandoned for want of provisions.[12] The *Trekh Sviatitelei*, which left the settlement on her return voyage a few days before Baranof's departure, was driven by heavy gales into Kamuishatzk Bay. There a large force of men was sent early in the following spring to repair the vessel, but she was found to be so badly damaged that her hull was set on fire, and only her iron-work was saved. At Voskressenski Bay Baranof was met by a messenger from Yakutat, who reported that twenty laborers and several women had perished of scurvy at the settlement during the past winter.

While hastening to the relief of the distressed settlers, the chief manager found time to visit Fort Konstantine on Nuchek Island, where the Lebedef-Lastochkin Company had hitherto maintained their principal depot. For several years no supplies had been forwarded to this place, and in consequence great dissatisfaction existed among the employees of the firm. Baranof found no great difficulty in inducing a majority of the Lebedef men to enter the service of the Shelikof Company, and the remainder were promised a passage to Okhotsk. At the same time the Chugatsches formally submitted to Baranof and furnished

[11] Two other bidarka fleets mustering 257 boats assembled during the same year at the village of Karluk, and after obtaining supplies of dried fish were despatched in the same direction. Each bidarka carried from 100 to 125 fish, but this food was used only in case of actual necessity. As a rule, fresh fish were caught and birds killed at every halting place. *Khlebnikof, Shizn. Baranova*, 34–5.

[12] The news was brought by one Radionof, who arrived at Kadiak from Cape St Elias in a bidar.

an additional quota of a hundred bidarkas to reënforce
his hunting parties, thus relieving him of all apprehensions of a native uprising west of Yakutat, and enabling
him to turn his undivided attention to the wants of
the new colony.

After relieving the existing distress and establishing order among the settlers, Baranof returned to Kadiak, arriving there on the first of October.   Shields,
who commanded the *Orel*, had in the mean time proceeded south-west from Ltua Bay with his fleet of
four hundred and fifty bidarkas, and succeeded in
reaching Norfolk Sound, where he soon collected two
thousand sea-otter skins.

We shall have occasion to refer later to the progress of the convict colony at Yakutat.   Shelikof
and his colleagues, when petitioning the empress that
a band of exiles should be sent to Alaska to aid in
developing the resources of Russian America, and a
party of clergymen to convert and educate the natives,
assured the government "that their wishes tended only
to add new possessions to Russia and new parishes to
the church."   "But," says Golovnin, who was instructed by the government to investigate the affairs
of the colony, "the clergy and the poor mechanics
had hardly arrived at Kadiak, when the former were
set to earn their bread by the sweat of their brow,
and the latter were distributed over different localities, wherever furs could be got to swell the profits
of the Shelikof Company.   Between 1794 and 1818
the missions received from the company neither bibles
nor new testaments, nor any other religious books,
not even spelling-books to teach the children, while
wax candles, wine, etc., necessary for the performance
of sacred ceremonies, could not be obtained from them.
But of the thirty-five families of mechanics only three
men and one woman remained in 1818.[13]   The re-

---

[13] About the year 1870 Ivan Petrof states that there are at Niniltchik,
on Cook Inlet, six families, including some forty souls, claiming to be descendants of these exiles.

mainder were killed or died from want and hardship,
while hunting for the company. For all this I am
in possession of written proofs. And thus Shelikof
showed to the world that between traders on a large
or small scale there is no difference. As the shopman
in the market makes the sign of the cross and calls
God to witness in order to sell his goods a few copeks
dearer, so Shelikof used the name of Christ and this
sacred faith to deceive the government and entice
thirty-five unfortunate families to the savage shores
of America, where they fell victims to his avarice and
that of his successors."[14]

All this is sufficiently bitter, and if any further
proof be wanted that Golovnin was somewhat biased,
his mention of Baranof, whom he describes as "a
man who became famous on account of his long residence among the savages, and still more so because
he, while enlightening them, grew wild himself and
sunk to a degree below the savage," is further evidence.[15] It is but due to the memory of Shelikof,
whose decease occurred in July 1795, to quote a few
lines from the letter of his widow, addressed on
November 22d of that year to the governor of
Tauris: "The administration of the colony has made
arrangements that these settlers shall not be hampered in their work of constructing the new village
by anxiety with regard to producing the necessary
provisions during the first year, and has provided
ample supplies of food to last them until they can
provide for themselves, as well as tools, etc., all of
which have been purchased at Okhotsk by my late
husband at his own expense. At the same time an
agent was appointed to attend to the issue of these
supplies, according to the wants of the people. But
finally they got up a conspiracy, and threatened to
take the agent's life unless he gave them guns and
ammunition to protect themselves against the sav-

[14] *Materialui Istor. Russ.*, i. 54.
[15] *Id.*, 53.

ages when they would reach the mainland, and that they would take possession of the ship and sail for the Kurile Islands, selecting one of their men as navigator. They had three great guns with ammunition, all ready for use, but the chief agent of the company discovered their conspiracy, and three of the ringleaders were, in accordance with the instructions of the commanding officer at Okhotsk, punished by flogging, and separated among the hunters at various stations." [16]

Knowing how he had compromised himself in his dealings with the turbulent traders on Cook Inlet by assuming official authority which did not belong to him, Baranof had to exert all his ingenuity, and probably resorted to threats and violence, in order to keep the knowledge of his proceedings from the priests, who were only too ready to meddle with the concerns of the Shelikof Company. [17] Though outwardly professing the veneration of an orthodox member of the Russian church for its ordained representatives, Baranof considered them as enemies and acted accordingly. He knew that in the pursuit of his business the full control of the natives was essential to his success, and he believed that every one of the missionaries would strive to obtain such control for himself in the name of the holy synod. In order to lessen the number of his enemies, he urged upon Ioassaf the necessity of sending out missionaries to the savage tribes of the mainland, from whom the light of Christianity was still entirely hidden. The chief of the mission expressed his full understanding of this necessity, but winter

---

[16] *Tikhmenef, Istor. Obos.*, ii. app. part ii. 109.

[17] The following is a list of members of this first mission: Archimandrite Ioássaf, drowned on the *Feniks* in 1799; Ieromonakh Juvenal, killed by the savages in northern America, as will be afterward related; Ieromonakh Makar, returned voluntarily to Okhotsk; Affanassic, returned to Irkutsk in 1825; Ierodiakon Stefan, drowned in the suite of the bishop; Nektar, sent to Irkutsk by Father Gideon in 1807; Monk German, still among the living in 1835; Monk Ioassaf, who died at Kadiak in 1823; and ten church servitors not belonging to the priesthood.

was then approaching fast and the journey to the continent was becoming dangerous. Thus Baranof was obliged to face his adversaries during the whole of a long arctic winter, and to counteract their intrigues as best he might.

The attitude assumed by the first apostles of Christianity in Alaska from the very beginning of their residence in America was decidedly hostile to all who managed and carried on business enterprises in the colonies. Previous to reaching their destination the members of this mission were detained for a whole winter in the wretched sea-port towns of eastern Siberia and Kamchatka, where they met with numbers of the former servants of the various trading companies, who were full of discontent and resentment, and painted to them in the blackest colors the condition of the country and the people inhabiting it. The result was that the priests finally sailed for the American coast imbued with a prejudice against everything and everybody belonging to the colonies. Being thus prepared to see nothing but evil, priestly ingenuity and craft succeeded in finding much more than had been discovered by their ignorant informers. In the correspondence transmitted by members of the mission to Shelikof, and to dignitaries of the synod, during this first period of their missionary work, they make the worst of everything.

The archimandrite was especially bitter in his denunciations of the chief manager, but there is little doubt that many of his accusations were unfounded.[13]

[13] Though the tone of his letters and reports is decidedly hostile to Baranof, the latter seems to have succeeded in concealing from the inquisitive clergy his wrongful assumption of authority in Cook Inlet, which would have exposed him to the most severe punishment by the authorities. I make the following extract from the letter of the archimandrite to Shelikof, written in May 1795: 'We have no proper church as yet, and though I personally urged Alexander Andreievitch [Baranof] to build a small church at this place as soon as possible, and offered a plan for a chapel only four fathoms long by a fathom and a half in width, the timber for it still remains uncut. Since my arrival at this harbor I have seen nothing but what seems to be in direct opposition to your kind intentions. The only thing which gives me satisfaction is the fact that the natives flock in from everywhere to become christianized, but the Russians not only make no effort to help

It must be admitted, however, that the ecclesiastics suffered many privations through the neglect of Baranof and the traders, who regarded them simply as intermeddlers, of whom they must rid themselves as speedily as possible. During their first winter the missionaries were without sufficient food and shelter;[19] no encouragement was afforded them in their work, and it was not until July 1796 that the first church was built in Kadiak, at Three Saints, though before that time it was claimed that twelve thousand natives had been baptized.

While making his report to Shélikof, the archiman-

in the work of enlightenment, but use every means to discourage them, and the cause of this is the vicious lives they have been leading from the first with American [native] women. I have barely succeeded in persuading a few hunters to get married, but the others will not even listen to such a proposal. Thus far I have not been enabled to discover whether it is Mr Baranof or his assistants who are endeavoring to cause ill-feeling against us and you. All I can say is that the hunters are incensed against you. All do their best to evade compliance with the written clauses of their contracts with you. Ships and other property of the company are neglected, and many say that the company's interests are opposed to those of the settlers, and try to persuade others to think the same.' *Tikhmenef, Istor. Obos.*, ii. app. part ii. 101–2.

[19] 'About the domestic arrangements,' continues Ioassaf, 'nothing good can be said. Since our arrival there has been a famine during the whole winter. Yukola [dried salmon] three years old is all that is offered us, and though we do not like dried fish, we are compelled to eat it. The laborers do nothing toward providing food. The nets were left on the ground near the beach all winter, being thoroughly spoiled. The dogs have eaten up two of the calves which we brought with us, and of the two sheep which remained to us on our arrival, one was devoured by dogs. The goats all perished. In accordance with your instructions, I was to accustom my clergymen to the food of the country, and to employ them at various kinds of labor, but this would have been done without your instructions. We are not troubled with an abundance of provisions, keeping our table upon the beach, picking up mussels, clams, and crabs. In addition to this, we have a little bread, and that will soon be exhausted. Baranof and his favorites do not suffer; for him they shoot birds, sea-lions, and seals. From the Alaskan peninsula they bring him reindeer meat. Milk he has always, even in the winter, two cows being reserved for his use alone. They used to give us milk enough for our tea, but at the present time, when ten cows have calved, we get only one tea-cupful a day, exclusive of fast-days. Our light is miserable, as we get nothing but whale-oil for that purpose. Then the winter was very cold, the roofs leaky, and the windows very bad; thus we passed the whole winter. I have never felt comfortable since my arrival here. I bore with our miserable accommodations as long as I could, and sent the brothers to the barracks where the working people live; but it would not do for me to go there in the position of dignity I hold here; and the barracks were full and even crowded. They had frequent assemblies and games there, and often whole nights were passed in singing and dancing. They kept it up every Sunday and holiday, and sometimes even on work-days. On Ash Wednesday they came to me and asked me to postpone the confession until evening, when they would have finished their games.' *Id.*, 102–4.

drite states that he could fill a book with the evil
doings and atrocities that came under his observation,
but that out of consideration for him he would not
lodge a formal complaint with the supreme church
authorities. He felt that even if Baranof knew that
he was writing the truth to the head of the company,
he would be prevented from making any further
progress in his work, and perhaps even endanger his
life. He expressed his firm belief that no admonition
of the managers by his superiors could do any good,
and that removal alone could remedy the evil. Should
that be considered impracticable, he would suffer in
silence, doing all the good that was possible under
such unfavorable circumstances, and patiently awaiting the time when providence would carry him and
his much-abused brethren back to Russia, beyond the
control of their 'untiring persecutor.' The reverend
correspondent likewise throws out hints of misman-
agement and peculation in business affairs.[20]

On the other hand, the letters of Baranof and his
chief assistants, written during the same period, display a marked forbearance in speaking of the missionaries and their doings.[21] The difficulties of Baranof's position during this winter of close companion-
ship with inquisitive, suspicious priests, rebellious
servants, and discontented natives cannot well be

[20] Ioassaf wrote: He (Baranof) has sold his tobacco at 400 roubles per
poud (40 lbs.) and more, though he had on hand over 20 pouds belonging to
the company. *Id.*, 105.

[21] This must of course be partly ascribed to policy on their part, but a
perusal of these documents impresses upon the reader the conviction that the
part which the traders were obliged to play in this controversy was more
difficult than that of the priests, and that the former were perfectly honest in
attempting to avoid all complications. The charges advanced by missionaries, of being starved and forced to pick up their food on the beach while
Baranof and his favorites feasted upon the fat of the land, is not sustained by
such credible witnesses as Lieutenants Khvostof and Davidof and other naval
officers then entering the employ of the Russian-American Company, who
all testified to the fact that Baranof and his favored leaders shared all privations with their subordinates. At the very time when Ioassaf complained
in his letter of Baranof's delay in erecting a church or chapel, the latter,
though lacking time, men, and means to employ in church building just then,
donated 1,500 roubles from his own salary for the purpose. *Id.*, i. 50, and ii.
app. 150-1.

exaggerated. No supplies of provisions had arrived with the missionaries, who, to a certain extent, were responsible for their own privations, having feasted and lived in too great abundance during their detention on the coast of Siberia and on the sea voyage.

In the spring of 1795 the missionaries, with one exception, proceeded to the mainland, there to labor with but indifferent success among the native tribes not previously approached by the pioneers of Muscovite civilization.

At Unalaska and the neighboring islands Father Makar, though meeting with little opposition from the few promyshleniki remaining there, labored with apparent success.[22] The natives were now thoroughly subdued, and hundreds of them had been carried away to join the hunting parties of Baranof. Their territory no longer afforded sites for profitable stations, and they were left almost to themselves. An indifference bordering on apathy had succeeded to the former warlike spirit of the Aleuts, who in earlier days had wreaked dire vengeance upon their Russian oppressors whenever opportunity offered. It is impossible to ascertain whether Makar was really an eloquent preacher of the gospel, or whether his success was solely due to circumstances; but success he certainly had. In a few years nearly all the inhabitants of the Aleutian Isles were baptized and duly reported to the holy synod as voluntary converts and good Christians. The circumstance that no attempt was made to translate the confession of faith, or any portion of the scripture or ritual, into the native language at that early time, suggests serious doubts as to the agency of eloquence and argument in this wholesale conversion. When Veniaminof entered upon his missionary career on the

[22] The father appears to have been a somewhat meddlesome ecclesiastic. In a copy of an imperial rescript issued a few years later, we read: 'The monk Makar, who has exceeded the bounds of his duties and meddled with affairs that did not concern him, is hereby informed that though we pardon him this time for absenting himself wilfully from his appointed post of duty, he must not repeat the offence, and must allow complaints made by the Aleutians to go through their proper channel.' *Id.*, 173.

islands twenty years later, he found the people Christians by name, but was compelled to begin from the foundation the work of enlightenment and explanation of the creed in which they had been baptized by Makar.

With the death of Shelikof the missionaries lost their principal support, and no further attempt was made to extend their operations until the archimandrite Ioassaf was recalled to Irkutsk by order of the synod, in order to be consecrated as bishop. He started upon his journey full of ambitious plans, and with the determination to make use of his new dignity in overcoming all opposition, real or imaginary, on the part of his persecutors. Visions of building up an ecclesiastical empire in Russian America may have gladdened his soul after years of suffering and humiliation; but whatever his ambitious dreams may have been, they must have lost much in scope and vividness long before he embarked in the *Feniks* a second time, not to return in splendor to the scene of former misery, but to find a watery grave at some unknown point within a few days' sail of his destination.

Prominent among the missionaries who accompanied the archimandrite was Father Juvenal, who in 1795 was sent to Yakutat Bay, probably to draw plans for Baranof, and on his return commenced to labor at Kadiak as a priest and teacher. "With the help of God," he writes from Three Saints Harbor on June 19, 1796, "a school was opened to-day at this place, the first since the attempt of the late Mr Shelikof to instruct the natives of this neighborhood. Eleven boys and several grown men were in attendance. When I read prayers they seemed very attentive, and were evidently deeply impressed, though they did not understand the language." On the following day two more youths were placed under his charge, and "when school was closed," continues the father, "I went to the river with my boys, and with

the help of God we caught one hundred and three salmon of large size, which some of the women assisted
us in cutting up ready for drying."[23]   Other scholars
were quickly enrolled, and though the pupils had an
unpleasant trick of running off without ceremony to
trade furs whenever opportunity offered, all went well
until the 12th of July, when Baranof arrived at the
settlement, with instructions from the bishop of
Irkutsk that Juvenal should proceed to Ilyamna station.

On the following sabbath the priest celebrated
divine service for the last time at Three Saints.   A
brief description of the ceremony may not be without
interest: "We had a very solemn and impressive
service this morning.   Mr Baranof and officers and
sailors from the ship attended, and also a large number of natives.   We had fine singing, and a congregation with great outward appearance of devotion.   I
could not help but marvel at Alexander Alexandre-
ievitch [Baranof], who stood there and listened and
crossed himself, gave the responses at the proper time,
and joined in the singing with the same hoarse voice
with which he was shouting obscene songs the night
before, when I saw him in the midst of a drunken
carousal with a woman seated in his lap.   I dispensed
with services in the afternoon, because the traders
were drunk again, and might have disturbed us and
disgusted the natives."

The next day Juvenal repaired to Baranof's tent to
inquire what disposition was to be made of the pupils
under his charge.   The reply was that they were to
be removed to Pavlovsk, where Father German had
arrived and opened a school for girls; he would doubtless be willing to take the boys also.

---

[23] *Jour.*, MS., 1-2.   Of the visit of some strangers who came from Tugi-
dak Island to trade, he relates the following: 'They asked me if I could cure
a man when he was very sick, and I answered that with the help of God I
might.   At this they shrugged their shoulders, and one man said: " We have
a shaman at home who once brought a dead man back to life; and he did it
all alone."'   *Id.*, 9.

After blessing his flock and taking leave of them one by one, the priest embarked for Pavlovsk on the 16th of July on board the brigantine *Catherine*, where, he tells us, the cabin being taken up by Baranof and his party, he was shown a small space in the hold between some bales of goods and a pile of dried fish. In this dark and noisome berth, by the light of a wretched lantern, he wrote a portion of his journal, often disturbed by the ribald songs which the chief manager's attendants sang for his amusement. On the second day of the voyage a strong head wind set in, accompanied with a heavy chopping sea. Baranof, being out of humor, sent for the father and asked him whether he had blessed the ship. On being told that he had done so, he was ordered with many curses to light a taper before an image of Nikolai Ugodnik, which hung in the cabin. Juvenal complied without a word, and then retired to his berth, which, foul as it was, he preferred to the company of the chief manager. The gale continued over night, and at daybreak the vessel was out of sight of land, whereupon in presence of the sailors and passengers Baranof spoke of the priest as a second Jonah, and observed that there were plenty of whales about. All this time the latter was unable to partake of food, and, as he says, was buried under a heap of dried fish whenever the vessel rolled heavily.

At Pavlovsk, Juvenal noticed the great activity in building, which was not even interrupted on the sabbath. On the fourth day after his arrival he took his leave of Baranof, who promised him a passage in his fleet of bidarkas as far as St George on the gulf of Kenaï, but told him that afterward he must depend on the Lebedef Company, whose traders, he added with a malicious grin, "were little better than robbers and murderers."[24]

[24] During his stay at Pavlovsk Juvenal was lodged in a half-finished hut intended for a salt-house, where swarms of mosquitoes deprived him of rest. Before his departure he had an interview with Father German, who, he says, was on the best terms with Baranof. When asked whether he had any ma-

After a tedious passage from island to island, sometimes meeting with long delays, the priest reached the Kaknu or Kenaï River, where was the nearest station of the Lebedef Company, on the 11th of August. Here, notwithstanding Baranof's warning, he met with the first signs of religious observance by promyshleniki during his travels in the colonies.[25] During his stay of about a fortnight he married several couples, baptized a number of infants and adults, and at intervals held divine service, which was well attended.[26]

Soon, however, the religious ardor cooled, and so little interest did the natives take in the missionary that, when ready to depart, he found it difficult to obtain men and bidarkas to take him across the inlet to his destination. At last one morning after service he appealed to the natives for men to assist him across the water, telling them that he must go to the Ilyamna country to preach the new word to the people, who had never yet heard it. Thereupon an old man arose and remarked that he ought not to go; that the Kenaïtze people had been the friends of the Russians for long years, and had a better right to have a priest among them than the Ilyamnas, who were very bad. The missionary, in his journal, confessed that he was puzzled for a fitting reply to this argument. On the 25th, however, he set out from the station, accompanied by two men from Chekituk village.

A delay was again occasioned by his guides indulging in a seal-hunt on Kalgin Island, situated midway

tron in charge of his school for girls, German laughed and said there was no need of one. 'I intended,' writes Juvenal, 'to recommend my boys at Three Saints Harbor to the special attention of Father German, but his repulsive manner caused me to change my intention, and now I pray that the poor little fellows may never be intrusted to his care.' *Id.*, 24–5.

[25] Juvenal writes: 'Stepan Laduiguin is the trader for the Lebedef-Lastochkin Company, and he has with him four other Russians and nearly a hundred Kenaïtzo, who are all Christians. Ignatiy Terentief, one of the Russians, reads prayers on the sabbath, but no priest has visited the place since the archimandrite's arbitration.' *Id.*, 40.

[26] During this time several shocks of earthquake occurred, and a stabbing affray between two natives, which was punished by flogging both offenders severely.

in the inlet, and the western shore was not reached till the 29th. On the 30th he writes: "This morning two natives came out of the forest and shouted to my companions. Two of the latter went out to meet them. There was a great deal of talking before the strangers concluded to come to our tents. When they came at last, and I was pointed out to them as the man who was to live among them, they wished to see my goods. I encountered some difficulty in making them understand that I am not here to trade and barter, and have nothing for sale. Finally, when they were told that I had come among them to make better men of them, one of them, named Katlewah, the brother of a chief, said he was glad of that, as they had many bad men among the Ilyamna people, especially his brother. The two savages have agreed to carry my chattels for me to their village, but, to satisfy Katlewah, I was compelled to open every bundle and show him the contents. I did not like the greedy glitter in his eye when he saw and felt of my vestments."

On the 3d of September the party reached Ilyamna village, after a fatiguing journey over the mountains and a canoe voyage on the lake. Shakmut, the chief, received the missionary with friendly words, interpreted by a boy named Nikita, who had been a hostage with the Russians. He invited him to his own house, and on the priest's expressing a wish for a separate residence, promised to have one built for him, and allowed him to retain Nikita in his service. Finding that the latter, though living with the Russians for years, had not been baptized, Juvenal performed that ceremony at the first opportunity, before the astonished natives, who regarded it as sorcery, and one asked whether Nikita would live many days.[27]

[27] Under date of September 5th, Juvenal writes: 'It will be a relief to get away from the crowded house of the chief, where persons of all ages and sexes mingle without any regard to decency or morals. To my utter astonishment Shakmut asked me last night to share the couch of one of his wives. He has three or four. I suppose such abomination is the custom of the coun-

Juvenal's success was not remarkable, to judge from his diary. One young woman asked to be baptized like the boy Nikita, expressing the hope that then she could also live in the new house with the missionary. An old woman brought two boys, stating that they were orphans who had nobody to care for them, and that she would like to see them baptized, "to change their luck." The chief Shakmut also promised to consider the question of embracing Christianity, and for some reason he did so promise in the presence of the whole tribe, and amidst great feasting and rejoicing. Two servants and one of his wives were included in the ceremony, the priest not daring to refuse them on the ground that they had received no instructions, for fear of losing the advantage which the chief's example might give him in his future work.[23]

The conversion of the chief had not, however, the desired effect; it only led to dissensions among the people, and when the priest began to tell the converts

---

try, and he intended no insult. God gave me grace to overcome my indignation, and decline the offer in a friendly and dignified manner. My first duty, when I have somewhat mastered the language, shall be to preach against such wicked practices, but I could not touch upon such subjects through a boy interpreter.' *Id.*, 55–6.

[23] Juvenal evidently had no faith in his convert, as evinced in the following extracts from his journal, p. 64–7: 'Shakmut comes regularly for instruction, but I have my doubts of his sincerity. In order to give more solemnity to the occasion, he has concluded to have two of his servants or slaves baptized also. They only come at his command, of course, but I must bear with a great deal until this conversion has become an accomplished fact. Katlewah, the chief's brother, called upon me to-day, and repeated that he was glad that Shakmut was to be baptized, for he was very bad, and if I made him a good man, he and all the Ilyamna people would rejoice and be baptized also. I do not like this way of testing the efficacy of Christianity; only a miracle of God could effect such a sudden change in Shakmut's heart.' It was making altogether too practical and literal a matter of conversion to suit the good Juvenal. On September 21st he writes: 'The great step which is to lay the foundation of future success in my labors has been taken. The chief of the Ilyamnas has been baptized, with two of his slaves and one of his wives. The latter came forward at the last moment, but I dared not refuse her for fear of stopping the whole ceremony. Shakmut was gorgeously arrayed in deerskin robes nearly covered with costly beads. Katlewah asked me if his brother would be allowed to wear such clothes as a Russian, and when I replied in the affirmative the fellow seemed disappointed. I do not like either of the brothers: it is difficult to say whether the new Christian or the pagan is the worse. I gave the name of Alexander to the chief, telling him that it was the name of his majesty, the emperor, at which he seemed to feel flattered.'

that they must put away their secondary wives, the chief and others began to plot his downfall. It had been a marvel to the savages that a man should put a bridle upon his passions and live in celibacy, but their wonder was mingled with feelings of respect. To overcome the influence which the missionary was gaining over some of his people, Shakmut, or Alexander as he was now christened, plotted to throw temptation in his way, and alas for Juvenal! whose priestly wrath had been so lately roused by the immorality of Baranof and his godless crew of promyshleniki, it must be related that he fell. In the dead of night, according to his own confession, an Ilyamna damsel captured him by storm.[29]

On the day after this incident, the outraged ecclesiastic received a visit from Katlewah, who expressed a wish to be baptized on the following sabbath. "I can tell by his manner," writes the priest on September 26th, "that he knows of my disgrace, though he did not say anything. When I walked to the forest to-day to cut some wood, I heard two girls laughing at me, behind my back; and in the morning, when I was making a wooden bolt for the door of my sleeping-room, a woman looked in and laughed right into my face. She may be the one who caused my fall, for it was dark and I never saw her countenance. Alexander visited me, also, and insisted upon having

[29] I quote from the journal, p. 69–70, the father's own account of the matter: 'September 25th. With a trembling hand I write the sad occurrences of the past day and night. Much rather I would leave the disgraceful story untold, but I must overcome my own shame and mortification, and write it down as a warning to other missionaries who may come after me. Last night I retired at my usual hour, after prayer with the boys who sleep in another room. In the middle of the night I awoke to find myself in the arms of a woman whose fiery embraces excited me to such an extent that I fell a victim to lust, and a grievous sin was committed before I could extricate myself. As soon as I regained my senses I drove the woman out, but I felt too guilty to be very harsh with her. What a terrible blow this is to all my recent hopes! How can I hold up my head among the people, who, of course, will hear of this affair? I am not sure, even, that the boys in the adjoining room were not awakened by the noise. God is my witness that I have set down the truth here in the face of anything that may be said about it hereafter. I have kept myself secluded to-day from everybody. I have not yet the strength to face the world.'

his wives baptized next Sunday. I had no spirit left
to contest the matter with him, and consented; but I
shall not shrink from my duty to make him relinquish
all but one wife when the proper time arrives. If I
wink at polygamy now, I shall be forever unable to
combat it. Perhaps it is only imagination, but I
think I can discover a lack of respect in Nikita's behavior toward me since yesterday." Continuing his
journal on the 27th, he adds: "My disgrace has become public already, and I am laughed at wherever I
go, especially by the women. Of course they do not
understand the sin, but rather look upon it as a good
joke. It will require great firmness on my part to
regain what respect I have lost for myself as well as
on behalf of the church. I have vowed to burn no
fuel in my bedroom during the whole winter, in order
to chastise my body—a mild punishment, indeed,
compared to the blackness of my sin."

The next day was Sunday. "With a heavy
heart," says Juvenal, "but with a firm purpose, I baptized Katlewah and his family, the three wives of
the chief, seven children, and one aged couple. Under any other circumstances such a rich harvest would
have filled me with joy, but I am filled with gloom."
In the evening he called on Alexander and found him
and his wives carousing together. Notwithstanding
his recent downfall, the priest's wrath was kindled, and
through Nikita he informed the chief that he must
marry one of his wives according to the rites of the
church, and put away the rest, or be forever damned.
Alexander now became angry in his turn and bade him
leave the house. On his way home he met Katlewah,"
who rated him soundly, declaring that he had lied to
them all, for "his brother was as bad as ever, and no
good had come of any of his baptisms."

The career of Father Juvenal was now ended, and
the little that remains to be said is best told in his own

---

[20] Baptized under the name of Gregor.

words : "September 29th. The chief and his brother have both been here this morning and abused me shamefully. Their language I could not understand, but they spat in my face, and what was worse, upon the sacred images on the walls. Katlewah seized my vestments and carried them off, and I was left bleeding from a blow struck with an ivory club [31] by the chief. Nikita has bandaged and washed my wounds; but from his anxious manner I can see that I am still in danger. The other boys have run away. My wound pains me so that I can scarcely—" Here the manuscript journal breaks off, and probably the moment after the last line was penned his assassins entered and completed their work by stabbing him to the heart. [32] This at least was his fate, as represented

[31] Such as are used to kill salmon and seals.

[32] Khlebnikof, the biographer of Baranof, simply states that Juvenal went among the Aglegmutes alone, and that it is not definitely known when or where he was killed by the savages. Veniaminof says: 'The cause of his death was not so much that he prohibited polygamy, as the fact that the chiefs and prominent natives, having given him their children to be educated at Kadiak, repented of their action, and failing to recover them, turned against him and finally slew him as a deceiver. They declare that, during the attack of the savages, Juvenal never thought of flight or self-defence, but surrendered himself into their hands without resistance, asking only for mercy for his companions. The natives relate that the missionary, after being killed, rose up and followed his murderers, asking, Why do you do this? Thereupon the savages, thinking he was still alive, fell upon and beat him; but he again arose and approached them. This happened several times. Finally they cut him in pieces, in order to get rid of him, and then the preacher of the word of God, who may be called a martyr, was silent. But the same natives tell us that, from the place where his remains lay, a column of smoke arose, reaching to heaven. How long this apparition lasted is not known.' *Zapiski, Oonalashk*, 155–6. Other Russian writers, as Berg and Davidof, affirm that he was killed near Lake Ilyamna, because he preached too vigorously against polygamy. Dall, *Alaska*, 317, whose work, so far as the historical part of it is concerned, is but a brief compendium carelessly compiled, says that he was killed while in the act of preaching to the natives. I have before me a translation of Juvenal's own journal, from June 19, 1796, to the time of his death, as handed by the boy Nikita to Veniaminof, and by him to Innokentius Shasnikof, the priest at Unalaska. The tenor of this document, the authenticity of which I have no reason to doubt, is such as to impress on the reader the conviction that Juvenal, with all his failings, was a man of higher character than his companions. He appears, however, to have been of weak intellect, and his blind trust in providence and the saints sometimes stands out in ludicrous contrast with his pitiful lack of success and self-command. When visiting Baranof to inquire as to the disposition of the scholars whom he must leave behind at Three Saints, he finds him seated in front of his tent while his servant was preparing tea. 'He did not ask me to be seated or to partake of tea,' writes the priest, 'though it was nearly a year since I had tasted any. He only asked me gruffly what I wanted so early in the morning.' After

by the boy Nikita, who escaped with the diary and
other papers to a Russian settlement, and delivered
them into the hands of Father Veniaminof on his first
visit to the Nushegak villages.

stating that the boys were to be intrusted to the charge of Father German, who
had opened a girls' school at Pavlovsk, Baranof indulged in some obscene
jokes, 'which put him into such good humor that he finally offered me some
tea. I felt that I ought to refuse under the circumstances, but my longing
for the beverage was too strong. I degraded myself before God and man for
the sake of a drink of tea. Refreshed, but ashamed of myself, I left the
wicked man to pray in my humble retreat for strength and pride in the sanctity of my calling.' p. 18-20. Nevertheless Juvenal's expressions are far
more elevated in tone, temper, and diction than those of the archimandrite,
a few of whose letters are still extant.

CHAPTER XVII.

THE RUSSIAN AMERICAN COMPANY.

1796-1799.

THREATENED EXHAUSTION OF THE SEAL-FISHERIES—SPECIAL PRIVILEGES
GIVEN TO SIBERIAN MERCHANTS—SHELIKOF PETITIONS FOR A GRANT OF
THE ENTIRE NORTH-WEST—HE IS SUPPORTED BY REZANOF—MUILNI-
KOF'S ENTERPRISE—THE UNITED AMERICAN COMPANY—ITS ACT OF CON-
SOLIDATION CONFIRMED BY IMPERIAL OUKAZ—AND ITS NAME CHANGED
TO THE RUSSIAN AMERICAN COMPANY—TEXT OF THE OUKAZ—OBLIGA-
TIONS OF THE COMPANY.

IT will be remembered that after Bering and Chirikof had discovered the Aleutian Islands and the
adjacent coast in 1741, their wealth in fur-bearing
animals was soon made known to Europe and northern Asia. Trading, or, as they were termed, 'contribution' companies were quickly formed; some of the
first vessels despatched from Okhotsk returned with
cargoes that enriched their owners by a single voyage;
and it was believed that in the far north a never-fail-
ing source of riches had been discovered, greater and
more certain than the mines of Española, which yielded
their millions in the time of Bobadilla, or those of
Castilla del Oro, where lay, as the great navigator
believed, the veritable Ophir of the days of Solomon.
Of course many of the fur-hunters found only a grave
where they had gone in quest of wealth; but, like the
Spaniards who followed Cortés and Pedro de Alvarado, they set little value on their lives or on those
of others. Moreover, the faint-hearted Aleuts offered
no such resistance as was encountered by the con-
querors of Mexico and Guatemala. The promyshleniki

could easily take by force what they had not the
money to buy, or what the natives did not care to
sell. They had no fear of punishment. Robbery,
rape, and even murder could be committed with impunity, for, to use their own phrase, "God was high
above, and the tzar was far away."

Thus for many years matters were allowed to take
their course; but toward the end of the eighteenth
century the threatened exhaustion of the known
sources of supply caused much uneasiness among the
Siberian merchants engaged in the fur trade, and
some of them endeavored to remedy the evil by solic-
iting special privileges from the government for the
exclusive right to certain islands, with the understanding that a fixed percentage of the gross yield—
usually one tenth—was to be paid into the public
treasury. Such privileges were granted freely enough,
but it was another matter to make the numerous
half-piratical traders, who roamed Bering Sea and
the North Pacific, respect or even pay the least attention to them.

The encounters which took place between rival companies have already been related, and now only two
remained—the Shelikof-Golikof and the Lebedef-
Lastochkin.   The former had established itself in
Kadiak by force of arms, and Shelikof, by greatly
exaggerating the importance of his conquest, and representing that he had added fifty thousand subjects
to the Russian empire[1] and as many converts to the
Greek church, had so worked upon the authorities at
St Petersburg that his petition for exclusive privileges
for his company was favorably received.   These privileges amounted in fact to a grant of all the Russian
discoveries in north-western America, and of the
islands that lay between them and the coast of Asia,

---

[1] There never were 50,000 natives at Kadiak at any period subsequent to
its conquest. Golovnin estimates the number at the time of Shelikof's landing at 15,000. See p. 306, note, this vol. While the census taken by Baranof's order, in the winter of 1795–0, showed only 6,206 natives. *Tikhmenef,
Istor. Obos.*, i. 61.

including also the Kurile Islands and the coast of
Kamchatka.

Nikolai Rezanof, of whom mention has already
been made, and who later becomes a prominent fig-
ure in the history of the colonies, making Shelikof's
acquaintance at St Petersburg, was somewhat impressed with the scope of his plans. A man of parts
and ambition, of noble birth but scant patrimony, he
solicited the hand of Shelikof's daughter and was
accepted. But the plans of Shelikof, bold as they
seemed to many, were thrown into the shade by
those of his son-in-law, who purposed to obtain for
himself and his partners in America rights similar
to those granted by the English government to the
East India Company. Matters prospered for a time.
Shares in the association were taken by members of
the nobility, and after much astute intrigue had been
brought to bear, Catherine II. was on the point of
granting a charter, when her decease occurred in
1796.

Meanwhile Shelikof had returned to Irkutsk,
where he died, as will be remembered, in 1795.
After this event, his wife Natalia, who had accompanied her husband in all his travels in the wilds of
Siberia and even to Kadiak, and had always successfully conducted her husband's business during his absence, at once undertook the management of affairs,
with Rezanof as chief adviser.

During the year 1797 an Irkutsk merchant named
Muilnikof organized a company, with a capital of
129,000 roubles, for the purpose of engaging in the
fur trade; but fearing that his capital was inadequate,
and that complications might ensue from the fact that
Shelikof's widow, who was to share in the enterprise,
was interested in other associations already permanently established, Muilnikof proposed to join himself
with the Shelikof Company. The offer was accepted,
an agreement made which included all the partners,
and on the 3d of August, 1798, an association, includ-

ing two smaller concerns, and known as the United American Company, was organized at Irkutsk,[2] with a capital of 724,000 roubles, divided into 724 shares of 1,000 roubles each. All hunters, or 'small traders' as they were more frequently called, in Russian America were invited to become partners in the company, on the same conditions as had been granted to other members, and were forbidden to hunt or trade in the territory claimed by the company without their permission.

If we can believe the report of the committee on the organization of the Russian American colonies, made by royal permission and extending back to the time of the earliest discoveries, the need of such an institution as the United American Company was greatly felt by the government. "Having received information from all sides," says this report, "of disorders, outrages, and oppressions of the natives, caused in the colonies by parties of Russian hunters, as well as of groundless claims advanced by foreign navigators to lands discovered by Russians, it had some reason to hope that placing the business of that distant region in the hands of one strong company would serve on the one hand to perpetuate Russian supremacy there, and on the other would prevent many disorders and preserve the fur trade, the principal wealth of the country, affording protection to the natives against violence and abuse, and tending toward a general improvement of their condition."

Nevertheless it was at first feared that the decease of Catherine II. would be a death-blow to the ambitious schemes of the Shelikof party, for it was known that her successor, Paul I., was opposed to them. But Rezanof never for a moment lost heart, and with the versatility of a true courtier, quickly adapted himself to the change of circumstances. He had been a

---

[2] The association included, besides the Shelikof, Golikof, and Muilnikof companies, the American and North-eastern and the Northern and Kurile companies. *Report on Russ. Amer. Colonies*, MS., vi. 13. The full text of the act of consolidation is given in *Golovnin, Materialui*, i. 55-63.

faithful servant to the pleasure-loving empress, and
he now became a constant companion and attendant
upon the feeble-minded man who wore the crown.
So successful were his efforts, that on the 11th of
August, 1799, the act of consolidation of the United
American Company was confirmed by imperial oukaz,
and the association then received the name of the
Russian American Company. "By the same oukaz,"[3]
continues the report above quoted, "the company

[3] The following is a literal translation of the oukaz granted by Paul I. to the
Russian American Company, taken from *Golovnin*, in *Materialui*, i. 77-80:
    'By the grace of a merciful God, we, Paul the First, emperor and autocrat
of all the Russias, etc.   To the Russian American Company under our highest
protection.   The benefits and advantages resulting to our empire from the
hunting and trading carried on by our loyal subjects in the north-eastern seas
and along the coasts of America have attracted our royal attention and consideration; therefore, having taken under our immediate protection a company
organized for the above-named purpose of carrying on hunting and trading,
we allow it to assume the appellation of "Russian American Company under
our highest protection;" and for the purpose of aiding the company in its enterprises, we allow the commanders of our land and sea forces to employ said
forces in the company's aid if occasion requires it, while for further relief and
assistance of said company, and having examined their rules and regulations,
we hereby declare it to be our highest imperial will to grant to this company
for a period of 20 years the following rights and privileges:
    'I. By the right of discovery in past times, by Russian navigators of the
north-eastern part of America, beginning from the 55th degree of north latitude and of the chain of islands extending from Kamchatka to the north to
America, and southward to Japan, and by right of possession of the same by
Russia, we most graciously permit the company to have the use of all hunting-
grounds and establishments now existing on the north-eastern [*sic*, this blun-
der is made all through the document] coast of America, from the above
mentioned 55th degree to Bering Strait, and on the same also on the Aleutian, Kurile, and other islands situated in the north-eastern ocean.
    'II. To make new discoveries not only north of the 55th degree of north
latitude, but farther to the south, and to occupy the new lands discovered,
as Russian possessions, according to prescribed rules, if they have not been
previously occupied by any other nation, or been dependent on another nation.
    'III. To use and profit by everything which has been or shall be dis-
covered in those localities, on the surface and in the bosom of the earth, without any competition by others.
    'IV. We most graciously permit this company to establish settlements in
future times, wherever they are wanted, according to their best knowledge
and belief, and fortify them to insure the safety of the inhabitants, and to
send ships to those shores with goods and hunters, without any obstacles on
the part of the government.
    'V. To extend their navigation to all adjoining nations and hold business
intercourse with all surrounding powers, upon obtaining their free consent for
the purpose, and under our highest protection, to enable them to prosecute
their enterprises with greater force and advantage.
    'VI. To employ for navigation, hunting, and all other business, free and
unsuspected people, having no illegal views or intentions. In consideration
of the distance of the localities where they will be sent, the provincial authorities will grant to all persons sent out as settlers, hunters, and in other ca-

was granted full privileges, for a period of twenty
years, on the coast of north-western America, beginning from latitude 55° north, and including the

pacities, passports for seven years. Serfs and house-servants will only be
employed by the company with the consent of their landholders, and government taxes will be paid for all serfs thus employed.

'VII. Though it is forbidden by our highest order to cut government
timber anywhere without the permission of the college of admiralty, this company is hereby permitted, on account of the distance of the admiralty from
Okhotsk, when it needs timber for repairs, and occasionally for the construction of new ships, to use freely such timber as is required.

'VIII. For shooting animals, for marine signals, and on all unexpected
emergencies on the mainland of America and on the islands, the company is
permitted to buy for cash, at cost price, from the government artillery magazine at Irkutsk yearly 40 or 50 pouds of powder, and from the Nertchinsk
mine 200 pouds of lead.

'IX. If one of the partners of the company becomes indebted to the government or to private persons, and is not in a condition to pay them from any
other property except what he holds in the company, such property cannot
be seized for the satisfaction of such debts, but the debtor shall not be permitted to use anything but the interest or dividends of such property until
the term of the company's privileges expires, when it will be at his or his
creditors' disposal.

'X. The exclusive right most graciously granted to the company for a
period of 20 years, to use and enjoy, in the above-described extent of country
and islands, all profits and advantages derived from hunting, trade, industries, and discovery of new lands, prohibiting the enjoyment of these profits
and advantages not only to those who would wish to sail to those countries
on their own account, but to all former hunters and trappers who have been
engaged in this trade, and have their vessels and furs at those places; and
other companies which may have been formed will not be allowed to continue their business unless they unite with the present company with their
free consent; but such private companies or traders as have their vessels in
those regions can either sell their property, or, with the company's consent,
remain until they have obtained a cargo, but no longer than is required for
the loading and return of their vessel; and after that nobody will have any
privileges but this one company, which will be protected in the enjoyment of
all the advantages mentioned.

'XI. Under our highest protection, the Russian American Company will
have full control over all above-mentioned localities, and exercise judicial
powers in minor cases. The company will also be permitted to use all local
facilities for fortifications in the defence of the country under their control
against foreign attacks. Only partners of the company shall be employed in
the administration of the new possessions in charge of the company.

'In conclusion of this our most gracious order for the benefit of the Russian American Company under highest protection, we enjoin all our military and civil authorites in the above-mentioned localities not only not to
prevent them from enjoying to the fullest extent the privileges granted by
us, but in case of need to protect them with all their power from loss or
injury, and to render them, upon application of the company's authorities, all
necessary aid, assistance, and protection. To give effect to this our most
gracious order, we subscribe it with our own hand and give orders to confirm
it with our imperial seal. Given at St Petersburg, in the year after the birth
of Christ 1799, the 27th day of December, in the fourth year of our reign.

'PAVL.'

Then follows a copy of the company's rules and regulations, for which the
emperor's approval was solicited before the oukaz was granted. At the
beginning of them is written in the emperor's own handwriting, 'Be it thus.'

chain of islands extending from Kamchatka northward to America and southward to Japan; the exclusive right to all enterprises, whether hunting, trading,
or building, and to new discoveries, with strict prohibition from profiting by any of these pursuits, not
only to all parties who might engage in them on their
own responsibility, but also to those who formerly
had ships and establishments there, except those who
have united with the new company." All who refused
to join the company, and had capital invested in fur
adventures, were allowed to carry on their business
only until their vessels returned to port.[4]

In addition to the original capital, a further issue of
one thousand shares was authorized; but it was forbidden that foreigners should be allowed to invest in
the enterprise. Subscriptions flowed in rapidly, and
the entire amount was quickly absorbed, most of it
probably in St Petersburg; for by oukaz of October
19, 1800, it was ordered that the headquarters of the
company, which had formerly been at Irkutsk, should
be transferred to that city. Two years later, the emperor, empress, and Grand Duke Constantine each subscribed for twenty shares, giving directions that the

[4] All the private trading and hunting parties in existence at the end of the
eighteenth century were merged into the Russian American Company, and
so far as is known, with little difficulty. Politofsky differs materially in his
description of the privileges granted by Paul I. to the Russian American
Company. First of all, he says they were conferred on the 8th of July, 1799,
while Dall, who follows Tikhmenef closely, though with frequent blunders,
gives June 8, 1799, as the date. According to the former authority, 'the
company was empowered to make discoveries not only above latitude 55°
north, but also south of that parallel, and to incorporate the lands thus discovered with the Russian possessions, provided that no other power had previously seized them or established a claim to them. It was empowered to
establish settlements wherever it was most convenient for its business, or
most advantageous to the country at large, and also to erect fortifications for
the protection of the inhabitants, and to make voyages to all neighboring
lands and nations, and maintain commercial intercourse with all surrounding
powers, with their free consent and under permission of the emperor. All
the locations selected as sites for settlements were to be respected as such. In conclusion, all military or civil authorities stationed at those places were enjoined, not only to
throw no obstacle in the way of enjoyment of all the rights and privileges
granted, but also to endeavor, as far as was in their power, to protect the
company against loss or injury, and to offer in this intercourse with the company's officers every assistance, protection, and means of defence.' *Istor. Obos.*,
Ross. Amerik Kom., 4-8.

dividends be devoted to charity. The company was
allowed to engage all classes of free labor, and to employ serfs with the consent of their masters;[5] but
nothing was mentioned in the text of the oukaz of
1799 as to the obligations of the company in relation
to the native inhabitants. The only regulations on
this subject are contained in the first paragraph of the
act of consolidation, in which "the company binds
itself," to quote the words of the report once more,
"to maintain a mission of the Græco-Catholic church
in America, members of which were to accompany all
trading and hunting expeditions, and voyages of discovery which were likely to bring them in contact
with known or unknown tribes, and to use every endeavor to christianize them and encourage their allegiance to Russia. They were to use efforts to promote
ship-building and domestic industries on the part of
Russian settlers who might take possession of uninhabited lands, as well as to encourage the introduction of agriculture and cattle-breeding on the American
islands and continent. They were also to keep constantly in view the maintenance of friendly relations
with the Americans and islanders, employing them at
their establishments and engaging in trade with them."

Thus was the famous Russian American Company
established on a firm basis, and little did Shelikof
dream, when representing an obscure company of Siberian merchants he founded on the island of Kadiak
the village of Three Saints, that he was laying the basis
of a monopoly which was destined, as we shall see later,
to hold sway over a territory almost as vast as was
then the European domain of the tzar.[6] As yet, how-

---

[5] After Shelikof's decease, his widow, being possessed of a small estate in
Russia, petitioned Count Zubof, one of the emperor's ministers, for permission
to transfer the serfs upon her estate to Alaska, to form there the nucleus of
an agricultural settlement. At the same time she entered into correspondence with the metropolitans of Moscow and Novgorod, and other church dignitaries, on the subject of missionary enterprise in the new colonies, and thus
secured their assistance in furthering the plans of the company. Count Zubof not only granted the request, but offered to send an additional force of a
hundred serfs from crown lands in Siberia for the same purpose.

[6] In 1821, when the charter of the company was renewed, as will be men-

ever, the boundaries of this territory were not clearly
defined, and its inhabitants were for the most part unsubdued.   The Aleuts were indeed held in subjection,
but none of the warlike tribes that peopled the peninsula and the adjoining continent had yet been conquered.   The Russian colonies at Yakutat and elsewhere on the mainland were constantly threatened,
and, as will presently be described, a settlement that
was founded about this time near the site where now
stands the capital of Alaska was attacked and destroyed by savages.

tioned in its place, the emperor issued a oukaz, in which the whole north west
coast of America north of 51° was declared Russian territory.

anof at this juncture bear evidence of his confidence. Early in March the new sloop *Konstantin* arrived at Kadiak from Prince William Sound, and was supplied with sails and rigging from the stores brought by Bocharof. On the 10th of April, Baranof set sail with the two vessels, manned by twenty-two Russians and accompanied by a fleet of nearly two hundred canoes. The course was along the coast of the Kenaï peninsula to Prince William Sound, where the expedition was joined by Baranof's most trusted assistant, Kuskof, with one hundred and fifty additional canoes which had wintered on Nuchek Island.

Misfortune attended Baranof's enterprise from its inception. On the 2d of May, while weathering Cape Suckling on the coast opposite Kayak, thirty of the canoes, containing two men each, were swallowed by the heavy seas into which even a moderate breeze raises these shallow waters. In a letter to his friend Delarof, Baranof tells of his further troubles: "While we were still mourning the loss of our hunters, night came on, and as I saw further indications of storm, I ordered all the canoes to make for the shore, accompanying them in person in my own bidarka. In the darkness we underestimated the distance, and when at last we reached the sandy beach, exhausted from continued paddling, we threw ourselves upon the sand overshadowed by dense forests. No sooner had we closed our eyes, than the dreaded war-cry of the Kolosh brought us again to our feet. The greatest consternation prevailed among the naturally timid Aleuts, who were filled with such dread of the well-known enemy as to think it useless to make any resistance. Many of them rushed into the forest, into the very hands of their assailants, instead of launching their canoes and putting to sea. I had only two Russians with me, and we fired our guns into the darkness wherever the cries of the Kolosh were loudest; but when our ammunition was expended, we did not know what execution we had done. A few of the native hunters who had been presented with fowling-pieces also made a feeble show of resistance; but what saved us from total destruction was the intervening darkness, which prevented our assailants from distinguishing friends from enemies. After an unequal contest, lasting over an hour, the Kolosh retired to the woods, while I and my assistants endeavored to rally our scattered men. By shouting to them in the Aleutian tongue, we succeeded in gathering the survivors, still hidden in the woods and among the driftwood lining the shore, and before morning departed from the inhospitable beach, leaving thirteen canoes, the owners of which had been killed or carried into captivity. The rising sun showed us the sloops in the offing, and we lost no time in seeking their welcome protection."

This attack by the natives, added to the loss at sea, had so reduced the force, that Kuskof advised a return to Prince William Sound; but Baranof was not to be thus thwarted. He pressed forward, travelling along the coast, chiefly by night, and daring to camp only on prominent points, where there was least danger of surprise. At last, on the 25th, the expedition entered the sheltered basin of Norfolk, or Sitka Sound. The towering heights were still covered with snow, almost to the water's edge, and the weather was stormy; rain, snow, and sleet alternating with furious gusts of wind. The landing was accomplished at a point still known as Old Sitka, about six miles north of the present town of that name. A large crowd of natives had assembled to watch the movements of the new-comers. A Sitkan chief, Katleut, or Katlean, whom Kuskof had met during his hunting expedition of the preceding summer, approached Baranof and demanded to know his intentions, telling him at the same time that a Boston ship was anchored a short distance to the southward, and that her captain had purchased many skins.

Baranof replied in a lengthy harangue, reciting the long-stereotyped European falsehood, that the em-

pcror of all the Russias, who was the lord of that
country, had sent him to establish a settlement for
trade, and to assure his new subjects of his fatherly
care and protection.   At the same time he asked for
the grant of a small piece of ground for the erection
of buildings, and for which he offered to pay in beads
and other trading goods.   The barter was concluded,
and Katleut even asserted that he could force the
other chiefs into the agreement.   A few hours afterward the sound of Russian axes was heard in the
virgin forest, the crash of falling timber was echoed
from the sides of Verstovoi, and all was bustle and
high determination.   The site bordered a shallow
stream alive with salmon.   One half of the company
were employed in building, while the remainder were
sent to hunt sea-otter in the vicinity.   On the following day the chief manager received a visit from the
Boston ship, which proved to be the *Caroline*, in
charge of Captain Cleveland, who stated that he had
only ten men before the mast, and that on account of
the fierce character of the natives he had found it
necessary to take great precautions.   He had placed
a screen of hides round the ship with the exception of
the stern, whence trade was carried on with the natives,[2] who could not see the deck, or know how few
men he had.   Two pieces of cannon were placed in
position, and on the taffrail was a pair of blunderbusses
on swivels.

The savages who then inhabited the neighborhood
of Norfolk Sound were among the most treacherous
and repulsive of all the Alaskan tribes.   "A more
hideous set of beings in the form of men and women,"

---

[2] Cleveland states that on the first day he bought 100 skins at the cheap
rate of two yards of broadcloth per skin.   On the second day he purchased
200.   During his stay at Norfolk Sound the natives made several attempts to
capture the vessel. *Voy.*, i. 92–5 (Boston ed., 1850).   On one occasion a native dressed in a bear-skin came down to the beach, on all fours, imitating
the movements of the animal, in order to decoy the crew on shore, while an
armed party lay in ambush close by.   A boat was lowered to take some of
the men in pursuit of the bear, but one of the ambushed party exposed himself,
and that gave the alarm. *Id.*, i. 105.

writes the captain, "I had never before seen. The
fantastic manner in which many of the faces of the
men were painted was probably intended to give
them a ferocious appearance; and some groups looked
really as if they had escaped from the dominions
of Satan himself. One had a perpendicular line
dividing the two sides of the face, one side of
which was painted red, the other black; with the hair
daubed with grease and red ochre, and filled with the
down of birds. Another had the face divided with a
horizontal line in the middle, and painted black and
white. The visage of a third was painted in checkers,
etc. Most of them had little mirrors; before the acquisition of which they must have been dependent
on each other for those correct touches of the pencil
which are so much in vogue, and which daily require
more time than the toilet of a Parisian belle."

From the ship *Enterprise*, which arrived at Kadiak
from New York[3] on the 24th of April, 1800, the chief
manager heard that hostilities had broken out in
Europe, that Spain had formed an alliance with
France, and that a Spanish frigate was to be sent to
Russian America. The news was received with no
little anxiety. At this time all the storehouses at
Three Saints were full of choice furs, which Baranof
now caused to be concealed in the adjacent islands.
"Truly," he writes, "if the terrible emergency should
arise, and the enemy come upon us, they cannot take
much more than our lives, and these are in God's
hands. It would take more than mortal eyes to discover where our precious skins are concealed."[4]

Several other American vessels, among them the
brig *Eliza*, under Captain Rowan, visited the bay during the summer, and absorbed the trade, while the

[3] Baranof purchased from her captain a quantity of goods, partly with a
view to prevent him from trading with the natives, and partly because the
Fenix being now given up for lost, no supplies could be expected for that
season. *Khlebnikof, Shizn. Baranova*, 63–4.

[4] *Id.*, 68.

Russians were preparing to occupy the field in the future. During the preceding winter the relations between the colonists and the natives had been peaceable, but there was much suffering on account of insufficient food and shelter. A fort was erected, and named after the archangel Michael,[5] in "the hope that the great champion of the Lord would protect the promyshleniki;" nevertheless, soon after the establishment of the settlement misfortune again reduced Baranof's force. On the 18th of July, he received news from an Aleutian party which had camped for the night on the tortuous passage connecting Norfolk Sound with Chatham Strait, that a number of the men had died from eating poisonous mussels. The passage was thereafter named Pogibshie, or Destruction Strait, which name has subsequently been changed by Americans to Peril Strait.

While Baranof was thus engaged in establishing his new colony, a block-house and stockade had been built by Polomoshnoi at Yakutat, or Bering Bay, for the reception of the Siberian convicts, or agricultural settlers, as they were called. The site for this settlement had been chosen by mistake. After his first visit to Prince William Sound, Baranof had recommended the country bordering on Comptroller Bay as probably adapted to agricultural pursuits. Cape Suckling, the western point of this bay, had been erroneously called Cape St Elias, the name applied to the south

---

[5] In a letter to Rodianof, agent at Nuchek, dated May 14, 1800, Baranof writes: 'We enjoyed good health and fair success during our winter there, and though we had some difficulties with the people, we finally established friendly intercourse with them. I resolved to establish a permanent settlement, and at once set to work to erect the necessary buildings, one of which was a two-story structure, 8 fathoms long and 4 wide, protected on all sides by palisades and two strong block-houses or towers. Another building I had put up for myself and future commanders, with the necessary accommodation for servants and officers, and there I have lived from the middle of February to the present date. A small temporary bath-house had been erected, wherein I passed the first part of the winter, a shed and sleeping-rooms for the members of the party, a blacksmith's shop, and temporary kitchen. One fortified block-house is not quite finished, while two others have been only just begun. The men here number 25 Russians and 55 Aleutian hunters.' *Tikhmenef, Istor. Obos.*, ii. app. part ii. 131.

point of Kayak Island by Bering, and in his recommendation Baranof spoke of the country about Cape St Elias. Subsequently the bay of Yakutat had been visited by Purtof and Kuskof; and as this affords the only good harbor on that part of the coast, and is overshadowed by the peak of St Elias, the proposed settlement had been located there in a desolate region of ice and rock, entirely unfit for occupation by man. Polomoshnoi only obeyed orders in locating the block-house there, but as soon as the buildings were completed, he returned to Kadiak to remonstrate against any attempts at founding an agricultural colony in such a place. He was ordered back, how-

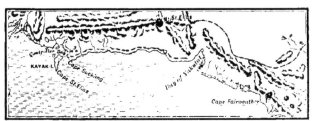

YAKUTAT BAY SETTLEMENT.

ever, by Baranof's representative, and sailed for his destination on the brig *Orel,* laden with provisions for the new settlement, in charge of Talin, a naval officer in the service of the company, but one who, like all of his profession, was little disposed to heed the chief manager's instructions, and when his vessel was lying in Norfolk Sound had threatened to hang Baranof from the mast-head if he dared to show himself on board. While beating against head winds, the ship was wrecked on the island of Sukluk (Montague), and Polomoshnoi, with five men, perished.[6]

[6] Four hundred sea-otter skins, valued at 22,000 roubles, were lost on this occasion, in addition to the rigging and anchors and ship's stores. Talin had

pany to send from Russia some one to relieve him.
As we shall see, this request was repeated several
times during a period of nearly twenty years before a
successor finally reached the colonies, though two were
appointed meanwhile, but were shipwrecked on the
way. There can be no doubt that the chief cause of
his dissatisfaction was the unpleasant relations with
the naval officers and the intrigues of the missionaries, though his failing health and the condition of
his finances were additional reasons.[7]

Believing the Sitka settlement to be now firmly
established and safe from hostile attacks, Baranof returned to Kadiak in the autumn of 1800. But prior
to his return he made an official visit to various settlements, an account of which I give in his own words.

Writing to Larionof, the agent at Unalaska, in July
of this year, he says: "On Kenaï Bay at Ilyamna
Lake the rebellious tribes have killed three of our
men since Lebedef's people departed. Our establishments on the gulf of Kenaï have been broken up three
times, and a conspiracy has been discovered to destroy
all places occupied by Russians, and to kill them as
well as the natives of Kadiak in their employ; and
we have not been able as yet entirely to suppress the
spirit of rebellion. But the saddest news of all, and
the most disastrous to us, is of the wreck of the *Feniks*,

[7] His pecuniary affairs at this time were in an unsatisfactory state. 'Of
9,000 roubles which I had left in the hands of Kretcheotzaff,' he writes, 'only
one half has been returned, and I have met with losses in other quarters. If
I were to return to Siberia now, I would not be a rouble better off than I was
when I came to this country. The glass factory in Irkutsk in which I had invested 4,000 roubles has fallen into decay, and the stock gone into possession of
my former partner, Lackman. I inquired concerning the sale of the property
of my late wife, but never received an answer. This is the way, my friend, all
the little property I had, and left in charge of my wife and friends, has been
scattered. Some of it has been absorbed by unjust claims advanced by Shar-
ikof and Lebedef. For this reason it would be advisable that I should return
hence before I am left entirely destitute in my old age. But unfortunately,
the shareholders have paid no attention to my demand for a successor, and
I cannot conscientiously abandon my position and duties without leaving some
one in my place, as such action might involve the company in inextricable
difficulties. For the proper management of affairs here, a man in the prime
of life, in the enjoyment of full health and all his faculties, is required, and not
a person worn out with hardship and fatigue, and with a temper soured by
adversity.'

and the loss of the whole cargo and all on board. For two months portions of the wreck have been cast on the beach in various localities, but the exact place of the disaster remains unknown.

"I set out in person in July, first for the gulf of Kenaï, to subdue the rebellious tribes, and the remnant of the Lebedef Company, who had killed over a hundred people between them, and had divided themselves into several bands of robbers. Many of them threatened our men on the Kaknu River, which station they had occupied after the breaking-up of the Lebedef Company, but fortunately the leaders of the conspiracy dispersed upon my arrival, and though the combination was not entirely dissolved, I succeeded in obtaining several hostages for the safety of our agent in command, Vassili Malakhof, but in the more distant settlements there is still a strong inclination to warfare and plunder. I remained there until the 15th of August, making necessary arrangements to insure the safety of the place by strengthening its fortifications. I also selected a more convenient site for the fort, made a plan in accordance with the local facilities, and left its execution to the agent Malakhof; and after collecting all the furs at the station, consisting chiefly of those of small land-animals, I proceeded to Fort Alexandroffsk at the entrance of the gulf. Here I furnished the agent Ostrogin with further instructions, and sailed again on the 30th of August, shaping my course for the redoubt at Voskressenski Bay. Thence I proceeded to Nuchek Island, where I made a searching investigation of everything, and established the fort St Konstantin upon a new site. I also had several interviews with the natives, and placed my assistant Kuskof in command of that region."

"Concerning the new settlement at Sitka," the manager says, for I cannot do better than permit him to continue his story, "I thought there would be no danger with proper protection from the larger

vessels, though the natives there possess large quantities of fire-arms and all kinds of ammunition, receiv-
.ing new supplies annually from the English and
from the republicans of Boston and America, whose
object is not permanent settlement on these shores,
but who have been in the habit of making trading
trips to these regions. It is to be hoped that the
fruits of the discoveries of Russian navigators may
not be enjoyed by European or other companies, de-
priving us of our hard-earned advantages. I trust
that God in his justice will allow us to enjoy the
fruits of our enterprise, and as, with his help, I, an
ignorant subject, have been able to add something to
the vast dominion of his imperial Majesty, we must
hope that we shall find the means to preserve our new
possessions intact, and make them profitable.

"At the settlement of Yakutat I found nothing but
trouble and disorder in every department. This was
partly owing to the old difficulties between Polomoshnoi[8] and your brother Stepan, who was appointed
assistant manager in 1796. During the first winter
thirteen of the twenty-five hunters and seven of the
settlers died of scurvy, besides women and children.
Polomoshnoi had written a whole ream of trash and
nonsense which he forwarded to Kadiak, the whole
report containing only what one settler had said of
another, what the settlers had said of the hunters, and
the threats made by the latter against his life. In
conclusion, he asked to be relieved. The wish was complied with; and Nikolai Moukhin, who was thought
to possess considerable administrative ability, was sent
as his substitute. I had all the property forwarded
to Yakutat on behalf of the settlers transferred to him,
though it was almost impossible to obtain any clear
statement with regard to it from the confused mass of
papers left by Polomoshnoi. His reports spoke of
many acts of cruelty and abuse committed by the
hunters, and he had even gone so far as to appoint a

[8] Baranof had not yet heard of Polomoshnoi's death.

commission to investigate the charges; but as the members of the commission were all ignorant settlers who were interested in the case, they did nothing beyond getting up a voluminous pile of testimony which amounts to nothing but empty words. Several times I was on the point of solving all difficulties by disbanding the settlement; but better thoughts prevailed, and remembering the importance of the success of this experiment to the company and to the country at large, I did my best to restore order and reconcile the parties involved.

"The tribes living in the vicinity of our Sitka settlement at first met us in a very friendly manner, but of late they have displayed some distrust, and when our men had formed a procession during holy week in honor of the emperor, they thought we were preparing for a fight, and seized our interpreter, who happened to be in the native village. The procession was conducted with great solemnity and pomp, and after it had been disbanded, our men went through some military evolutions, all of which had been witnessed by the chiefs of the savages, who listened frowningly to our discharges of musketry and artillery; but all this display did not induce them to give up the interpreter, and some property which they had stolen; and I found it necessary to assure them that we were not afraid of them. Therefore, on the third day I proceeded to the principal village with twenty-two men, landed fearlessly on the beach, and placed two small cannon in front of their houses. Over three hundred armed men surrounded us, but we marched directly to the house where the prisoner was reported to be. We fired a few blank volleys to keep the crowd in awe, and seized a few men who seemed inclined to offer resistance. Our determined attitude held the people in check, and when we had accomplished our object and released the prisoner, they began to ridicule the affair, bandying words with our men, and offering them food. I rejoiced in having accomplished my end without bloodshed, and made up my mind not to allow the slightest offence on their part to pass unnoticed in the future."

The admixture of business and piety in this despatch is somewhat noteworthy. "With God's help," he writes, "our men killed 40 sea-lions and 150 seals during the winter." Speaking of the hunter Mikhaïl, whom he had ordered to travel around Kadiak "for the purpose of taking a census of that island, and to make presents to the leading men among the Aleuts of tobacco and other trifles," he remarks, "I thought this course of action best, in view of the misfortune which had happened last year, as I wrote to you from Sitka; and with God's help, he succeeded so well in his mission that the necessary number of men were obtained in all districts, from the first to the last, even to bird-hunting parties."

Again, in a letter to Larionof, dated March 22, 1801, the chief manager thus expresses his gratitude: "The All-creator of the world, in his infinite mercy, has overlooked and forgiven our sins, and tempered the cruel blows of misfortune with success in sea-otter hunting. In the three years which have elapsed since the arrival of the last transport, we have collected over 4,000 skins of sea-otters—males, females, and yearlings, besides cubs. The skins secured at Nuchek and Sitka will probably amount to nearly 4,000, with the help of God. On the other hand, the trappers have had but little success, on account of the unfavorable weather during the winter; and, as you see from the statement, only 1,500 skins were obtained from that source, while in former years from 2,000 to 2,500 was the average number."[9]

Baranof's complaints of foreign encroachment appear to have been well grounded. Within a few leagues of Sitka the captains of three Boston ships secured 2,000 skins, though paying very high prices, each one trying to outbid the other. For a sin-

---

[9] In 1800 the skins obtained from Sitka amounted to 2,600, and for the whole colony to 3,300. *Khlebnikof, Shizn. Baranova*, 62.

gle skin they gave cloth worth twenty-eight roubles, or three coats of frieze lined with cotton. In the same neighborhood two skins were formerly bartered for cloth valued at ten and a half roubles. "The Americans," writes the chief manager, "who have been acquainted with these tribes for two or three years, and have sent from six to eight ships each year, speak of the trade as follows: 'The American republic is greatly in need of Chinese goods, the Chinese teas, the various silk materials and other products of that country, which had formerly to be purchased for coin, the Spanish silver dollar exclusively, but since these shores have been discovered, with their abundance of furs, they were no longer obliged to take coin with them, but loaded their vessels with full cargoes of European goods and products of their own country, which are easier obtained than coin.'" After touching on the political complications that marked the close of the eighteenth century, Baranof continues: "The resources of this region are such that millions may be made there for our country with proper management in the future, but for over ten years from six to ten English and American vessels have called here every year. It is safe to calculate an average of 2,000 skins on eight, or say six vessels, which would make 12,000 a year, and if we even take 10,000 as a minimum, it would amount in ten years to 100,000 skins, which at the price at Canton of 45 roubles per skin would amount to 4,500,000 roubles."[10]

For the next year and a half, little worthy of record occurred in connection with the affairs of the Russian American Company. A number of agriculturists and mechanics, placed at the disposal of the company by Count Zubof, arrived at Kadiak, together with a reën-

[10] *Id.*, ii. app. part ii. 145–8. The total value of furs shipped by the She-likof-Golikof Company between 1786 and 1797 was only 1,479,600 roubles. *Berg, Kronol. Ist.*, 169.

forcement of missionaries. The chief manager has
little to report, save that he has succeeded in bringing
into friendly relations with the Russians a number of
tribes, among whom, as he supposed, were the Kolosh.
The question of boundaries between the Russian and
British American possessions had been mooted, however, almost from the time that Spain ceded Nootka
to the English, and Baranof feared that his people
might be driven from their settlements,[11] although
their right of discovery and occupation north of the
55th parallel left little room for dispute. He begs
the governor of Irkutsk to intercede with the emperor,
more especially in relation to the establishment of an
agricultural settlement, for it was useless to select a
site until some definite action was taken,[12] and the
colony at Cape St Elias was of no benefit.

[11] The English claimed Ltua Bay, and even the gulf of Kenaï and Prince
William Sound.
[12] In this despatch Baranof says: 'Our greatest need is now skilled navigators, since of five vessels in American waters only one has an experienced
master, and he is in poor health.'

CHAPTER XIX.

THE SITKA MASSACRE.

1802.

Baranof's hope that the Kolosh were at length finally pacified proved to be ill founded. Although he was not aware of it, disaffection had long been rife among the warlike nations of Sitka and of the mainland, in the vicinity of the Yakutat settlement. It is said that the hostile spirit was fostered by the English and American traders, who supplied the savages with fire-arms, ammunition, and intoxicating drink. Rumors had reached the commanders of both Sitka and Yakutat that an organized attack was contemplated on the Russian strongholds; but as the chiefs in their vicinity continued to profess friendship, and as traffic was carried on as usual, the agents paid little heed to the repeated warnings. No change was made in the daily routine about the settlement. Parties were sent out to cut timber in the forests, and to hunt on the islands and bays. Sentries were posted in accordance with Baranof's instructions, but as the force was small in either place only the sick and disabled were selected for such duty, and it was therefore performed in the most inefficient manner. In the mean

time, the savages had matured their plans. Allies
had been secured from all the villages throughout the
Alexander Archipelago, and from the populous valley
of the Stakhin River, and during the summer of 1802
the blow was struck which swept from earth the infant colony.

The exact date of the Sitka massacre is not known;
the only survivors were Russian laborers and natives,
who were so terrified as to have taken no note of time.
It is certain, however, that the event occurred in the
month of June. The best statements of this incident
are contained in depositions made by the few survivors
in the office of the company's agent at Kadiak.[1] They
were rude, ignorant men, and their ideas and words
are crude; but they are better for the purpose than
mine would be, and I will not mar their testimony by
another rendering.

Abrossin Plotnikof, a hunter, who was among those
who were rescued, testified as follows: " In this present
year, 1802, about the 24th day of June—I do not remember the exact date, but it was a holiday—about
two o'clock in the afternoon, I went to the river to
look after our calves, as I had been detailed by the
commander of the fort, Vassili Medvednikof, to take
care of the cattle. On returning soon after, I noticed
at the fort a great multitude of Kolosh people, who
had not only surrounded the barracks below, but were
already climbing over the balcony and to the roof with
guns and cannon; and standing upon a little knoll in
front of the out-houses was the Sitka *toyon*, or chief,
Mikhaïl, giving orders to those who were around the
barracks, and shouting to some people in canoes not far
away, to make haste and assist in the fight. In
answer to his shouts, sixty-two canoes emerged from
behind points of rocks. Even if I had reached the
barracks, they were already closed and barricaded,

---

[1] These survivors were carried to Kadiak by Captain Barber, the commander of an English vessel, who, as will be seen, played a somewhat am-
biguous role in the tragedy.

and there was no safety outside; therefore I rushed
away to the cattle-yard, where I had a gun.   I only
waited to tell a girl, who was employed in the yard,
to take her little child and fly to the woods, when,
seizing my gun, I closed up the shed.   Very soon
after this four Kolosh came to the door and knocked
three times.   As soon as I ran out of the shed they
seized me by the coat and took my gun from me.
I was compelled to leave both in their hands, and
jumping through a window, ran past the fort and hid
in the thick underbrush of the forest, though two
Kolosh ran after me, but could not find me in the
woods.   Soon after, I emerged from the underbrush,
and approached the barracks to see if the attack had
been repulsed, but I saw that not only the barracks,
but the ship recently built, the warehouse and sheds,
the cattle-sheds, bath-house, and other small buildings
had been set on fire, and were already in full blaze.
The sea-otter skins and other property of the company,
as well as the private property of the commander Medvednikof and the hunters, the savages were throwing to the ground from the balcony on the water side,
while others seized them and carried them to the
canoes, which were close to the fort."

After mentioning that there were sixteen men in
the barracks, and giving the names of others who were
absent on hunting or fishing expeditions, he continues:
"All at once I saw two Kolosh running toward me
armed with guns and lances, and I was compelled to
hide again in the woods.   I threw myself down among
the underbrush on the edge of the forest, covering
myself with pieces of bark.   From there I saw
Nakvassin drop from the upper balcony and run
toward the woods; but when nearly across the open
space he fell to the ground, and four warriors rushed
up and carried him back to the barracks on the points
of their lances and cut off his head.   Kabanof was
dragged from the barracks into the street, where the
Kolosh pierced him with their lances; but how the

other Russians who were there came to their end I
do not know.   The slaughter and incendiarism were
continued by the savages until the evening, but finally
I stole out among the ruins and ashes, and in my
wanderings came across some of our cows, and saw
that even the poor dumb animals had not escaped the
blood-thirsty fiends, having spears stuck in their sides.
Exercising all my strength, I was barely able to pull
out some of the spears, when I was observed by two
Kolosh, and compelled to leave the cows to their fate
and hide again in the woods.

"I passed the night not far from the ruins of the
fort.   In the morning I heard the report of a cannon
and looked out of the brush, but could see nobody,
and not wishing to expose myself again to further
danger, went higher up the mountain through the
forest.   While advancing cautiously through the
woods, I met two other persons who were in the
same condition as myself: a girl from the Chiniatz
village, Kadiak, with an infant on her breast, and a
man from Kiliuda village, who had been left behind
by the hunting party on account of sickness.   I took
them both with me to the mountain, but each night
I went to the ruins of the fort with my companions,
and bewailed the fate of the slain.   In this miserable condition we remained for eight days, without
anything to eat and nothing but water to drink.
About noon of the last day we heard from the mountain two cannon-shots, which raised some hope in me,
and I told my companions to follow me at a little
distance, and then went down toward the river
through the woods to hide myself near the shore, and
see whether there was a ship in the bay.   When I
reached the beach I saw behind a small island a vessel which looked to me like our *Ekaterina*, but when
I came to our harbor which overlooked the entire
bay I found that it was not the *Ekaterina*, but an
English ship.

"I then ascended the rock where a tent had been

set up when the chief manager was present, and shouted for help. Some Kolosh, who were near the river, heard my voice, and six of them had almost reached me before I saw them, and I barely succeeded in escaping from them and hiding in the woods. Thus I had been chased three times by the savages. They drove me to another point on the beach, near the cape, where again I hailed the ship, and to my great joy a boat put off from the vessel to the place where I was standing. I had barely time to jump into it when the Kolosh in pursuit of me came in sight again, but when they saw I was already in the boat, they went away again. The commander of the vessel was in the boat, and when we had got on board, I gave him a full account of the sad disaster, and asked him to save the girl with her infant son, and the man whom I had left ashore, and showed them the place where I had told the girl and man to hide. The captain at once despatched an armed yawl, and fortunately we hit upon the very spot where they were hiding, and they were taken into the boat and brought on board the ship. The boat was sent off again immediately to the other side of the bay, and soon returned, to my great astonishment, with Baturin, another Russian, whom I recognized with unspeakable joy, and we soon related to each other our experience.

"We asked the commander of the ship to escort us to the site of the destroyed fort, to see if anything had been spared by the savages. He very kindly consented, had the yawl manned again, got in himself, and took me with him. When we arrived at the ruins he examined the bodies of the dead, all of which were without heads, except Kabanof, and we buried them. Of property, we found nothing but the melted barrel of a brass gun, and a broken cannon, which we picked up and brought to the ship. When we had been on board the ship three days, two bidarkas came from the shore with the Sitkan chief, Mikhail, and

his nephew. The former asked the captain if there
were any Russians on board, and whether he wished to
trade. The captain said nothing of our presence, and
with friendly words coaxed him on board, together
with his nephew, and the Kolosh girl who had been
in Kuzmichef's service at the settlement. At our
request, the captain seized the chief and his nephew,
and ordered them to be kept in confinement, ironed
hand and foot, until all the persons captured at the
time of the destruction of the settlement had been
given up. The chief told his men who had remained
in the bidarkas to go and bring them. After that
they began to restore our servant-girls and children,
not all at once, however, but one by one. Finally,
the captain told the chief that if he did not give up at
once all the · prisoners in his hands, he would hang
him, and in order to frighten him, the necessary
preparations for the execution were made.

"In the mean time two other English ships entered
the bay and anchored close to each other. With the
captain of one of them we were somewhat acquainted,
as he had once wintered with his vessel near our fort.
This was the *Abetz*.[2] The Kolosh put off to the two
ships in many canoes, and when the commander of the
Abetz learned of our misfortunes, he held a consultation with the captains of the other vessels. As the
savages approached in their canoes he fired grape-shot
at them from the cannon, destroying several. Some
of the occupants reached the shore, while many were
drowned. Several of the Kolosh the captain of the
Abetz kept as prisoners, and by that means succeeded

---

[2] Probably the *Alert*, Captain Ebbets, from Boston. Plotnikof was evidently unable to distinguish captains' and ships' names, or even nationalities.
The ship commanded by Barber must have been the *Unicorn*, mentioned in
the list of vessels wintering on the coast in 1801, in *Sturgis' Narr.*, MS., 7,
as hailing from London. The *Alert* first appears in the Sturgis list in 1802,
but as it registered there with 2,000 sea-otter skins on board, the vessel must
have reached the coast previous to that time. In the list of north-west
traders made by James G. Swan, I find the ship *Alert*, Captain Bowles, in
1799, while it occurs again in 1801 under command of Captain Ebbets. The
Unicorn, Captain Barber, must have escaped Mr Swan's notice, though she
made several visits to the coast.

in obtaining the release of a few more of the captured women. As soon as the Kolosh discovered what had been done, they would not visit the ships any more; but from the girls we learned that they held prisoner one of our men, Taradanof. We asked the captain not to release the chief; and when the Kolosh saw that he and his nephew were not set at liberty, they brought us Taradanof, four more women, and a large number of sea-otter skins. After taking Taradanof and the women on board, the captain released the chief and his nephew, though we entreated him not to do so, but to take them to Kadiak. Both at Sitka and on the voyage the captain supplied us with clothing and abundant food. The commanders of the other vessels also made us presents of clothing, as we had lost everything."

Of another statement concerning this affair, I will make an abstract. Ekaterina, wife of the Russian Zakhar Lebedef, testified as follows: "She was in the street of Fort Sv Mikhaïl at noon—the day and month she did not know—near the ladder which led to the upper story where the commander Medvednikof lived. She heard a Russian shouting, but could not distinguish the words. A man named Tumakaief ran from the kitchen and told her to hasten to the barracks, as the Kolosh were coming with guns. While he was still speaking, all the Russians and women who had been in the street ran into the barracks. The doors were then barricaded; but from the windows we saw an immense crowd of Kolosh approaching, and they soon surrounded the barracks, armed with guns and lances."

The witness then gives the names of those who were within the barracks, and also of those who were absent, agreeing in this part of her statement with Plotnikof, and continues: "When the Kolosh came up they at once rushed at the windows and began a continuous fire, while the doors were soon broken down in spite of those inside. Among the first who were hit were the commander and Tumakof; others were also wounded, when the rest were ordered to the upper story, but though they kept up a constant fire, they could not do much. When the Kolosh broke into the building, Tumakof, though wounded, fired the cannon at the entrance and killed a few Kolosh; whereupon the remainder retreated a little. It was soon evident that there was not ammunition enough for the cannon in the lower story, and to get a new supply, one of the men broke through the ceiling between the upper and lower stories, when flames came through the opening and suffocating smoke. When the fire spread in the lower story the women were thrust into the basement; but soon afterward some of the Russians again fired the cannon, and the concussion broke the door leading from the basement into the street. The women then ran out and were seized by the Kolosh and carried to the canoes which lay close by. Thence they could see the Russians jumping down into the street when the fire drove them out. There they were caught and pierced with lances."[3]

[3] *Tikhmenef, Istor. Obos.*, ii. app. part ii. 174–9. The account of Sturgis, captain of the *Caroline*, for veracity is a fair specimen of the information given of the Russians by American and English ship captains of that day. Knowing the facts, it is not possible that the writer intended to tell the truth. 'In the year 1799,' he says, 'the Russians from Kamchatka had formed an establishment at Norfolk Sound, consisting of 30 Russians and 700 or 800 natives of Kadiak and Unalaska, for the purpose of killing sea-otters and other animals. They had built a strong fort, contrary to the wishes of the natives, who had notwithstanding conducted themselves in a peaceable manner, probably awed by the superior power of the invaders. Much to their discredit, the Russians did not adopt the same conciliatory conduct, but on some real or pretended suspicions of a conspiracy, pursued the most sanguinary course toward these people, some of whom were massacred, and others sent into captivity to Kadiak Island. Stimulated to revenge by the loss of friends and relatives, and finding their stores of wealth, and almost of subsistence, seized by strangers settled amongst them contrary to their wishes, the natives formed a plan to attack the fort, and either exterminate their oppressors at a blow or perish in the attempt. They succeeded, got possession of the fort by surprise, and instantly put to death several men in the garrison... Previous to this, the ship *Jenny*, of Boston, had been at Norfolk Sound, where seven of the men deserted and took refuge with the Russians. The natives knew this, and willing to make a just distinction between those whom they considered as commercial friends and their arbitrary oppressors, they sent a message requesting the Americans to make them a friendly visit at their village. Six of them accepted the invitation; the other was out with a

When all was over, the witness was taken to the winter village of the Kolosh, where she was treated as a slave. During her presence there, a messenger was captured, from whom the savages learned of the approach of a large Aleutian hunting party under Kuskof. An armed force was sent to overtake and

party of Kadiak natives hunting. When they arrived at the village, the Indians communicated to them their designs, and requested their assistance. This they declined giving, and were then assured that no injury should be offered to them, but were at the same time informed that they would be detained at the village to prevent any information being given to the Russians of what was intended. From the time of their successful attack on the Russians, the Indians constantly protected and supplied the Americans until two American and one English ship arrived, about twenty days later. They were then permitted to go where they chose.' This portion of Sturgis' narrative is partly confirmed by the mention of one Englishman as having perished with the Russians, in the narrative of the widow Lebedef: 'Such conduct towards their countrymen merited the most friendly return on the part of the Americans, and policy as well as justice forbade any attempt to avenge the cause of the Russians; but unfortunately the men and officers were of a different opinion. I am inclined to suppose that they were in this instance too much influenced by the master of the English ship, who was induced from motives of interest to take part with the Russians. He was bound for Kadiak, and knew that whatever prisoners might be rescued would be forwarded in his ship. This he expected would ingratiate him with the Russians, and procure him commercial advantages with them. At a meeting of the officers of the different vessels, it was determined to seize the native chiefs, who were alongside in the most friendly manner, and to keep them as hostages until the Kadiak women and other prisoners on shore were delivered up. In pursuance of this resolve, several natives who chanced to be on the deck were immediately secured, and an attempt was made to seize those in the canoes, who however fled to the shore. They were fired on from the ships, and to the eternal disgrace of their civilized visitors, numbers were killed...The captive chiefs were now told that unless all the prisoners on shore were delivered up, they must expect no mercy. One of the natives attempted to escape, but failed, and in the attempt was slightly wounded. He was immediately singled out as a proper object for vengeance. After a mock-trial, he was placed, as was the custom in naval executions, on a gun on the forecastle with a halter from the yard-arm around his neck. The gun was fired, and he strung up in the smoke of it.' Mr Sturgis here indulges in a discussion of the atrocity of killing 'peaceable Indians,' and inserts a speech supposed to have been made by the condemned savage, which would do honor to the fictitious redskinned heroes of Cooper in both eloquence and logic, and then continues: ' I have before observed that this speech had no effect. The man was executed. After several days, some of the Kadiak prisoners were liberated, put on board the English vessel, and sent to their former place of residence.' Narr., MS., 19–24. I have not been able to discover the name of the second American vessel, but have convinced myself that Mr Sturgis was not well informed as to this occurrence, and that the pretended speech is pure invention.

Lisiansky, in his story of the Sitka massacre, says: 'Among the assailants were three seamen belonging to the United States, who, having deserted from their ship, had entered into the service of the Russians, and then took part against them. These double traitors were among the most active in the plot. They contrived combustible wads, which they lighted, and threw upon the buildings where they knew the gunpowder was kept, which took fire and were blown up. Every person who was found in the fort was put to death.

destroy them, but they returned without having accomplished their object. After many days the widow Lebedef and two native women, together with fifty sea-otter skins stolen from the Russians, were placed on board an English ship and finally brought to Kadiak. While on her way to the ship in a canoe, a savage seated close by the woman whispered to her that during the attack upon Kuskof's party only ten natives had been killed.

On account of the importance of the event, I give one more narrative of the massacre, that of Baranof's biographer, Khlebnikof, a patient investigator, though of course somewhat biased in favor of his country-men. He relates that "on Sunday, the 18th or 19th of June,[4] after dinner, Medvednikof sent off a few men to fish, others to look after the nets in the river, and some of the women went to the woods to pick berries. Only fifteen Russians remained in the garri-son, resting from their labor without the slightest sus-picion. A few of these and some of the women were outside of the barracks.

"The Kolosh women living with the Russians had in-formed their countrymen, not only of the number of people in the garrison, but of all precautionary meas-ures and means of defence, and the Kolosh chose a holiday for the attack. They suddenly emerged noiselessly from the shelter of the impenetrable for-ests, armed with guns, spears, and daggers. Their faces were covered with masks representing the heads

Not content with this, the Sitcans dispersed in search both of Russians and Aleuts, and had many opportunities of exercising their barbarity. Two Russians in particular were put to the most excruciating torture. The place was so rich in merchandise, that two thousand sea-otter skins and other articles of value were saved by the Sitcans from the conflagration.' *Voy.*, 219-20, London ed., 1814.

Davidof says: 'At the station there lived several sailors who had deserted from a United States ship and had been allowed to stay and work for their subsistence. These made joint cause with the savages, set fire to the bar-racks, and fired upon the Russians at the time of the attack by the Kolosh.' *Dvukr*, ii. iii.

[4] That all the narrators of the events just decribed are in error as to date is evident from Baranof's own diary, in which it is stated that the *Unicorn* arrived at Kadiak on June 24th.

of animals, and smeared with red and other paint; their hair was tied up and powdered with eagle down. Some of the masks were shaped in imitation of ferocious animals with gleaming teeth and of monstrous beings. They were not observed until they were close to the barracks; and the people lounging about the door had barely time to rally and run into the building when the savages, surrounding them in a moment with wild and savage yells, opened a heavy fire from their guns at the windows. A terrific uproar was continued in imitation of the cries of the animals represented by their masks, with the object of inspiring greater terror.

"Medvednikof had only time to hurry down from the upper story, and bravely attempted to repulse the sudden attack with the twelve men at his disposal. But the wailing of the women, and the frightened cries of the children, added to the confusion, and at the same time nerved the defenders to do their utmost. The assailants broke into the door of the vestibule, cut through the inside door, and kept up a wild but continuous fire. Finally the last door of the barracks was broken in, the last weak barrier which protected the besieged, and in the savages poured. Suddenly the report of a cannon was heard. Those within range threw themselves down, while others ran away in terror. A few more well directed and rapid discharges, and it might have been possible to frighten away the enemy, who were numerous but cowardly. The bold defenders Medvednikof, Tumakof, and Shashin were killed, and others dangerously wounded. The women in the upper story, crazed by fright, crowded with their children to the trap-door over the stairway. Another cannon-shot was heard, and the trap-door gave way. The women were precipitated into the street, and in a moment were seized and carried off to the boats."

Meanwhile the savages had set fire to the building. "The flames increased," continues Khlebnikof, "in the

upper story of the barracks, and the Russians still
fighting there, suffocated in the dense smoke and
heat, jumped from the balcony to the ground, in the
hope of gaining the shelter of the woods. But the
enraged Kolosh rushed after them with hideous cries,
thrust their lances through them, and dragged them
about for a long time to increase their suffering, and
then, with curses and foul abuse, slowly cut off the
heads of the dying men.

"Skaoushleoot, the false friend of Baranof, who
had been named Mikhaïlof by the Russians, stood at
the time of the attack upon a knoll opposite the
agent's house, and having given the signal for the attack, shouted to the canoes with terrible yells to hasten to the slaughter. Amid fierce outcries, about
sixty of these instantly appeared round the point,
filled with armed men who, as soon as they landed,
made a rush for the barracks. The number of assailants may be estimated, without exaggeration, at over
a thousand, and the few brave defenders could not
long hold out against them. They fell, struck with bullets, daggers, and lances, amid the flames and in torture, but with honor. They were sacrificed for their
country. The hordes of Kolosh then poured into the
upper story, and carried away through the smoke and
flames furs, trading goods, and articles belonging to
the murdered men, throwing them to the ground over
the balcony, while others seized the booty and carried it off to the canoes. In the mean time, not only
the barracks, but the commander's house, the warehouse, and other buildings, as well as a small vessel
just completed, had been burned; and as the flames,
fanned by the wind, leaped upward amid the unearthly
howls of the mad, hurrying savages, the spectacle
became hideous and awe-inspiring."[5]

When the massacre occurred the chief manager was
at Afognak Island; but on hearing that Barber had

[5] *Mater. Ist. Russ. Zass.*, 46–7.

brought with him three Russians, two Aleuts, and eighteen women whom he had rescued from the Kolosh at Sitka, he returned in all haste to Kadiak. Instead of landing the released prisoners at once, Captain Barber, under the idea that there was war between England and Russia, cleared his decks for action, prepared his twenty guns for service, and armed his men. At the same time he declared that from motives of humanity he had rescued the prisoners from the hands of savages, fed and clothed them, and neglected his business; and he demanded as compensation 50,000 roubles in cash, or an equivalent in furs at prices to be fixed by himself. Baranof learned, however, that Barber had not only paid no ransom, but had even appropriated a large number of sea-otter skins of which the savages had robbed the Russian magazine. His only expense had been in clothing the captives, and feeding them on the way to Kadiak. The demand was of course refused, whereupon the captain threatened to use force if it were not satisfied within a month. Baranof was somewhat disconcerted. He was without news from Europe, and unaware of any declaration of war, but he prepared his settlement for defence as far as lay in his power, and remonstrated with Barber on the injustice of his claims. At last, after much haggling and repeated threats on the part of the Englishman, a compromise was arrived at, and the British philanthropist departed after receiving furs to the value of 10,000 roubles.[6]

The loss of Fort Sv Mikhaïl was a heavy blow to the Russians. Baranof saw at once that his plans for an advance beyond Sitka to the eastward must be abandoned until the Russians had been avenged, and

---

[6] *Baranof, Correspondence*, MS., 20-1. Sturgis makes no mention of the captain's demand for compensation, and probably knew nothing about it, though it is mentioned by all the leading authorities. Khlebnikof states that Baranof took a receipt from the captain in order to explain his action to the Russian American Company. *Shizn. Baranova*, 70.

to do this he felt himself powerless.   His loss in men
had been considerable, and in property enormous.
Moreover, he knew not in what light the misfortune,
occurring as it did during his absence, would be
viewed by the company.

Before the close of the year matters assumed a
brighter aspect.   On the 13th of September the brig
Alexandr arrived from Okhotsk, and on the 1st of
November the brig *Elizaveta* under Lieutenant
Khvostof, the two vessels having on board a hundred
and twenty hunters and laborers, and an immense
stock of provisions and trading goods.[7]

By the *Elizaveta* Baranof received secret instructions from the managers of the company,[8] that were
of considerable importance, as they touched on points
that subsequently arose between the governments of
Russia, England, Spain, and the United States, in
regard to territorial claims.   He was directed to push
forward his settlements to the 55th parallel, to lay
claim to Nootka Sound, and to establish forts and
garrisons,[9] with a view to obtain from the English
government a settlement of the boundary question.[10]
All explorations to the northward were to cease
meanwhile, unless the advance traders of the company
should come in contact with Englishmen, in which
case a line of posts must be constructed.   He was

[7] Baranof now learned for the first time that his old enemy Ioassaf had
perished on board the *Feniks*, with the crew and passengers, numbering 90
souls.

[8] The original instructions have been preserved in the archives of the Russian American Company, now deposited in the department of state in Washington.

[9] If natives already occupied the most convenient sites, Baranof was permitted to form settlements at the same points, provided he obtained their
consent by purchase or by making presents.   In *Tikhménef, Istor. Obos.*, i.
117-18, is a list of the fortified stations occupied by the company in 1803.   They
were twelve in number, and included, besides those at Pavlovsk and Three
Saints, three on the gulf of Kenaï Bay—forts St George, St Paul, and St
Nicholas—two in the Chugatsch territory—one named Fort Constantine and
Helen at Nuchek, and the other at Port Delarof—two on Yakutat Bay, and
one each at Cape St Elias, Afognak Island, and Cape Kenaï, the last being
named Fort Alexander.   Most of them were armed with three-pounder pivot
guns, and with due precautions were strong enough to resist the attacks of
hostile natives.

[10] At the 50th parallel, if possible.

instructed to avoid disputes as to boundary lines, and should they become unavoidable, to declare that, while insisting on the rights of Russia, he was not authorized to treat on such a subject, and that the government of Great Britain must address the tzar directly.[11]

The instructions then touch on the political changes which had occurred in Europe. Baranof learns for the first time that "the French nation had been universally acknowledged as a republic, that the wise administration of the first consul had put an end to the shedding of blood, and that a universal peace had been declared." Little did the managers of the Russian American Company dream how soon this universal peace would be followed by Austerlitz and Friedland. Allusion is also made to Nelson's appearance in the Baltic after the battle of Copenhagen; and though harmony was now restored between England and Russia, Baranof is cautioned that such misunderstandings might arise again, and is ordered to collect all the furs gathered at Pavlovsk and its vicinity, or to ship them to Siberia without delay. In future a naval officer was to be sent with each transport to take charge of the vessel on the return voyage.

With regard to the navigator Shields, the managers write that, "though they have no reason to doubt his zeal, his kinship with the English may lead him to act to their advantage, and therefore advise Baranof to use every precaution, to watch his every step, and to keep the board informed, endeavoring at the same time not to irritate him with suspicions, and not only to abstain from the slightest provocation of a quarrel with him, but to treat him kindly and ply him with promises of reward from the government and pecuniary recognition from the company, in order to attach him the more firmly to the Russians, and that, under the fatherly rule of his imperial Majesty, this

[11] The managers remark that in *Vancouver's Voyage* it is stated that some of Baranof's traders had given charts of the Russian voyages to the English, and forbid any repetition of this practice.

foreigner may feel to the fullest extent the blessings
of his fate, and see no reason to seek his fortune elsewhere."

In conclusion, Baranof is enjoined to maintain peace
and good feeling among all, as a necessary condition
to the success of the great and promising enterprise
on which the company has just entered. The execution of all plans is left to him as chief manager of the
Russian American possessions, "under the conviction
that he will devote his strength and labors to the
service of the emperor, and thus make known his name
in Russian history." [12]

From Unalaska also had come good news, though
not unmixed with evil tidings. In May the councillor
Banner[13] arrived with intelligence that the Russian
American Company had obtained a new charter and
fresh privileges. Baranof had been appointed a shareholder, and by permission of the emperor Alexander
was allowed to wear the gold medal of the order of
St Vladimir, previously bestowed on him by Paul I.
The day on which he heard of his advancement he
counted as one of the happiest of his life. "I went

---

[12] Baranof is informed that the government had views concerning America
that must be kept a profound secret, and is instructed to send his despatches
direct to the board of managers, instead of through the authorities at Okhotsk,
with whom no secret was safe. As a proof of this, a copy of *Shelikof's Travels*
was enclosed, which consisted merely of his journal, presented confidentially
to the governor of Siberia, and on his removal stolen from the chancelry, and,
contrary to the wishes of the deceased, printed in Moscow, thus exposing
state secrets, especially the location of tablets claiming possession of the
country for Russia. Baranof is ordered to cause the immediate removal of
these tablets to such points as he may select, and in future to address everything pertaining to discoveries direct to the managers, in special reports,
marked 'secret.' The document is signed by the directors Mikhail Buldakof,
Eustrate Delarof, and Ivan Shelikof, and approved by a committee of the
shareholders assembled at the office of the minister of commerce, Count Nikolai
Petrovich Rumiantzof.

[13] Ivan Ivanovich Banner had been formerly in the government service in
the province of Irkutsk as provincial inspector in Zashciversk. On leaving
the service, he was engaged by the company to proceed to Bering Bay with a
colony of agriculturists. The vessel was injured on the voyage, and detained
for nearly a year on one of the Kurile Islands. At Unalaska the vessel was
also detained by Larionof, and as the plan of a settlement in that region had
been abandoned, Banner was ordered to Kadiak, where he remained until
his death in 1816. He was favorably mentioned by Langsdorff, Rezanof,
Campbell, and other visitors to the island during his residence there of twelve
years. *Id.*, 66.

to the barracks," he says, "where the imperial orders and documents concerning my promotion were read out, and also the new charter and privileges granted by highest order. The undeserved favors which our great monarch has thus showered upon me, almost overwhelmed me. I prayed from the bottom of my heart that God's blessings might fall upon him. As a small token of my gratitude, I donated a thousand roubles for the establishment of a school here for the instruction of the children of the Russians and the natives. On the occasion of this holiday I killed a sheep which had been on the island from our first settlement. What gluttony!"

From Larionof, who had been appointed agent at Unalaska in 1797, the chief manager received letters, in which the condition of affairs was depicted in gloomy colors. Supplies of goods and provisions were nearly exhausted,[14] and no vessels had arrived; while scurvy and other diseases were playing havoc among the islanders and the few discontented hunters who still remained.

It is probable that Baranof now proposed to abandon this settlement; for in April 1803, he ordered Banner to sail for Unalaska in the *Olga*, and ship thence, in the *Petr y Pavl*, all the men that could be spared, the furs and trading goods in the storehouses, and all the provisions, except what were needed to supply the islanders until the next visit. He was then to take his best seamen and proceed for the hunting season to the islands of St Paul and St George, which had not been visited for many years, and where a vast number of skins must have been accumulated by the natives.

At Kadiak also much dissatisfaction was caused about this time by a change in the relations between

---

[14] Langsdorff says that during his stay at Unalaska, in 1805, Larionof assured him that for five years he had seldom tasted bread. Some time before he had procured five or six pouds of meal from Okhotsk, but only on rare occasions was bread or pastry made of it. *Voy.*, part ii. 30.

enkof, bound for the Sitka coast, by way of Ledianof
(Cross) Sound, and Baranof in person sailed two days
later with the sloops *Ekaterina* and *Alexandr*, leaving
Banner in charge at St Paul. On arriving at Yakutat, he found that Kuskof had strictly obeyed his
orders, and that two craft lay on the shore ready to be
launched. The vessels were named the *Yermak* and
the *Rostislaf*.

CHAPTER XX.

SITKA RECAPTURED.

1803-1805.

The 'Nadeshda' and 'Neva' Sail from Kronstadt—Lisiansky Arrives at Norfolk Sound in the 'Neva'—Baranof Sets Forth from Yakutat—His Narrow Escape from Shipwreck—He Joins Forces with Lisiansky—Fruitless Negotiations—Defeat of the Russians—The Fortress Bombarded—And Evacuated by the Savages—The Natives Massacre their Children—Lisiansky's Visit to Kadiak—His Description of the Settlements—A Kolosh Embassy—A Dinner Party at Novo Arkhangelsk—The 'Neva's' Homeward Voyage—Bibliography.

Before proceeding further with the narrative of Baranof's operations, it is necessary to give some account of an expedition which had previously sailed from St Petersburg. While he was yet smarting under the loss inflicted by the savages of Sitka, and looking about in vain for men and means to avenge himself, a young naval officer in that city was setting in motion a chain of events that were destined to aid in the accomplishment of the chief manager's wishes.

During the years 1798–9, Lieutenant Krusenstern, of the Russian navy, sailed for Canton on board an English merchant vessel, for the purpose of becoming acquainted with the navigation of the China Sea. There he noticed the arrival of an English trading vessel[1] from the American coast, and the disposal of her cargo of furs for 60,000 piastres. On his return to Russia, Krusenstern presented a memorial to the

---

[1] Probably Meares' ship.

minister of marine,[2] proposing the despatch direct from Kronstadt to the Russian American colonies of two ships, fitted with all the material needed for the construction and equipment of vessels, and having on board a force of shipwrights and skilled workmen, and a supply of charts, instruments, and nautical works.

The trade with China was then conducted by way of Okhotsk and Kiakhta, thus entailing a loss in time of more than two years with each cargo. If suitable vessels could be built on the American coast, or the adjacent islands, furs shipped thence direct to Canton, the proceeds expended in the purchase of Chinese goods for shipment to Russia, the vessels touching at Manila, Batavia, or some port in the East Indies to complete their freight, a commerce might be developed which erelong would place the Russian American Company beyond the competition of the English and Dutch East India companies.

Such was Krusenstern's project; and though, as he says, there was nothing novel about the idea, it does not seem to have occurred to the managers of the company. The memorial met with the approval of the minister of marine, who discussed the matter with the minister of commerce; and within a few months, the young officer was summoned to St Petersburg, and, much to his astonishment, informed that the emperor had selected him to carry his own plan into execution.

Captain Lisiansky, who had served with Krusenstern on board the English fleet during the American war of independence, was appointed second in command, and to him was intrusted the purchase of suitable vessels. Two ships, renamed the *Nadeshda*, or *Hope*, and the *Neva*, were secured in London for £17,000

---

[2] An abstract of the memorial was first presented to Count Kuschelef, who returned a discouraging answer. On the accession of Alexander I., Admiral Mordvinof was appointed minister of marine, and to him the memorial was presented in January 1802, with a favorable result. *Krusenstern's Voy. round World*, introd., p. xxix.-xxx.

sterling, and an additional sum of £5,000 was immediately expended for repairs.[3] On their arrival at Kronstadt further repairs were found necessary, and it was not until late in the summer of 1803 that the expedition was ready for sea.

Meanwhile Krusenstern was informed that advantage would be taken of the opportunity to despatch an embassy to Japan, with a view to opening the ports of that country to Russian commerce. Rezanof was appointed ambassador, and was intrusted with an autograph letter addressed by the tzar to the mikado, and with presents for that dignitary. To Rezanof was probably due, in part, the favor with which Krusenstern's project was regarded, for, as we have seen, he had great influence at court. Moreover, the dowry of his wife, who had died soon after her marriage, was entirely invested in the stock of the Russian American Company.

About a month before the departure of the expedition, the commander had the honor of receiving the tzar on board his vessel. "The object of his visit," says Krusenstern, "was to see the two ships which were to carry the Russian flag for the first time round the world—an event which, after a hundred years' improvement in Russia, was reserved for the reign of Alexander. He noticed everything with the greatest attention, as well with the ships themselves as with the different articles which were brought from England for the voyage. He conversed with the commanders, and attended for some time with pleasure to the work which was going on on board the ship."[4]

On the 7th of August, exactly one year after Krusenstern had received his appointment, the vessels

---

[3] *Id.*, 3. Tikhmenef, *Istor. Obos.*, i. 98, says the *Nadeshda* was purchased for 82,024 roubles, and the *Neva* for 89,914 roubles, in parchment money. These figures are certainly inaccurate, for parchment money was at a very heavy discount.

[4] Krusenstern had now an opportunity of thanking the tzar in person for assigning to his wife, for twelve years, the income of an estate amounting to 1,500 roubles a year, in order, as the emperor said, to set his mind perfectly at ease with respect to the welfare of his family. *Id.*, i. 7.

sailed from Kronstadt, supplied with two or three
years' provisions, and having on board a hundred and
thirty-nine persons. The *Neva* was placed in charge
of Lisiansky, while on board the *Nadeshda* were the
commander, the ambassador and his suite, the naturalist Langsdorff, and two sons of the counsellor Kotzebue, one of whom afterward became famous as an
explorer in the north-west.[5]

As only one ship was allowed by the mikado to call
yearly at Japan,[6] it was arranged that they should
part company at the Sandwich Islands, the *Nadeshda*
sailing for Japan, thence for Kadiak, and afterward for
Kamchatka, there to winter, while the *Neva* sailed
direct for the harbor of Three Saints. In the following
summer both were to proceed to Canton freighted
with furs, and after taking in a cargo of Chinese
wares to return to Kronstadt.

After calling at Copenhagen and Falmouth, the
vessels sailed for the island of Teneriffe, and thence
for Santa Catharina, on the coast of Brazil, where they
were repaired and refitted. Here disputes broke out
between the members of the embassy and the naval
commanders, Rezanof attempting to control the movements of the expedition by virtue of his rank and
social position. In April 1804 the two ships rounded
Cape Horn. Explorations among the South Sea Islands caused further delay, and it was not until the
second week in June that the expedition sailed from
the Hawaiian Islands. The programme of the voyage was now somewhat altered, the *Nadeshda*, before
proceeding to Japan, steering for Petropavlovsk, where

  [5] The *Nadeshda* was a vessel of 450 tons, and had 64 persons on board.
The complement of the *Neva*, a 370-ton ship, consisted of 8 officers and 46
sailors and petty officers. A list of the officers, the ambassador's suite, and
the scientific men who accompanied the expedition is given in *Id.*, 16–18.
With two exceptions all the members of the embassy returned to St Petersburg, after leaving the *Nadeshda* at Kamchatka in 1805.
  [6] An embassy sent to Japan in 1792 had been favorably received, permission being given for one Russian vessel to be admitted each year to the
port of Nangasaki, for trading purposes; but until 1803 no use appears to
have been made of this concession.

for the present we will leave her, while the *Neva* was headed for Kadiak.

On the 13th of July, 1804, Lisiansky sighted Pavlovsk, or, as we shall now call it, St Paul Harbor, where he thus describes his reception: "Shortly after midnight, two large leathern boats came to our assistance, in consequence of a letter I had sent the day before, by means of a small bidarka, to announce our arrival, in one of which was Captain Bander,[7] deputy commander of the Russian establishment here. The weather was so thick and dark that he found us merely by the noise we made in furling our sails. His stay with us was short, but he left his pilot on board, who brought the vessel into the harbor about two o'clock in the afternoon. On passing the fort, we were saluted by eleven guns; and as soon as the anchor was down, Mr. Bander returned, accompanied by several Russians, who were eager to congratulate us on our happy arrival. It is not easy to express what I felt on this occasion. Being the first Russian that had hitherto performed so long and tedious a voyage, a degree of religious fervor mixed itself with the delight and satisfaction of my mind."[8]

Lisiansky hoped that his hardships for that year at least were over, and that he would have time to repair and refit after his long voyage; but no sooner had he landed, than Banner placed in his hands a communication from Baranof relating the destruction of the Sitka settlement,[9] and begging assistance in conquering the savages and rebuilding the fort. Convinced of the importance of recovering this point, he complied at once with the request. Only the most necessary repairs were made, and after being detained for a few days by unfavorable weather, the *Neva* sailed from Kadiak on the 15th of August, and five

[7] Banner. Langsdorff makes the same mistake in his *Voy. and Trav.*, part ii. 56.

[8] *Lisiansky's Voy. round World*, 142-3.

[9] Lisiansky had heard a rumor of the disaster during his brief stay at the Sandwich Islands.

days later entered Sitka Sound, where the *Alexandr*
and *Ekaterina* were found at anchor, awaiting the
arrival of Baranof, who was then engaged in a hunting expedition. From one of the officers it was ascertained that the natives had taken up their position
on a bluff, a few miles distant, where they had fortified themselves, and were resolved to try issue with
the Russians.

Relating his impressions of the surrounding country,
Lisiansky says: "On our entrance into Sitca Sound
to the place where we now were, there was not to be
seen on the shore the least vestige of habitation.
Nothing presented itself to our view but impenetrable woods reaching from the water-side to the very
tops of the mountains. I never saw a country so
wild and gloomy; it appeared more adapted for the
residence of wild beasts than of men."

On the 25th of August, the chief manager sailed
from Yakutat on board the *Yermak*, and on the following day his boats and bidarkas entered Ledianof
Sound. A swift current runs by these shores, and
great care was needed to keep the vessels on their
course. Moreover, the fog which overhangs the sound
at all seasons of the year completely hid the boats from
sight. A strong tide was setting in, which carried
the *Yermak* away from the remainder of the flotilla,
and soon all the vessels were rapidly closing in with
the shore. Presently the wind calmed, the sails hung
to the mast, the boats would not obey the rudder, and
the depth of water prevented them from anchoring.
There appeared to be no hope of keeping off the
beach, where the Kolosh might be upon them at any
moment. "There was nothing to be done," says
Khlebnikof, "but to leave everything to providence."[10]

[10] The Russians appear to have been somewhat unmindful of the maxim
on providence and self-help. A laughable story is told of a skipper who, being caught in a squall about this year, and his vessel thrown on her beam-ends,
was roused from his slumbers by the water coming into his berth, and by one
of the mates who came to warn him of the danger. 'Now the ship is in

The chief manager preserved the greatest calmness, and by his demeanor inspired his frightened men with some confidence. Thus encouraged, their exertions never relaxed, and from time to time they would obtain glimpses of each other through the fog, as they continued to keep off the dreaded shore. Baranof writes of this incident: "What a position to be in; working desperately to hold our own between steep cliffs and rapid currents! At last the tide turned, and we were drawn toward the opposite shore. At the same time a breeze sprung up and allowed the hoisting of sail, while the fog dispersed. But nothing seemed to be in our favor that day. Soon the breeze freshened into a gale, threatening the expedition with another danger. The ships barely escaped stranding, as they tacked frequently and cleared the strait in the teeth of the storm. The bidarkas were scattered over the sound, and some sought shelter under the rocks, trusting rather to the protection of providence from the savages than risking exposure to the merciless elements. Finally the prayers of so many anxious souls were heard, and with almost superhuman exertion a sheltered bay was reached, and the boats anchored, the *Rostislaf* coming in last. The *Yermak* had lost a skiff, the *Rostislaf* a considerable part of her rigging, while one of the bidarkas went down in the storm."[11]

Without further incident worthy of mention, Baranof arrived at Sitka Sound on the 19th of September, and on the following day went on board the *Neva* to consult with Lisiansky. "Hearing nothing," writes the latter, "of the hunters who had been separated

God's hands,' he exclaimed, as he turned over in his bed, and commencing to pray, there remained until one of the officers had sense enough to let go the main-sail, when the ship righted.

[11] Langsdorff, who passed through this channel in a bidarka, in company with the navigator De Wolf, says: 'At this point the force of the current and tide is considerable. The passage is only 150 toises wide, while the average depth is 200 fathoms, with rocks coming up within 5 feet at low tide.' De Wolf remarks that nowhere in his travels has he met with anything to compare with the violence of the current. *Khlebnikof, Shizn. Baranova*, 80–1.

in the gale, an armed vessel was on the 23d sent in search of them, and everything in the mean time prepared for their reception, in a small bay opposite to us. At eight o'clock in the evening, sixty bidarkas belonging to this party, among whom were twenty Russians, arrived, under the command of Mr Kooskoff, who, on passing us, fired a salute of muskets, in answer to which I ordered two rockets to be sent up. Expecting more of these bidarkas in the course of the night, we hung out a lantern to each top-gallant mast-head of our vessel.

"The next morning, as soon as it was light, observing the shore to the extent of three hundred yards completely covered with the hunting-boats, we sent our launch armed with four swivels, to cruise on the sound, to prevent them from being attacked by the Sitcans; and shortly after I went with some of my officers on shore, where the picture that presented itself to our view was new to us.

"Of the numerous families of hunters several had already fixed their tents; others were busy in erecting them. Some were hanging up their clothes to dry, some kindling a fire, some cooking victuals; some again, overcome with fatigue, had stretched themselves on the ground, expecting, amidst this clash of sounds and hum of men, to take a little repose; whilst at a distance boats were seen arriving every moment, and by adding to the numbers, increasing the interest of the scene. On coming out of the barge we were met by at least five hundred of these, our new countrymen, among whom were many toyons."

On the 28th of September the united squadron moved out of Krestovsky Bay, the *Neva* being towed by over one hundred canoes. In the evening an anchorage was found near the high bluff upon which the Sitkans' stronghold was situated. All night the weird song of the chaman was heard by the Russians, but no opposition was offered, when on michaelmas day of 1804 Baranof and his party landed near the site of the modern town of Sitka.[12]

At dusk an envoy from the Kolosh came to the Russians with friendly overtures. He was told that conditions of peace could be made only with the chiefs. The next morning he reappeared in company with a hostage, whom he delivered up, but received the same answer. At noon thirty armed savages approached, and halting just beyond musket-shot, commenced to parley. Baranof's terms were that the Russians should be allowed to retain permanent possession of the bluff, and that two additional hostages should be given. To this the Kolosh would not consent, and soon afterward withdrew, being warned through the interpreters that the ships would be immediately moved close to their fort, and that they had only themselves to blame for what might follow.

On the 1st of October four of the ships were drawn up in line before the enemy's fort,[13] in readiness for action, and a white flag hoisted on board the *Neva*. As no response was made, the order was given to open fire, and Lieutenant Arbusof, with two boats and a field-piece, was instructed to destroy the canoes which lay on the beach, and to set fire to a large barn near the shore, which was supposed to be the storehouse of the Kolosh. Finding that he could do little damage in his boats, Arbusof landed and marched toward the fort, whereupon Baranof went to his support with a hundred and fifty men and several guns. The surrounding woods were so dense that the two parties

---

[12] This was the spot selected by Baranof on his first appearance on Norfolk Sound, but another site was chosen on account of the disinclination of the natives to see a Russian settlement established there.

[13] Khlebnikof gives Sept. 20th as the date. *Shizn. Baranova*, 85. This fort was in the shape of an irregular polygon, its longest side facing the sea. It was protected by a breastwork two logs in thickness, and about six feet high. Around and above it tangled brush-wood was piled. Grape-shot did little damage, even at the distance of a cable's length. There were two embrasures for cannon in the side facing the sea, and two gates facing the forest. Within were fourteen large huts, or, as they were called by the natives, barabaras. Judging from the quantity of provisions and domestic implements found there, it must have contained at least 800 warriors. *Lisiansky's Voy. round World*, 163, where a plan of the fort is given.

could not see each other as they advanced; their
progress was slow, and night was upon them when
they reached the stronghold. Meanwhile the savages
remained perfectly quiet, except that occasionally a
musket-shot was fired, probably as a signal. Mistaking
this inaction for timidity, Baranof rashly ordered his
men to carry the fort by storm. He was met by the
savages in a compact body, and a well-directed fire
was opened on his men, causing a stampede among
the natives, who were dragging along the guns. Left
with a mere handful of sailors and promyshleniki, the
commander was forced to retire. The Kolosh then
rushed forth in pursuit. The Russians fought gal-
lantly, and succeeded in saving their field-pieces, though
with the loss of ten killed and twenty-six wounded,
among the latter being the chief manager, who was
shot through the arm with a musket-ball.[14] As they
neared the shore, their retreat was covered by the
guns of the flotilla, but for which circumstance it is
probable that none would have escaped, and that Baranof's career would now have been brought to a close.

The following day Lisiansky was requested by
Baranof to take charge of the expedition. He at once
opened a brisk fire on the fort. In the afternoon,
messengers were sent by the Kolosh to sue for peace,
with the promise to give as hostages some members
of the most prominent families, and to liberate all the
Kadiak natives who were detained as prisoners. The
overture was favorably received, and on this and the
three following days a number of hostages were delivered into the hands of the Russians. Meanwhile the
evacuation of the fort was demanded, and to show
that he was in earnest, Lisiansky moved his ship farther in shore. To this the chief toyon consented
after a brief negotiation.

[14] Of the *Neva's* men alone two were killed, and a lieutenant (Povalishin),
a master's mate, a surgeon's mate, a quartermaster, and ten sailors of the
sixteen who accompanied them, were wounded. Of the two that were killed,
one was immediately held up on the spears of the savages. *Id.*, 158.

On the morning of the 6th, an interpreter was sent to ask whether the Kolosh were ready to abandon their stronghold. He was answered that they would do so at high water. At noon the tide was at its height, and as there was no sign of preparation for departure, the savages were again hailed, and no answer being returned, fire was opened from the *Neva*. During the day a raft was constructed, on which the guns could be brought close up to the fort. Toward evening two large canoes appeared, one of them belonging to an old man, "who," says Lisiansky, "like another Charon, had in general brought the hostages to us." He was advised to return and persuade his countrymen to retire at once if they valued their safety. To this he consented, and it was arranged that if he were successful, it should be made known to the Russians by a certain signal.[15] Two or three hours later the signal was heard and was answered by a cheer from those on board the vessels. Then far into the night a strange chant was wafted on the still air from the encampment of the savages, expressing their relief, as the interpreters said, that now their lives were no longer in peril.

But the chant had other significance. At daylight no sound was heard from shore, nor was any living creature in sight, save flocks of carrion birds hovering around the fort. The Kolosh had fled to the woods, and within the stronghold lay the dead bodies of their children, slaughtered lest their cries should betray the lurking place of the fugitives.[16] The fort-

[15] Shouting thrice the word "oo," meaning "end."

[16] Thirty of the Kolosh warriors were also found dead in the fort. It was at first supposed that the survivors had crossed the mountains to Khusnoffsky Sound, but soon afterward they attacked a party of Aleuts a few versts distant, killing nine of them. *Khlebnikof, Shizn. Baranova*, 87–8. Lisiansky thinks that their flight was due to fear of vengeance, on account of their late cruelty and perfidy, but that if ammunition had not failed them, they would have defended themselves to the last extremity. He is of opinion that if Baranof had adopted his suggestion to harass the enemy from the ships, and cut off their water supply and their communication with the sea, the fort might have been captured by the Russians without the loss of a single man. The Kolosh left behind them a quantity of provisions and more than twenty large canoes. *Voy. round World*, 102–4.

ress was then burned to the ground, and the construction of magazines was immediately commenced, together with spacious barracks and a residence for the chief manager.   The buildings were surrounded with a stockade, block-houses being erected at each corner, and a stronghold was thus formed that was believed to be impregnable against the attacks of the Kolosh. To this settlement was given the name of Novo Arkhangelsk. Under the bluff were anchored all the vessels, with the exception of the despatch boat *Rostislaf* and the *Neva*, both of which sailed for Kadiak, Lisiansky purposing to winter there, and after taking in supplies, to return in the spring to Sitka Sound, whence he proposed to sail for Canton.[17]

During his stay in Kadiak, Lisiansky visited several of the settlements on that island, concerning which he gives some interesting details. The entire population apart from the Russians he estimates at only four thousand,[18] and remarks that according to the report of the oldest inhabitants it had decreased by one half since the arrival of the Russians. The wholesale mortality which had thus prevailed since Shelikof landed there in 1784 was mainly due to diseases introduced by the invaders, and to the severe toil and hardship to which the natives were exposed during the long hunting expeditions required of them by

[17] Banner was ordered to supply the *Neva* with all the fish and game needed, and all the cattle that could be spared. On board the ship were two Kolosh prisoners. Baranof sent instructions to keep them confined in the stockade at St Paul, and make them work along with the Aleuts, who were placed there for punishment. *Khlebnikof, Shizn. Baranova*, 89.

[18] His calculation is based on the number of barabaras in the several districts, and these he found to be 202. Allowing 18 persons to each barabara, we have a total of 3,636, the remainder consisting of Aleuts in the company's service. *Voy. round World*, 193. This is probably near the truth, for a census list lodged in the office of the directors at St Petersburg in 1804 gives 4,834 as the population of Kadiak and the adjacent islands about that date, against 6,519 in 1795. Delarof in 1790 places the number as low as 3,000, and Baranof and Banner in 1805 state that there were only 450 men in Kadiak capable of labor. Langsdorff, who was at Kadiak in the latter year, is inclined to believe that the number of men fit for work or hunting did not exceed 500. *Voy. and Trav.*, part ii. 60.

their task-masters.[19]   Other causes were the destruction of the sea-otter, on which they had been accustomed to rely for food during winter, and their neglect to lay in a stock of dried salmon for the season of scarcity.   In winter and early spring the islanders lived mainly on shell-fish, and this in a country where, between the months of May and October, salmon could be taken out of the rivers by hand, and sea-bears[20] could catch them in their paws so easily that they devoured only the head, and threw away the remainder.

On visiting Igak on the 24th of March, 1805, Lisiansky reports that he found all the people in search of shell-fish along the beach, only the young children being left in the eleven filthy barabaras which formed that settlement.   "After dinner," he writes, "the chief with his wife came to pay me a visit.   On entering my room they crossed themselves several times, and then sat down on the floor and begged snuff.   In the course of conversation their poverty was mentioned, when I endeavored to convince them that their extreme indolence was the cause of it; and I suggested various ways by which they might improve their situation and render life more comfortable.   I advised them to build better habitations, to lay in regularly a sufficient stock of winter provisions, which they almost always neglect, to attend more to the article of cleanliness, and lastly, to cultivate differ-

[19] Langsdorff declares that he has seen the promyshleniki put the natives to a horrible death from mere caprice. Speaking of the overseers, he terms them 'Siberian malefactors or adventurers.' Both these statements are denied by Lisiansky, who affirms that the exiles sent to Kadiak were employed only as common laborers. 'That mistakes of this nature should be made by Langsdorff,' he remarks. 'is not to be wondered at, when we find him thus speaking of himself: "To examine a country accurately, three things are requisite, not one of which I at this time enjoyed—leisure, serenity of mind, and convenience." To this might be added, that he was but a short time in the country of which he speaks, and was ignorant of the language both of the natives and of the Russians.' *Voy. round World*, 215, note.

[20] Called by the Russians *kotik*, and belonging to the seal genus, though differing materially from the *phoca vitulina*, or common seal. *Langsdorff's Voy.*, part ii. 22. Lisiansky makes a ridiculous mistake on this point. He says that the wild beasts, and especially bears, go into the river and catch these fish with their paws. *Voy. round World*, 192.

ent culinary plants near their houses, by which they would be relieved from the trouble of collecting wild roots and herbs, which were neither so palatable nor so nutritious." [21]

At Killuda Bay, a few versts south-west of Igak, Lisiansky landed at a settlement, " in which," he says, "we found only women and children, the men belonging to it having been absent with Baranof since the preceding spring. Not having laid in provisions in sufficient quantity for the winter, these poor wretches were literally half starved. Wishing to afford them what was in my power, I distributed among them the stock of dried fish I had in the boats, and left this abode of wretchedness with no very pleasurable sensations. It was indeed a heart-rending scene to see these emaciated beings crawling out of their huts to thank me for the trifling relief I had afforded them. Though the weather was the next morning very disagreeable, I went to Drunkard's Bay, where I witnessed the same meagre traits of poverty. Of the inhabitants I purchased several curiosities, consisting of images dressed in different forms. The best were cut out of bone. They are used here as dolls. Indeed, the women who have no children keep them, I was told, to represent the wished-for infant offspring, and amuse themselves with them, as if they were real infants.

"On the 1st of April we proceeded to the harbor of Three Saints, where we arrived in the afternoon. In our way we visited a village called the Fugitive, which was in a thriving condition. The inhabitants appeared much healthier than those of Ihack[22] or Killuden,[23] and lived better. On our arrival, the

[21] *Id.*, 173-4. Two days later Lisiansky received a visit from a Russian who had lived in Unalaska. He reported that a volcanic island had appeared above the sea in the middle of April 1797. The news was brought by some Aleutian fishermen, who observed a great smoke issuing from the waters. The land gradually rose above the surface, and in May of the following year an eruption occurred which was distinctly visible at a settlement on Makushin Bay, 45 miles distant. In 1799 the island was 12 miles in circumference.

[22] Igak.

[23] Killuda.

chief's wife brought us a basin of berries, mixed with rancid whale oil, begging us to refresh ourselves. This delicate mess, produced at a time when the berries are not in season, is regarded by the islanders as no small proof of opulence. I gave this treat, however, to my Aleutians; and after distributing tobacco and other trifles among the family, took my leave.

"The next morning, as soon as my arrival at the harbor of Three Saints was known in the neighborhood, several of the toyons came together to see me. After the usual compliments, and a treat of snuff on my part,[24] the conversation began on the common topic of poverty, when I endeavored, with some earnestness, to persuade them to throw off the sloth and idleness so visible amongst them, and exert themselves; and I stated, as I had done in a previous instance, the many comforts they would derive from habits of industry, of which they were at present perfectly destitute. The toyons listened attentively to my advice, and assured me that they should be happy to follow it, but that there were many circumstances to prevent them; and I must confess I blushed when I heard that the principal of these was the high price fixed by the Russian Company on every necessary article, and especially its iron instruments, which rendered it impossible for the islanders to purchase them. While this is the case, what improvement can be expected in these people?"

On the 6th Lisiansky and his party visited a settlement on the adjacent island of Sitkhalidak, with regard to which I give one more quotation. "Toward evening," he continues, "the weather becoming cold, we made a fire in the middle of our barabara, which was soon surrounded by the inhabitants, young and old They were very much amused at seeing us drinking tea; but I have no doubt were still more gratified when I ordered some dried fish to be distributed

[24] Snuff is the best treat that can be offered to these people, who will often go twenty miles out of their way to get merely a pinch or two of it. *Id.*, 179.

amongst them, which was a rarity at this season of
the year.   The master and mistress of the house were
invited to partake of our beverage, and they seemed
to plume themselves upon the circumstance, as if distinguished by it from the rest of the party.   During
our tea repast, the family were at their supper, which
was served up in the following manner: The cook
having filled a wooden bowl with dried fish, presented
it to the master of the house, who, after eating as
much as he could, gave the rest to his wife.   The
other dishes were served up in similar order, beginning with the oldest of the family, who, when he
had eaten his fill, gave the dish to the next in age,
and he again to the next; and thus it passed in rota-
tion till it came to the youngest, whose patience, as
the family was numerous, must have been a little exhausted.   Perceiving, at length, that our companions
were becoming drowsy, I advised them to go to rest,
which they did, wishing us several times a good night,
and expressing how satisfied they were with our kindness.

"The next morning when I arose at daylight, and
was proceeding to take a walk, I found all the men
sitting on the roofs of their houses.   This is their favorite recreation after sleeping; though they are also
fond of sitting on the beach, and looking for hours together at the sea, when they have nothing else to do.
In this practice they resemble more a herd of beasts
than an association of reasonable beings endowed with
the gift of speech   Indeed, these savages, when assembled together, appear to have no delight in the oral intercourse that generally distinguishes the human race;
for they never converse; on the contrary, a stupid
silence reigns amongst them.   I had many opportunities of noticing individuals of every age and degree;
and I am persuaded that the simplicity of their character exceeds that of any other people, and that a long
time must elapse before it will undergo any very perceptible change.   It is true, that on my entering their

houses, some sort of ceremony was always observed by them; but by degrees even this so completely disappeared, that an Aleutian would undress himself to a state of nudity, without at all regarding my presence; though at the same moment he considered me as the greatest personage on the island."

On the 14th of June the *Neva* sailed from St Paul, and on the 22d of the same month entered the harbor of Novo Arkhangelsk. During Lisiansky's absence matters had prospered with the new settlement. Eight substantial buildings had been completed; the fort was also finished and mounted with cannon; a number of kitchen-gardens were under cultivation, and the live-stock were thriving. All winter the Kolosh had avoided the neighborhood, and only now and then a few small canoes appeared, whose inmates carefully scanned the movements of the Russians and then vanished quickly from sight.

On the 2d of July an interpreter was despatched by Baranof to inform them that the *Neva* had arrived with the hostages who had been delivered up on the cessation of hostilities.[25] The demoralized savages had scattered during the winter, but now were assembling once more, and had built another fort on the western shore of Chatham Strait, opposite the village of Houtshnoo. The report was current that other tribes also were fortifying their villages, and it was feared that in time the colony would again be surrounded with dangerous neighbors. The messenger was sent back with the answer that the toyons required some assurance of good faith before placing themselves in the power of the Russians, and was again despatched on the same errand, with presents and promises of kind treatment.

[25] While waiting for a reply from the enemy, Lisiansky caused a survey to be made of Norfolk Sound, and especially of the island upon which Mount Edgecumbe is situated. To this he gave the name of Kruze, now Kruzof, in honor of an admiral of that name to whom he was indebted for his preferment. *Id.*, 220–1.

On the afternoon of the 16th five canoes were seen
approaching the fort, and as they drew near it became
known that they contained the messenger and an embassy from the Kolosh. The Chugatsches in Baranof's
camp were ordered to conduct them to the fort, playing the part of gentlemen ushers, as Lisiansky remarks, and donning their holiday apparel, set forth to
meet them. Some were attired only in a threadbare
vest, some few in a pair of ragged breeches, while by
others an old hat, or a powdering of eagle down on the
hair, was considered a full-dress suit for a gentleman.
When close to the beach the embassy stopped, and
the savages on shore and in boat executed a dance and
song, the toyon of the Kolosh being conspicuous for
his nimble capering. The canoes were then pulled on
shore by the Chugatsches, their inmates remaining
seated, while the gentleman ushers entertained them
with a second performance.

At length the ambassador and his suite were lifted
from their boats and carried to their apartments,
where a feast had been prepared for them. On the
following day they paid a visit to the *Neva*, and were
regaled with tea and brandy. The envoy in chief was
invited into the cabin, where his son, who had been
held as a hostage, was brought into his presence.[26] He
was surprised at the cheerful and well-fed appearance
of the lad, and expressed his gratitude to the captain,
but no sign of affection was shown by child or parent.
After more singing and dancing, the savages returned
on shore,[27] and in the afternoon held an interview

[26] Among the hostages were three creole youths, to whom were given the
names of Andrei Klimovsky, Ivan Chernof, and Gerassin Kondakof. One of
them was the ambassador's son, but, as Lisiansky says, was afterward exchanged for a younger brother, who probably received the same name. They
were subsequently placed in the school of navigation by the board of managers,
and were finally returned to the colonies. Klimoffsky became a captain and
commanded several vessels, while the others were appointed mates in the
company's service. Kondakof died in 1820 and Klimoffsky in 1831. *Baranof,
Shizn.*, 90. The third, Chernof, survived the transfer of Alaska to the United
States, dying in the year 1877. His two sons still navigate the waters of
Alaska.

[27] Lisiansky says: 'These people are so fond of dancing, that I never saw
three of them together without their feet being in motion. Before the de-

with Baranof, who presented to each a cloak [28] and a pewter medal, the latter in token of peace. Brandy was produced, the terms of the treaty were arranged,[29] and all were invited to a banquet at the residence of the chief manager. The place of honor was of course given to the envoy's wife, whose evening costume was a piece of red cloth thrown over her shoulders, and a thick coating of black paint on her face. Her coiffure was composed entirely of soot, and for ornament she wore a round piece of wood in the lower lip. It was observed that during her frequent sips of fire-water she was extremely careful of this feature, which projected at right angles from the chin, and was regarded as her greatest charm. Late at night the ambassador, his spouse, and suite were again carried to their apartments, none of them being sober enough to stand on their feet. The next day they took their leave, the chief of the embassy being presented with a staff on which were the Russian arms, wrought in copper, decorated with ribbons and eagle down. This he was told to present to his countrymen as a token of friendship.[30]

After the conclusion of the treaty with the Kolosh, Lisiansky made ready for sea, and on the 1st of September, 1805, sailed for Canton with a cargo valued at more than four hundred and fifty thousand roubles.[31]

parture of the ambassador I allowed him to fire off one of our twelve-pounders, which he did with a firmness I little expected, exhibiting no surprise either at the report of the cannon or its motion.' *Voy. round World*, 223–4.

[28] To the ambassador was given a mantle of fine red cloth trimmed with ermine, and to the rest cloaks of common blue cloth.

[29] I have been unable to find any account of the terms of this treaty. Neither Lisiansky nor Baranof has a word to say about it in their reports of the affair.

[30] Returning to the fort on August 16th, after an excursion to the summit of Mount Edgecumbe, Lisiansky found the ambassador there. He had returned to announce to the Russians his appointment as chief toyon in place of Kotlean. His new dignity had so elated his pride that he no longer deigned to use his legs, except when dancing, but was invariably carried on the shoulders of his attendants. *Id.*, 232.

[31] Including 3,000 sea-otter and more than 150,000 small skins. *Khlebnikof, Shizn. Baranova*, 90. This authority gives August 20th as the time of the *Neva's* departure. With regard to date, he is constantly at variance with Lisiansky, who has been accepted as the chief authority for the statements made in this chapter.

Here he arrived early in December of the same
year,[32] calling at Macao, where he met with Captain
Krusenstern, who had arrived in the *Nadeshda* on his
homeward voyage, Rezanof meanwhile having sailed
in another vessel for Alaska.   After much vexatious
delay, caused by the Chinese officials, the furs were
landed and sold,[33] a cargo of tea, nankeens, and other
goods purchased with the proceeds, and on the 4th
of August, 1806, the *Neva* cast anchor at Kronstadt.

As soon as the news of her return was known in
St Petersburg the vessel was thronged with persons
of every rank, and for many days her commander
was so much occupied with answering their questions
and listening to their compliments that, as he says, he
had barely time to eat or sleep.   Among those who
visited the ship were the emperor and the empress's
mother.   The former complimented Lisiansky on
the appearance of the *Neva*, and observed that her
crew looked better than when they had left the shores
of Russia,[34] while the latter spoke a few kind words
to all on board, and afterward sent presents to each
of the officers and sailors.

On the 19th of the same month the *Nadeshda*
arrived, having accomplished her voyage round the
world in three years and twelve days, with the loss of
only one man.[35]

The two commanders received the order of St
Vladimir of the third class, and a pension of 3,000
roubles a year for life.[36]   The other officers were pro-

---

[32] During the voyage, it was discovered that a large portion of the skins
were in an advanced stage of decomposition.   Several days were occupied in
sorting them and throwing overboard those that were entirely spoiled.   The
loss was estimated at 200,000 roubles. *Lisiansky's Voy. round World,* 264–6.

[33] The *Nadeshda* was also detained at Macao by the authorities.   Both
cargoes were sold at low prices.

[34] Among the refreshments served to the emperor was some Russian salt
beef, 'which,' Lisiansky says, 'had stood the test of the entire voyage, and
was nevertheless more juicy and less salt than the Irish beef which he had
lately purchased at Falmouth.'

[35] Rezanof's cook, who, as Krusenstern affirms, was in an advanced stage
of consumption when he went on board the ship. *Voy. round World,* 404,
note.

[36] Lisiansky also received many valuable presents from the royal family.

moted one step, with pensions of 500 to 1,000 roubles; and to the petty officers and sailors were given pensions of 50 to 75 roubles, with permission to retire from the service if they so desired.[37] Lisiansky was raised to the rank of commander in the imperial navy, but no further promotion appears to have been conferred on Krusenstern.[38] ⋅ He had failed in his mis-

[37] *Id.*, introd. xxx.-xxxi., note; *Lisiansky, Voy. round World*, 318. Langsdorff and the scientific men who accompanied him received pensions of 300 ducats a year.

[38] The principal sources of information as to the recapture of Sitka and the incidents in connection with the voyage of the *Nadeshda* and *Neva* are *A Voyage round the World*, in 1803–6, with plates and charts, by *Urey Lisiansky* (translated from the Russian, London, 1814); *Voyages and Travels in Various Parts of the World*, in 1803–7, with sixteen plates, by G. H. von Langsdorff (in two parts, St Petersburg, 1811, and London, 1813); and *Voyage round the World*, in 1803–6, by A. J. von Krusenstern (3 vols, with atlas and maps, St Petersburg, 1810–14; 2 vols. London, 1813, and Paris, 1820). Lisiansky's account of the taking of the Kolosh stronghold is probably the most reliable version of this event, and is to be preferred to that of Khlebnikof, as the former was an eye-witness of all that transpired, took a leading part in the operations of the expedition, and writes without any of the bias shown by Baranof's biographer, though perhaps taking a little too much credit for his own share in the achievement. The first seven chapters and a part of the eighth describe the voyage of the *Neva* from Kronstadt to Kadiak, and contain some interesting particulars about the natives of the Sandwich Islands, where the ship called on her passage. In the remainder of cap. viii. and in ix.–xii., we have an account of his travels and observations in Alaska, and of the recapture of Sitka. In the rest of the work he relates his homeward voyage. The book is entertaining, written in an easy and natural style, and evidently with more regard to truth than effect. Lisiansky was a native of Nagin, where he was born of noble parents, on the 2d of April, 1773. After completing his education at the naval academy at Kronstadt, he was appointed, when fifteen years of age, a midshipman in the Russian navy, in which capacity he served during the war with Sweden, being present at the battle of Revel, in 1790. Later, he took service in the English navy, where he first met with Krusenstern, and after travelling in the United States, returned to Russia in 1800, where he was appointed to the command of a frigate, and made a knight of the order of St George of the fourth class.

Krusenstern, although in command of the expedition, never visited the north-west; but, as we have seen, the despatch of the expedition was due to his efforts. The narrative of his voyage in the *Nadeshda* is full of interest, and by no means justifies the first part of the motto which appears on the title-page: 'Les marins écrivent mal, mais avec assez de candeur.' Between the years 1824 and 1835 he published in St Petersburg, in 3 vols, an *Atlas de l'Océan Pacifique*, together with his *Recueil des Mémoires Hydrographiques*, and in 1836 his *Supplémens au Recueil de Mémoires Hydrographiques pour servir d'analyse et d'explication à l'Atlas de l'Océan Pacifique*. These works are very favorably noticed in the *Jour. Royal Geog. Soc. of London*, 1837, vii. 406–9, wherein is a list of the more important errors contained in Arrowsmith's chart of the Pacific, which, it was claimed, had been corrected up to the year 1832, and was then considered the best in Europe. Among others is the location of the island of St Paul. 'The *Supplémens*,' says the *Journal of the London Geographical Society*, 'registers all the discoveries and newly determined positions that have been made in the lapse of the last thirteen years,

sion; but, as we shall see later, through no fault of his own.

during which more has been done towards obtaining a correct knowledge of those seas than at any time since the voyages of Cook and La Pérouse.'

Langsdorff's work is the least valuable of the three. As a savant he was superficial; as a chronicler he was biased. In neither capacity does he add much to what was already known of Russian America. The first part contains a narrative of his voyage to Kamchatka, thence to Japan, and back to Petropovlovsk, the incidents of which are also related in Krusenstern's work. The first five and the eleventh and twelfth chapters of the second part relate to Alaska, and the remainder of the work is taken up with his visit to California and his homeward journey. His statements as to the condition of the natives and the promyshleniki appear to be greatly exaggerated. They are not indorsed by any of the Alaskan annalists, and though Lisiansky gives some color to them, they are strongly at variance with the reports of Rezanof, who was a keen and impartial observer. A proof of the little value set on Langsdorff's services is the smallness of the pension granted to him on his return. He received, as will be remembered, but 300 ducats a year, and the like sum was given to his assistants, while the lieutenants and surgeons of the expedition were awarded pensions of 1,000 roubles.

CHAPTER XXI.

REZANOF'S VISIT.

1804-1806.

VOYAGE OF THE 'NADESHDA'—A RUSSIAN EMBASSY DISMISSED BY THE JAPAN-
ESE—REZANOF AT ST PAUL ISLAND—WHOLESALE SLAUGHTER OF FUR-
SEALS—THE AMBASSADOR'S LETTER TO THE EMPEROR—THE ENVOY PRO-
CEEDS TO KADIAK—AND THENCE TO NOVO ARKHANGELSK—HIS REPORT
TO THE RUSSIAN AMERICAN COMPANY—FURTHER TROUBLE WITH THE
KOLOSH—THE AMBASSADOR'S INSTRUCTIONS TO THE CHIEF MANAGER—
EVIL TIDINGS FROM KADIAK—REZANOF'S VOYAGE TO CALIFORNIA—HIS
COMPLAINTS AGAINST NAVAL OFFICERS—HIS OPINION OF THE MISSION-
ARIES—HIS LAST JOURNEY.

A FORTNIGHT before the *Neva* sailed for Canton, the
Elizaveta arrived at Novo Arkhangelsk, together with
two American ships, one of them, named the *Juno*,
laden with provisions, calling for repairs. A few days
later the company's brig *Maria* entered the harbor,
having on board as passengers lieutenants Kvostof
and Davidof, the naturalist Langsdorff, and the ambassador Rezanof, who was destined to play an important part in the development of the Russian
American colonies. Before proceeding further, it
may be well to mention briefly the voyage of the
Nadeshda from the time of her parting company
with her consort, and the envoy's operations before
landing at Novo Arkhangelsk.

After a passage of thirty-five days from the Sandwich Islands, the vessel arrived at Petropavlovsk on
the 14th of July, 1804. Here Rezanof assumed full
control. The ship, after being unrigged and repaired,
was again ready for sea at the end of August, but

was weather-bound until the 6th of the following
month, when she sailed from the coast of Kamchatka,
well equipped, and with an ample stock of provisions.[1]

Arriving at Nangasaki on October 8th, after a
rough passage, Rezanof was detained for several
months by the frivolous trifling of the Japanese authorities.   At length, on the 30th of March, 1805, a
plenipotentiary arrived from Jeddo, and "on the 3d
of April," writes Krusenstern, "it was concluded that
the ambassador should pay the representative of the
Japanese emperor, a European, and not a Japanese,
compliment.   This latter, indeed, is of so debasing a
nature, that even the very lowest of Europeans could
not submit to it; but he was obliged to appear without his sword or shoes, nor would they allow him a
chair or any kind of European seat, but reduced him
to the necessity of sitting in front of the governor and
the plenipotentiary, on the floor, with his feet tucked
under him, an attitude by no means the most convenient.

"On the 4th of April Rezanof had his first audience,
to which he was conveyed in a large boat adorned
with flags and curtains.   On this occasion, merely an
exchange of compliments took place, and a few insignificant questions were put to him.   The second audience was conducted with the same ceremonies, and
here the negotiation terminated; the necessary documents being delivered into his hands, which contained
an order that no Russian ship should again come to
Japan; and the presents, and even the letter from
the emperor of Russia, were all refused."[2]

---

[1] Krusenstern writes: 'I doubt whether any ship ever sailed from this
harbor so well provisioned as we were; and shall mention the chief articles
we were furnished with, in order to show what Kamchatka was competent
to provide.   We had seven large live oxen, a considerable provision of salted
and dried fish, a great supply of vegetables, several casks of salt fish for
the crew, and three large barrels of wild garlic (as an anti-scorbutic and a
substitute for sourkrout).   Besides these, we received several delicacies for
our own table, such as salted reindeer and game, argali or wild sheep, salted
wild geese, etc., for all which we were indebted to the governor, who, if I
may be allowed the expression, employed all Kamchatka to our advantage.'
Voy. round World, i. 215-16.

[2] *Id.*, i. 284-5.   'Should any Japanese hereafter be cast upon the coast of

In sore disgust, Rezanof ordered th captain of thee *Nadeshda* to weigh anchor on the morning of the 17th of April. After being engaged for several weeks in exploring expeditions among the Japanese, Kurile, and Saghalin Islands, the ship again cast anchor off Petropavlovsk on the 5th of June. Here Rezanof engaged a passage on board the brig *Maria* for Kadiak, the *Nadeshda* sailing a month later, and after further explorations, arriving at Macao on the 20th of November.

Dismissing the members of his embassy with the exception of Langsdorff, the plenipotentiary sailed from Petropavlovsk on the 24th of June, and about three weeks later landed at the island of St Paul. Here he met with sufficient evidences of carelessness and waste. The skins of the fur-seal were scattered about over beach and bluff in various stages of decomposition. The storehouses were full, but only a small part of their contents was in a marketable state. As many as thirty thousand had been killed for their flesh alone, the skins having been left on the spot or thrown into the sea. After questioning the Aleutian laborers and Russian overseers, Rezanof came to the conclusion that unless an end were put to this wanton destruction, a few years more would witness the extirpation of the fur-seal.

On the 25th of July the *Maria* entered Beaver Bay, on the eastern side of Unalaska, and thence, with a few companions, Rezanof proceeded on foot over the rough mountain trail to the company's station at Illiuliuk.[3]

Russia,' continues Krusenstern, 'they were to be delivered over to the Dutch, who would send them by way of Batavia to Nangasaki. Further: we were forbidden from making any presents, or purchasing anything for money, as well as from visiting or receiving the visit of the Dutch factor. On the other hand, it was declared that the repairs of the ship and the supply of provisions were to be taken into the imperial account; that she should be provided with everything for two months; and that the emperor had sent 2,000 sacks of salt, each weighing 30 pounds, and 100 sacks of rice, each of 150 pounds weight, besides 2,000 pieces of capock or silk wadding.'

[3] The natives of the settlement on Beaver Bay (Borka) still relate incidents of this journey, transmitted to them by their fathers. They told Mr

From this settlement Rezanof despatched his first
official letter.   After making brief mention of his voyage, he writes:[4] "The multitude of seals in which St
Paul abounds is incredible; the shores are covered
with them.   They are easily caught, and as we were
short of provisions, eighteen were killed for us in half
an hour.   But at the same time we were informed
that they had decreased in number ninety per cent
since earlier times.   These islands would be an inexhaustible source of wealth were it not for the Bostonians, who undermine our trade with China in furs, of
which they obtain large numbers on our American
coast.   As over a million had already been killed, I
gave orders to stop the slaughter at once, in order to
prevent their total extirmination, and to employ the
men in collecting walrus tusks, as there is a small isl-
and near St Paul covered with walrus.

" I take the liberty, as a faithful subject of your imperial Majesty, of declaring my opinion that it is very
necessary to take a stronger hold of this country.   It
is certain that we shall leave it empty-handed, since
from fifteen to twenty ships come here annually from
Boston to trade.   In the first place, the company
should build a small stanch brig, and send out heavy
ordnance for her armament.   This would compel the
Bostonians to keep away, and the Chinese would get
no furs but ours.   Secondly, the establishment of the
company's business on so large a scale requires great
expenditure, and the trade in furs alone cannot support
it.   The American colonies can never be fully developed as long as bread, the principal staple of food,
has to be shipped from Okhotsk.   To this end it is

Petroff, during his visit in 1878, that when this greatest and mightiest of all
Russians who had ever visited their country passed over the trail connecting
the head of Beaver Bay with Illiuliuk settlement, the obsequious promyshleniki had engaged numbers of natives to carry pieces of board or plank in advance
of the ambassador to be laid over rivulets and damp places, and thereby save
his excellency from wetting his feet.   The natives, who think nothing of
wading through water for hours at a time, were evidently deeply impressed with
this extraordinary precaution.

[4] He was authorized to address his despatches directly to the emperor, a
privilege seldom granted to a Russian subject.

necessary to intercede with the Spanish government
for permission to purchase on the Philippine Islands,
or in Chili, the produce of those countries. There we
could obtain breadstuffs, sugar, and rum at low prices
for bills of exchange in piastres, and in sufficient quantity to supply all Kamchatka; while in the mean time
we are developing our colonies in America, and after
building ships there could compel the Japanese to open
their ports to our trade.

"I hope that your imperial Majesty will not consider it a crime on my part, if, after being reënforced
by my distinguished coöperators, Lieutenants Khvostof and Davidof, and having the ship repaired and
newly armed, I push on next year to the coast of
Japan, there to destroy the settlement at Matsmai,
drive the Japanese from Saghalin Island, and frighten
them away from the whole coast and the Kurile Islands, breaking up their fisheries, and thereby depriv-
ing 200,000 people of food, which will force them all
the sooner to open their ports. I have heard that
they have been bold enough to erect a factory at Oor-
upa Island, one of our Kuriles.

"Here at Unalaska, I have succeeded in impressing
the islanders with your Majesty's fatherly care for
their welfare. I asked them if they were satisfied
with their agent Mr Larionof, and if they suffered
oppression. They all answered unanimously that he
had been a father to them. I questioned also the
chiefs of more distant villages, and they all answered
the same. Finally I assembled the whole population,
and persuaded them to tell me without fear whether
they had cause for complaint, informing them that my
advent among them was the consequence of your imperial Majesty's anxiety for their well-being. They
answered that they had only one request to make, and
that not of me, but of the agent, and when I inquired
what that request was, assuring them that it should
be granted, they answered that they wished him to
be as good to them in the future as he had been in

the past, for they had been perfectly quiet and happy, and received such remuneration for their labor as had been mutually agreed upon. I gave to the agent Larionof, in the name of your imperial Majesty, a gold medal, and to the interpreter Pankof a silver medal, and told the chiefs that these men had been rewarded solely on the strength of their unanimous favorable answers to my questions. At the same time I inflicted exemplary punishment upon the trader Kulikalof, who had been summoned from Atkha Island for cruelly beating a native woman and her infant son. After assembling all the chiefs and other natives, and the Russians and sailors from the vessel, I had the culprit put in irons and sent him off to Irkutsk by the transport then about to sail, to be turned over to the courts of justice; after which I explained to the islanders that before your imperial Majesty all subjects were equal, and then turning to the Russian hunters, I assured them that every act of violence would be as severely punished. "

On the 25th of July, the *Maria* sailed from Unalaska, and a week latter anchored in the harbor of St Paul. Upon landing, Rezanof, as the plenipotentiary of the Russian emperor, was saluted with salvos of artillery and received with hearty welcome.[5] His report on the condition of affairs was satisfactory, and he speaks in high terms of Banner, who was still in charge of the colony.[6]

form, who had ranged themselves along the stockade. At the landing place, he was met by three Russian clergymen and conducted by them to the church. Here a te deum was offered up by the whole population upon the happy arrival of so distinguished a personage. *Langsdorff's Voy.*, part ii. 57.

[d] At this time it consisted of about 30 buildings, apart from the habitations of the natives. *Id.*, 66. Of the condition of the natives, Langsdorff gives a very unfavorable account. 'They are at present,' he says, 'so completely the slaves of the company, that they hold of them their baidars, their clothing, and even the bone with which their javelins are pointed, and the whole produce of their hunting parties is entirely at their disposal. It is revolting to a mind of any feeling to see these poor creatures half starved and almost naked, as if they were in a house of correction, when at the same time the warehouses of the company are full of clothing and provisions. Nor is this the case with the natives alone: the Russian promüschleniks are not in a much better situation. They are extremely ill-treated, and kept at

During his brief stay he took measures to improve
the moral condition of the settlement. In a building
which had been erected during the preceding winter
by Lisiansky, he laid the foundation for a library,
with books forwarded for the purpose from St Petersburg.[7] He urged upon the promyshleniki and natives
in the service of the company the benefit to be
derived from sending their children to the school,
which for some years had been sparsely attended.
At the same time he induced the wife of Banner to
take into her house a certain number of young girls
to be trained in housekeeping.

Arriving at Novo Arkhangelsk near the end of
August, Rezanof and his party were provided with
the best accommodation at the disposal of the chief
manager, and with such rough and scant fare as his
stores could furnish. "We all live poorly," writes
the former, a few weeks later, in his first report to
the Russian American Company; "but worse than
all lives the founder of this place, in a miserable hut,
so damp that the floor is always wet, and during the
constant heavy rains the place leaks like a sieve.
Wonderful man! He only cares for the comfort of
others, and is very neglectful of himself. Once I
found his bed floating in the water, and asked him
whether the wind had not torn off a board somewhere

their work till their strength is entirely exhausted; if they are ill, they must
never hope for medical assistance or support in any other way; while as
little attention at the same time is paid to their minds as to their bodies.
The bad quality of their food, which consists chiefly of the flesh of whales
and sea-dogs, the moist, foggy climate, the dirtiness of their habitations in
the barracks, the want of a proper change of linen and clothing, all these are
circumstances sufficient to undermine the strongest constitution. *Id.*, 71-2.
Langsdorff's statements, though supported in part by those of Lisiansky,
which I have already quoted, are probably exaggerated.

[7] Previous to his departure from St Petersburg, Rezanof received portraits
in oil of the imperial family, and of scientific men, the latter presenting their
likenesses 'with the sole object of awakening in the untutored mind of the
American savage an understanding of true art.' One of these donations was
made by State Counsellor Von Fuchs, director of the Moscow Academy of
Sciences, who accompanied his gift with a letter, in which he spoke of Rezanof as the 'worthy successor of all the great discoverers of the world—the
Russian Columbus.' Petroff during his wanderings in Alaska saw the portrait of Fuchs doing duty as saint in the corner of a smoky dwelling of a
native up Cook Inlet.

HIST. ALASKA. 29

from the side of the hut. 'No,' he answered quietly, 'it
is only the old leak,' and turned again to his occupation.
I tell you, gentlemen, that Baranof is an original, and
at the same time a very happy production of nature.
His name is heard on the whole western coast, down
to California. The Bostonians esteem him and respect
him, and the savage tribes, in their dread of him, offer
their friendship from the most distant regions." Rezanof then informs the directors that both Baranof
and Kuskof desire to leave the country, and declares
that in the existing state of affairs a new man could be
of no use, for, in the time that he would require to become acquainted with his duties, the company would
inevitably suffer considerable loss, and might be deprived of all its possessions.

In their last communication, the directors had informed their plenipotentiary that they purposed to establish trading-posts in Tonquin, Cochin China, Bur-
mah, and elsewhere in the farther Indies. But Rezanof, although a man of sanguine temperament, was
of opinion that, with the resources at his command,
such a project was simply chimerical. He does not appear, however, to have abandoned his intention of
forcing the Japanese to open their ports, although he
states that the company is in no condition to extend
its operations beyond north-western America.[8]

[8] He had intended that a flotilla should be built at Novo Arkhangelsk for
his Japanese expedition, but in view of the poverty-stricken condition of the
settlement, contented himself with ordering a launch made for the *Juno*. The
craft was significantly named the *Avos* (Perhaps), and Davidof was appointed her commander, Kvosdof taking charge of the *Juno*. On his arrival at
Okhotsk, in September 1806, Rezanof procured a new armament for the *Juno*
and the *Avos* for the expedition to the Japanese coast. The commanders
of the two vessels were instructed to seize everything in such Japanese settlements as were accessible, taking care at the same time to capture alive as
large a number as possible of skilled artisans, who might be useful in the
American colonies. Having long since revolved the plan of this enterprise
in his mind, he had instructed Baranof to prepare quarters for such compulsory immigrants on an island in Sitka Bay, which has since borne the name
of Japanovsky, though the envoy's plan was never carried out. Feeling that
he was acting rashly, and without the sanction of the imperial government,
Rezanof was somewhat uneasy, and changed the tenor of his instructions several times before finally delivering them to Kvosdof and Davidof. The two

"The Kolosh appear to be subdued," continues the envoy, "but for how long? They have been armed by the Bostonians with the best guns and pistols, and have even falconets. All along the sound they have erected forts. The fierceness and treachery once exhibited by the natives have taught us all the greatest caution. Our cannon are always loaded, and not only are sentries with loaded guns posted everywhere, but arms of all kinds are the chief furniture of our rooms. Every evening, after sundown, signals are maintained throughout the night, and a watchword is passed from post to post until daylight. Perfect military discipline is enforced, and we are ready at any moment to receive the savages, who are in the habit of profiting by the darkness and gloom of night to make their attacks."

Rezanof's fears were not ill-founded. About the very time that his report was written a rumor reached Novo Arkhangelsk, which was afterward confirmed, that the Yakutat colony had been destroyed by the Kolosh, and all the Russians, except the commander's wife and children, together with a number of Aleuts, massacred.[9] Encouraged by this success, the savages determined to attack the Russian settlements lying farther to the north. Embarking in eight large warcanoes, they proceeded to the mouth of the Copper River, where, leaving six of their vessels, they despatched the other two to the Konstantinovski Redoubt, on Nuchek Island. Their chief, Fedor, a godson of Baranof, and a man well known to the promyshleniki, appeared boldly before Ouvarof, the commander of the station, declaring that he wished to trade with the Chugatsches. Ouvarof gave him permission, and

officers by no means liked the part they were to play in the proposed undertaking, but being accustomed to implicit obedience of orders, they did their best in carrying out the work of destruction. This course of action subsequently involved them in serious difficulties with the Okhotsk authorities, resulting in imprisonment, privation, and suffering. *Tikhmenef*, i. 154-160.

[9] The news was sent by Ivan Repin, the company's agent at Konstantinovsk Redoubt, on Nuchek Island. His letter was sent to Kadiak, and dated September 24, 1805. *Tikhmenef, Istor. Obos.*, ii. app. part ii. 195.

witnessed the usual preliminary dances and festivity. On one of the canoes kept in reserve there was, however, a captive Chugatsch, who succeeded in escaping, and informed Ouvarof of the real object of the Kolosh. Thereupon the Russian commander seized the chief, and told him that his plan had been revealed. In the mean time the native allies, hearing of the matter, had taken the remainder of the Kolosh to their village under pretence of inviting them to a feast, and had there massacred almost the entire party. Among the few that escaped was Fedor, who carried to the party at Copper River the news of their comrades' fate. Fearing that the Chugatsches would soon be upon them, the panic-stricken Kolosh at once put to sea, and while attempting to cross the bar in the teeth of a gale, the bidarkas were dashed to pieces and their inmates drowned. Thus was the Yakutat massacre avenged without the loss of a single man on the side of the Russians.[10]

During a brief sojourn in London, in 1803, while the *Nadeshda* was lying at Falmouth, Rezanof visited Newgate prison, where he saw four hundred convicts awaiting transportation to Botany Bay. Thus was suggested to him the idea of petitioning the crown that a number of exiles be sent out yearly to reënforce the sparsely peopled colonies of Russian America. He recommends that those selected be chiefly mechanics and laborers, and that it be understood that none should have permission to return, in order that society might be permanently rid of a portion of its dangerous members; while the criminals, being fairly treated and having no hope of escape, would be of great benefit in building up the settlements.

For several months after Rezanof's arrival at Novo Arkhangelsk, formal councils were convened for the purpose of discussing measures for the welfare of the

[10] *Khlebnikof, Shizn. Baranova,* 102-5. The number of Kolosh who perished was about 200, of whom 70 were massacred at Nuchek Island.

colonies.[11]   At their meetings Baranof and his chief
assistants were always present, but the plenipotentiary
was doubtless the guiding spirit.   At the close of
their deliberations the latter handed to the chief manager a list of instructions for his guidance, which,
though some of them were for the time impracticable,
show a keen insight into the wants of the colony.   He
recommends that special attention be paid to the
training of mechanics and tradesmen; that the garrison be recruited from friendly natives and native
youths reared at the company's expense; that young
men be trained in the schools of the colony to fill positions as book-keepers, clerks, and agents; that a fund
be provided for the support of the aged and disabled;
that, in view of the scarcity of shipwrights, ships be
purchased from foreigners whenever opportunity may
offer, even at a sacrifice, and that for this purpose
credits be established with banking houses in London
and Amsterdam; and that in order to insure a sufficient supply of bread-stuffs, trade be established with
California, New Albion, and the Philippine Islands.[12]

"Upon the fur trade alone," he writes in a letter
to the directors, "the company cannot subsist, and it
is absolutely necessary to organize without delay a
business of a general character—a trade with other
countries to which the road is open from the colony.
This is all the more necessary, as the number of fur-
bearing animals decreases from year to year.   If Baranof had not returned to Novo Arkhangelsk, but given
up the enterprise there as lost, the effect upon the

[11] The first of them appears to have been held on the 1st of September,
1805.   On this occasion the envoy, after examining the reports of Baranof,
said: 'The organization of the company is complete and in perfect working
order; all matters connected with trade, actual settlement, and general economy are flourishing; the inhabitants are being instructed in the necessary
industries, trades, and manufactures; the business connections are being constantly extended; the administration of justice is efficient; the navigation of
the company's vessels is intrusted to tried seamen, and youths are being trained
to succeed them when required; the fighting establishment is strong, and
ready for any emergency; and the relations with friendly tribes of the natives
are of a satisfactory character, and likely to be permanent.' *Id.*, 91-2.
[12] The principal items in these instructions are given in *Tikhmenef, Istor.
Obos.*, i. 142-4.

company would have been to carry the value of the
shares, not up into the thousands as in former years,
but down to about 280 roubles. In that case the hunter who receives his half-share, or 140 roubles, would
work for nothing, as his expenses for food and drink
alone exceed that sum each year. According to my
calculation, the annual expenses of the hunter, at the
present high prices, cannot amount to less than 317
roubles."

The prices of all imported commodities throughout
Russian America were, at this period, so extravagant that the promyshleniki were always hopelessly
in debt to their employers. They were not allowed
to leave the country until their obligation was can-
celled; and he was considered a fortunate man who,
after many years of exile and privation, could return
to his native country to end his days, broken in
health and spirit, and without a rouble in his pocket.
Bread-stuffs could be brought from Boston at lower
rates than from Okhotsk, while at Petropavlovsk
trade was in the hands of a few monopolists. As an
illustration of the condition of affairs at the latter port,
it may be mentioned that the mere sale of the *Nadeshda's* surplus supplies, during Rezanof's visit, caused
the leading articles of consumption to fall in price from
fifty to seventy per cent.[13]

Such was the dearth of provisions in Novo Arkhangelsk at the approach of winter, that early in
October Baranof was compelled to purchase the *Juno's*
cargo of provisions, which was sold, together with the
ship, for the sum of sixty-seven thousand piastres.[14]
On the 15th of the month the vessel was despatched

[13] Linen fell from 14 to 7 roubles a piece, sugar from 140 to 48 roubles a
poud, brandy from 20 to 8 roubles a quart, and tobacco from 2½ roubles to 75
kopeks a pound. *Id.*, 132.

[14] The provisions obtained by this purchase consisted of 19 casks of salt
pork, 42 casks of salted beef, 1,955 gals. of molasses, 2,983 lbs. of powdered
sugar, 315 lbs. loaf-sugar, 4,343 lbs. of rice, 11 casks of fine wheat flour,
7,332 lbs. of biscuit. *Langsdorff's Voy.*, part ii. 89-90. Payment was made
in furs to the amount of 31,250 piastres, and the remainder in drafts on
directors in St Petersburg. A small vessel was also given to the captain in
which to ship his crew and furs.

to Kadiak for further supplies, and a few weeks later
returned laden with dried fish and oil for the use of
the natives.

The tidings from St Paul were almost as disastrous
as was the news which Captain Barber brought from
Novo Arkhangelsk to the chief manager, some three
years before. The *Elizaveta*, despatched to Kadiak
for provisions soon after Rezanof's arrival, had been
wrecked during a heavy storm; six large bidarkas,
laden with furs, had foundered during the same gale;
of a party which had left Norfolk Sound under
Demianenkof, more than two hundred had perished at
sea; and finally the destruction of the Yakutat settlement was confirmed.

The details of the disaster which overtook Demianenkof and his party are as follow: He had left
Novo Arkhangelsk with the intention of proceeding
to Kadiak, and not many days after his departure
heard rumors of the Yakutat massacre, and of the
intention of the Kolosh to attack his party also. He
at once adopted extraordinary precautions, travelling
only at night, and hiding by day in the dense forests
lining the shore. When he had reached a point about
forty miles distant from Yakutat, he timed the departure of his command so as to reach the settlement at
midnight. As they cautiously approached the shore,
after ten hours of hard paddling, they were soon convinced that the reports of disaster were true. Of all
the buildings, not one log was left standing upon
another. Ashes, the remains of destroyed implements
and of other property, covered the whole village site.
The frightened Aleutian hunters, though almost exhausted, refused to land, and after a brief consultation
a majority of the force concluded to proceed without
delay to the island of Kyak, a hundred and fifty
miles away; but the inmates of thirty of the bidarkas,
exhausted with their long toil, landed on the beach
near by, preferring the chances of death or captivity
to further exertion. The coast between Yakutat and

Prince William Sound consists of steep cliffs and great
bodies of glacier ice, affording no landing places,
even to canoes, for nearly the whole distance.   As
fate ordained, those who had chosen almost certain
death at the hand of the Kolosh were saved, and
finally reached their destination without being molested; but as soon as the landing had been effected, a
terrible gale sprung up, during which all their companions at sea perished.   The following morning the
shore was lined with corpses and the shattered remnants of bidarkas.

The winter was passed by Rezanof and his companions in great discomfort, on account of constant
rain and snow storms, and though the stores of the
Juno had appeared ample for the season, a scarcity of
provisions was felt by the Russians as early as the
beginning of February.[15]   At length the envoy, tired
of his dismal abode, ordered the *Juno* to be again
made ready for sea, having resolved to proceed to the
coast of California, there to negotiate with the governor for a constant exchange of commodities.   With
difficulty a small crew was mustered from a command
weakened by disease and privation, and even these
were so emaciated that Rezanof would not allow them
to be seen by the Californian officials until they had
been plentifully fed and brought into better condition.
The details of Rezanof's visit to San Francisco, which
after lengthy negotiations resulted in the accomplish-
men of its object, are related elsewhere.[16]   It is sufficient to state, at present, that the *Juno* returned to
Novo Arkhangelsk on the 19th of June, with a cargo
of 671 fanegas of wheat, 117 of oats, 140 of pease and
beans, and a large quantity of flour, tallow, salt, and

---

[15] Langsdorff gives a sensational account of the suffering among the colonists at Novo Arkhangelsk during this winter, and of the spread of scorbutic
diseases.   Some of his statements appear false on their face.   For instance,
he says that the houses of the promyshleniki and native laborers were only
warmed 'by their own fetid breath'—and this in a settlement surrounded
on all sides by dense forests. *Voy.*, part ii. 93–95.

[16] *Hist. Cal.*, ii. 64 et seq., this series.

other supplies, valued at 5,587 piastres, payment having been made chiefly in Russian manufactured goods.

Rezanof had now fulfilled his mission to the best of his power, and five days later sailed for Okhotsk on board the *Juno*, intending to proceed thence overland to St Petersburg, and report in person to the emperor his achievements and his plans for the future, and to ask of his sovereign permission to bring to its legitimate end his romantic episode with Doña Concepcion de Argüello, of which mention is made in another volume.[17]   His sojourn in the north-west had wrought many changes for the better, and though his relations with Baranof and his subordinates were always friendly, the envoy was even more bitter than the chief manager in his complaints of the treatment which he received at the hands of the naval officers.   Describing an interview with one of them, he says: "A man dressed in a black coat and vest approached me and shook hands.   I asked him, 'Who are you?'   He answered, 'I am Lieutenant Sookin of the Russian navy, commanding the ship *Elizaveta*.'   I replied that I was chamberlain of the Russian court and commander of all America.   I expressed my displeasure at his appearance, and ordered him to return to shore and present his report to me, dressed in proper uniform.   He complied with my orders very unwillingly."   For this conduct Rezanof threatened to send the lieutenant back to Russia, but Baranof asked that he be allowed to remain and earn his pay, for he had already received for doing nothing the sum of five thousand roubles, "of which amount," says Rezanof, "he had expended three thousand roubles in rum.   I saw him but five times during the whole winter, always in his room, dividing his time between sleeping and drinking, though his quiet consumption of the liquor disturbs nobody and injures only his own health.   He is so unobtrusive that we scarcely notice his presence.

[17] *Id.*, 68 et seq.

His log-books and reports will convince you of the
insufficiency of his nautical knowledge. On shore he
spends much time inditing ungrammatical letters to
the chief manager, and thus far has spent eighteen
months' salary in purchasing rum. He is like a useless sea-sprite, to whom, however, the chief manager
does not dare to intrust a vessel; therefore I have concluded to send him back to you, leaving it to you to
settle his accounts."

The next officer discussed is Lieutenant Mashin,
"who," says Rezanof, "has asked to be relieved. The
history of his services has been given to you by the
chief manager. I will only remark that by his consumption of brandy he has contributed considerably
to the profits of the company, and therefore gratitude
prevents me from keeping him in the service. He
lives in the same house with Sookin. Their tastes
and recreations are the same, but I am told that they
live in a very original and independent way. They do
nothing together. They sleep by turns; they promenade one after the other, and care so little about
past, present, or future, that they find no topics upon
which to converse." [18]

[18] During the winter of 1805–6, Lieutenant Khvostof was debited in the
company's books with 9½ buckets (19 gallons) of French brandy, and 2½
buckets of alcohol. *Tikhmenef*, ii. app. part ii. 248. Khvostof and Davidof
were both drowned while crossing the Neva in a small boat by night. The
accident was probably due to a joint debauch. *Dvukratnoe Puteshestvie v
Ameriku Morskikh Offitzerov Khvostova i Davidova*, app.—two voyages to
America by the naval officers, Khvostof and Davidof, written by the latter.
2 vols. 1810 and 1812, Naval Printing Office, St Petersburg. This work
contains a detailed and for the most part clear and impartial account of the
voyages and experience of two naval officers in the service of the Russian
American Company. Both were men of culture and education, and were the
first to avail themselves of the privilege granted by an imperial oukaz, which
permitted officers of the navy to enter into temporary engagements with the
Russian American Company, without losing rank or pay in the public service. Their departure from St Petersburg took place in April 1802, and the
first two chapters are devoted to the overland journey to Okhotsk, where
they arrived in August of the same year. The next two chapters contain the
departure from Okhotsk, the journey to Kadiak, an interview with Baranof,
a brief review of the company's history and business, and the return voyage
to Okhotsk in June 1803. Thence they returned to St Petersburg overland,
arriving there in January 1804. An appendix to the first volume contains a
short biographical sketch of both travellers, a letter addressed to them jointly
by Rezanof, whom they accompanied on his mission to Japan, and concludes

Of the missionaries and their labors Rezanof has little good to report. He remarks that their so-called conversion was merely a name, and that the ceremony of baptism had not affected their morals or customs. He states that the Russian priests did not follow the example of the Jesuits in their missionary work, that they did not enter into the plans of the government and the company, that they lived in idleness, or busied themselves only in meddling with the company's affairs, often causing disturbance between officers and servants at the various stations. He complains that through lack of zeal few took the trouble to acquire the native language, and states incidentally that the late bishop Ioassaf had received fifteen shares of stock in the Russian American Company—a circumstance which explains the tenor of the prelate's reports.[19]

On the 24th of September, 1806, Rezanof left Okhotsk on his homeward journey. Prompted by remarkable activity of mind and body, he travelled rapidly; but, weakened as he was by the hardships, anxiety, and trouble of the past three years, the journey had a fatal effect upon his health. While crossing rivers, over the thin ice just forming, it frequently happened that he was not only drenched, but obliged to camp in the snow afterward. About

with two poems in praise of the achievements of Davidof and Khvostof, and alluding to their tragic death.

The second volume is devoted entirely to a detailed description of Kadiak and the settlements on Cook Inlet, and at Novo Arkhangelsk, with historical sketches of the colonies and the Russian American Company, and a review of the manners and customs of the natives, and the way in which they were managed by the Russians. Attached to this volume are two brief vocabularies of the Kolosh and Kenaïski languages, of little value to the philologist on account of numerous mistakes. Sokolof subsequently reviewed Khvostof and Davidof at length in the *Morskoi Sbornik*. He confined himself chiefly to Khvostof, whom he describes as a talented, amiable individual, though imbittered in mind by misfortune and dissipation, and feeling great enmity toward Rezanof. When the latter sailed in the *Juno* for California to save the people of Novo Arkhangelsk from starvation, Khvostof complained that he was 'taking them into a tropical latitude at the most dangerous season of the year.' *Morskoi Sb.*, ix. 349-58.

[19] Dall, *Alaska*, 316, speaks of Ioassof as an Augustine friar. It is difficult to conceive whence he obtained this information, as there is but one monastic order in all Russia—that of St Basilius.

sixty miles east of the Aldana, he was attacked with
a violent fever and carried unconscious into a Yakout
hut. A few days after he became convalescent, he
pushed on to Yakutat before recovering his strength.
Here again he was prostrated, and again continued
his journey; but his career was now at an end, and
on the 1st of March, 1807, the plenipotentiary breathed
his last at Krasnoyarsk, in eastern Siberia.[20]

[20] Tikhmenef reflects thus on Rezanof's death: ' The company lost in him
a spirit most active in its organization, and in the development of the colonies
under its control. Having acquainted himself on the spot with the requirements of the country, and having made the most earnest efforts to establish
relations with adjoining countries, Rezanof could not brook delay on his
homeward journey, where he expected, to plead personally the company's
cause before the imperial throne. There can be no doubt that his influence, so
far as it reached, has been wholly beneficial. We do not know what plans
were seething in his active brain, ready to be laid before the company's directors and the government upon his return to the capital. If Rezanof's life had
not ended so prematurely, some of his plans would certainly have been brought
to successful issue at a much earlier period than we can now hope for, while
others would not have suffered total neglect at the hands of the authorities.
We cannot fail to see that he was no idle dreamer, though his efforts for the
public welfare were not much appreciated during his life-time, being frequently
spoken of in a deprecating manner. A few looked on him as a visionary, capable only of concocting schemes on paper, but at the same time hardships,
disasters, and opposition could not prevent him from following his course and
pursuing the object of his life. The honesty and amiability of his character
were universally acknowledged, and though he failed to accomplish much
that he proposed, he probably did more than any of his assailants.' *Istor.
Obos.*, i. 102–3.

CHAPTER XXII.

THREE years had now elapsed since the chief manager had sailed from Kadiak, and at the end of September 1806 he returned to St Paul, leaving Kuskof in command at Novo Arkhangelsk, with instructions to hasten the completion of certain buildings and ships then in course of construction. In March 1807 a fine brig named the *Sitka* was launched, and two months later she arrived at Kadiak. During the following summer a three-masted vessel of three hundred tons, christened the *Otkrytie*, or *Discovery*, was also built at Novo Arkhangelsk, and at the same time the keel was laid for a schooner, to be named in honor of the discoverer Chirikof.[1] A few days after the arrival of the *Sitka*, the English ship *Myrtle* anchored in the harbor of St Paul, in charge of Captain Barber, of whom mention has been made in connection

---

[1] On the completion of each vessel, the builder received a gratuity of 1,000 roubles from the company. Chirikof, it will be remembered, was in command of the first Russian vessel that visited the farther north-west coast of America.

with the Sitka massacre. Although no friendly feeling existed between him and Baranof, so greatly was the latter in need of vessels, that the ship was purchased, together with her cargo,[2] and renamed the *Kadiak*.

In September 1807 the *Neva* arrived at Novo Arkhangelsk on her second voyage from Kronstadt,[3] in command of Lieutenant Hagemeister, who, as we shall see, was appointed some years later Baranof's successor, and in the following spring the ship was added to the company's fleet. By this vessel the chief manager received news that the imperial government had bestowed on him, as an additional reward, the order of St Anne of the third class, while on Kuskof was conferred the rank of commercial councillor.

Meanwhile the *Kadiak* had been despatched to Yakutat by way of Novo Arkhangelsk, her commander being instructed to rescue the survivors of the massacre who were still in the hands of the Kolosh. A foreign flag was hoisted in order to deceive the savages, and thus two of them were induced to board the ship, and were secured. Negotiations were then opened, and the commander's widow and children with several others were released from captivity.[4]

[2] The ship for 42,000 piastres, and the cargo of furs, provisions, arms, and ammunition for 63,675 roubles. Barber received his pay in drafts on the board of managers, and demanded to be placed at Okhotsk on one of the company's vessels in order to proceed to St Petersburg overland. He sailed on the *Sitka* the following autumn, but owing to the lateness of the season, the vessel proceeded to Petropavlovsk. Here she was loaded with goods for Nishe Kamchatsk, but was totally wrecked at the mouth of Kamchatka River on the 15th of October, 1807. The crew and passengers were saved. *Khlebnikof, Shizn. Baranova*, 117-18.

[3] In August 1806 it had been resolved at a meeting of the shareholders to send the *Neva* once more to the colonies. Hagemeister and the other officers were engaged for a period of four years. *Tikhmenef, Istor. Obos.*, i. 164.

[4] During the preceding year Baranof had sent Captain Campbell, an American, upon the same errand, but he succeeded only in securing two hostages and releasing one Aleut and his wife. The former were transferred to Kadiak and baptized, receiving the names of Kalistrat and Gideon. They afterward returned to Sitka, where they were employed as interpreters. Kalistrat died in 1832, and Gideon several years later. *Khlebnikof, Shizn.*

During the winter of 1806–7, the Kolosh again assumed a threatening attitude, encouraged chiefly by the absence of Baranof. Reports of intended attacks reached Kuskof at various times. Under pretext of engaging in herring fishery, they assembled on the islands of Norfolk Sound, with more than four hundred large war-canoes, while the number of warriors was not less than two thousand. The Kolosh women, who cohabited with the promyshleniki of the garrison, aided in spreading alarm by exaggerated reports of the intentions of their countrymen. Deeds of violence were of daily occurrence, and at last a party of Aleutian fishermen were captured and killed. Prompt action was now required; but as the Russians were not strong enough to attack the enemy, or even sustain a siege, Kuskof resolved to try the effect of peaceful measures. He invited to the fort the most powerful of the chiefs, feasted them, flattered them, plied them with rum, and by a liberal distribution of presents, finally induced them to leave the neighborhood.[5]

The year 1809 witnessed the most formidable of the many conspiracies hatched by the promyshleniki and Siberian ex-convicts against the chief manager. A few headstrong ruffians of the latter class, having been detained for some time at Kamchatka on their journey to America, had there learned the details of Benyovsky's famous exploits, doubtless exaggerated and embellished by transmission from one generation to another. One of these unruly spirits, Naplavkof, who had been originally exiled to Siberia and subsequently permitted to enter the company's service, conceived the idea of imitating the venturesome Pole, and forming a secret society for the purpose of over-

Baranova, 119–20. In 1835 Baron Wrangell, then chief manager, recommended that a pension be given to Gideon for his long services.

[5] In a private letter to Baranof, Kuskof reports that the success of his manœuvres was due to the efforts of a Kolosh girl sent by him into the hostile camp to create dissensions among the leaders.

throwing existing authority. His most trusted confidant was a peasant named Popof. By the time
these two worthies reached Novo Arkhangelsk, they
had admitted into their confidence eight or ten others,
assuring them that as soon as the first blow was
struck the whole colony would rise in revolt.

The object of the conspiracy was to put to death the
chief manager, who had now returned to Novo Arkhangelsk, and seize the arsenal and fort on some day
when Naplavkof, who was then acting as a subaltern
officer in the garrison, should be on duty. The conspirators then intended to plunder the storehouses
and barracks, and to load the ship *Otkrytie* with provisions and the most valuable of the goods. Each of the
conspirators was to select one of the women for his
mistress, and in addition, fifteen female natives were
to be taken as servants. On leaving Novo Arkhangelsk they purposed to sail for Easter Island, or to
some uninhabited spot still farther south, where they
could form a settlement, calling on the way at the
Hawaiian Islands to exchange their furs for provisions
and other necessaries.[6]

Few as were the conspirators in number, no less than
three of them, each independently of the others, revealed the secret to Baranof. Two of these traitors
were Poles, named Leshchinsky and Berezovsky; the
third a Russian, called Sidorof. From these men the
chief manager learned that the party met at Leshchinsky's quarters, and that all the members were
about to sign a written pledge, wherein each agreed to
carry out the plans of the rest, and to subscribe to a code
of rules and regulations. In expectation of this event,
Baranof ordered Leshchinsky to keep him informed
when the date was fixed for the proposed meeting, and

---

[6] Khlebnikof gives to this plot a tinge of romance. He says that, taking advantage of the war then raging in Europe, the conspirators purposed to form
a colonial confederation, capture Siberia, and establish a great republic of
hunters and traders. *Shizn. Baranova*, 128. He gives no authority, however,
for stating that such a foolhardy enterprise was conceived by Naplavkof and
his gang.

supplied him with a keg of brandy, wherewith to make merry with his comrades.

On the 6th of August the conspirators met at the usual rendezvous, which was close to the residence of the chief manager, in order to affix their signatures to an agreement drawn up by Popof from Naplavkof's dictation. When the object of the meeting had been accomplished, and the brandy freely handed round, Leshchinsky, according to a preconcerted signal, began to sing, whereupon Baranof, with a large force of armed men, rushed into the building. Naplavkof, a sabre in one hand and a loaded pistol in the other, made a show of resistance, while Popof hastily thrust the document into the oven. So sudden was the onslaught, however, that all the party were seized and bound before they could make use of their weapons. The document was recovered, almost intact, but the only additional information obtained from it was that Popof had been elected chief of the society under the assumed name of Khounshim, and that it had been agreed to do nothing until a hunting party, which contained some of their number, should return from Chatham Strait. The ringleaders and four others were ironed, placed under guard, and finally sent to Kamchatka for trial; and thus ended the plot, without further result than to increase the chief manager's desire to be relieved from office.[7]

---

[7] Baranof soon afterward forwarded an urgent letter to the board of directors, asking to be relieved. Captain V. M. Golovnin, of the sloop-of-war *Diana*, in speaking of this conspiracy, remarks: 'The Russian American Company's commissioner at Kamchatka, Khlebnikof, an honorable man, obtained from the leader of this conspiracy all the details, and finding that they had been suffering from hunger, cruel labor, and inhuman treatment by the officials, desired, in the interest of the company's good name and perhaps its existence, to conceal the whole proceedings from the government, to which end he wrote a letter to the directors of the company, dated July 8, 1810, wherein he declared that if Naplavkof and his companions were tried in any open court, they could reveal truths of a character most damaging to the company; therefore he asked them to drop the matter. But the directors did not approve of Khlebnikof's opinion, and replied, under date of September 29, 1810, that he must bring the offenders to justice, but make every effort to manage the affair to the advantage of the company, that is, to punish the conspirators while at the same time concealing the shortcomings of the company.' *Voy.*, 78–9.

Baranof's wish was not fulfilled until several years later, though, as we shall see, through no neglect on the part of the directors. There were none of his subordinates to whom he dared to intrust the control of affairs, and he had no alternative but to remain until a successor should arrive. Meanwhile he was relieved for a time from all anxiety as to further revolt among Russians or Kolosh by the arrival, in June 1810, of the sloop-of-war *Diana*, commanded by Captain Golovnin.[8]

The captain, who, like other naval officers, was not predisposed in the company's favor, thus describes his arrival: "It was 10 P. M., and dark. We fired a gun to call the pilot; lights were hung out, and we lay at anchor until midnight; we could then hear the noise of oars, but it was too dark to see the boat. At last Russian voices became audible, and we could doubt no longer that some of the company's promyshleniki were approaching, but for all that we did not neglect any precautionary measures. It was well known to me that this class of the company's servants consisted chiefly of criminals; and also that this class of scoundrels, having come from exile under false promises and expectations, found life in America even worse than that of a Siberian convict, and therefore were always ready to profit by any opportunity to throw off the yoke of the Russian American Company. They would not have hesitated even to surprise a ship of war and take possession of the country. All arms were kept at hand, and the crew on the alert. I then hailed the boat. They stated in reply that they were sixteen unarmed men, who had been sent by the chief manager to our assistance. I ordered them to board, and while they were standing in line I questioned them, the answers being evidently given in fear. During this time the officers of the *Diana* stood motionless at their posts. Not a voice was heard but my

_____

[8] The *Diana* had been expected the previous year. She reached Petropavlovsk in the autumn of 1809, and wintered there.

own and that of their spokesman. They had never witnessed such discipline before, and, as I subsequently heard, were laboring under the belief that they had been captured by some European man-of-war, on which I alone could speak Russian. But as soon as I had learned all I cared to know, I told them they might talk to their countrymen, and when they heard the Russian language spoken on all sides, they were almost beside themselves with joy. Only then they confessed that they had come armed with pistols, spears, and guns, which, suspecting us to be English, they had concealed in the bottom of the boat."

On the following morning the *Diana* was towed to the anchorage under the fort and saluted with eleven guns. After a ridiculous discussion between Baranof and Golovnin as to the number of guns to which each was entitled, the salute was returned. The captain was then invited to dinner, together with his officers and the commanders of several American vessels then in port. He thus relates his impressions: "In the fort we could see nothing remarkable. It consisted of strong wooden bastions and palisades. The houses, barrack magazines, and manager's residence were built of exceedingly thick logs. In Baranof's house the furniture and finishing were of fine workmanship and very costly, having been brought from St Petersburg and England; but what astonished me most was the large library in nearly all European languages, and the collection of fine paintings—this in a country where probably only Baranof can appreciate a picture, and no travellers are apt to call except the skippers of American trading vessels. Mr Baranof explained that the paintings had been presented to the company at the time of its organization, and that the directors had considered it best to send them to the colonies; with a smile, he added that it would have been wiser to send out physicians, as there was not one in the colonies, nor even a surgeon or apothecary.[9] I asked Mr Baranof how the directors could neglect to send surgeons to a country the climate of which was conducive to all kinds of diseases, and where men may at any time be wounded by savages and need surgical treatment. 'I do not know,' he said, 'whether the directors trouble themselves to think about it; but we doctor ourselves a little, and if a man is wounded so as to require an operation, he must die.' Mr Baranof treated us to an excellent dinner, during which we had music which was not bad."

During his stay in Russian America, Golovnin displayed in a somewhat ridiculous aspect his jealousy of the Russian American Company and of foreign traders. A short time before, the American ship *Enterprise*, in charge of Captain Ebbets, had arrived at Novo Arkhangelsk, laden with trading goods. The captain handed to the chief manager a despatch from the owner of the vessel, John Jacob Astor, wherein the latter stated that "for twenty-five years he had been established in New York and engaged in foreign trade; that he had done business with the Canadian Company and exchanged goods with Europe and Canton, and that he now sent his first ship to the north-west coast of America in charge of Captain Ebbets."

If we can believe the chief manager's biographer, Dashkof, the Russian consul-general for the United States,[10] being informed that Baranof was in want of supplies, had been recommended to inquire of Astor what was most needed, and by his advice had purchased a full cargo for the colonies. "I was very glad to oblige Mr Dashkof," continues the New York merchant, "and have loaded the ship with such useful commodities as will be best adapted to trade in the

---

[9] Baranof was of course aware that there was a hospital at St Paul. See Campbell's *Voy. round World*, 101, where the town is called Alexandria. Probably the chief manager was amusing himself and his guests at the expense of the captain.

[10] Afterward envoy plenipotentiary to the United States, and counsellor of state. *Khlebnikof, Shizn. Baranova*, 136.

colonies.   I send the vessel direct, giving full power
to Captain Ebbets to make agreements and contracts,
if he should see fit, and I am prepared to send, each
year, two or three vessels specially for that trade."

Baranof purchased goods of Ebbets to the amount
of twenty-seven thousand piastres, but declined to
buy the entire cargo.   In reply to Astor's letter, he
wrote that "he had reason to believe from private information that he would soon receive supplies, and
that he could not make contracts for the future, as he
expected to be relieved.   But he would always be
able to take the cargoes of one or two vessels each
year, if the price were not too high."

The *Enterprise* was now despatched with furs to
Canton, the proceeds to be invested in Chinese goods,
and after a prosperous voyage Ebbets returned in
May 1811.   He had sold his peltry at fair rates,
and purchased his cargo at low prices.[11]   Baranof inspected the bills of sale and the papers relating to
the several transactions, and so pleased was he with
the result, that he soon afterward despatched the
vessel on a second trip to Canton, with a cargo of
English goods which had been purchased during her
absence.

All this appears to be a very simple and straightforward transaction, though doubtless matters were
concealed by the chief manager's biographer which he
did not care to bring to light.   But now let us hear
Golovnin's account of the matter.   "Ebbets brought
a despatch from Dashkof," writes the captain of the
Diana, "with a contract with Astor, and a second
letter written by Astor himself with similar proposals, in terms very flattering to the chief manager,
calling him 'governor,' 'count,' and 'your excellency'
on nearly every line, and showing that even the republicans know how to bestow titles when their in-

[11] The terms of his contract with Baranof, the prices which he obtained
for the furs, and the goods bought with the proceeds are mentioned in *Id.*,
138-9.

terest requires it." He then makes the questionable statement that the letter was written in French, and that as Ebbets understood only English, and there were no interpreters, matters were at a stand-still when the *Diana* arrived. "An American sailor," he continues, "who was teaching English to the boys at Kadiak, without understanding Russian, a Prussian skipper of one of the company's vessels, and a relative of Baranof's who had picked up a few hundred English words, composed, previous to our arrival, the diplomatic corps of the Russian American Company; but as the first two were absent, and the third could only speak of subjects at which he could point with his fingers, Baranof could not communicate with the foreigners. Ebbets had already decided to leave without accomplishing anything, but when he heard that we could speak both English and French, he asked for our coöperation, which was freely promised, myself and Lieutenant Ricord acting as interpreters. We translated all the letters and documents and drew up the contracts."

Golovnin, in his account of these transactions, claims to have discovered that some deep-laid plan was contemplated by Astor, and thus gives his reasons for such an assertion: "Ebbets, desiring to let me know how much it had cost Astor to complete the *Enterprise* and fit her out for the expedition, gave me three books to look over. Two of them contained the accounts mentioned, but the third was evidently given by mistake, and contained supplementary instructions to Ebbets, in which he was directed to call at certain Spanish ports on the American coast and endeavor to trade with the inhabitants. If he succeeded, he was to go to Novo Arkhangelsk in ballast and trade with Baranof, and in case the latter should ask why he brought no goods, he must give as an excuse that he had heard the colonies were fully supplied. He was also told to obtain most minute details of the trade and condition of the Russian colonies, their strength and means of protection, the actual power of Baranof, and the relations between the company and the government. In brief, Astor wished to ascertain the feasibility of a seizure of the colonies by the United States. I returned the books to Ebbets without saying anything, but immediately wrote down the gist of the instructions and laid them before Baranof, who thought it best to forward them to the board of managers, who, with their usual policy, will no doubt, in course of time, make the best use of this information for themselves."

Whether the captain's view of the matter was right or wrong, he does not appear to have been actuated by very patriotic motives; for, without heeding Baranof's urgent request to prolong his stay in the colonies on account of the danger threatened from English privateers, he at once took on board a cargo of furs and trading goods for the company's commissioner in Kamchatka, and was ready for sea on the 2d of August. On that day Captain Winship, a Boston trader, entered the outer harbor in the ship *O'Cain*.[12] Ebbets, anxious to communicate with the new-comer, sent off a boat, which was stopped by a shot from the *Diana*, much to Baranof's satisfaction, who was glad to see the Russian authority maintained in this manner. Golovnin afterward sent a formal communication to Ebbets and Winship, stating that no one must communicate with an incoming ship until the harbor authorities had done their duty.

---

[12] During Rezanof's absence in California, Winship arrived in the *Enterprise* at Novo Arkhangelsk, and with him Baranof concluded a contract for hunting sea-otter on the coast of California. Winship was furnished with 50 bidarkas, under command of a trusted friend of Baranof, Pavl Slobodchikof, who subsequently was in captivity in Lower California. The agreement was made for a period of from 10 to 14 months. There appears to have been some disagreement between Slobodchikof and Winship, as the former, after a successful hunt all along the California coast, left the ship at the island of Cerros, where he purchased of an American skipper a small schooner for 150 sea-otters, naming her the *Nikolai*. On this craft, with a crew of two Americans and three Kanakas, he sailed for the Sandwich Islands, and thence for Novo Arkhangelsk. Winship did not reach the latter port until September of the following year. This enterprise resulted in the collection of 4,820 sea-otter skins. *Id.*, 107–8.

Late in August 1812, the American ship *Beaver*, fitted out by Astor, arrived at Novo Arkhangelsk, having on board his confidential agent, Wilson B. Hunt, who was instructed to treat with Baranof for the establishment of permanent relations between the American and Russian fur companies. Hunt executed his commission with some difficulty. He succeeded, however, in disposing of his cargo on advantageous terms, but was obliged to go to the Prybilof Islands for his payment in seal skins.

Considering the relations that were now established between Baranof and Astor, one may indulge in some speculation as to what would have been the result of this alliance had the enterprise of the latter been successful.[13] In that case, the Hudson's Bay Company would probably not have remained the chief factor in shaping the destinies of the north-west coast, and the British flag might not to-day float over the province of British Columbia. But it is probable that the shrewd New York merchant was out-matched by the chief manager, whom Irving describes at random as "a rough, rugged, hospitable, hard-drinking old Russian; somewhat of a soldier, somewhat of a trader, above all, a boon companion of the old roistering school, with a strong cross of the bear, but as keen, not to say crafty, at a bargain as the most arrant water-drinker."

Nevertheless, Astor had no cause for complaint against the Russian American Company. After abandoning his trading-post at the mouth of the Columbia, on the outbreak of war in 1812, his claim for damages was not disputed. His agent, Russell Far-

---

[13] The first cargo forwarded by Astor under the new agreement was lost by the wreck of the *Lark* at the Sandwich Islands in 1813. During this year Baranof purchased two foreign vessels, the *Atahualpa*, and her consort, the *Lady*. The *Atahualpa* was an old visitor on the north-west coast, appearing first in Sturgis' list of north-west traders in 1801, being then commanded by Captain Wild (Wildes according to Swan). The sale was effected by Captain Bennet, who in 1813 commanded the *Atahualpa*. The price agreed upon was 31,000 piastres for the cargo and 20,000 fur-seal skins for the vessel. *Sturgis' Remarks*, MS.; *Baranof, Shizn.*, 155. The *Atahualpa*, a three-master, was re-named the *Bering*, and the *Lady*, a brig, received the name *Ilmen*. Both were subsequently wrecked at the Sandwich Islands.

num, being despatched to Astoria, found that the person whose evidence was necessary to prove the claim had gone the previous year to Novo Arkhangelsk. After waiting a year for a vessel, the agent followed him, only to find that he had crossed over to Kamchatka. Reaching Bering Strait, Farnum made the passage between the ice-floes in an open boat, and at length overtook the man of whom he was in search. After obtaining the necessary proof, he made his way through Siberia and northern Russia to St Petersburg. "There," says Thomas Gray, who, while residing at Keokuk in 1830, heard the story from Farnum's own lips, and recently furnished me with a statement of his adventures,[14] "he met the head of the Russian Fur Company, adjusted the claim, and received an order on the London branch of a Russian bank in favor of Astor for the amount." Farnum returned to New York, and after an absence of three years, presented himself to the astonished Astor, who had long since given him up for lost.[15]

On the day of Winship's arrival at Novo Arkhangelsk, the *Juno* returned from a cruise in the interior channels of the Alexander Archipelago, where she had been attacked by the Kolosh. Several of the crew had been wounded, and were treated by the surgeon of the *Diana*. After remaining in port for nearly a month, the vessel sailed for Petropavlovsk, on what proved to be her last voyage. "Sailing from

[14] Mr Gray was kind enough to call at my Library and hand me a copy of the *St Louis Republican*, dated October 18, 1883, in which is a copy of his letter to Dr O. W. Stevens, acting president of the Missouri Historical Society in that city, containing a narrative of Farnum's adventures. In his letter, Gray, who now resides in San Francisco, writes: 'I desire to communicate what I know of this matter to a person who is writing a work on the Pacific coast, and that he may not have to depend solely upon my say so, I should be glad to have the testimony of others, as far as they know anything relating to the same.' His statement is corroborated by several persons. One of them, Mr Richard Dowling, then in his 79th year, and a resident of St Louis from the time when it contained only 1,700 inhabitants, relates further incidents of Farnum's adventures.

[15] Astor gave Farnum an interest in the business of which he was then the head, and this he retained until his death at St Louis in 1832. *Id.*

Novo Arkhangelsk," writes her captain in his log-book on the 14th of November, "with the ship placed under my charge, I find myself in sight of land in the most miserable condition. For three months we have been battling with continuous gales, and for nineteen days we have been within sight of the coast, with only three good sailors on board, and those entirely exhausted, and five young apprentices who have been intrusted to my care. Two of the latter who are more robust than the others are doing sailors' duty, while the rest can only assist at the rudder and in pumping the ship, for we are making five inches of water per hour. They help me to haul the log and to keep my journal. The management of the ship with these eight persons is exceedingly difficult; the remainder of my command—"[16] With this broken sentence the report ends.

The gale continued, and a few days afterward the greater part of the bulwarks were carried away, the rudder was unshipped, and the *Juno* drifted in shore. Anchor was cast in thirty fathoms, but still the vessel drifted helplessly shoreward; a second anchor was thrown out, but this also gave way, and now the ship was dashed on a reef parallel with the coast. Here she lay till the incoming tide cast her on an inner reef. All through this chill November night the men stood waiting for death, lashed to the rigging, and drenched with the ice-cold waves. One huge breaker swept away six of the company, among whom was the captain, and even their fate was a merciful one, for when the vessel was finally carried into the mouth of the river Viliuya, only four reached the land out of twenty-two men who had sailed from Novo Arkhangelsk.

Six hours after being cast on shore the vessel broke to pieces. One of the survivors was struck by a falling mast. He was wrapped in such articles of

---

[16] *Sitka Archives, Log-books,* iii.

clothing as his shipmates could spare; but knowing that he could not live, crept to a projecting rock and threw himself headlong into the waves. His comrades tried to save him, and twice he was almost within reach. Then the recoil of a wave carried him beyond their grasp, and he was seen no more.

The three Russians now set forth on their way along the bleak Kamchatka coast, with little hope of meeting any living creature, save the wolves and bears which infested that wintry solitude. Their sufferings during this journey I shall not attempt to describe. All that men can suffer from cold and hunger they endured. Crawling gaunt and half naked to the banks of a neighboring stream, they were fortunate enough to catch some fish, and near by a few sables, which furnished food and clothing; and thus toward Christmas of 1811 they made their way to Petropavlovsk.[17]

[17] *Khlebnikof, Shizn. Baranova*, 141–3. When the news was received at Petropavlovsk, the commissioner of the company at once repaired to the scene of the wreck. Search was made through the adjacent woods, but no trace of any human being was found. The beach was strewn with corpses, all of which had their arms or legs broken.

CHAPTER XXIII.

FOREIGN VENTURES AND THE ROSS COLONY.

1803-1841.

BARANOF'S WANT OF MEANS—O'CAIN'S EXPEDITION TO CALIFORNIA—AND
TO JAPAN—THE 'MERCURY' AT SAN DIEGO—TRADING CONTRACTS WITH
AMERICAN SKIPPERS—KUSKOF ON THE COAST OF NEW ALBION—THE
ROSS COLONY FOUNDED—SEAL-HUNTING ON THE COAST OF CALIFORNIA—
SHIP-BUILDING—AGRICULTURE—SHIPMENTS OF CEREALS TO NOVO ARK-
HANGELSK—HORTICULTURE—STOCK-RAISING—LOSSES INCURRED BY THE
COMPANY—HUNTING-POST ESTABLISHED AT THE FARALLONES—FAILURE
OF THE ENTERPRISE—SALE OF THE COLONY'S EFFECTS.

NOTWITHSTANDING frequent losses by shipwreck, Baranof was now well supplied with sea-going craft, and
had more vessels at his disposal than he could use for
hunting expeditions. He had not forgotten, however,
the secret instructions received from the directors of
the company in November 1803, and for several years
had been pushing forward his settlements toward the
south. The rich hunting-grounds on the coast of California had long since attracted his attention, and he
had made several efforts, though with little success,
to avail himself of this source of wealth, and to open
up a trade with the Spanish colonies.

The only obstacle that now lay in the path of the
chief manager was want of means. Men were not
lacking, nor ships; but supplies were forwarded to
him in such meagre quantity and at such exorbitant
rates that, as will be remembered, want was a familiar
guest in the Russian settlements. The resources of
the Russian American Company's territory, bountiful
though they were, had thus far served at best only to

supply the few needs of the settlers, to furnish small dividends to the shareholders, and to satisfy in part the greed of the company's agents.

In 1803 the vessels that arrived at Okhotsk from Alaska were freighted with furs valued at 2,500,000 roubles.[1] Other large shipments followed, among them being one by the *Neva*, in 1805, valued at 500,000 roubles. Nevertheless, Baranof did not venture to draw on St Petersburg for the means wherewith to carry out his instructions. " 'There is another cargo with half a million,' you will say," writes Rezanof to the directors in November of this year, " 'and where is the threatened want of means?' But I must answer you, gentlemen, that in your extensive business this is only a short palliative, the drawing of a breath, and no permanent relief. Patience! and you will agree with me."[2]

A few days before the chief manager received his secret despatch, the American ship *O'Cain*, or as it was called by the Russians the *Boston*, arrived at Kadiak, in command of Captain O'Cain, whom the former had previously met as mate of the *Enterprise*. After an exchange of trading goods for furs, to the value of 10,000 roubles, O'Cain proposed that Baranof should furnish him with Aleutian hunters and bidarkas for an expedition to the coast of California. The latter was disposed to listen favorably to such a proposition, for during this and the two preceding years the destruction of seals in Russian America had been on an enormous scale, and, as we have seen, a few months later orders were given by Rezanof that the slaughter should cease for a time. After some negotiation an agreement was concluded, and twenty bidarkas were fitted out and placed in charge of Shutzof,[3] a tried servant of the company. Shutzof

[1] Between 1801 and 1804 the company accumulated about 800,000 skins, many of which were spoiled through want of care in dressing. *Tikhmenef, Istor. Obos.*, i. 93–4.

[2] *Id.*, app. part ii. 201. The letter was dated from Novo Arkhangelsk.

[3] Sixteen years later the widow of this man petitioned the company for a pension, basing her claim on the assertion that her husband had 'opened to the Russian American Company, and to the Russian empire, the valuable trade

was ordered to observe closely all parts of the coast
which he might visit, to mark the number and character of the inhabitants, and to procure information of
all hunting-grounds which might in the future be utilized by the company without the assistance of foreigners.   He was instructed also to observe the sea-
ports that were frequented by Americans for purposes
of trade, and to ascertain the prices of provisions and
other products of the country.

The *Boston* sailed from Kadiak on the 26th of October, and after calling at San Diego, proceeded to the
bay of San Quintin in Lower California, where
O'Cain[4] made his headquarters, sending out hunting
parties in various directions, until the 1st of March of
the following year.   The number of furs secured was
eleven hundred, and Shutzof reported that the American captain, trading on his own account with the missionaries and soldiers, had obtained seven hundred
additional skins at prices ranging from three to four
piastres.   Thus was inaugurated a series of hunting
expeditions beyond the borders of the Russian colonies, which continued for many years with varying
success.

In August 1806 O'Cain returned to Alaska, arriving at Novo Arkhangelsk on board the *Eclipse*.
Touching at the Hawaiian Islands on his voyage, he
had found there a crew of Japanese sailors who had
been picked up at sea.   He now proposed to the chief
manager to supply him with a cargo of furs for Canton, and that, having taken on board the shipwrecked
sailors, he should proceed thence to Japan, with a
view to opening the Japanese ports to the Russians.
As the captain had before proved faithful to his trust,
Baranof consented, and a few weeks later the vessel
set sail, with a cargo[5] valued at three hundred and

of California.' *Archives Russian American Company*, 1819 (Letter Books,
vol. iii.)

[4] For further mention of O'Cain's voyage, see *Hist. Cal.*, ii. 25–6, this series.

[5] Including 1,800 sea-otter, 103,000 marten, 2,500 beaver, and other skins.
Khlebnikof, Shizn. Baranova, 111.   The terms of the contract between O'Cain
and Baranof are given in *Id.*, 109–10.

ten thousand roubles. The expedition proved a complete failure. The furs were sold at Canton at low prices, and Chinese goods purchased with the proceeds.[6] On entering the harbor of Nangasaki under Russian colors, the ship was immediately surrounded with hundreds of row-boats and towed to the anchorage ground. Soon afterward a Dutch official came on board, and finding that neither captain nor crew were Russian, ordered them to haul down their flag. As the Japanese would not listen to his proposals, O'Cain informed them that he was in need of provisions and fresh water. Supplies were delivered to him in abundance free of charge; but on the third day after his arrival, he was towed out to sea under a strong guard, with orders never to enter a Japanese port again. The *Eclipse* was then headed for Petropavlovsk, where half her cargo was transferred to the care of the Russian commissioner, and sailing thence for Kadiak, was wrecked on the voyage at the island of Sannakh. Only the captain and four others were saved, and with the assistance of some natives from Unalaska, made their way to St Paul.[7]

The result of O'Cain's hunting expedition to the coast of California had been so satisfactory that Baranof resolved to profit by every opportunity of repeating the experiment. Through captains Ebbets and Meek it had become known among American skippers that money could be made in this way, and several of the north-west traders were only too willing to make the attempt. In May 1808 a contract was entered into with Captain George Ayres, of the ship *Mercury* from Boston. Ayres was furnished with twenty-five

---

[6] Baranof, in his reports, hints at sharp practice on the part of O'Cain. The price obtained for sea-otter skins was only 13½ piastres each, while martens brought only 40 cents, beavers 3 piastres, etc. The whole cargo was sold for 155,000 roubles, just one half the estimated value. With this sum the captain purchased 3,000 sacks of rice, 280 chests of tea, and 25,000 packages of various Chinese goods. *Id.*, 112.

[7] An account of this shipwreck is given by Campbell, one of the survivors, in his *Voy. round World*, 42 et seq. (Edinburgh, 1810). He calls St Paul 'Alexandria.'

bidarkas for the purpose of hunting in the vicinity of islands 'not previously known.' Baranof engaged to furnish the Aleuts with subsistence, and no party was to be sent out without an armed escort. For any native hunter killed or captured while hunting, Ayres promised to pay 250 piastres toward the support of his family. The ship was to return within ten or twelve months, and the proceeds of the trip were to be equally divided, the furs being valued by the chief manager. For the labor of the Aleuts, Ayres was to deduct from his share three and a half piastres for each sea-otter, a piastre and a half for each fur-seal, and one piastre for each beaver.

The *Mercury* sailed from Kadiak on the 8th of July, Shutzof being in charge of the hunters. At Charlotte and adjacent islands Ayres bought a number of sea-otter furs from the natives, paying for each a can of powder, and at the mouth of the Columbia[8] Shutzof purchased five hundred and eighty beaver skins. In September the vessel entered the harbor of Trinidad, but meeting with little trade, the captain sailed for Bodega Bay, and thence for San Francisco and San Diego. From the latter port hunting parties were sent out during the winter, and the ship returned the following year with more than two thousand skins.

Between 1809 and 1812 Baranof made six additional contracts with American masters, the result being that over eight thousand sea-otter skins, procured outside the limit of the company's possessions, were delivered to the chief manager as his share of the proceeds.[9] These transactions were approved by

---

[8] 'Here,' says Khlebnikof, 'the party met with two United States officials and a number of soldiers, who were already putting up barracks. The officials had given medals to the savages, bearing the portrait of Washington.' *Shizn. Baranova*, 123. This occurred in August 1808, and as Lewis and Clarke left the mouth of the Columbia in 1806, and Astoria was not established until 1811, it remains to be shown who these officials were. Doubtless they were not United States officers and soldiers, but traders.

[9] In 1809, Captain John Winship on the ship *O'Cain* was furnished with 50 bidarkas, the company's share being 2,728 sea-otter skins. In 1810, Nathan Winship of the *Albatross* hunted with 68 bidarkas, the company's

the directors, but the frequent purchases of entire cargoes of goods and provisions, for which payment was usually made in fur-seal skins, were regarded with less favor. Twice in succession shrewd Yankee skippers succeeded in selling their skins to the commissioner at Kamchatka or Okhotsk at a higher valuation than had been placed upon them by Baranof in the original transaction; and finally a peremptory order was issued by the board of directors to make no more payments in kind, but to give drafts on the home office at St Petersburg.

After his return from California, Rezanof had never ceased to urge on the chief manager the importance of establishing, on the shore of New Albion,[10] a station for hunting, trading, and agricultural purposes. It is probable that his plans were even more ambitious than those contained in the company's private instructions to Baranof, and that he purposed gradually to push forward the Russian colonies toward the mouth of the Columbia, and in time even to wrest from Spain a portion of California.

Baranof did all that lay in his power. In October 1808 Kuskof was sent to the coast of New Albion on board the ship *Kadiak*, the schooner *Nikolai* having been despatched southward a fortnight earlier. The latter was wrecked at the mouth of Gray Harbor, where she had been ordered to join her consort; and though no lives were lost, the men were held captives by the Indians, a few of them being rescued by an American vessel, in which they returned to Novo Ark-

share amounting only to 560 skins. In the same year Davis of the *Isabella* hunted with 48 bidarkas, the company receiving 2,488 skins. In 1811, Meek of the *Amethyst* was supplied with 52 bidarkas, the company's share of the result being 721 sea-otter. In the same year Blanchard of the *Catherine* hunted with 50 bidarkas, and returned 750 sea-otter. In 1812, Captain Wittemore of the *Charon* was supplied with hunters, and returned to the company 896 sea-otters as its share.

[10] The term 'New Albion' was of somewhat vague significance. Its southern limit was anywhere between San Diego and Point Reyes, near which, it will be remembered, Drake landed in 1579, at the bay which now bears his name, and called the country 'New Albion.'

hangelsk two years later.   Contrary winds prevented
the *Kadiak* from entering the harbor, and Kuskof
proceeded to Bodega Bay, where he arrived at the
close of the year.   Returning after a twelve months'
voyage with more than two thousand otter skins,[11] he
laid before Baranof information of the greatest importance. He reported that sea-otter and fish abounded
on the whole coast, that he had found many places
well adapted for agriculture and ship-building, and that
the whole country north of San Francisco Bay was
unoccupied by any European power.

The chief manager finally resolved to delay no longer
the execution of his plans in that direction, although
he did not receive positive instructions to found such
a colony until several years later.   He gave orders to
collect all the men who might be of use in forming a
permanent settlement, including ex-convicts from the
agricultural provinces of Russia, and others skilled in
agriculture and stock-raising ; and in 1810 despatched
Kuskof on a second trip to the coast of New Albion,
with orders to make further explorations.   This expedition was unsuccessful.   Calling at Queen Charlotte Islands, his men were attacked by savages, and
after losing eight of his hunters, he was compelled to return to Novo Arkhangelsk,[12] whence he was again sent
in the same direction in the schooner *Chirikof* early in
1811.   Of his voyage little is known,[13] but anchoring
in Bodega Bay, which he re-named Rumiantzof, he
found its vicinity not adapted to his purpose, and selecting another location eighteen miles to the north-

[11] For further details of this voyage and a map of Bodega Bay, see *Hist.
Cal.*, ii. 80–2, this series.

[12] *Tikhmenef, Istor. Obos.*, i. 208.   Kuskof sailed on board the *Juno* two
years before she was wrecked.

[13] Khlebnikof, *Zapiski* in *Materialui*, 137–9, gives Jan. 22d as the date of
the *Chirikof's* departure, and says that Bodega Bay was reached a month later,
but that finding there a scarcity of sea-otter, Kuskof sent twenty-two bidarkas to San Francisco Bay, where they met a party of Aleuts under command
of Terepanoff with forty-eight bidarkas, and one belonging to Winship's expedition with sixty-eight bidarkas.   Kuskof's men secured 1,160 sea-otter
and 78 yearlings within three months.   In order to drive them away, the
Spaniards placed guards at all the points where the Aleuts were accustomed
to procure fresh water.

ward, purchased a tract of land from the natives. On his return to Novo Arkhangelsk he was ordered to proceed at once to this site with a large party of Russians and Aleuts, and was furnished with an ample store of supplies for the use of the proposed settlement. Of the colony founded by Kuskof, in 1812, a full description is given elsewhere;[14] it remains only to make brief mention of it, and to give a few details as to the industrial progress of an enterprise which the company had long desired to establish.

During the year a fort, mounted with ten guns, was erected on a bluff about a hundred feet above the sea; other buildings were added, and on September 10th, or, according to the Russian calendar, on August 30th, the new colony was named Ross—the root of the modern word Russia.[15]

Thus at length a foothold was gained on the shore of New Albion, but the result disappointed all expectation. The hunting-grounds on the neighboring coast to which the Russians had access were soon exhausted; while as a site for ship-building and agriculture, it met with little success.[16] Between 1812 and 1823 only about 1,100 large sea-otter skins and some 250 yearlings were secured, and of these at least two thirds were obtained during the first four years of this period, the seals rapidly disappearing from the neighborhood. In 1824, the treaty between Russia and the United States permitted the Russians to send

[14] *Hist. Cal.*, ii., cap. xiv.–xxviii., and iv., cap. vi., this series. On p. 300, vol. ii., is a map of the region.

[15] The fort was surrounded with a palisade, enclosing a space of about 42 by 49 fathoms. The other buildings included the commandant's house, barracks, storehouses, magazines, barns, shops, bath-house, tannery, and windmill. All were not completed until 1814. *Khlebnikof, Zapiski* in *Materialui*, 138.

[16] As early as 1818, Hagemeister writes in his report: 'As to agriculture in the colony of Ross, I am obliged to destroy the hopes that have been entertained. The main obstacle consists in not having competent workmen. Those sent from Novo Arkhangelsk are, with a few exceptions, the scum of the scum. The Aleuts are also unfitted for this kind of work, and long training is necessary to prepare them for their new occupation. Meanwhile the Russian American Company loses the advantage that would be gained by employing them in seal hunting.' *Zavalishin, Koloniy Ross*, 21-2.

out hunting parties to all portions of the Oregon coast
and inland waters for a period of ten years; but this
had no bearing on California. During this time about
1,800 sea-otter, 2,700 fur-seals, and a few yearlings
were delivered by the Aleutian hunters as the company's share. Nevertheless, even for the greater portion of this decade, the business was unprofitable.[17]

From 1816 to 1824 four vessels, with an aggregate
capacity of 720 tons, were built at a cost of more than
150,000 roubles.[18] An experienced ship-carpenter
from Novo Arkhangelsk superintended their construction, and for a time it was thought that the oak, pine,
and cedar found in the neighborhood were well adapted
for the purpose. The result proved most unsatisfactory, however. The wood was cut when in the sap;
soon the timbers began to rot, and within six years after
being launched not one of the ships was seaworthy.

But it was mainly with a view to agricultural purposes, as we have seen, that the site of the Ross colony was selected. Although it was no doubt the
best one that the Russians found available, the location had many disadvantages. The spot was surrounded with hills, densely wooded at a distance of
one mile from the sea; the level ground contained
numerous gulches; the most fertile portions of it were
difficult of access, some of them being at a distance of
three versts from the fort; the summer fogs caused
the ripening grain to rust, while squirrels and gophers
spread havoc among the growing crops.

Farming was carried on by private individuals, as
well as by the company's agents, but by neither with
system. The ploughs in use were of all patterns—
Russian, Siberian, Finnish, and Californian. The
shares of many of them were merely a pointed piece

---

[17] A statement of each year's catch is given in *Tikhmenef, Istor. Obos.*, i.
357.

[18] The *Rumiantzof*, of 160 tons, completed in 1818 at a cost of 20,212 roubles; the *Buldakof*, of 200 tons, launched in 1820, the expense being
59,404 roubles; the *Volga*, of 160 tons, finished in 1822, at a cost of 36,189
roubles; and the *Kiakhta*, of about 200 tons, launched in 1834, at an expense
of 35,248 roubles. *Khlebnikof, Zapiski* in *Materialui*, 149-50.

of thick bar-iron, and where the soil was rocky and no plough could be used, Indians were employed to dig up the ground with spades. Each one farmed as seemed best in his own eyes, and the usual result was, of course, failure. Between 1815 and 1829 about 4,800 pouds of wheat and 740 of barley were sown, and over 25,000 pouds of wheat and 3,600 of barley harvested. Thus the average yield for both these cereals was little more than five-fold; while in 1823, the most prosperous of the intervening years, it did not exceed ten or eleven fold, and in bad seasons fell as low as two or three fold. Not until 1826 were any considerable shipments of grain made to Novo Arkhangelsk, and from that date to 1833 only 6,000 pouds were forwarded.[19]

During his visit to the colony in the latter year, Baron Wrangell selected a new site for agricultural purposes, near the mouth of the Slavianka (Russian) River, midway between the Ross settlement and Bodega Bay. About 400 pouds of wheat were sown, together with a small quantity of barley; and besides what was required for home consumption and for seed, there remained as the result of the harvest about 4,500 pouds of wheat and 450 of barley for shipment to Novo Arkhangelsk. The next year's crop was almost as satisfactory, but that of 1835 was a partial, and of 1836 a total failure. From the latter date until 1840 the surplus of wheat at both settlements amounted to about 10,000 pouds, in addition to a few hundred pouds of other cereals.

Other branches of husbandry were introduced, but with little better result, for there were none who thoroughly understood the business. The first peach-tree was brought from San Francisco in 1814, on board the *Chirikof*, and six years later yielded fruit.

[19] In 1833 wheat yielded only 8 to 1. *Vallejo, Informe Reservado*, MS. In a few choice localities the yield was sometimes as high as 15 to 1 of wheat, and of barley 19 to 1. In *Hist. Cal.*, ii. 636, this series, is a list of the provisions obtained by the company in California between 1817 and 1825.

In 1817 the grape-vine was introduced from Lima, and in 1820 apple, pear, and cherry trees were planted. The vines began to bear in 1823, and the fruit trees not till five years later, and then in small quantity. Melons and pumpkins were planted by Kuskof, who also raised large quantities of beets, cabbages, potatoes, lettuce, pease, beans, radishes, and turnips. The two last were large in size but poor in flavor. Vegetables, however, gave the most abundant crop, and after supplying the wants of the colony and of vessels that touched at the Ross settlement, a surplus was available for shipment to Novo Arkhangelsk.[20]

The industry of stock-raising was somewhat more successful, though restricted by want of pasture, all the best land being under cultivation. The cattle were left to roam among the mountain ranges, and many were slaughtered by Indians or fell a prey to wild beasts.[21] Nevertheless, between 1817 and 1829 the number of horned cattle that could be mustered at the settlement increased from 61 to 521, of horses from 10 to 253, and of sheep from 161 to 614. During the interval a considerable quantity of live-stock was purchased from the natives, and a few at the San Francisco mission, but more were slaughtered for home consumption, for the use of the company's vessels, or for shipment to Alaska. During 1826 and the three succeeding years, more than 450 pouds of salt beef were forwarded to Novo Arkhangelsk. Tallow was produced at the rate of 10 to 15 pouds a year. Of butter over 400 pouds were made between 1825 and 1829, two thirds of it being shipped to Novo Arkhangelsk. Hides were made into sole and upper leather, the tanner being an Aleut from Kadiak, who

---

[20] Tikhmenef, *Istor. Obos.*, i. 210, states that potatoes grew twice a year, and yielded eleven-fold, as many as 250 being found to the hill in some instances. This is not confirmed by Khlebnikof.

[21] During Kuskof's residence at Ross colony, an ox returned to the settlement covered with blood, and with pieces of flesh torn out of its sides. The horns were also blood-stained. Oxen grew to an enormous size, one that was placed on board the Kutusof in 1817 giving 920 lbs. of clear meat. *Khlebnikof, Zapiski* in *Materialui*, 153.

had learned his business from the Russians. An attempt was also made to manufacture blankets, but the wool was of poor quality, and there was no one who understood how to construct a loom.

Between 1825 and 1830 the expense of maintaining the Ross settlement was about 45,000 roubles a year, while the average receipts were less than 13,000 roubles.[22] In later years, though the shipments of produce were on a larger scale, the hunting-grounds became almost worthless. Meanwhile the outlay was largely increased, and during the last four years of its existence the colony was maintained at a total cost of about 288,000 roubles, while the returns were less than 105,000 roubles, leaving a net loss of more than 45,000 roubles a year.

Trade was carried on to a small extent with the Spaniards at San Francisco even before the treaty of 1824, though before that date the Russians were not allowed to enter the harbor for hunting purposes. At the Farallones, however, a station was established, which for a time was fairly profitable.[23] From 1812

[22] Consisting of 8,745 roubles' worth of produce and 4,138 of furs. *Tikhmenef, Istor. Obos.*, i. 359.

[23] The men sent to this station were relieved at intervals, as want of proper food, shelter, fuel, and wholesome water caused sickness and death among them. Zakhar Chichinof, who was one of a party sent to the Farallones in 1819, thus relates his experience: 'A schooner took us down to the islands, but we had to cruise around for over a week before we could make a landing. We had a few planks with us and some canvas, and with that scanty material and some sea-lion skins we built huts for shelter. We had a little drift-wood, and used to burn the fat of sea-lions and seals for cooking purposes. When we landed we had about 120 lbs. of flour and 10 or 12 lbs. of tea, and, as we were nine persons, the provisions did not last long, and we were soon reduced to sea-lion, seal, and fish. The water was very bad also, being taken from hollow places in the rocks, where it stood all the year round. We had no fire-arms; the sea-lions were killed with clubs and spears. The sea-lion meat was salted down in barrels and boxes, which we had brought with us, and in holes in the rocks. Once only, about six months after we landed on the islands, one of the company's brigs came and took away the salted meat and a lot of fur-seal skins, and then went on her way, leaving us about 100 lbs. of flour, a few pounds of tea, and some salt. About a month afterward the scurvy broke out among us, and in a short time all were sick except myself. My father and two others were all that kept at work, and they were growing weaker every day. Two of the Aleuts died a month after the disease broke out. All the next winter we passed there in great misery, and when spring came the men were too weak to kill sea-lions, and all we could do was to crawl around the cliffs and gather some sea-birds' eggs, and suck them raw.' *Adventures, MS.*, 6–8.

to 1818, about 8,400 fur-seal skins were obtained there, and it is stated that, before their occupation by the Russians, as many as 10,000 were taken on these islands in a single autumn. Later the supply was gradually exhausted, but the ground was not finally abandoned until 1840, the few Aleuts left there in charge of a single Russian being employed in shooting and drying sea-gulls for use at the Ross colony and in gathering sea-birds' eggs.[24]

One of the greatest obstacles to the prosperity of the Ross settlement was that the colonists held no secure title to their possessions. The land had been purchased from the Indians for a trifle; but the Spaniards had never recognized their ownership, and at this time laid claim to the entire coast as far as the strait of San Juan de Fuca. Of the disputes that arose on this point, an account is given in another volume.[25] As early as 1820 the company offered to surrender the colony if restrictions on trade were removed, for they had already begun to despair of its success. In 1838, after the failure of Wrangell's mission to Mexico, of which mention is made in connection with my *History of California*, it became evident that the days of the colony were numbered. Already American immigrants had taken up land within ten leagues of the settlement, and others proposed to establish themselves still nearer to Ross. In vain an appeal was made to the vice-chancellor at St Petersburg. His decision was that no claim could be advanced, "other than right to possession of the land already occupied and of the buildings erected thereon."

This was a death-blow to the company's hopes. After two unsuccessful attempts to sell the establishment, first to the Hudson's Bay Company and then to General Vallejo,[26] the entire property at Ross and

---

[24] The average number of birds obtained was 5,000 to 10,000 a year, but in 1828, 50,000 were killed. *Khlebnikof, Zapiski* in *Materialui*, 157.

[25] *Hist. Cal.*, ii. 303 et seq., this series.

[26] See *Douglas, Journal*, MS., 16, and *Vallejo. Doc.*, MS., x. 60-2.

Bodega, apart from the real estate, including all improvements, agricultural implements, 1,700 head of cattle, 940 horses, and 900 sheep, was sold to John A. Sutter in September 1841, for $30,000, the amount being payable in yearly instalments,[27] and two thirds of it in produce, to be delivered at San Francisco, freight and duty free.[28]

Thus ended, in loss and failure, the company's schemes of colonization on the coast of New Albion. The experiment had been for thirty years a constant source of expense and vexation; but if the Russians could have maintained their foothold, results might have followed, more brilliant than even Rezanof contemplated. Within a few years after their departure, gold-bearing sands were discovered beyond the ranges of hills which separated from an interior valley the abandoned site of Ross.

[27] Extending over four years, the first two of $5,000 and the others of $10,000 each. *Ross, Contrat de Vente*, MS., 1841, of which there is a copy in Spanish in *Dept. St. Pap.*, MS., vi. 108-9.

[28] Tikhmenef, *Istor. Obos.*, i. 366, states that payment was guaranteed by the Mexican government, but such was not the fact. The Bodega property, two ranchos belonging to Tschernich and Khlebnikof, and an establishment at New Helvetia, were left in the hands of the company's agents as security. *Ross, Contrat de Vente*, MS. The last payment was not made until about 1850. For further particulars on this matter, see *Hist. Cal.*, iv. cap. vi., this series.

CHAPTER XXIV.

As only casual mention of the Ross settlement will
be required in the remainder of this volume, I have
thought it best to complete the brief record of its
operations before proceeding further. I shall now
refer to other and earlier attempts at foreign colonization; for, as we have seen, the company's plans were
far-reaching, and extended not only to both shores of
the Pacific, but to the islands that lay between.

In 1808 Captain Hagemeister sailed for the
Sandwich Islands in charge of the *Neva*, with instructions to establish a colony there, and to survey
the field with a view to future occupation by the Russians.[1] Arriving at a harbor on the southern side of

---

[1] Campbell, *Voy. round World*, 118, states that the *Neva* had a crew of
seventy-five men belonging to the Russian navy. He was one of those who
survived the wreck of the *Eclipse*, in 1807. Though an illiterate seaman, his
story is interesting, and in the main worthy of credit. He writes appar-

Oahu, the ship was boarded by a large canoe, in which was seated, dressed in European costume, King Kamehameha, then the potentate of the Hawaiian group. "Immediately on his coming on board," says Campbell, a Scotch sailor who acted as Hagemeister's interpreter, "the king entered into earnest conversation with the captain. Among other questions, he asked whether the ship was English or American. Being informed that she was Russian, he answered, 'Meitei, meitei,' or 'Very good.' A handsome scarlet cloak, edged and ornamented with ermine, was presented to him from the governor of the Aleutian Islands. After trying it on, he gave it to his attendants to be taken ashore. I never saw him use it afterwards. In other canoes came Tamena, one of his queens, Crymakoo, his brother-in-law, and other chiefs of inferior rank."[2]

Through fear of British intervention, or for other reasons not specified by the chroniclers of the time, no attempt was made to found a settlement,[3] though, if we

ently without bias, and speaks very favorably of his reception in Alaska and in the Hawaiian Islands. His work was noticed in the Edinburgh Review, vol. ix.

[2] *Id.*, 127. In Campbell's work, *Washington Irving's Astoria, Vancouver's Voy.*, and *Kotzebue, Voy. of Discov.* (London, 1821), the king is called Tamaahmaah; in *Meares' Voy.*, Tomyhomyhaw; in *Portlock's Voy.*, Comaamaa; in *Langsdorff's Voy.*, Tomoona; in *Lisiansky, Voy. round World*, Hameamea. How the monarch received so many aliases does not appear, for in Samwell's account of Captain Cook's death (Samwell was the surgeon of the *Discovery*), his name is spelled Tameamea. In the Hawaiian dialect consonants are often substituted for each other, a guttural even taking the place of a lingual when rendered into English characters, as in this instance. Kamehameha I., surnamed the conqueror, was already known by fame throughout Europe. In the Nuuanu Valley, it will be remembered, he routed the army of the king of Oahu, and drove hundreds of the enemy over a neighboring pali, at the foot of which their bones lie bleaching to this day. The spot is but a few miles from Honolulu.

[3] Baranof certainly instructed Hagemeister to found a settlement, and a copy of his instructions has been preserved in the *Sitka Archives*, but no mention of this is made in the captain's report. It is probable that he was prevented by fear of British opposition, for on August 6th of the following year, Kamehameha wrote to George III. proposing to acknowledge him as his sovereign, and asking that the Islands be placed under British protection. The request was granted. Tikhmenef, *Istor. Obos.*, i. 166, says that as soon as a rumor spread throughout the Islands that a vessel had been sent from Novo Arkhangelsk for the purpose of founding a settlement, an English frigate called there to ascertain the truth of the matter. This statement is not indorsed, however, by Campbell, who remained in the Islands for more than a year after the departure of the *Neva*. Tikhmenef would have us believe that Hagemeister was ordered to make a tour of the Russian colonies, and

can believe Kamehameha, Hagemeister tried to bring
the natives of Oahu under subjection by threatening
that ships of war should be sent against them.[4]   After
calling at other islands in the Hawaiian group, and
bartering seal skins and walrus tusks for salt, sandal-
wood, and pearls, the captain sailed for Kamchatka,
and thence for Novo Arkhangelsk, setting forth on
his homeward voyage the following year.[5]   In his
report to Baranof, whom, as we shall see later, he
succeeded in office, he states that taro, maize, and
sugar could be purchased at moderate prices in Oahu
and the neighboring islands, but that European goods
were held at extravagant rates.

The control of the company's affairs had long been
felt as too severe a strain by the chief manager, who
was now more than sixty years of age.   He had several times requested that a successor be appointed, and
twice his request had been granted, but on both occasions the official who was sent to relieve him died on
the way.   In October 1811 the brig *Maria* returned
to Kadiak, having sailed from Okhotsk during the previous year.   In this vessel Collegiate Assessor Koch,
who had been appointed Baranof's assistant with a
view to succeeding him, had taken passage, but during
the voyage he fell sick, and breathed his last at Petropavlovsk.   The news of his death was doubly sad to
Baranof, who had been on terms of intimacy with the
deceased for many years.[6]   By the *Maria* the chief

then to ascertain the exact location of certain islands lying between the
Japanese and Hawaiian groups, discovered in the seventeenth century, his
visit to Oahu being merely with a view to trade.

[4] See the king's address to Kotzebue, as related in his *Voy. of Discov.*, i.
303.

[5] After wintering at Kadiak, he was sent to Petropavlovsk, with a cargo
of furs valued at over 750,000 roubles.

[6] Ivan Gavrilovich Koch, a native of Hamburg, entered the Russian military service as a surgeon in 1769.   He did duty during the siege and capture
of Bender in 1770, and throughout the Turkish war of that period until the
conclusion of peace.   In 1783 he was promoted to the rank of staff surgeon
and attached to the Irkutsk district.   In 1784 he was transferred to the
civil service, with the rank of collegiate assessor, and sent to Okhotsk as commandant of the garrison, which position he filled with credit until 1795.   For
distinguished services, he was decorated with the order of St Vladimir.   During the following years he made several official visits to Irkutsk, and was

manager received authority from the board of directors
to establish a permanent settlement on the coast of
New Albion wherever he might think best. Meanwhile he did not neglect to forward another petition
to St Petersburg, asking that his resignation be accepted; but once more he was disappointed. Early
in the month of January 1813, the inhabitants of
Novo Arkhangelsk were surprised by the arrival of a
small boat containing a few Russian sailors, half dead
from cold and hunger. They brought the unwelcome
news that the *Neva*, which had sailed from Okhotsk
under command of Lieutenant Podushkin, had been
wrecked in the vicinity of Mount Edgecumbe. One
of those who perished on board this craft was Collegiate Counsellor Bornovolokof, who had been appointed
Baranof's successor.[7]

In December of this year the *Ilmen* was despatched
to Ross with a cargo of goods and provisions. On
board the vessel was a hunting party under the leadership of Tarakanof, and a man named Eliot, or Eliot de
Castro, who had volunteered to conduct the trade
with the missionaries on the Californian coast, claiming long acquaintance with the fathers.[8]

The ship left Sitka in December 1813. On her arrival at Bodega, the Aleutian hunters were divided

appointed assistant on the general staff and commissary-general. He retired
with full pay in 1902. *Khlebnikof, Shizn. Baranova*, 145–6.
  [7] The wreck occurred on the 9th of January. Bornovolokof, the pilot
Kalinin, the wife and son of the mate Nerodof, the boatswain, 27 promyshleniki, and 4 women were drowned. The survivors were Lieutenant Podushkin, the mate Nerodof, cadet Terpigoref, a quartermaster, and 21 promyshleniki. Three of the latter died soon afterward. During the voyage from
Okhotsk 15 men had died from sickness. *Id.*, 149–50. See also *Berg, Shipwreck of the Neva*, and *Golovnin Korablekrush*, iv. The survivors reported that
the brig *Alexandr*, which had sailed from Novo Arkhangelsk in June of the
preceding year, with over 8,000 sea-otter skins, under command of master
Petrof, had also been wrecked on the Kurile Islands.
  [8] Eliot is mentioned by Kotzebue in the first volume of his voyage as Eliot
de Castro, a native of Portugal, and is so called by several other writers. In
the argument between him and Baranof, which has been preserved in the
Sitka Archives, the document is signed 'John Eliot,' and he is spoken of in the
indorsement as an American. vi. 113. In *Guerra, Doc. Hist. Cal.*, ii. 74–83,
I find a number of statements relating to Eliot, but in no instance does the
name of Castro occur. It is always Eliot or Don Juan Eliot.

into detachments and scattered over the sea-otter
grounds.   Seal were not plentiful, and though for a
time the Aleuts escaped the vigilance of the Spanish
soldiery, the largest detachment, together with Eliot
and Tarakanof, were surprised by a troop of horse
in the vicinity of San Luis Obispo and taken to the
presidio of Santa Barbara.[9]

Eliot and his companions remained captives until
1815, when all who had not taken unto themselves
Indian wives were delivered to Lieutenant Kotzebue,
who visited the California coast during his voyage of
exploration in the brig *Rurik*.[10]

The *Rurik*, a vessel of one hundred and eighty tons,
was built and equipped by Count Romanof, for the purpose of exploring the supposed north-west passage by
way of Davis Strait or Hudson Bay; but as an expedition was being fitted out in England for the same purpose, it was determined to attempt the passage from
the eastward.   Otto von Kotzebue, who a few years
before had sailed with Krusenstern on board the
Neva, as will be remembered, was placed in command.
Sailing from Kronstadt on the 30th of July, 1815,[11]
the brig arrived at Petropavlovsk after an uneventful
voyage lasting nearly a year, and thence was headed
for Bering Strait.   Proceeding in a north-easterly direction, the commander, after touching at St Lawrence Island, entered a large inlet, through the center
of which passed the arctic circle, and whose waters
extended to the eastward as far as the eye could
reach, the current running strong into the entrance.

---

[9] In Tarakanof's official report of the matter, Cape Concepcion is mentioned
as the scene of this incident.

[10] In the course of his transactions with the missionaries, Eliot had sold
goods to the amount of more than ten thousand piastres, for which he received
payment in cash, grain, and otter skins, and transmitted the proceeds to
Kuskof at Ross.

[11] The naval officers who accompanied Kotzebue were lieutenants Zok-
harin and Schischmaref, the scientists Chamisso and Wormskloid, Dr Eschscholtz, and the artist Choris. *Kotzebue's Voy. of Discov.*, i. introd. 90-1.
Among the subordinate officers were the mates Petrof and Khramchemka, who
subsequently figured prominently in the annals of Alaskan explorations.
The vessel carried the imperial flag and was mounted with eight guns.

From a small neighboring hill on the southern shore
no land could be seen on the horizon, while high
mountains lay to the north.   Here, thought the Russians, is the channel that connects the two oceans, the
quest of which has for three centuries baffled the
greatest navigators in Europe. On the following day,
the 2d of August, the vessel continued her course,
and from the mast-head nothing but open sea appeared to the eastward.   Toward sundown land was
in sight in several directions, but at noon on the 3d
the opening was still five miles in width.[12]   On the

KOTZEBUE SOUND.

4th the search was continued in boats, for now the
water was shoaling rapidly, and after proceeding fourteen miles farther, only a small open space was visible to the eastward.[13]   A few days later the party
set forth on their return to the *Rurik*, but were
driven back to shore by a violent storm.

   "It seemed," says Kotzebue, "as if fortune had sent
this storm to enable us to make a very remarkable

[12] On this day an island was discovered, to which was given the name of
Chamisso. *Id.*, i. 213.
[13] Probably the head of Eschscholtz, or perhaps Schischmaref Bay.

discovery, which we owe to Dr Eschscholtz. We had climbed much about during our stay, without discovering that we were on real icebergs. The doctor, who had extended his excursions, found part of the bank broken down, and saw, to his astonishment, that the interior of the mountain consisted purely of ice. At this news, we all went, provided with shovels and crows, to examine this phenomenon more closely, and soon arrived at a place where the back rises almost perpendicularly out of the sea to a height of a hundred feet; and then runs off, rising still higher. We saw masses of the purest ice, of the height of a hundred feet, which are under a cover of moss and grass, and could not have been produced but by some terrible revolution.[14] The place, which by some accident had fallen in and is now exposed to the sun and air, melts away, and a good deal of water flows into the sea. An indisputable proof that what we saw was real ice is the quantity of mammoths' teeth and bones which were exposed to view by the melting, and among which I myself found a very fine tooth. We could not assign any reason for a strong smell, like that of burnt horn, which we perceived in this place."

On the 11th of August the *Rurik* left the inlet which now bears the name of Kotzebue Sound,[15] and sailed for St Lawrence Island and thence for Una-

[14] 'This result of a terrible revolution,' remarks the *London Quarterly Review*, 'is considered by Chamisso, the naturalist, to be similar to the ground ice, covered with vegetation, at the mouth of the Lena, out of which the mammoth, the skeleton of which is now in St Petersburg, was thawed. He makes the height of it to be 80 feet at most; and the length of the profile, in which the ice is exposed to sight, about a musket-shot. We have little doubt that both Kotzebue and Chamisso are mistaken with regard to the formation of this ice mountain. The terrible revolution of nature is sheer nonsense; and the ground ice of the Lena is cast up from the sea, and afterward buried by the alluvial soil brought down by the floods in the same manner as the huge blocks which Captain Parry found on the beach of Melville Island; this operation, however, could not take place on the face of the promontory in the tranquil sound of Kotzebue. What they discovered (without suspecting it) was, in fact, a real iceberg, which had been formed in the manner in which all icebergs are.' xxvi. 352 (1822).

[15] This name was not given until after Kotzebue's return to Russia; but other points were named by him after members of the expedition, Eschscholtz Bay being one of them. Cape Krusenstern, on the northern shore of the sound, was so called after the captain of the *Nadeshda*.

laska, where the commander gave orders to the agent of the Russian American Company to have men, boats, and supplies in readiness for the following summer, when he purposed to make a thorough exploration of the farther north-west.　Remaining only long enough for needed repairs, he proceeded to San Francisco without having attempted to explore, according to his instructions, the coast of Alaska southward from Norton Sound, then a *terra incognita*, but, as it proved, one of the richest portions of the territory.[16] After sharing in a conference touching the affairs of the Ross colony, at which Kuskof and the governor of California were present, as is mentioned elsewhere,[17] he sailed for the Sandwich Islands, taking on board Eliot and three of his fellow-captives.

Landing at the island of Hawaii, Kotzebue was met by Kamehameha, who was now king of the entire group, and thus describes his reception: "I now stood at the side of the celebrated Tamaahmaah, who has attracted the attention of all Europe, and who inspired me with the greatest confidence by his unreserved and friendly behavior.　He conducted me to his straw palace, which, according to the custom of the country, consisted only of one spacious apartment; and, like all the houses here, afforded a free draught both to the land and sea breezes.　They offered us European chairs very neatly made, placed a mahogany table before us, and we were then in possession of all the furniture of the palace.　Tamaahmaah's dress, which consisted of a white shirt, blue pantaloons, a red waistcoat, and a colored neckcloth, surprised me

[16] Kotzebue probably made a great mistake when he omitted the exploration of this portion of the coast of Alaska, of which nothing more was known than when Cook left it between his Shoalness and Point Shallow (Cape Romanof and the mouth of the Kuskokvim).　Captain Golovnin, of the sloop-of-war *Diana*, had definite instruction to survey it, but was prevented by his captivity among the Japanese.　Count Romanof had given this instruction to Golovnin, and when the latter set out upon his second voyage around the world, in the sloop-of-war *Kamchatka*, he received a letter from the minister of marine, who requested him to survey the coast north of Alaska Peninsula provided that Kotzebue had not already done so.

[17] *Hist. Cal.*, ii. 31, this series.

very much, for I had formed very different notions of the royal attire. The distinguished personages present at our audience, who had all seated themselves on the ground, wore a still more singular costume than the king; for their black frocks looked very ludicrous on the naked body. One of the ministers had the waist half-way up his back; the coat had been buttoned with the greatest difficulty; he perspired freely in his tight state costume, and his distress was evident; but fashion would not permit him to relieve himself of the inconvenience. The sentinels at the door were quite naked; a cartridge-box and a pair of pistols were tied round their waist, and they held a musket in their hand.

"After the king had poured out some very good wine, and had himself drunk to our health, I made him acquainted with my intention of taking in fresh provisions, water, and wood. A young man of the name of Cook, the only white whom the king had about him, acted as interpreter. Tamaahmaah desired him to say to me as follows: 'I learn that you are the commander of a ship of war, and are engaged in a voyage similar to those of Cook and Vancouver, and consequently do not engage in trade; it is therefore my intention not to carry on any trade with you, but to provide you gratis with everything that my islands produce. I shall now beg you to inform me whether it is with the consent of your emperor that his subjects begin to disturb me in my old age. Since Tamaahmaah has been king of these islands, no European has had cause to complain of having suffered injustice here. I have made my islands an asylum for all nations, and honestly supplied with provisions every ship that desired them.'"

After alluding to the trouble caused by Hagemeister and his party, the king continues: "A Russian physician, named Scheffer, who came here some months ago, pretended that he had been sent by the Emperor Alexander to botanize on my islands. I

not only gave him this permission, but also promised
him every assistance; and made him a present of a
piece of land, with peasants, so that he could never
want for provisions. What was the consequence of
my hospitality? Even before he left Owhyee,[18] he
repaid my kindness with ingratitude, which I bore
patiently. Then, according to his own desire, he
travelled from one place to another; and at last
settled in the fruitful island of Woahoo,[19] where he
proved himself to be my most inveterate enemy;
destroying our sanctuary, the Morai; and exciting
against me, in the island of Atooi,[20] King Tamary,
who had submitted to my power years before. Scheffer is there at this very moment and threatens my
islands."

"I assured Tamaahmaah," continues Kotzebue,
"that the bad conduct of the Russians here must not
be ascribed to the will of our emperor, who never commanded his subjects to do an unjust act; but that
the extent of his empire prevented him from being
immediately informed of bad actions, which, however,
were not allowed to remain unpunished when they
came to his knowledge. The king seemed very
much pleased on my assuring him that our sovereign
never intended to conquer his islands; the glasses
were immediately filled, to drink the emperor's
health, and Kamehameha was even more cordial than
before."

Eliot, who before his captivity had lived for two
years in the Sandwich Islands as physician and chief
favorite to the king, remained at Hawaii in his former
position; and taking his leave in the middle of December, Kotzebue sailed in a south-westerly direction.
On the 1st of January, 1817, he discovered a low
wooded islet, to which was given the name of New
Year's Island. Three days later a chain of islands
was sighted, extending as far as the eye could reach,

[18] Hawaii.   [19] Oahu.   [20] Kauai.

the spaces between being filled with reefs.[21] After some weeks had been spent amid these and other groups in the Caroline Archipelago, the *Rurik* was again headed for Unalaska, her commander purposing to continue his explorations in search of a northeast passage. But this was not to be. On the 11th of April, when in latitude 44° 30' N. and longitude 181° 8' W., a violent storm arose, and during the following night increased to a hurricane. "The waves, which before ran high," says Kotzebue, for I cannot do better than use his own words, "rose in immense masses, such as I had never yet seen; the *Rurik* suffered beyond description. Immediately after midnight the fury of the hurricane rose to such a degree, that it tore the tops of the waves from the sea, and drove them in the form of a thick rain over the surface of the ocean. Nobody who has not witnessed such a scene can form an adequate idea of it. It seems as if a direful revolution was at that moment destroying the whole stupendous fabric of nature.

"I had just relieved Lieutenant Schischmareff. Besides myself, there were four sailors on the deck, of whom two were holding the helm; the rest of the crew I had, for greater security, sent into the hold. At four o'clock in the morning I was just looking at the height of a foaming wave, when it suddenly took its direction to the *Rurik*, and in the same moment threw me down senseless. The violent pain which I felt on recovering was heightened by the melancholy sight of my ship, whose fate would be inevitable if the hurricane should rage for another hour; for not a corner of it had escaped the ravages of that furious wave. The first thing I saw was the broken bowsprit; and an idea may be formed of the violence of the water, which at once dashed in pieces a beam of two feet in diameter.

[21] Whether these are the islands that were sighted by Captain Marshall in 1788 is uncertain. At least, Kotzebue was the first to ascertain their exact position.

The loss was the more important, as the two masts could not long withstand the tossing of the ship, and then deliverance would be impossible. The gigantic wave broke the leg of one of my sailors; a subaltern officer was thrown into the sea, but saved himself with much presence of mind by seizing the rope which hung behind the ship; the steering-wheel was broken, the two sailors who held it were much hurt, and I myself thrown violently with my breast against a corner, suffered severe pain, and was obliged to keep my bed for several days."

When the storm had moderated the vessel was put in order, and reached Unalaska in safety, though heavy weather prevailed during the rest of the voyage.[22] She was then unrigged, unloaded, careened, and repaired, and within a month was again ready for sea. Boats, provisions, and a party of Aleuts, together with two interpreters from Kadiak, were provided by the agent, as Kotzebue had directed,[23] and on the 29th of June the *Rurik* again sailed on her voyage northward.[24] On the 10th of July St Lawrence Island was sighted, and here the commander ascertained that ice-floes had surrounded it on the south-east until three days before. Anchoring at midnight off its northern promontory, he found an unbroken ice-pack toward the north and east.

There was now no hope of passing Bering Strait until the end of the month, when, as Kotzebue thought,

[22] *Kotzebue's Voy. of Discov.*, ii. 160–1. The author remarks: 'I would advise no one to visit this ocean so early in the year, for the storms are frightful.'

[23] Kotzebue was furnished with an order from the directors of the Russian American Company requiring Kriukof, then agent at Unalaska, to supply the expedition with all that was needed, and declares that he received every courtesy and assistance at the hands of the agent.

[24] On the *Rurik* was a boy named Kadu, whom Kotzebue had taken on board at one of the Caroline Islands. He appeared to be contented on reaching Unalaska, though he was disappointed at not finding there any cocoa-nut or bread-fruit trees, and did not approve of the Aleutian mode of living under ground. He asked whether people lived so at St Petersburg. Gazing at the oxen on board the vessel, he expressed his joy that the meat consumed by the crew was the flesh of these animals. Being asked his reason, he confessed that he thought the Russians were cannibals, that he regarded himself as a portion of the ship's provisions, and looked forward in horror to the moment when they might be in want of food. *Id.*, 166.

the season would be too far advanced for a successful voyage. Moreover, his health was shattered; his breathing was difficult; he was suffering from spasms in the chest, fainting fits, and hemorrhage of the lungs. The surgeon of the vessel declared that to remain longer in the neighborhood of the ice would cost him his life. "More than once," he says, "I resolved to brave death, but I felt that I must suppress my ambition. I signified to the crew, in writing, that my ill health obliged me to return to Oonalaska. The moment I signed the paper was the most painful in my life, for with this stroke of the pen I gave up the ardent and long-cherished wish of my heart."

Returning by way of the Sandwich Islands, Kotzebue reached Hawaii on the 27th of September. Here he was greeted by Kamehameha and his old acquaintance, Eliot de Castro. Sailing thence to Oahu, he found six American ships at anchor, and one—the *Kadiak*—belonging to the Russian American Company, hauled up on the beach. In this vessel Sheffer had reached Oahu, after being expelled from Kauai, where he intended to found a settlement. A few days later the *Boston* arrived on her way to Canton, with a cargo of furs shipped from Novo Arkhangelsk.

Calling at St Helena on his homeward voyage, Kotzebue met with a most surly reception from the British naval officers who kept guard over the rock where the captive emperor was then entombed alive, his craft being fired upon without apparent cause.[25] His reception in England was more cordial. During a visit to London, where business compelled him to spend a few days on his way to Kronstadt, he was introduced to the Prince Regent and to the Archduke Nikolai Pavlovitch. On the 23d of July, 1818, the *Rurik* sailed past the port of Revel, and now, after an

---

[25] Kotzebue's purpose in calling at St Helena was to give the Russian commissary, Count Balleman, an opportunity to send letters to his countrymen. Three shots were fired at the *Rurik*, one of them passing between her masts. *Id.*, 255.

absence of three years, Kotzebue once more beheld his native city.   A week later the vessel cast anchor in the Neva, opposite the palace of Count Romanof.[26]

Before making further mention of Sheffer's exploits in the Hawaiian Islands, it is necessary to refer to incidents which preceded the voyage of the *Rurik.*   In April 1814 one of Baranof's American friends, Captain Bennett, who had sold him two vessels and their cargoes, offered to accept fur-seal skins in part payment, but having none of the required kind on hand at Novo Arkhangelsk, the chief manager induced Bennett to proceed in the *Bering* to the island of St Paul in search of them, and at the same time to take a cargo of furs, worth half a million roubles, to be landed at Okhotsk.   There he took on board a number of the company's hunters who were awaiting passage, and a large mail of the company's despatches. He then sailed for the Sandwich Islands, where it had been arranged that he should purchase a cargo of taro,

[26] In his *Voyage of Discovery into the South Sea and Beering's Straits, for the Purpose of Exploring a North-east Passage* (3 vols., Berlin, 1819, and London, 1821), the author, after a lengthy introduction, devotes the first seven chapters of the first volume to his journey from Kronstadt to Kotzebue Sound, the eighth to his trip from the latter part to Unalaska, and the ninth and tenth to his visit to California and the Sandwich Islands.   In the eleventh chapter, which opens the second volume, we have an account of his explorations in the Caroline Archipelago.   Then follow his second voyage northward, and his homeward journey, occupying the four next chapters.   The remainder of the work is taken up with an *Analysis of the Islands Discovered by the Rurik in the Great Ocean* (written by Krusenstern), a short paper on the *Diseases of the Crew during the Three Years of the Voyage, by Frederick Eschscholtz, M.D.* (the ship's physician), and the *Remarks and Opinions of the Naturalist of the Expedition, Adelbert von Chamisso.*   In his preface, Chamisso remarks that he recognizes only the German edition, ' for the various foreign subjects of which he had to treat have made him too sensible how difficult it is, when aiming at brevity to avoid obscurity, for him to answer for translations of which he cannot judge.'   The precaution was justified, for in the English translation by H. E. Lloyd are many errors, caused probably by the extreme haste with which the work was rendered.   A few years later Kotzebue published in two volumes his *New Voyage round the World in the Years 1823-26.*   I have before me only the English translation (London, 1830).   As on this occasion he visited Novo Arkhangelsk, California, and the Sandwich Islands, we shall hear of him again.   Three years after completing his second voyage, he retired to his estate in Esthonia, where his decease occurred in 1846.   His sons and grandsons held positions in Unalaska in the service of the Russian American Company, until it was disincorporated, and several remained there after the purchase of Alaska by the United States.   The last of them died in 1861.

salt, and other provisions.   Having exhausted the resources of Hawaii, he proceeded to Kauai, where, the
captain being on shore, the ship was struck by a sudden
squall, and vessel and cargo were cast on the beach.
King Tomari, who was then in power at Kauai, though
subject to Kamehameha's authority, offered Bennett
every assistance in collecting his cargo; but when all
that could be saved had been secured beyond reach of
the waves, he coolly appropriated it as a perquisite of
the owner of the soil.   The captain and some of his
crew soon afterward made their way back to Alaska.

At the time when the *Rurik* left Kronstadt the
imperial government was fitting out two vessels, the
Suvarof and *Kutusof*, for an expedition to Russian
America.   They were placed in charge of Captain
Lozaref,[27] and the *Suvarof* with the commander on
board sailed from Kronstadt on the 8th of October,
1813, arriving at Novo Arkhangelsk in November of
the following year.   Lozaref, in common with all the
naval officers, was prejudiced against Baranof.   Disputes between the two men arose at once, and ceased
only when the ship set sail from Novo Arkhangelsk.[28]

[27] Krusenstern, who was now an admiral, recommended Kotzebue for the position, but the Russian American Company, which was to pay a part of the
expenses, objected on the ground of his youth.   The other officers were
lieutenants Unkovsky and Schveikovsky; the mates Rossysky and Dr
Sylva; cadet Samsonof, Dr Sheffer, and the supercargo Molvee.   The crew
consisted of 23 naval seamen, 9 merchant sailors, and 7 laborers of the company. *Tikhmenef, Istor. Obos.*, i. 183.

[28] On his return to St Petersburg, Lozaref was tried before a naval court
of inquiry on charges preferred by the board of managers of the
Russian American Company.   He was charged with immorality, with
returning from Novo Arkhangelsk without the company's supercargo,
the boy Molvee being deemed too young for such a position, without
the physician appointed to the vessel, without bills of lading or any
despatches from Baranof, and without the chief manager's permission.
To this the captain replied that he had repeatedly asked for orders, and
finally sailed, and made his way back around Cape Horn with all speed.
He also stated that the misunderstanding arose from his refusal to sanction
Baranof's action in seizing the brig *Pedler* belonging to Astor.   On that
occasion Lozaref stated that Baranof's anger was so great that he trained
the guns of the fort upon the *Suvarof*, and threatened to sink her.   Lozaref
was also charged with having sold at Lima 60,000 roubles' worth of furs belonging to the company.   This he denied, but stated that he sold to the
viceroy of Peru a few black-bear skins for the manufacture of shakoes for
his soldiers, and received 22 piastras each for the skins.   The other charges
were of a similar nature. *Zeleniy, Corr.*, MS., in *Sitka Archives*, iii.

Lozaref desired to pass the winter at Novo Ark-hangelsk, and to land his cargo and repair the vessel, but Baranof insisted that he should make a winter voyage to the Prybilof Islands for a cargo of furs, as there was not enough peltry at Novo Arkhangelsk to complete his freight. The captain then put to sea, but returned almost immediately, under pretence that the ship was leaking, and remained in port until the following May, when he finally executed the chief manager's orders. Soon after his return he again set sail on the 24th of July, leaving the anchorage hurriedly and without waiting for the mail prepared by Baranof for the home office of the company. Enraged at this, the chief manager despatched a fleet bidarka after the retreating ship, and threatened to open fire on her, but did not execute his threat. The *Suvarof* then proceeded on her voyage to St Petersburg, calling at San Francisco and at the port of Callao, where a part of the cargo was exchanged for Russian products.[29]

One of the officers of the *Suvarof* was the German doctor, Sheffer, who, having quarrelled with the commander, had for that reason found favor in the eyes of Baranof. Sheffer remained at Novo Arkhangelsk, and being a plausible adventurer, and somewhat of a linguist, succeeded in convincing the autocrat of the colonies that he was the man to carry out his schemes of colonization in the Hawaiian Islands.

Bennett, who had now returned to Novo Arkhangelsk, urged Baranof to demand the return of the *Bering's* cargo, but the latter would not consent to use force for such a purpose, as he had frequently exchanged presents and friendly messages with Kamehameha through their mutual acquaintances among the American north-west traders. He decided, therefore, to send Sheffer to the Sandwich Islands as a pas-

[29] In 1815 Baranof despatched another cargo of furs, valued at 800,000 roubles, to Kiakhta, in the *Maria*, master Petrof. The vessel was wrecked at Okhotsk, but most of the cargo was saved. *Khlebnikof, Shizn. Baranova*, 160.

senger in a foreign vessel, with instructions to open
negotiations with the Hawaiian monarch.   The doctor
sailed on the *Isabella*, which left Novo Arkhangelsk
on the 5th of October, 1815, and it was arranged that
the *Otkrytie*, commanded by Lieutenant Podushkin,
should follow in the spring with a number of native
mechanics and laborers for the purpose of establishing
a settlement.

On arriving at Hawaii, Sheffer presented himself at
once before Kamehameha and delivered letters and
presents from Baranof, at the same time complaining
of King Tomari for seizing the cargo of the *Bering*.
The king promised redress, and appeared to listen
favorably to the doctor's proposals to establish more
intimate relations with the chief manager of the
Russian American Company.   He even assigned to
Sheffer several pieces of land, whereon to make experiments in the planting of grain and vegetables.   One
of them was situated on the island of Kauai, the
domain of King Tomari.   Though Sheffer continued
in favor for a time, he found that he could not compete with the Englishmen and Americans, who were
already established at Kamehameha's court, and resolved to try his fortune with Tomari.   During the
first week of his stay in Kauai, it was his good fortune
to cure the queen of an intermittent fever and the
king of dropsy.   The German adventurer was now in
the good graces of his intended victim, and in a few
weeks an agreement was drawn up to serve as the
basis for a formal treaty, subject to the approval of
the Russian government.

It was stipulated that the *Bering's* cargo should be
returned to the Russians, with the exception of a few
articles which the king required, and for which he
bound himself to pay in sandal-wood; that Tomari
should send annually to the colonies a cargo of dried
taro root; that all the sandal-wood on the islands subject to Tomari should be placed at Sheffer's disposal,
to be sold only to the Russian American Company;

and that the company should have the right to establish stations or factories in any part of the king's
possessions.   As an offset to these favors, the doctor
pledged himself to furnish five hundred men, and some
armed vessels, for the purpose of assisting in the overthrow of Kamehameha, and of placing Tomari on his
throne.   The troops were to be under Sheffer's command, and in case of success, one half of the island
of Hawaii was to be ceded to the company.   Finally
Tomari and all his people were to be placed under the
protection of Russia.   In order more firmly to establish the king's confidence in his authority, Sheffer at
once bought an American schooner for $5,000, and
agreed to purchase a ship for the sum of $40,000, pay-
ment to be made in furs, which he promised to order
from Novo Arkhangelsk.[30]

In the mean time, Sheffer's intrigues had been
watched by American and English traders, and by the
Europeans settled on the islands under Kamehameha's
protection.   They took care to magnify the danger in
the eyes of the latter, urging him to enter on a campaign against Sheffer and the would-be rebel Tomari.
Though opposed to open hostility, Kamehameha's

[30] Sheffer was of course playing upon the king's ambition to serve his own.
He was certainly a bold man, a true adventurer, and one who led an exceedingly checkered life.   He was born in Russia, of German parents, the date of
his birth being uncertain, and entered public life as a surgeon in the Moscow
police.   In 1812 he was engaged in constructing balloons to watch the movements of Napoleon's invading army.   In 1813 he was detailed as medical
officer of the ship *Suvarof*.   We have seen how he left the ship at Novo Ark-
bangelsk, but it remains to record the doctor's strange career after the col-
lapse of the Sandwich Island scheme.   On making his escape from Oahu, he
proceeded to Canton, and thence to St Petersburg.   Here he made to the
imperial government the most vivid representations of the advantages to be
gained by taking possession of the Sandwich Islands.   The minister for interior affairs requested the managers of the Russian American Company to
express their opinion on the subject, and they reported unfavorably.   The
emperor's ministers could not blind themselves to the fact that Russia did not
then possess a navy which could support such an enterprise against the objection of the great maritime powers, and the doctor was doomed to disappointment.   He left Russia in disgrace, and was lost to view for a short time,
until he finally turned up again in Brazil, where he managed to ingratiate himself with Dom Pedro I., who conferred upon him the high-sounding title of
Count von Frankenthal, and intrusted him with a commission to Germany to
recruit men for the imperial body-guard.   Sheffer finally died peaceably in
Germany, at a very advanced age.

repeated orders to Tomari finally resulted in an estrangement between him and the German doctor, who by this time had succeeded in establishing plantations on various points of the Islands, and had erected buildings for his own accommodation, for the mechanics and laborers who had now arrived in the *Otkrytie,* and for housing the crops intended for shipment to Novo Arkhangelsk. The unfriendly feeling thus engendered increased in intensity until the Russians and Aleuts were looked upon by the Hawaiians as enemies, and were compelled to adopt measures for their defence. A few slender fortifications were erected at Wymea, the ruins of which remain to the present day.

As soon as Baranof ascertained that this, the pet scheme of his old age, must fail, he lost no time in forwarding orders to Sheffer to give up everything, and to save what he could out of the wreck which was impending. By this time news had also been received of the refusal. on the part of the imperial government to sanction the scheme of annexation. The doctor's position became more critical every day. From Novo Arkhangelsk he could expect no further support, while on the Islands the Americans and English became constantly more aggressive. A small Russian station on the island of Hawaii was sacked by sailors from an American ship, and they even threatened to destroy the company's plantations on Kauai. A report was also started that American men-of-war were on their way to the Islands. Some of the Americans in the company's service became disaffected, one of them, Captain Wosdwith, who commanded the *Ilmen,* purposely running his vessel on the beach and joining the adversaries of Sheffer.

By this time the ire of Tomari's subjects had been roused against the intruders, and they forced the Russians to abandon their settlements and to seek refuge on board the *Kadiak,* which was anchored off the island. When the fugitives left the beach it was discovered that the boat had been scuttled; the crew, however, reached the vessel by swimming. The natives now turned the guns of the fort against them and endeavored to sink the ship. The shot fell harmless, but it was discovered that the vessel had sprung a-leak, and that the water was gaining rapidly. In this predicament, an effort was made to get off the *Ilmen*, which succeeded. The American captain of the *Kadiak* was then transferred to the *Ilmen* by Sheffer, and sent to Novo Arkhangelsk to carry to Baranof the news of the failure of his enterprise, a duty which the doctor did not wish to undertake in person. After a brief stay at Kamehameha's court, exposed to constant annoyance from foreigners, accompanied with threats of personal violence, Sheffer finally escaped to China on board an American vessel, leaving the rest of his countrymen, and the Aleuts sent from Novo Arkhangelsk, to labor on the plantations. Of these Tarakanof took charge, and finally succeeded in securing their return [31] in 1818, by engaging himself and his men to an American skipper to hunt sea-otter for a brief season on the Californian coast. Thus ended the attempt at colonization in the Hawaiian Islands, whereby nothing was gained, and a loss of two hundred and fifty thousand roubles was incurred by the Russian American Company.[32]

[31] Tarakanof, whom Kotzbue met in Oahu, where Kamehameha then held his court, declared that the men escaped almost by a miracle, as Tomari might easily have killed all the party. Only three of them were shot. *Kotzebue's Voy. of Discov.*, ii. 197.

[32] Kamehameha expected that the Russians would take revenge for the treatment of Sheffer and his party, until Captain Golovnin's arrival in 1818. After that year the company's vessels again visited the Sandwich Islands, but at long intervals. Occasional intercourse was also maintained through American ships. The produce of the Islands, consisting of cocoa-nuts, rum, taro, and rope of cocoa-palm fibre, was exchanged for peltry and piastres. *Lutke*, in *Materialui, Istor. Russ.*, part iv. 146-7. One of Baranof's plans for the establishment of trade with the Philippine Islands also failed of success. For this purpose he sent one of his confidential clerks to Manila in the *Ilmen*. On his return he reported that the Spanish authorities were strongly opposed to extending their trade with foreigners.

CHAPTER XXV.

CLOSE OF BARANOF'S ADMINISTRATION.

1819–1821.

HAGEMEISTER SAILS FOR NOVO ARKHANGELSK—HE SUPERSEDES BARANOF—
TRANSFER OF THE COMPANY'S EFFECTS—THE ACCOUNTS IN GOOD ORDER—
SICKNESS OF THE EX-MANAGER—BARANOF TAKES LEAVE OF THE COL-
ONIES—HIS DEATH—REMARKS OF KHLEDNIKOF AND OTHERS ON BAR-
ANOF—KORASOKOVSKY'S EXPEDITION TO THE KUSKOKVIM—ROQUEFEUIL'S
VOYAGE—MASSACRE OF HIS HUNTERS—FURTHER EXPLORATIONS—DIV-
IDENDS AND INCREASE OF CAPITAL—COMMERCE—DECREASE IN THE
YIELD OF FURS—THE COMPANY'S SERVANTS.

IN 1815 an expedition to Alaska was fitted out by
the imperial government in conjunction with the
Russian American Company, and Hagemeister, whose
voyage in the *Neva* has been mentioned, was placed
in command. A vessel, renamed the *Kutusof*,[1] was
purchased at Havre for £6,000 sterling, and in July
of the following year was ready for sea, when Lozaref
returned to Kronstadt in the *Suvarof*. On his arrival, the directors resolved to delay the departure
of the expedition until after the decision of the
naval court of inquiry, held to investigate the charges
made against him by the chief manager.[2] When
the judgment was made known, the directors added
to Hagemeister's instructions a clause authorizing
him to assume control in place of Baranof, if he
should find it necessary.

The *Suvarof* arrived at Novo Arkhangelsk on the
23d of July, and her consort, the *Kutusof*, on the

[1] Of 525 tons.
[2] See chap. xxiv., this vol., note 28.

·20th of November, 1817.[3]   Both vessels had been detained at Lima, whence the former had sailed direct for
Alaska, while the latter visited other Peruvian ports,
and also Bodega and San Francisco, where large quantities of provisions were purchased.   For these supplies Baranof expressed his thanks, but complained
bitterly of the company's refusal to listen to his renewed request to be relieved, declaring most emphatically that he was no longer able to bear the burden
of his responsibility. Hagemeister meanwhile did
not choose to reveal the extent of the powers conferred on him, but began at once quietly to investigate the state of affairs in the colonies and the exact
status of the company's business.   During the whole
winter he kept his orders concealed from Baranof,
who, though almost prostrated with disease, labored
assiduously in surrendering the affairs of the company.   He was now failing in mind as well as in bod-
ily health, one of the symptoms of his approaching
imbecility being his sudden attachment to the church.
He kept constantly about him the priest who had
established the first church at Novo Arkhangelsk
during the preceding summer, and urged by his spirit-
ual adviser, made large donations for religious purposes.

Hagemeister was impressed with the great respon-
siblities that awaited him, and hesitated long before
consenting to assume the burden.   At last he saw a
way out of the difficulty.   Yanovsky, the first lieutenant of the *Suvarof*, had become enamored of Baranof's daughter, the offspring of a connection with a
native woman, and had obtained his consent to become his son-in-law.   Hagemeister's consent was also
necessary, and this was granted on condition that
Yanovsky should remain at Novo Arkhangelsk for
two years and represent him as chief manager.

[3] Tikhmenef, *Istor. Obos.*, i. 200, gives the dates of the arrival of the *Suvarof*
and *Kutusof* as the 22d of July and the 22d of November. These given in
the text are taken from the books of the company preserved in the *Sitka
Archives.*

At last, on the 11th of January, 1818, Hagemeister suddenly laid before Baranof his orders, and three days later despatched the *Suvarof* to St Petersburg with a report of his proceedings. This surprise prostrated the deposed autocrat. The fulfilment of his long-cherished desire came upon him too suddenly. He could not in reason have expected a successor until the next ship arrived from St Petersburg. Whatever may have been Hagemeister's motive, the effect certainly was to shorten the days of Baranof, who deserved more consideration. After displaying his instructions, the former at once gave a peremptory order that all the books and property should be immediately delivered to the company's commissioner, Khlebnikof. Making a supreme effort, Baranof rose from his bed on the day of the *Suvarof's* departure and began the transfer of the company's effects,[4] a task which was not completed for several months. The property at Novo Arkhangelsk alone was estimated by Khlebnikof at two and a half millions of roubles. In addition to two hundred thousand roubles' worth of furs shipped on the *Suvarof*, there still remained in the storehouses skins to the value of nine hundred thousand roubles. The buildings were all in excellent condition, as were the sea-going vessels. In all the complicated accounts of this vast business, Khlebnikof failed to find a single discrepancy.[5] The cash accounts, involving millions, were in perfect order; in the item of strong liquors there was a small quantity not accounted for, but this had been caused by the hospitalities extended to naval officers and other visitors. Among the many who had been with him for long years, Baranof knew no one to whom he could intrust the irksome duty which now fell to his lot, but labored from morn-

[4] A list of the principal articles is given in *Khlebnikof, Zapiski*, in *Materialui*, 23-4.

[5] *Khlebnikof, Shizn. Baranova*, 174; *Tikhmenef, Istor. Obos.*, i. 243, 245, The latter states that the value of property transferred exceeded that which appeared on paper.

ing to night, overcoming his weakness with stimulants. At length the task was finished, and in September 1818 he delivered a full statement of the
company's affairs to his son-in-law. "I recommend
to your special care," he said, "the people who have
learned to love me, and who under judicious treatment will be just as well disposed toward those who
shall watch over them in the future."

Nearly forty years had now elapsed since Baranof
had left his native land; nearly thirty since he had
first landed at Kadiak. He was ill requited for his
long and faithful service. To him was due, more than
to all others, the success of the Russian colonies in
America; by him they had been founded and fostered,
and but for him they would never have been established, or would have had, at best, a brief and troubled
existence. Here, amid these wintry solitudes, he had
raised towns and villages, built a fleet of sea-going
ships, and laid a basis of trade with American and
Asiatic ports. All this he had accomplished while
paying regular dividends to shareholders; and now
in his old age he was cast adrift and called to render
an account as an unfaithful steward. He was already
in his seventy-second year. Where should he be-
take him during the brief span of life that yet remained?

Bitter as was the humiliation which Baranof suffered, he could not at once tear himself away from the
land which he loved so well. He resolved first to pay a
visit to Kadiak, meet once more the tried friends and
servants who were yet living there, and take a last
glance at the settlements, where first he had planted
his country's flag. He would then bid good-by to all,
and join his brother at Izhiga, in Kamchatka, the only
one of his kin that now survived.[8] Finally, his
old acquaintance, Captain V. M. Golovnin, who about

<hr>

[8] At one time he purposed to sail for the Sandwich Islands and end his
days at the court of Kamehameha, with whom he was still on friendly terms.
Khlebnikof, Shizn. Baranova, 174-5.

this time had returned to Novo Arkhangelsk, urged him to return to Russia, where he could still be of great service to the company by giving advice to the managers on colonial affairs. The prospect of continued usefulness and perhaps the hope of receiving reward for past services, then much needed by the ex-manager, decided him to accept this advice. The period of general leave-taking preceding his departure was a severe ordeal. He was frequently found in tears, and the symptoms of disease increased as he was submitted again and again to the trial of bidding farewell to the men with whom he had been intimately associated for more than a generation, and to the children who had learned to love him from their infancy.

At length, on the 27th of November, 1818, he embarked on the *Kutusof*, and as the vessel entered the waters of the sound, he gazed for the last time on the settlement which was entirely of his own creation. After touching at Umata, the vessel arrived on the 7th of March at Batavia, where she was detained for thirty-six days. No more unfortunate choice could have been made for so prolonged a visit than amidst the pestilential climate of that Dutch colony. Tired of the confinement of his cabin, the ex-manager insisted upon living on shore, spending his whole time in the hostelry just outside the settlement; thence he was carried almost lifeless on board the ship, which now put to sea; on the 16th of April, 1819, he breathed his last; on the following day his obsequies were performed, and in the strait of Sunda the waters of the Indian Ocean closed over the remains of Alexandr Andreïevich Baranof.

With all his faults, and they were neither few nor small, it must be admitted that in many respects Baranof had no equal among his successors. "I saw him in his seventieth year," writes his biographer, Khlebnikof, "and even then life and energy sparkled in his eye...He never knew what avarice was, and never hoarded riches. He did not wait until his death

to make provision for the living, and gave freely to
all who had any claims upon him. Some said that
he had large deposits in foreign banks, but no proof
of this was to be found when he died. He always
lived on his means, and never drew his balance from
the company while he was in their service. From
Shelikof he had received ten shares, and by the Shelikof Company he was allowed twenty shares more.
Of these he gave away a considerable portion to his
fellow-laborers Banner and Kuskof, who were rather
poorly paid. There are not a few now living in the
colonies whom he helped out of difficulty, and many a
remittance he sent to Russia to the relatives of persons who had died, or were by misfortune prevented
from supporting those dependent upon them. An
example of this occurred in the case of Mr Koch, who
was sent out to relieve him but died on the way. He
had assisted him formerly both with money and influence, and after his' death sent large remittances to his
family." [7]

[7] 'Every one looked to him as chief manager,' remarks Khlebnikof.
Shizn. Baranova, 197–8. 'There were two classes to be provided for—the
Russians and the natives. The latter never troubled themselves about the
future, as long as they had a fish to eat; but Baranof, with his good warm
heart, looked into the future for them. On one occasion all kinds of provisions were giving out, even the supply of fish dwindling away. He did not
sleep at night, when the wind was blowing, thinking of the ships on the way
to him, laden with what was needed so much. Had he known at this time
that, at the very moment when he was praying for the arrival of a ship on
the coast of America, the vessel which he expected was breaking to pieces on
the rocky shore of Kamchatka, even his stout heart might have trembled.
Baranof was never at his wit's end nor faint-hearted. When he heard at the
same time of the wreck of the *Elizaveta*, Demianenkof's disaster, and the
Yakutat massacre, all he said was, "My God! how can we repair all these disasters!"' Among the many instances related by Khlebnikof of Baranof's
business ability the following may be mentioned: In 1802 he received by the
Elizaveta a cargo worth only 20,000 roubles, a great part of which was useless for his purpose. Baranof went round the different stations to collect
goods to be exchanged for furs and to pay the hunters. Meeting with little
success, he sent out Aleuts to shoot or trap sea-birds, and of their skins he
had fanciful parkas (cloaks) made, which greatly pleased the natives, and
were readily accepted in payment for furs.

Although the author's name does not appear on the title-page of the
*Shizneopissanie Alexandra Andreievitcha Baranova Glavnago Pravitelia Ros-
siyskich Koloniy v Amerike* (Biography of Alexander Andreievich Baranof,
Chief Manager of the Russian Colonies in America), Naval Printing Office,
St Petersburg, 1835, it is evident from the introduction that the work was
written by Kyrill Khlebnikof. It was dedicated to his Excellency the Ad-

One of the officers of the sloop-of-war *Kamchatka*, in which vessel Golovnin arrived at Novo Arkhangelsk, a short time before Baranof's departure, thus relates his impressions: "We had just cast anchor in port, and were sitting down to dinner when Baranof was announced. The life and actions of this extraordinary man had excited in me a great curiosity to see him. He is much below medium height. His face is covered with wrinkles, and he is perfectly bald; but for all that he looks younger than his years, considering his hard and troubled life. The next day we were invited to dine with him. After dinner singers were introduced, who, to please the late manager, spared neither their own lungs nor our ears. When they sang his favorite song, 'The spirit of Russian hunters

miral, Member of the Privy Council, Knight of all Russian Orders, Count Nikolai Semenovitch Mordvinoff. Khlebnikof held a prominent position under the Russian American Company for many years, and devoted much time and study to the colonies. His biography of Baranof is very complete though tinged with admiration. Baranof was so thoroughly identified with all that was accomplished by the Russians on the American coast from 1790 to 1818, that his biography furnishes a complete history of the enterprise up to that time. His numerous thrilling adventures, his firm but sometimes cruel mode of dealing with the savages and his own followers—but little above the former in the scale of civilization—his vast plans for extending the field of the company's operations over half the Pacific Ocean, are ably and clearly portrayed. The relations between the Russian fur-trader and the Californian authorities, and his ventures in the Sandwich Islands, occupy considerable space in this volume.

Khlebnikof's letters on America, forming part iii. of the *Materialui dlia Istoriy Russkikh Zasseleniy po Beregam Vostochnavo Okeana* (Material for the History of the Russian Settlements on the Shores of the Eastern Ocean), Printing Office of the Ministerium of Marine, St Petersburg, 1861, bear no date, but were apparently written in 1829 or 1830. This work is a collection of papers published in the *Morskoi Sbornik*, the organ of the Russian Naval Department, on the then all-absorbing topic of the Russian Colonies. The contents of the collection are: I. Instructions of the Russian marine minister to Captain Golovnin, 1817. II. Communication from the marine minister, Marquis de Traverse, to Baron Testel, governor general of Siberia, 1817. III. Communication in reply, 1817. IV. Letter of Captain Golovnin to the governor of Siberia, 1817. V. Report of the commanding officer at Okhotsk to the civil governor of Irkutsk, 1815. VI. Letters of the post commander of Okhotsk on the oppression of Aleutian employees by the company. VII. Letter of Captain Golovnin on the condition of the Russian American Company, 1818. VIII. Review of the Russian colonies in North America by Captain Golovnin. IX. Letters of Khlebnikof on America, divided into two parts—the northern colonies and the Ross settlement, containing minute and reliable data on both subjects. X. Translations and extracts from the works of the following authors: Khlebnikof, Davidof, Krusenstern, Lisiansky, Kotzebue. Golovnin, Lozaref, Lütke, Langsdorff, Roquefeuil, Belcher, La Place, Mofras, Simpson, and Kellett. Statistical tables are appended to the collection.

devised,' he stood in their midst and rehearsed with them their common deeds in the New World. I must add here a word as to his mode of life. He rises early, and eats only once during the day, having no certain time for his meal. It may be said that in this respect he resembles Suvarof, but I believe Baranof never resembled anybody, except perhaps Cortés or Pizarro.[8] His former condition had caused him to adopt a custom of which he could never wean himself— that of keeping around him a crowd of madcaps, who were greatly attached to him, and ready, as the saying is, to go through fire and water for him. To these people he often gave feasts, when each one could drink as much as he pleased, and this explains the enormous consumption of rum which Baranof was in no condition to buy, and had to procure at the company's expense."[9]

It is probable that the words which Washington Irving puts into the mouth of Astor's agent, when he "found this hyperborean veteran ensconced in a fort which crested the whole of a high rocky promontory," are but too near the truth. "He is continually giving entertainments by way of parade," says Mr Hunt, "and if you do not drink raw rum, and boiling punch as strong as sulphur, he will insult you as soon as he gets drunk, which will be very shortly after sitting down to table.

"As to any 'temperance captain,'" continues Irving, "who stood fast to his faith and refused to give up his sobriety, he might go elsewhere for a market, for he stood no chance with the governor. Rarely, however, did any cold-water caitiff of the kind darken the door of Baranof; the coasting captains knew too well his humor and their own interests; they joined in his revels; they drank and sang and whooped and hic-

---

[8] In what respect the writer does not explain.

[9] *Tikhmenef, Istor. Obos.*, i. 244–5. The officer remarks, that during his whole term of administration he had exhibited a rare disinterestedness, and though he had every chance of enriching himself, had never taken advantage of his position.

cuped, until they all got 'half-seas-over,' and then affairs went on swimmingly.

"An awful warning to all 'flinchers' occurred shortly before Hunt's arrival. A young naval officer had recently been sent out by the emperor to take command of one of the company's vessels. The governor, as usual, had him at his 'prosnics,'[10] and plied him with fiery potations. The young man stood on the defensive, until the old count's ire was completely kindled; he carried his point and made the greenhorn tipsy, willy nilly. In proportion as they grew fuddled, they grew noisy; they quarrelled in their cups; the youngster paid Baranof in his own coin, by rating him soundly; in reward for which, when sober, he was taken the rounds of four pickets, and received seventy-nine lashes, taled out with Russian punctuality of punishment.

"Such was the old grizzled bear with whom Mr Hunt had to do his business. How he managed to cope with his humor, whether he pledged himself in raw rum and blazing punch, and 'clinked' the can with him as they made their bargains, does not appear upon record; we must infer, however, from his general observations on the absolute sway of this hard-drinking potentate, that he had to conform to the customs of his court, and that their business transactions presented a maudlin mixture of punch and peltry."[11]

Before taking final leave of Baranof, I will give one more quotation from a manuscript in my possession, from the dictation of one formerly in the service of the Russian American Company, who arrived at Novo Arkhangelsk in 1817, for the purpose of rejoining his father, who had been sent to the Ross colony. "On the day after our arrival, Mr Baranof sent for me. He was a small man, of yellow complexion, and

[10] Carousals.
[11] Astoria, 465-7. Irving states that in 1812 the fort at Novo Arkhangelsk mounted 100 guns; but one must, of course, allow for the vivid imagination of the novelist. There were but 50 cannon as late as 1817. Golovnin, in Materialui, Istor. Russ., part iv. 101.

with very little hair on his head.   He spoke to me
very kindly, and promised to send me to Mr Kuskof
as soon as any of the company's ships were going in
his direction.   Then he told me I could stay at his
house and help the woman who was his housekeeper.
He had several women about his house, young and
old, and one daughter about seventeen years of age,
for whom he kept a German governess.   The mother
had been a Kolosh woman, but she died before I
came to Novo Arkhangelsk.

"Baranof was often sick, and sometimes very cross,
but his daughter could always put him in good humor by playing on the piano.   I have seen him send
every one out of the house in a heavy snow-storm
when his anger was roused, but half an hour later he
sent messengers to call back the women and servants,
and gave each one an order on the store for whatever
they wished.   Then he would send for liquor and order a feast to be prepared, and call for his singers to
amuse him while he was eating.   After his meal he
was apt to get drunk on such occasions, and would
try to make all around him drunk.   Most of the people in the house liked to see him in a rage, because
they knew that a carousal would follow.   As soon as
he began to feel the effect of drink he always sent his
daughter away, but all the other women were required
to stay with him and share in the revelry.

"One night Baranof came into the kitchen for some
purpose, and saw the German governess taking a glass
of rum.   He was so enraged that he struck her on
the head and drove her out of the house.   On the next
day he sent for her, made her some presents, and apol-
ogized for striking her.   He said that she might drink
now and then, but must never let his daughter see it.
The governess promised to abstain from dram-drinking
in the presence of her pupil, and remained with her
until she was married to a young naval officer,[12] who

[12] Yanovsky.

had arrived from St Petersburg on board a man-of-
war."[13]

Here we have probably a truthful picture of Baranof's household during the last years of his residence at Novo Arkhangelsk.   At this period he displayed only too often the darker phase of his character,
for the use of stimulants had now sapped the vigor of
his manhood, and in their use alone could he find
temporary relief from his constitutional fits of melancholy.   That he indulged too freely in strong drink
has never been disputed by his friends; but that he
was, as some chronicles allege, a cruel and vindictive
man, has never been proven by his enemies.   It
must be remembered that drunkenness was then a
vice far more common among the Russians than it is
to-day, and that it is now more prevalent in Russia
than in any civilized country in the world.   The as-
persions made on Baranof's character by missionaries
and naval officers have already been noticed.   They
need no further comment.   When we read the pages
of Father Juvenal's manuscript, and the remarks of
such men as Lieutenant Kotzebue, in whose work he
is spoken of as "a monster who purchases every gain
with the blood of his fellow-creatures," we can but
wish that they had formed a truer estimate of one
whose memory is still held in respect by his fellow-
countrymen.

While Baranof was still at Novo Arkhangelsk,

[13] *Adventures of Zakhar Chichinof*, MS., 2-4. Chichinof was a native of
Yakutak, where he was born in 1802. When eight years of age he went
to Kadiak, and was placed in the school of Father German, or Germanius,
under whose care he remained until the year 1817, learning to read, write,
and cipher. His father removed to Novo Arkhangelsk, where his son followed him in the autumn, earning his passage by acting as servant to
Hagemeister, who was a passenger on the same vessel. 'Hagemeister was
very proud,' remarks Chichinof, 'and used to kick me for not taking off my
cap before going into the cabin.' Hearing that his father had joined the Ross
colony, he presented to Baranof a letter from the missionary, requesting that
he be allowed to see his parent as soon as possible. It will be remembered
that, on his arrival at Ross, he was sent to the Farallon Islands, where he was
employed to keep accounts. Chichinof was a resident of St Paul, Kadiak,
in 1878, in which year he related to my agent, partly from memory and
partly from his journal, the incidents contained in my manuscript.

and probably under his direction, a force was despatched by land to make a thorough exploration of the territory north of Bristol Bay, and to establish a permanent station on the Nushagak River. The expedition formed on Cook Inlet, in charge of one Korasakovsky, who was well acquainted with the natives of this portion of Alaska.[14] Proceeding to lake Ilyamna, the party descended the river Kuichak to Bristol Bay, and following the coast, reached the mouth of the Nushagak, where the leader left be-

PLAN OF EXPEDITION.

hind him a portion of his command with instructions to build a fort, while he went on with the remainder to the mouth of the river Tugiak, far to the westward, where the sloop *Konstantin* was to meet him

[14] A curious superstition is alluded to in Korasakovsky's instructions. From early times a belief had existed among the promyshleniki and others, that somewhere in the interior, on the banks of the river named the Khinveren, there lived white people with long beards, the descendants, probably, of some of Deshnef's companions who were reported to have been lost on the American coast in 1648. Others ascribed their origin to the members of Chirikof's crew lost on the coast of America. How firm a hold this childish belief had taken on the minds even of those in authority, is evidenced by the fact that Korasakovsky was instructed to search for the mysterious white men of the interior. *Tikhmenef, Istor. Obos.*, i. 249.

an Indian, who was apparently unarmed. A few minutes later a musket-shot was heard, followed immediately by a volley. The captain instantly turned back, but seeing the Aleuts running toward the beach without offering resistance, he hid himself in a thicket which lined the shore, and made signals for a boat to come off to his rescue. As soon as his signal was answered, he stripped and swam off toward the ship, holding his watch between his teeth. As the boat approached, the savages opened fire on her, and wounded four out of a crew of seven, but Roquefeuil was finally rescued. Meanwhile the sailors returned the fire, and a lieutenant was sent with two sail-boats to rescue the survivors. Seven men were lifted out of their torn and sinking bidarkas, two of them being at the point of death, four severely wounded, and from a small hole in the rocks crept forth seven others, who all escaped unhurt. On the 19th a strong party was sent on shore to search for more survivors, but without success. Most of the bidarkas were recovered, a few muskets were picked up near the beach, and nineteen Aleuts lay dead within the encampment, the only traces of the fight being a few discharged pistols and broken spears.[18]

On Roquefeuil's return to Novo Arkhangelsk, Hagemeister offered him an opportunity to retrieve his losses by joining one of the Russian hunting parties then engaged among the islands, but the crew refused to receive on board any more Aleuts, or to engage a second time in the dangerous service of escorting them. The captain resolved, therefore, to confine himself to trading; and after repairing damages, he again sailed for the Alexander Archipelago. Hoping

---

[18] Roquefeuil, *Id.*, i. 71, states that of 47 Aleuts, 20 were killed, and 25 escaped or were picked up by the boats, the fate of the other two being unknown. Of the survivors, 12 were wounded, most of them seriously. Only one Kaigan was found dead on the scene of the massacre. In the accounts of the Russian American Company, contained in the *Sitka Archives*, vi., an entry speaks of 23 natives (20 men and 3 women) who had lost their lives on this occasion, and for each of whom Roquefeuil was made to pay $90, under the terms of his contract.

to deceive the savages, and capture some of their chiefs, to be held for ransom, he had painted his ship and changed the rigging; but his trouble was in vain; the ruse did not deceive the Kaigans, and not a canoe came near his craft.[19]

Roquefeuil then sailed for San Francisco to procure a cargo of grain with which to settle his indebtedness to the company. There he was detained by the authorities for more than a month, but finally obtained Governor Sola's permission to trade, chiefly through the intervention of Golovnin, who was then at the same port. Returning once more to Novo Arkhangelsk, he found that Hagemeister was willing to accept a small cash payment in behalf of the relatives of the Aleutian hunters, and after landing his bread-stuffs, took his final leave on the 13th of December. We may presume that he was not very deeply impressed with the advantages of the fur trade on the upper north-west coast.

The end of the period for which the company's charter had been granted was now approaching. Anxious to make all possible progress, both in discovery and exploration, the directors ordered expeditions to be despatched in various directions, and at the same time new buildings were erected in nearly all the settlements. Two attempts had already been made to explore the head waters of the Copper River, but in both instances the leaders had been killed by the Atnas. From the Nikolaievsk redoubt another expedition was despatched, under command of Malakhof, for the purpose of exploring the country north of Cook Inlet.[20] From Petropavlovsk the company sent

[19] At about the same time the Boston ship *Brutus*, Captain Nye, had some difficulty with the Kolosh in the archipelago, during which a few of the latter were killed. Captain Young was cruising in the same vicinity for the Russian American Company in the brig *Finland*, but was not attacked. The result of his expedition was by no means satisfactory, however, for only 400 sea-otter were obtained with a force of 70 bidarkas.

[20] In the *Sitka Archives*, x., is a report transmitted by Malakhof to Yanovsky, describing the journey undertaken in accordance with his instruc-

the sloop *Dobroie Namerenie* (Good Intent) to explore the Arctic coast. This craft sailed in 1818, but was delayed at the mouth of the Anadir River, and did not return till three years later. No report of the expedition is extant, but the voyage was continued at least as far as East Cape.[21]

The efforts made by the company at the same time to explore the Asiatic coast south of Kamchatka, and especially the mouths of the Amoor, do not properly fall within the scope of this volume, but serve to show that the monopoly was straining every nerve to obtain a renewal of its privileges.

After reorganizing the affairs of the colony[22] and visiting the different settlements, Hagemeister sailed on board the *Kutusof* for Kronstadt,[23] where he arrived

---

tions. In this document, which does not bear the impress of reliability, Malakhof states that, striking eastward from the Kuskokvim across a chain of mountains, he found himself on the banks of a large river thickly dotted with native settlements, and flowing northward. It is not safe to assume that he reached the Yukon, as the time occupied in his exploration was altogether too short for such a journey. He probably heard from the natives on the Kuskokvim of the existence of a large river toward the north.

[21] Lieutenant Hooper of the royal navy, in his description of the voyage of the *Plover*, states that he saw near East Cape a cross on which was inscribed in Russian: 'In this place was buried the body of carpenter Stepan Naumof of the sloop *Good Intent*, August 12, 1821.' *Tents of the Tuski*, 151.

[22] Among other measures, he ordered that the promyshleniki should receive, instead of their usual remuneration from half-shares, a salary of 300 roubles a year, and one poud of flour per month. This system was first recommended by Rezanof. He also instructed the officials to provide each of the Aleuts with seal-skins for bidarkas, a whale-bladder coat, and a bird-skin parka, for which they were to pay only one fifth of the regular price. From the pay of those who were indebted to the company, only one third must be deducted. All skins brought in by hunters were to be marked in their presence with the company's stamp, and with initials indicating their quality and grade. *Khlebnikof, Zapiski in Materialui*, 25–8. Tikhmenef says that Hagemeister proposed to fix the pay of hunters at 350 roubles, but that the directors would not consent. He also states that the latter made other regulations, which were approved by the general administration for the guidance of officials in Kadiak, Novo Arkhangelsk, Unalaska, and Ross, and revised regulations for foreign vessels visiting Novo Arkhangelsk. *Tikhmenef, Istor. Obos.*, i. 246. In his remarks on Novo Arkhangelsk, Golovnin says: 'Perhaps the directors do not know of the loss which the company suffers from contrabandists, and of the injury done to the colony and its inhabitants.' He recommends that the matter be brought to the notice of the government. *Id.*, 251.

[23] When the *Kutusof* arrived, an English ship of 600 tons, purchased by the company and renamed the *Borodino*, was being fitted out for another naval expedition, the command being intrusted to Lieutenant Ponafidin, formerly of the *Suvarof*. The complement of the *Borodino* consisted of 12

on the 7th of September, 1819. Calling at Batavia, he purchased an assortment of goods to the amount of two hundred thousand roubles, and the value of his cargo of furs was estimated at a million. The vessel was at once refitted, and again despatched to the colonies about a year later under command of Lieutenant Dokhturof, who subsequently became famous in Russian naval annals.[24] Arriving at Novo Arkhangelsk in October 1821, after calling at several Californian ports, she returned the following year with another cargo of furs valued at over a million.

As we have now come to the close of the first term for which the privileges of the Russian American Company were granted, I will give a brief account of its operations during this period, or so much of them as can be obtained from the records which have come down to us. The original capital of 723,000 roubles was increased by the subscriptions of new shareholders to 1,238,740 roubles; and the net earnings between 1797 and 1820, the first years including the operations of the Shelikof-Golikof Company, were 7,685,608 roubles. Of this sum about 4,250,000 roubles were distributed as dividends, and the remainder added to the capital, which amounted in 1820 to about 4,570,000 roubles.[25] Meanwhile, furs were sold or exchanged for other commodities at Kiakhta to the amount of 16,376,696 roubles,[26] and at Canton through foreign

officers and petty officers, and 79 seamen of the navy. She had also 33 laborers on board. *Tikhmenef, Istor. Obos.*, i. 201; *Sitka Archives*, i. Of the officers of this expedition, Chistiakof and Zarembo were afterward prominently connected with the development of the Russian colonies. On Hagemeister's return the directors ordered Ponafidin to call at Rio de Janeiro, and then at Manila, where commodities could be purchased at low rates. As a mercantile speculation the enterprise proved a success, but it cost the lives of many of the crew. Disease broke out soon after leaving the latter port, and 40 of the crew fell victims to fever. On his return from the colonies in 1821, Ponafidin was temporarily suspended from duty.

[24] With Dokhturof sailed 42 seamen of the navy, 28 laborers, and 3 creole youths who had completed their education in St Petersburg.

[25] Divided in 1820 into 7,713 shares, and distributed among 630 shareholders. *Tikhmenef, Istor. Obos.*, i. 255-6. The figures given are in paper roubles, then worth about 20 cents.

[26] At Kiakhta furs were usually exchanged for tea, Chinese cloth, and some-

vessels to the amount of 3,648,002 roubles.   Of the company's transactions elsewhere we have no complete records.

Notwithstanding the large shipments of furs made during the first twenty years of the company's existence, the yield had greatly diminished since the first years of Baranof's administration.   In the gulf of Kenaï, where Delarof had obtained 3,000 skins during his first year's hunting, the catch decreased, until in 1812 it amounted only to 100.   In Chugatsch Bay, where seal had before been plentiful, the yield fell off in the same year to 50 skins.   Between that point and Novo Arkhangelsk sea-otter abounded when the Russians first took possession, but five years later they had almost disappeared.   In Otter Bay, Queen Charlotte Island, and Nootka Sound they were still plentiful, but the Americans absorbed most of this trade, bartering fire-arms and rum with the Kolosh in return for skins, of which they obtained about 8,000 a year, while the Russians tried in vain to compete with them.

In Novo Arkhangelsk, which had now become the commercial centre of Russian America, there were, in 1818, 620 inhabitants, of whom more than 400 were male adults.   Of the servants of the company, 190 were at that time engaged on shares, and 101 on fixed salaries.   The income of the chief manager was 7,800 roubles a year; that of the head clerk from 3,000 to 4,000, of a trading skipper about the same, an assistant clerk or priest 600, and an Aleutian or creole hunter from 60 to 150 roubles.   The total sum paid yearly at Novo Arkhangelsk on account of shares, salaries, premiums, and pensions, was about 120,000 roubles.

It will be seen that, with a few exceptions, the company's servants had little chance to enrich themselves

times for silk or sugar.   Sea-otter skins were valued at 110 to 124 roubles, fur-seal 5 to 7 roubles, and fox skins from 2 roubles and 20 kopeks to 13 roubles in tea, according to quality. *Id.*, 234.

during their sojourn in the farther north-west. Moreover, the necessaries of life often became so scarce that they were beyond reach of most of the colonists.[27] There were some exceptions, however. Bread, for instance, was usually sold to married men, at least after Hagemeister's arrival, at cost, and in sufficient quantity. To laborers goods were issued from the stores, on a written order from the chief manager, and charged to their accounts once a month or once in three months. On these occasions they received a present of a small quantity of flour or other provisions.

[27] *Khlebnikof, Zapiski* in *Materialui*, 245. There are no data as to the prices at which goods were furnished to employees in 1818; but in previous years they were often purchased by the chief manager at very high rates, and of course retailed at a profit. In 1805, $25 per barrel was paid to Captain Wolf for salt beef, and the same price per cental for common soap; in 1808, $7.50 per cental was paid to Ayres for wheat, and $50 per cental for tobacco. In 1810, $16.80 per cental was paid to Davis for white sugar; and in 1811, $15 to Ebbets for brown sugar. *Id.*, 14.

CHAPTER XXVI.

SECOND PERIOD OF THE RUSSIAN AMERICAN COMPANY'S OPERATIONS.

1821–1842.

GOLOVNIN'S REPORT ON THE COLONIES—THE COMPANY'S CHARTER RE-
NEWED—NEW PRIVILEGES GRANTED—MOURAVIEF APPOINTED GOVER-
NOR—ALASKA DIVIDED INTO DISTRICTS—THREATENED STARVATION—
CHISTIAKOF SUPERSEDES MOURAVIEF—FOREIGN TRADE PROHIBITED—
THE ANGLO-RUSSIAN AND RUSSO-AMERICAN TREATIES—MORE EXPLOR-
ATIONS—WRANGELL'S ADMINISTRATION—HE IS SUCCEEDED BY KUP-
RIANOF—DISPUTES WITH THE HUDSON'S BAY COMPANY—THEIR ADJUST-
MENT—FORT STIKEEN—ETHOLEN APPOINTED GOVERNOR—A SMALL-POX
EPIDEMIC—STATISTICAL.

AT the end of the twenty years for which the exclusive privileges of the Russian American Company
were granted, we find this powerful monopoly firmly
established in the favor of the imperial government,
many nobles of high rank and several members of
the royal family being among the shareholders. The
company already occupied nearly all that portion of the
American continent and the adjacent islands south
of the Yukon River now comprised in the territory
of Alaska. The country north of Cook Inlet and
Prince William Sound, and the Alexander Archipelago north of Dixon Sound, was also universally
acknowledged as belonging to Russia, though her
right was not established by treaty until some years
later. With an imposing list of permanent stations
represented as forts and redoubts, with a long list of
tribes converted to Christianity and brought under
subjection, the directors now sought to obtain, not

only a renewal of the favors already granted, but important additions to their privileges.

Aware that such a request would be made, the government had instructed Captain Golovnin to inquire into the condition of the settlements during his cruise in the *Kamchatka*.[1] His report was by no means favorable. "Three things are wanting," he says, "in the organization of the company's colonies: a clearer definition of the duties belonging to the various officers, a distinction of rank, and a regular uniform, so that foreigners visiting these parts may see something indicating the existence of forts and troops belonging to the Russian sceptre—something resembling a regular garrison. At present they can come to no other conclusion than that these stations are but temporary fortifications erected by hunters as a defence against savages." The captain expresses almost unqualified condemnation of the treatment of creoles and hired laborers, but concludes his report with the following words: "I consider it my duty to remark that these abuses occurred before Lieutenant Hagemeister's accession to office. Though he has but recently assumed control, and their entire abolition cannot yet be expected, the measures which he has already adopted for improving the condition of natives and promyshleniki promise complete success in the near future."[2]

It was of course to be expected that Golovnin, being a naval officer, should condemn Baranof's administration, and speak in favor of Hagemeister. Some of his suggestions were adopted, but notwithstanding his adverse criticism, an imperial oukaz was issued, in September 1821, granting exclusive privileges to the company for another period of twenty years.[3]

[1] The instructions for his guidance were framed by the marquis de Traverse, minister of marine. They are given in the *Materialui Istor. Russ.*, part i. 1-2.

[2] In a letter to Captain Etholen, Alexander Kashevarof, a creole educated at St Petersburg at the company's expense, declares that the last paragraph was added to the report after the directors had read the proofs, and at their special solicitation. *Russ. Amer. Co. Archives*, i.i.

[3] A few days before the oukaz was issued, a communication from the

This document was introduced by the following words, which are in strong contrast with the tenor of the captain's report: "The Russian American Company, under our highest protection, having enjoyed the privileges most graciously granted by us in the year 1799, has to the fullest extent justified our hopes and fulfilled our expectations, in extending navigation and discovery as well as the commerce of our empire, in addition to bringing considerable immediate profit to the shareholders in the enterprise. In consideration of this, and desiring to continue and confirm its existence, we renew the privileges given to it, with some necessary changes and additions, for twenty years from this time; and having made for its guidance certain rules, we hereby lay them before the governing senate, with our orders to promulgate the same, to be submitted to us for signature."

In the new charter, the text of which included twenty paragraphs, the jurisdiction of the company was established over all the territory from the northern cape of Vancouver Island, in latitude 51° N., to Bering Strait and beyond, and to all islands belonging to that coast as well as to those between it and the coast of eastern Siberia, also to the Kurile Islands, where they were allowed to trade as far as the island of Ourupa, to the exclusion of other Russian subjects and of foreigners. It was granted the right to all that existed in those regions, on the surface as well as in the bosom of the earth, without regard to the claims of others. Communication could be carried on

---

emperor, containing 63 paragraphs, was laid before the senate, wherein were regulations for the management of the company's business and for the general administration of colonial affairs. It was called forth by representations made by the company as to losses suffered from the illicit trade of foreigners, and was accompanied by the following letter: 'From information laid before us, we have learned that the trade of our subjects on the Aleutian Islands and on the north-west coast of America in our possession, is suffering from the existence of illegitimate traffic in the same localities, and that the chief reason for this has been the absence of definite rules and regulations for commerce and navigation on the coasts mentioned, as well as on the shore of eastern Siberia, and the Kurile Islands. To remedy this fault, we hereby transmit to the senate the much-needed rules and regulations.' *Tikhmenef, Istor. Obos.,* i. app. 27.

by sea between the colonies and adjoining regions belonging to foreign powers, but only with the consent
of their rulers.

Considering the vast territory controlled by the
company, and the large numbers of its inhabitants, the
government saw fit to confer certain rank and official
standing on the company's servants. The chief
manager was to be placed on the same footing as the
governors of Siberia; government officials of the military, naval, and civil service were allowed to enter
the company's service, retaining half their former pay,
and without losing their turn for promotion; all officials
in the company's employ, not previously invested with
rank, were to be promoted to that of collegiate assessor
after two years' service in the colonies; all servants
of the company were exempt from conscription, and
all officials and agents from the payment of taxes.
Employés were granted the right of complaining to
the senate for injustice or abuse on the part of the
company, the complaint to be made within six months
after the occurrence; right of appeal to the senate
from the decision of the company's authorities was
also given, the appeal to be made within the same
period.

If the company's shares should fall fifty per cent in
market value, the government was to assume the responsibility and sell them at auction. The right to
change the relations of the company was given to the
larger assembly of the shareholders, subject to appeal
to the senate, and permission was granted to the
board of directors to despatch vessels from Kronstadt
to the colonies with cargoes of Russian and foreign
commodities free of duty, and also to ship goods to the
colonies on government vessels at low rates. Finally,
all military, naval, and other officers were enjoined
to aid the company, and to insist on the strict
observance of these rights by Russian subjects and
foreigners. Most of the privileges contained in the

oukaz of 1799 were also renewed in the charter of 1821.[4]

The regulations appended to this charter were very voluminous, referring to the treatment of the natives, the obligation of the company to maintain churches and schools at its own expense, and to provide for the importation of supplies in sufficient quantity, the rights and privileges of creoles, and the rights and duties of shareholders and of the company's officials. It was provided that the chief manager must be selected from the naval service, and rank not lower than captain of the second class; the assistant manager must also be a naval officer; the board of directors, each of whom must hold not less than twenty-five shares, was to consist of four members, to be elected by the assembly of shareholders, and all the transactions of the company were to be subject to the supervision of the minister of finance, to whom detailed reports were to be submitted.

The first step taken by the board of directors, after obtaining their second charter, was the election of a successor to Hagemeister, or rather his representative Yanovsky, who, having married Baranof's daughter, was not considered free from the taint thrown upon the latter's fame by Golovnin. M. N. Mouravief, a captain in the navy and a scion of an old family belonging to the Russian nobility, was the one selected, and his appointment being confirmed, he sailed for Novo Arkhangelsk during the year 1821. He at once took measures to reconstruct the garrison, to repair the fortifications of all the settlements, and to erect new buildings wherever they were required.[5]

Mouravief at once saw the absurdity of Baranof's

---

[4] Among others were those of making settlements in regions adjacent to their territory, not occupied by foreign nations, and of engaging laborers for a term of seven years in any part of the empire, the company assuming the payment of their taxes. Capital invested by shareholders was also exempt, as before, from attachment, though dividends could be appropriated in payment of debts.

[5] It is related that he added more buildings to the company's stations than any subsequent manager.

policy in keeping the Kolosh at a distance from Novo Arkhangelsk. Up to this time they had been compelled to live on the islands north and south of the settle- ment, and this arrangement, intended to insure the safety of the Russians, had only served to increase the danger of hostile attack.   Away from all commu- nication and supervision, they had been at liberty to plot mischief at leisure, while they were kept informed of all that occurred in the garrison by the females of their tribe, whose intercourse with the promyshleniki was never interrupted.   The result was, that murder and robbery were committed with impunity on de- tached parties of laborers and fishermen.   Mouravief, taking advantage of the presence of the well armed ship which brought him to the colonies, summoned the chiefs of the Sitkas, and told them that they might return with their people to their former village adjoining the fort. The permission was gladly accepted, and the removal effected within a few days.   Mean- while the palisade separating the native huts from the company's precincts had been strengthened, and a heavy gate built, through which no savage was allowed to enter without a permit.   On certain days, they might, at a stated hour, visit the enclosed space for the purpose of disposing of game, fish, furs, and other commodities.   Before sunset the streets were patrolled by an armed guard, and all the natives kept out from that time until daylight; sentries were doubled and kept vigilant by a half-hourly exchange of signals. These regulations were found so satisfactory that they were continued by Mouravief's successors, and to a certain extent even by the American troops who took charge of the territory after its transfer in 1867.

The chief manager, or governor as he was now styled, also issued orders that the garrisons should be placed under strict discipline at all the outlying sta- tions; but only in Kadiak could this be done, for at other points the force was too small to allow of mili- tary organization.   He then made a tour of inspection through the colonies, visiting all the stations except those at Atkha and Atoo, and on his return divided the colonies into districts. The Sitka district included the mainland of Russian America from Mount St Elias as far as latitude 54° 40′ N., together with the islands along the adjacent shore. The Kadiak district embraced the coast and the islands on the gulfs of Kenaï and Chugatsch, the Alaska peninsula as far south as Shumagin Island, the Kadiak, Ookamok, Semidi, and all adjacent islands, the shores of Bristol Bay, and the coast between the mouths of the Nushagak and Kuskokvim rivers. In the Mikhaïlof district were included the basins of the Kvichak and Kuskokvim rivers, and the coast lying between Norton Sound and Bering Strait. The Unalaska district comprised all of the Alaska peninsula not included in the district of Kadiak, and the Lissiev, Sannakh, and Prybilof islands. The Atkha district consisted of the Andreanofsky group and the Blishic, Krissie, and Commander islands, and the Kurile district of the islands of that name lying between Ourupa and the Kamchatka peninsula.[6]

Soon after Mouravief's arrival, the colonies were once more threatened with starvation, a danger which was due to the following incidents: In the summer of 1821 supplies were despatched from Kronstadt in the *Rurik*, which had been placed at the company's disposal at the conclusion of Kotzebue's voyage, and in the *Elizaveta*, a Hamburg ship. The command of the *Rurik* and of the expedition was given to Master Klotchkof. The *Elizaveta* was intrusted to Acting Master Kisslakovsky.[7] While rounding the Cape of Good Hope, the two craft met with a hurricane, dur-

---

[6] The head office of the colonies was of course at Novo Arkhangelsk. There was also an office at St Paul in Kadiak. The other districts were managed by agents selected by the colonial administration. *Golovnin, Obsor. Russ. Kol.* in *Materialui*, 51–2.

[7] Their cargoes consisted of goods for the colonies and of rye flour for Okhotsk. *Tikhmenef, Istor. Obos.*, i. 335.

ing which the *Elizaveta* lost several sails and sprung a-leak, whereupon both vessels were headed for Simon Bay. On again putting to sea, after repairs had been made at great expense, it was found that the ship still leaked, and it was thought best to return to port, sell the *Elizaveta*, and transfer her crew to the *Rurik*, which arrived at Novo Arkhangelsk in November 1822. As most of the supplies had been given in payment for repairs, the governor detained her in the colonies, having no other vessel at his disposal fitted for a long voyage in search of provisions.

When informed of this disaster, the directors at once ordered the purchase of a ship of four hundred tons in New Bedford, Massachusetts. The craft was renamed the *Elena*, and placed under command of Lieutenant Chistiakof, who had before made the voyage from Kronstadt to Novo Arkhangelsk. A few days before the vessel was ready for sea a general assembly of shareholders was held, at which one of the directors[8] stated that, as several rich cargoes had recently been despatched to the colonies, goods and provisions must have accumulated there in great quantity, and that there was no necessity to despatch another vessel round the world. The majority of the shareholders present adopted this view of the matter, and the expedition was abandoned for the time.

Thus in the year 1823 it became known throughout the settlements that supplies need not be expected from home during that and the following year. At the same time a despatch was received from the company's commissioner in California, stating that, on account of a failure of crops and for other reasons, it would be impossible to forward the usual quantity of bread-stuffs from that country. The colonies were now in evil case, and starvation, or at best the prospect of living for a time on seal flesh, appeared to be inevitable, for already the storehouses were almost

[8] Named Prokofeief. *Id.*, 337.

empty.   Mouravief at once sent an urgent appeal to the managers, and meanwhile despatched Lieutenant Etholen to the Sandwich Islands in the brig *Golovnin* for a cargo of provisions, the *Rurik* being then engaged in the intercolonial trade.   Calling at San Francisco on his voyage, Etholin succeeded, notwithstanding the dearth, in bartering furs for a large quantity of wheat[9] at moderate rates.   Proceeding thence to the Sandwich Islands, where he found the price of most commodities extremely high, he purchased at a fair price an American brig named the *Arab*, with her cargo of provisions and trading goods,[10] the captain agreeing to take his craft to Novo Arkhangelsk. Both vessels arrived safely, and in time to prevent any serious suffering among the colonists.   A few months later the stock of provisions was further increased by the cargo of the *Rurik*, which was sent to the Sandwich Islands with the crew of the *Arab*, after calling at California ports during the voyage, and returned with a moderate supply.[11]

As in this instance, the colonies had frequently been relieved from want by trade with foreigners; and indeed, this was too often the only means of averting starvation.   Even between 1818 and 1822, when supplies were comparatively abundant, goods, consisting mainly of provisions, were obtained by traffic with American and English masters to the value of more

[9] He paid also 5,000 piastres in cash, and secured altogether 1,900 fanegas. The entire crop in California for 1823 was only 50,000 fanegas. See *Hist. Cal.*, ii. 403, this series.

[10] The brig was renamed the *Baikal.* Tikhmenef, *Istor. Obos.*, i. 338, claims that the company realized a large profit on this transaction, but his explanation of the matter is somewhat vague.

[11] The goods purchased in the Sandwich Islands were 1,000 lbs. of salt, 1,270 lbs. of biscuit, 500 lbs. of sperm candles, 217 gals. of rum, 133 gals. of brandy, 30 kegs of cocoanuts, and 18 kegs of tar, for which were given in exchange 2,000 fur-seal skins and 300 Spanish piastres. *Khlebnikof, Zapiski* in *Materialui*, 85. In 1825 fur-seal skins were bartered in the Sandwich Islands by the captain of one of the company's ships on the basis of $1.75 per skin. *Id.*, 88. This seems an extravagent price, when, as will be remembered, the price at Kiakhta was only 5 to 7 roubles in scrip ($1 to $1.40); but it was the usual rate at which furs were exchanged at Novo Arkhangelsk with American and English skippers. See *Id.*, 75-6, where a list is given of goods exchanged in trade with foreigners between 1818 and 1822.

than three hundred thousand roubles in scrip.[12] The supplies shipped by the company were never more than sufficient for the actual needs of the settlements, and if a ship were lost, her cargo was seldom replaced. The Aleuts were, of course, the principal sufferers, often perishing during their hunting expeditions from hunger and exposure. But what mattered the lives of the Aleuts? It were better that hundreds of them should perish for lack of food than that the shareholders should suffer from want of dividends.

The governor's appeal was, however, too urgent to be neglected, and, on the 31st of July, 1824, the *Elena* sailed from Kronstadt with a cargo of supplies, arriving at Novo Arkhangelsk a year later.[13] The ship was again placed in charge of Lieutenant Chistiakof,[14] who was directed to relieve Mouravief, the latter returning home on board the same vessel.[15]

It is probable that the only reason for Mouravief's recall was some slight disobedience of orders, coupled with the failure of the hunting expeditions sent out by his direction. About the close of the year 1822 the Russian sloop of war *Apollon* had arrived at Novo Arkhangelsk, with instructions that all trade with foreigners should cease, and for two years the interdict remained in force.[16] Willing as he was to obey

[12] The paper rouble, worth at this time about 20 cents, though its value was of course fluctuating, is always the one spoken of in this volume, unless the silver rouble (worth about 75 cents) is specified.

[13] The *Elena* returned to the colonies in 1828, with a cargo worth 500,000 roubles. Among those on board was the creole Kashevarof. We again hear of this vessel at Novo Arkhangelsk in 1836, on which occasion she brought out Lieutenant Mashin and Master Khalizof. In August of the following year the *Nikolai* was despatched from Kronstadt. Among her passengers was the creole Arkhimandritof. *Tikhmenef, Istor. Obos.*, i. 347–50. Kashevarof and Arkhimandritof had been educated at the company's expense, the latter at the imperial school of navigation, and both afterward did good service as navigators, and the former as an explorer.

[14] In the instructions given to Chistiakof, it was stated that the frigate *Kreisser* and the sloop-of-war *Ladoga* had been sent to the colonies to prevent all foreign trade which might be injurious to the colonies, especially that of exchanging fire-arms and munitions of war with the natives in return for peltry. *Id.*, 339–40.

[15] With a cargo of furs valued at 150,000 roubles, and 10,000 pouds of sugar purchased in Brazil. *Id.*, 340.

[16] When it was removed, in 1824, the company was relieved from its obli-

even this ill-advised order, he was sometimes compelled
to enter into transactions that were necessary to the
very existence of the Ross colony, to which he must
now look for supplies in case of need.[17] Of sea-otter,
the catch during the four years of Mouravief's administration was little more than fifteen hundred
skins[18]—a grievous contrast with the condition of this
industry in the days of Baranof, who, it is related,
could estimate, almost exactly, the number of furs
which could be collected in each section of his hunting grounds.[19]

Not satisfied with prohibiting foreign trade, the
Russian government issued an order forbidding the
approach of any foreign vessel within thirty leagues
of the coast. In 1822 the sloops-of-war *Kreisser* and
Ladoga arrived in the colonies from St Petersburg,
having been sent out to enforce the provisions of the
oukaz, and remained in colonial waters for two years.[20]

gation to furnish provisions in its own vessels for Petropavlovsk and Okhotsk.
Dok. Com. Russ. Amer. Kol., i. 35.

[17] About this period trade with California became very considerable.
From the company's books we find that between 1817 and 1825 eleven vessels
visited San Francisco, Santa Cruz, and Monterey, exchanging furs for provisions.

[18] The catch for each year between 1818 and 1825 is given in *Khlebnikof,
Zapiski* in *Materialui*, 73.

[19] In 1829 the catch had become so small that little hunting was allowed,
and payment was made to the captains of trading vessels in bills of exchange
instead of furs. *Tikhmenef, Istor. Obos.*, i. 341.

[20] A second voyage round the world was made by Otto von Kotzebue during the years 1823-1826. A new ship, the *Predpriatie* (Enterprise), carrying
24 guns, was fitted out for this undertaking. There were on board the naturalists Eschscholtz and Lenz, the astronomer Preuss, and the mineralogist Hoffman. *Kotzebue's New Voy. round World*, i. introd. The commander received
general instructions to protect the interests of the Russian American Company. He sailed from St Petersburg on the 28th of July. 1823, and after a
prolonged sojourn at Rio Janeiro, and a quick trip around Cape Horn, put
into Concepcion Bay, Chile, which country had become republican since his
last visit. Owing to intrigues between the different parties, he was not so well
received as on the former occasion. In his journal he asserted that a plot had
been formed to capture him and his officers, and that two Chilian men-of-war
attempted to prevent the sailing of the *Predpriatie*, which vessel next visited
the Sandwich Islands, and the groups in the Caroline Archipelago discovered
during the voyage of the *Rurik*. The expedition finally reached Petropavlovsk
and Kamchatka on the 8th of June, 1824, and sailed for Novo Arkhangelsk
on the 10th of August. Thence Kotzebue again proceeded to the Sandwich
Islands and the coast of California, where he greatly increased the difficulties
then arising between the Russian and Californian authorities in regard to the
continued occupation of the Ross colony. In his report upon the matter, he

The shareholders soon began to see the folly of · their senseless agitation against traffic with foreigners; receipts fell off to an alarming extent, and it became evident that something must be done to avert the dissolution of the company. At a general meeting, one of the directors, named Prokofief, laid before them the report of Mouravief in relation to the evil effects of the imperial order, and stated that a famine would have ensued in all the colonies if the governor had obeyed the spirit as well as the letter of his instructions. He pointed out to them how much Baranof owed to his unfettered intercourse with foreign traders in developing the resources of the colonies. He also showed them the enormous expense of expeditions sent direct from Kronstadt, and the advantage of purchasing goods from foreign skippers who came to the company's ports at their own risk and expense. His appeal was successful, and a resolution was adopted by the assembly petitioning the government to reopen to foreign vessels the port of Novo Arkhangelsk. The request was granted, and the consequence was that under Chistiakof's management there was a great improvement in the company's affairs.

While the company's business was thus progressing satisfactorily, a cloud arose in the diplomatic horizon, which at one time threatened the very existence of the colonies. As soon as the arbitrary measure of Russia became known to English and American northwest traders, protestations and complaints were forwarded to their respective governments. The matter was discussed with some heat in the United States congress, causing voluminous diplomatic correspondence. In the mean time some traffic was carried on under protest, and the matter was finally settled by the Anglo-Russian and Russo-American treaties of 1824 and 1825, when the eastern and southern

---

sided clearly with the Californian authorities and against the company. He returned to Novo Arkhangelsk on the 23d of February, 1825, and sailed on his homeward voyage in the autumn of the following year.

boundaries were then established as they remain to the present day, the limit of Russia's territory being fixed at latitude 54° 40'. The clause relating to the boundary between the Portland Canal and Mount St Elias furnishes an instance of the absurdity of legislation by diplomates in regard to regions of which they were entirely ignorant. At some time in the future this work will have to be undone, and another line agreed upon, as it is impossible to follow in reality the wording of the treaty.[21]

The convention between the Russian and English governments was concluded in February 1825. The commissioners on the part of Russia were the same

[21] I insert here an extract from the treaty with the United States of the 17th of April, 1824, as published by the Russian government: 'I. With mutual consent, it is hereby established that in all parts of the great ocean commonly known as the Pacific Ocean, or its adjoining seas to the south, the citizens and subjects of the high contracting powers may engage freely and without opposition in navigation or fishing, and enjoy the right to establish themselves on the coasts of such regions as are not already occupied for the purpose of trading with the natives, subject to the rules and regulations mentioned in subsequent clauses. II. In order to prevent such privileges from serving as a pretext for engaging in illegitimate traffic, it is agreed that the citizens of the United States cannot land at places where Russian settlements are located, without the permission of the local agent or commander, and that in the same manner Russian subjects cannot land without permission in the settlements of the United States on the north-west coast. III. It is also agreed that from this time forth citizens of the United States, or persons under protection of those states, will establish no settlements on the north-west coast of America, or any of the adjoining islands north of latitude 54° 40' N., and that Russian subjects will establish no settlements to the south of the same parallel. IV. It is provided, however, that for a period of ten years, to commence from the signing of this treaty, the ships of both powers, or the subjects belonging to either, shall be allowed to enter without restriction all interior waters, bays, coves, and harbors of either country, for the purpose of fishing and trading with the native inhabitants of the country. V. From the trade permitted in the preceding paragraphs are excepted all spirituous liquors, fire and small arms, powder, and munitions of war of all kinds, which both contracting powers agree not to sell or to allow their citizens or subjects to sell to the native inhabitants. It is also agreed that this prohibition shall not serve as a pretext for searching vessels or detaining them, or for the seizure of goods, or for violent measures against the commanders or crews of the vessels engaged in such traffic, since the high contracting powers reserve to themselves the right of meting out punishments or imposing fines for infraction of this article on their respective citizens and subjects. VI. As soon as this treaty is ratified in due form, on the one hand by his Majesty the emperor of all the Russias, and on the other by the president of the United States with consent of the senate, the ratifications shall be exchanged at Washington within ten months of the date hereto subscribed, or sooner if possible, in confirmation of which the respective plenipotentiaries have appended their signatures and their respective seals and stamps. St Petersburg, April 5th (17th), in the year 1824, after the birth of Christ, 1824.' *Tikhmenef, Istor. Obos.*, i. app. 62-3.

as those who concluded the American treaty, while Great Britain was represented by Lord Stratford Canning, a privy councillor. The third article contains the boundary clause which was subsequently inserted in the Russo-American treaty at the cession of Alaska, and is thus worded: "The boundary line between the possessions of the high contracting powers on the coast of the mainland and the islands of north-western America is established as follows: beginning at the southernmost point of the islands named Prince of Wales, which point is situated in latitude 54° 40′ N. and between the 131st and 133d degrees of western longitude, the line extends north along a sound known as Portland Canal, to a point on the mainland where it crosses the 56th degree of north latitude. Hence the boundary line follows the chain of mountains running parallel with the coast to the point of intersection with the 141st degree of longitude west from Greenwich, and finally from this point of intersection on the same meridian to the Arctic Sea, forming the boundary between the Russian and British possessions on the mainland of north-western America." [22]

[22] The first and second articles are substantially the same as in the treaty with the United States. The fourth article stipulates that, 'with regard to the boundary lines established in the preceding article, it is understood that the island named Prince of Wales belongs entirely to Russia, and that whenever the summits of the mountains running parallel with the coast from 56° of N. lat. to the point of intersection with the 141st meridian shall be more than ten leagues from the shore, the boundary line of the British possessions shall run parallel with the coast line at a distance not greater than ten leagues, the land between such line and the coast to belong to Russia.' Article v. provides that the contracting powers must not establish settlements within each other's territory. Article vi. stipulates that the subjects of Great Britain shall be forever at liberty to pass to and from the ocean by way of rivers and streams emptying into the Pacific Ocean and cutting through the coast strip in Russian possession described above. Article vii. provides for free navigation and right of fishery by the subjects of both powers for ten years in the harbors, bays, and channels. Clause viii. provides that the port of Novo Arkhangelsk shall be open to the trade and to the ships of British subjects for ten years counting from the day of ratification, and that if any other power should obtain this privilege for a longer period, the time shall be extended to Great Britain. Article ix. provides that the free trade granted in previous paragraphs shall not extend to spirituous liquors, powder or other munitions of war, which shall not be sold to any of the native inhabitants. By article x. Russian and British ships were permitted to enter any harbor in distress or for repairs,

It was further provided in these conventions that citizens of the United States and subjects of Great Britain should have the right of free navigation, fishery, and trade in the Alaskan waters for a period of ten years, but that the trading-posts of either contracting power could not be visited by subjects or citizens of the other without the consent of the officer in command; that at the end of ten years this right might be abrogated by Russia; that in the mean while arms, ammunition, and spirituous liquors were in no case to be sold to the natives, and that British subjects should always have the privilege of passing to and fro on rivers and streams flowing into the Pacific and cutting the strip of coast already described.

The news of these treaties, which was not received until after Chistiakof had taken command, aroused a storm of remonstrance on the part of the Russian American Company. The imperial government was besieged with petitions to abrogate the clauses granting free trade and navigation to Americans and Englishmen for a period of ten years. It was represented as a most flagrant violation of the rights granted by the imperial government, the result of which would inevitably be the dissolution of the company. The most active promoter of this agitation was Admiral N. P. Mordvinof, a shareholder of the company, who, in a letter to the minister for foreign affairs, defended the sanctity of the company's privileges, pointing out that the vague wording of some of the treaty clauses would lead to many misunderstandings. During the lifetime of Alexander, no attention was paid to these complaints; but after Nicholas had ascended the throne, negotiations were inaugurated with the British and United States governments for an abolition

provisions, or material, without payment of duty or port charges, but if the captain of such vessel was obliged to sell a portion of his cargo to cover the expenses incurred, he was to conform to local regulations of trade. Clause xi. provides that in case of any complaint of the violation of this treaty, the civil and military authorities of either contracting power should not be allowed to resort to arbitrary or forcible measures, but that the matter must be referred to the respective courts at St Petersburg and St James's. *Id.*, 64-6.

of the treaty. The first proposals met with a firm refusal in both countries, but to appease the shareholders a supplementary oukaz was issued, stating that the privileges of navigation and trade extended to foreigners would be confined to the strip of coast between the British possessions and the 141st meridian. The standpoint of Russia on this question was communicated to all the representatives of that nation abroad, and as the north-west trade was then in its decline, no further complications ensued, and no attempt was ever made to apply the provisions of the convention to the islands and coasts of western Alaska.

KURILE ISLANDS.

While the directors of the company were loud in their remonstrance against foreign encroachment, they did not hesitate themselves to establish settlements in regions to which they had no valid claim. A committee established by the company at Petropavlovsk in November 1830 ordered that an expedition be sent to the Kurile Islands. A settlement on Ourupa Island, abandoned in 1805, had been rebuilt in 1828, and during that and the following year furs to the value of eight hundred thousand roubles had been obtained. In 1830 a ship was despatched from Novo Arkhangelsk with a party of hunters, well supplied with provisions and material, to form a colony on Simusir Isl-

and.   The natives were not numerous, numbering in
1812 only sixty-seven souls for the entire group, and
the Russians found no difficulty in annexing their territory to the possessions of the company.[23]

· During the second term of the Russian American
Company's existence, several important expeditions
were undertaken.   Within the colonies, explorations
were continued by Mouravief, the principal one being
under command of Khramchenko, Etholen, and Master
Vassilaief, who sailed from Novo Arkhangelsk in the
brig *Golovnin* and the schooner *Baranof*, in June
1822, and remained absent for two years.   A detailed
survey was made on this occasion of the coasts from
Bristol Bay westward to the mouth of the Kuskokvim.   Norton Sound was also explored along its eastern and northern coast, the deep indentation on the
north shore being named Golovnin.   Many prominent points were definitely located with the help of
astronomical observations, but the coast between
Stuart Island and the Kuskokvim was again neglected, as it had been by all previous explorers.   To this
expedition we owe the only charts now existing of
the coast between Bristol Bay and Cape Newenham.[24]

In 1826 the Russian government despatched an
exploring expedition in command of Captain Lütke,
who arrived at Novo Arkhangelsk in June of the
following year.[25]   After remaining in port for a

[23] Before the annexation of the Kurile Islands each native paid an annual
tribute of 41 sea-otter, 23 fox skins, and 74 kopeks in money.

[24] From the reports in the *Sitka Archives*, it appears that Khramchenko
and Vassilaief were always quarrelling, Etholen serving as arbitrator.   It is
perhaps owing to this circumstance that Etholen's name alone appears on the
charts compiled during the progress of the explorations, though the work of
surveying was accomplished almost exclusively by his colleagues.   We find
several capes named Etholen, and also one strait between Unalaska Island and
the mainland.   The name of Vassilaief, who subsequently did much good
work in inland exploration, does not appear on any map or chart except in
connection with a submerged rock in Kadiak Harbor, upon which the mari-
ner's craft happened to strike. *Sitka Archives* (log-book), ix.

[25] In the *Materialui, Istor. Russ.*, part iv. 133–41, is a description, by the
captain, of Novo Arkhangelsk, its inhabitants, and their mode of life at the
time of his visit.

month, the captain proceeded to Unalaska and the Prybilof Islands, making also a careful survey of the northern coast of the Alaska peninsula, naming the various points, and finally visiting St Matthew Island and Petropavlovsk before proceeding south for the winter.[26] Two other vessels belonging to the expedition, the *Krotky* and the *Möller*, sailed in 1828, the former commanded by Hagemeister, the latter by Captain Staniukovich. Both officers made important surveys of the coasts of Bering Sea, which was visited about the same time by Captain Beechey in the ship *Blossom*.

In 1829 Chistiakof ordered an inland exploration to the north of the Nushagak River, in charge of Vassilaief, the creole Alexander Kolmakof being one of the party. The expedition was organized on Kadiak Island, and crossing the peninsula ascended the Nushagak to the region of the lakes, and thence reached the Kuskokvim. Kolmakof on this occasion selected the site for a trading-post, built by him two or three years later; and in 1841 a redoubt was constructed and named after him, near the junction of the Kvigin and Kuskokvim rivers. The furs brought back were fox and sable of fine quality, and the establishment of a permanent station in the interior was determined. On his return, Vassilaief laid before the governor a plan for establishing communication with Norton Sound by way of the route which he had discovered. On the Kuskokvim he had met with natives living on the lower Yukon and the shores of Norton Sound who assured him that the transit from one river basin to the other was short and easy of accomplishment.

In 1830 the brig *Chichagof* was despatched northward in charge of midshipman Etholen, with instruc-

[26] During this cruise, Lütke named port Moller on the Alaska peninsula, port Haiden, Cape Seniavin, and Hagemeister Island. He also made a minute survey of the vicinity of Cape Chukotsk on the coast of Asia. The scientists Kitlitz, Postels, and Mertens sailed in the *Seniavin*. All three published reports of their investigations.

tions to explore Norton Sound and proceed thence to
Bering Strait, touching at St Lawrence, Asiak, and
Ookivok islands.   Ookivok the midshipman found to
be an entirely barren island; and "one wonders," he
writes in his report, "how people could ever settle
upon it, but the countless number of walrus around
its shores soon solves the riddle.   The savages who
hunt these animals receive in exchange from the inhabitants of the mainland all the necessaries of life,
and gain their subsistence easily."   At St Lawrence
Etholen found five native villages, the inhabitants of
which also lived chiefly by hunting walrus.   On his
return to Novo Arkhangelsk, he reported that it would
be beneficial to the company's trade to establish a fort
on or near Stuart Island at the entrance of Norton
Sound.[27]

On the arrival in the colonies of Baron Ferdinand P.
von Wrangell, who was appointed Chistiakof's successor,[28] explorations were made on a larger scale.   After
examining the reports of Vassilaief's and Etholen's
expeditions, Wrangell came to the conclusion that communication between Bering Bay and Norton Sound
could be established overland.   For this purpose he
ordered Lieutenant Tebenkof to proceed to the latter
point in the sloop *Ourupa*.   Tebenkof erected a fortification with the consent of the natives, who promised
to trade with the Russians, and gave to the settlement
and to the island on which it was founded the name
of Mikhaielovsk.[29]   When the necessary buildings had

[27] *Tikhmenef, Istor. Obos.*, i. 283–5.   In 1831 and 1837 careful explorations
were also made of the Alaska peninsula and the adjacent islands.

[28] Though Chistiakof had given complete satisfaction to the managers, they
resolved to relieve him at the end of his term and appoint a man of scientific
attainments, and one higher in social and official rank.   From the beginning
of his administration, Chistiakof had endeavored to persuade the managers
that their interests would be served by removing the seat of authority from
Novo Arkhangelsk to St Paul.   So repeated and urgent were his representations, that the assembly of shareholders finally passed a resolution authorizing
the change.   Before the removal could be effected, however, Chistiakof was
relieved, and the project abandoned.

[29] It narrowly escaped destruction in 1836 from an attack of the natives,
an account of which is given in *Zagoskin, Peshekhodnaia Opiss Chasty Russ.
Vlad. v Amer.*, part i. 28–9; and *Tikhmenef, Istor. Obos.*, i. 287–8.   According

been completed preparations were begun for the inland explorations included in the governor's instructions.

A native of the colonies, a creole named Andreï Glazanof, who had been instructed in the use of astronomical instruments, and was familiar with various dialects of the Innuit language, was selected to take charge of the expedition.[30] The plan first adopted was to proceed to the mouth of the river Pastol, making the portage across a low divide to the Yukon; but rumors being heard of hostile intent on the part of the natives in that region, it was found impossible to secure a guide. Three natives were therefore secured to guide the party to the banks of the Yukon in a north-easterly direction, and on the 30th of December, 1833, the explorers left the road with two sleds, each drawn by five dogs, and a small quantity of provisions and trading goods, the men carrying their own guns, knapsacks, and clothing. They travelled on the ice, following the coast in a northerly direction until reaching the village of Kigikhtowik, whence on the following day they struck eastward. After crossing several ranges of hills with great difficulty, Glazanof arrived on the banks of the Anvik. His progress was much impeded by the condition of the ice on the rivers, and within two weeks his provisions were exhausted. In the hope of finding natives, his party proceeded up the Anvik into the mountains, but finding it impossible to reach their hunting-grounds, was forced to return, subsisting on a small quantity of

to the former authority, the settlement contained, about the year 1843, a barrack, a house for the managing agent, two magazines, a shed, bath-house, and kitchen, all occupying a space of 20 fathoms square, enclosed with a stockade 15 feet high, and protected by two block-houses, mounted with six three-pounders. Outside the stockade was a blacksmith's shop, a house for native visitors, and a chapel.

[30] He was accompanied by four volunteers, Vassili Donskoi, Vassili Dershabin, Ivan Balachef, and Jacob Knagge. Donskoi died from the effect of injuries received during the journey. Dershabin and Balachef remained in the company's service; the former was finally killed in the Nulato massacre, together with Lieutenant Barnard of the English navy, while Balachef served at the stations on Cook Inlet, where his children are still living. *Wrangell, Statist. und Ethnog.*, 138–9.

frozen fish taken from the Indian caches. On the 17th of January the explorers stumbled on a subterranean dwelling occupied by a native couple and their three children. Here they were treated to an ample meal of rotten fish, and found an opportunity to mend their broken sleds and snow-shoes.

A week later Glazanof and his men, now completely exhausted, arrived at the mouth of the Anvik, where they found a native village, the inhabitants of which, at the first sight of the Russians, began to prepare for defence, but a messenger being sent forward unarmed, succeeded in persuading them as to Glazanof's peaceable intentions, whereupon a cordial invitation was extended to the way-worn travellers to rest and recuperate their strength. One of the subterranean dwellings was vacated by its occupants to accommodate the guests, and after taking due precautions, Glazanof proceeded to the *kashim*, or council-house, a large structure containing several hundred people. He addressed the multitude, and less by his eloquence probably than by a judicious distribution of tobacco, succeeded in gaining their friendship. Presents of fish blubber, bear meat, and other food were laid before him, and he was told that if he had other wants they should be at once supplied. Here the party remained for some time, in friendly intercourse with the natives, and finally proceeded down the Yukon, as their new friends dissuaded them from attempting the portage route to the Kuskokvim.[31]

The subsequent explorations of Glazanof and his party were confined to the delta of the Yukon, the dense population of which astonished the Russians. His diary, which has been preserved, is full of the most minute observations of the topography and ethnology of this region, which modern investigations

[31] Glazanof questioned two natives who arrived during his presence at Anvik from the Chageluk River, and obtained from them a description of the country between the two rivers. These men evidently described the longest portage route, without mentioning another by which communiction can be effected in two days with the greatest ease. *Id.*, 148-9.

prove to be remarkably accurate. At one mouth
of the Yukon, named the Kashunok, he met with
two natives from the Kuskokvim, who had been baptized by Kolmakof in the year 1832. They described the ceremony to the other natives, who were
so much pleased with it that they requested Glazanof
to baptize them also; but he declared that he had no
authority to do so. A large number of these Indians
agreed to accompany the Russians on their return to
Mikhaielovsk, on condition that the guides who had

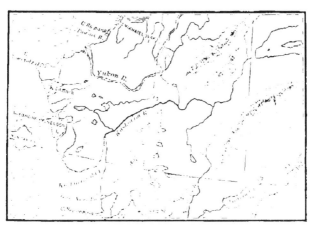

PLAN OF EXPEDITION.

accompanied them thus far be left as hostages; but
having acquired a good hold on the people, Glazanof resolved to push on to the Kuskokvim, which he reached
on the 19th of February. Here he was met by a
party of natives returning to their homes from the
Yukon. They told him that they had intended to
visit Kolmakof, but that he had returned to the Nushagak, leaving behind his interpreter Lukin. On the
following day the expedition proceeded up the Kus-

kokvim, and on the 21st arrived at the village called
Kvigym Painagmute, where they found Lukin in a
log house built by Kalmakof. Glazanof was now informed of a portage route along a tributary of the
Kuskokvim, from which it was possible in one day to
reach a stream emptying into Cook Inlet, but he tried
in vain to obtain guides to lead him in that direction.
The natives assured him that several parties of their
countrymen had been killed by the inhabitants of the
intervening mountains, and Lukin confirmed these
sensational reports, stating that he himself had failed
in a similar attempt. Glazanof then resolved to proceed alone, but being unacquainted with the country
and having lost his compass, shaped his course too
much to the north, and found himself involved in a
network of lakes and streams without provisions, and
in a country destitute of animal life at that season
of year. His men were reduced to the most cruel
straits, and obliged to eat their dog-harness, boots,
and seal-skin provision bags. Finally, after wandering about until the 19th of March, they once more
found themselves upon the banks of the Kuskokvim,
and soon afterward met Lukin, who had returned from
a journey into the mountains. Accompanied by him,
and several friendly natives who furnished them with
ample supplies, Glazanof's men at last regained the
banks of the Yukon, and thence crossed over to the
Mikhaielovsk settlement.[32]

In 1838, after Wrangell had been relieved from office, an expedition was fitted out by the Russian American Company to explore the arctic coast of America
eastward from Kotzebue Sound. A creole named
Alexander Kashevarof, a native of Kadiak, who was
thoroughly conversant with various Innuit dialects,
was appointed to command the force, the party, which
was composed mainly of creoles and Aleuts, being

[32] The time occupied by Glazanof in this remarkable journey was 104 days,
and according to his calculation the distance traversed was 1,500 miles. *Id.*,
152-60.

taken northward on the brig *Polyfem.* The skipper, who was a Russian, Chernof by name,[33] was instructed to pass through Bering Strait, to proceed thence north-eastward as far as possible, and to land Kashevarof with one bidar and five three-hatch bidarkas at the furthermost point reached by the vessel. The Eskimos living on the coast opposed Kashevarof's progress, and as he advanced slowly through the shallow sea wash-ing the arctic shore, hostile bands began to gather in rapidly increasing numbers, until, when still a hun-dred miles west of Cape Beechey, the creole found himself compelled to turn back before an armed body outnumbering the explorers twenty to one. On his return journey, he was attacked at various times, but finally regained Norton Sound, where he found Chernof awaiting him.

In the same year, Malakhof ascended the Yukon River as far as the present site of Nulato, where he built a small block-house. In want of provisions, and with only two men, he was obliged temporarily to abandon the building and repair to Mikhaielovsk for supplies. During his absence the Indians living in the neighborhood burned the building.

In 1842 Lieutenant Zagoskin of the imperial navy set forth for Norton Sound and Mikhaielovsk, purpos-ing to make an inland exploration of the northern territory. His work was confined chiefly to the mid-dle course of the Kuskokvim, and the lower course and northern tributaries of the Yukon, especially the Koyukuk, which he followed to its head waters and to the divide which separates it from the streams running into Kotzebue Sound. At Nulato he was assisted by Derzhavin in building a new fort. Zagoskin's ex-ploration was performed conscientiously and well. Wherever we find mistakes, we may ascribe them to his imperfect instruments and to local obstacles. He gathered most valuable trading statistics for the com-

[33] The sons of Chernof are now living on Afognak Island, engaged as ship-builders and navigators, and in comfortable circumstances.

pany, and ingratiated himself with all the tribes with
which he came in contact. His expedition was not
completed until 1844, when he returned to Russia to
superintend the publication of his notes.[34]

It had been Wrangell's desire to explore the arctic
coast of the Russian possessions, but complications
constantly arising with the Mexican authorities in
California required his personal attention. Figueroa,
then governor of California, had addressed to him
several letters, demanding the abandonment of the
Ross settlement. The latter always had the excuse
that he was not authorized to treat on so weighty a
subject; but when the end of his term was approaching, he received news of Figueroa's death, and resolved
to proceed homeward by way of Mexico, in order to
negotiate with the authorities at the capital of the new
republic, visiting on his way the Ross settlement. In
the harbor of San Blas he met with the company's ship
Sitka, having on board his successor, Captain Kuprianof. To him he surrendered his office, and soon afterward proceeded to Mexico. His negotiations with
the Mexican government on behalf of the Ross colony
and their failure are related in connection with my
History of California.[35]

[34] An account of this expedition will be found in *Peshekhodnaia Opiss
Chasty Russkikh Vladaniy v Amerika, Lieutenant A Zagoskin v 1842, 1843 i
1844 godakh*, or *Explorations on Foot of Parts of the Russian Possessions in
America, by Lieutenant A Zagoskin 1842-4* (in two parts, St Petersburg, 1847).
This work is a very complete description of the journeys undertaken by
Lieutenant Zagoskin of the imperial navy in the service of the Russian
American Company, between 1842 and 1844. The field of his operations
includes the territory north and east of Norton Sound and drained by the
Yukon and Kuskokvim. The entries of Zagoskin's journal are given for the
most part in full, with astronomical observations, etc., interspersed occasionally with historical sketches of various localities, and finishing with a review
of all the native tribes which came within his observation, and very complete vocabularies of their respective languages. An excellent chart is
appended to the work.
[35] Vol. iv., cap. vi. The *Statistische und Ethnographische nachrichten über
die Russischen Besitzungen*, or *Statistical and Ethnographical Statements concerning the Russian Possessions*, collected by Baron Wrangell, and edited by
E. K. von Baer, appeared in 1839 as the first volume of a series published by
the imperial academy of sciences at St Petersburg, under the title of *Beiträge
zur Kenntniss des Russischen Reiches*, or *Contributions to the Knowledge of the*

During Wrangell's administration a serious dispute arose with the Hudson's Bay Company, which was then extending its operations over the whole north-west, establishing forts at every available point on river and sea-coast, and which a few years later entirely outbid the Russian American Company in the trade of the Alexander Archipelago.   Taking advantage of the clause in the Anglo-Russian treaty of 1825, providing for the free navigation of streams crossing Russian territory in their course from the British possessions to the sea, the English company had pushed forward its trading-posts to the upper course of the Stikeen, and in 1833 fitted out the brig *Dryad* for the purpose of establishing a permanent station on that river. Information of this design had been conveyed to Wrangell during the preceding year, and he at once notified the managers at St Petersburg, asking them to induce the imperial government to rescind the clause under which the Hudson's Bay Company intended to encroach on Russian territory.   As a further motive for this request, he reported that the English company had violated the agreement to abstain from selling fire-arms and spirituous liquor to the natives.   The emperor granted the petition, and the British and United States governments were duly notified of the fact.   Both protested through their ministers at St Petersburg, but in vain; the reply of the Russian foreign office being that the objectionable clause would terminate in the following year. Without waiting to be informed of the success or failure of his application, Wrangell despatched two armed vessels, under command of Lieutenant Dionysi Zarembo, to the mouth of the Stikeen.   Here the latter established a fortified station on a small peninsula,

Russian Empire. In the preface the question is discussed whether the Alaskans were benefited or otherwise by the Russian occupation.   The first three sections contain valuable statistical and historical information.   Then follow linguistic studies by Wrangell and Kostromitinof, the journal of skipper Glazanof, the exploration of the Copper River, and the characteristics of the Aleuts, the last being by Veniaminof, and miscellaneous remarks by the editor.

the neck of which was flooded at high water, and named the fort St Dionysi.[36]

These warlike preparations remained unknown to the officials of the Hudson's Bay Company, and when the *Dryad* approached the mouth of the Stikeen, the men crowding her deck were surprised by a puff of white smoke and a loud report from the densely wooded shore, followed by several shots from a vessel in the offing. The brig was at once put about, but anchored just out of range, whereupon a boat was sent from shore carrying Lieutenant Zarembo, who, in the name of the governor of the Russian colonies and the emperor of Russia, protested against the entrance of an English vessel into a river belonging to Russian territory. All appeals on the part of the Hudson's Bay Company's agents were ineffectual. They were informed that if they desired to save themselves, their property, and their vessel, they must weigh anchor as once, and after a brief delay the *Dryad* sailed for Fort Vancouver.

The authorities of the Hudson's Bay Company lost no time in sending reports of this affair to London, accompanied with a statement that the loss incurred through this interference with their project amounted to £20,000 sterling. The British government immediately demanded satisfaction from Russia, but the matter was not finally settled until 1839, when a commission met in London to arrange the points of dispute between the two corporations, and in a few weeks solved difficulties which experienced diplomates had failed to unravel in as many years. The claim of the Hudson's Bay Company was waived on condition that the Russian company grant a lease to the former of all their continental territory lying between Cape Spencer and latitude 54° 40'. The annual rental was fixed at two thousand land-otter skins,[37] and

---

[36] This fort was built on the site of an Indian village near the town of Wrangell. The logs used for its foundation can be seen at the present day.
[37] A fur much used in the Russian army for trimming officers' uniforms.

at the same time the English company agreed to supply the colonies with a large quantity of provisions at moderate rates.[38] The abandonment of the Ross colony, whence the Russians obtained most of their supplies, was now merely a question of time, and the agreement appears to have given satisfaction to both parties, for at the end of the term the lease was renewed for a period of ten years, and twice again for periods of four years.

On the 1st of June, 1840, a salute of seven guns was fired as the British flag was hoisted from Fort St Dionysi, or Fort Stikeen, as it was renamed by Sir James Douglas, who then represented the Hudson's Bay Company, and during a previous visit had appointed John McLoughlin, junior, to the command.[39] Having arrived at Novo Arkhangelsk on April 25th of the same year, Sir James says, that "he had held daily conference with the governor in a frank and open manner, so as to dissipate all semblance of reserve, and establish intercourse on a basis of mutual confidence. The question of boundary was settled in a manner that will prevent any future misunderstanding.... They wish to sell Bodega[40] for $30,000, with a stock of 1,500 sheep, 2,000 neat-cattle, and 1,000 horses and mules, with important land fenced in, with barns, thrashing-floor, etc., sufficient to raise 3,000 fanegas of wheat. They of course cannot sell the soil, but merely the improvements, which we can hold only through a native. We concluded to write to Mr McLoughlin on this subject, so that he may write

[38] Including 14,000 pouds of wheat at 80 cents per poud, 498 of flour at $1.45, 404 each of pease and groats at 96 cents, 922 of salt beef at 75 cents, 498 of butter at $4.05, and 92 pouds of ham at 12 cents per lb. *Tikhmenef, Istor. Obos.*, i. 351. In *Finlayson's Vancouver Island and N. W. Coast*, MS., 12, it is stated that the Hudson's Bay Company also agreed to supply trading goods. Dall, *Alaska*, 338, gives 1837 as the date of the agreement, but on what authority I am unable to ascertain. The correct date is given in *Wrangell, Statist. und Ethnog.* 322 (St Petersburg, 1839), and by Tikhmenef and others.

[39] In the same year a fort was built by the Hudson's Bay Company on the Taku River. *Douglas, Jour.*, MS., 27–44; *Finlayson's Vancouver Island and N. W. Coast*, MS., 13. It was abandoned in 1843.

[40] Ross.

to Mr Etholen in reply in the autumn by the steam
vessel, or appoint an agent to settle with the commandant at Bodega."[41]   What might have been the
result if England, with her powerful navy and all-
grasping policy, had now gained a foothold in California on the eve of the gold discovery!

Almost as soon as the Hudson's Bay Company's
men had established themselves at Fort Stikeen, hostilities were commenced by the natives.   In 1840 an
attempt was made to scale the stockade; in 1841 the
Indians destroyed the aqueduct which supplied the
fort with fresh water, and the beleaguered garrison
only saved themselves by seizing one of their chiefs,
whom they held as hostage.   In the following year a
more serious attack was threatened, which would probably have been carried out successfully but for the
timely arrival of two armed vessels from Novo Arkhangelsk in charge of Sir George Simpson, the governor of the company's territories, whose statement I
will give in his own words.

"By daybreak on Monday the 25th of April, we
were in Wrangell's Straits, and toward evening, as we
approached Stikeen, my apprehensions were awakened
by observing the two national flags, the Russian and
the English, hoisted half-mast high, while, on landing
about seven, my worst fears were realized by hearing
of the tragical end of Mr John McLoughlin, jun.,
the gentleman recently in charge.   On the night of
the 20th a dispute had arisen in the fort, while some
of the men, as I was grieved to hear, were in a state
of intoxication; and several shots were fired, by one
of which Mr McLoughlin fell.   My arrival with two
vessels at this critical juncture was most opportune,
for otherwise the fort might probably have fallen a
sacrifice to the savages, who were assembled round it
to the number of about two thousand, justly thinking
that the place could make but a feeble resistance, de-

prived as it was of its head, and garrisoned by men in a state of complete insubordination." [42]

A few days later Simpson returned to Novo Arkhangelsk, in order to discuss with Etholen, who in 1840 had relieved Kuprianof as governor, [43] the difficulties constantly arising between the Russian and Hudson's Bay Company's agents with regard to trade on the Alexander Archipelago. Though Etholen was unyielding in other matters, he was quite willing to join Simpson in his efforts to suppress traffic in spirituous liquors among the Kolosh, [44] and an agreement to this effect was signed by the representatives of both companies on the 13th of May, 1842. [45] The evil was

[42] *Narr. Jour. round World.*, ii. 181. 'If the fort had fallen,' continues Simpson, 'not only the whites, 22 in number, would have been destroyed, but the stock of ammunition and stores would have made the captors dangerous to the other establishments on the coast.'

[43] He arrived in the *Nikolai I.*, which again sailed from Kronstadt for the colonies in August 1839, with a cargo worth 500,000 roubles. Etholen, who, as we have seen, had before done good service in the colonies, was accompanied by his wife, an accomplished lady, a native of Finland. Calling at Rio Janeiro, he purchased for the company a brig, which he renamed the *Grand Duke Konstantin*, and loaded her with a cargo of Brazilian produce. Both vessels arrived at Novo Arkhangelsk May 1, 1840. *Tikhmenef, Istor. Obos.*, i. 350.

[44] 'At the post on Stakhin River the Indians were buying liquor and fighting all the time among themselves just outside the fort. A big hogshead of liquor four feet high was emptied in one day on the occasion of a feast. There were always four watchmen around, in the night especially. It was terrible; but they got plenty of beaver skin.' *Mrs Harvey's Life of McLoughlin*, MS., 19-20.

[45] This document was handed as evidence to a select committee of the house of commons in June 1857. The following is a copy of the original: 'With a view effectually to guard against the injurious consequences that arise from the use of spirituous liquors in the Indian trade on the north-west coast, it is hereby agreed by Sir George Simpson, governor in chief of Rupert's Land, acting on behalf of the honorable Hudson's Bay Company, and his Excellency Adolphus Etholen, captain in the imperial navy and governor of the Russian American colonies on the north-west coast of America, acting on behalf of the Russian American Company, that no spirituous liquors shall be sold or given to Indians in barter, as presents, or on any pretence or consideration whatsoever, by any of the officers or servants belonging or attached to any of the establishments or vessels belonging to either concern, or by any other person or persons acting on their behalf on any part of the north-west coast of America to the northward of latitude 50°, unless competition in trade should render it necessary, with a view to the protection of the interests of the Hudson's Bay Company, to discontinue this agreement in so far as the same relates to or is applicable to that part of the coast southward of lat. 54° 40'; this agreement to take effect from the date thereof at New Arkhangel, or wherever else the Russian American Company have dealings with Indians on the northwest

felt in all parts of the archipelago, and nowhere more than at the capital.

"Some reformation certainly was wanted in this respect," writes Simpson, " for of all the drunken as well as of all the dirty places that I had visited, New Archangel was the worst. On the holidays in particular, of which, Sundays included, there are one hundred and sixty-five in the year, men, women, and even children were to be seen staggering about in all directions. The common houses are nothing but wooden hovels huddled together without order or design in nasty alleys, the hot-beds of such odors as are themselves sufficient, independently of any other cause, to breed all sorts of fevers. In a word, while the inhabitant do all that they can to poison the atmosphere, the place itself appears to have been planned for the express purpose of checking ventilation."

The Indian villages in the neighborhood of Novo Arkhangelsk had suffered severely a few years before, when during Kuprianof's administration the small-pox epidemic appeared for the first time among the natives of Alaska. The disease broke out in 1836, among the Kolosh tribes near the southern boundary, and was probably introduced by Indians from the British possessions. During the first year the settlement of Tongass suffered most severely, two hundred and fifty dying in a settlement numbering nine hundred inhabitants. From Tongass the contagion rapidly spread over all the Kolosh settlements of the Alexander Archipelago. The filthy dwellings of the Kolosh fostered the germs of the disease, and the mortality was appalling, fifty to sixty per cent of the population being swept away. From the outlying settlements the scourge was introduced to Novo Arkhangelsk, and here as elsewhere a large portion of the native popula-

coast, and from the date of the receipt of a copy thereof at the establishments of Takoo, Stikine, Fort Simpson, and Fort McLoughlin.' *Report on Hudson Bay Co.* (1857), 369.

tion perished, while the promyshleniki, almost as filthy as the natives in their habits, escaped with comparatively small loss. Kuprianof did all in his power to check the epidemic, enforcing vaccination wherever it could be enforced, and keeping the whole medical staff of the company in the field, surgeons, stewards, and medical apprentices. Dr Blaschke, a German, who was in charge of the medical service, stated officially that three thousand natives died before any vaccination was attempted, and that for an entire year its effect was barely perceptible.[46]

In 1838 the doctor proceeded to Unalaska in the *Polyfem*, then en route to the Arctic. The disease broke out on that island immediately after his arrival, and it was some time before the superstitious Aleuts could be made to understand that Blaschke had come among them to cure and not to kill. They consented to vaccination only after a most peremptory order had been issued by the commander of the district.[47] All the villages in the Unalaska district were

[46] Chichinof, who travelled in the Kenaï district in 1836, says that in some of the villages the inhabitants had fled, leaving only the sick and dead, the latter in various stages of decomposition. *Adventures*, MS., 29. Markof, in *Voy.* (by Sokolof), MS., 7-9, says: 'The disease came northward from the Columbia, and was carried from village to village by Kolosh traders. At one time, at Khutznu village, they found the place deserted, and dozens of corpses lying around, rotting away. They threw some earth over the bodies, and were on the point of leaving again, when an old man appeared and said that all the people who had escaped the disease had moved into a temporary camp in the woods, and that they were afraid to come to the village, but would willingly be vaccinated. When my father and a surgeon's apprentice who was doing the vaccinating had followed the old man a short distance into the woods, they found themselves surrounded by a crowd of men, including one of the most powerful shamans. The shaman was exhorting the people to save themselves and their families from certain death by killing the vaccinators and burning their bodies, and a large fire for that purpose had already been started. The surgeon's apprentice gave himself up for lost, knelt down, and began to pray and make the sign of the cross, believing himself about to die. My father, however, began to talk to the men, showed them the marks of vaccination on his own arm and on that of his companion, and called upon some of the Khutznu men, who had been to Novo Arkhangelsk, to say whether they had seen any of the Russians or creoles die of the disease.' The above statement was made in Russian to my agent, during his stay at Sitka in July 1878. Tikhmenef states that the number of deaths in all the districts was not less than 4,000, and that the epidemic disappeared in 1840. *Istor. Obos.*, i. 312. Vaccination has since been performed on all children on reaching a certain age. *Dok. Kom. Russ. Amer. Kol.*, i. 83.

[47] *Blaschke, Report* in *Morskoi Sbornik* (1848), 115-24.

visited by the vaccinators, and parties were sent on the same errand of mercy to the Alaska peninsula, to Bristol Bay, and Cook Inlet.[48] In nearly every instance the outbreak of the epidemic could be traced to the arrival of persons from sections of the colonies already affected, a circumstance which greatly increased the difficulties with which the medical men had to battle in treating and protecting the natives. From the coast villages the disease spread into the interior, decimating or depopulating entire settlements. From Bristol Bay it advanced northward to the Kuskokvim and the Yukon, and raged fiercely among the dense population of the Yukon delta and Norton Sound. To this day the islands and coasts are dotted with numerous village sites, the inhabitants of which were carried off to the last individual during this dreadful period. In many instances the dead were left in their dwellings, which thus served as their graves, and skeletons can still be found in many of these ruined habitations.

One of the effects of the small-pox epidemic was a general distress in the outlying settlements, caused by the death of so many heads of families. Large issues of provisions were made to widows and orphans for several years; and when it was reported to Etholen that in the various districts there existed many villages where only a few male youths of tender age survived to take care of the women and children, and where constant aid from the company would be required for some time to come, he framed measures for the consolidation of small villages into large central settlements, where people might help each other in case of distress. His plan was not perfected un-

[48] The villages in the Unalaska district at that time numbered nine; one on Unalaska Island, two on Akun, one each at Avatanok, Tigalda, Ulga, Unalga, and Unimak, three on the Alaska peninsula, two on Unmak, and one on each of the Pribylof Islands. The service was performed on the Alaska peninsula by surgeon's apprentice Malakhof, with one interpreter as assistant. Surgeon's apprentice Fomin, and Orlof, interpreter, were sent to Bristol Bay. A trader named Malakhof was intrusted with the vaccination on Cook Inlet. *Id.*, 116–17.

til 1844, and though it met with violent opposition
on the part of the natives who were to be benefited
by it, it was finally carried out, and fulfilled the most
sanguine expectations of the governor.

Notwithstanding the loss of life that occurred during the years 1836–1839, the population of the colonies
amounted, according to a census taken in 1841, to 7,580
souls, a decrease since 1822, when the first regular census was taken, of 706, and since 1819 of 1,439 persons.[49]
There were in 1841 714 Russians or Europeans of
foreign birth, 1,351 creoles, and 5,417 Indians.[50] Between 1830 and 1840 the number of Aleuts decreased from 6,864 to 4,007, but the loss was in part
compensated by the increase in the Russian and creole
population, the fecundity among the latter class being
much greater than among the natives, as they received
better food and clothing, and were exempt from enforced service on hunting expeditions.

Although the yield of the various hunting-grounds
decreased considerably during the second term of the
Russian American Company's existence, it was still
on a large scale. Between 1821 and 1842 there were
shipped from the colonies over 25,000 sea-otter, 458,000
fur-seal, 162,000 beaver, 160,000 fox skins, 138,000
pounds of whalebone, and 260,000 pounds of walrus
tusks.[51] At the time of Simpson's visit to the colonies in 1842, the catch of sea-otter at Kadiak, Una-

---

[49] *Dok. Kom. Russ. Amer. Kol.*, i. 40. Yermolof, in *L'Amerique Russ.*,
89, gives 11,259 as the population in 1836, without counting the Indians of
the interior, who were more or less subject to the company's authority, and
who, he says, numbered about 40,000. The St Petersburger Calendar of 1837,
p. 132, places the entire population as high as 100,000, but both these estimates are no doubt exaggerated.

[50] There were also 95 natives of the Kurile Islands. Of the Indians, 4,163
were Aleuts, 967 Kenaïtze, and 287 Chugaches. Wrangell says there were,
in 1836, 730 Russians, 1,142 Creoles, and 9,082 Indians, and points with pride
to the increase of 295 souls which had occurred during his administration.
Statist. und Ethnog., 327.

[51] Also 29,442 otter skins, 23,506 sea-otter tails, 5,355 bear, 4,253 lynx,
1,564 glutton, 15,481 mink, 15,666 sable, 4,491 musk-rat, and 201 wolf skins.
Tikhmenef, Istor. Obos., i. 327. Veniaminof, *Zapiski*, in a table at the end
of vol. ii., gives the yield of the Prybilof Islands alone, between 1817 and
1837, at 578,224 fur-seals. Of the whale fisheries mention will be made
later.

laska, and Atkha, then the principal hunting-grounds, did not exceed 1,000 a year. Of course the diminished yield was attended with a corresponding increase in price, six or seven blankets being given for a good sea-otter skin, and thirteen for the best, while as much as two hundred roubles in cash was asked for a single fur of the choicest quality.[52] Moreover, the natives were not slow to better the instruction which had accompanied the progress of civilization in the far north-west. They had learned how to cheat, and could already outcheat the Russians. "One favorite artifice," relates Simpson, "is to stretch the tails of land-otters into those of sea-otters. Again, when a skin is rejected as being deficient in size or defective in quality, it is immediately, according to circumstances, enlarged or colored or pressed to order, and is then submitted as a virgin article to the buyer's criticism by a different customer."

It is somewhat remarkable that the decline in the leading industry of the colonies and the increase in the value of furs was not attended with a corresponding reduction of dividends. Between 1821 and 1841 about 8,500,000 roubles were distributed among the shareholders,[53] or nearly double the sum disbursed during the company's first term. The directors were, however, often in sore need of funds, and sometimes could only declare a dividend by charging it to the earnings of future years. During this period the gross revenues exceeded 61,400,000 roubles, and in 1841 the capital had been increased to about 6,200,000 roubles, which was represented mainly by trading goods, provisions, material, implements, furs, sea-going vessels, and real estate in Russia, the amount of cash on hand at that date being less than 50,000 roubles.

[52] Besides this no bargain was concluded without other trifles being thrown in. *Belcher's Narr. Voy. round World*, ii. 101.

[53] A list of these dividends is given in *Tikhmenef, Istor. Obos.*, i. 378. They were paid every two years, and varied from 168 to 88 roubles per share. For 1822-3 and 1840-1 no dividends were declared.

Large quantities of furs were still exchanged at Kiakhta for teas and Chinese cloths, which were afterward sold at Moscow and at the fair at Nijinei-Novgorod, the remainder of the furs and all the walrus tusks and whalebone being marketed at St Petersburg.

The contract with the Hudson's Bay Company and the reopening of intercourse with foreigners, though limited to the port of Novo Arkhangelsk, were of great benefit to the shareholders. In 1822 and 1823, when the prohibition against foreign traffic was in force, the company suffered a clear loss of 85,000 roubles in silver, while for the two following years the dividend was the largest paid during the second term, amounting to nearly 45 silver roubles per share. Although furs were bartered with English and American skippers at half or less than half the prices current in Russia, the loss was more than counterbalanced by the cheaper rates at which provisions and trading goods could be obtained.[54] Moreover, the freight charged on the Hudson's Bay Company's vessels, accordingly to the terms of the contract, was 50 to 78 silver roubles per ton, while from Kronstadt it was 180 to 254, and by way of Siberia 540 to 630 roubles in silver. Between 1821 and 1840 twelve expeditions were despatched from Kronstadt to the colonies with supplies, and yet more than once the governor was compelled to send vessels to Chile for cargoes of breadstuffs.[55]

[54] For the inhabitants of Novo Arkhangelsk alone, and for the crews of the company's vessels sailing from that port, there were imported, in 1831, 6,000 pouds of grain, 900 of salt beef, 500 of dried beef, and a sufficient quantity of butter and other provisions. Two years later wheat flour was selling at 14 roubles a poud, salt beef at 6 to 12, butter at 28, tea at 280, white sugar at 65, and tobacco at 50 to 60 roubles a poud. *Wrangell, Statist. und Ethnog.*, 12, 24-5.

[55] *Dok. Kom. Russ. Amer. Kol.*, i. 36. The *Baikal* was sent to Chile in 1829, in charge of Etholin. Russian manufactures were then introduced for the first time into Chilian markets, and met with ready sale at profitable rates. Etholen purchased 9,340 pouds of wheat, at prices much lower than those prevailing at Okhotsk or even in California. *Tikhmenef, Istor. Obos.*, i. 344-5. Several regulations made during the company's second term, whereby expenses could be reduced, are mentioned in *Id.*, 373-4.

The expense of supporting the colonies, apart from the sums required for the home office, taxes, and other items, increased from about 676,000 roubles, scrip, in 1821, to over 1,219,000 roubles in 1841, and amounted for the whole period to nearly 18,000,000 roubles. The increase was due mainly to the necessity of establishing more stations as seal became scarce near the settlements, and of increasing the pay of employees. "The salaries of the officers," remarks Simpson during his stay at Novo Arkhangelsk, "independently of such pay as they may have, according to their rank in the imperial navy, range between three thousand and twelve thousand roubles a year, the rouble being, as nearly as possible, equal to the franc; while they are, moreover, provided with firewood and candles, with a room for each, and a servant and a kitchen between two. Generally speaking, the officers are extravagant, those of five thousand roubles and upwards spending nearly the whole, and the others getting into debt, as a kind of mortgage on their future promotion.

" For the amount of business done, the men, as well as the officers, appear to be unnecessarily numerous, amounting this season to nearly five hundred, who, with their families, make about one thousand two hundred souls as the population of the establishment.[56] Among the servants are some excellent tradesmen, such as engineers, armorers, tin-smiths, cabinet-makers, jewellers, watchmakers, tailors, cobblers, builders, etc., receiving generally about three hundred and fifty roubles a year; they have come originally on engagements of seven years; but most of them, by drinking or by indulging in other extravagance,[57] contrive

[56] These figures probably include only the employees and their families. In *Finlayson's Vancouver Island and N. W. Coast*, MS., 10, it is stated that in 1840 Sitka was garrisoned by over 500 troops.

[57] 'Spirits, which cost the company at Montreal $2 per gallon, were sold in the interior to their servants at $8 per quart. At this rate the company could not lose anything by increasing the salaries of drinking men.' *Dunn's Oregon and British N. Amer. Fur Trade*, 25 (Philadelphia, 1845).

to be so regularly in debt as to become fixtures for life." [58]

[58] In his *Narrative of a Journey round the World* during the years 1841 and 1842, Sir George Simpson gives some interesting descriptions of Novo Arkhangelsk and its inhabitants, from which I shall give one or two extracts later. He appears to have been a keen observer, and his work was evidently written without bias. Travelling as the representative of the Hudson's Bay Company, he made the journey overland from Boston to Fort Vancouver. Thence, after a visit to Novo Arkhangelsk, he sailed for California and the Sandwich Islands. Returning to Novo Arkhangelsk in the spring of 1842, he soon afterward sailed for Okhotsk, and traversing Siberia and European Russia, arrived at London in October of the same year, the entire journey occupying 19 months and 26 days.

CHAPTER XXVII.

THE RUSSIAN AMERICAN COMPANY'S LAST TERM.

1842-1866.

THE CHARTER RENEWED—ITS PROVISIONS—THE AFFAIR AT PETROPAV-
LOVSK—OUTBREAKS AMONG THE NATIVES—THE NULATO MASSACRE—
A SECOND MASSACRE THREATENED AT NOVO ARKHANGELSK—EXPLOR-
ATIONS—THE WESTERN UNION TELEGRAPH COMPANY—WESTDAHL'S
EXPERIENCE—THE COMPANY REQUESTS ANOTHER RENEWAL OF ITS
CHARTER—NEGOTIATIONS WITH THE IMPERIAL GOVERNMENT—THEIR
FAILURE—POPULATION—FOOD SUPPLIES—THE YIELD OF FURS—WHAL-
ING—DIVIDENDS—TRADE—BIBLIOGRAPHICAL.

AT the request of the directors, and after a careful investigation into the condition of the colonies,
the imperial council at St Petersburg decided, on the
5th of March,[1] 1841, to renew the charter of the
Russian American Company for a further period of
twenty years. "In the variety and extent of its
operations," declare the members of the council, "no
other company can compare with it. In addition to
a commercial and industrial monopoly, the government has invested it with a portion of its own powers
in governing the vast and distant territory over which
it now holds control. A change in this system would
now be of doubtful benefit. To open our ports to all
hunters promiscuously would be a death-blow to the
fur trade while the government, having transferred to
the company the control of the colonies, could not now
resume it without great expense and trouble, and would
have to create new financial resources for such a pur-

---

[1] *Dok. Kom. Russ. Amer. Kol.*, i. 40; the 7th according to *Tikhmenef, Istor.
Obos.*, i. 385.

pose." This opinion, together with a charter defining the privileges and duties of the company, was delivered to the tzar and received his signature on the 11th of October, 1844.

The new charter did not differ in its main features from that of 1821, though the boundary was of course changed in accordance with the English and American treaties. None of the company's rights were curtailed, and the additional privileges were granted of trading with certain ports in China, and of shipping tea direct from Shanghai to St Petersburg. The board of managers, through its agent the governor of the colonies, was recognized as the supreme power, though appeal could be made to the emperor through the minister of finance. A colonial council was established, consisting of the deputy governor and four naval officers, or officials of the company, with criminal jurisdiction in all but capital cases. Much indulgence was shown to naval, military, and civil officers, who while in the company's service received half-pay, and did not forfeit their right of promotion, their time of service being counted double.[2]

The sale of fire-arms, ammunition, and spirituous liquor to the natives was still forbidden; and this prohibition was followed by an order from the governor that no intoxicating drink should be sold in the colonies. It is related that when this order was read to the servants of the company many of them could not refrain from tears. The temperance cause had but few advocates in Russian America. One of the men, named Markof, who in 1845 sailed from Novo Arkhangelsk for San Francisco, thus relates his experience: "How easily and willingly the labor of getting the ship under way was performed! Each sailor had it in his mind that he could enjoy himself for his trouble in the first tap-room in California. In the

[2] The provisions of the charter of 1844 are given at length in *Dok. Kom. Russ. Amer. Kol.*, i. 49–60; and in *Tikhmenef, Istor. Obos.*, ii. app. part i. 11–74.

evening we could only see the outlines of our former home, traced in black, indistinct shapes against the darkening sky. 'The devil must have planted these cursed sea-otters in these out-of-the-way regions, said one of the sailors; 'as far as we can see land up and down the coast, not a single rum-shop is to be found.' 'Yes,' answered another, 'but I remember Father Baranof. There was a time when a camp-kettle was set out brimming full, and he would shout, "Drink, children!" and he would join himself in a merry song. Those were better days,' continued he, with his eyes fixed on the waning land; 'but now what times have we! We can do nothing but work, and when that is done, we promenade, or smoke in the barrack. What a life!' 'You see,' replied his comrade, 'in this country we all have to join the temperance society.' 'What is that?' 'I don't know exactly: it is some kind of a sect. I belonged to it once, but it is so long ago I forget. I can make no reckoning of time when I get no drinks to count by; but I remember we all had to pay a beaver skin apiece.' 'A beaver skin apiece! That is a big price to pay for the privilege of drinking nothing but water. I'll have nothing to do with any such sect. There was that German Mukolof; he joined the sect, and in a few weeks he was dead. God knows where he is now'—crossing himself: 'I don't think there is much room for Dutchmen in heaven; so many Russians go there.'"[8]

As soon as war between England and Russia became a certainty, representatives of the Russian American and Hudson's Bay companies met in London to consult on the exigences of the case. It was agreed that both companies should petition their governments for a convention of neutrality, that should include the Russian and English possessions on the

[8] *Ruskie na Vostotchnom*, etc., or The Russians on the Eastern Ocean (2d ed., St Petersburg, 1856), 59–60, 102–4. Markof adds that, on reaching San Francisco, the first building which they entered was a drinking-saloon, kept by one of Napoleon's veterans who had served in the campaign of 1812.

north-west coast of America, the parties being allowed to trade freely with each other, while forbearing to furnish aid to the squadrons of Russia or of the allies. The powers at war, considering this a small matter, and wishing to keep their hands free in other quarters, consented to sanction the agreement. A few English cruisers appeared at the entrance of Sitka Bay at various times, but finding no vessels of war in port, nor any evidence of a violation of the agreement, inflicted no damage.[4] The company suffered some loss, however, by the bombardment of Petropavlovsk in 1854,[5] and through its destruction in the following year, on which occasion the allies burned the government buildings, plundered the Greek-catholic church, broke all the windows in the town,[6] and captured a vessel belonging to the Russian American Company. A part of the allied forces then sailed for Ourup, and bombarded the Russian settlement on that island, burned all the buildings, seized the furs and papers belonging to the company,[7] and hoisted the union-jack, the tricolor, and a sign-post declaring that they took possession of the territory on behalf of England and France. These proceedings were sufficiently disgraceful—the most disgraceful

[4] This was either a fortunate accident or was due to the vigilance of the Russians. In 1852 the frigates *Aurora* and *Diana*, the corvette *Navarin*, and the transport *Niemen* were despatched from Kronstadt to Kamchatka. *Morskoi Sbornik*, x. 21–8. The *Diana* and a corvette (probably the *Navarin*) were expected to rendezvous at Novo Arkhangelsk. *Saint Amant. Voy. en Cal. et dans l'Oregon* (Paris, 1854), 637. At this time the fort of Novo Arkhangelsk was mounted with 70 guns, including two of very long range, and was garrisoned by 250 to 300 men, well commanded, but poorly armed. Of 483 rifles sent from Tobolsk, between 1851 and 1854, only 161 were fit for use. *Sitka Archives*, ii. 83.

[5] After the failure of the attack which followed the bombardment the English admiral Price committed suicide. When informed of this the Russians would not believe it, but ascribed his death to a well aimed shot from the shore batteries. *Morskoi Sbornik*, xlv. 1, 2, 23. By oukaz of Dec. 2, 1849, Okhotsk was closed as a naval station and the force transferred to Petropavlovsk. *Id.*, clv. 7.

[6] In *Rodgers' Letters*, MS., ii., it is stated that, in 1856, few houses were left standing at Petropavlovsk, but that the English behaved well, while the French rioted in destruction.

[7] The natives of the Kurile Islands reported sea-otter plentiful on some of the group. In 1853, 108 skins were shipped from Ourup, and 200 retained for future shipment. *Sitka Archives*, ii. 65.

affair, perhaps, of the whole war, if we except the
Sinope massacre; but yet more disgraceful was the
conduct of the English government which sanctioned
them, on the ground that the convention of neutrality
extended only to the north-west coast of America, and
not to all the company's territory.

Though no attack was made, during the war, on
the Alaskan settlements, the Russians suffered more
severely about this date from outbreaks among the
natives than at any time since the Sitka massacre.
In 1851 the fort at Nulato was surprised by Indians,
and most of the inmates butchered.   Among the vic-

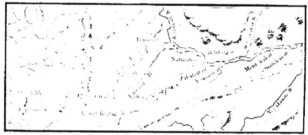

PLAN OF NULATO.

tims were the commandant Derzhavin and Lieutenant
Barnard, an English naval officer on board the *Enterprise*, despatched in search of Sir John Franklin
and his party.[8]   In that year Barnard was sent to investigate the truth of certain rumors as to the murder of a party of his countrymen near Lake Mintokh,
and in his blunt English fashion announced that he
intended to send for the chief of the Koyukans,

[8] In July 1850 the *Herald, Plover,* and *Investigator,* all despatched in search
of Franklin and his party, met in Kotzebue Sound.   While anchored off
Chamisso Island during the previous year, the captain of one of these vessels
caused search to be made for a cask of flour buried there by Beechey, 23 years
before.   It was found to be in good condition, and a dinner party was given,
at which cakes and pastry made of the flour formed part of the fare. *Seeman's
Narr. Voy. Herald,* ii. 100, 179; *Hooper's Tents of the Tuski,* 213.

named Larion, who was then holding festival at his village a few leagues distant. But, as Dall remarks, this man "was not accustomed to be sent for. When the Russians desired to see him, they respectfully requested the honor of his presence." Now Larion was a great chief, and also a shaman, and his ire was thoroughly roused at the insult. Moreover, there was another cause of provocation. One of his daughters had for some time been living with Derzhavin as a concubine. This was perfectly legitimate and seemly according to the native and even the Russian code of morals; but a second daughter had recently found favor in the eyes of the commandant, and when the shaman demanded, in person, the surrender of at least one of his children, Derzhavin coolly answered that he had at the fort a visitor, who must also be provided with a concubine. After his departure perhaps one of the damsels might be restored.

A council was called, and Larion swore that the salmon should have blood to drink before they went back to the sea. At this moment a dog-sled appeared in sight on the Yukon, by the side of which walked a Russian and a Nulato workman. Soon afterward the sled was drawn up on the bank for the purpose of cooking the mid-day meal, and while the Nulato was searching for water, a party of Indians stole up steathily behind the Russian, and stunning him with a blow on the head, beat in his skull with their clubs. His flesh was then cut in strips, roasted, and devoured, and the Koyukans set forth at once for Nulato. Half a mile from the fort were three large buildings, in which were many Nulato families. These were set on fire, and their occupants were either smothered in the smoke or fell beneath the knives and arrows of the savages, one man only making his escape to the mountains, and a few women being spared to serve as slaves.

The Koyukans then advanced on the fort, where most of the inmates were yet asleep, and all were unconscious of the impending danger. Derzhavin, who had just risen, was stabbed in the back and fell dead without a struggle. Barnard, who was reading in bed, grasped his gun and fired two shots, but each time the barrel was struck upward and the balls lodged in the ceiling, whereupon he was stabbed in the stomach, his intestines protruding from the wound. The workmen, who lived in a separate building in which were two Russians and a few creoles, had now taken the alarm and barricaded the door. Muskets were fired at the savages, but without effect, and were answered by a flight of arrows. At length one of them fell, whereupon the entire party at once took to flight, carrying with them their booty and prisoners.[9] A new fort surrounded with a stockade was built two or three years later on the spot where it now stands, and within a hundred yards of it is a cross that marks the resting-place of Barnard and Derzhavin.

In the following year a party of Kolosh destroyed the buildings at the hot springs near the Ozerskoi re-

[9] Dall, *Alaska*, 48–51, is probably the best authority on the Nulato massacre, though, as I have before remarked, he is extremely inaccurate in matters relating to the history of Alaska. I have accepted some portions of his narrative, and the remainder is taken principally from the statement of one who was present at the massacre and from which the following is an extract: 'When the Koyukans had gathered about 100 warriors they started down stream, journeying only by night. Finally they camped on the shore of a lake, about half a day's travel from the river, and the same distance from the fort. Several small parties and some women were then sent forward to the redoubt, to trade and act as spies. On the third day some of them returned, and during the night we advanced to within a short distance of Nulato. At daybreak the attack was made, our men being assisted by the spies who had remained in the fort. This was the first war-party that I had ever joined, and I was very much frightened, and fired my musket at random. When I entered the redoubt the victims were all dead, and our people were engaged in collecting the plunder, of which my share was two silver-mounted pistols and a box of beads; but afterward I heard Larion boast repeatedly that he killed both Deriabin and the English officer with his own hand, and there were none to contradict him.' This statement was made on the 15th of January, 1879, by Ivan Konnygen, a native of the village of Unalakleet, near Mikhaielovsk. My agent obtained the information from Konnygen, who was a prisoner at San Quentin, where he went by the name of Korrigan. At the time of the massacre he was a suitor for one of Larion's daughters. Tikhmenef, *Istor. Obos.*, ii. 202, mentions only three victims—Deriabin, Barnard, and one Aleut. He also states that the reason for the attack was the protection given by the Russians to some of the Nulato people who had incurred the wrath of the Koyukans. Russian authorities appear to be ill informed on this matter or to have purposely misrepresented it. In *Dok. Kom. Russ. Amer. Kol.*, i. 80, it is merely stated that the attack was repulsed.

doubt. The inmates were stripped of all that they possessed, even to their shirts, and in this plight made their way across the mountains to the capital.[10] In 1855 the Andreief station, south of Fort Michaielovsk, was destroyed by Indians, two of the company's servants being slaughtered.[11] In the same year an attack was made on Novo Arkhangelsk. The Sitkan Kolosh, without apparent provocation, fell upon a sentry who was guarding the wood-piles of the company and wounded him with spears. The governor demanded the surrender of the guilty individuals, but was answered with threats. Two cannon-shot were then fired, whereupon the savages made a rush for the fort and began to chop down the palisade. A sharp fire of musketry and artillery was opened on them, but without effect. Some tried to force themselves through the embrasures; others broke in the door of a church, built outside the stockade for the use of natives, and returned the fusillade from the windows. If the Kolosh had been in possession of a few pieces of cannon, it is not improbable that there might have been a repetition of the Sitka massacre. For two hours they stood their ground, but after losing more than a hundred of their number,[12] were forced to capitulate and give hostages to the Russians. A strict surveillance was thenceforth kept over the independent native tribes, and no serious émeutes occurred.

[10] About 5,000 roubles was distributed among them as compensation. *Sitka Archives*, ii. 107. One of them, an invalid, is supposed to have perished, as nothing was heard of him. *Ward's Three Weeks at Sitka*, MS., 43. During the same year 35 Stikeens were massacred by the Kolosh, while on a visit to Novo Arkhangelsk in sight of the town. On another occasion several of them were smothered while taking a steam bath, the Kolosh closing all the openings. *Id.*, 63–4. In October 1853 a creole and an Aleut, while hunting deer near the Ozerskoi redoubt, were murdered by Kolosh. *Sitka Archives*, ii. 69.

[11] *Tikhmenef, Istor. Obos.*, ii. 202–3. In *Id.*, 339, is a list of the stations under the control. Among them was Nulato.

[12] *Dok. Kom. Russ. Amer. Kol.*, i. 81, where it is stated that two of the defenders were killed and 19 wounded. *Tikhmenef, Istor. Obos.*, ii. 208, places the losses of the Russians at the same figures, and that of the Kolosh at 60 killed and wounded. Otherwise there is no material difference in these two accounts of the affair. A description of it is also given in the *Adventures of Zakhar Chichinof*, MS., 41–6. Chichinof was an eye-witness, as was also Charles Kruger, in 1885 a resident of San Francisco.

After his return from the colonies, Tebenkof, who succeeded Etholen as governor, published, in 1852, an atlas, in which the results were exhibited of all the explorations of the previous twelve years, together with many of former periods.[13] To mention the discoveries of all the exploring parties that were despatched during the company's third term would serve but to tax the reader's patience.[14] More interesting are the operations of the scientific corps that sailed from Stuart Island on the 17th of September, 1865, under the auspices of the Western Union Telegraph Company.

It was intended by the managers to build an overland line to Europe through Alaska, across Bering Strait, and through Siberia by way of the Amoor River.[15] The coöperation of the Russian government was obtained, and a party of explorers organized for mak-

[13] It was published in 1852, named *The North-western Coast of America, from Bering Straits to Cape Corrientes and the Atlantic Islands, with the Addition of a Few Points on the North-eastern Coast of Asia.* The maps, which numbered 39, were engraved at Novo Arkhangelsk by the creole Terentief. The discoveries up to 1842 have already been related. In 1843 two parties explored the Sustchina and Copper rivers for the purpose of extending trade with the natives. During Tebenkof's administration, explorations included the coast from Anchor Point in Kenaï Bay to Sukli Island in Chugasch Bay, the whole of Kadiak and the smaller islands to the south of it, Voskreasenski Bay, Andreianof, Afognak, Unmak, Unalaska, Shumagin, Ourup, and other islands; the shores of Baranof and Cruzof islands from Cape Ommaney to Mount Edgecumbe, Norton Bay, and Bering and Kurile straits. *Tikhmenef, Istor. Obos.,* ii. 247–8; *Dok. Kom. Russ. Amer. Kol.,* i. 98.

[14] In this connection may be mentioned the exploration of the Aleutian Islands, made by Lieutenant Gibson in the United States schooner *Fenimore Cooper,* in 1856, as mentioned in the *Rogers Letters,* MS., ii. (Washington, D. C.), Blake's survey of the Stikeen River, as related in his *Russian America,* 1–2, and Kennicott and Kirby's journeys from the Mackenzie River to the Yukon, as narrated in the *Smithsonian Reports,* 1861, 39–40, and 1864, 416–20. Kennicott was appointed director of the scientific corps, in connection with the Western Union Telegraph Company, but died a few months before the expedition set forth. *Dall's Alaska,* 4–5.

[15] The project is credited to Major Collins, to whom the Russian government gave the privilege of constructing, maintaining, and working a line from the mouth of the Amoor to the boundary between Russian territory and British America. He was allowed to erect block-houses and other necessary defences. He might cut timber, open roads, navigate rivers, and in fact do almost anything except organize a new empire. *Knox., Russ. Amer. Tel.,* 242. In 1862 a committee of the U. S. Senate reported in favor of a survey for a line via Siberia. *U. S. Sen. Com., Report,* 37th cong., 2d sess., xiii. In the same year the U. S. Minister in Russia was ordered to favor the enterprise. *U. S. Sen. Ex. Doc.,* 37th cong., 2d sess., x.

ing preliminary surveys on the American continent and in Siberia. Captain C. S. Bulkley was appointed to superintend the expedition, and for this purpose proceeded to Novo Arkhangelsk in the spring of 1865. A steamer, three barks, and other craft were purchased for the use of the members, and with the permission of the secretary of the treasury several revenue officers participated in the enterprise. One vessel sailed for British Columbia, the intention being to penetrate from the head waters of the Frazer River to those of the Yukon; another to Novo Arkhangelsk, a third to Fort Mikhaielovsk, and a fourth to the mouth of the Anadir River in Siberia. In the following year explorations were continued; but in 1867, a few months after the first pole was raised,[16] the company, after having incurred an expense of three millions of dollars, abandoned the enterprise and recalled its explorers, finding that the line could not compete with the Atlantic cable. The details of their operations do not concern the purposes of this volume, but we have some interesting descriptions, which will be mentioned later, of the condition of the Russian settlements, especially in the work of Dall, who was appointed director of the scientific corps.

I shall venture also to give a brief extract from a statement made in 1878 by Ferdinand Westdahl, who who was employed to survey Norton Sound and other points for the purpose of determining their exact position on the company's chart, and had not then heard of his recall: "We lay at Unalakleet until February, when we went into the field and continued to work on the line, putting up some 30 miles—the posts only—for we had no wire. The country is a complete bog. If you dig down on the hills there two feet, you strike ice. We dug three holes with crow-

---

[16] On the 1st of January, 1867, after breakfast, the party went out in a body and raised the first telegraph pole, ornamented with the flags of the United States, the telegraph expedition, the masonic fraternity, and the scientific corps A salute of 36 guns was fired. *Dall's Alaska*, 59.

bars. In many places we found snow 15 feet in depth to leeward of a hill. Our poles were on an average 15 feet long, but on the leeward side we had to make them 24 feet long. We should have made them all 24 or 30 feet long, but that the timber was too short. We dug them three feet into the ground, which consists of frozen dirt. In summer when the surface thawed, we found many of them, which we supposed to be very firmly erected, entirely loose.

"The men were very contented. They were of course exposed to severe cold, and we had the thermometer as low as 68° below zero, but we did not suffer in the least. We were dressed in furs like Indians, and slept in open camps. For rations we had only beans and graham flour. We also obtained seal-oil from the Indians, and sometimes frozen fish. This was just the kind of food that we needed in such a climate. When we started forth on journeys, we used to cook an entire sack of beans into bean soup. Before it was entirely cold, we would pour it into a bag, let it freeze, and take it with us. When we camped at night, we took out an axe, chopped off a little, made our fire, and our supper was ready immediately."[17]

In 1860 the general administration of the Russian American Company submitted to the minister of finance a draught of a new charter, together with a request that the privileges be renewed for a further term of twenty years, to commence from the 1st of January 1862.[18] In the following year Captain Golovnin was sent to Novo Arkhangelsk, with instructions to make a thorough investigation into the condition

[17] This statement was made to me personally, on June 7, 1878, by Mr Westdahl, on board Ellicott's steam-launch, near Anderson Island in Puget Sound.

[18] This was approved at a general assembly of shareholders. The few additional privileges and changes requested are mentioned in *Dok. Kom. Ross. Amer. Kol.*, i. 144-53, and in Politoffsky, *Istor. Obos. Ross. Amer. Kom.*, 162-3.

of the company's affairs and report thereon to the
government. His report was in the main favorable,
though suggesting many changes and containing much
adverse criticism. It was followed by a reply from
the creole Kashevarof, exposing abuses which had
hitherto been kept secret; and the statements of the
latter being indorsed by Baron Wrangell, the government refused to renew the charter, except on such
conditions as the company was not willing to accept.
In 1865 meetings of the imperial council were held at
which these conditions were determined, and in the
same year they were approved by the president and
submitted to the general administration. Some of
them were extremely unpalatable, especially those
requiring that the Aleuts and other dependent tribes
be exempt from enforced labor, and that all the inhabitants of Russian America be allowed to engage,
without distinction or restriction, in whatever industry they preferred except that of fur-hunting.[19] After
much intrigue, some concessions were obtained from
government, and a subsidy was even promised,[20]
but no satisfactory arrangement was made, though
negotiations were continued almost until the transfer
of the territory to the United States.

During the debates which occurred in congress on
the purchase question, and in the comments of the
press on the same subject, it has frequently been
stated that, in 1866, the charter of the Russian
American Company was about to expire. It had already expired on the 1st of January 1862, and about
two years later Prince Maksutof, an officer appointed
by the imperial government,[21] took charge of the company's affairs. That the renewal of the charter was
contemplated, however, appears in the following ex-

[19] The full text of the imperial council's decision is given in Politoffsky,
Istor. Obos. Ross. Amer. Kom., 147–54.
[20] *Id.*, 154–7.
[21] He commanded a battery at the attack on Petropavlovsk in 1854, and
was wounded while loading a cannon with his own hands. *Du Hailly, L'Ex-
péd. de Petropavlovsk*, in *Revue des deux Mondes*, Aug. 1, 1858.

tract from a decision of the imperial council, confirmed by its president, the grand duke Constantine, on April 2, 1866: "The company is allowed to increase its working capital by the issue of new shares, but at the final settlement of the company's business, within twenty years hence or later, all claims must be satisfied at the company's expense, without assistance from the government."

Though the abuses mentioned by Kashevarof were no doubt sufficiently culpable, it would seem that the treatment of the natives was somewhat less severe than during the two first terms of the company's existence. The number of Aleuts, which in 1840 had decreased, it will be remembered, to 4,007, was in 1860 about 4,400,[22] the entire Indian population subject to the company having increased during the same time from about 5,400 to over 7,600. Meanwhile the Russian population had increased to 784, and the creoles mustered nearly 1,700, the whole population of the colonies being about 12,000, a gain of more than 58 per cent since the census of 1841.[23]

The increase in the native population was due in part to their being better fed and housed than in former years. Though except for a scant crop of vegetables raised chiefly at Kadiak, nearly all food supplies, with the exception of fish and game, were imported, the company not only supplied fair rations of flour, fish, sugar, tea, and other provisions

[22] In 1849 it had reached 4,322, but the following year fell to 4,084. This was caused by an outbreak of the measles in the Sitka and Unalaska districts. *Dok. Kom. Ross. Amer. Kol.*, i. 131. In *Davidson's Report Coast Survey*, 1867, the number is given at 4,268. Dall, *Alaska*, 350, after an amusing exhibition of indignant philanthropy on stilts, states that their number had decreased about this date to 1,500. To point ont any more of Mr Dall's blunders in the so-called historical portion of his work is a task for which I have neither space nor inclination.

[23] *Golovnin, Obsor. Ross. Kol.*, in *Materialui*, i. app. 151. Tikhmenef, *Istor. Obos.*, ii. 264, gives the entire population in 1860 at 12,028, including 784 Russians and 1,676 creoles, the remainder being Indians. Among the Russians he includes 208 women, but most of these were probably their creole or Indian wives. His figures coincide somewhat suspiciously with those of Golovnin.

to its servants,[24] but sold flour to them at a small fixed price,[25] and often at a heavy loss.[26] Fish was of course the staple food, and was supplied to servants free of charge, those who received less than 1,000 roubles a year being allowed to draw each day their dole of bread and fish, of pease or gruel twice a week, of salt beef on holidays, and of game when it was plentiful, from the public kitchen; while married men could receive an equivalent in money.[27] The Aleuts and others employed on hunting expeditions also received a liberal supply of food and warm clothing, and were allowed higher rates for their furs.[28]

At the beginning of the company's third term, rules were established for the preservation of fur-bearing animals by a system of alternation at the various hunt-

[24] At the Mikhaielovsk redoubt they received in 1866 about 50 pounds of flour, a pound of tea, and three pounds of sugar a month, in addition to their pay of one rouble a day. *Dall's Alaska*, 12. In the *Sitka Archives*, ii. 17, 1854, it is stated that after Voievodsky's arrival, the ration of flour was increased from 40 to 60 pounds, and that to reimburse the company, two hours were added to each day's work during the summer months. Besides these rations, servants received an allowance of fish. In *Id.*, ii. 71, it is mentioned that 71,500 salmon were salted at the Ozerskoi redoubt. It does not appear that the laborer could purchase much for his wages, for according to the company's price list for 1860, woollen shirts were sold at Novo Arkhangelsk for 123 roubles a dozen, blankets for about 21 roubles each, boots of second quality for 15 roubles a pair, and tobacco at 67½ roubles a poud. *Tikhmenef, Istor. Obos.*, ii. 234–5.

[25] Five roubles (scrip) per poud for rye and common wheat flour, and 10 for fine white flour. The company refused to sell it, or sold it in very small quantities, to those who were not in their service, on the ground that they were compelled to keep on hand a two-years supply. *Golovnin, Obsor. Ross. Kol.*, in *Materialui*, 56.

[26] In 1856 rye flour imported from Russia cost the company 9.42 roubles per poud, in 1857, 7.05, and in 1859, 6.47 roubles (scrip). Of course breadstuffs were obtained at cheaper rates when California began to export cereals.

[27] Beef from Ayan sold in the colonies at 25 kopeks, or 5 cents, per pound, and even at that price was beyond the means of the poor, at least of the poor who had families. California salt beef sold for about double that price. Hogs were raised to some extent, but as they were fed mainly on fish, their meat was unsavory. Chickens, also fed partly on fish, sold at Novo Arkhangelsk for 5 to 7 roubles each, and eggs at about 6 roubles a dozen. Rum was issued to the servants at the rate of eight gills a year; but after fatiguing labor and in bad weather a further allowance was issued, so that they usually received one or two gills a week. When one had need of a laborer or craftsman, he would usually pay in rum, which could be obtained by those in office for one tenth of the price at which it was given in payment. Thus, for making a pair of boots, a bottle of rum which had cost only 3½ roubles, would often be accepted in lieu of 30 or 35 roubles, scrip. *Id.*, 58–9.

[28] A table of the prices paid by the company between 1836 and 1855 is given in *Id.*, app. 180–5.

ing-grounds, those which were threatened with exhaustion being allowed to lie undisturbed for a period of ten years. The increase which occurred after this regulation in the number of fur-seals was remarkable, especially at the Prybilof group. In 1851, 30,000 could be killed annually at St Paul Island alone, and in 1861 as many as 70,000, without fear of exhausting the supply. Between 1842 and 1861 shipments of furs from the colonies included about 25,600 sea-otter, 338,600 fur-seal, 161,000 beaver, and 129,600 fox skins.[29] It will be observed that these figures show a considerable decrease from the quantity forwarded during the period 1821–1842. This was caused mainly by the encroachments of foreign traders, and especially of American whaling-vessels, whose masters often touched at various points in the Russian possessions during their voyage, and paid much higher prices for furs than those fixed by the company's tariff. Another reason was the growth of intertribal traffic, clothing worn by the natives far in the interior and made up by Aleutian women being bartered for small skins, oil, and bone.[30]

In 1826 Chistiakof wrote to the directors, asking that an experienced whaler be sent to the colonies.

[29] Id., app. 158 et seq. During the company's third term the supply of fox skins became much smaller and their quality poorer. Etholen forbade shooting them in the Unalaska and Kadiak districts, though traps might still be used. Tikhmenef, Istor. Obos., ii. 219. Ward, Three Weeks in Sitka, MS., 28(1853), says that about 50,000 skins a year were received at the warehouse in Novo Arkhangelsk. From Kadiak, shipments between 1842 and 1861 included 5,809 sea-otter, 85,381 beaver, 14,298 sable skins, and 1,296 pouds of walrus tusks. From St Paul Island, during the same period, there were shipped 277,778 fur-seal, 10,508 fox skins, and 104 pouds of walrus tusks. Tikhmenef, Istor. Obos., ii. 190,200. For the quantities forwarded from other points, see Id., ii. 179, 181 6, 226. Probably the largest cargo of furs ever shipped from the colonies was that of the Cesarevitch, despatched from Novo Arkhangelsk to Ayan in 1857. It contained 458 packages, was valued 2,004,919 roubles, and insured by the company's agent in London for £100,000. Sitka Archives (1857), i. 169, 243.

[30] In Whymper's Trav. and Advent. in Alaska, 162, it is stated that this trade was carried on by the Tchuktchis, who crossed from Siberia by way of Bering Strait, and exchanged their reindeer skins for these commodities with the Kaneaks and Malemutes, whom they met at Port Clarence. Mr Whymper did not seem to be aware that the Tchuktchis or Chugasches and the Malemutes both belonged to the family of Koniagas. For a description of these tribes, see my Native Races, passim.

No further steps were taken in the matter until 1833, when an American named Barton arrived at Novo Arkhangelsk, under a five-years contract to engage in this industry, and to instruct the natives in harpooning and in rendering oil. He met with little success, for the method employed by the Aleuts of shooting the whales with spears or arrows, and waiting until the carcass was washed ashore, was found easier and less dangerous. Moreover, the company had neither funds nor vessels to spare for the active prosecution of this industry, as trade with California and the Hawaiian Islands was now on a large scale, and severely taxed the company's resources. For several years, therefore, the whale-fisheries were left in the hands of foreigners, since without the coöperation of the Russian government the directors had no power to prevent their intrusion.

In 1842 Etholen transmitted a report from Captain Kadlikof, commanding the company's ship *Naslednik Alexandr*, wherein the latter stated that he had spoken an American whaler north of the Aleutian Islands, and had learned from the captain that he had sailed together with 30 other whalers for Bering Sea. He also mentioned that, the preceding year, he had been in the same waters with 50 other vessels, and that he alone had killed 13 whales, yielding 1,600 barrels of oil. Upon this report Etholen based a request that the imperial government should send armed cruisers for the preservation of Bering sea as a *mare clausum*. Etholen's efforts were assisted by the board of managers, but did not meet with immediate success, the minister for foreign affairs replying that the treaty between Russia and the United States gave to American citizens the right to engage in fishing over the whole extent of the Pacific Ocean. Etholen, however, would not allow the matter to rest, but continued his correspondence on the subject, urging that so lucrative an industry should be placed in the hands of Russians, instead of being left entirely to Americans.

The government at length referred the matter to a committee, composed of officals of the navy department, who reported that the cost of fitting out a cruiser for the protection of Bering Sea against foreign whalers would be 200,000 roubles in silver, and the cost of maintaining such a craft 85,000 roubles a year. To this a recommendation was added that if the company were willing to assume the expenditure, a cruiser should at once be placed at their disposal. Though the directors would not consent to this outlay, complaints of the doings of American whalers were forwarded from time to time, referring chiefly to the practice of landing on the Aleutian Islands and other portions of the coast for the purpose of trying out blubber, on which occasions a wanton destruction of fuel took place, causing great hardship to the inhabitants, who depended entirely on the scant supplies of drift-wood. It was not until 1850 that an armed corvette was finally ordered to cruise in the north Pacific.

In the mean time Tebenkof took up the matter, and forwarded proposals to the company for the establishment at various points of whaling stations, provided with whale-boats and improved appliances, and in charge of experienced American whalers to be engaged by the company for a term of years. In the year 1850 it was estimated that 300, and in later years as many as 500 or 600 whalers annually visited the Arctic Ocean, the Okhotsk and Bering seas,[31] and Alaskan waters, carrying off the stores of dried fish reserved for hunting parties, and bartering liquor, arms, and powder with the natives for furs. In 1849 a whaling enterprise was established at Åbo under the name of the Russian Finland Whaling Company, with a capital of 200,000 roubles in silver, one half of which was

---

[31] In 1854 there were 525; in 1855, 468; in 1856, 366; and in some years 600 foreign whalers. *Dok. Kom. Ross. Amer. Kol.*, i. 116. In *Seeman's Narr. Voy. Herald* (London, 1853), ii. 94, it is stated that in 1849–50 the American whaling fleet in the Arctic consisted of 290 vessels, with 8,970 seamen, and that the catch yielded about $6,367,000 worth of oil and $2,075,000 worth of bone.

furnished by the Russian American Company. The
corporation received from the government a donation
of 20,000 roubles, and a premium of 10,000 roubles
each for the first four vessels equipped for this purpose,
and was permitted to import material, implements,
and stores, and to export its products, duty free, for a
period of twelve years.[32]

During the few years of the Russian Finland
Whaling Company's existence, six vessels were fitted
out, but the losses incurred and the difficulty in selling cargoes during the war with England and France
caused the enterprise to prove unprofitable.[33]   In 1854
the shareholders resolved to go into liquidation, and
were enabled to settle their liabilities in full by a
special grant from the imperial treasury, made on
account of losses incurred during the war.   Thus the
whale fisheries were again left in the hands of foreigners, who, before long, caused their entire destruction
in the sea of Okhotsk.

In consequence of the political complications then
arising in Europe, no successor was appointed at the
close of Tebenkof's administration in 1850, until four
years later, when Captain Voievodsky was elected
governor.   He was succeeded in 1859 by the mining
engineer Furuhelm, the interval between Tebenkof

[32] *Sgibnef*, in *Morskoi Sbornik*, ciii. 8, 89, 90; *Tikhmenef, Istor. Obos.*, ii.
app. 1-11, where further particulars of the charter are given.   The value of
every tenth whale killed was to be delivered to the Russian American Company, to reimburse the natives for the loss caused by this enterprise.

[33] The *Suomi*, the first of the company's ships, a 500-ton vessel built at
Abo and fitted out in Bremen, obtained, during her cruise in 1853, 1,500
barrels of oil and 21,400 lbs. whalebone.   Her cargo was sold for 80,000 roubles, yielding a profit of 13,600 roubles.   The second one, the *Turko*, secured
only one whale during her first cruise, but in the following year was more
successful.   In 1854 the *Aian* wintered at Petropavlovsk, being intended to
sail with the *Turko* for Bremen, but was captured and burnt by the allied
fleet.   *Tikhmenef, Istor. Obos.*, ii. 139–53; *Morskoi Sbornik*, xxiii. 5, 29–30;
Sitka Archives (1854), ii. 110. Tikhmenef gives a full description of the operations of the Russian Finland Whaling Company.   In the *Morskoi Sbornik*,
xxiii. 4, 45, 47, it is stated that in 1854 a private whaling company was
established at Helsingfors under the auspices of the Russian American Company, and despatched a brig to Kamchatka by way of New Zealand.   We
have no further details of its operations.

and Voievodsky's administrations being filled by the
temporary appointment of lieutenants Rosenburg
and Rudakof, who managed the company's affairs
during the first years of the Russo-Turkish war.

Notwithstanding some unfavorable features and the
interruption to trade caused by the war of 1853, there
was a considerable increase in dividends during the
company's last term, the amount disbursed being about
10,210,000 roubles, a gain of nearly 17 per cent
over the sum distributed in the previous twenty
years. At the close of the term the fixed and working capital of the company amounted to more than
13,600,000 roubles.[34] The receipts from all sources
exceeded 75,770,000 roubles, of which amount over
23,755,300 was required for the support of the colonies, and nearly 11,366,000 roubles for the general
administration, including, among other items, pensions
and rewards to officials and servants.[35]

The entire amount received from sales of tea, which,
as in former years, was mainly purchased at Kiakhta
and marketed in Russia, exceeded 27,000,000 roubles.
The profits on these transactions were greatly reduced
when, on the application of a few Moscow manufact-
urers, a rule was established that the company's agents
should be required to accept Russian manufactured
goods in part payment; the more so as these were
always of inferior quality. Between 1835 and 1841
the company's profits on each chest of tea were from

---

[34] The items and also the rate of each year's dividend are given in *Tikh-menef, Istor. Obos.*, ii. 281-2, and are in silver roubles, but have been reduced to roubles in scrip, as this kind of money is the one usually mentioned in the text of this volume. The figures given in *Dok. Kom. Ross. Amer. Kol.*, i. 100, differ somewhat from Tikhmenef's.

[35] A colonial pension fund was created in 1851 by a tax on the sale of liquor, but about two years later there was a deficit, which was made good by an appropriation from the company. *Sitka Archives*, 1854, ii. 85. Rewards were on a liberal scale. For 1853 they amounted at Novo Arkhangelsk alone to 26,555 roubles. *Id.*, 73. The total number of the company's servants on the 1st of January, 1861, including a portion of the Siberian line battalion, was 847. *Golovnin, Obsor. Ross. Kol.*, in *Materialui*, app. 145. This of course does not include the hunters. Ward states that the governor received 35,000 roubles a year, and his assistant 12,000. *Three Weeks in Sitka*, MS., 79.

187 to 300 roubles; in 1845 it was less than 23 roubles. The loss fell entirely on the company, or more probably on the company's servants. Two years after permission was given to send cargoes of tea from Shanghai to Russia, annual shipments were made of 4,000 chests; and yet cloths manufactured at Moscow could be bought cheaper at Shanghai than in the former city.[36]

The discovery of gold in California was of course followed by a marked revival of trade with that country. One cargo of almost worthless goods, that had been in the company's storehouses for years, was disposed of in San Francisco at fabulous rates. Other ventures were less successful, though most of them were profitable.[37] In 1851 a party of San Francisco capitalists, among whom were Messrs Sanderson and J. Mora Moss, made a contract with Rosenberg for 250 tons of ice to be shipped from Novo Arkhangelsk at $75 per ton. The shipment was made in February 1852, and in October of the same year the price was reduced to $35 per ton, and the quantity forwarded increased to 1,000 tons, a contract to this effect being made for three years. Later the price was further reduced and the quantity again increased. Between 1852 and 1859 there were shipped from Novo Arkhangelsk 13,960 tons, and from Kadiak 7,403 tons.[38] The ice was procured from two lakes, one of them near Novo Arkhangelsk and the other on Wood Island, near Kadiak, five buildings being erected for its storage[39] with a total capacity of 12,000 tons.[40]

[36] Dok. Kom. Ross. Amer. Kol., i. 99; Golovnin, Obsor. Ross. Kol., in Materialui, 121-2. The company was allowed to ship tea by water only on condition that they would not undersell the Kiakhta merchants.

[37] There was also a small but profitable trade with New York during the company's third term. In 1857, 7,500 fur-seals and 4,000 beaver skins were shipped to that port. Sitka Archives, i. 308.

[38] An account of each year's shipments is given in Id., 186-8. It is there stated that 20,554 tons were sold in San Francisco, netting $121,956.

[39] Three at Novo Arkhangelsk and two at Kadiak, all built in 1852-3. Sitka Archives, i. 188. In Id., 9, it is stated that one ice-house was built in each of the years 1852, 1853, and 1856. Ward, in his Three Weeks in Sitka, MS., 10, says that an ice-house was built in 1853 at the edge of the lake, but mentions no other.

[40] According to the opinion of an American engineer in the company's em-

Rails were laid to connect the ice-houses with the
wharves, these being the first tracks constructed in
Russian America. I append in a note[41] a few remarks

ploy, the lake on Wood Island alone could furnish 30,000 tons a year. *Tikhmenef, Istor. Obos.*, ii. 198.

[41] Among the principal sources of information as to the affairs of the Russian American Company, may be mentioned first the *Doklad Komiteta ob
Ustroistva Russkikh Amerikanskikh Koloni*, or Report of the Committee on
the Reorganization of the Russian American Colonies, St Petersburg, 1863–
4, 2 vols. The question of what was to be done with the Russian possessions
in America at the expiration of the absolute control of the Russian American
Company was referred to a mixed committee of fourteen, composed of government officials, men of science, and members of the company. This committee presented an elaborate report based upon the information they had
gathered from the works of Khlebnikof, Tikhmenef, and others, and from
private individuals, which was published in the present work, together
with the following additional documents: 1. A separate opinion of Actual State Counsellor Kostlivtzof, a member of the committee; 2. Explanations as to the conclusions of the committee by the general administration of the Russian American Company; 3. A letter of a member of the
general administration, Admiral Etholin; 4. A communication from the general administration on the financial condition of the company; 5. Report of
an inspection of the Russian American colonies in 1860 and 1861 by Kostlivtzof; 6. Report on the same subject by Captain Golovnin; 7. Remarks of
the general administration on Kostlivtzof's report; 8. Reply of the company
to the opinion of the minister of marine concerning its privileges; 9. Letter
on the same subject by Adjutant General Wrangell, member of the privy
council; 10. Letter of Furuhilm on the mining interests of the Russian
American colonies; 11. Letter of Captain Wehrman on the condition of the
Russian American Company and the trade with the arctic regions; 12. Extracts from a communication of the company to the committee on the organization of the Russian American colonies. The work has few historical data
not contained in the work of Tikhmenef, but throws light on the circumstances which led to the sale of Alaska to the United States, and is probably
more reliable in matters of detail.

At the time when the third term of the exclusive privileges granted to the
Russian American Company was about to expire, the subject of renewing or
revoking its charter was generally discussed, both in commercial and government circles. Tikhmenef undertook the task of compiling a complete history
of the colonies and of the company, and as he was afforded every facility by
the directors, the different departments of the government, and the holy synod,
he succeeded admirably. The work covers a period of 75 years, and is
enriched with a large number of verbal copies of original documents and letters by Baranof, Shelikof, Ioassaff, Rezanof, and others who played a prominent part in the development of the Russian colonies in America. The various
imperial edicts and charters of the company are also given in full, as well as
comprehensive statistics of population, commerce, and industries. The volumes are handsomely printed, and adorned with excellent charts, steel en-
gravings, and autographs of Shelikof, Baranof, and Rezanof. It is entitled
Istoricheskoie Obosrenie Obrazovania Rossiysko Amerikanskoi Kompani, or
Historical Review of the Origin of the Russian American Company (2 vols.,
St Petersburg, 1861). Of the *Materialui dlia Istori Russkikh Zasseleni*, or
Material for the History of the Russian Settlements, mention has before
been made.

The *Kratkoie Istoricheskoie Obozrénie Obrazovania i deistvy Rossiisko-Amer-
ikanskoi Kompani s'samago Nachala Uchrezdenia Onoi i do Nastoiastcharo
Vremeni*, or Short Historical Account of the Establishment and Operations
of the Russian American Company from its First Beginning down to

of a bibliograhical nature on authorities for annals of the company.

the Present Time, by Lieutenant General Politoffsky (St Petersburg, 1861), covers only the ground occupied by Tikhmenef and others, but in a later edition contains the negotiations between the company and the imperial government, not to be found in any of the authors quoted in this volume. The above authorities together with Khlebnikof, Veniaminof, and Zavalishin are the principal sources of information concerning the Russian American Company, apart from the Sitka and Alaska archives, though many items of interest may be gleaned from Markof, Davidof, Lisiansky, Wrangell, Belcher, Simpson, and from the manuscripts quoted in this volume.

Worthy of mention also is the *Khronologicheskaia Istoria Otkrytia Aleutskikh Ostrovov ili Podvigi Rossiyskago Kupechestva ss Prisovokupleniem Istoricheskago Izvestia o Miakhovoi Torgovla*, or Chronological History of the Discovery of the Aleutian Islands or the Achievements of the Russian Merchants, with an additional Historical Review of the Fur Trade. (Gretsch Printing Office, St Petersburg, 1823.) The author of this work, who is not named on the title-page, is Vassili Berg, and the volume is dedicated to the vice-admiral and chief of the naval staff of his imperial Majesty, Anton Vassilievitch Von Moller. The writer, who was a member of the Imperial Academy of Sciences, has collected with great care and arranged chronologically the accounts of all voyages of Russian fur traders and hunters from Okhotsk and Kamchatka to the islands and coasts of Bering Sea, between 1743 and 1805, as found in the original journals and archives of Siberian towns.

CHAPTER XXVIII.

ALASKA AS A UNITED STATES COLONY.

1867–1883.

MOTIVES FOR THE TRANSFER BY THE RUSSIAN GOVERNMENT—NEGOTIA-
TIONS COMMENCED—SENATOR COLE'S EFFORTS—THE TREATY SIGNED
AND RATIFIED—REASONS FOR AND AGAINST THE PURCHASE—THE TER-
RITORY AS AN INVESTMENT—ITS FORMAL CESSION—INFLUX OF AMER-
ICAN ADVENTURERS—MEASURES IN CONGRESS—A COUNTRY WITHOUT
LAW OR PROTECTION—EVIL EFFECT OF THE MILITARY OCCUPATION—
AN EMEUTE AT SITKA—FURTHER TROUBLES WITH THE NATIVES—THEIR
CAUSE—HOOTCHENOO OR MOLASSES-RUM—REVENUE—SUGGESTIONS FOR
A CIVIL GOVERNMENT—WANT OF MAIL FACILITIES—SURVEYS AND EX-
PLORATIONS.

FROM the day on which the term of the Russian
American Company's third charter expired, the great
monopoly ceased to enjoy, except on sufferance, any
rights or privileges other than those common to all
Russian subjects. It retained, of course, its personal
property and the real estate actually in use, but after
the company refused to accept the terms of the imperial government, operations were continued only
pending the disposition of its effects and the winding-
up of its affairs. Expenses were curtailed, some of
the trading posts abandoned, and the control of the
colonies placed in charge of an officer appointed by
the company.

But Russia had no desire to retain control of this
territory, separated as it was from the seat of government by a wide tract of tempestuous ocean and by
the breadth of her vast empire. Long before the
Crimean war, the question had been mooted of plac-

ing Alaska under imperial rule, but it was decided that the expense of protecting this vast territory, and of maintaining there the costly machinery of a colonial government, was not justified by the prospect of an adequate return.   The bombardment of Petropavlovsk and other incidents of the war had confirmed this impression, and the day seemed not far distant when the long-threatened struggle would begin with England for supremacy in central Asia.   In such an event Russia would need all her resources.   Already her railroads had been built and her wars conducted mainly with borrowed capital.   In case of another war with the greatest moneyed power and the greatest maritime power in the world, neither men, ships, nor money could be spared for the protection of Russian America.   Moreover, Russia had never occupied, and had never wished to occupy, this territory. For two thirds of a century she had been represented there, as we have seen, almost entirely by a fur and trading company under the protection of government. In a measure it had controlled, or endeavored to conrol, the affairs of that company, and among its stockholders were several members of the royal family; but Alaska had been originally granted to the Russian American Company by imperial oukaz, and by imperial oukaz the charter had been twice renewed. Now that the company had declined to accept a fourth charter on the terms proposed, something must be done with the territory, and Russia would lose no actual portion of her empire in ceding it to a republic with which she was on friendly terms, and whose domain seemed destined to spread over the entire continent.

The exact date at which negotiations were commenced for the transfer is difficult to determine; but we know that at Kadiak it was regarded almost as a certainty not later than 1861,[1] and that at Washington

---

[1] According to Chichinof, *Adventures*, MS., 48, the manager of this district declared that arrangements with the United States were almost com.

it was discussed at least as early as 1859. In December of the latter year, during Buchanan's administration, Mr Gwin, then senator for California, held several interviews with the Russian minister, in the course of which he stated, though not officially, that the United States would be willing to pay five million dollars for Alaska. The assistant secretary of state also affirmed that the president was in favor of the purchase, and that if a favorable answer were returned by the Russian government, he would lay the matter before the cabinet. A few months later a despatch was received from Prince Gortschakof stating that the sum offered was entirely inadequate; but that the minister of finance was about to inquire into the condition of the territory, after which Russia would be in a condition to treat.[2]

On the 1st of January, 1860, the company's capital was estimated at about four million four hundred thousand dollars,[3] but it was represented almost entirely by furs, goods, real estate, improvements, and sea-going vessels, which would realize, of course, but a small part of the value placed on them. In view of this fact, and of the uncertainty as to the renewal of the charter, it is not improbable that a positive offer of five million dollars might have been accepted, but for the outbreak of the civil war, which for several years put an end to further negotiations.

Among those who most desired the transfer were the people of Washington Territory, many of whom had been employed in the fisheries of the British provinces, and wished for right of fishery among the rich salmon, cod, and halibut grounds of the Alaskan coast.[4] In the winter of 1866 a memorial was adopted

pleted, but nothing more was heard of the matter at Kadiak until a few weeks before the transfer occurred.

[2] *Sumner's Speech, Cess. Russ. Amer.*, 8 (Washington, 1867). Sumner remarks that Buchanan employed as his intermediary a known sympathizer with slavery, and one who afterward became a rebel.

[3] Politoffsky, *Istor. Obos. Ross. Amer. Kom.*, 162, gives it at 5,907,859.08 roubles, silver.

[4] In *Rept. Com. For. Aff.* in *House Com. Rept.* 40th cong. 2d sess., No. 37,

by the legislature of this territory, "in reference to the cod and other fisheries,"[5] and after being presented to the president, was delivered to the Russian minister, with some comments on the necessity of an arrangement that would avoid difficulties between the two powers.

A few weeks later other influences were brought to bear. The lease of territory which, it will be remembered, had been granted by the Russian American Company to the Hudson's Bay Company in 1837, and several times renewed, would expire in June 1868. Could not the control of this valuable slip of earth be obtained for a trading company to be organized on the Pacific coast, together with a license to gather furs in portions of the Russian territory? Mr Cole, senator for California, sought to obtain these privileges on behalf of certain parties in that state, and thus, as Sumner remarks, "the mighty Hudson's Bay Company, with its headquarters in London, was to give way to an American company, with its headquarters in California." The minister of the United States at St Petersburg was addressed on the subject, but replied that the Russian American Company was then in correspondence with the Hudson's Bay Company as to the renewal of their lease, and that no action could be taken until some definite answer were received. Meanwhile the Russian minister at Washington,[6] with whom Cole had held several interviews, returned to St Petersburg on leave of absence, promising to do his best to maintain friendly relations between the two powers.

If at this juncture a prompt and satisfactory an-

p. 11, it is stated that the people of Washington Territory 'entered into competition unsuccessfully with the subjects of Great Britain and Russia, who had obtained from their respective governments a virtual monopoly of the seas and coast above the parallel of 49° north latitude.' The committee did not seem to be aware that the Russians made little use of their fisheries except for local consumption, and that even the whale-fisheries were mainly in the hands of Americans.

[5] A copy of it is given in *Sumner's Speech*, 8-9.

[6] Baron Edward de Stoeckl.

HIST. ALASKA. 38

swer had been returned by the Hudson's Bay Company, Alaska might at this day have been one of the numerous colonies of Great Britain, instead of being, as in fact it became for a time, the only colony belonging to the United States. But no answer came, or none that was acceptable; nor at the beginning of 1867 had any agreement been made by the Russian American Company with the imperial government as to the renewal of its charter.

In February of this year, when the Russian minister was about to return to Washington, the archduke Constantine gave him power to treat for the sale of the territory. On his arrival, negotiations were at once opened for this purpose. On the 23d of March he received a note from the secretary of state offering to add, subject to the president's approval, two hundred thousand dollars to the sum of seven million dollars before proposed, on condition that the cession be "free and unencumbered by any reservations, privileges, franchises, grants, or possessions by any associated companies, whether corporate or incorporate, Russian or any other."[7] Two days later an answer was returned, stating that the minister believed himself authorized to accept these terms. On the 29th final instructions were received by cable from St Petersburg. On the same day a note was addressed by the minister to the secretary of state, informing him that the tsar consented to the cession of Russian America for the stipulated sum of seven million two hundred thousand dollars in gold. At four o'clock the next morning the treaty was signed by the two parties without further phrase or negotiation. In May the treaty was ratified,[8] and on June 20, 1867, the usual proclamation was issued by the president of the United States.

---

[7] *William H. Seward's Letter to Edward de Stoeckl*, in *Rept.*, ut supra, 52.

[8] On May 27th, or according to the Russian calendar, on May 15th, Seward received from Stoeckl, who was then at New York, a despatch, stating that the treaty had been ratified at St Petersburg. On the 28th Stoeckl was in Washington, and on the same day the treaty was ratified by the government of the United States. *Rept.*, ut supra, 53.

Such in brief is the history of this treaty, which for years was published and republished, discussed and rediscussed, throughout the United States.[9] As there is no principle involved, nor any interesting information connected therewith, it is not necessary here to enter upon an analysis or elucidation of these discussions. The circumstances which led to the transfer are still supposed by many to be enshrouded in mystery, but I can assure the reader that there is no mystery about it. In diplomatic circles, even so simple a transaction as buying a piece of ground must not be allowed consummation without the usual wise winks, whisperings, and circumlocution.

Some of the reasons which probably induced Russia to cede her American possessions have already been mentioned. The motives which led the United States government to purchase them are thus stated in a report of the committee on foreign affairs, published May 18, 1868: "They were, first, the laudable desire of citizens of the Pacific coast to share in the prolific fisheries of the oceans, seas, bays, and rivers of the western world; the refusal of Russia to renew the charter of the Russian American Fur Company in 1866; the friendship of Russia for the United States; the necessity of preventing the transfer, by any possible chance, of the north-west coast of America to an unfriendly power;[10] the creation of new industrial interests on the Pacific necessary to the supremacy of our empire on the sea and land; and finally, to facilitate and secure the advantages of an unlimited American commerce with the friendly powers of Japan and China."

Here we have probably a fair statement of the case in favor of the purchase question, howsoever senseless

[9] Copies of it are to be found in *Mess. and Doc. Dept. State*, I., 40th cong. 2d sess. 388–90, in *Dall's Alaska*, 360–2, among other works, and in countless newspapers and periodicals.

[10] In *Sumner's Speech*, 10–11, is a clear and logical discussion on the relation of former treaties between England and Russia as to the transfer of Alaska; and in *Hansard, Deb.* ccxv. 1487–8, and ccxvi. 1157 (1867), are some remarks made in the British House of Commons on this point.

and illogical some of the reasons cited may appear.
On the other side, we have some cogent arguments in
the minority report, where it is remarked that "a contract
is entered into by the president, acting through the secretary of state, to purchase of the Russian government
the territory of Alaska. The contract contained stipulations which were well understood by Baron Stoeckl,
the agent of the Russian government. Those stipulations were such as the negotiators could not enforce,
but which were necessary to be complied with before
the treaty could become valid or binding. The stipulations were, first, that the treaty should be ratified
by the senate; and second, that the legislative power
should vote the necessary appropriation. The first
stipulation was complied with, and the second is the
one now being considered. Each stipulation was independent of the other, and required independent powers to carry it into execution. The treaty-making
power can no more bind congress to pass a law than
congress can bind it to make a treaty. They are
independent departments, and were designed to act as
checks rather than be subservient to each other.

"As was well said by Judge McLean,...'a treaty
is the supreme law of the land only when the treaty-
making power can carry it into effect. A treaty
which stipulates for the payment of moneys under-
takes to do that which the treaty-making power cannot do; therefore, the treaty is not the supreme law
of the land. A foreign government may be presumed
to know that the power of appropriating money belongs to congress.'"[11]

The unseemly haste with which the treaty was con-
summated, and the reluctance with which the purchase
money was afterward voted by congress, add to the
pertinence of these remarks; and the mistrust as to
the expenditure of public funds was not dispelled by

[11] In the minority report it is complained that in answer to a resolution
that all correspondence and information in possession of the executive be laid
before the house of representatives, 300 pages mainly of irrelevant matter
were produced.

the report of the committee on public expenditure published at Washington in February 1869.[12] Moreover, it was well known to all American citizens that the president of the United States, or his representative, had no more right to use the public money for the purchase of Alaska without a vote of congress, than had the queen of England to demand from her people the price of her daily breakfast without the consent of parliament.

Nevertheless, experience has proved that the territory was well worth the sum paid for it, though at first it was believed to be almost valueless. And this is the real reason of the purchase; it was thought to be a good bargain, and so it was bought, though cash on hand was not over plentiful at the time. A special agent of the treasury, in a report dated November 30, 1869, estimates the compounded interest of the purchase money for twenty-five years at $23,701,792.14, and adds to this sum $12,500,000 as the probable expense, caused by the transfer, to the army and navy departments for the same period, thus making the total cost, including the principal, $43,401,792.14 for the first quarter of a century. He is of opinion, however, that $75,000 to $100,000 a year might be derived from what he terms the 'seal-fisheries,' and perhaps $5,000 to $10,000 from customs. "As a financial measure," he remarks, "it might not be the worst

---

[12] In this report we have a copy of the treasury warrant delivered to Stoeckl, and of his receipt. From the statements of all the witnesses, no evidence of bribery was elicited when the facts were sifted from rumor and hearsay, unless the offer by the Russian minister of $3,000 in gold to the principal proprietor of the *Washington Daily Chronicle*, and the payment of $1,000 in greenbacks to a representative of the California press, be so regarded. The fees paid to counsel were very moderate. William H. Seward, one of the witnesses, denied most emphatically 'all knowledge whatever of any payments or distribution of any part of said money other than to the representative of the Russian government, or of any payments other than trifling sums for printing, purchasing, and distributing documents by and from the state department pertaining to Alaska.' Such a statement, however, proves nothing, as there were doubtless several thousand others, at Washington and elsewhere, who knew of no bribery or corruption in the matter. In the *Bancroft Library Scraps*, and in *Honcharenko's Scrap Book*, i. passim, there are some amusing discussions and comments on the disposition of the purchase money.

policy to abandon the territory for the present."[13] The agent appears to have been somewhat astray in his estimates, for between 1871 and 1883 about $5,000,000 were paid into the United States treasury as rent of the Prybilof Islands and tax on seal-skins alone. It is true that the military occupation, while it lasted, was somewhat expensive, and that buildings which cost many thousands of dollars were afterward sold for a few hundreds; but, as we shall see, troops were not needed in Alaska, and the cost of maintaining the single war-vessel which was occasionally stationed at Sitka after their withdrawal cannot have been excessive.

Seward, who visited Alaska a short time before the agent's report was published,[14] and who delivered a speech at Sitka in August 1869, remarks: "Mr Sumner, in his elaborate and magnificent oration, although he spake only from historical accounts, has not exaggerated—no man can exaggerate—the marine treasures of the territory. Besides the whale, which everywhere and at all times is seen enjoying his robust exercise, and the sea-otter, the fur-seal, the hair-seal, and the walrus found in the waters which imbosom the western islands, those waters, as well as the seas of the eastern archipelago, are found teeming with the salmon, cod, and other fishes adapted to the support of human and animal life. Indeed, what I have seen here has almost made me a convert to the theory of some naturalists, that the waters of the globe are filled with stores for the sustenance of ani-

[13] *McIntyre's Rept.* in *Sen. Ex. Doc.*, 41st cong. 2d sess., No. 32, p. 34. He states that the entire number of voters in the territory does not exceed 125, and reports against the establishment of a territorial government.

[14] He arrived at Sitka on board the *Active* on July 30, 1869, and witnessed the eclipse that occurred a few days later near Davidson's camp on the Chilkat. Seward was on his way up the river when the eclipse occurred. The day was cloudy, and the sun was first observed by an Indian, who remarked that it 'was very sick and wanted to go to sleep.' The Indians refused to row any farther, and the party went ashore and lighted a fire in a dell near the river bank. In the evening Seward's party reached the professor's camp, to which they had been invited. *Honcharenko's Scrap Book*, i. 72.

mal life surpassing the available productions of the land."[15]

Of the resources of Alaska, mention will be made later. At present her furs and fisheries are of course the chief attractions; but it is not improbable that in the distant future the sale of her mining and timber lands will yield to the United States an annual income larger than the amount of the purchase money. The Russian American Company, besides supporting its numerous and expensive establishments, paid into the imperial treasury between 1841 and 1862 over 4,400,000 roubles in duties,[16] to stockholders more than 2,700,000, and for churches, schools, and benevolent institutions about 553,000 roubles. There appears no valid reason, therefore, why Alaska should not have been a source of profit to the United States, except perhaps that this was the first experiment made in the colonization, and it is to be hoped the last in the military occupation, of a territory which, as will be related, the attorney-general declared in 1873 to be 'Indian country.'

On Friday, the 18th of October, 1867, the Russian and United States commissioners, Captain Alexei Pestchourof and General L. H. Rousseau, escorted by a company of the ninth infantry, landed at Novo Arkhangelsk, or Sitka,[17] from the United States steamer *John L. Stephens.* Marching to the governor's residence, they were drawn up side by side with the Russian garrison on the summit of the rock where floated the Russian flag; "whereupon," writes an eye-witness of the proceedings, "Captain Pestchourof ordered the

[15] *Speeches of William H. Seward in Alaska, Van., and Or.* 6 (Washington, 1869).
[16] On tea forwarded from Shanghai and Kiakhta. *Tikhmenef, Istor. Obos.,* ii. 280.
[17] I find no evidence as to the exact date when the name of Novo Arkhangelsk was changed to that of Sitka. Simpson, writing in 1847, uses both words. *Jour. round World,* ii. 180-1. Though the latter is used by writers before his time, it was probably about this date that it first came generally into use.

Russian flag hauled down, and thereby, with brief declaration, transferred and delivered the territory of Alaska to the United States; the garrisons presented arms, and the Russian batteries and our men of war fired the international salute; a brief reply of acceptance was made as the stars and stripes were run up and similarly saluted, and we stood upon the soil of the United States."[18]

Thus, without further ceremony, without even banqueting or speech-making, this vast area of land, belonging by right to neither, was transferred from one European race to the offshoot of another. No sooner had the transfer been made than General Davis demanded the barracks for his troops, taking possession, moreover, of all the buildings, and this although the improvements of whatever kind were beyond doubt the property of the Russian American Company, the Russian government having no right whatever to transfer them. Thus the inhabitants were turned into the streets, only a few of them obtaining two or three days' grace in which to find shelter for their families and remove their effects.

Within a few weeks after the American flag was raised over the fort at Sitka, stores, drinking-saloons, and restaurants were opened, vacant lots were staked out, were covered with frame shanties, and changed hands at prices that promised to make the frontage of the one street which the capital contained alone worth the purchase money of the territory. To this new domain flocked men in all conditions of life—speculators, politicians, office-hunters, tradesmen, even laborers. Nor were there wanting loafers, harlots,

---

[18] *Bloodgood's Eight Months at Sitka*, in *Overland Monthly*, Feb. 1869. In *Whymper's Alaska*, 105–6, and in some of the Pacific coast newspapers, it is stated that the Russian flag, when being lowered, clung to the yard-arm. The following extract from the *Albany State Rights Democrat*, March 26, 1873, will serve as a fair specimen of the nonsense published on this matter: 'A sailor was ordered up the flagstaff, and had actually to cut the flag into shreds before he could take it down. When the American flag reached the top of the staff, it hung lifeless, until, at the first boom of the saluting Russian artillery, it gave a convulsive shudder, and at the second gun it shook out its starry folds and proudly floated in the breeze.'

gamblers, and divers other classes of free white Europeans never seen in these parts before; for of such is our superior civilization. A charter was framed for the so-called city, laws were drawn up, and an election held, at which a hundred votes were polled for almost as many candidates.[19] The claims of squatters were put on record; judgment was passed in cases where liberty and even life were at stake; questions were decided which involved nice points of international law; and all this was done with utter indifference to the military authorities, then the only legal tribunal in the territory.

Two generations had passed away since Baranof and his countrymen had built the fort, or as it is now termed the castle, of Sitka. During all these years the Russians had known little and cared for little beyond the dull routine of their daily labor and their daily life. It is probable that the appearance of the first steam-vessel in Alaskan waters caused no less sensation among them than did the news of Austerlitz, of Eylau, or of Waterloo. Apart from the higher officials, they belonged for the most part to the uneducated classes. If poorly paid, they had been better fed and clad and housed than others of their class. They were a law-abiding, if not a God-fearing, community. During the long term of the company's dominion there had been no overt resistance to authority, except in the two instances already mentioned in this volume. They had been accustomed to submit without a murmur to the dictates of the governor, from whom there was no appeal, save to a court from whose seat they were separated by more than one third of the earth's circumference. This, however, was under what might be called a half-savage régime.

[19] Mr Dodge, collector of customs, was the first mayor of Sitka. Soon after the purchase, the following ticket was elected: For mayor, W. H. Wood; for councilmen, J. A. Fuller, C. A. Kinkaid, Frank Mahoney, Isaac Bergman, and J. Helstedt; for recorder, G. R. McKnight; for surveyor, J. A. Fuller; and for constable, P. B. Ryan. In 1882, Wood was practising law in San Francisco, Fuller lived at Napa, Kinkaid at Portland, Or., McKnight at Key West, Fla., and Helstedt still kept a store at Sitka.

But now all was changed. Speculation and lawlessness were rife, and the veriest necessaries sold at
prices beyond reach of the poor. The natives were
not slow to take advantage of their opportunity, and
refused to sell the Russians game or fish at former
rates;[20] while the Americans refused to accept the
parchment money which formed their circulating
medium[21] in payment for goods, except at a heavy discount. No wonder that few of the Russians cared to
take advantage of the clause in the treaty which provides that, "with the exception of the uncivilized
native tribes, the inhabitants of the ceded territory
shall be admitted to the enjoyment of all the rights,
advantages, and immunities of citizens of the United
States, and shall be maintained and protected in the
free enjoyment of their liberty, property, and religion."
The company and the imperial government gave
them at least protection, sufficient means of livelihood,
schools, a church; but in this vast territory there
never existed, since 1867, other than a semblance
even of military law. There was not in 1883 legal
protection for person or property, nor, apart from a
few regulations as to commerce and navigation, had
any important act been passed by congress, save those
that relate to the preservation of seals, the collection
of revenue, and the sale of fire-arms and fire-water.

"The inhabitants of the ceded territory, according
to their choice, reserving their natural allegiance, may
return to Russia within three years," read the words
of the treaty. Within a few weeks, or perhaps months,
after the transfer, there were not more than a dozen

---

[20] The situation was rendered worse by certain agitators, prominent among
whom was Honcharenko, who, on July 1, 1868, published an address in the
Alaska Herald, advising the Aleuts and Russo-Americans, as he termed
them, not to work for less than five dollars a day in gold. On September
23d of this year Andrei Popof was admitted to citizenship—the first Russian who changed his nationality.

[21] Usually in pieces two inches square, which passed current for about
eight cents when two corners were cut off, and for four cents when all the
corners were lopped. The soldiers, after clipping the lower part of the four-
cent pieces, passed them off for eight cents until the fraud was discovered.

Russians left at Sitka, the remainder having been
sent home by way of California, or round the Horn.[22]
Five years later, the population was composed of a few
creoles of the poorer class, a handful of American soldiers, perhaps a score of American civilians, a few
Aleuts, and a few Kolosh.

Toward the creoles and Indians the policy of the
United States has thus far been severely negative;
and, to put the matter in its most favorable light, I
cannot do better than quote the words of the creole
Kostromitin, who in 1878 was a resident of Unalaska,
being at that date an octogenarian. "I am glad," he
says, "that I lived to see the Americans in the country. The Aleuts are better off now than they were
under the Russians. The first Russians who came
here killed our men and took away our women and
all our possessions; and afterward, when the Russian
American Company came, they made all the Aleuts
like slaves, and sent them to hunt far away, where
many were drowned and many killed by savage natives, and others stopped in strange places and never
came back. The old company gave us fish for nothing,
but we could have got plenty of it for ourselves if we
had been allowed to stay at home and provide for our
families. Often they would not sell us flour or tea,
even if we had skins to pay for it. Now we must pay
for everything, but we can buy what we like. God
will not give me many days to live, but I am satisfied."[23] We shall see presently that Kostromitin's
satisfaction was not shared by a majority of his countrymen.

In many sessions of congress bills have been introduced relating to Alaska, of which some have provoked discussion, many have been tabled, and a few
have passed into law. The only measures to which

[22] *Kruger's* MS. Mr Chas Kruger was for more than 15 years a trusted
employé of the Russian American Co.
[23] *Early Times in Aleut Isl.*, MS., 15-16. Kostromitin was then living at
the village of Makushin.

reference is needed at present are the act of congress approved July 27, 1868, whereby, among other provisions, a collection district was established in that territory;[24] two bills introduced in 1869 and 1870 to provide for a temporary government in Alaska, both of which were referred, though neither passed; some futile attempts to extend the United States land laws over the territory;[25] and certain regulations as to the importation, sale, and manufacture of liquor.[26]

It is worthy of note, that in a territory which has belonged to the United States for more than half a generation, and whose area is more than double that of the largest state in the Union, no legal title could be obtained to land, other than to small tracts deeded to the Russians at the time of the purchase, except by special act of congress, and not a single acre had as yet been surveyed for preëmption.[27]   "Claims of preëmption and settlements," remarks Seward, "are not only without the sanction of law, but are in direct violation of laws applicable to the public domain.   Military force may be used to remove intruders if necessary."[28]

As there was no legal title to land in Alaska, there could be neither legal conveyance nor mortgage, though conveyances were made occasionally, and recorded by

[24] See *Cong. Globe*, 1867–8, app. 567–8. A list of the various sub-districts, with their locations in 1869, is given in *Bryant* and *McIntyre, Rept. Alaska*, 2–24, in *Sen. Ex. Doc., 41st Cong., 2d Sess.*, No. 32; and of the collectors, their duties, etc., in *Morris, Rept. Alaska*, 15–19, in *Sen. Ex. Doc., 45th Cong. 3d Sess.*, No. 59.

[25] A bill was introduced for this purpose in 1871. See *House Jour., 41st Cong. 3d Sess.*, 549.

[26] Contained in section 3 of the act of July 27, 1868, and amended by act of March 3, 1873, extending over the territory sections 20 and 21 of the act of June 30, 1834, regulating trade and intercourse with Indian tribes, the sections being those relating to the manufacture and introduction of liquor. See *Cong. Globe*, 1872–3, app. 274.

[27] *H. Ex. Doc., 45th Cong. 2d Sess.*, viii. 155, 217, and *45th Cong. 3l Sess.*, ix. 146. According to the latter, no survey had been made up to June 30, 1878, and none but special and local surveys appear to have been made since that date. A survey was proposed as early as 1867. *Id., 40th Cong. 2d Sess.*, ix. No. 80. For report on quantity and quality of land, see *Zabriskie's Land Laws*, 880–1.

[28] Letter of William H. Seward to Gen. Grant, Oct. 28, 1867, in *Morris, Rept. Alaska*, 119. The secretary requests that Grant cause instructions to this effect to be forwarded to General Rousseau at Sitka. See also *Beardslee's Rept. Alaska*, in *Sen. Ex. Doc., 40th Cong. 2d Sess.*, no. 103, p. 14.

the deputy collectors at Wrangell and Sitka, the parties concerned taking their own risk as to whether the transaction might at some distant day be legalized.

Miners and others whose entire possessions might lie within the territory, and who might have become residents, could not bequeath their property, whether real or personal,[29] for there were no probate courts, nor any authority whereby estates could be administered. Debts could not be collected except through the summary process by which disputes are sometimes settled in mining camps.[30] In short, there was neither civil nor criminal jurisdiction[31] in any part of Alaska. Even murder might be committed, and there was no redress within that colony. Thus it was that "the inhabitants of the

[29] In Nov. 1877 the postmaster at Sitka died intestate. Soon after his death his creditors arrived from Oregon, and a general scramble took place for his property. The creditors, of course, took the lion's share, the widow what they vouchsafed to leave her, and the two young children of the deceased by a former wife were left to the charity of strangers. *Morris's Rept. Alaska*, 120, in *Sen. Ex. Doc., 45th Cong. 2d Sess.*, no. 59, p. 120.

[30] To quote the words of a memorial addressed by the inhabitants of southeastern Alaska, in 1881, to the president and congress of the United States: 'There are no courts of record, by which title to property may be established, or conflicting claims adjudicated, or estates administered, or naturalization and other privileges acquired, or debts collected, or the commercial advantages of laws secured. And persons accused of crimes and misdemeanors are subject to the arbitrary will of a military or naval commander—thrown into prison and kept there for months without trial, or punishment by imprisonment upon simple accusation and without verdict of a jury—all in plain violation of the constitution of the United States.' The following is an extract from a letter addressed July 11, 1881, by the secretary of the navy to Commander Glass of the *Jamestown*, then stationed at Sitka, relating to parties arrested for certain disorders: 'In the absence of any legally constituted judicial tribunals, the peace and good order of society demand that the naval authority in control of the territory should interpose its power to maintain the protection of the lives, persons, and property of individuals within its reach.'

[31] The only offences that could be committed apparently were those which violate the act of July 27, 1868, 'to extend the laws of the United States relating to customs, commerce, and navigation over the territory ceded to the United States by Russia, to establish a collection district therein, and for other purposes' (the other purposes relating to the sale, importation, and use of fire-arms, ammunition, and distilled liquors, and the protection of fur-bearing animals). In such cases it is provided, by section 7 of the same act, that the offender shall be prosecuted in any U. S. district court of California or Oregon, or in one of the district courts of Washington Territory. In 1872 a bill was introduced 'further to provide for the punishment of offences committed in the district of Alaska.' *U. S. Sen. Jour., 42d Cong. 2d Sess.*, 400–1. And one in the same year 'authorizing the secretary of the interior to take jurisdiction over the people of Alaska called Indians, and for other purposes.' *House Jour., 42d Cong. 2d Sess.*, 609.

ceded territory were admitted to the enjoyment of all
the rights, advantages, and immunities of citizens of
the United States."

What shall we do with Alaska? was one of the first
questions asked after the transfer of the territory—
make of it a penal colony?[32] Perhaps it had been
better so. At no period in the annals of Alaska were
there so many Indian émeutes as during the few years
of the military occupation; at no period were lust,
theft, and drunkenness more prevalent among Indians
and white persons alike. After the withdrawal of the
troops, in June 1877,[33] disturbances among the natives became fewer in number and less serious in character, and it is probable that many lives would have
been saved if no United States soldier had ever set
foot in the territory.

"I am compelled to say," writes William S. Dodge,
collector of customs, to Vincent Colyer, special Indian commissioner, in 1869, "that the conduct of certain military and naval officers and soldiers has been
bad and demoralizing in the extreme: not only con-
taminating the Indians, but in fact demoralizing and
making the inhabitants of Sitka what Dante charac-
terized Italy—'A grand house of ill-fame.' I speak
only of things as seen and felt at Sitka.

"First. The demoralizing influence originated in the
fact that the garrison was located in the heart of the
town.

"Secondly. The great mass of the soldiers were
either desperate or very immoral men.

"Thirdly. Some of the officers did not carry out
military discipline in that just way which the regula-

[32] The question was seriously mooted by Nordhoff, in a magazine article
entitled 'What shall we do with Scroggs? Scroggs is the American Ginx's
baby;' and by certain of the San Francisco and Sacramento papers.

[33] *Gen. Orders, Dept. Cal.*, May 23, 1877. In *Rept. Sec. War*, I., *44th
Cong. 1st Sess.*, 47, the statement shows 46 men at Fort Wrangell, and
in *Id.*, 124, it is mentioned that companies F and L of the fourth artillery
were stationed at Sitka. It is worthy of remark that the secretary, while
stating that there was an improvement in the morale of the army, says that
out of a force of 25,000 the number of deserters in 1874-5 was 2,100 less
than during the previous year.

tions contemplate. They gave too great license to bad men; and the deepest evil to all, and out of which other great evils resulted, was an indiscriminate pass system at night. Many has been the night when soldiers have taken possession of a Russian house, and frightened and browbeaten the women into compliance with their lustful passions.

"Many is the night I have been called upon after midnight, by men and women, Russian and Aleutian, in their night-clothes, to protect them against the malice of the soldiers. In instances where the guilty parties could be recognized, they have been punished; but generally they have not been recognized, and therefore escaped punishment.

"Fourthly. The conduct of some of the officers has been so demoralizing that it was next to impossible to keep discipline among the soldiers.... Officers have carried on with the same high hand among the Russian people; and were the testimony of citizens to be taken, many instances of real infamy and wrongs would come to light.

"For a long time some of the officers drank immoderately of liquor, and it is telling the simple truth when I say that one or two of them have been drunk for a week at a time. The soldiers saw this, the Indians saw it; and as 'ayas tyhus,' or 'big chiefs,' as they called the officers, drank, they thought that they too must get intoxicated. Then came the distrust of American justice when they found themselves in the guard-house, but never saw the officers in when in a like condition."[34]

[34] *Sec. of Interior Rept., 41st Cong. 2d Sess.*, 1030–1, where it is stated that within six months after the arrival of the troops at Sitka nearly the whole Sitka tribe, some 1,200 in number, were suffering from venereal diseases. It is probable, however, that most of them had such diseases long before a United States soldier set foot in the territory. Colyer remarks: 'I have spoken of the ill effects of the near proximity of soldiers to the Indian villages, and of the demoralizing effects upon both. It is the same in all Indian countries. It appears to be worse here because more needless. Nowhere else that I have visited is the absolute uselessness of soldiers so apparent as in Alaska....The soldiers will have whiskey, and the Indians are equally fond of it. The free use of this by both soldiers and Indians, together with the other

"An effort is being made to have the military return to Alaska," writes the deputy collector of customs from Fort Wrangell, in October 1877, "and in the name of humanity and common sense I ask, What for ? Is it for the best interests of the territory that they should return ? Look at the past for an answer. Whenever did they do anything for the country or the people in it that deserves praise ? Did they encourage enterprise and assist in the developing of the resources of the country ? No! It stands recorded that they foiled the developing of it, and placed restrictions on enterprise and improvements. Did they seek the enlightenment of the Indian, and endeavor to elevate him to a higher moral standard ? On this point let the Indians themselves testify."[35]

There were in 1869 five hundred soldiers stationed in Alaska, while it was admitted by many of the officers that two hundred were sufficient, and it had already become apparent to civilians that none were really needed. In a country where there are few roads, and where communication is almost entirely by water, three or four revenue cutters and the presence of a single war-vessel would have prevented smuggling and lawlessness far more effectually than any force of troops.[36]

debaucheries between them, rapidly demoralizes both.' *Rept. Ind. Affairs*, 1869, 556. In 1869 some soldiers were drummed out of the service for robbing the Greek church at Sitka, and for other crimes. *Id.*, 557. For further though less reliable details as to the misconduct of the military, see *Honcharenko's Scrap Book*, i. passim.

[35] Letter to *Puget Sound Argus*, published Nov. 23, 1877, of which there is a copy in *Morris's Rept.*, app. 153. A statement as to the result of military rule is given by three chiefs among the Wrangell Indians.

[36] Captain White, in a letter to the secretary of the treasury, remarks: 'From my own personal observation and the experience gained in my former cruise to this portion of Alaska, embracing the waters of the Alexandrian Archipelago, and extending from latitude N. 54° 40' to latitude N. 60°, I have no hesitation in respectfully stating that even for armed vessels of the deepest draught there is no difficulty in approaching, within easy shelling distance, any of the villages and completely destroying them.' *Morris's Report, Alaska*, 139. Morris is of opinion that vessels intended to be permanently stationed on the coast of Alaska should be of not less than 500 tons burden; but, as White remarks, a small vessel properly armed and equipped could accomplish all that a larger and more heavily armed one could, with the added advantage of celerity of movement and quickness of evolution. On the withdrawal of the troops in 1877 three revenue cutters were stationed in Alaska.

Notwithstanding all that has been said against the régime of the Russian American Company, it must be admitted that there were more troubles with the natives in the ten years during which American troops were stationed in Alaska than in any decade of the Russian occupation.

"When the territory was transferred to the United States," writes Bryant, "the natives had no knowledge of the people with whom they were to deal; and having been prejudiced by the parties then residing among them, some of the more warlike chiefs were in favor of driving out the 'Boston men,' as they termed us."[37] The discontent arose, not from any antagonism to the Americans, but from the fact that the territory had been sold without their consent, and that they had received none of the proceeds of the sale. The Russians, they argued, had been allowed to occupy the territory partly for mutual benefit, but their forefathers had dwelt in Alaska long before any white man had set foot in America. Why had not the $7,200,000 been paid to them instead of to the Russians?

But long before the purchase, as the reader will remember, the natives received better prices for their peltry from the Americans than from the Russians, and when it was found, after the transfer, that still higher rates and greater variety of products could be obtained, their antipathy rapidly disappeared. Thus for a time there was no difficulty; Aleut and Thlinkeet became friends of the 'Boston men,'[38] and so it might have continued but for an untoward incident.

On New-Year's day, 1869, a Chilkat chief,[39] Chol-

---

[37] *Bryant's Rept.*, 14.

[38] The U. S. military force sent to Cook Inlet in 1868 was instructed to 'beware of the northern Indians as savage, treacherous, and warlike.' That character the natives of Cook Inlet do not deserve. The troops found them truthful, by no means warlike though good hunters, and thieves only under great temptation. When the soldiers were shipwrecked and at their mercy, they did not steal from them, but caught fish for their subsistence. *Wythe's Cook Inlet*, 65.

[39] The Chilkats are a Thlinkeet tribe.

cheka by name, was invited to dinner by General
Davis, then in command of the district. After doing
ample justice to the general's hospitality, he was presented with two bottles of American whiskey, and on
taking his leave, felt that he was not only every
inch a chief, but as good and great a man as any who
claimed possession of his country. On reaching the
foot of the castle stairs, attired in a cast-off army uniform, and with bottles in hand, he stalked majesti-
cally across the part of the parade-ground reserved
for officers, and was challenged by the sentry. Ignoring such paltry presence, Cholcheka went on his way
toward the stockade, at the gate of which was a
second sentry, and refusing to turn back, he received
a kick as he passed out. Now a kick to a Chilkat
chief, and especially to one who dons the United
States uniform, has just dined with the general in
command, and has a bottle of whiskey in each hand,
is a sore indignity. With the aid of one Sitka Jack,
then a well known character among the townsfolk, he
wrested the rifle from the soldier's grasp, and entered
the Indian village close at hand.

The guard was at once turned out, and "ordered,"
writes Davis in his report of January 5, 1869, "to
follow him into the village, and arrest him and his
party. He resisted by opening a fire upon the guard.
The guard returned it, but finding the Indians too
strong for them, retreated back into the garrison. As
the chief himself was reported probably killed in the
mêlée, and the whole tribe of Sitkas, among whom he
was staying, was thrown into a great state of excitement, I thought it prudent to order a strong guard
out for the night, and to take no further action until
morning, as the night was very dark, thus giving
them time to reflect.

"I called the principal Sitka chiefs together, and
they disclaimed any participation in the affair, and
said they did not desire to fight either the troops or
the Chilkahts, and that they had already hoisted white

flags over their cabins.   I then demanded the surrender of the Chilkaht chief, who, after considerable delay
and some show of fight on the part of about fifty of
his warriors, came in and gave himself up.   A few
minutes' talk with him sufficed to convince me that he
was bent on war, and I would have had to fight but
for the Sitkas refusing to join in his design.   I confined him and his principal confederates in the guard-
house, where he still remains."[40]

In a few days Cholcheka and his party were liberated, and here it was supposed the matter would
end; but, as it proved, this, the first difficulty between
the Indians and the military, was fraught with evil
consequences, and all on account of a United States
general making an Indian drunk, and then having two
of his people killed.   And this from his own showing;
we never hear the other side of these stories.   "On
the 25th of December last," continues Davis, in a
report dated March 9, 1869, "a couple of white
men, named Maager and Walker, left Sitka in a
small boat on a trading expedition in Chatham Straits.
About one week after their departure the difficulty
between the Chilcot chief and a few of his followers occurred at this place, as heretofore reported.
It appears that during this difficulty a party of
eight Kake Indians were at the Sitka village, and
one of them was shot by a sentinel while attempting
to escape from the village in a canoe, contrary to orders and an understanding with the peaceable portion
of the Indians.   The parties thus attempting to escape
were run down by small boats from the *Saginaw* and
the revenue cutter *Reliance*, and brought back.   As
they were unarmed, they were permitted to go about
their business.   They remained some days among the
Sitkas, and after the Chilcot chief was restored to

[40] *Sec. Interior, Rept.*, *41st Cong. 2d Sess.*, 1028.   In his letter to Vincent
Colyer, dated Nov. 10, 1869, Dodge says that the kicking was witnessed by
a little Russian girl. *Id.*, 1031.   Two Indians were killed in the fray, and one
soldier severely wounded.

liberty, it is reported they tried to get him to join them in a general fight against the whites. From the best information I can get, he declined to do so. They then left for their homes, and en route murdered Maager and Walker in the most brutal manner."[41]

It was not yet known to the military authorities, or, if it were, the fact was ignored, that among the Thlinkeet tribes, when a member has suffered death or injury from violence, his comrades require payment in money or goods, and in default of it, never fail to retaliate. The present of a few blankets or other articles to the relatives of those who fell in the émeute at Sitka would probably have prevented the troubles that ensued.[42] It is certain that it would at least have prevented the mutilation and murder of Maager and Walker.

Davis had now, as he thought, no alternative. He sailed for Kou Island, the territory of the Kakes, on board the *Saginaw*, intending to obtain the surrender of the murderers, or to seize some of their chiefs as hostages. On his arrival he found that the whole tribe had disappeared, dreading the vengeance that might overtake them; whereupon he ordered their villages to be razed to the ground and all their property to be destroyed.

Henceforth troubles with the Indians continued throughout and after the military occupation.[43] On

---

[41] *Army and Navy Jour.*, March 1, 1869. A copy of Gen. Davis' report was furnished to this publication from the headquarters of the military division of the Pacific.

[42] Five months after the émeute occurred, a party of Chilkats boarded a vessel, and demanded money or life. Guaranty was given for payment, and on the refusal of the commander at Sitka to furnish the sum agreed on, it was paid by the owner, Frank K. Louthan, a Sitka merchant, who says, in a letter to Vincent Colyer, in 1869: 'My own experience has taught me that an immediate settlement for any mortal or other injury inflicted is the most judicious course to pursue with the Kolosh Indians.' *Rept. Ind. Affairs, Alaska*, in *Rept. Ind. Comm.*, 1869, p. 573.

[43] Professor Davidson of the coast survey went to the Chilkat River to observe the solar eclipse on August 9, 1869. He was warned that the Chilkat Indians had just been provoked to hostility, but did not heed the warning, and the party returned safe. The observation was made near a populous village, and when it took place the Indians gradually disappeared and fled into the woods in silent dismay. They had not believed Davidson's predic-

Christmas night of 1869 it was reported to the officer in command at Fort Wrangell that a Stikeen named Lowan, or Siwau,[44] had bitten off the finger of the wife of the quartermaster sergeant. A detachment was sent to arrest him, in charge of Lieutenant Loucks, who states that he entered the Indian's house with twelve men, eight being posted outside, and instructions given to fire at a given signal. "I tapped Siwau on the shoulder," reports the lieutenant, "saying that I wanted him to come with me. He arose from his sitting posture and said he would put on his vest; after that he wished to get his coat. Feeling convinced that this was merely to gain time, and that he wished to trifle with me, I began to be more urgent. Siwau appeared less and less inclined to come away with me, and in this the latter part of the parley he became impudent and menacing in raising his hands as if to strike me. I admonished him against such actions, and tried my utmost to avoid extreme measures in arresting him. About this time Esteen, probably apprehending danger to his brother, Siwau, rushed forward in front of the detachment, extending his arms theatrically, and exclaiming, as I supposed under the circumstances, 'Shoot; kill me; I am not afraid.' Siwau, seeing this, also rushed upon the detachment, endeavoring to snatch a musket away from one of the men on the right of the detachment. Still wishing to avoid loss of life if possible, I tried to give him two or three sabre-cuts over the head to stun without killing him. In doing this I had given the preconcerted signal, by raising my hand, to fire. I should judge about six or eight shots were fired during the mêlée, and only ceasing by the Indian Siwau falling at the feet of the detachment dead."

The officer returned to his quarters and dismissed his men, supposing that no further trouble would

tion the day before, and its fulfilment probably caused the safety of the party. *Rept. Coast Survey*, 1869, 177-9.

[44] Both names are used in the official reports on this matter.

occur; but an hour later shots were heard from the direction of the store of the post-trader, and taking with him a single private, Loucks ran toward the spot. On his way he stumbled across an object near the plank walk laid between the store and the garrison quarters. It was the post-trader's partner, Leon Smith, lying on his breast with arms extended, a revolver near his right hand, fourteeen bullet wounds in his left side just below the heart, and three in the left wrist. A few hours later he died an extremely painful death, and it was ascertained that the murder had been committed by an Indian named Scutdoo.

Immediately after reveillé Loucks was sent with twenty men to demand the surrender of the murderer; to summon the chiefs of the tribe to the post, and to state that if the culprit were not delivered up at mid-day at latest, fire would be opened on the Indian village outside the stockade. At noon there were no indications that the demand would be complied with, but there were very strong indications that the Indians intended to fight.[45] After consulting with his fellow-officers and waiting for two hours more, in the hope that the natives would change their determination, Lieutenant Borrowe of the second artillery, then in command, ordered his battery to open with solid shot on the murderer's house. Several shot passed through the building, but the Indians maintained their position and returned the fire. Later a fusillade was opened by the Indians from the hills in rear of the post, but being answered with canister, they quickly dispersed.

Firing was continued on both sides until dark. "The next morning, just at daybreak," reports Borrowe, "they opened on the garrison from the ranch with musketry, which was immediately replied to, and seeing that they were determined not only to resist, but

---

[45] Some of them were observed carrying away their goods to a place of safety. *Lieutenant Borrowe's Rept.* in *Sen. Ex. Doc., 41st Cong. 2d Sess.*, no. 67.

had become the assailants, I resolved to shell them, but having only solid shot for the six-pounder, and the distance being too great for canister, I still continued the fire from that gun with shot and from the mountain howitzer with shell."

During the afternoon messengers were sent under a flag of truce to request a parley. The reply was, that until the murderer was surrendered "talk was useless." " Soon after," continues Borrowe, " the chiefs were seen coming over, and a party behind them with the murderer, who was easily recognized by his dress. Just as they were leaving the ranch a scuffle, evidently prearranged, took place, and the prisoner escaped, and was seen making for the bush, no attempt to rearrest him being made." On arriving at the post the chiefs were informed that if Scutdoo were not delivered up before six o'clock the next evening their village and its occupants would be destroyed. At nine P. M. on the 26th the murderer was surrendered; on the 28th he was tried by court-martial, and at noon on the following day he was hanged.[46]

The prompt action of Lieutenant Borrowe was approved by General Davis, but it would appear that the matter might have been settled without the murder of an Indian, a white man, and the bombardment of an Indian village, especially as the general admits that Siwau was drunk when he bit off the woman's finger. This skilful and gentlemanly performance of the lieutenant, who with twenty armed men could not arrest a drunken and defenceless Indian without first cutting him on the head with a sabre, and then allowing him to be shot, was a fitting supplement to that of his general. The killing of Siwau was no less a murder than was the assassination of the white man. For that murder vengeance must be taken, in accordance with Indian notions of justice, and the post-trader's assassi-

---

[46] A full report of the affair at Fort Wrangell is contained in *Id.*, the report of Lieutenant Loucks which follows, and the proceedings of the court-martial which are appended.

nation was the act of vengeance as inflicted by Scutdoo. After listening with perfect calmness to his sentence, the prisoner exclaimed, "Very well," and said that " he would see Mr Smith in the other world, and, as it were, explain to him how it all happened; that he did not intend to kill him particularly; had it been any one else, it would have been all the same."[47]

There is abundant testimony as to the peaceful character of the Indians at Fort Wrangell. Leon Smith himself says, in a letter to Vincent Colyer, written about three months before his death, "I have found them to be quiet, and they seem well disposed toward the whites;" and in the same letter remarks that "the Stick (Stikeen)[48] tribe are a very honest tribe, and partial to the whites." These statements are indorsed by others. Moreover, from the reports of several reliable witnesses it appears that the Wrangell Indians were far more industrious, if not more intelligent, than the United States soldiers.[49]

From the official reports of the officers in command at Sitka and Fort Wrangell, it will be seen that the conduct of the troops was sufficiently atrocious, and of course they put the matter in its most favorable light. "If," writes the Christian missionary society's superintendent of Indian missions[50] to Vincent Colyer, in 1870, "the United States government did but know half, I am sure they would shrink from being identified with such abominations, and the cause of so much misery. I hope and pray that in God's good providence the soldiers will be moved away from Fort

[47] See report of proceedings of court-martial. Scutdoo admitted that he was the murderer, and was identified by the chiefs.
[48] A Thlinkeet tribe. The word is variously spelled. For the location of the tribe, see my *Native Races*, i. 96, 143.
[49] 'The majority of these Indians are very industrious, and are always anxious to get employment,' writes W. Wall, interpreter at Wrangell. 'They are of a very superior intelligence,' says William S. Dodge, collector of customs. *Colyer's Rept.*, app. D.
[50] The Rev. W. Duncan, superintendent in British Columbia, near the boundary line of Alaska. *Id.*, p. 10.

Tongas and Fort Wrangel, where there are no whites to protect."[51]

It is unnecessary to relate in detail all the outrages that called forth this well deserved remark and justified it in later years. I will mention only three instances. At Sitka, a Chilkat was deliberately shot dead by a civilian in 1869 for breaking the glass of a show-case;[52] three were wounded in 1872 by United States soldiers in an affray caused by the

[51] The superintendent is wrong on this point. There was a small number of white people at each of these posts.

[52] Probably by James C. Parker, an employee of the post-trader. Parker was tried by a court-martial. The finding of the court was, that 'after a careful examination of the witnesses who have been called before the board, the board has not been able to determine, further than through the inferences of circumstantial evidence, who shot the Chilkat Indian. The circumstantial evidence points to an employee of the post-trader, Mr Parker, as the person who did the shooting; the breaking of a show-case for the purpose of stealing being, as far as the board can determine, the circumstance which led to the shooting, and the board is of the opinion that if there were no more reasons for shooting than those brought out in evidence, the act was not justifiable.' The evidence was at least such as would have endangered Parker's neck if he had been living in British Columbia. Colonel W. H. Dennison, then in command of the post, testified: 'I was in the sutler's [post-trader's] store at about 4 o'clock in the afternoon. Mr Parker, who is employed in the store, came in very much excited, and asked Mr Southan [the sutler] where his rifle was. Mr Southan asked Mr Parker to the purport as to whether he had seen the Indian. Mr Parker replied that he had. While Mr Parker was looking around for the rifle and changing his shoes, Mr Southan told him two or three times not to take the rifle. Some one else sitting by the stove told Mr Parker to take the pistol instead of the rifle. Mr Parker said the pistol was not sure enough; "I am going to take the rifle to bring the Indian back." He took the Henry rifle, went out of the front door, and walked up toward the Indian market-house, and came back in about ten minutes. Mr Southan asked him if he had gotten the Indian. Mr Parker replied that "that was a very hard question to ask a man."' When asked whether, as commanding officer, he had taken any action in the case, the colonel answered: 'I took none more than to investigate and satisfy myself that no soldier of my command was engaged in the shooting.' Southan stated that the damage to the show-case was trifling, and that Parker asked for the rifle, saying that he was in pursuit of the Indian who had broken the show-case window. Private John McKenzie testified that there was no one with Parker at the time, private Alonzo Ramsey, that he saw Parker chase the Indian, return to the store for the rifle, go outside the stockade, and disappear behind a neighboring hill near the Greek church. A few minutes later Ramsey heard three shots fired, and from the direction of the smoke supposed that Parker had discharged his gun. Immediately after the shooting the Indian stated to his brother that the shots were fired at him by Parker in rear of the Greek church, on the hill near the stockade. *Sec. Interior Rept., 41st Cong. 2d Sess.*, app. R, 1047. A few weeks before this incident, Lieutenant Cowan of the revenue service was shot dead in a saloon by a discharged soldier. The bullet was intended for Colonel Dennison, who was with Cowan at the time.

accidental breaking of an egg;[53] and an Indian chief,
being sent on board a steamer from Fort Wrangell in
1875, as a witness against some military prisoners, met
with such ill usage that he cut his throat, his servant
afterward attempting to blow up the steamer by
throwing a large can of powder into one of the fur-
naces, and his tribe threatening war on hearing of
their chief's suicide.

After the withdrawal of the troops there was no
power or authority in the land to punish wrong-doers,
and a serious outbreak was of course anticipated; but
none occurred. In August 1877 there were at most
but fifteen American citizens and five Russians remaining at Sitka, with their wives and families, at
the mercy of the hundreds of Kolosh who inhabited
the adjoining village. They were in hourly fear of
their lives, as they saw drunken men staggering past
their residences at all hours of the day and night; but
that for two years at least, the Indians caused further
trouble, apart from being noisy, boisterous, sometimes
insolent, sometimes guilty of petty theft, and always
drunk when they could obtain liquor, there is no
evidence. Much indignation was expressed by the
newspapers of the Pacific coast as to the indifference
with which a handful of loafers and office-seeking politicians—American citizens they were called—were
abandoned to their fate.[54] In a San Francisco publication issued November 2, 1877, it is even stated
that the timely arrival of a revenue cutter alone saved
Sitka from demolition and the white population from

[53] Two soldiers were bargaining with an Indian woman for a basket of
eggs, and broke one of them, for which the woman demanded payment. A
scuffle followed, and soon the tribe gathered in the parade-ground. One of
them shot at the sentry, whereupon the troops were put under arms. *Alaska
Her.*, July 24, 1872; *Portland Bull.*, July 15, 1872; *S. F. Bulletin*, August
1, 1872.

[54] Among others, see the *S. F. Bulletin*, Sept. 24, 1877, Oct. 30. 1877,
Jan. 22, 1878; *Chronicle*, Oct. 31, 1877, Jan. 26, 1878; *Call*, Jan. 23, 1878.
In the *San Francisco Post*, October 31, 1877, it is justly remarked that 'the
clamor for troops to hold the Indians in check is a shallow pretext, prompted
by a dozen contractors, and the agents of a steamship line that has lost its
traffic.'

slaughter; but now let us hear the official reports of the revenue officers themselves on this matter.

Captain White of the *Corwin*, ordered to Sitka soon after the withdrawal of the military, writes, on August 12, 1877: "After diligent inquiries and careful observation since our arrival here, I have not discovered any breach of the public peace, nor has my attention been called to any particular act, save a few petty trespasses committed by the Indians, half-breeds, and white men as well."[55]

In September of this year there was much needless alarm at Sitka. It was reported that Sitka Jack, then the chief of his tribe, had invited a large number of the Kolosh from the districts north of the capital to be present at a grand festival which was to commence on the 1st of October. Liquor would of course flow plentifully, and it was feared that the festival

[55] *Morris's Rept.*, 127. The vessel was sent at the request of Major Berry, collector of customs, and William Gouverneur Morris, special agent of the treasury department, and author of the report. The cruise of the *Corwin* in Alaska and the N. W. Arctic in 1881, as related, *House Ex. Doc.* (published in separate form, Washington, 1883), is too well known to the reader to require comment. Mention of this cruise is made in the *S. F. Bulletin*, Sept. 23–29 and Oct. 22, 1881. On August 12th of this year, Capt. Hooper of the *Corwin* succeeded, after much difficulty, in reaching Wrangell Land. The island was christened New Columbia, the American flag hoisted, a record of the *Corwin's* visit and a copy of the *New York Herald* were placed in a bottle and secured to the flag-pole, and the flag saluted. The decision of the court of inquiry held at Washington, as to the members of the *Jeanette* expedition, is published in *Id.*, Feb. 19, 1883. During her cruise the *Corwin* destroyed the Indian village of Hootchenoo on the Alaska coast, two miles from North Port. The incident is thus described in *Id.*, Nov. 13, 1882: 'The tribe had seized and held two white men and a steam-launch, which had been sent out with a tug after whales. The launch was provided with a bomb-gun, upon firing which an explosion occurred, and an Indian chief who was assisted on board the launch was killed. The tribe surrounded and captured the launch with two white men, and nearly succeeded in getting possession of the tug. The latter, however, got away and steamed to Sitka. The *Corwin*, with Capt. Merriman and sixty sailors and marines, was despatched to Hoochenoo. Capt. Merriman demanded the surrender of the launch and prisoners, and the Indians demanded 200 blankets in compensation for the death of the chief. Captain Merriman put in a counterclaim for 400 blankets as compensation for the seizure of the launch and men. The Indians refused, and the next morning a Gatling gun was played on the Indian canoes on the beach. A force was afterward landed, which destroyed all of them. The Indians afterward fled to the woods and the village was shelled, the huts remaining standing after the shelling, being looted and burned to the ground.' The cruise of the United States relief steamer *Rodgers* is mentioned in *Id.*, Nov. 9, 14, 17, 1881, and the wreck of the *Vigilant* in *Id.*, Aug. 15, 1881.

would end in the sack of the town and the massacre
of its inhabitants.   The revenue steamer *Wolcott* was
therefore ordered to Sitka from Port Townsend, and
on the 18th of October her commander thus reports
to the secretary of the treasury: "The situation of
affairs here remains unchanged since the cutter *Corwin*
left.   The festival among the Indians is nothing new;
they have continued this fashion of holding an annual
celebration similar to this one for years, and I learn
from a reliable source that no trouble has ever come
of it, or is there likely to now.   They are noisy and
boisterous in their mirth, and assume immense airs,
and swagger around with some insolence, but never
make any threats.   Sitka Jack, the chief of the Sitka
Indians, has recently built him a new house, and cele-
brates the event on this occasion by inviting the relatives of his wife, numbering about thirty persons,
from the Chilkaht tribe.   These are all the Indians
from abroad, which, with the five hundred Sitka Indians, comprise the total number present.   With the
exception of the noise and mirth incident to these
festivities, I am assured by the chiefs that there shall
be no disturbance."[56]   And there was none; nor has
there since been any very serious trouble.   In 1879
émeutes were threatened at Sitka and Fort Wrangell,
but both were prevented, the former by the arrival of
the British man-of-war *Osprey*, and the latter, which
was merely a fray between two hostile tribes, by the
arrival of a party of armed men from the United
States steamer *Jamestown*.[57]   Since that time there
have been occasional murders and attempts at murder,
but less frequently, in proportion to the population,

---

[56] *Id.*, 128.   Captain Selden, who wrote this report, was of opinion that the
Sitkas, being entirely dependent on the sea-coast for the means of subsistence, and knowing the certainty of punishment if they displayed hostility toward the whites, feared the consequences too much to commit any
depredations.   The only depredations which they committed, worthy of mention, were carrying off the doors and windows of the government buildings,
and tearing away a part of the stockade for firewood.
[57] An account of the former affair is given in *Beardslee's Rept. Affairs,
Alaska*, 4-6, and of the latter in the *S. F. Bulletin* of Feb. 2, 1880.

than has been the case in some of the states and territories of the Pacific coast.

Considering that since the withdrawal of the troops the natives have been for the most part masters of the situation, they appear to have shown more forbearance than could reasonably be expected. It is true that they have often assumed an arrogant tone, have sometimes demanded and occasionally received blackmail from the white man when trouble was threatened;[58] but this is not surprising. They had been accustomed to stern treatment under Russian rule, to brutal treatment under American rule, and now that there was no rule, they found themselves living in company with Americans, Russians, creoles, Chinamen, Eskimos, men of all races, creeds, and colors, in a condition of primitive republican simplicity. They vastly outnumbered those of all other nationalities. Notwithstanding the regulations as to the sale of fire-arms, ammunition, and spirituous liquor, the Indians could always obtain these articles in exchange for peltry and other wares. They were seldom free from the craze of strong drink, and strong drink of the vilest description; the imported liquor sold to them was the cheapest and most poisonous compound manufactured in the United States, and the soldiers had taught them how to make a still more abominable compound for themselves.

Nearly all the troubles that have occurred with Indians, since the time of the purchase, may be traced directly or indirectly to the abuse of liquor. During the régime of the Russian American Company, rum was sold to them only on special occasions, and then in moderate quantities, but afterward the supply was limited only by the means of the purchaser. The excitement of a drunken and lascivious debauch became the one object in life for which the Indians lived, the one object for which they worked. While sober

[58] See the report of the commander of the *Osprey*, published in the *S. F. Bulletin*, March 18, 1879.

they were tractable and sometimes industrious, and
if they had sufficient self-denial, would remain sober
long enough to earn money for a prolonged carousal.
They would then plan their prasnik, as they termed
it, deliberately, and of malice aforethought, and enjoy
it as deliberately as did the English farm-laborer in
the seventeenth century, when spirits were cheap and
untaxed, and when for a single shilling he could soak
his brains in alcohol for a week at a time at one of the
road-side taverns, where signs informed the wayfarer
that he could get well drunk for a penny, dead-drunk
for twopence, and without further expense sleep off
the effects of his orgy on the clean straw provided for
him in the cellar.

Soon after the purchase, an order was issued by the
president of the United States[59] that all distilled
spirits should be sent to department headquarters at
Sitka and placed under control of General Davis—a
wise proceeding, if we may judge from results—but
the injunction was of no avail. In 1869 confiscated
liquor was sold at auction by the collector of the port
in the streets of Sitka. In the same year nine hundred
gallons of pure alcohol, landed from the steamer *Newbern* and marked 'coal oil,' were seized by the inspector; but for each gallon of alcohol or alcoholic
liquor confiscated by the revenue officers, probably ten
were smuggled into the territory,[60] or were delivered
under some pretext, at the sutler's stores. By the
Newbern were also forwarded to Tongass and Fort
Wrangell, during the same trip, ten barrels of distilled
spirits, twenty of ale, and a large number of cases of
porter and wine. The ship's papers showed that they
were for the use of the officers; but as there were only
four officers at Tongass and a single company of troops
at Fort Wrangell, there is no doubt that they were

[59] Under act of congress. See *Colyer's Rept.*, 537, and app. H, 585.
[60] 'During the summer season,' writes Morris, on April 14, 1877, 'the Alaskan coast swarms with small vessels and canoes, navigated by desperate and
lawless men, bent upon smuggling, illicit barter, and that especial curse to
the natives—trading in ardent spirits.' *Rept.*, 23.

intended for sale at the Indian villages adjoining these posts.[61]

In answer to a letter from the secretary of war in 1873, the attorney general of the United States declared officially that "Alaska was to be regarded as Indian country, and that no spirituous liquors or wines could be introduced into the territory without an order by the war department for that purpose."[62] In 1875 all permits for the sale of spirituous liquors in Alaska were revoked,[63] and during the two remaining years of the military occupation, we learn of no serious disturbances among the natives.

The disorders that followed the withdrawal of the troops were due quite as much to white men as to Indians; and by both, the revenue laws and revenue officers were held in contempt. Of the disgraceful scenes that then ensued, I will give a single instance. Early in 1878 there were about two hundred and fifty miners at Fort Wrangell, waiting until the ice should form on the Stikeen River or navigation should become practicable. In a report dated February 23d of that year, the deputy collector of customs at Wrangell says: "While I was at Sitka another thing occurred at this port that puts to shame anything that has happened heretofore. A gang of rowdies and bummers have, for the past three months, been in the habit of getting on a drunken spree, and then at midnight going about the town making the most hideous noises imaginable, disturbing everybody, and insulting those who complain of these doings. On the night of February 16th the incarnate devils started out about midnight, and after raising a commotion

[61] *Id.*, 537–8. The spirits were afterward sent to Sitka, through the interference of Colyer.

[62] Letter of Geo. H. Williams to W. W. Belknap, in *Sen. Ex. Doc., 43d Cong. 2d Sess.*, 24. In Oct. 1874 the deputy collector at Wrangell was arrested by order of the officer in command for violating the rules on the importation of liquor. *Alaska Her.*, Oct. 28th. On Jan. 7, 1875, the district court at Portland, *in re* John A. Carr on *habeas corpus*, held Carr to answer on a similar charge, and fixed his bail at $2,500. *Portland Oregonian*, Jan. 8, 1875.

[63] *Gen. Orders, Dept. Col.*, Jan. 21, 1875.

all over town, visited a house occupied by an Indian woman, gave her whiskey that made her beastly drunk, and then left. Shortly after their departure the house occupied by the woman was discovered to be in flames, and ere any assistance could be rendered the poor woman was burned to death."[64] It was feared that two months later there might be a thousand miners congregated at Wrangell; and the population of the Indian village was about double that number. As there was a plentiful supply of whiskey for the former, and of hootchenoo, or molasses-rum, for the latter, serious troubles were anticipated.

During the last five months of 1877, there were delivered at Sitka, from the steamer which carried the United States mail from Portland, 4,889 gallons of molasses, and at Fort Wrangell 1,635 gallons. Large quantities were also landed from other vessels, all for the purpose of making hootchenoo, the other ingredients used being flour, dried apples or rice, yeast powder, and sometimes hops. Sufficient water is added to make a thin batter, and after fermentation has taken place, a sour, muddy, highly alcoholic liquor is produced, of abominable taste and odor.[65] From one gallon of the mixture nearly a gallon of hootchenoo is distilled, a pint of which is quite sufficient to craze the strongest brain.

Before the time of the purchase the art of making molasses-rum was unknown to the natives, but after the military occupation many of the soldiers became proprietors of hootchenoo stills, while others were in the habit of repairing for their morning dram to the Indian village outside the stockade at Sitka, where this liquor was sold at ten cents a glass.[66] Occasional

[64] Report of I. C. Dennis in *Morris's Rept.*, 4–5. The deputy collector states that he intends to stop the liquor traffic.

[65] The process is described in *Morris's Rept.*, 61–2. Petroff says that in 1880 the natives used Sandwich Island sugar for this purpose. *Pop. Alaska*, 13. Beardslee states that in 1879 a number of hootchenoo distilleries near Sitka were broken up. *Rept. Affairs, Alaska*, 16.

[66] *Morris's Rept.*, 62; and letter of I. C. Dennis in *Puget Sound Argus*, Nov. 23, 1877. 'And yet,' remarks the deputy collector, 'white men were ar-

raids were made on the distilleries, and the proceeds detained until it could be settled by the proper authorities what should be done with them. What was done with them was seldom known, but it is certain that no real effort was made to check this evil, though pretended restrictions were sometimes placed on vendors of raw sugar and molasses.

At least, a considerable amount of revenue might have been derived from this source, enough, perhaps, if honestly collected, to offset a large part of the excess in disbursements over receipts, which has occurred each year since Sitka was declared a port of entry. Between July 1, 1869, and May 1, 1878, the receipts of the customs district of Alaska from all sources were $57,464.95, while the disbursements for the same period were $116,074.87. The operations of the Alaska Commercial Company, of which mention will be made later, were confined almost entirely to the Prybilof Islands, and have yielded an income to the United States sufficient to pay good interest on the purchase money. But the rent paid for the fur-seal islands since 1871, apart from the tax on furs, has barely covered the deficit of revenue in other portions of the territory. Under these circumstances, it was recommended by the secretary of the treasury, in December 1877, that Sitka should be abolished as a port of entry,[67] or, in other words, that Alaska should be left to take care of itself.

It would seem that a territory which for the five years ending May 1, 1876, paid into the United States treasury as rent for the Prybilof Islands, and tax on seal skins, more than $1,700,000,[63] or nearly four and three quarters per cent a year on the purchase money,

rested, confined, and prosecuted on a charge of having introduced at Wrangell a bottle of liquor.

[67] Rept. in House Ex. Doc., 45th Cong. 2d Sess., xxx. The receipts and disbursements of the customs district of Alaska between July 1, 1869, and May 1, 1878, are given in detail, for each year, in Morris's Rept., 11–12.

[63] Fernando Wood's Rept., Alaska Com. Co., in House Com. Repts, 44th Cong. 1st Sess., app. C, 19.

deserved a better fate.   It is at least the only territory
that yields, or ever has yielded, any direct revenue; and
yet, notwithstanding all the bills and petitions laid before congress for its organization, it was without government, and almost without protection.

" I recommend civil government," writes General
Howard to the secretary of war, in 1875, "by attaching
Alaska to Washington Territory as a county, as the
simplest solution of all difficulties in the case."[69]   In a
despatch to the secretary of the navy, dated January
22, 1880, the commander of the *Jamestown*, then stationed at Sitka, remarks: "A court should be established possessing full power to summon a jury and try
and settle all minor cases of delinquency on the spot,
and with power to make arrests and inflict punishment
of fine or imprisonment.   For offences of magnitude
this court should have full power to take all testimony,
which should be received by the United States court
at Portland as final. . . . The land here should be surveyed and existing titles perfected and protected, and
it made possible to transfer real estate."[70]   " Either
the civil laws of the United States should be extended over the Indians," remarks Colyer, "or a code

[69] In the same year a bill was introduced by Senator Mitchell, and one in
1876 by Delegate Garfielde (from Washington Ter.), for this purpose. In
Cong. Globe, 1875–6, 194, it is stated that the latter bill was referred to committee, but nothing came of either of them. In 1867 a bill to organize the
territory was introduced by James M. Ashley, *House Jour.*, *40th Cong. 1st
Sess.*, 269, and one in 1871 to provide a 'temporary civil organization for the
territory.' *U. S. Sen. Jour.*, 566, and *House Rept.*, 2944. In 1880 a bill was
before congress for organizing the territory. On December 13, 1881, it was
resolved in the senate, 'that the committee on territories be instructed to inquire as to the expediency of organizing civil government in Alaska.' *U. S.
Sen. Jour.*, *47th Cong. 1st Sess.*, 96. In the same session a senate joint resolution authorizing the president to declare martial law in Alaska was read
twice and referred, *Id.*, 1281; and a bill for establishing courts of justice
and record in the territory was read twice, referred, and reported on unfavorably. *Id.*, 1162. During this session a petition of the citizens of south-
eastern Alaska for a territorial government, a resolution of the San Francisco
board of trade in favor of the introduction of civil law, and a memorial of the
Portland (Or.) board of trade in favor of the establishment of territorial government were presented, of course with the usual result.

[70] *Beardslee's Rept.*, 34. On page 14 of this report Beardslee says: 'There
are a number of miners, mining engineers, and others, etc., who are desirous
of settling in Sitka and bringing their families. If they could preëmpt land
here, or purchase land and houses from the government, the place would take
a step forward; this they cannot do.'

of laws at once adopted defining crime and providing a judiciary and a police force to execute it."[71] "What this country wants is law, and without it she will never flourish and prosper," remarks I. C. Dennis, on resigning his position as deputy collector at Wrangell in 1878. "I have acted in the capacity of arbitrator, adjudicator, and peace-maker until forbearance has ceased to be a virtue. Within the past month one thousand complaints by Indians have been laid before me for settlement, and as I am neither Indian agent nor justice of the peace, I decline the honor of patching up Indian troubles."

The main obstacle in the establishment of some form of civil government for Alaska appears to have been the difficulty in reconciling the conflicting claims of the several sections, separated as they are by a vast extent of territory, and having few interests in common. South-eastern Alaska has mines, timber, and fisheries, though it is not probable that any of these resources except the last will receive much attention in the near future. On Cook Inlet in Kadiak, on the Alaskan peninsula, and on the Aleutian Islands there are also mines and fisheries, but fur-hunting is still the leading industry. In the far north, on the banks of the Yukon, now almost deserted by white men, salmon canneries may be established at no distant day, which will rival those of the Columbia River; while at the Prybilof Islands, the catch of fur-seals produces at present a larger aggregate of wealth than all the other industries of the territory combined.

In 1883 Alaska was but a customs district, with a collector and a few deputies. For laws, the territory had the regulations made by the secretary of the treasury; and for protection, the presence of a single war-vessel, the crew of which was sometimes employed as a police force among the settlements of the Alexander Archipelago.

[71] *Rept.*, 560-1. Colyer recommends that the savage tribes be put on reservations, but this would seem impracticable.

From St Paul to Sitka the distance is but five hundred and fifty miles, and from Iluiliuk in Unalaska about a thousand miles; and yet the deputies at both of these stations could rarely report to the collector except by way of San Francisco, nearly twenty degrees to the south of either point. The mail service established between Sitka and Port Townsend extended only to Fort Wrangell and Harrisburg, and in some parts of the territory the visit of a whaling-vessel or revenue cutter afforded until recently the only means of communication with the outside world.[72]

Among the wants of Alaska, remarks a special agent of the census of 1880, are "a gradual but systematic exploration of the interior, and an immediate survey of the coast and harbors of the region now constantly frequented by trading and fishing vessels, in order to prevent the alarmingly frequent occurrence of wrecks upon unknown rocks and shoals."[73] The navigation of the Alaskan coast is in many parts extremely intricate, and as yet reliable charts exist only for a few sections. Some progress has been made in this direction, however, since the purchase, and as I have already observed, we may in the remote future possess reliable charts for the entire coast and more definite information as to the interior.

In 1867 an expedition organized by the treasury department sailed from San Francisco on board the revenue steamer *Lincoln,* and during the summer passed several months in exploring and obtaining information concerning the newly purchased country.

[72] In 1869 the United States senate resolved that the committee on post-offices inquire as to the expediency of establishing a mail service between Portland and Alaska. *Sen. Jour., 41st Cong. 1st Sess.,* p. 77. Mail statistics for 1876-7 are given by the postmaster-gen. in *Rept., 44th Cong. 2d Sess.,* and in *House Ex. Doc., 45th Cong. 2d Sess.,* vii. part ii. There are no overland mails. During the latter part of the Russian occupation there appears to have been regular overland communication. In 1857 the agent at Saint Michael was instructed to send an overland mail to Sitka by way of Cook Inlet and Kadiak. In the previous year the mail had arrived safely and in good order. *Sitka Archives,* i. 264.

[73] *Ivan Petroff,* in *Internat. Rev.,* Feb. 1882, 122-3.

Among the members was George Davidson, who was placed in charge of the coast survey party, and whose report was printed by order of congress, and forms a most valuable memoir.[74]

In 1869 a party was sent to the Yukon River, in charge of Charles W. Raymond, for the purpose of ascertaining the amount of the Hudson's Bay Company's trade in that district, and the quantity of goods forwarded from British territory; also to obtain information concerning the sources of the Yukon and its tributaries, and the disposition of the tribes in its neighborhood.[75] In 1871–2 W. H. Dall surveyed the Aleutian and Shumagin Islands and located several new harbors.[76] In 1879 a valuable set of charts of Sitka Sound was forwarded to the bureau of navigation by L. A. Beardslee, the commander of the *Jamestown.*[77] Thus some little effort has been made toward the survey and exploration of the territory, if none as yet toward its development.

[74] *U. S. Coast Survey, 40th Cong. 2d Sess.*, app. 18, p. 187. The personnel of the expedition is given in *Id.*, 198–9. The most interesting parts of the report, relating to climate, vegetable productions, fisheries, timber, and fur-bearing animals, were republished in the *Coast Pilot of Alaska* (Washington, 1869). Some valuable collections in natural history and ethnology were supplied by Davidson and others to the Smithsonian Institution. *Smithsonian Rept.*, 1867, p. 43.

[75] The report is published in *Sen. Doc., 42d Cong. 1st Sess.*, 12. In 1880 a partial exploration of the Chilkat River was made by a private party. An account of it is given in *Bancroft Library Scraps*, 190–2.

[76] Fourteen according to *Rept. Coast Survey*, 1872, 49, but most of them were known before, at least to the Russians. In *Id.*, 1873, 122, is given the height of a number of mountains as estimated by Dall, who gives as the height of Mount Shishaldin in Oonimak, 8,683 feet. Alphonse Pinart, a French scientist, attempted its ascent in September 1872, but after attaining, as he relates, a height of 8,782 feet, was confronted by almost perpendicular walls of ice. *Voy.*, 13. During a canoe voyage from Unalaska to Kadiak, he stopped at an island which he calls Vozoychenski (probably Voznessensky), where he met an Aleut, who was said to be 120 years of age, and remembered the time the Russians took possession of the country. *Id.*, 15.

[77] Beardslee claims that his officers discovered a better channel into Sitka Harbor than any before known. *Rept. Affairs, Alaska*, 9.

CHAPTER XXIX.

COMMERCE, REVENUE, AND FURS.

1868-1884.

THE exports from California to Siberia amounted
for the year ending June 30, 1883, to a very large
sum, and were greatly in excess of the amount for the
previous year. The imports for 1883 were valued at
$2,887,200, and never exceeded in any year $3,000,-
000. There is probably no country in the world holding commercial relations with which the balance of
trade is so largely in favor of the United States.

The commerce between Alaska and other portions
of the Pacific coast is insignificant, but will probably
increase now that congress has put that territory
within pale of the law. As is the case with Siberia,
however, imports are largely in excess of exports.

During the existence of the Russian American
Company it will be remembered that trade became
every term more considerable, and yielded each year
a moderate revenue to the imperial government.
There is little doubt that, were any considerable

portions of the territory surveyed and open to preëmption, its resources are sufficient, apart from the seal-grounds, to attract capital and population, and hence to develop traffic. For a year or two after the military occupation there was a fair amount of commerce, but subsequently for a time the fees and duties of the entire district about sufficed to pay the salary of a single deputy collector.

The following figures require little comment: For the six months ending July 1, 1868, the imports on which duty was paid were valued at more than $26,-000; for the twelve months ending March 1, 1878, at $3,295, the decrease meanwhile being gradual. For the year ending December 31, 1870, fines, penalties, and forfeitures amounted to nearly $9,000; for the year ending December 31, 1877, to $10. During 1876 there were no fines, and the revenue collections for that year amounted to $1,417.81,[1] while the cost of collecting this sum, apart from the expense of maintaining revenue cutters, was $11,195. Thus the cost of collection was to receipts about in the ratio of eight to one. And yet the year 1876 compares very favorably with other years. In 1872, for instance, excluding fines, the cost of collecting one dollar of revenue was fifty dollars, and in 1873 sixty dollars.[2] These figures do not, of course, include the royalty on fur-seals, or the rent paid by the Alaska Commercial Company for the lease of the Pribylof Islands.

The total value of domestic exports from Alaska, excluding peltry, was, for 1880, about $90,000, and will no doubt increase when the fisheries are more largely utilized. The value of domestic imports depends partly on the demand at the various mining districts, and especially at the Cassiar district in British Columbia, for which Wrangell is the distributing

---

[1] For duties $724.43, and for tonnage tax $693.38. *Morris's Rept.*, 11. Marine hospital collections for 1876 amounted to $331.70, and this is included by the collector as a part of the revenue.

[2] *Id.*, 11-12. Statistics as to trade will be found in the *Com. and Nav. Repts.*

point, and is therefore fluctuating. In occasional years it reaches or exceeds $350,000,[3] and may average about $300,000, the principal commodities being California flour, tea, coarse sugar, and tobacco. The demand is about equally divided between eastern and western Alaska, the latter having imported from San Francisco in 1880 nearly 20,000 barrels of flour.[4]

It is worthy of note that a territory which absorbs this amount of produce should import so trifling a quantity of duty-paying goods, and that the cost of collecting the duty on these goods should be three or four times their value, and at least eight times that of the revenue collected. Moreover, it is difficult to account for the fact that fines, penalties, and forfeitures should have decreased from $8,843 in 1870 to $2,921 in 1872, increased to $5,814 the following year, and fallen to nothing in 1876. Hootchenoo distilleries were in full blast, it will be remembered, almost throughout the military occupation; there is no evidence that there was less smuggling in 1872 than in 1870; and there is no evidence that there was less smuggling in 1876 than in 1873. On the contrary, there is strong evidence that smuggling was steadily on the increase during and after the military occupation.

The fact that imports of duty-paying goods decreased from $26,000 for the six months ending July 1, 1868, to about $3,000 for the year ending March 1, 1878, and that, meanwhile, trade had been so honestly conducted that there was no longer occasion for fines, penalties, or forfeitures, is a matter that invites investigation. Apart from the negligence of officials, to use no stronger phrase, it is certain that powerful factors have been at work to cause this anomaly, and the main factor is probably the operations of the Hudson's Bay Company.

[3] The value of merchandise that passed through Wrangell alone in 1874 was more than $156,000. *Alaska Her.*, March 15, 1875.

[4] Besides 3,432 cases of hard bread, 733 chests of tea, and 2,943 half-barrels of sugar. *Petroff's Pop. Alaska*, 86. At least 50,000 lbs. of leaf-tobacco were also imported, a part of which came from San Francisco.

When governor of this corporation, Sir George Simpson declared that, without the strip of coast leased to it by the Russian American Company, the interior would be "comparatively useless to England." It will be remembered that, by the Anglo-Russian treaty of 1825, the boundary between the Russian and British possessions was one drawn between the Portland canal and Mount St Elias, and following the trend of the coast range, or at a distance of thirty miles from the sea. By the same treaty it was provided that British subjects should forever enjoy right of navigation on the rivers and streams which cross this line in their course toward the north Pacific. The latter clause was repeated in the treaties of commerce and navigation between Russia and Great Britain in 1843 and 1859.

As the Hudson's Bay Company surrendered most of its possessions to the British government in 1869,[5] and is now merely a private trading corporation, there can bo no doubt that its pretensions are barred by the clause in the treaty of 1867, which declares the cession of Alaska to be free of encumbrance through privileges granted to any association or to any parties except individual property holders. It is also improbable that its employés, or other British subjects, will continue to enjoy right of navigation on the rivers and streams which cross the boundary line.

"In succeeding to the Russian possessions," remarks Sumner, "it does not follow that the United States succeed to ancient obligations assumed by Russia, as if, according to a phrase of the common law, they 'are covenants running with the land.' If these stipulations are in the nature of servitudes, they depend for their duration on the sovereignty of Russia, and are personal or national rather than territorial. So at least I am inclined to believe. But it is hardly profitable to speculate on a point of so little practicable value. Even if 'running with the land,' these servi-

[5] For £300,000 sterling.

tudes can be terminated at the expiration of ten years from the last treaty, by a notice, which equitably the United States may give so as to take effect on the 12th of January, 1869. Meanwhile, during this brief period, it will be easy by act of congress in advance to limit importations at Sitka, so that this 'free port' shall not be made the channel or doorway by which British goods may be introduced into the United States free of duty."[6]

In the customs regulations it is provided that "no duty shall be levied or collected on the importation of peltries brought into the territories of the United States, nor on the proper goods and effects, of whatever nature, of Indians passing or repassing the boundary line aforesaid, unless the same be goods in bales or other large packages unusual among Indians, which shall not be considered as goods belonging to Indians, nor be entitled to the exemption from duty aforesaid."

When we consider that five or six revenue officers, hampered with such restrictions, and some of them a thousand miles apart, collect the customs of a territory whose coast line is more than twice as great as that of the United States,[7] it is not surprising that the results should be nugatory. There is probably no better opportunity for smuggling in any part of the world than amidst the tortuous channels of the Alexander Archipelago and among the Aleutian Islands. Hundreds of bidarkas laden with blankets, molasses, sugar, fire-arms, and other commodities purchased from the Hudson's Bay Company's agents, escape the vigilance of the revenue-cutters, or if detected, the wares are passed off as the "proper

[6] *Speech on Cess. Russ. Amer.*, 11. In the president's message in *Sen. Ex. Doc., 40th Cong. 3d Sess., No. 42*, complaints are made of the encroachments of the Hudson's Bay Company on the trade of Alaska. Ex-Collector Berry states that, after the cession, the company established a town eight or ten miles from the mouth of the Stikeen River, and at the head of tide-water, for the purpose of unloading vessels from Victoria, B. C., at that point, and thus evading custom dues. *Developments, Alaska*, MS., 3.

[7] The coast line of Alaska, including the islands, is 26,000 miles, and of the United States 10,000 miles. *Seward's Our North Pac. States*, 3.

goods and effects of Indians." Among Indians, blankets are still the principal currency, as they were during the régime of the Russian American Company. Blankets of Pacific coast manufacture are sold to-day to a small extent in England, and to a considerable extent in the states and territories east of the Rocky Mountains; but so successful has been this illicit traffic, that a few years ago none but Hudson's Bay Company blankets were to be found among the Indians of Alaska.

Of smuggling among white men, two instances may be mentioned—those of one Charles V. Baranovich, a trader at Karta Bay,[8] and of the Rev. William Duncan, an Episcopalian missionary and teacher, magistrate, and trader at Metlahkatlah, in British Columbia, near the Alaskan border. Baranovich was accused in 1875 of smuggling blankets, hard-bread, and flour. The evidence was conclusive, but there was no jurisdiction in Alaska, and it was not considered worth the expense to indict him in the courts of Oregon or Washington Territory. In the following year, the Rev. W. Duncan was known to have held complicity with smugglers of blankets, silk goods, fire-arms, and molasses.[9] Mr Duncan is criticised perhaps a little too severely by William Gouverneur Morris, a late agent of the treasury department,[10] but it would seem alien to the functions of a missionary to transgress or to connive at the transgression of the United States revenue laws. The expense at which the revenue laws have been administered, and the contempt in which they are held, need no further comment.

Let us now consider the resources of a territory which contains but a few score of American citizens,

[8] Prince of Wales Island.
[9] The evidence in the latter case appears to be sufficiently conclusive. See *Morris's Rept.*, 38-9. Duncan's bidarka fleet, on its way from Metlahkatlah, was chased by Deputy Collector Dennis. Collector M. P. Berry, who ordered the chase, paid the expense out of his own pocket, as for some reason it was disallowed by the accounting officers of the department.
[10] Duncan is complimented very highly in *Colyer's Rept.*, 558-9.

and which was declared 'Indian country' by an ex-attorney-general of the United States. They consist of furs, fisheries, timber, mines, and as some would have us believe, agriculture. The last three are as yet but little utilized, and will be mentioned later. The fur-seal trade, which is at present the most important industry, is now in the hands of the Alaska Commercial Company, of which I shall make some mention before proceeding further.

When negotiations for the sale of the Russian possessions were drawing to a close, a party of San Francisco merchants, among whom was J. Mora Moss, obtained from Prince Maksutof a promise to transfer to them all the property of the Russian American Company; but no contract was signed.

Among those who landed from the *John L. Stephens* at the time of the transfer, however, was a merchant named Hutchinson, who proceeded at once to the castle and made arrangements with the ex-governor to dispose of a portion of the company's vessels and other property to the firm of Hutchinson, Kohl, and Company,[11] on better terms than those offered by Moss and his colleagues. His offer was accepted. A fur-trader named Boscovitch also purchased about sixteen thousand fur-seal skins at forty cents apiece, which were shipped to Victoria and sold for two or three dollars each.[12] Other portions of the company's assets were disposed of to various parties, most of them at rates very much below their value.

In 1869 the Alaska Commercial Company was incorporated, with a capital of $2,000,000. In 1870 a law was passed by congress for the protection of fur-bearing animals,[13] and a lease of the Prybilof or Seal

---

[11] As to the amount of his purchases, there are no reliable data.

[12] Thereupon Boscovitch tried to secure the remainder of the skins; but meanwhile the governor had received orders not to part with them. Among the stock in the warehouses were 80,000 dried fur-seal skins.

[13] For reports, bills, discussions, and investigations concerning the seal-hunting grounds of Alaska, see *Sen. Ex. Doc., 41st Cong. 2d Sess.*, 1; *Sen. Rept., 41st Cong. 2d Sess.*, 47, p. 228–30, and *Cong. Globe*, 1869–70, app. 555–9, 675.

islands granted to the company for a term of twenty years.[14] In 1872 the company purchased the property and interest of Hutchinson, Kohl, & Company.

Apart from the seal islands, the industries of the territory are open to the public, and for the stations which the company has established on the Aleutian Islands and on the peninsula north and west of Kadiak, no special privileges are claimed.

It was estimated by the secretary of the treasury, before the lease was granted, that the cost of maintaining at the expense of the United States a revenue-cutter and a detachment of twenty troops, and of paying the salaries of officials, would amount to $371,200 a year, while a private company could save nearly half that sum.[15]

" The plan I propose," remarked one of the stock-holders[16] to the chairman of committee on commerce in the house of representatives, "asks for no expenditure of money, nor the exercise of any doubtful or unusual power of the government. On the other hand, it will abolish the entire expense of the military and naval establishments, which have already cost the government so much at a time when it could be least afforded; and in the next place, it will put into the treasury $150,000 per annum net revenue at a time when it is most needed."

It must be admitted even by its enemies that the Alaska Commercial Company has thus far more than fulfilled its promise. Instead of $150,000 a year, the

---

[14] Morris, *Rept.*, 151-2, makes the following absurd statement: In 1868-9 there were four or five companies engaged in killing seals on these islands, as fast as they could hire Aleuts to do the work. Among them was an eastern firm that was too religious to allow seals to be killed on the sabbath, but did not hesitate to supply whiskey to the Aleuts in payment for skins. Captain J W. White, of the revenue marine, stopped this wholesale slaughter, which threatened the extermination of the fur-seal, and ordered all the whiskey-barrels to be broken open, and their contents poured on the ground. The Aleuts lapped up the pools of whiskey as dogs lap water. There were but two companies engaged in killing seals on the Prybilof islands in 1868-9, and otherwise the statement is pure fiction.

[15] It was supposed that loss by shipwreck would entail an additional expense of about $168,000. The number of revenue-cutters which the United States proposed to lose each year is not stated in the secretary's report.

[16] Nathan F. Dixon.

average revenue between 1870 and 1883 was about $317,000, and meanwhile the supply of fur-seals increased.[17]

By the act approved July 1, 1870, "to prevent the extermination of fur-bearing animals in Alaska," it was provided that fur-seals should be killed at the Prybilof Islands only during the months of June, July, September, and October, except such as might be required for the food and clothing of the natives; that the slaughter should be restricted to males at least twelve months old; that the number killed each year for their skins should not exceed 75,000 at St Paul and 25,000 at St George Island; and that the use of fire-arms or other weapons tending to drive the seals away should not be permitted. It was estimated by H. W. Elliott, a treasury agent, from surveys made in 1872–3, that only one eighteenth of the aggregate supply was contained at the latter island, and that to secure there 25,000 seals within the time allotted would be a difficult task. Through his efforts the act of 1870 was amended,[18] and the secretary of the treasury authorized to determine the relative number to be killed at each island from season to season. The time for killing was also extended to the first half of the month of August.

According to the terms of its contract, the company was required to pay a fixed rental of $55,000 a year, a tax of $2.62½ on each fur-seal skin, and 55 cents per gallon on all the seal-oil shipped from the Prybilof Islands; to furnish annually to the natives, free of charge, 25,000 dried salmon and 60 cords of fire-wood, together with salt and barrels for preserving seal-meat; and to maintain a school on each island for at least eight months in the year. As the market value of seal-oil ranged from 35 to 55 cents per gallon, the company could not save it except at a loss, and it was

[17] After the indiscriminate slaughter in 1868–9 seals disappeared rapidly from the Prybilof Islands, but two or three years later began to return in vast numbers.

[18] By act approved March 24, 1874.

allowed to go to waste. Though the tax was afterward abolished in consideration of a payment to the natives of 10 cents per gallon, the production of oil was still found to be unprofitable, and shipments have never been considerable.[19]

In the regulations of the Alaska Commercial Company, prescribed in January 1872,[20] are certain provisions as to the remuneration and treatment of the natives, which, together with the obligations of its contract with government, appear to have been faithfully carried out. The Aleuts are to be paid forty cents for each skin delivered, and for other labor a sum to be agreed upon between the company's agents and the parties employed. The working parties are to be under control of native chiefs, and no compulsory labor is to be required. Goods are to be sold at rates not more than twenty-five per cent above the wholesale price in San Francisco, salmon, fuel, and oil being furnished gratis. Widows and orphans at either island are to be supported if necessary at the company's expense. Medicines and medical attendance are to be provided for all free of expense. Free transportation and subsistence on the company's vessels must be furnished to those who any time wish to remove to any island on the Aleutian group. Finally, the agents and employés of the company are strictly enjoined at all times to "treat the inhabitants of the islands with the utmost kindness, and endeavor to preserve amicable relations with them. Force is never to be used against them, except in defense of life, or to prevent

[19] It was alleged in 1876, that the 100,000 seals killed each year would yield at least 200,000 gallons of oil, that if the tax had been maintained it would have yielded $110,000 a year to government, and that the oil would have sold in London for 95 cents per gallon. It is well known that the seals whose fur is most valuable give the least oil, and the average yield is probably nearer half a gallon than two gallons per seal. Moreover, the oil that sells in London for 95 cents a gallon is not fur-seal but hair-seal oil. The former has sometimes no marketable value, and apart from tax, the highest price paid for it never exceeds the cost of production, freight, and other charges. See *House Com. Repts.*, *44th Cong. 1st Sess.*, 623, p. 9.

[20] A copy of them, and also of the 'Act to prevent the extermination of fur-bearing animals in Alaska,' may be found in *Elliott's Seal-Islands, Alaska*, 153-6.

the wanton destruction of valuable property. The agents and servants of the company are expected to instruct the native people in household economy, and by precept and example illustrate to them the principles and benefits of a higher civilization."

The workmen keep a tally of their number of skins, and at the close of each day's labor give the result to their chief. When the skins are afterward counted by the company's agent at the salt-houses, it is seldom that any discrepancy is found. Once a month, or sometimes more frequently, the sum due for the catch is paid to the chiefs, by whom a portion is distributed among the men, the remainder being reserved until the final settlement, which takes place at the end of the season. First-class workmen can thus earn, including extra work, about $450[21] for three or four months' labor, and considering that they are supplied gratis the year round with house-room,[22] fuel, oil, and their staple article of food, it would seem that their condition is much better than that of the majority of laborers in other parts of the world. Not a few of them save money, though thrift is a rare virtue among the Aleuts, and the company allows good interest to those who deposit their savings,[23] some having several thousand dollars to their credit.[24]

Complaints have been made from time to time of

[21] At 40 cents per skin, the payment for the 75,000 skins taken at St Paul Island in 1872 amounted to $30,000, and including extra work, to $30,637.37. This was divided into 74 shares, though in fact only 56 men were at work, portions being reserved for the church, the priest, widows, and orphans. The shares were thus divided: 37 first-class shares at $451.22; 23 second-class shares at $406.08; 4 third-class shares at $360.97; 10 fourth-class shares at $315.85. *Id.*, 25–6. First-class shares are given to those who have worked regularly and are of good standing in the community; second-class to those who have worked irregularly or for a portion of the time; third-class to those who have been idle and worked only when they felt disposed, and fourth-class to boys. *Testimony of Charles Bryant*, in *House Com. Repts., 44th Cong. 1st Sess.*, 623, p. 97.

[22] In 1876 dwellings had been erected on both islands, one for each family. They were lined inside and filled in between the lining and weather-boarding. Stoves were also provided free of expense. *Testimony of John F. Miller*, in *Id.*, 30.

[23] Nine per cent was the rate paid in 1880.

[24] In 1875, eighty natives at St Paul were credited with $34,715.24. *Id.*, 31.

the treatment of natives by the Alaska Commercial Company. Even before its incorporation the commissioner of Indian affairs lamented that the relations of Hutchinson, Kohl, & Company with the Aleuts were merely those of traders, and "in the name of humanity" trusted that the bill which passed the house of representatives in 1868, and which "would virtually reduce the Indians of Alaska to a condition of serfdom," would not become law. What relations other than those of traders he expected to exist between the Aleuts and Hutchinson, Kohl, & Company the commissioner does not state. It is certain, however, that at the Prybilof Islands the treatment of the former has been in marked and favorable contrast with that which they received elsewhere during the military occupation or during the régime of the Russian American Company.

The entire population of the Prybilof Islands numbered, in 1880, nearly four hundred persons,[25] all but eighteen of them being Aleuts. Until these islands were leased to the Alaska Commercial Company, most of the natives lived in sod huts, some of them partly under ground. The fat of seals and a small quantity of drift-wood found on the northern shore of St Paul Island formed their only fuel, and when these failed, they passed the remainder of the long drear winter huddled together beneath seal-skins, in the warmest corner of their dark and noisome dwellings. Now there is in their midst neither poverty, suffering, nor crime,[26] and the villages at St Paul and St George will compare not unfavorably with those of equal size, even in the eastern states. The streets are regularly laid out; each family lives in a comfortable frame dwelling; there are churches and school-houses at both

[25] At St Paul there were 298, including 14 white persons, 128 male and 156 female Aleuts; at St George the population was 92, including 4 whites, 35 male Aleuts and 53 females, an increase of 30 or 40 souls since 1873. *Elliott's Seal-Islands, Alaska*, 20.

[26] There are no policemen nor courts of justice, and since 1870 there has not been a single instance where the presence of a justice of the peace was needed. *Id.*, 22.

from the government for seal-fishing on the Saint George's and Saint Paul's islands."

In the fourth section of the act of July 1, 1870, for the protection of the seal-islands, it is ordered that the secretary of the treasury shall immediately lease the Prybilof Islands "to proper and responsible parties, to the best advantage of the United States, having due regard to the interests of the government, the native inhabitants, the parties heretofore engaged in the trade, and the protection of the seal-fisheries, for a term of twenty years from the 1st day of May, 1870." In the sixth section it is provided "that the annual rental to be reserved by said lease shall be not less than fifty thousand dollars per annum, to be secured by deposit of United States bonds to that amount, and in addition thereto a revenue tax or duty of two dollars is hereby laid upon each fur-seal skin taken from said islands during the continuance of such lease."

On the 8th of July, 1870, an advertisement was published by order of the secretary of the treasury, stating that bids would be received for a period of twelve days, and among them was one from Louis Goldstone, offering to pay, in addition to $55,000 of rental, 2.62\frac{1}{2}$ for each seal-skin and 55 cents for each gallon of seal-oil. Goldstone represented three parties in California, among whom was the "American Russian Commercial Company," which withdrew about the time that the bids were opened, notice to that effect being immediately sent to Mr Boutwell.

After considering all the proposals, together with the character, fitness, and financial responsibility of the parties, the secretary decided that the Alaska Commercial Company best fulfilled the conditions named in the act, and could give the surest guarantee of a faithful and intelligent performance of their contract. He therefore awarded to them the lease on the same terms as were offered by Goldstone, the company agreeing, moreover, to furnish food and fuel, and to maintain free schools for the use of their native employés on the Prybilof Islands.

Such, in brief, is the story of this transaction—one that, like the purchase, is supposed to be deeply shrouded in mystery, but was in fact a very straight forward, business-like proceeding.

Mr Boutwell, in giving his testimony before the committee, stated that the lease was assigned by his direction, after such investigation as was thought necessary on the question of granting to the Alaska Commercial Company the preference. The matter had been first submitted to the attorney-general, who had also been asked whether, in his opinion, it was the duty of the secretary to give public notice of the passage of the bill, and to invite proposals. The reply was that the company was entitled to preference only so far as the secretary should consider them to have peculiar facilities for the performance of the contract, and that the invitation for public bids was a matter that lay very much within his own discretion. If the terms which the company offered were as favorable to the government, to the inhabitants of the seal-islands, and to the protection of the seal-fisheries as those which could be obtained in any other quarter, or nearly so, "then, under the provisions of the act, they would be entitled to a preference." [30]

General Miller testified that the Alaska Commercial Company offered for the lease as much as any other proper and responsible party, and in addition, the considerations above mentioned. The proposals were merely invited by the secretary for his own information, and he had of course the power to reject any or all of them, as he saw fit. Being asked whether, if the contract had been let to other parties, they could have fulfilled it satisfactorily, General Miller replied

[30] *Id.*, 49-50. Mr Boutwell's testimony was confirmed by that of W. A. Richardson, assistant secretary, by whom the contract was signed, the former being absent from Washington at the time. Mr Richardson states that Boutwell was very much opposed to leasing the seal-islands at all, but the law having been passed, and the attorney-general having rendered his opinion, there was no alternative. *Id.*, 60.

that it would have been very difficult for them to do so. They could not have obtained at the islands the use of a single building, nor any of the appliances needed for carrying on the business, since all of them belonged to the Alaska Commercial Company,[31] a member of which had also made contracts with the natives for their labor. To build salt-houses, boats, dwelling-houses, and procure what else was needed, would require much time and capital, whereas the company had already on hand everything that was necessary. Hence they were better fitted to carry on the business than were other parties.

In addition to the above reasons for granting the lease to this company, it may be stated that among its stockholders were three firms, certain of whose members had more experience in fur-sealing and the fur-seal business than any of the remaining applicants, their names being Williams, Haven, and Company of New London, John Parrott and Company of San Francisco, and Hutchinson, Kohl, and Company. These firms afterward consolidated and formed the nucleus of the present Alaska Commercial Company, the first of them being the oldest and most successful of all firms connected with the American fur trade. At the time when the lease was assigned, this association represented a capital of nine millions of dollars, and owned no less than fifty trading posts in various parts of Alaska.

As to the bid tendered by Louis Goldstone, it remains only to be said that, on the withdrawal of the American Russian Commercial Company, the secretary of the treasury considered it thereby invalidated, probably not deeming Mr Goldstone and his colleagues "proper and responsible parties," "having due regard to the interests of the government." Certain it is that the offer made by Goldstone was suspiciously liberal—more liberal than the law required,

---

[31] Being transferred by Mr Hutchinson to the firm of Hutchinson, Kohl, and Company, and by the latter to the Alaska Commercial Company. Testimony of H. M. Hutchinson, in *Id.*, pp. 112, 118.

though less so than the terms ultimately proposed by the Alaska Commercial Company. The action taken by the secretary gave sore offence to Goldstone and his associates, by some of whom a pamphlet was published, entitled the *History of the Wrongs of Alaska*,[32] a memorial being also forwarded to the representatives and referred to committee, in which it was alleged that the lease had been illegally assigned. The statement was afterward retracted, as having been made under a misapprehension of the facts, and the memorial withdrawn.[33]

If any other evidence be needed, in addition to the statements already mentioned, we have the testimony of the Hon. B. H. Bristow, of which more later, Joseph S. Moore, and other responsible gentlemen, whose answers before the committee were unanimously in favor of the company. Finally, we have the report of the members of the committee themselves, who "concur in the opinion that the lease with the Alaska Commercial Company was made in pursuance of the law; that it was made in the interest of the United States, and properly granted to the Alaska Commercial Company; that the interest of the United States was properly protected in all the requirements of the law; and that the lessees have faithfully complied with their part of the contract."

[32] A copy of it will be found in *House Ex. Doc., 44th Cong. 1st Sess.*, no. 83, p. 152-71.
[33] A copy of the letter will be found in *House Com. Repts., 44th Cong. 1st Sess.*, 623, p. 136. It reads as follows:

SAN FRANCISCO, CAL., Dec. 15, 1871.

HONORED SIR: During the last session of Congress a memorial was prepared by the undersigned and associates and presented to the House, and referred to your committee, in which it was alleged that the lease to the Alaska Commercial Company by the United States, for the islands of St Paul and St George, Alaska, August 3, 1870, was illegally obtained by said company from the Secretary of the Treasury, and ought to have been awarded to the undersigned and associates. I now desire to withdraw said memorial. The allegations contained therein, having been made under a misapprehension of facts, are therefore untrue. The undersigned, representing the memorialists, as an act of justice to the Secretary of the Treasury and all concerned, begs to withdraw all statements of complaint contained in said memorial.

I have the honor to be, sir, your obedient servant,
LOUIS GOLDSTONE.
HON. JOHN A. BINGHAM, Chairman Judiciary Committee House of Representatives, Washington, D. C.

Among the papers submitted to the committee of ways and means were two communications from Robert Desty of San Francisco. In the first one, dated February 28, 1876, he cites a number of charges against the company,[34] which then solicited an investigation, and which he compares to a "thief who aims to keep himself always ready to be searched, depending on having the search directed by himself." He also states that he has delivered to Senator Jones, of Nevada, certain documents relating to Alaska, to which he refers the committee. "I am not a trader," writes Desty, "never was, and never likely to be, have no interest in Alaska, but for many years I have been a close student of its affairs, and have contributed some to writing up its resources, which I believe to be greatly underrated by the company; and desiring to see an honest administration of the affairs of government, I took the liberty thus to address you."

From Desty's second communication, dated May 1, 1876, I will give a few extracts, which may serve to explain the *History of the Wrongs of Alaska* and the newspaper comments to which it gave rise. "Some time since I forwarded to you a collection of documents, and a written statement of the affairs of the Alaska Commercial Company. Since that time I have taken especial pains to investigate as far as I was able the matters involved therein, and I have become convinced that most of the charges against the company are not founded on facts which can be proved.

"Having written nearly all the newspaper articles which have appeared in the San Francisco papers during the last seven years against the Alaska Commercial Company, and being the author, in print, of most of the charges which have been published against that company...I deem it incumbent on me to make the following statement...Being a poor man, and a writer, I wrote upon this subject such things as I was required to write by those who employed me; and

[34] They are given in *Id.*, p. 139–43.

being a radical in politics, of the French school, I was the more easily deceived, and more readily accepted the statements which charged oppression and wrongful acts upon the part of this powerful company as true, and wrote them up with all the vigor and zeal I possessed, induced by my natural desire to protect the weak against the strong.

"It is well known that there has existed in this city for several years a combination of individuals, mostly fur-dealers, who singly and together, under various names, have made common cause against the Alaska Commercial Company. For a time they took the name of the 'Alaska Traders' Protective Association;' lately they have assumed the name, 'The Anti-Monopoly Association of the Pacific Coast.'[35]

"It was in the interest of this combination, as I now discover, that I was employed to write, and the alleged facts and charges which I have from time to time written and published against the company were furnished by one and another of these parties.[36]

"The pamphlet called the *History of the Wrongs of Alaska* was mostly composed of statements and charges made by me in the *Alaska Herald* and other sources—the articles written by me and published in the *Alaska Herald* and other San Francisco papers,[37] and in the New York and Chicago papers.

"The object and purpose of all these various publications on the part of this combination was to raise a clamor against the Alaska Commercial Company, and by charging fraud and oppression continually, make the company so odious to the public that congress would take action towards the abrogation of its contract of lease for the Seal Islands.

[35] The names of the members, according to Desty's information, are given in *Id.*, 141. Desty states that he was himself invited to become a member, but declined.

[36] 'And others in written memoranda furnished by the pen of Honcharenko, and which I elaborated into the articles which appeared in print.'

[37] Desty states that Honcharenko was never in Alaska, and that the *Alaska Herald* was published for several years in San Francisco, and supported by the combination and their sympathizers.

"I now desire to retract all I have written against the company, and this I do freely and voluntarily, without fear or compulsion of any sort, but as an act of simple justice."

Desty's communications, for whatever they were worth, were put on file as evidence. Their worth is probably known to those who were residents of San Francisco when the suit of Thomas Taylor and others versus the Alaska Commercial Company and others was tried in 1871,[38] and they are mentioned in these pages merely to explain in part the adverse comments that have appeared in the press and in various pamphlets.

Perhaps the most valuable testimony educed during the investigation was that of B. H. Bristow. "I understand you to say," remarked a member of the sub-committee, "that you have instituted all the inquiries that you deem necessary, but that you have not found anything against the company that is reliable?" "Yes, sir," replied the secretary of the treasury, "all that I thought necessary—indeed, all that I could; for, to speak the plain truth, when it came to my knowledge that the company was making a very large profit out of the matter,[39] I felt that the government was not getting as much as it ought to have, and I wanted to find some way of getting a share of the profits for the government; but I found myself confronted with the law and this contract, and I saw no reason to believe that the company were not carrying out their contract in good faith, whatever may be the suspicions by which they are surrounded."

The only charge worthy of mention that was brought home to the Alaska Commercial Company was a dis-

[38] A portion of the evidence in this case, of which I have a copy, will be found in the *Alaska Com. Co.*, MS.

[39] Miller testified that the company lost money the first year, but the second year made a small profit, that for the third year the dividend was ten per cent, and for 1875 fifteen per cent. *House Com. Repts.*, *44th Cong. 1st Sess.*, 623, p. 37, where are given the names of the stockholders in 1876.

crepancy of $1,467.37 [40] between the accounts kept by
the custom-house and those of the company; and in
the opinion of the official appointed to examine the
company's books, this was due to an error of the government agents.

In 1869 the value of a fur-seal skin in London, the
world's mart for peltry, did not exceed three or four
dollars, but at that date the tax was one dollar per
skin.   In 1876 a first-class skin delivered in London
cost the company six to six and a half dollars; its
market value at that date before being dressed or
dyed was about fifteen dollars, and in 1881 twenty
dollars.   The enhanced price is due in part to better
preservation, but more to whim of fashion.

The demand for furs is of course controlled by fashion.   As men wear beaver hats in summer, so do
women seal-skin sacks.   Among others, furriers regulate fashion.   "When I was in London," remarks
Miller, "I talked with all the great furriers, and
they were delighted to know that they could calculate with reasonable certainty upon the number of
skins that were to be put upon the market each year.
The furriers influence fashion.   The value of this
article is subject to the caprice of fashion, but the furriers themselves aid in making the fashions, and they
make the fashion for an article that will pay."

Among the charges brought against the Alaska
Commercial Company was that of taking more than the
number of skins allowed by law.   It is unnecessary to
discuss this charge.   As a fact, they usually take one
or two hundred less than the number prescribed, and
not until 1881 did the number of accepted skins
amount to a hundred thousand. [41]   "If we overran the

[40] The amount of tax on 539 skins at $2.62½ each.
[41] *Elliott's Seal Islands, Alaska*, 169.   The list of the treasury agent is the
official indorsement of the company's catch.   The skins are shipped to San
Francisco, where they are counted.   'As it never happened before, until the
season of 1881,' remarks Elliott, 'that the two counts at San Francisco and St
Paul have agreed to a unit, the company has given strict and imperative
orders that no more than 99,500 or 99,850 shall be annually taken by its

market to any appreciable extent," stated Miller, in evidence, "it would certainly knock the price down, and it would do it because it disturbs the present equilibrium."

At the Prybilof Islands the government has what may be termed a stock-farm, which yields an income of more than $300,000 a year. The advantages of leasing these islands to responsible parties are thus stated by Henry W. Elliott, formerly a treasury agent, who inspected the seal-grounds in 1876:

"First. When the government took possession of these interests, in 1868 and 1869, the gross value of a seal-skin laid down in the best market, at London, was less in some instances, and in others but slightly above, the present tax and royalty paid upon it by the Alaska Commercial Company.

"Second. Through the action of the intelligent business men who took the contract from the government, in stimulating and encouraging the dressers of the raw material, and in taking sedulous care that nothing but good skins should leave the islands, and in combination with leaders of fashion abroad, the demand for the fur, by this manipulation and management, has been wonderfully increased.

"Third. As matters now stand, the greatest and best interests of the lessees are identical with those of the government; what injures one injures the other. In other words, both strive to guard against anything that shall interfere with the preservation of the seal-life in its original integrity, and both having it to their interest if possible to increase that life; if the lessees had it in their power, which they certainly have not, to ruin these interests by a few seasons of rapacity, they are so bonded and so environed that prudence prevents it.

agents from the seal-islands. Taking the full quota for this season of 1881 was contrary to its express direction.' In the *Rept. on Finances*, in *House Ex. Doc.*, *47th Cong. 2d Sess.*, 47, the secretary of the treasury states that in 1882 the Alaska Commercial Co. took 'nearly the maximum number of seal-skins permitted under its lease, paid the tax thereon, as well as the rent of the islands, and otherwise performed its duties under its lease.'

"Fourth. The frequent changes in the office of the
secretary of the treasury, who has very properly the
absolute control of the business as it stands, do not
permit upon his part of that close, careful scrutiny
which is exercised by the lessees, who, unlike him,
have but their one purpose to carry out. The character of the leading men among them is enough to
assure the public that the business is in responsible
hands, and in the care of persons who will use every
effort for its preservation and its perpetuation...As
matters are now conducted, there is no room for any
scandal—not one single transaction on the islands but
what is as clear to investigation and accountability
as the light of the noon-day sun; what is done is
known to everybody, and the tax now laid by the
government upon and paid into the treasury every
year by the Alaska Commercial Company yields
alone a handsome rate of interest on the entire purchase money expended for the ownership of all
Alaska."[42]

It is probable that the lease of the Prybilof Islands
has been a much more profitable transaction, both for
the government and the Alaska Commercial Company, than was anticipated at the time when it was
signed. In 1871 Hutchinson, Kohl, & Company
obtained a lease of Bering, Copper, and Robben
islands on very much more favorable terms. The
rental was but five thousand roubles in silver, and the
royalty two roubles. The minimum number of skins
that should be taken was fixed at one thousand, but
otherwise there was no limit.[43]

In many parts of Alaska there were, in the time of
the Russian American Company, as the reader will

[42] *Seal Islands, Alaska*, 26-7. 'It is frequently urged with great persistency, by misinformed or malicious authority,' continues Elliott, 'that the
lessees can and do take thousands of skins in excess of the law, and this catch
in excess is shipped *sub rosa* to Japan from the Pribylov Islands.' To show
the impossibility of such action on the part of the company, he then states
the conditions under which the skins are taken.
[43] A copy of the lease is given in *House Com. Repts.*, *44th Cong. 1st Sess.*,
623, app. B.

remember, seal-grounds of great value, but where to-day the catch is inconsiderable. In the south Pacific there were, less than fifty years ago, rookeries frequented by millions of seals, and which now yield but five to ten thousand skins a year. That the same fate would have overtaken the Prybilof Islands, but for the intervention of congress; that, instead of the five millions of fur-seals which at present make these islands their summer resort, there would have been but a few thousands, cannot reasonably be doubted.[44] They return each year only because they are not allowed to be disturbed by the sound of fire-arms or by other means, much care and method being used during the slaughtering season.

When they come in from the north Pacific in early summer, the seals usually select their landing-places on the south and south-eastern shores of the Prybilof Islands, mainly, as is supposed, because the winds, blowing at that season usually from the north and west, carry out to sea the scent of their old rookeries. During the month of May only a few hundreds of full-grown males are to be seen on the grounds, but about the first week in June, when banks of gray fog begin to enshroud the islands, the males swarm in daily by thousands, and choose locations for their harems close to high-water mark.

Toward the end of the month the females arrive, and meanwhile a constant fight has been going on between the new-comers and those already in the field, during which the latter, exhausted by repeated conflicts, are often driven higher up the rookery and away from the water-line. The contests are only among the full-grown males,[45] which dispute in single combat the choicest spots; and veterans have been known to fight thirty or forty pitched battles in order

[44] About 3,000,000 are full-grown females. Where they all harbor during the rest of the year is not known, but it is believed that they spend the winter south of the Aleutian Islands, in places where fish are abundant. *Hittell's Com. and Ind., Pac. Coast*, 332.
[45] Eight years old or more.

to maintain their ground until the arrival of the females, when it seems to be understood that those who have held their own shall not be disturbed for the season.[46]

The combatants approach warily and with averted gaze. When at close quarters they make feints or passes like pugilists in the ring, their heads darting in and out and their eyes gleaming with a lurid light. After much preliminary roaring and writhing, they seize each other with their long canine teeth, and when the grip is relaxed, the skin and blubber of one or both are scarred with furrows, the blood streaming down meanwhile, and the conflict being perhaps the most singular that man can witness.

"Thus," as Elliott remarks, "about two thirds of all the males which are born, and they are equal in numbers to the females born, are never permitted by the remaining third, strongest by natural selection, to land upon the same breeding-ground with the females, which always herd thereupon en masse. Hence, the great band of bachelor seals, or holluschickie,[47] so fitly termed, when it visits the island is obliged to live apart entirely, sometimes, and in some places, miles away from the rookeries; and in this admirably perfect method of nature are those seals which can be properly killed without injury to the rookeries selected and held aside, so that the natives can visit and take them without disturbing, in the least degree, the entire quiet of the breeding-grounds, where the stock is perpetuated."

To the bachelor seals remains the choice of taking up their abode—in technical phrase, 'hauling up'— in rear of the rookeries, or on what are termed the free beaches. For the former purpose a path is left through the married-quarters by which they pass in ceaseless files, day or night, at will. No well con-

[46] Elliott states that he has seen a veteran seal fight 40 or 50 battles and beat off all his assailants, coming out of the campaign with the loss of an eye, and covered with raw and festering scars. *Seal Islands, Alaska,* 32.

[47] A Russian word for bachelors.

ducted holluschick is molested on the way, but woe
to him that keeps not straight on his path, or looks
askant and sniffs in the neighborhood of a harem.
Loss of flipper or of life is the sure penalty.

During the early part of the season, the bachelor seals
that select as their ground the free beaches haul up[43]
within a few rods of high-water mark, and to effect
their capture great caution is required.   At the first
glimpse of dawn, a party of natives is sent to the
spot whence the seals are to be driven to the slaugh-
tering-ground, and while their victims are still dozing,
creep stealthily between them and the surf.   When
roused, they find themselves cut off from retreat to
the sea, and crawl or lope in the direction in which
they are guided by the Aleuts, who, brandishing their
clubs, but as noiselessly as possible, walk slowly on
the flank and in rear of the drove.   In this manner, under favorable circumstances, several thousand
fur-seals may be driven by a dozen men, but usually
only a few hundred are taken at a time.

From the hauling-grounds to the killing-grounds
the seals are driven at the rate of about half a mile
an hour, with frequent halts to allow time to cool, as
heating injures the quality of the fur.   During the
'drive,' as it is termed, they never show fight, unless
it should happen that a few veterans are among the
drove.   When the men think it time to halt, they
drop back a few paces, whereupon the holluschickie
stop, and pant, and fan themselves.   The clattering
of a few bones or a shout from their drivers causes
them instantly to resume their march to the slaughtering-grounds.[49]

About seven o'clock the seals are secured in the
slaughtering corral, which is always close to one of the

<hr/>

[48] A phrase applied to the action of seals when they land from the surf and
drag themselves over the beach.

[49] The 'drive' to Lukannon on St Paul Island occupies about two hours,
to Tolstoi on the same island two and a half to three hours, while to Zoltoi,
on St George Island, the distance from the beach is trifling.   These are the
principal slaughtering-grounds. *Id.*, 71 (note).   Opposite that page is a plate
representing a drove on its way to the killing-grounds.

Alaska Commercial Company's villages.   Here they
are allowed to cool until the men have breakfasted, after
which all the Aleuts come forth, armed with bludgeons,
clubs,[50] and stabbing and skinning knives.   At a given
signal the men step into the corral, from which a
hundred or a hundred and fifty are driven at a time,
and surrounded, the circle narrowing until the seals
are huddled together and within reach of the clubs.
The chief then selects those which are doomed, and
a single blow of the club, which will stun and not
kill, is dealt to all.   If the day happen to be warm
and fair, the skin will spoil, unless removed, sometimes
within half an hour,[51] and always within an hour and
a half after the death of the seal.   To avoid waste,
therefore, and to allow those whose furs have been
injured during the harem fights a chance to escape,
the fatal blow is not struck until later, when a single
well aimed stroke of the bludgeon crushes in the slender bones of the victim's skull and stretches him lifeless.[52]

The skins are taken to the salt-house, where they
are carefully examined, and those which are damaged,
the number seldom exceeding one per cent, are rejected.
They are then salted on the fleshy side, and, in sealing
phrase, piled, fat to fat, in 'kenches,'[53] after which
salt is thrown on the outer edges and kept in place by
sliding planks.   In two or three weeks they are pickled,
when they are taken, as required, rolled into bundles
of two, with the fur outward, and are tightly corded.
They are then ready for shipment to San Francisco,
where they are counted by the government agent and
thence forwarded to London in casks containing each
forty to eighty skins.[54]

The method of dressing and dyeing the skins is a

[50] The bludgeons are of hickory, and the clubs five or six feet in length,
and three inches in diameter at the head.
[51] Elliott states that this occurs, but is a rare occurrence.
[52] The blows are usually repeated two or three times.
[53] Large bins.
[54] The average weight of a skin thus pickled is 6 to 10 lbs.   A table of
the weight, size, and growth of the fur-seal at the Prybilof Islands is given
in *Id.*, 46.

trade secret, and for some reason this branch of industry appears to be almost concentrated in London.   Although artisans have been engaged, and dye-stuffs and even water imported from England by the French, furs prepared by artisans of the latter nation are not considered equal to those prepared in London.   The processes previous to that of dyeing, wherein the secret lies, are very simple.   In order to rid it of greasy particles, the skin is first soaked in warm water, and after being scraped clean, again soaked in warm water containing rose-wood or mahogany sawdust.   The fleshy side of the skin is then shaved, in order to cut off the roots of the coarser hairs, which fall out, leaving only the soft fur, which is then ready for the dyeing process.[55]

Whatever has been or may be alleged against the Alaska Commercial Company, it cannot be said with truth that it has diminished the world's wealth.   During the first term of the Russian American Company's existence, the entire catch of fur-seals at the Pribylof Islands was estimated at a little over 1,000,000, during the second term at less than 460,000, and during the third term at about 340,000, each term extending over about twenty years, and almost each year showing a diminution in the supply.   The waste of skins caused through fault of curing has already been mentioned.[56]   In 1868 the slaughter exceeded 240,000, and, as we have seen, the rookeries were threatened with extermination.   In 1883 about 100,000 were killed; their value was greatly enhanced, and during the portion of the company's lease that had then expired the supply was gradually on the increase.

The catch of sea-otter now averages 5,000 to 6,000 a year, or more than double the number secured be-

[55] *Hittell's Com. and Ind. Pac. Coast*, 335.   The price of a good finished skin in London was, in 1881, about $40.

[56] Elliott remarks that the method of curing in early times was to peg them out when green on the ground, or stretch them on a wooden frame.   About 750,000 were spoiled in 1803.

fore the purchase; and their skins are worth in London from $75 to $100.[57]   This industry furnishes profitable employment for a few months in the year to several thousand Aleuts, the skin being the most valuable of all peltry, excepting perhaps the pelt of the black fox.

Silver-gray and black fox-skins were first introduced to fashion, it will be remembered, at St Petersburg.[58] Of either the catch is inconsiderable, that of the silver fox seldom exceeding one hundred, while the appearance of a black fox-skin in the market is of very rare occurrence.   Blue fox-skins are taken to the number of about 2,000.   The red fox has little commercial value.   Of marten and beaver skins considerable shipments are made; but of these, as of other land peltry, the principal supply comes from the Hudson's Bay Company.

[57] For 1879 the catch was 900 in the Kadiak district, and 4,850 in the Unalaska district, the latter including the Shumagin Islands. *Petroff's Pop. Alaska*, 66.
[58] This vol., p. 253.

CHAPTER XXX.

FISHERIES.

1867-1884.

SALMON PACKING—PRICE AND WEIGHT OF THE RAW FISH—YUKON-RIVER
SALMON—ALASKAN CANNERIES—DOMESTIC CONSUMPTION AND WASTE—
THE COD-BANKS OF ALASKA—LARGE INCREASE IN THE CATCH OF COD-
FISH—AND DECREASE IN ITS VALUE—THE HALIBUT-FISHERIES—HER-
RING AND HERRING-OIL—MACKEREL—THE EULACHON OR CANDLE-FISH—
VALUE AND PROSPECTS OF THE ALASKAN FISHERIES—WHALING ENTER-
PRISE—THE NORTH PACIFIC WHALING FLEET—GRADUAL DECREASE
IN THE CATCH—THREATENED EXHAUSTION OF THE WHALING-GROUNDS.

"IN their public prayers," remarks John Adams, "it
is said that the Dutch ask of the supreme being that
it may please him to bless the government, the states,
the lords, and the fisheries." In 1776 the fisheries of
Alaska were unknown to John Adams and to the
Dutch, nor were the Russians aware of their value,
even at the time of the transfer, though it is not improbable that, a generation hence, the waters of this
territory may be one of the main sources of the world's
supply.

There is, of course, no immediate prospect that the
fisheries of Alaska will be extensively utilized unless
other sources of supply should begin to fail. It is a
little significant, however, that the salmon-pack should
have increased from about 8,000 cases in 1880[1] to
36,000 in 1883, the yield in the latter year being
worth about $180,000,[2] while during the interval the

---

[1] *Hittell's Com. and Ind. Pac. Coast*, 375. There were also shipped in 1880
500,000 lbs of salted salmon.
[2] *San Fran. Bulletin*, April 12, 1884. A case contains four dozen one-pound
tins, the value of which is estimated at $1.25 per dozen.

market for canned salmon had become greatly over-stocked. More than 36,000 cases are often shipped by a single cannery on the Columbia, although the price paid per fish in 1883 was on the Columbia seventy cents, and at the Alaska canneries from one cent to five cents.

The average weight of salmon caught in Alaskan rivers, after being cleaned, exceeds fifteen pounds,[3] while on the Columbia it is less than twenty pounds. The flavor of the best fish caught in the former locality is only excelled by that of Scotch and Norwegian salmon, which are considered superior to any in the world. The more northerly the waters in which salmon are taken, the better their flavor. The king salmon, the largest and choicest of the species found in Alaska, not unfrequently attains a weight of eighty and sometimes of a hundred pounds, its range being from the Alexander Archipelago to the Yukon. It is known to ascend that river for more than a thousand miles,[4] the run commencing about the middle of June and lasting till the end of August. So choice is its flavor, that during the régime of the Russian American Company, several barrels of the salted fish were shipped each season to St Petersburg for the use of the friends of the company's officials.[5]

The run of salmon on the Yukon is immense, but lasting as it does only for about six weeks, is at present considered of too brief duration to warrant the investment of capital. The fact that the mouth of the Yukon is not navigable for sea-going vessels is a

[3] In *Morris's Rept.*, *Alaska*, 113, it is stated that at Cook's Inlet they average 60 lbs, and that some have been caught weighing 120 lbs. The statement would be true if it were applied only to king salmon, but is much above the figures for the average catch.

[4] Beyond the site of Fort Yukon.

[5] *U. S. Agric. Rept.* (1870), *41st Cong. 3d Sess.*, 382-3. The more common species have the same range, but their run commences a few days later and they remain longer. A king salmon when dried will make on an average about 20 lbs of *ukali*, as the dried fish was termed by the Indians. In the report the weight of the common species is given at 10 to 30 lbs, and when cleaned and smoked 2 or 3 lbs. These figures are too low. Probably the Aleut process of curing is the one mentioned.

further obstacle. In other rivers and streams of Alaska, however, salmon are almost equally abundant, and it is possible that the proprietors of the Columbia River canneries may find competition from these sources increase more rapidly than they anticipate.

About the year 1868 a cannery was built at Klowak, on Prince of Wales Island, probably the first one in Alaska, and afterward became the property of the San Francisco firm of Sisson, Wallace, and Company, who incorporated under the laws of California, taking the name of the North Pacific and Trading Company.[6] In 1878 Cutting and Company, also of San Francisco, established a cannery near the site of Fort Sv Mikhaïl, or, as it is now termed, old Sitka,[7] and although they did not commence operations until late in the season, their first pack was about five thousand cases.[8] On account of an accident, this cannery was afterward removed to a favorable site on Cook Inlet. In 1883 the Alaska Salmon Packing and Fur Company was incorporated, among its purposes being the canning, salting, and smoking of fish at the lake and harbor of Naha. Small canneries have also been established at other points, and it is worthy of note that they should find the industry remunerative, while, on account of low prices, the canneries of the Columbia, with their superior appliances, have almost ceased to be profitable.

The chief obstacles in the way of the canneries are the shortness of the season, the difficulty in obtaining labor, the great cost of supplies, the want of communication, and the fact that no title can be obtained to land. That raw fish will continue to be cheaper, because more abundant and more easily caught than

---

[6] Morris states that the first year's operations satisfied the firm that the enterprise would be successful. *Rept.*, 115.

[7] Five miles from the present town of Sitka.

[8] *Berry's Developments, Alaska*, MS., 12. Berry states that the firm did not lose money the first season. In *Sen. Ex. Doc., 46th Cong. 2d Sess.*, 105, p. 13, it is stated that the total shipments for 1879 were 6,000 cases, and a large quantity of salted salmon in barrels. At that date there were two other firms in operation.

elsewhere in the world, there is little doubt. It would seem that as salmon can be bought from the natives in Alaska at less than one fifteenth of the price paid on the Columbia, and as Alaska salmon is preferred in the eastern states and in Europe to Columbia River salmon, these difficulties will in time be overcome. Moreover, it is probable that the demand for canned salmon will gradually increase, and that its present low marketable value will not long continue, for few more nourishing and palatable articles of food can be bought at the price, and the entire pack of Alaska would not yet furnish breakfast for the population of London for a single day.

The quantity of salmon shipped from Alaska is of course but a small portion of the annual catch, for this is the staple food of the 30,000 or 35,000 Indians who inhabit the territory.[9] A 30 or 40-pound fish will weigh but four or five pounds when prepared by their wasteful process for winter use, and it is estimated that they take 10,000,000 or 12,000,000 salmons a year, probably at least thrice the number required to supply the demand of all the canneries on the Pacific coast.[10]

The cod-banks of Alaska, like the salmon fisheries, are admitted to be the most extensive known to the world, and only in the waters near this territory, and perhaps three or four degrees farther south, is the *gadus morrhua*, or true cod, known to exist on the Pacific coast. The banks extend at intervals from the Shumagin Islands northward and westward to the ice-line of the Bering Sea, eastward to Cook Inlet, and southward to the strait of San Juan de Fuca,[11] those near

[9] According to the census of 1880 the entire population was 33,426, of whom 430 were white persons, 1,756 creoles, and the remainder Indians.

[10] The Pacific coast pack was estimated, for 1881, at 44,440,000 lbs. *Hittell's Com. and Ind. Pac. Coast*, 380.

[11] *U. S. Agric. Rept.*, 1870, 375. Dodge states that the cod fisheries extend to Bering Strait, and even to the Arctic Ocean. *Morris's Rept.*, 113. A few stragglers may find their way through the strait during summer, but lat. 59° N., which is about the line reached in mid-winter by floating ice, is practically the limit.

are considered the best, but in the neighborhood of Sitka they are perhaps most abundant. At the latter point a canoe load can easily be secured within half an hour. Though a few barrels may occasionally find their way to San Francisco, the Alaska herring has as yet no commercial value except for its oil, for the production of which an establishment was in operation at Prince Frederick Sound in 1883, about 20,000 gallons being obtained in that year.[21] It is admitted that, in bulk and flavor, those taken at Unalaska and elsewhere are quite equal to imported herring, and there appears no good reason why they should not, if properly cured, find a profitable market on this coast.

Mackerel, equal in size and flavor to those captured in Atlantic waters, are found in the bays and straits of the Aleutian and Shumagin islands, and when shipped to San Francisco have met with ready sale, sometimes realizing as much as $24 per barrel. It is probable that, when the range and distribution of this favorite food-fish is better ascertained, a thriving industry may be established in connection with other branches of fishery.

The eulachon, or candle-fish, as it is often termed, a small silvery fish, seldom exceeding fifteen inches in length, and in appearance resembling a smelt, abounds in river and stream as far south as latitude 49°. It is most abundant in Alaskan waters, where for the three or four weeks during which the season lasts, the run is more marvellous even than that of salmon. The eulachon is the fattest of known fish, and the oil tried out from it is sold to the Indians on the Nass River near the Alaskan border[22] at profitable rates.[23] When dried, it serves as a torch, burning with a clear bright flame. Hence its name of candle-fish. When smoked

[21] Besides 3,000 gals of whale oil and 12,000 of dog-fish oil. This industry was established by the North-west Trading Company of Portland. The company has another station at Cordova Bay, where it was proposed to commence work in 1882. *Hittell's Com. and Ind. Pac. Coast*, 357.

[22] The eulachon is also plentiful in the Fraser and Columbia rivers.

[23] About $1 per gal. in 1881. *Id.*, 355. Hittell states that the oil possesses valuable medicinal qualities.

and prepared for table by broiling or steaming, it is equal in flavor to the finest quality of eastern mackerel, and when pickled and shipped to San Francisco, finds a ready market.

On the Nass River, eulachon are usually caught in wicker baskets, and after being dried or smoked are stored up for future use. The fishing commences about the end of March; and in connection with it is a curious custom which prevails elsewhere among the natives and in other branches of fishery. The first eulachon caught is addressed as a chief, and the natives gathering round him, tender profuse apologies that they should be compelled to destroy his kindred in order to supply their wants. Then follows a feast, with speeches, songs, dancing, and of course drinking, after which fishing commences in earnest and continues until all have procured a sufficient stock.

I have mentioned only the varieties that, with the exception perhaps of the white fish, have or are likely to have any commercial value, but in few parts of the world are other kinds more abundant. Among them may be mentioned the tom-cod, smelt, salmon-trout, and grayling,[24] all of which are found in Alaskan waters, the first three being of excellent quality.

The value of all the Alaskan fisheries, in which phrase is included the seal-hunting grounds, was estimated in the census of 1880 at $2,661,640, of which sum fur-seal skins and other pelagic peltry were valued at $2,096,500, and the fisheries proper at $565,140. What will be the commercial value of these fisheries, when, as will probably be the case at no very distant day, the Pacific states and territories are peopled with 15,000,000 instead of 1,500,000 people, and are threaded with railroads almost as com-

---

[24] The tom-cod resembles the eastern fish of that name, but is much better flavored. Smelt are plentiful near Sitka and elsewhere. Salmon-trout of excellent flavor are taken in the smaller rivers and streams. The grayling is of poor quality. Pike are taken in the lakes and ponds of northern Alaska, but are of little value as a table-fish, and are mainly used for dog-feed.

pletely as are now the western states of America?
But when this shall happen, there will doubtless be
more frequent communication with Mexico and Central
and South America; for already Pacific coast manufactures have found a foothold in all these countries,
and it is predicted by political economists that the
manufactures of this coast will exceed both mining
and agriculture in aggregate wealth. The fur-seal
industry is the only one at present utilized to any
considerable extent, but it is not improbable that,
even before the close of this century, the fisheries may
become more valuable than are now the fur-seal
grounds.

Of whaling enterprise in the neighborhood of the
Alaskan coast, mention has already been made; but a
few statements that will serve to explain the enormous decrease that has occurred in the catch within
the last three decades may not be out of place.

Of the six or seven hundred American whalers that
were fitted out for the season of 1857, at least one
half, including most of the larger vessels, were engaged in the north Pacific.[25] The presence of so vast a
fleet tended of course to exhaust the whaling-grounds
or to drive the fish into other waters, for no permanent
whaling-grounds exist on any portions of the globe
except in those encircled by ice for about ten months
in the year. In the seas of Greenland, not many
years ago, whales were rarely to be seen; in 1870 they
were fairly plentiful. The sea of Okhotsk and the
waters in the neighborhood of the Aleutian Islands
were a few decades ago favorite hunting-grounds,[26]
but are now almost depleted, while in 1870 the coast
of New Siberia was swarming with whales. Schools

[25] Including of course the Bering Sea. *Zabriskie's Land Laws*, 882.
[26] Davidson says that in 1868 whales were as plentiful near the Aleutian
group as in the Arctic, but that the shoal waters of the latter greatly facili-
tated their pursuit. *Scient. Exped.*, 476. It would seem that, if they were
as plentiful off the Aleutian Islands as the professor would have us believe,
they would have been taken in greater number. The Aleuts found no difficulty in catching them.

of sperm-whale are occasionally seen between the Alaska Peninsula and Prince William Sound, and the hump-back sometimes makes its appearance as far north as Baranof Island. Between Bristol Bay and Bering Strait a fair catch is sometimes taken, but most of the vessels forming what is termed the north Pacific whaling fleet, now pass into the Arctic Ocean in quest of their prey.[27] Probably not more than eight or ten of them are employed on the whaling grounds of the Alaskan coast.

In 1881 the whaling fleet of the north Pacific mustered only thirty, and in the following year forty craft, of which four were steamers.[28] The catch for 1881 was one of the most profitable that has occurred since the date of the transfer, being valued at $1,139,-000, or an average of about $57,000 for each vessel,[29] some of them returning with cargoes worth $75,000, and few with cargoes worth less than $30,000. In 1883 the catch was inconsiderable, several of the whalers returning 'clean,' and few making a profit for their owners.

The threatened destruction of these fisheries is a matter that seems to deserve some attention. In 1850, as will be remembered, it was estimated that 300 whaling vessels visited Alaskan waters, and the Okhotsk and Bering seas.[30] Two years later the value of the catch of the north Pacific fleet was more than $14,000,000.[31] After 1852 it gradually decreased, until in 1862 it was less than $800,000; for 1867 the amount was about $3,200,000; in 1881 it had again fallen to $1,139,000;

[27] *Sen. Ex. Doc., 42d Cong. 2d Sess.*, 34, p. 2–3. It is there stated that of 28 right whales caught near the coast of Alaska during one season eleven were lost.

[28] A steam whaler was despatched from San Francisco for the first time in 1880. *Hittell's Com. and Ind. Pac. Coast*, 347.

[29] Including 354,000 lbs of whalebone worth $2 to $2.50 per lb., 21,000 bbls of oil at about 35 cents per gallon, and 15,000 lbs of ivory at 60 cents per lb. *Id.*, 348.

[30] P. 584, this vol. They were not of course all American vessels.

[31] The fleet for that year consisted of 278 ships. *Sen. Ex. Doc., 42d Cong. 2d Sess.*, 34, p. 4.

and for the season of 1883 there was a still further reduction.[32]

The whaling-grounds of the north Pacific, though of course open to all nations, are now in the hands of Americans, and were so practically before the purchase.[33] It is probable that the United States will continue to enjoy a virtual monopoly of this industry, for under present conditions it will erelong cease to be profitable.

[32] In *Id.*, 4–5, the value is stated of each year's catch between 1845 and 1867.

[33] In 1864 there were only 14 whalers, in 1865, 18, and in 1866, 9 vessels sailing under other flags. *Id.*, 5.

CHAPTER XXXI.

SETTLEMENTS, AGRICULTURE, SHIP-BUILDING, AND MINING.

1794-1884.

IN May, 1794, Vancouver visited a settlement at Cook Inlet, which he thus describes: "We met some Russians, who came to welcome and conduct us to their dwelling by a very indifferent path, which was rendered more disagreeable by a most intolerable stench, the worst excepting that of the skunk I had ever the inconvenience of experiencing; occasioned, I believe, by a deposit made during the winter of an immense collection of all kinds of filth, offal, etc., that had now become a fluid mass of putrid matter, just without the rails of the Russian factory, over which these noxious exhalations spread, and seemed to become a greater nuisance by their combination with the effluvia arising from their houses."

Cleanliness and comfort were little regarded by the early settlers in Alaska. It will be remembered that Rezanof, calling on the chief manager in 1805, found him occupying a hut at Sitka, in which the bed was often afloat, and a leak in the roof was considered too trivial a matter to need attention. As late as 1841,

Simpson, who visited the settlement during his voyage round the world, declared it, as the reader will remember, the dirtiest and most wretched place that he had ever seen.[1] Nevertheless, it continued to increase rapidly. On the site where the first colonists pitched their tents and lived in constant fear of the Kolosh, there stood, in 1845, besides other buildings, a spacious residence for the governor, a well furnished club-house for the lower officials, barracks for laborers and soldiers, an arsenal, a library, an observatory,[2] and the churches, schools, and hospital of which mention will be made later. A wharf, with a stone foundation, and on which were several storehouses, led out into deep water, and the fort, from which floated the flag of the Russian American Company, was mounted with two rows of cannon, which commanded all portions of the town.[3]

[1] There was, however, a considerable improvement in the condition of the settlement before this date. Belcher gives a detailed description of Sitka at the time of his visit, in 1837, in which he notes the solidity of its buildings and fortifications, and its excellent ship-yard and arsenal. *Narr. Voy. round World*, i. 95–9. On the evening before Belcher's departure, Kouprianof, who was then chief manager, gave a ball at which the former remarks that the women, though almost self-taught, danced with as much ease and grace as those who had been trained in European capitals. He speaks very favorably of Madame Kouprianof, and states that the wife of Baron Wrangell was the first Russian woman who came to Alaska. *Id.*, i. 103–6. Davis, who arrived at Sitka on board the *Louisa* in 1831 (the first year of Wrangell's administration), speaks of the wives and daughters of the Russian officials as being exceedingly beautiful. *Glimpses of the Past in Cal.*, MS., i. 2; but he was a mere boy at the time, and probably exaggerates, for in the *Sitka Archives*, MS., of this date but two women are mentioned as living at Sitka.
[2] The observatory was built at the company's expense, and its reports were published by the academy of sciences at St Petersburg. *Dok. Kom. Russ. Amer. Kol.*, i. 98. It was erected on one of the islands in Sitka Bay. *Ward's Three Weeks in Sitka*, MS., 28.
[3] *Markof, Russkie na Vostotchnom Okeana*, 54–6 (St. Petersburg, 1856, 2d ed.) Tikhmenef states that the number of guns in position was 60, and that there were 87 others in the arsenal and elsewhere, of all sizes, from 80-pound mortars down to one-pound falconets. *Istor. Obos.*, ii. 328. Ward, who was at Sitka in 1853, says that the chief manager's residence was a very large two-story building, the lower part of which was used for his private apartments, offices, etc., while the upper floor was used for public receptions, balls, and dinner-parties. On the 4th of July, 1853, at which date an American bark was lying in the harbor, and several Americans were on a visit to the settlement, a salute of 13 guns was fired, and in the evening there was a dinner-party, at which champagne flowed freely and complimentary speeches were made. *Three Weeks in Sitka*, MS., 13–14, 17–18. Many of the officers and officials in the company's service could speak English.

Such was Sitka about the middle of the present century, when its inhabitants mustered about one thousand souls; and there are to-day on the Pacific coast few more busy communities than that which peopled the capital of Alaska toward the close of the Russian occupation. After the withdrawal of the Russian employés who departed for their native land, and of American speculators who departed with

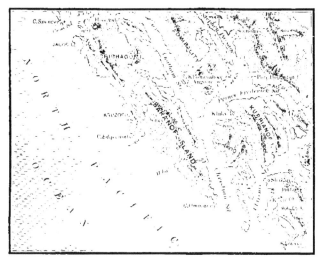

BARANOF AND KRUZOF ISLANDS.

empty pockets, the settlement gradually fell into decay, and soon was but the ghost of its former self. In 1875 the population had decreased to one half; in 1883 it was little more;[4] many of the dwellings were tenantless; the harbor was almost deserted, and the arrival

---

[4] In the *S. F. Bulletin* of Oct. 3, 1882, it is given at 560, of whom 250 were white people and 410 Indians. Most of the latter were probably creoles. In 1869 the Indian village adjoining Sitka contained 56 houses, with about 1,200 inmates.

or departure of the mail steamer was the sole incident
that roused from their lethargy the people of the
once thriving town of Novo Arkhangelsk.

With the exception of the fort, or castle, which
crowns a rock about a hundred feet in height, and is
reached by a steep flight of steps, the buildings occupy
a low and narrow strip of land at the base of Mount
Verstovoi. On Kruzof Island, at the entrance of the
bay, is Mount Edgecumbe, the prominent landmark
of this portion of the coast. In the bay are several
islets, which partly screen from view the portion of
Baranof Island on which Sitka is built, until the vessel arrives within a few cables' length. On landing,
one notices unmistakable signs of decay. Many of
the houses are falling into ruins; and some of them,
being built of logs and their lower portion continually
water-soaked, are settling down on their foundations.
After passing the fort we come to a better class of
buildings, prominent among which is the Greek church,[5]
with its dome and roof painted an emerald green.
Beyond this are the club-house, the principal school-
house, and the hospital; then come a score or two of
huts, and then the forest, through which is cut for a
short distance a path, the second road made in Alaska
before the purchase.[6]

Of social life at Sitka, before the transfer, some interesting records have been handed down to us by
travellers, and by the annalists of the Russian American Company, among whom were several of the company's servants. Officers and officials had cast in
their lot in this the Ultima Thule of the known world,
far removed from all centres of civilization, and from
all civilizing influences. Some were of noble birth,
and had passed their youth and early manhood among
the cultured circles of St Petersburg; but here, amidst

---

[5] Adjacent to this building is the Lutheran chapel, which in 1877 was
vacant.

[6] *Whymper's Alaska*, 97–8. Other roads have been built since that date.
Until 1867 Sitka had no regular communication with any point outside of
Alaska. In the following year it was made a port of entry.

this waste, there was for many years no society, no home circle, no topic even for conversation. How best should they beguile the long years of their banishment, the tedium of barrack life, the drear monotony of their voluntary servitude? No wonder that many fell victims to gambling and strong drink, sank even to yet lower depths, and gradually debased themselves oftentimes below the level of the savage.

To remedy this state of affairs, and especially to provide comfortable accommodation for unmarried officers and officials of the higher rank,[7] Etholen, during the first year of his administration,[8] established at Sitka a social club, furnished with reading, billiard, card, and supper rooms. Here the members entertained visitors, when the hospitalities tendered by the governor were intermitted. Until the transfer, this institution was conducted on the system adopted at its foundation, and wrought much benefit in the colony, save, perhaps, in the cause of temperance—a virtue which the Russians were loath to practise. "Russian hospitality is proverbial," remarks Whymper, "and we all somewhat suffered therefrom. The first phrase of their language acquired by us was 'petnatchit copla'—fifteen drops. Now this quantity—in words so modest—usually meant a good half-tumbler of some unmitigated spirit, ranging from cognac to raw vodhka, and which was pressed upon us on every available occasion. To refuse was simply to insult your host. Then memory refuses to retain the number of times we had to drink tea, which was served sometimes in tumblers, sometimes in cups. I need not say the oft-described samovar was in every household. Several entertainments—balls, suppers, and a fête in the club-gardens—were organized for our benefit, and a number of visitors came off daily to our fleet of four vessels."[9]

[7] The distinction of 'honorable' and 'very honorable'—potchetnui and pol-upotchetnui—was made according to rank. The very honorables were naval officers and the higher officials; the honorables, petty officers, clerks, book-keepers, and the like.
[8] On the 5th of November, 1840. *Tikhmenef, Istor. Obos.*, ii. 244.
[9] *Alaska*, 101-2. This occurred in 1865, during Maksutof's administra-

At all seasons of the year the tables of the social club and of the higher class of employés were supplied with venison or other game, with chickens, pork, vegetables, berries, and of course with fish. A similar diet was provided for the lower officials, while the staple food of the laborers was for about nine months in the year fresh fish, and for the remaining three, salt fish.[10]

There was little variation in the routine of life at Sitka. Employés, other than the higher officials, were required to rise at 5 A. M., and to work in summer for about twelve hours a day; at reveillé and at 8 P. M. the drums beat; at 9 lights were extinguished, and at half-hour intervals during the night bells were tolled, the sentries responding at each stroke.[11]   For the higher officials there were card-

tion. Simpson, who took leave of Etholin in 1842, remarks: 'The farewell dinner, to which about thirty of us sat down, exceeded in sumptuousness anything that I had yet seen, even at the same hospitable board. The glass, the plate, and the appointments in general were very costly; the viands were excellent; and Governor Etholine played the part of host to perfection.' *Narr. Jour. round World*, ii. 212. On festive occasions, as on the emperor's birthday, etc., the officials and native chiefs dined with the governor, after divine service. All wore full dress and decorations. *Ward's Three Weeks in Sitka*, MS., 29 et seq.

[10] The Kolosh supplied the market with deer, fish, clams, and berries. *Wrangell, Statist. und Ethnog.*, 12–13. Beef and mutton were rarely seen, even on the tables of the higher officials, and as late as 1876 could not be had at the one restaurant then open at Sitka, though according to the *Alaska Times* of Oct. 31, 1868, the market price of beef was 15 to 30 cents per lb. At the latter date eggs were selling at $1.50 per doz., and scarce at that. Milk was $1 to $1.50 per gal.; coffee 18 to 33 cents; ham and fresh pork 25 cents; and fish 6 cents per lb. In this year speculation was rife at Sitka, town lots being held, says Whymper, at $10,000. In May 1878 the Rev. John G. Brady, writing from Sitka to the Rev. Sheldon Jackson, says: 'This part of Alaska abounds in food. Yesterday I bought four codfish for ten cents, and a string of black bass for five cents. A silver salmon, weighing thirty-eight to forty pounds, is sold for fifteen or twenty cents. Last week I bought fifteen dozen fresh clams for ten cents, and about twenty pounds of halibut for the same price. Ducks, geese, grouse, and snipe are abundant and cheap. A good ham of venison will bring fifty cents.' *Jackson's Alaska*, 209–10.

[11] *Ward's Three Weeks in Sitka*, MS., 41. This precaution was needed to provide against surprise from the Kolosh. Even after the purchase they were admitted only at 9 A. M. in order to exchange their peltry for other wares, and at 3 P. M. were driven out at the point of the bayonet if necessary. About 15 versts to the south-east of Sitka was the Ozerskoi redoubt, built as a protection against the Kolosh at the outlet of a lake seven miles in length. In 1853 there were six or eight houses, and a dam with fish-traps had been constructed at the mouth of the lake, the catch being marketed at Sitka. *Id.; Tikhmenef, Istor. Obos.*, ii. 332–3.

parties, dance-parties, or drinking-parties at the club-rooms, varied occasionally with an amateur theatrical entertainment, and when there was no other recourse the evening hours were passed at the library.

The Sitka library, which, it will be remembered, Rezanof founded in 1805, contained in 1835 about 1,700 volumes in the Russian and other languages, in addition to 400 periodicals and pamphlets, and a valuable collection of charts.[12] Of any printed local literature before the purchase we have no records.

On the 1st of March, 1868, the first newspaper concerning Alaska, styled the *Alaska Herald*, was published in San Francisco by a Pole named Agapius Honcharenko,[13] and contained the first part of a Russian translation of the United States constitution. It was issued semi-monthly, printed in Russian and English, and about twelve months after its first appearance, claimed a circulation of fifteen hundred copies.[14] During the same year the *Alaska Coast Pilot* was published by the United States Coast Survey, and also the *Sitka Times*, which was at first issued in manuscript, and had but an ephemeral existence.[15]

Near the mainland, a little more than a hundred miles to the south-east of Sitka, is Fort Wrangell,

[12] *Wrangell, Statist. und Ethnog.*, 17. Of the books, 600 were Russian, 300 French, 130 German, 35 English, 30 Latin, and the rest Swedish, Dutch, Spanish, and Italian. *Khlebnikof, Zapiski*, in *Materialui*, 116.

[13] Who gives his autobiography as follows: 'I was born in the government of Kieff Aug. 19, 1832, and educated in Kieff. In 1857 I left Russia and was appointed to service with the Russian embassy to Greece. On the 2d of Feb. 1860, I was arrested in Athens for advocating the liberation of serfs, but succeeded in escaping to England and subsequently to America, where I was employed by the American Bible Society. I came to San Francisco in 1867. I was much persecuted by the representatives of Russia abroad.' *Alaska Herald*, Dec. 15, 1868.

[14] On May 2, 1868, the first number of *Free Press and Alaska Herald* was first issued, and Honcharenko's name does not appear on the sheet. On June 1st of the same year the *Herald* again appeared under its old name, with Honcharenko as proprietor, and in May 1872 passed into the hands of A. A. Stickney. The Russian articles were frequently repeated through three or four numbers.

[15] It was issued weekly in MS. by T. G. Murphy, and contained advertisements and unimportant local items. The first printed number was published on April 29, 1869, and the last on September 13, 1870.

built on an island of the same name, and situated
about a hundred and thirty miles north of the boundary line of British Columbia, at the head of ship
navigation on the route to the Cassiar mining district.
While the mines were prosperous, this was, during a
few months in the year, the busiest town in Alaska,
the miners who ascended the Stikeen[16] each spring to
the number of about four thousand, and returned in
the autumn, averaging in good seasons as much as
fifteen hundred dollars per capita, and leaving most
of their earnings among the store and saloon keepers.
The fort is now deserted, and the town nearly so, except by Indians.   The government buildings, which
cost the United States a hundred and fifty thousand
dollars, were sold in 1877 for a few hundreds.   The
main street is choked with decaying logs and stumps,
and is passable only by a narrow plank sidewalk.
Most of the habitations contain but one room, with
sleeping-berths arranged round the walls and a stove
in the centre, and many of them have neither windows
nor openings, except for the chimney and a single
door.   Nevertheless, in these comfortless abodes several hundreds of white men were content to pass the
long winter months in former years, and a few score
still remain, who have not yet lost their faith in the
mines.

"Fort Wrangell," writes one who visited that settlement in 1883, "is a fit introduction to Alaska.   It
is most weird and wild of aspect.   It is the key-note
to the sublime and lonely scenery of the north.   It is
situated at the foot of conical hills, at the head of a
gloomy harbor filled with gloomy islands.   Frowning
cliffs, beetling crags stretch away on all sides surrounding it.   Lofty promontories guard it, backed by
range after range of sharp volcanic peaks, which in
turn are lost against lines of snowy mountains.   It is

---

[16] As far as Telegraph Point, a distance of about 130 miles.   Thence a land
journey awaited them of about 180 miles to the lower and 240 miles to the
upper gold-fields.   This was usually made on foot.

the home of storms. You see that in the broken
pines on the cliff sides, in the fierce, wave-swept rocks,
in the lowering mountains, and in the sullen skies.
There is not a bright touch in it—not in its straggling
lines of native huts, each with its demon-like totem
beside its threshold; nor in the fort, for that is dilapidated and fast sinking into decay; not even in the
flag, for the blue is a nondescript tint, and the glory
of the stars has long since departed." [17]

On a small island at the mouth of the Portland
Canal, and close to the southern boundary of Alaska,
is Fort Tongass, the first military post established by
the United States government after the purchase.
The site was well chosen, containing a plentiful supply
of timber and pasture, while fish and game abound in
the neighborhood.

At the foot of a perpendicular bluff fifteen hundred
feet in height, and about two hundred miles north of
Sitka, is the town of Harrisburg, or Juneau, the latter name, and the name now commonly in use, being
that of one of the discoverers of a mining district,[18] of
which mention will be made later. In 1883 this was
probably the most thriving settlement in Alaska, containing in winter about a thousand inhabitants, and
before that date the mail service between Port Townsend, Wrangell, and Sitka had been extended to Harrisburg, the last being the most northerly point from
which the United States mails were distributed.

Passing from the Alexander Archipelago westward
to Cook Inlet and Kadiak, we find at the former point
few remaining traces of Russian civilization. A short
distance from Port Chatham is the settlement of Seldovia,[19] with about seventy native and creole hunters,

---

[17] *Overland Monthly*, March, 1884.

[18] In the *S. F. Bulletin*, Feb. 1, 1883, it is stated that Juno (Juneau)
was one of the discoverers of the district, and that it was also called Rock-
well, the name of the acting officer of the *Jamestown*.

[19] Between Port Chatham and Seldovia is Alexandrovsk, a settlement with
about 40 hunters.

and a few leagues north of it the village of Ninilchik, where dwell thirty Russian and creole descendants of the colonial citizens, who subsist mainly by agriculture and stock-raising. Close to it is the mouth of a small river, the waters of which discharge, or are rather filtered into the sea through the bar that chokes its outlet. In former years this was a favorite spawning-ground for salmon, which still attempt to leap the bar in vast numbers, many of them failing to gain the stream beyond, and being gathered up by the settlers, who select only the choicest.[20]

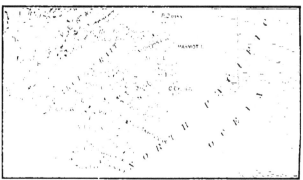

MAP OF KADIAK AND ADJACENT ISLANDS.

The islands of Kadiak and Afognak, 'the garden spots of Alaska,' as they are termed, enjoy more sunshine and fair weather than any portion of the territory, with the exception, perhaps, of some favored localities on Cook Inlet. Here are found, in parts, rich pastures dotted with woodlands,[21] and covered, during summer, with a carpet of wild flowers. When the Russians were compelled to remove their capital from Saint Paul to Sitka, they did so with extreme re-

[20] *Petroff's Pop. Alaska*, 37, where is a description of other settlements in Cook Inlet.
[21] The timber is much inferior to that in the neighborhood of Sitka. *Davidson's Sci. Exped.*, 473.

luctance, for the former, as Dall remarks, "deserves far more than Sitka the honor of being the capital."[22]

The village of Saint Paul, or Kadiak, contained in 1880 about four hundred inhabitants,[23] a large proportion of whom were creoles. Here were built the stores and warehouses of the Alaska Commercial Company, the Western Fur and Trading Company,[24] and the barracks formerly occupied by the United States troops. While a garrison was stationed at this point, bridges were built across the rivulets that intersect the village, and culverts to drain the neighboring lakes and marshes; but so little enterprise had the inhabitants that after the withdrawal of the soldiers no attempt was made to keep them in repair. The culverts were washed away, and the bridges allowed to rot, except those which were used for fire-wood. The houses are built of logs, the crevices being filled with moss, but are clean and comfortable. The people are probably better circumstanced than those of their own status in other portions of America. Labor is in demand and fairly paid; food is cheap and abundant; there are no paupers in their midst, no lawyers or tax collectors; and all are at liberty to make use of unoccupied land.

At Wood Island, opposite to Saint Paul, is a thriving settlement, the inhabitants of which support themselves in summer by hunting, and in winter by cutting

---

[22] In 1874 the Icelandic Society in Milwaukee sent a petition to the president of the United States, asking that facilities be afforded for exploring portions of Alaska, with a view to colonization. Three commissioners were appointed by the society, and a sloop of war placed at their disposal, in which the party was conveyed to Cook Inlet. Finding there no suitable location, they were taken to St Paul. Here they found plenty of pasture and tillable land, and were so well pleased that they made no further search. Two of them remained until the following summer to make preparations for the reception of their countrymen, but a winter's residence in their adopted country appears to have disgusted them. The winter of 1874–5 was exceptionally severe, and an outbreak of measles spread havoc among the natives. The commissioners returned in July, and nothing came of the matter. *Bancroft Library Scraps*, 232. See also *Sec. U. S. Navy Rept., 43d Cong. 2d Sess.*, p. 14–15.

[23] Petroff gives the population at only 288, but his estimate was made somewhat earlier.

[24] Afterward removed to St Paul Island.

and storing ice.   In order to develop the latter industry was built the first road constructed in Alaska,
comprising the circuit of the island, a distance of
about thirteen miles.

A few versts farther to the north-west is Spruce
Island, on which is a village containing about eighty
creoles. "Here," says Tikhmenef, "died the last member of the first clerical mission, the monk Herman,
and was buried side by side with the Hieromonakh
Joassaf.   During his life-time Father Herman built
near his dwelling a school for the daughters of the
natives, and also cultivated potatoes"!

The village of Three Saints, where, it will be remembered, Shelikof landed from a vessel of that name in
1784, and founded the pioneer colony in Russian
America, now contains about three hundred inhabitants.   There were in Shelikof's days the finest sea-
otter grounds, and are now perhaps the finest halibut
grounds in Alaska.

The village of Afognak, on the island of the same
name, separated by a narrow channel from the northern
shore of Kadiak, is one of the most thriving settlements
in Alaska.   Though mountainous, and in some parts
thickly wooded, the cutting of timber and fire-wood
being one of the chief industries, it contains many spots
suitable for pasture and agriculture.   Boat-building
is also a profitable occupation.   Many of the inhabitants, who now muster about three hundred and fifty,
live in substantial frame houses, this being one of the
few places in the territory where any considerable
number of dwellings other than log huts are to be
found.[25]

The principal port in the Aleutian group is Illiuliuk,
or, as it is sometimes called, Unalaska,[26] on the island

---

[25] For a short description of the remaining settlements in the Kadiak and
other districts as they were at the time of the last census, see *Petroff's Pop.
Alaska*, passim.   Want of space forbids my mentioning any but the more
prominent settlements, and those about which there is something of interest
to relate.

[26] Spelt also Oonalashka, and otherwise.

of the latter name. Its main recommendation is that it possesses one of the best harbors in Alaska, and it is probable that it will always remain, as it is to-day, the chief centre of trade for this district. Nevertheless, the population of Illiuliuk is little more than four hundred, and of the island from six to seven hundred. Most of them are hunters by occupation, for so rugged is the coast and so deeply indented that there is little room for other pursuits.[27] Brought frequently into contact with foreigners, and especially with Americans, they are perhaps among the most enlightened

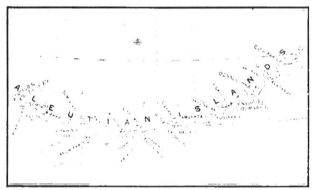

ALEUTIAN ISLANDS.

of their race. More than half of them can read and write, and it is said that on festive occasions, as on the 4th of July, their exploits in wrestling, dancing, and foot-racing surpass anything that can be witnessed elsewhere in the territory.

Under the volcano of Makushin, in a small settlement of the same name on the western coast of Unalaska, lived, in 1880, a man named Peter Kostromitin,

[27] *Id.*, and *Tikhmenef, Istor. Obos.*, ii. 303. The island of Sannakh and its vicinity is their favorite hunting ground.

who witnessed, about sixty years before that date, a
volcanic eruption, during which a new island made its
appearance to the north of Oumnak.[28]   On the 10th
of March, 1825, a violent disturbance occurred at
Oonimak, which is thus described by Veniaminof:
"After a prolonged subterraneous noise, resembling a
cannonade, which lasted almost an entire day, and was
heard at Unalaska, the north-eastern mountain chain
of Oonimak opened in the middle of the day, in five
or more places, for a considerable distance, accompanied with eruptions of flame and great quantities of
black ashes, which covered the whole extent of
Alaska[29] to the depth of several inches.   In the
neighboring localities on the peninsula it was dark for
three or four hours.   On this occasion the ice and
snow lying on the top of the chain melted, and a considerable stream flowed from it for several days, the
width of which was five to ten versts.   These waters
ran down the eastern side of the island in such volume
that the sea in the vicinity was of a mud color until
late in the autumn."[30]   Some of the islands on the
coast of Alaska are unmistakably of volcanic origin,
and it is the received opinion of geologists that the
greater portion of the Alaskan peninsula is being
gradually raised by Plutonic action.   Nevertheless,
though between 1700 and 1867 many earthquakes
and violent eruptions are reported,[31] none of them
have proved very destructive, the last severe earthquake shock having occurred in 1880, and being severely felt at Sitka, though causing no damage worthy
of mention.

[28] I have an account of this phenomenon as related by Kostromitin in his
Early Times, MS., 6–10, but it will not bear quoting.   There is no doubt,
however, that he witnessed it.
[29] The peninsula, of course.
[30] *Zapiski ob Ost. Ounalashk*, i. 35–6.   In *Id.*, i. 37–9, 205–7, are accounts
of other eruptions and earthquakes.   See also *Tikhmenef, Istor. Obos.*, ii. 295,
312, 330, and *Whymper's Alaska*, 105.
[31] A list of them is given in *Dall's Alaska*, 466–470.   Grewink, the Russian geographer, laid down between Cook Inlet and the island of Attoo, 48
active volcanoes.   *Davidson's Sci. Exped.*, 475.

Of the Innuit races that people the neighborhood of Bristol Bay and the Kuskovkim Valley, no mention is required in this chapter. Sailing in a north-easterly direction from the Prybilof Islands we find, close to the southern shore of Norton Sound, the old port and trading post of Mikhaïelovsk, or as it is now termed St Michael,[32] founded, as will be remembered, by Tebenkof, during Wrangell's administration. Here was the chief mart of trade in the district of the Yukon, for no sea-going vessel can enter the mouth of this vast river, the volume of whose waters is said to be greater than that of the Mississippi. Of St Michael, Whymper remarks: "It is not merely the best point for a vessel to touch at in order to land goods for the interior, including that great tract of country watered by the Yukon, but it has been and is, to a great extent, a central port for Indian trade, and for the collection of furs from distant and interior posts. The inhabitants of the fort—all servants of the company—were a very mixed crowd, including pure Russians and Finlanders, Yakutz from Eastern Siberia, Aleuts from the islands, and creoles from all parts. They were not a very satisfactory body of men; in point of fact, it is said that some of them had been criminals, who had been convicted at St Petersburg, and offered the alternative of going to prison or into the service of the Russian American Company! We found them—as did Zagoskin years before—much given to laziness and drunkenness. Fortunately their opportunity for this latter indulgence was limited, usually to one bout a year, on the arrival of the Russian ship from Sitka with their supplies; while the 'provalishik,' Mr Stephanoff, the commander of this fort, who had charge of the whole district, stood no nonsense with them, and was ever ready to make them yield assistance. His arguments were of a forcible character. I believe the knout

[32] For a description of this post as it now exists, see *S. F. Chronicle*, June 26, 1881, and *S. F. Bulletin*, Aug. 16, 1881.

formed no part of his establishment, but he used his fists with great effect!"[33]

Since the purchase little attention has been given to the Yukon district, or to the territory of the Ingaliks.[34] At St Michael and an adjoining Innuit village, at Nulato, and at Fort Yukon, the total population mustered, in 1879, only three hundred and eighty souls, of whom all but eleven were natives. The site of Fort Yukon on the verge of the Arctic zone, where the thermometer sometimes rises above 100° of Fahrenheit in summer and sinks occasionally to 55° below zero in winter,[35] was in 1867 one of the cleanliest of the Russian settlements. At this, the northernmost point in Alaska inhabited by white men, the Russians appear to have established friendly relations with the natives. "Each male," says Whymper, "on arrival at the fort, received a present of a small cake of tobacco and a clay pipe; and those who were out of provisions drew a daily ration of moose-meat from the commander, which rather taxed the resources of the establishment." Game and fish were the principal diet of both Russians and natives, for during the greater portion of the year, bread and vegetables were seldom to be had, though it has frequently been stated that vegetables can be raised in abundance during the brief hot summer of the Yukon valley.

[33] *Alaska*, 152–4. Dall, who passed through this settlement about the same time, says: 'Stepánoff has been in office about four years. He is a middle-aged man of great energy and iron will, with the Russian fondness for strong liquor, and with ungovernable passions in certain directions. He has a soldier's contempt for making money by small ways, a certain code of honor of his own, is generous in his own way, and seldom does a mean thing when he is sober, but nevertheless is a good deal of a brute. He will gamble and drink in the most democratic way with his workmen, and bears no malice for a black eye when received in a drunken brawl; but woe to the unfortunate who infringes discipline while he is sober, for he shall certainly receive his reward, and Stepánoff often says of his men, when speaking to an American, "You can expect nothing good of this rabble: they left Russia because they were not wanted there."'
[34] The natives that inhabit the far interior.
[35] Dall's figures are 112°+ and 69°− as extremes. *Alaska*, 105.

A vast amount of nonsense, as Whymper remarks, has been published and republished in the United States on the agricultural resources of Alaska. Dall, for instance, assures us that potatoes, turnips, lettuce, and other garden vegetables were raised at Fort Yukon,[36] but his statement lacks confirmation.

Berries and the hardier class of vegetables are the only produce of which the soil is capable, even in favored localities, and though numberless and patient attempts were made to raise cereals, during and after the Russian occupation, nearly all proved a failure. A scant crop of barley may mature in a few localities in exceptional seasons, and both wheat and barley will grow in many portions of the territory, but barley seldom kernels, and wheat never.[37] Potatoes, cabbages, turnips, lettuce, radishes, and horse-radish are produced in many parts of the territory, but cabbages often fail to head. On Kadiak, Afognak, and Prince of Wales islands, at Fort Wrangell and Bristol Bay, potatoes of fair quality can be raised in favorable seasons, but are often a partial or total failure, and when they mature are, in common with other vegetables, for the most part watery.[38]

A fair crop of hay is often secured at Kadiak[39] and at some other points, where cattle and sheep are raised. Live-stock were supplied to some of the Aleuts free of charge early during the company's régime, but most

[36] *Ibid.*

[37] Oats were raised near Ninilchik Bay (between the redoubt St Nikolaï and Kachekmak Bay) in 1855. *Tikhmenef, Istor. Obos.*, ii. 322–3. Petroff says that in 1880 potatoes and turnips, the latter of excellent quality, were raised there. *Pop. Alaska*, 37.

[38] Khlebnikof, *Zapiski*, in *Materialui*, 126–7, claims that mealy and good-flavored potatoes were raised at Sitka on ground manured with sea-weed, the crop being in some places 12 or 14 to one, but there is no confirmation of this statement. Wrangell states that in 1831, 2,424 pouds were raised at Sitka. *Statist. und Ethnog.*, 12–13; but says nothing as to their quality. According to *Petroff's Pop. Alaska*, 76, nearly 100 acres of potatoes and turnips were raised at Afognak in 1880. Tikhmenef says that attempts to raise vegetables on the Prybilof Islands usually failed. *Istor. Obos.*, ii. 310; but in *Elliott's Seal-Islands, Alaska*, 12, it is mentioned that lettuce, turnips, and radishes were raised at St Paul Island in 1880.

[39] Golovnin, in *Materialui*, 54, says that the Aleuts were too lazy to turn the hay or place it under shelter.

of them perished from want of care.   The Aleuts, being accustomed to a diet of fish, did not relish milk or
flesh, and regarded animals as a nuisance.   The cows
were kept in corners used for storing salmon, and
knocked down with their horns the poles on which the
fish were suspended, trampling them under foot;[40] while
pigs undermined the natives' huts by scratching out
the earth in search of refuse, and goats climbed on the
roofs and tore away the thatch.

The cattle sent to Alaska during the Russian occupation were of the hardiest Siberian stock, but even in
1883 the herds seldom mustered more than twenty
head; though beef-cattle are often sent from San
Francisco to fatten at Kadiak or the Aleutian Islands,
and are slaughtered in October.   Horses and mules
are of course little valued in a territory where there
are few roads, and where, as in Venice, travel is almost entirely by water.   Sheep thrive well during the
short, hot summer, especially on the nutritious grasses
of the Kadiak pastures, and at this season their mutton is of choice quality; but in winter they are crowded
together in dark, sheltered corners, whence they crawl
out, in early spring, weak and emaciated.[41]

Among the resources of the territory, timber will
probably be an important factor in the future, though
of course in the distant future; for, so long as the immense forests of Oregon, Washington Territory, and
British Columbia are available, those of Alaska can

[40] As early as 1795 there was a small supply of live-stock in Alaska, and in
that year cows were sent from Kadiak to Unalaska.   No butter was made in
the Russian colonies until 1831, when 20 pouds were produced.   *Veniaminof,
Zapiski, Ost. Ounalashk*, 71.   In 1833 the Russian American Company had 220
head of horned cattle, apart from those at the Ross colony.   *Wrangell, Statist. und Ethnog.*, 18.   In 1823 a pair of pigs was landed at Chemobura Island
(between Sannakh and Deer islands); in 1826 they had increased to more
than a hundred.   Chickens were kept by many Russians and Aleuts, but in
small number.   Two pairs of ducks were landed at Unalaska in 1833, and in
the following year had increased to 100.

[41] A few years ago Falkner, Bell & Co. of San Francisco sent about 150
sheep of the hardiest breed, in charge of a Scotch shepherd, to Colma, Kadiak,
a spot formerly selected by the Russians for farming purposes.   The flock
thrived remarkably in summer, but most of them perished during winter.

have little commercial value. There are at present no exports of lumber, or none worthy of mention, while several cargoes are shipped yearly to the Aleutian Islands from Puget Sound, and even from San Francisco.

Forests clothe the valleys and mountain sides of the Alexander Archipelago and the mainland adjacent, and are found at intervals throughout the territory between Cross Sound and the Kenaï Peninsula. Thence the timber belt extends westward and northward at a distance of fifty to more than one hundred miles from the coast, as far as the valley of the Yukon. A little beyond this point the timber line practically ceases, though clumps of stunted trees are met with along the banks of rivers that discharge into Kotzebue Sound and even into the Arctic.

Spruce is the most abundant timber in Alaska, and attains its largest growth in the islands of the Alexander Archipelago. On account of the slow growth of the trees, the boards, after being put through the saw-mill, are found to be full of knots, and when subjected to heat, exude gum or resin. Hence they are not in demand for cabinet or other work where paint or varnish is applied. The hemlock-spruce is plentiful, and its bark may be in demand for tanneries, when, as is already threatened, the supplies of California oak bark become exhausted. The white spruce abounds in the Yukon district, and for spars has no superior, though for masts most of it is too slender. Houses built of this material will last, when the logs are seasoned, for more than twenty years, and when green for about fifteen years.

The most valuable timber is yellow cedar, which is found on some of the islands in the Alexander Archipelago and in the neighborhood of Sitka, and frequently attains a height of one hundred feet, with a diameter of five or six feet.[42] This wood is in

---

[42] Davidson, *Sci. Exped.*, 471, says that trees have been found near Sitka 175 feet in height.

demand by ship-builders and cabinet-makers on account of its fine texture, durable quality, and aromatic odor. The clumps of birch, poplar, maple, willow, and alder found in some parts of the territory have little value, though the inner bark of the willow is used for making twine for fishing-nets, and both willow and alder bark are used for coloring deer-skins.[43]

There were, in 1880, only three saw-mills in operation throughout the territory—one at Sitka, one near the northern point of Prince of Wales Island, and one at Wood Island. All of them were closed during a portion of the year. The first two were established mainly to supply the limited demand for lumber at Fort Wrangell and Sitka, and the last principally for the making of sawdust for use in packing ice. In this and other branches of industry, as in the manufacture of bricks, flour, leather, machinery, and especially in ship-building, there is less activity in Alaska at the present day than there was during the Russian occupation.[44]

During the company's second term ship-building was a prominent industry. In 1821, the company's fleet, apart from a few small craft, consisted only of ten sea-going vessels, whose total measurement was

[43] For further particulars as to the timber resources of Alaska, see *Golovnin*, in *Materialui*, 110; *Morris's Rept. Alaska*, 109–111; *Petroff's Pop. Alaska*, 5, 73–4.

[44] In 1833 a saw-mill was established at the Ozerskoi redoubt—the second that was built on the Pacific coast—the first having been erected by the Hudson's Bay Company on the Columbia. *Wrangell, Statist. und Ethnog.*, 14. During Voievodsky's administration it was worked by steam power. *Tikhmenef, Istor. Obos.*, ii. 245. In 1853 there was a saw-mill at Sitka, but it was so badly managed that lumber cost the company $25 to $30 per M, though the forest was close at hand. *Ward's Three Weeks in Sitka*, MS., 12. A saw-mill was also erected on the Kirenskoy River near Sitka. *Golovnin*, in *Materialui*, 72. At Karluck, Sitka, and Ooyak Bay, on the west coast of Kadiak, were small tanneries. *Id.*, 74; *Tikhmenef, Istor. Obos.*, ii. 246; *Davidson's Sci. Exped.*, 473. There was also a flouring-mill at Sitka, and several brick-yards and machine-shops in various parts of the colonies. With the exception of lumber, few of these branches of manufacture are now carried on. At Atkha grass cloth and other articles manufactured of grass are produced, as mats, baskets, and cigar-holders, of superior workmanship. A number of Indian carvings and manufactures were collected for the centennial exhibition by Mr J. G. Swan, special commissioner for Indian affairs. A description of them is published in his *Alaska Ind. Manuf.*, 7–8.

1,376 tons.[45]   Between that date and 1829, the *Urup*,
a four-hundred-ton ship, and several smaller craft were
built.[46] In 1834 Wrangell ordered the colonial ship-
yards to be abandoned, with the exception of the one
at Sitka, where all the conveniences could be obtained,
and good mechanics were employed.[47] About the
year 1839 the brig *Promissel*, and between that date
and 1842 the steamer *Nikolai I.*, of sixty horse-power,
and the steam-tug *Muir*, of eight horse-power, the first
vessels of the kind ever launched on colonial waters,
were constructed at the port.[48] The machinery for
the *Nikolai I.* was imported from Boston, but everything needed for the tug was manufactured at Novo
Arkhangelsk, under the superintendence of the ma-
chinist Muir, after whom the craft was named.[49]

Although other sea-going craft were built in the
colonies between 1821 and 1842, while at least four
were constructed for the company elsewhere, and several purchased, there were at the latter date only
fifteen vessels belonging to Alaskan waters;[50] many

[45] Between 1799 and 1821 five vessels were purchased by the company's
agents at Kronsdadt, eight in the colonies, and fifteen were built at the colonial dock at Okhotsk. During the same period sixteen were wrecked, five
were condemned, and three were sold. *Tikhmenef, Istor. Obos.*, i. 235. In 1817–
19 the schooners *Platof* and *Baranof* were built at Novo Arkhangelsk, and
the brigantine *Romanzof* and brig *Buldakof* at Bodega.

[46] *Lütke*, in *Materialui, Istor. Russ.*, part iv. 135; *Tikhmenef, Istor. Obos.*,
i. 330. The latter states that the *Urup* was a 300-ton ship, and that three
other vessels, the schooner *Aktzia*, 50 tons, the brig *Polyfem*, 180 tons, and
the sloop *Sitka*, 230 tons, were built for the company at Okhotsk, between
1829 and 1832.

[47] The work was carried on under the superintendence of a native of St
Paul, the Creole Netzvetoff, who had learned his business in St Petersburg.
For the ribs, a kind of cypress was used, which was called *dushnoie derevo*,
fragrant wood, and was well adapted for the purpose on account of its den-
sity, dryness, and remarkable lightness. The outside planking was of larch,
and the upper works of hemlock; the latter, however, is not very durable, as
it grows in damp soil. *Wrangell, Statist. und Ethnog.*, 20.

[48] Simpson, who sailed in the *Nikolai I.* to Fort Stikeen and back, states
that she made six to seven knots an hour, and had most of her machinery on
deck. *Narr. Voy. round World*, ii. 184. Besides the above-named vessels,
the company caused to be built at Abo the sailing ships *Nikolai I.*, 400 tons,
and *Crown Prince Alexander*, 300 tons.

[49] A considerable business was also done at Novo Arkhangelsk in repairing vessels. During Wrangell's administration an American ship was
retimbered at the wharf, and for some years later there was no other dock in
which vessels sailing in neighboring waters could be repaired.

[50] A list of 13 vessels lying at Sitka in April, 1842, is given in *Simpson's
Jour. round World*, ii. 198–9. Most of them belonged to the company.

losses having occurred from shipwreck,[51] and some after a few voyages proving worthless except for store-ships. It was found that vessels could be purchased from foreigners, and especially from Americans, to better advantage than they could be built in the colonies, and it is probable that the managers would have saved money if no attempt at ship-building had been made in Russian America, except perhaps for intercolonial traffic. During the last term little was attempted in this direction. In 1860 the company's fleet consisted of only three steamers, four sailing ships, two barks, two brigs, and one schooner,[52] or twelve vessels in all, of which but two were constructed in the colonies. The schooner was built at Sitka in 1848, at a cost of more than three thousand roubles per ton; while one of the barks, purchased in the Sandwich Islands during the same year, and built at Salem, Massachusetts, in 1845, cost only about eighteen hundred roubles a ton, and the other sailing craft were purchased at about the same rate.

Since the time of the purchase, only a few small coasting vessels have been built,[53] though attempts have been made to obtain from congress grants of land and the right of cutting timber in certain locali-

[51] The navigation of some portions of the Alaskan coast is exceedingly dangerous, and the danger is increased by the want of reliable charts. At the time of the purchase the charts then in existence were merely sectional, including those of La Pérouse, Vancouver, Tebenkof, Lütke, Kashevarof, Tikhmenef, and others. Tebenkof's were probably the best, though far from being complete, and several others are of considerable value. Since the purchase, better progress has been made in this direction, but the work has been of the same fragmentary nature. We may hope, however, that at no distant day we shall have some approach to accurate charts of the entire Alaskan coast. The coast-survey chart of 1868 is almost worthless so far as inland navigation is concerned, for few of the shoals and rocks appear on it. In *Morris's Rept., Alaska*, 56, is a partial list of the wrecks that have occurred in south-eastern Alaska during recent years. Two U. S. ships of war have also been lost in Alaskan waters. In 1878 there was not a single light-house in the territory. In *Id.*, 21, several points are mentioned where light-houses should be erected, and further mention of this matter is made in *U. S. Finance Rept., 1868*, 391-4, and *Sen. Ex. Doc., 40th Cong. 3d Sess.*, 53.

[52] Also a steam-tug completed at Sitka in 1860. The list is given in *Golovnin*, in *Materialui*, app., 152-5, where the armament and cost of each are stated.

[53] And a small stern-wheel steamer for trade on the Yukon and other rivers, built in 1869.

ties,[54] ostensibly for ship-building purposes. To procure at a nominal price a few thousand acres of the best timber-lands in Alaska, on condition of building a vessel or two, would doubtless be a profitable speculation, but thus far no sale or lease of timber-lands has been made. It is not improbable, however, that at no very distant day ship-building may again rank among the foremost industries in Alaska, for coal, iron,[55] and suitable timber are found in several portions of the territory, within easy access of navigable water.

Lignitic, bituminous, and anthracite coal,[56] but especially lignite, are found in many portions of Alaska, from Prince of Wales Island to the banks of the Yukon, and even on the shore of the Arctic Ocean,[57] the best veins being found in southern and western Alaska and the adjacent islands.

Coal-mining in Alaska was first begun about the middle of the present century near the mouth of Cook Inlet, or Kenaï Bay, at a point that still bears the name of Coal Harbor.[58] Machinery was erected and run by steam power; a force of laborers was obtained in Siberia; several experienced miners were brought from

[54] In 1874, Senator Hager presented a petition, signed by Thomas Burling, W. F. Babcock, John Parrott, and others, asking for the privilege of cutting timber for ship-building on government lands in the neighborhood of Prince Edward Island, where pine and yellow cedar are plentiful. They offered to pay for the privilege, and to purchase the land as it was cleared. During the same year, Representative Piper introduced a bill, granting to certain parties the right to purchase, at $1.25 per acre, the island of Kou, north of Clarence Strait, for ship-building purposes, and the privilege of taking up as much more land as might be required. This modest demand, under which all the best timber-lands in the territory might have been appropriated, was afterward limited to 100,000 acres. An account of the second bill introduced by Piper, on Dec. 20, 1876, is given in *Morris's Rept. Alaska*, 107-9.

[55] Iron is found in many portions of Alaska, but no deposit has yet been discovered that will pay for working, under present conditions.

[56] Dall remarks that the specimens of anthracite coal found in Alaska may owe their quality to local metamorphism of the rocks by heat, rather than to the general character of any large deposit. *Alaska*, 475.

[57] In 1878 a vein was opened beyond Cape Lisburn by Captain Hooper of the revenue marine, who claims that the coal mined easily and was fit for the use of steamers. *Petroff's Pop. Alaska*, 74. In 1866 Dall inspected a coal deposit near Nulato, but found it to be of inconsiderable extent. *Alaska*, 56-7. In *Id.*, 473-4, is a list of the principal coal districts known in 1870.

[58] On the north side of English Bay.

Germany, and every available man in the Siberian line battalion, then stationed at Sitka, was sent to aid in the work. The prospect of furnishing the company's steamers with coal obtained in the colonies, and of selling the surplus at high prices in San Francisco and elsewhere, acted as a powerful incentive. In 1857 shafts had been sunk and a drift run into the vein for a distance of nearly 1,700 feet, nearly all of which was in coal. During this and the three following years, over 2,700 tons were mined, the value of which was estimated at nearly 46,000 roubles, but the result was a net loss. The thickness of the vein was found to vary from nine to twelve feet, carrying 70 per cent of mineral, and its extent was practically unlimited; but the coal was found to be entirely unfit for the use of steamers, and a shipment of 500 tons forwarded to San Francisco realized only twelve and a half roubles per ton, or considerably less than cost.[59]

It was hoped that as greater depth was attained the vein at Coal Harbor would improve in strength and quality, but there is no sufficient evidence that, in this or other portions of Alaska, any considerable quantity of marketable coal has yet been produced except for local consumption. Nevertheless, there is little doubt that it exists,[60] though whether in deposits large enough to be of commercial value is a matter

[59] *Tikhmenef, Istor. Obos.*, ii. 250; *Kostlírtzof, Report*, 29–30; *Dok. Kom. Russ. Amer. Kol.*, i. 94. *Golovnin*, in *Materialui*, 108–9. According to the last of these authorities, it was already known that coal-veins existed on the Alaska peninsula, at Kadiak, the smaller islands adjoining, and elsewhere. In *Rogers, Letters*, MS., ii., we find the following, under date June 26, 1855: 'Lütke says: "On dit qu'il y a dans l'île d'Akoun des couches de charbon de terre."' In the *Sitka Archives*, MS., 1857, ii. 278, it is stated that the work of getting out coal was very difficult on account of local circumstances.
[60] Captain White, in *Morris's Rept. Alaska*, 103, states that Cook Inlet coal is well suited for the use of steamers, that it leaves a clear, white ash, and does not coke. In *Dall's Alaska*, 475, are analyses of coal from Cook Inlet, Nanaimo, Bellingham Bay, and Coose Bay. The analysis of Alaskan coal was made by Professor J. S. Newberry of the school of mines, Columbia College, New York. It was found to contain 49.89 per cent of fixed carbon, 39.87 of volatile conbustible matter, 1.25 of moisture, 1.20 of sulphur, and 7.82 of ash. Its character was lignitic. The professor remarks: 'This coal is fully equal to any found on the west coast, not excepting those of Vancouver Island and Bellingham Bay.' For a description of the Nanaimo mines (Vanc. Isl.), see my *Hist. Brit. Columb.*, 569 et seq.

that has yet to be determined. Most of the coal so far discovered in the territory belongs to the tertiary system, and is deficient in thickness of seam.. North of Coal Harbor, deposits are found almost as far as Cape Ninilchik, but here as elsewhere they seldom exceed seven feet of solid coal in thickness, and are more frequently less than three feet. It is well known that a vein of the latter kind, when situated at a distance from market, is almost worthless.

At Oonga and several other points persistent attempts have been made to work the mines at a profit, but as yet without success. The coal was not in demand except for local consumption. When used by steamers, it was found to burn so rapidly as to eat into the iron and endanger the boilers, so that many vessels sailing for Alaska bring with them their own fuel, or are supplied from tenders laden in British Columbia.[61]

It must be admitted, however, the mining prospect in Alaska is far from discouraging. Petroleum of good quality has been found floating on the surface of a lake near Katmai in the Alaska Peninsula.[62] Long before the purchase native copper was obtained from the Indians on the Atna or Copper River, being found occasionally in masses weighing more than thirty pounds. At Karta Bay, on Prince of Wales Island, there is a valuable copper mine, which was sold a few years ago to a San Francisco company.[63]

[61] In a despatch from Santa Bárbara, published in the *San Francisco Bulletin* of June 8, 1877, it is stated that three miles from the Oonga mine is one known as the Big Bonanza with a vein 30 feet thick, of which 15 are solid coal; that $10 per ton had been offered for the coal delivered in San Franciso; that it was considered equal to the best English and Scotch coal; and that the entire coal-fields of this district comprised 1,280 acres, and would suffice to supply California for generations. This may serve as a specimen of the nonsense which has been published in some of the newspapers of this coast as to Alaskan industries, though many valuable items have appeared in them at intervals since the purchase. There appears to be little probability that either Alaskan coal or Alaskan timber will find a more general market on the Pacific coast so long as there remain nearer and better sources of supply.

[62] In *Morris's Rept. Alaska*, 103, it is stated that large deposits of petroleum have been found on Copper River.

[63] *Id.*, 102. Morris states that he saw sacks of the ore and found it exceedingly rich. Metallic copper is found on Oonga and the north end of Admi-

Cinnabar is known to exist in the islands of the Alexander Archipelago, but the exact locality is as yet a secret. ·Lead has been found on Baranof, Wrangell, and Kadiak islands, but not in large deposits. Native sulphur is very plentiful, and this metal is nearly always found in solution at the mineral springs with which the territory abounds.

Among the lead and copper deposits is sometimes found a small percentage of silver,[64] but if there be any valuable silver mines in the territory they are not yet discovered.

From Golovnin Sound it was reported, in 1881, that silver ore, assaying a hundred and fifty dollars a ton, and easily worked, had been discovered so near to tide-water, and in such abundance, that vessels could be loaded with it as readily as with ballast. On May 5th of that year a schooner was despatched to the sound by way of St Michael, and on her return it was reported that the value of the mine had been not a whit exaggerated, but that it was thirty miles from tide-water.[65] Of the 'mountain of silver' that was supposed to exist in this neighborhood nothing further has yet been heard.

Gold-mining has been a little more successful. In 1880, a former state geologist of California remarked that "the gold of Alaska was still in the ground, all save a few thousand ounces gathered here and there from the more accessible veins and gravel-beds of the islands and the mountains along the coast."[66] In 1883 there were in operation several quartz and placer mines, which gave fair returns, and in south-eastern Alaska

ralty Islands. The blue carbonate occurs on the Kuskovkim and near Cape Romanzof, and sulphurets on the north coast of the peninsula. *Dall's Alaska*, 477.

[64] A piece of ore taken from a mine near Fort Wrangell, in 1873, assayed 26 per cent in copper, 20 per cent in lead, and about $7 per ton in silver. This was of course a choice specimen.

[65] *S. F. Bulletin*, Oct. 31, 1881. The truth appears to be that near the sound were base metal mines containing, in spots, a fair percentage of silver.

[66] Letter of John Muir, in *Id.*, Jan. 10, 1880. The letter contains an interesting and probably reliable account of the mines in Alaska at that date.

a trace of gold could be obtained from the sands of almost every stream that discharges into the Pacific.

Of the Stikeen River, or Cassiar, mines brief mention will be made in the volume on British Columbia, to which territory they belong.

Harrisburg was, in 1883, the mining centre of Alaska. On Douglas Island, separated from the town by a channel two miles in width, are several promising quartz and surface mines. Among the former, the Treadwell claim, owned by San Francisco capitalists, was the only one thoroughly developed. Four tunnels had been run into the ledge, and a large body of low-grade ore exposed. A five-stamp mill was in operation, and several bullion shipments were made during the year.

Of the Takoo district, on the Takoo River, a few miles from Harrisburg, great expectations were held, but as yet they have not been realized.[67]

On the 30th of January, 1877, the Alaska Gold and Silver Mining Company[68] was incorporated, the location being about fourteen miles to the south-east of Sitka. In 1880 rock was extracted from the ledge on three levels, averaging about $12 per ton, and at that date a considerable body of ore had been exposed. "The ledge is well defined," writes Walter, a practical mining engineer, in 1878, "runs east and west, and is about 15 feet wide, with a fissure vein from $3\frac{1}{2}$ to 4 feet in width. The rock is bluish gold-bearing quartz, and lies in a slate formation." A ten-stamp water-power mill was erected,[69] and the returns were for a time satisfactory, but the expense of operating a quartz mine under such conditions as at present exist in the territory forbids the working of

---

[67] Mention of this district is made in *Id.*, June 29, July 7, and Aug. 11, 1871.

[68] Their claim is usually called the Stewart tunnel.

[69] *Morris's Rept. Alaska*, 99. During a conversation held at my Library on Feb. 3, 1879, M. P. Berry stated that the mill did not do much in the aggregate. 'They have plenty of rock,' he remarked, 'and what milling they did showed pretty well. But the wheel did not carry the water nor the water the wheel.' *Developments in Alaska*, MS., 11-12.

veins that in more favored localities would be fairly
profitable.   That valuable gold deposits exist is not
disputed; but in a mountainous and densely wooded
territory such as is Alaska, and especially southern
Alaska, where the richest veins have been found,
mines are neglected which elsewhere on this coast
would not lack capital for their development.[70]

[70] Among other points gold has been discovered near the junction of the
Yukon and Pelly rivers. Some of it was assayed in 1883 by H. G. Hanks,
state mineralogist of California, who reported that about one tenth of its
weight consisted of a coating of rust, which made it almost indifferent to the
action of quicksilver.

CHAPTER XXXII.

CHURCHES, SCHOOLS, AND HOSPITALS.

1795-1884.

Glottof, it is claimed, one of the discoverers of the Aleutian Islands, baptized at Oumnak in 1759 the first native admitted into the fold of the Greek church. He was a chieftain's son, and a large cross was erected on the spot where the ceremony was performed; but timber was scarce in those treeless regions, and soon after the Russian occupation the wood was used for making sleighs.[1] Until nearly half a century after Glottof's visit neither Aleuts nor Koniagas received any regular religious instruction, though Shelikof, as will be remembered, affirmed that he converted forty heathen soon after the conquest of Kadiak.

The labors of the first missionaries sent forth to Alaska have already been related. In 1795, or perhaps a year or two later, a chapel was built at Saint Paul—the first in Russian America. At Sitka no church was built until 1817, religious ceremonies being usually performed by one of the officials of the

---

[1] *Veniaminof, Zapiski*, 151-2. The boy was taken to Petropavlovsk, where he learned the Russian language, and returned with the dignity of toyon over all the islands under the jurisdiction of Kamchatka.

Russian American Company, though meanwhile a priest occasionally visited this settlement, and baptisms were not infrequent.[2] In this year an ecclesiastic named Sokolof arrived, and a temporary building was at once erected, the altar being built of timbers cast ashore after the wreck of the *Neva*, "among which," wrote Baranof, "shone the image of Saint Michael." The vessels and utensils were of silver, fashioned by colonial craftsmen, and the robes and draperies of Chinese silk.

In 1819 a church named Saint Peter's was built at Saint Paul Island, and one at Saint George named after Saint George the Victor, in 1833; at the village of Unalaska a church was dedicated in 1826,[3] and in the same year a chapel, named Saint Nikolai, was built at Oumnak, where, as Veniaminof would have us believe, sickness attacked the Russians, who made sacrilegious use of the cross, while, for many years later, the Aleuts did not dare to gather sticks or boards in the neighborhood of this sanctuary.

A clause in the charter granted to the Russian American Company in 1821 provided that church establishments should be supported throughout the colonies,[4] and by order of the holy synod, in 1840,

---

[2] In the *Alaska Archives*, MS., 1–13, is a list of all the baptisms performed at Sitka between 1805 and 1819.

[3] In 1808 a log chapel was built at Unalaska and torn down in 1826. *Veniaminof, Zapiski*, 162.

[4] As an illustration of the condition of the colonial clergy at the end of Chistiakof's administration, may be mentioned the trial for sorcery of Feodor Bashmakof, a servitor at Novo Arkhangelsk in 1829. The charge was preferred by one Terenty Lestnikof to the effect that Bashmakof, a native Kolosh, baptized at Novo Arkhangelsk in November 1805, educated at the parish school, and admitted to the subordinate priesthood in January 1827, had been observed by competent witnesses in the act of assisting at certain pagan rites intended to effect the cure of a sick native, and had been seen ' to go through the motions and steps of chamans or sorcerers in the service of Satan,' and also of having at various times desecrated an orthodox shrine by taking pagan charms into the holy water blessed by the benediction of the priest, and of receiving payment in furs for such sacrilegious action. In the opinion of Veniaminof, which was afterward approved by the holy synod, Bashmakof sinned more from ignorance than from malice, and he was discharged with a severe reprimand. Though informed that he was free to return to Novo Arkhangelsk, Bashmakof voluntarily entered the convent of the Ascension at Nerchinsk. The proceedings in this case display a remarkable degree of leniency on the part of the higher Russian

at which date there were four churches and eight
chapels in Russian America, they were formed into
a diocese, which included the Okhotsk and Kamchatka precincts, the first bishop, afterward met-
ropolitan of Moscow, being Father Veniaminof,
whom Sir Edward Belcher, writing in 1837, describes
as "a very formidable, athletic man, about forty-five
years of age, and standing in his boots about six feet
three inches; quite herculean, and very clever."[5]
"When he preached the word of God," says Kostromitin, who was baptized by Father Joassaf in 1801,
"all the people listened, and listened without moving,
until he stopped. Nobody thought of fishing or
hunting while he spoke, and nobody felt hungry or
thirsty as long as he was speaking—not even little
children."[6]

clergy, and are in remarkable contrast with the tribunals of the Roman
Catholic church in similar cases. It is doubtful, however, whether Bashmakof's retirement to one of the most desolate convents in Siberia was
entirely a voluntary act. *Bashmakof, Sorcery Trial*, MS.
   [5] *Narr. Voy. round World*, 98.
   [6] *Early Times in Aleut. Islands*, MS., 5. Miracles were ascribed to him
by the superstitious, among whom was Kostromitin. There is no doubt,
however, that the bishop was a true and faithful pastor, though his writings
show that he himself shared the superstition common to his church. In his
Zapiski ob Ostrovakh Ounalashkinskavo Otdiala Sostavlennuia, or *Letters concerning the Islands of the Unalaska District*, published at the expense of the
Russian American Company, St Petersburg, 3 vols., 1840, Veniaminof shows
that he had become thoroughly acquainted with the Aleuts, their language,
customs, and history, and his work is the most reliable book on the subject.
It includes history, meteorology, geography, natural history, and ethnology;
but historical material seems to have been scarce, or was perhaps slighted
by the author. The second volume is devoted principally to the manners and
customs of the ancient and modern Aleuts, to legends and tales preserved
among them by tradition, and to their relations with the Russian American
Company, and contains a number of meteorological and statistical tables. The
third volume is confined to a review of the Aleuts of the Atkha District, the
Kolosh, and their respective dialects. The work on the Aleutian Islands was
partially reproduced in German, in *Erenan, Archiv fein wissenschaftliche kunde
von Russland*, ii. 459, 1842. His *Opuit Gramatiki Aleutsko-Lissievskavo Yazuika*, or *Attempt at a Grammar of the Lissiev-Aleutian Language*, St Petersburg, 1846, is confined to one dialect of the Aleutian language, spoken on
the Lissiev group, comprising the islands between 159° and 169° w., and
with a population of about 2,000 souls. The work is elaborate, though in
some cases the author seems to have made more of the language than there
really was, and made inflections of which the Aleuts had previously known
nothing. To indicate the pronunciation, the characters of the Ciryllic alpha-
bet are used. The vocabulary annexed to the volume is complete but not
conveniently arranged, as the Russian words refer only in numbers to the
other portion. The *Oukazanie Puti v Tzarstvie Nebesnoie, Po-outchenie na
Aleutsko-Lissievskom Yazuika ssokhinennoie Svestchennikom Ioannom Veniam-

During Veniaminof's administration a Lutheran clergyman was welcomed at Sitka,[7] and the same spirit of toleration was extended later to the Jesuits, several Poles of that order being transferred from Canada. On the 13th of October, 1867, the first service at which an American officiated[8] was held at Sitka, the congregation being composed of Russians, Finns, and Kolosh.

In 1861 there were in the Russian American colonies seven churches and thirty-five chapels, several of them, including the cathedral, being built and kept in repair by the Russian American Company. All were maintained by the contributions of parishioners and the sale of candles and tapers.[9] About this date the aggregate capital of the churches exceeded two hundred and fifty-five thousand roubles, the funds being held by the company's treasurer and interest allowed at five per cent.[10]

The Sitka cathedral contained three altars, which were separated from the body of the church by a partition, the doors of which were gilt, and the pilasters mounted with gold capitals. There were eight silver candlesticks more than four feet in height, and a silver chandelier hanging from the centre of the dome

inovaim, or Guide on the Road to the Heavenly Kingdom, for instruction in the Lisniev-Aleut Language, Complied by the Priest, Ioann Veniaminof, was published by the holy synod of Russia, and was a translation from the Russian into Aleut by Veniaminof, and printed in Church-Slavic characters, which are better adapted to express Aleutian words.

[7] Simpson's Narr. Journey round World, ii. 193. In 1857 Mr Winter, pastor of the Lutheran church at Sitka, received a gift of 1,200 roubles from the Russian American Company, and during the same year was reëngaged at a salary of 2,000 roubles a year. Sitka Archives, 1857, i. 316, 394. In 1853 his flock numbered 120 to 150 souls. Ward's Three Weeks in Sitka, MS., 70.

[8] Mr Rayner, an army chaplain.

[9] Golovnin, in Materialui, 75. In Dok. Kom. Russ. Amer. Kol., 76, and in Tikhmenef, Istor. Obos., ii. 270, nine churches are mentioned.

[10] The contributions were made partly in money and partly in furs, the company allowing the church 7 roubles, 14 kopeks, to 14 roubles, 29 kopeks, for sea-otter skins. The revenue from candles amounted to 5,500 roubles a year. The company incurred an expense of 32,938 roubles a year on church account. See Golovnin, 75, where are given the salaries of the bishop and officials. The residence of the bishop was built by the company at an expense of 30,000 roubles. Tikhmenef, Istor. Obos., ii. 268.

which was supported by a number of columns of the Byzantine order. On the altar was a miniature tomb of the saviour in gold and silver. The vestments and implements were also rich in gold and jewels. The books were bound in gold and crimson velvet, and adorned with miniatures of the evangelists set in diamonds. The communion cup was of gold, and similarly embellished; the mitre was covered with pearls, rubies, emeralds, and diamonds. The building was dedicated to Saint Michael.[11]

Veniaminof, after acquiring the Aleutian language, translated into it a number of books touching on the doctrines of his church; but with this exception few of the ecclesiastics understood the native dialects, while the interpreters had little knowledge of Russian. Between 1841 and 1860, 4,700 Indians were baptized,[12] and if we can believe Veniaminof, some of them were converted. "I do not mean," he writes, "that they knew how to make the sign of the cross, and to bow, and mutter some prayer. No! Some of them can pray from their soul, not exhibiting themselves in the church and before the people, but often in the seclusion of their chamber, with closed doors."[13] The bishop, who on his appointment adopted the title of Innokenty, according to the custom of his church, labored with marked success among the Kolosh. Before his arrival they had resisted all efforts at conversion, those who were baptized submitting to the ceremony only because they received presents of more or less value.[14]

[11] *Ward's Three Weeks in Sitka*, MS., 29–31, 35–37. The cathedral was roofed with iron, and the belfry and chimes cost 8,500 roubles in silver. *Tikhmenef, Istor. Obos.*, ii. 268. The church at St Paul, Kadiak, is built of hewn timber, the interstices being filled with moss. The interior is well but plainly furnished. *Glidden's Trip to Alaska*, MS., 13.

[12] A list of the converts is given in *Golovnin*, in *Materialui*, 147–150. Tikhmenef claims that in 1827 there were in the colonies 8,532 Christians, of whom more than 7,000 were Indians. *Istor. Obos.*, i. 296.

[13] As a proof that the teaching of the priests was not without effect, it is stated in *Id.*, 303, that in 1827 the number of illegitimate births among the Aleuts was seven, while from that year till 1839 it averaged only one.

[14] In the record of baptisms at Sitka, in the *Alaska Archives*, MS., 1–13, translated from original documents in the *Sitka Church Archives*, MS., men-

It must be admitted that the Greek church was a failure throughout Russian America. We have seen in what disrespect the priests were held by their own countrymen in the time of Baranof, and it is nowhere recorded, except by the priests themselves, that, with the single exception of Veniaminof, the teaching of the ecclesiastics made much impression on the natives. They squatted and smoked during service, listened, bowed, crossed themselves, and laughed so uproariously that the officiating priest was often interrupted in his solemn duty. They cared not for religion, or at least not for the doctrines of the Greek clergy. "If," writes Golovnin, "the object of a missionary be only the baptizing of a few natives yearly, to show the country that the number of conversions increases, and in visiting so many times a year such of the villages as are situated in close proximity to redoubts and trading posts, then the colonial missionaries perform their duty with more or less zeal; but if the missionary's duty is to spread among the pagans the teachings of an evangelist, and to strive by word and example to soften their hearts, to help them in their need, to administer to their physical and moral diseases, to persuade them gradually to lead a settled and industrious life, and above all to labor for the education of the children, and at last make the savages themselves wish for conversion, then not one of our former or present missionaries has fulfilled his duty." [15]

In 1880 the Russian church claimed 10,950 members, but this number is probably at least 2,500 in excess of the actual figures. The bishop of the diocese

tion is made of these presents, which consisted usually of tobacco, calico, knives, cutlasses, and blankets. Sometimes a rifle was given. Care was taken that the convert did not present himself a second time for baptism.

[15] If we can believe Simpson, Dall, and others who travelled in Alaska, negligence was not the only fault of which the missionaries were guilty. The latter remarks that all whom he met in Alaska were inveterate topers, and mentions the case of one who had been engaged for seven years as a missionary on the Yukon, and who thanked God that he then had an opportunity of returning to Russia, where a glass of rum could be had for 25 kopeks. *Alaska*, 226.

usually resides in San Francisco, whence he controls affairs and supplies the funds needed by the various parishes.[16] Service is at present conducted in Alaska both in the Russian and Aleutian languages, but the more distant settlements are visited only once a year by a regularly ordained priest, by whom baptisms and marriages are celebrated and the sacrament administered to those who desire it.

When Alaska was transferred to the United States, it was expected that the religious training of the Indians would not be neglected, but ten years passed by and little was done. In 1877, however, a presbyterian mission was established at Sitka. Two years later a catholic mission was established at Fort Wrangell,[17] but met with little success. Credit is also due to the Church Missionary Society of London and to the methodist church of Canada, both of which have their representatives on the borders of Alaska.[18] For several years protestant missionaries of several denominations, and especially the presbyterians, have, amid great discouragement, labored earnestly, and not in vain, to introduce their faith among the natives of Alaska. Meanwhile their efforts in the cause of education have been no less persistent.

[16] On the 12th of July, 1882, the bishop of the Greek church was drowned within twelve miles of Fort St Michael, either by accident or while under temporary aberration. The body was found. *S. F. Chronicle*, Aug. 15, Oct. 30, 1882.

[17] *Jackson's Alaska*, 227. 'The catholics are invading our ground,' writes Mr McFarland from Fort Wrangell in May 1879. 'Among the passengers on the *Olympia* a week ago was a Romish bishop and priest. They at once established a mission. The bishop made an attack on Mr Young the following sabbath morning. He was trying to get the people to make the sign of the cross, but none would respond save Shustaks, the wicked chief. This made the bishop angry, and he broke out as follows: "Why don't you do as I told you? Are you afraid of Mr Young? You are not Mr Young's slaves. He is not a true minister, anyway. No man can be a true minister and have a wife. Look at me; I am a true minister; I am all the same as Jesus Christ, and I don't have any wife."' *Id.* The reader will find many instances of such unseemly squabbles in my *History of British Columbia*, passim.

[18] William Duncan, of the Church Missionary Society of London, of whose complicity in smuggling operations mention has been made, built up the Indian village of Metlahkatlah. About 1877 it contained 1,000 inhabitants. The Rev. Thomas Crosby labored principally at Fort Simpson. Churches and schools were of course established at both points. *Jackson's Alaska*, 294, 302, et seq.

Of the members of the Greek church only a small proportion among the natives can read and write, though in villages where parish churches have been established, perhaps thirty per cent of the inhabitants have acquired the rudiments of an education. It was claimed by Veniaminof that in some localities all the Aleuts except young children could read fluently, but there is no evidence to support this statement. It was not until 1848 that printed books were issued in the Kadiak language, and for several years later none were circulated among the Kolosh. Those which afterward made their appearance contained only translations of prayers, hymns, anthems, of two of the gospels, the decalogue, and a small collection of words and conversational phrases.[19]

For half a century after the Russian occupation, educational matters were little more advanced than in the days of Shelikof, who established at Three Saints, in 1785, the first school in Russian America, and himself instructed the pupils, in his own language, in arithmetic and the precepts of christianity. The labors of Fathers Juvenal and German in this connection have already been mentioned. In 1817, and probably for some years later, the latter was still in charge of a mission school at Yelovoi Island. In 1805 Rezanof established a school for boys at Saint Paul, and during his visit a girls' school was opened at this settlement,[20] but both fell into decay after the envoy's departure, and were finally closed.

A few years later a school was opened at Sitka by Baranof, but the instruction was very inefficient until 1833, when Etholin took charge of it and somewhat improved its condition. At the end of their course, the pupils served the company in various capacities.[21]

[19] On the 15th of April, 1857, Voievodsky promises to send vocabularies from all the stations of the Russian American Company. *Sitka Archives*, MS., 1857, i. 111.

[20] In charge of Mrs Banner. It opened with 16 creole girls, four of whom were sent to St Petersburg for further instruction. *Tikhmenef, Istor. Obos.*, i. 140.

[21] Of those who left in 1837, four became sailors, four clerks, five mechanics, and three apprentices on board ship. *Golovnin, in Materialui*, 80-1.

In 1839 an institution was established at Sitka at which the orphan daughters of the company's employés were educated at the company's expense. In 1860 there were 22 inmates, and the expense for that year was 6,364 roubles.[22] About the same date a similar institution was opened for boys, to which were admitted orphans, and the children of laborers and of inferior officials. All were taught to read and write, and there was a small class in arithmetic and grammar. Their training of course included religious instruction. In 1860 there were 27 pupils, most of whom were intended for mechanical pursuits.[23]

It was not until 1841 that any attempt was made, even at Sitka, to provide the means for a higher class of education. In that year a church school was opened, which, in 1845, was raised to the rank of a seminary. "This institution was kept in good order," writes Ward in 1853, "the dormitories and class-rooms being plainly but neatly furnished. One room contained good philosophical apparatus, including air-pumps, batteries, pulleys, levers, etc., and another a good-sized library of Slavonic and Russian books."[24] The course included the Russian and English languages, the elements of the pure mathematics, mechanics and astronomy, navigation, history, geography, and book-keeping.[25]

In 1858, when the seat of the bishopric of Kamchatka was transferred to Yakoutsk, a vicariate being established for the colonies, the seminary was also removed to Yakoutsk. Soon afterward a school was

[22] Apart from fuel and lights, which were furnished in kind. The institution had a special fund obtained from the sale of the pupils' handiwork, from which each one received on marriage 150 to 300 roubles for her trousseau. *Id.*, 84.

[23] On the 1st of May, 1853, this school had 33 pupils, and a year later 26. *Sitka Archives*, MS., 1854, ii. 61.

[24] *Three Weeks in Sitka*, MS., 25. On the 29th of October, 1857, Voievodsky acknowledges the receipt from the educational bureau of the holy synod of 7,071 roubles, 50 kopeks, in silver, to be invested for the maintenance of the seminary. *Sitka Archives*, MS., 1857, i. 362.

[25] Ward also states that the higher classes studied Latin and Greek, but there is no mention of this in the Russian authorities.

established under the name of the General Colonial
Institute, for the sons of officials who had rendered
faithful service to the company, all who could read
and write the Russian language and understood the
first four rules of arithmetic being admitted free to
lectures on the governor's recommendation. The
course of instruction was almost identical with that
of the three-class graduating schools in Siberia, and
differed little from the curriculum of the academy.[26]
Navigation, commercial branches, and the English
language were taught by naval officers and others selected from the company's employés. The children
of officials were usually supported at the company's
expense, in which case they were required, after graduating, to enter its service for a term of ten years,
receiving a small salary,[27] 500 roubles for outfit, and
honorable rank at the end of six years' service. Instruction in theology and the Church-Slavic language
was also given to those destined for the church, their
expenses being paid from the church funds. Though
the sum disbursed by the company for the support of
this school exceeded 24,000 roubles a year,[28] in addition to 3,750 roubles contributed by the holy synod,
there were at its opening but 12 pupils, and in 1862
the number was only 27. It would appear indeed to
have been founded mainly for the benefit of the
teachers, who received 13,450 roubles out of the funds
furnished by the company, the sum expended for all
other purposes being less that 11,000 roubles.

The most successful school in other portions of the
colonies was the one founded at Unalaska, by Veniaminof. In 1860, after it had been in existence for

---

[26] A plan of the studies for each of the three classes is given in *Kostlirtzof, Report*, 1860, app., 38.

[27] Only 100 to 350 roubles (scrip) a year according to *Dall, Alaska*, 352; but as I have before mentioned, Dall's historical summary is not very reliable. He states, for instance, that the compulsory term of service was 15 years, while 10 are mentioned by *Golovnin*, in *Materialui*, 81, and *Tikhmenef, Istor. Obos.*, ii. 275.

[28] The exact amount, according to Golovnin, was 24,377 roubles and 77 kopeks. Tikhmenef, whose work was published in the same year, gives it at 7,000 roubles silver, which would be 26,250 roubles in scrip.

35 years, there were 93 pupils of both sexes. At the same date one of the Kadiak schools was re-opened, and there were primary schools on the island of Amla, in the Atkha district, at the Nushagak and Kvikh-pak missions, and at Bering Island, but all with a meagre attendance. There was also a school-house on the lower Yukon, but with no pupils.[20]

After the purchase, even the few traces of enlight-enment which the Russians had left behind were in danger of being obliterated, for the Russian schools were closed, and for years there were none to take their place. In 1869, Vincent Colyer, secretary of the board of Indian commissioners, visited Alaska, and mainly through his exertions the sum of $50,000 was appropriated by congress for school purposes; but there was no one to administer the fund, and it re-mained intact. According to the terms of the contract, two schools were maintained among the Aleuts, but they existed only in name, and no further provision was made by the United States government. It is somewhat remarkable that a nation which ranks among the foremost in wealth, culture, and charity, a nation whose boast it is that education is free to all her children, should have left the inhabitants of this territory for more than half a generation in outer darkness. To quote the words of the Rev. Shel-don Jackson, superintendent of presbyterian missions in the territories, "Russia gave them government, schools, and the Greek religion, but when the country passed from their possession they withdrew their rul-ers, priests, and teachers, while the United States did not send any others to take their places. Alaska, to-

---

[20] As to the discipline and hours of study enforced in these schools, we have few records. It is probable, however, that in the institute they were about the same as in the naval school at Petropavlovsk, where the pupils rose at 5.30 and retired at 9. At 6.30 there was inspection, after which came breakfast and preparation for classes, which lasted from 8 to 11. Then drill and play till noon—the dinner hour, which was followed by two more hours of play, and three of lectures or recitations. At 5 a meal of bread and milk was served, and at 8 supper, the interval being taken up with lessons and drill. *Morskoi Sbornik*, xxi. 44, 159–64. In the colonies the principal food of the students was salt fish.

day, has neither courts, rulers, ministers, nor teachers. The only thing the United States have done for them has been to introduce whiskey." [30]

Under the auspices of the presbyterian mission, a school was established at Fort Wrangell, which in 1877 had about 30 pupils, and a home for the rescue of young girls who would else have been sold into prostitution by their parents; while at Sitka a school was opened on the 17th of April, 1878, 50 scholars being present the first day, and 60 the following year. [31] All this was accomplished with very slender funds. About the same date there were twenty-two children in attendance at the two schools which the United States government promised to support, but which are in fact supported at the expense of the Alaska Commercial Company. [32]

During infancy, the natives of Alaska receive little care or supervision from their parents. Until seven or eight years of age they are more frequently naked than clad at all seasons of the year, often sleeping almost without shelter and with insufficient covering. Under these conditions, living, as they do, in a country where snow is perpetually in sight, and where rain, sleet, and fog are almost incessant, they grow up for the most part a weakly and puny race. Even where the skies are less inclement, this is still the case. The climate of the Aleutian Islands does not differ essentially from that of some portions of northern Scotland, [33] and yet there are few more effeminate speci-

[30] *U. S. Educ. Rept., 1877*, p. xxxii. The above is an extract from a letter published in the report.

[31] *Jackson's Alaska*, 206, 215, 217, 228, 251. In this work will be found a full and interesting account of the operations of the presbyterian mission. The home had at first a sore struggle for existence.

[32] There were also schools at Unalaska and Belkovsky, but the attendance was less than ten of both sexes. There were no schools at the missions of the Yukon, Nushagak, and Kenaï. In a village surrounding the first of these settlements, Petroff states that, apart from the attachés of the church, he found but one man who could speak the Russian language. *Pop. Alaska*, 79.

[33] The mean annual temperature of northern Scotland varies from 42° to 48°, and of the Aleutian district from 36° to 40°. The average rainfall in Unalaska is probably little more than 40 inches, while in Stirlingshire it is

mens of humanity than the Aleut, and none more hardy than the Scotch highlander.

At Sitka, though the rains are excessive, averaging nearly 83 inches in the year,[34] the days on which snow falls are seldom more than thirty; and, remarks Dall, "the average of many years' observations places the mean winter temperature about 33 Fahrenheit, which is nearly that of Mannheim on the Rhine, and warmer than Munich, Vienna, or Berlin. It is about the same as that of Washington, 1,095 miles farther south, and warmer than New York, Philadelphia, or Baltimore. At Nulato the mean winter temperature is 14 below zero, at Fort Yukon about 17, while at both points the thermometer reaches 100 in summer."

The census of 1880 gives the population of Alaska at 33,426,[35] and this is probably little more than half the number of inhabitants living during the early period of the Russian occupation. Many causes were at work to produce this result. Slavery in its worst form existed among the Alaskans. "A full third of the large population of this coast," writes Simpson, "are slaves of the most helpless and abject description. Some of them are prisoners taken in war, but the majority have been born in bondage. These wretches are the constant victims of cruelty, and often the instruments of malice or revenge. If ordered to kill a man, they must do it or lose their own life."[36] The earth huts of the Aleuts were without ovens. There was always a scarcity of wood and often of food. Sometimes

43 inches, in Bute about 46, and in the town of Inverness, in the same latitude as Kadiak, it was 49.9 in 1821 and 47.59 in 1822. *Dall's Alaska*, 445-6.

[34] The average of twelve years, as given in *Davidson's Sci. Exped.*, 481-2. The greatest rainfall during this period was 95.8 inches in 1861, and the least 58.06 in 1853. During August, September, and October, 1867, there were 52 inches.

[35] Of whom 24,161 lived west of Prince William Sound, 500 near the sound, and 5,517 in south-eastern Alaska. *Petroff's Pop. Alaska*, 85.

[36] *Simpson's Narr. Jour. round World*, i. 211. The custom of killing slaves at the death of a chief prevails among the Kolosh, and in late years the Russians had been in the habit of purchasing the victims selected for sacrifice. *Bloodgood*, in *Overland Monthly*, Feb. 1869.

their only diet was rotten fish, but those employed by
the company were well fed, housed, and clad.

Among the most fatal diseases were consumption,
gastric, bilious, typhus, and other fevers, syphilis, and
scrofula.[37] For the sick there were hospitals at Sitka
and Saint Paul. In 1860 the former accommodated
1,400 patients, and was maintained at an expense of
about 45,000 roubles; the latter had 550 patients, and
the outlay was in a greater ratio.[38] There was also a
hospital for the treatment of skin diseases at the sulphur springs near Sitka.[39] The steam bath was the

---

[37] 'In former times syphilitic diseases were very general among the Aleuts,
but now they hardly exist on the islands. Now and then the disease is
brought to Kadiak by crews of the company's vessels which winter there, but
it is met with more and more rarely, because now the commanders of vessels
are strictly enjoined to inspect their crew on arrival in port. At Novo Arkhangelsk, on the contrary, this disease is yet very common in spite of all pre-
ventive measures taken by the colonial government. It is communicated
to the Russians by the Kolosh, who in their turn are infected by their countrymen who live along the sounds, where it is carried by foreign ships which
carry on a contraband trade with the Kolosh. The Kolosh look at this disease with great indifference; they believe it to be an unavoidable evil, and
take no measures whatever for its cure. Nearly all the women who practise
prostitution in secret around the environs of Novo Arkhangelsk are affected
by this disease. At one time the syphilitic disease prevailed to such an extent among the soldiers and laborers at Novo Arkhangelsk, that for its possible prevention the then newly arrived administrator general (governor) felt
compelled to resort to the strongest measures. He caused to be torn down
at once all huts erected near the harbor, on the beach as well as in the woods,
where the traffic of prostitution was secretly carried on.' *Golovnin*, in *Materialui*, 87. 'After consumption, perhaps the largest list of death causes will be
laid at the door of scrofulous diseases, taking the form of malignant ulcers,
which eat into the vitals and destroy them. It renders whole settlements
sometimes lepers in the eyes of the civilized visitor; and it is hard to find a
settlement in the whole country where at least one or more of the families
therein have not got the singularly prominent scars peculiar to the disease.'
Petroff's Pop. Alaska, 83. In 1843-4, there was another outbreak of small-
pox among the Aleuts, but as most of them had been vaccinated, it was not
very destructive. Simpson states that hæmoptysis was a common complaint.
Jour. round World, ii. 190.
[38] *Dok. Kom. Russ. Amer. Kol.*, ii. 136; *Kostlivtzof*, in *Materialui*, app.,
41-2. 'In its wards,' writes Simpson, 'and, in short, in all the requisite appointments, the Sitka hospital would be no disgrace to England.' It had 40
beds. Near each was a table on which glasses and medicines were placed.
The diet was usually salt beef or fish, the soup made from them, mush of
rice or groats, bread, and tea. Of 1,400 patients admitted into the Sitka
hospital in 1860, only 22 died.
[39] There were three large springs close to each other. The temperature
was between 50 and 52° of Réaumur. *Golovnin*, in *Materialui*, 92-3. Dall gives
it at 122° of Fahrenheit, which would be only 40 of Réaumur. *Alaska*, 353.
The waters were impregnated with sulphur, iron, manganese, and chlorine,
97 per cent of the mineral matter being sulphur. During a visit to Atkha in

great panacea of the natives, who before the Russian occupation had no medicine, nor even knew of any medicinal herb.

Sick, aged, and disabled servants were provided for by the company, one half per cent of its profits being appropriated for this purpose after 1802. In later years a tax of ten roubles was levied on each keg of liquor, and of one rouble on each pound of tea sold by the company. From the funds thus raised the deserving poor were pensioned by the government, and in 1860 there were 375 persons in the receipt of pensions, the aggregate amount of which was 30,000 roubles a year. The pensioners were lodged at the company's expense, and the needy were also supplied with food from the public kitchen. Those who wished it were made colonial citizens, a class composed mainly of Russians and creoles. They were exempt from taxation, and had the privilege of reëntering the company's service at will.[40]

Creoles—by which term is always meant the offspring of Russians or Siberians and native women, none being the children of natives and of Russian women—had all the rights of Russian subjects, and were exempt from taxation or enforced service. Many were educated at the company's expense, and were afterward employed in various capacities, some of them, among whom was Veniaminof, being trained for the priesthood.[41]

The churches, schools, and hospitals of Alaska under the Russian régime were supported mainly at the expense of the Russian American Company. At present they exist on charity—charity so cold, that when

1873, Dall observed springs there the temperature of which was 192°. Near them were the ruins of deserted bath-houses. *Rept. Coast Survey* (1873), 114.

[40] There were no beggars in Alaska until after the purchase. The Aleuts supported their own poor. On returning from their expeditions, the hunters always gave a part of their spoils to the young, sick, and aged, who were told to go and help themselves from the bidarka, the owner of which was content with what remained. It was a rare thing among them for any one to ask assistance. He received it as his right. *Golovnin*, in *Materialui*, 93–4.

[41] *Tikhmenef, Istor. Obos.*, app. part i. 55; *Dok. Kom. Russ. Amer. Kol.*, i. 108–9; *Yermoloff, L'Amérique Russe*, 95.

the sum of fifty thousand dollars was voted by congress for educational purposes, there were found none to administer it. What shall we do with the people of Alaska now that they are manumitted? Let them sit and gaze seaward with a steadfast stare, awaiting the arrival of the steamer which, bearing the United States flag, brings to them month by month their supply of hootchenoo!

"Thirteen governments," wrote John Adams, in 1786, "founded on the natural authority of the people alone, without a pretence of miracle or mystery, and which are destined to spread over the northern part of that whole quarter of the globe, are a great point gained in favor of the rights of mankind." "Your best work and most important endowment," said Charles Sumner, addressing the United States senate in 1867, "will be the republican government, which, looking to a long future, you will organize with schools free to all, and with equal laws, before which every citizen will stand erect in the consciousness of manhood. Here will be a motive power, without which coal itself will be insufficient. Here will be a source of wealth more inexhaustible than any fisheries. Bestow such a government, and you will bestow what is better than all you can receive, whether quintals of fish, sands of gold, choicest fur, or most beautiful ivory."[42]

[42] 'If,' remarks J. Ross Browne, 'Mr Secretary Seward had accomplished nothing more in the course of his official career than the acquisition of Alaska, he would for that act alone be entitled not only to the thanks of every citizen of the Pacific coast, already awarded him, but to the gratitude of millions yet unborn, by whom the boundless domain of the west is destined to be peopled.' *Report on the Mineral Resources of the States and Territories West of the Rocky Mountains*, 598. It would be difficult, at this juncture, to find out in what respect the millions born, or to be born, have thus far been so greatly benefited by the transfer.

Elsewhere I have given a brief bibliography of Alaska up to the year 1867. After the purchase there are no complete records. The United States government documents and a number of publications have been consulted for the closing chapters of this volume. Among the newspapers, the *San Francisco Bulletin, Call, Chronicle*, and *Alta*, the *Portland West Shore, Bee, Herald, Oregonian*, and *Deutche Zeitung*, and the *Alaska Herald* may be specially mentioned. Among the government documents that furnish information is the report of *William Gouverneur Morris*, late collector at Sitka. The report is somewhat biased, and contains many errors, of which I will quote one. 'The Russians exercised over the inhabitants of Alaska despotic sway, and held them in absolute subjection. They treated them as brutes, and flogged them unmercifully for theft and petty misdemeanors. They punished crime promptly with severe corporal chastisement or imprisonment, and regarded the Indians as not more than one degree removed from dumb beasts. They held the power of life and death over their subjects. They had over two thousand soldiers, employés, and retainers ready to do the bidding of the local supreme authority. Ships of war were always at hand to bombard the villages into submission.' p. 126. The reader will remember that no Russian vessel of war appeared in Alaskan waters until the year 1850. p. 584, this vol. Notwithstanding errors, the report is very able, and many were sorry to hear that the decease of William Gouverneur Morris occurred early in 1884. The report of *Vincent Colyer on the Indian Tribes and their Surroundings in Alaska Territory* furnishes valuable information, as do those of *L. A. Beardslee on the Condition of Affairs in Alaska*, in *Sen. Ex. Doc., 44th Cong. 2d Sess.*, 105, and of *Bryant and McIntyre*, in *Sen. Ex. Doc., 41st Cong. 2d Sess.*, 32. *Henry W. Elliott's Report on the Seal Islands of Alaska* in the *Tenth Census of the United States* is probably the most reliable publication on the Pribylof Islands, notwithstanding the abuse that has been freely bestowed on that gentleman. From *Davidson's Coast Pilot of Alaska, Sheldon Jackson's Alaska, and Missions on the North Pacific Coast*, and *Hittell's Commerce and Industries of the Pacific Coast*, items of interest have also been gathered. Among the most valuable works published on Alaska during recent years are those of Alphonse L. Pinart, including the *Voyages à la Côte Nord-Ouest de l'Amérique; Voyage à la Côte Nord-Ouest d'Amérique d'Ounalashka à Kadiak;* and *Notes sur les Koloches.* As their contents are of a scientific nature, no use has been made of them in this volume.

For further references to authorities consulted for the last five chapters, see *Morris' Rept. Alaska*, 4–7, 10–19, 21–30, 36–41, 55–6, 59–63, 83–4, 90–4, 103–32; *Colyer's Rept. Ind. Aff.*, 537–9, 542, 554, 556, 568–9, 572, 590; *Bryant and McIntyre's Rept. Alaska*, 2–41; *Elliott's Seal Islands, Alaska*, 20–2, 24–7, 105–8; *U. S. Sen. Doc., 40th Cong., 3d Sess.*, Nos. 42, 53; *41st Cong., 2d Sess.*, 67, 68; *42d Cong., 1st Sess.*, 12; *44th Cong., 1st Sess.*, 12, 33, 48; *44th Cong., 2d Sess.*, 14; *House Ex. Doc., 40th Cong., 2d Sess.*, 80, 103; *41st Cong., 2d Sess.*, 36; *41st Cong., 3d Sess.*, 108, 122; *42d Cong., 1st Sess.*, 5; *42d Cong., 2d Sess.*, 20, 197; *44th Cong., 1st Sess.*, 43, 83; *45th Cong., 2d Sess.*, 155, 217; *45th Cong., 3d Sess.*, 146; *Senate Jour., 40th Cong., 2d Sess.*, pp. 1097, 1221; *42d Cong., 2d Sess.*, 1224; *43d Cong., 1st Sess.*, 963; *44th Cong., 1st Sess.*, 1047; *House Jour., 41st Cong., 2d Sess.*, 1334–5; *42d Cong., 2d Sess.*, 1160; *43d Cong., 1st Sess.*, 1362, 1427; *44th Cong., 1st Sess.*, 1361; *45th Cong., 2d Sess.*, 1508–9; *Sen. Repts., 41st Cong., 2d Sess.*, No. 47, pp. 228–30; *House Comm. Repts., 40th Cong., 2d Sess.*, No. 37; *40th Cong., 3d Sess.*, 35; *44th Cong., 1st Sess.*, 623; *House Misc. Doc., 40th Cong., 2d Sess.*, Nos. 130–1, 161; *42d Cong., 1st Sess.*, 5; *Mess. and Doc.*, 1867, i. pp. 475–88; 1868–9 (abridgment), 852–8; *Coast Survey Rept.*, 1867–8, pp. 41, 187, 264; 1872, 49; 1873, 59–60, 122; 1874, 42; 1875, 5–6, 64–6, 78; *Agr. Rept.*, 1868, pp. 172–89; *Fin. Rept.*, 1868, pp. 391–4; *Sec. Int. Rept., 44th Cong., 1st Sess.*, i. pp. 704–7; *Post. Rept., 44th Cong., 2d Sess.*, p. 41; *Land Off. Rept.*, 1869, pp. 201–7; *Rept. on Ind. Aff.*, 1868, pp. 308–17; 1869, 41–2, 105–9; *Educ. Rept., 41st Cong., 3d Sess.*, pp. 336–7, 345; *43d Cong., 1st Sess.*, 424; *44th Cong., 1st Sess.*, 463–6; *Cong. Globe*, 1867–8, app., pp. 567–8; 1868–9, i. 100, 340–3; 1869–70, app. 558–9, 675; 1871–2, app. 695; 1872–3, app. 274; *Hansard's Parl. Deb.*, ccxv. 1487–8, ccxvi. 1157; *Sumner's Cess. Russ. Amer.*, 8–13, 28–48; *Seward's Our N. Pac. States*, 3–16; *Zabriskie, Land Laws*, 874–84, 887; *Petroff's Pop. Alaska*, 15–86; *Davidson Scient. Exped.*, 471–7, 481–2; *Smithsonian Rept.*, 1867, 43–4; *Whymper's Alaska*, 86–8, 103–6; 253, 258, 274–5; *Jackson's Alaska*, 15–24, 41–6, 49–50, 129–30, 140–327; *Dall's Alaska*, 56–7; 102–5, 181–2, 192–3, 204, 226, 251; *Hittell's Com. and Ind. Pac. Coast*, 330–6, 375–6; *Browne's Mineral Res.*, 597–604; *Rouhaud, Les Régions Nouvelles*, 6; *Brockett's Our Western Empire*, 1271–5, 1277, 1279, 1281; *McCabe's Our Country and Its Res.*, 1081–2; *Pierrepont's Fifth Avenue to Alaska*, 149–217; *Niebaum's State-*

ment, MS., 3–18, 23–5, 44–61; *Berry's Devel. in Alaska*, MS., 2–13, 16–17; *Bancroft's Library Scraps*, 19–21, 25–9, 36–7, 55–63, 65–6, 72–3, 86, 125, 128, 134–45, 191–2, 196, 198, 211, 229, 232, 266–7; *Honcharenko, Scrap-book*, i. 10, 14, 26, 34, 43, 45, 47, 51–4, 60, 74–6, 80–1, 86–8, 99–101, 145; ii. 2, 8, 10–14, 23–4, 32–7, 112–13, 115; *Army and Navy Journal*, May 1, 1869; *Harper's Mag.*, July, 1867, 170–85; *N. Y. Forest and Stream*, July 24, Aug. 14, Dec. 18, 1879, Mar. 4, 18, Apr. 22, May 13, June 24, July 8, Aug. 20, 1880, Jan. 6, 20, 27, 1881; *Alaska Herald*, June 1, 15, Aug. 1, 15, Sept. 1, Nov. 1, Dec. 1, 15, 1868, Feb. 1, Mar. 1, June 15, July 1, 15, Sept. 1, Oct. 1, 22, Nov. 20, 1869, Feb. 1, Oct. 1, 1870, July 15, Aug. 18, Oct. 20, Nov. 1, 1871, Feb. 15, July 24, 1872, Oct. 24, Nov. 25, 1873, Mar. 1, May 28, 1874, Jan. 15, Mar. 15, Apr. 1, Oct. 1, 1875; *Sitka Times*, Apr. 30, May 14, June 4, July 30, Aug. 13, Sept. 1, 11, 25, Oct. 23, Nov. 13, Dec. 4, 1869, Jan. 15, Mar. 5, Apr. 16, June 11, 1870; *S. F. Overland Monthly* (1869), ii. 175–86, (1870) v. 297–301; *Com. Herald*, Apr. 14, 1868, Jan. 30, Apr. 30, 1869, Apr. 22, 29, 1870, Nov. 5, 1874; *Mining and Sci. Press*, Apr. 20, 1872, Jan. 18, June 28, Aug. 2, Sept. 20, 27, 1873, July 27, 1878; *Alta*, June 1, 27, July 2, 14, 20, Aug. 1, Oct. 18, Nov. 3, 14, 16, 25, 29, 1867, Jan. 14, Mar. 27, Aug. 9, Oct. 20, Dec. 18, 1868, Feb. 25, 27, Mar. 19, Sept. 1, Nov. 17, 1869, Mar. 22, 24, Oct. 9, 1870, July 3, 1871, Aug. 6, Sept. 5, 1873; Feb. 2, 1874, June 21, 1875; *Bulletin*, July 13, 1867, May 2, 18, Aug. 1, 27, 1868, Jan. 30, Feb. 2, Apr. 13, Dec. 10, 21, 1869, Jan. 6, 1870, Jan. 26, Feb. 20, June 15, Oct. 5, 12, 1871, Aug. 1, 1872, Nov. 3, 1873, Feb. 16, 1875, June 22, 1877, Sept. 5, 1878, Mar. 18, Apr. 10, Oct. 30, 1879, Jan. 10, Feb. 2, Mar. 23, 1880, July 13, 21, 25, Aug. 11, 16, 26, Sept. 23, 26, 27, Oct. 1, 25, 27, 31, Nov. 25, Dec. 21, 1881, May 11, 23, 24, 27, 1882, Apr. 20, May 3, Aug. 1, 2, Oct. 6, Nov. 28, Dec. 29, 1883; *Call*, Nov. 14, 1867, Mar. 19, Aug. 17, Sept. 25, Oct. 17, 1869, Feb. 16, 1870, Mar. 25, 1871, June 9, Sept. 25, 1877; *Chronicle*, Sept. 2, Nov. 25, 1868, Aug. 6, 1872, July 21, 1873, Nov. 19, 1874, Sept. 15, 1875, Sept. 28, Dec. 14, 1877, Jan. 26, 1878, Dec. 31, 1879, Nov. 17, Dec. 21, 1880, June 26, 1881, Oct. 30, 1882; *Post*, Mar. 13, 1872, May 2, 9, 24, 28, July 1, 1873, Jan. 2, Sept. 24, Nov. 18, 1874, Feb. 26, Apr. 22, 1876, Feb. 14, Oct. 31, 1877; *Sacramento Union*, May 6, Nov. 25, 1867, July 17, 1868, Mar. 27, Apr. 14, Oct. 18, 1869, July 9, 1870, Sept. 9, Oct. 5, 24, 1871, Apr. 11, 1879; *Sacramento Bee*, Feb. 2, 1874, Feb. 22, 1879, Aug. 21, 1880; Portland *West Shore*, May, June, 1876, June, 1878, Oct., Nov., 1879, Jan., 1880; *Deutche Zeitung*, Feb. 6, 1875, Feb. 22, Mar. 1, 1879; *Oregonian*, Sept. 28, 1877, Feb. 22, Mar. 22, Apr. 19, July 19, Aug. 23, 1879, Dec. 3, 1883; *Telegram*, Feb. 6, Mar. 17, 20, May 5, July 9, 10, 16, 1879; Olympia *Courier*, Mar. 24, May 26, Aug. 11, 18, 1882; *Standard*, Jan. 6, Nov. 24, 1877; Seattle *Intelligencer*, Feb. 7, Apr. 24, Dec. 4, 1880; Port Townsend *Argus*, Mar. 13, May 22, July 31, Sept. 4, 1879; Victoria *British Colonist*, Jan. 8, 29, Feb. 12, 1879.

CHAPTER XXXIII.

ALASKA AS A CIVIL AND JUDICIAL DISTRICT.

1883-1885.

THE ORGANIC ACT—A PHANTOM OF CIVIL GOVERNMENT—PROPOSED INDIAN
RESERVATIONS—EDUCATIONAL MATTERS—APPOINTMENT OF UNITED
STATES OFFICIALS—REPORT OF GOVERNOR KINKEAD—HIS SUCCESSOR
APPOINTED—SCHWATKA'S VOYAGE ON A RAFT—EVERETTE'S EXPLORA-
TION—STONEY'S EXPEDITION—MINING ON THE YUKON AND ITS TRIBUTA-
RIES—THE TAKOO MINES—THE TREADWELL LODE—FISHERIES—COM-
MERCE AND NAVIGATION.

THE little that is to be said as to the action of congress concerning Alaska during the opening years of
the present decade, and for several previous years,
may be summed up almost in ten words.   Appropriations were made for the salaries and expenses of agents
at the fur-seal grounds,[1] and, as will presently appear,
these salaries and expenses were voted with no nig-
gard hand.   Yet, during the long period that had
now elapsed since the purchase of Russian America,
petitions without number had been presented to congress, asking for some form of civil government.   At
one time the few Russian residents still remaining in
Alaska were about to petition the tzar to secure for
them the privileges and immunities of citizens of the
United States, as guaranteed by the treaty.   On
another occasion the commander of a Russian man-of-

[1] On the 3d of March, 1881, the sum of $8,000 was appropriated for the
repair and preservation of public buildings. *U. S. Stat., 46th Cong. 3d Sess.*,
436.   In 1882 a few postal routes were established, as will be mentioned
presently.   With these exceptions, nothing was done in congress concerning
Alaska, the salaries of the agents passing among the appropriations for the
miscellaneous civil expenses of each year.

war, stationed on the Pacific coast, had determined
to visit Sitka in order to inquire into the condition of
his countrymen, to whom had been granted neither
protection nor civil rights of any description.   Each
year the president of the United States called attention to the matter, and almost every year resolutions
and bills were introduced in the senate for this purpose, but without result.   Most of them were tabled;
a few were passed to committee, and all were rejected.
It was admitted that, as an abstract proposition, the
Russians and creoles of this *Ultima Thule* were entitled
to protection; but abstract justice was now somewhat
out of date in congressional circles.   Moreover, there
were many conflicting interests to be considered, some
parties desiring that settlement should be encouraged,
and others wishing to retain as much of the mainland
as possible for a stock-farm, and being therefore opposed to any legislation that would cause an influx of
settlers, as was the case some thirty years ago with
the Hudson's Bay Company in Vancouver Island and
New Caledonia.   Meanwhile the outside world knew
nothing of Alaska.   During this interregnum, if we may
believe Major Morris, dozens of letters were addressed
to the "United States Consul at Sitka," and many governors of states and territories sent copies of their
thanksgiving proclamations to the "Governor of
Alaska Territory," years before that country enjoyed
the presence of any such official.[2]

At length, on the 4th of December, 1883, Senator
Harrison introduced a bill to provide a civil government for Alaska, which, with some amendments,
passed both houses, receiving the president's signature on the 17th of May, 1884.   Thus, after many
years of waiting, this long-mooted measure took effect.

By the provisions of what we will call the organic
act, Alaska was organized as a civil and judicial district, its seat being temporarily established at Sitka.
A governor was to be appointed, who should perform

[2] *Scidmore's Alaska,* 228.

generally such duties as belonged to the chief magistrate of a territory, and make an annual report to the president of his official acts, of the condition of the district with reference to its resources, industries, and population. and of the administration of civil government therein, the president having the power to confirm or annul any of his proceedings.[3] A district court was to be established, with the civil and criminal jurisdiction of United States district and circuit courts, the judge to hold at least two terms in each year—one at Sitka, beginning the first Monday in May, and the other at Wrangell, beginning the first Monday in November—together with special sessions as they might be required for the despatch of business, at such times and places as were deemed necessary. The clerk of the court was to be ex officio secretary and treasurer of the district, recorder of deeds, mortgages, certificates of mining claims, and contracts relating to real estate, and also registrar of wills.[4] A marshal was to be appointed, having the general authority and powers of United States marshals, with the right of appointing four deputies, who were to reside respectively in the towns of Sitka, Wrangell, Unalaska, and Juneau, and to perform the duties of constables under the laws of Oregon.

There were also to be appointed four commissioners, one to reside in each of the four towns above mentioned, and having the jurisdiction and powers of

[3] It was also a part of the governor's duties to inquire from time to time into the operations of the Alaska Commercial Co., reporting thereon to congress, and mentioning all violations of the contract existing between the company and the United States. How the governor was to inquire from time to time is not explained in the text of the act, but on this matter he remarks in his report to the president: 'The fur-seal islands are 1,500 miles to the westward of Sitka. To reach them the government must furnish transportation to enable the governor to make such inquiries....The United States ship now at this station might be detailed for the purpose, carrying such officers of the civil government as might be necessary to gain the required information.' S. F. Bulletin, Dec. 18, 1884.

[4] He must establish offices at Sitka and Wrangell for the safe-keeping of all official records. Separate offices might also be established, at the discretion of the court, at Wrangell, Unalaska, and Juneau, for the recording of such instruments as pertained to the several natural divisions of the district, their limits to be defined by the court.

commissioners of United States circuit courts, together with those conferred on justices of the peace under the laws of Oregon. They were also to have jurisdiction, subject to the supervision of the district judge, in all testamentary and probate matters, and for this purpose their courts were to be opened at stated terms as courts of record.[5] The general laws of Oregon, as they were then in force, were to be the law of the district, so far as they were applicable, and did not conflict with the provisions of the act or with the laws of the United States. But the district court was to have exclusive jurisdiction in all equity suits, in all capital criminal cases, and in those involving questions of title to land or mining rights. In civil cases, issues of fact might be determined by a jury at the request of either party, and appeal lay from the decision of the commissioners to the district court, in cases where the amount involved was $200 or more, and in criminal cases where the sentence was imprisonment,[6] or a fine exceeding $100.

Alaska was created a land district, with a United States land-office, to be located at Sitka. The commissioner residing at that point, the clerk, and the marshal were to hold office respectively as registrar, receiver of public moneys, and surveyor-general of the district. The laws of the United States relating to mining claims, and the rights incident thereto, were to be in full force, subject to such regulations as might be made by the secretary for the interior.[7] Nothing

[5] They had power to grant writs of habeas corpus, the writs being returnable before the district judge, and like proceedings could be taken thereon as though they had been granted by said judge. They had, moreover, the powers of notaries public, and must keep a record of all deeds and other instruments acknowledged before them, relating to the title to or transfer of property within their district, this record to be open to public inspection. They must also keep a list of all fines and forfeitures received by them, paying over the amount quarterly to the clerk of the district court.

[6] The jail in the town of Sitka was to be repaired and made suitable for a penitentiary. For this purpose $1,000 was appropriated. *U. S. Stat.*, *48th Cong. 1st Sess.*, 179.

[7] Provided that persons then in possession should not be disturbed in the use or occupation of their lands, though the terms under which they might acquire title were reserved for future legislation. Persons who had located

contained in the act, however, was to be so construed
as to put in force within the district the general land
laws of the United States.

The governor, judge, district attorney, clerk, marshal, and commissioners were to be appointed by the
president, and to hold office for four years, or until
their successors were appointed. The salaries of the
governor and judge were to be each $3,000 a year, and
of the district attorney, clerk, and marshal each $2,500
a year. The commissioners were to receive the fees
usually pertaining to their office, and to justices of the
peace in Oregon, together with such fees for recording instruments as are allowed by that state, and, in
addition, a fixed salary of $1,000 a year.[8] The deputy
marshals were to receive salaries of $750 a year, be-
sides the usual fees of constables in Oregon.

The attorney-general was directed at once to compile and cause to be printed, in pamphlet form, so
much of the laws of the United States as was applicable to the duties of the several officials.[9] The secretary for the interior was ordered to select two of the
officials to be appointed under the act, who, with the
governor, should constitute a commission "to examine
into and report upon the condition of the Indians residing in said territory, what lands, if any, should be
reserved for their use, what provision shall be made
for their education, what rights of occupation by settlers should be recognized," and other matters that
might enable congress to determine the limitations and
conditions to be imposed when the land laws of the
United States should be extended to the district. He
was also required to make temporary provision for the

mines or mineral privileges under the laws of the U. S., or who had occupied,
improved, or exercised rights of ownership over such lands, were to be allowed to perfect their titles. Lands occupied as missionary stations, not
exceeding 640 acres to each station, with the improvements thereon, were also
to be continued in the occupancy of the societies holding them.

[8] Each of the commissioners was required to file a bond in the penal sum
of $3,000, and the clerk in the sum of $10,000.

[9] The sum of $500 was afterward appropriated for the purpose of printing
200 copies of the compiled laws, to be distributed among the officials. *U. S.
Stat., 48th Cong. 1st Sess.*, 223.

education of all children of school age without regard
to race, until a permanent school system should be
established, and for this purpose the sum of $25,000
was appropriated. Finally the manufacture, importation, and sale of intoxicating liquors, except for
medicinal, mechanical, and scientific purposes, were
forbidden, under the penalties provided in the revised
statutes of the United States.[10]

As a land purchase, Alaska had thus far proved a paying investment,[11] though still undeveloped; and yet it
was but a phantom of a government which congress now
somewhat reluctantly bestowed upon it, a government
without representative institutions, or the privilege
of sending a delegate to congress. Meanwhile Russians, creoles, and Americans, who, year by year, had
become more dissatisfied with the shadow of republican administration, expressed their contempt in no
measured phrase for the dilatory action of the national
legislature. Thankful for small mercies, however, they
still waited and hoped, believing that south-eastern
Alaska would, even in their generation, contain settlers enough to warrant the erection of a territory,
though phantom rule might yet prevail in the unpeo-
pled solitudes of the north. At least one step was
gained, now that the drear interregnum of military
occupation or revenue-cutter rule, in the land which
the attorney-general declared to be Indian territory,
had given place to the semblance of civil law.

As to the condition, training, and proposed reservations for Indians mentioned somewhat neatly in the
text of the act, it is probable that the natives would
be only too glad to be left alone as severely in the future as they have been in the past. Considering that
they received no portion of the purchase money of their
native soil, and, as yet, have reaped no benefit from that

[10] Section 1955. For text of the act providing a civil government for
Alaska, see *U. S. Stat.*, *48th Cong. 1st Sess.*, 24-9; *Scidmore's Alaska*, 323-6.
[11] The interest on $7,200,000 invested in U. S. four-per-cent bonds at $1.23
would be about $235,000. The Alaska Commercial Company pays for its
lease and royalty about $317,000 a year.

purchase, save the art of manufacturing hootchenoo, it would appear that this favor might at least be conceded. After the close of the military occupation, Indian outbreaks were of rare occurrence, as I have already mentioned, and in almost every instance were provoked by the misconduct of the white population.[12] What will be the result should they be placed on reservations, and under such treatment as seems in store for them, is a question that the future may solve. At present they are the most contented of all the native tribes under American domination.[13]

[12] See pp. 618-24, this vol. The latest instance of any serious trouble with the natives occurred in October 1882. On the 23d of that month the superintendent of a fishing station at Killisnoo, belonging to the Northwest Trading Company, arrived at Sitka and requested protection from Capt. Merriman, the commander of the U. S. steamer *Adams*. He reported that on the previous night, while the company's whaling-boat was fishing at Hootsnoo (Kootzenoo) lagoon, a bomb, shot from the boat at a whale, accidentally killed one of the native crew, who happened to be a shaman. For this the Indians demanded 200 blankets, and at the same time seized the boat, nets, whaling gear, and steam-launch belonging to the company, overpowering the two white men in the boat, whom they held as prisoners. The tribe of Hoodsinoos, to which the shaman belonged, then threatened, if payment was not made, to burn the company's store and buildings, destroy all their boats, and put to death their captives. As the *Adams* was too large for such service, the *Corwin* was despatched to the scene of the disturbance with Merriman on board; whereupon the prisoners and property were at once surrendered and some of the ringleaders captured. But in addition, Merriman demanded 400 blankets as a punishment, and also as a guarantee for future good behavior. This being refused, their canoes were destroyed; and the tribe being still refractory, their summer camp at Killisnoo was burned. The cutter then steamed out of the Kootzenoo lagoon, and a few hours later shelled their main village, a party of marines landing under cover of the guns and setting fire to the houses, excepting those of friendly Indians. Reports of Lieut M. A. Healy, commanding the *Corwin*, and Collector Wm C. Morris, in *House Ex. Doc.*, 9, parts 2-4, *47th Cong. 2d Sess.*, 9. With this exception, I find no mention of any serious Indian disturbance during recent years. In the spring of 1885 a party of 30 mining prospectors, bound for some point on the Yukon, was stopped by the Chilkats, who demanded toll for admission into their country. *S. F. Chronicle*, May 30, 1885. But no trouble arose out of this matter.

[13] 'They are very cheerful and fond of dancing,' remarks J. C. Glidden, who in the winter of 1870-1 was in charge of a vessel bound for Kadiak and Afognak, 'especially when they have plenty of kvass. More than half a century has elapsed without a murder being committed on these islands, and when one was committed, the inhabitants were horrified at the deed. A visit to some of our cities would cause them to regard such deeds with the equanimity of civilized communities.'

In a *Trip to Alaska*, by J. C. Glidden, MS., I have been supplied with a very interesting manuscript, though one which I cannot use to advantage in this volume, as the subject-matter refers mainly to topics of which I have treated in my *Native Races*. During his visit the author attended divine service at the chapel at St Paul, Kadiak, built, as the reader will remember, about the year 1795, and the first in Russian America. His observations are worthy of

In considering the other provisions of the Harrison bill, it must be admitted that in one respect they were most liberal. For the salaries of the government officials of Alaska, with its handful of white inhabitants, there was appropriated, in 1884, the sum of $20,500, while for each of the territories of Washington, Wyoming, Idaho, Montana, and New Mexico the appropriation for the same purpose was less than $14,000.[14] Moreover, there were appointed, ostensibly for the protection of the seal fisheries of Alaska, four government agents, whose joint salaries and expenses amounted for this year to $13,350, the chief agent receiving a larger stipend than fell to the share of the governor;[15] and to enable the secretary of the treasury to use revenue steamers "for the protection of the interests of government," was voted a further sum of $15,000. But outside of the seal islands the government had no interests to protect, for, as we have seen, apart from the rent and royalty paid for these islands, the income derived from the entire district was altogether inappreciable.

Thus we have, as the expenses of the so-called government of this district, an appropriation for the year of 1884 of about $50,000, or nearly four times the amount voted for any territory in the union, and this for the salaries and allowances of less than a score of officials, four of whom receive the lion's share for keeping watch over the Prybilof Islands, and whose operations have as yet resulted merely in the

note. 'It is built of hewn timber,' he says, 'the interstices being filled with moss. The interior was well but plainly finished. There were no seats, all the audience standing during the services, which were conducted in Russian by a priest whom we termed "the second mate of the church." The utmost decorum prevailed. Each individual, upon entering, went down on the hands and knees, putting the top of the head on the floor. This was repeated a number of times. Upon rising and during service they crossed themselves frequently. All were dressed in their best apparel, that of the young children being elaborately ornamented with glass beads. Near the close of the services the priest placed a large book upon a desk, on the cover of which was a metallic cross. All the worshippers reverently kissed the sacred symbol as they filed past it in line; those who were not tall enough to reach it being lifted to the requisite height by their parents or friends.'

[14] U. S. Stat., 48th Cong. 1st Sess., 178-9.
[15] Three thousand six hundred and fifty dollars. Id., 206.

finding of one slight discrepancy in the tale of skins, and that due to the mistake of one of the agents.[16] After all, it is a far-away country, and government could well enough afford to be liberal. Nevertheless, why it is that the services of four highly paid agents and of a revenue-cutter should be at all needed in counting the tale of skins has never yet been explained. It would appear that such surveillance is wasted on a company which has paid within the past fifteen years about the sum of $5,000,000 into the United States treasury, and that, too, when it is directly against the interests of the company to slaughter more than the prescribed number of fur-seals. Concerning the duties of these agents, however, the statute is singularly reticent. Alaska has been usually regarded by government servants as a place in which to save money, wear out old clothes, and as there were no amusements, no newspapers, and but a single monthly mail,[17] to study fortitude in the endurance of their high honors, and to show themselves indeed patriots on small pay.

The appropriation of $25,000 for educational purposes has thus far been of no practical benefit, for, as with the one of double that amount made some years before, it seemed no one's business to administer it. No public schools were established as contemplated by the provisions of the act, and up to the close of 1884 neither reports nor suggestions had been made as to the disposition of the fund. In July 1884 a further sum of $15,000 was appropriated by congress

[16] See p. 651, this vol.

[17] In an act making appropriations for the postal service, approved July 5, 1884, it is provided that for the fiscal year ending June 30, 1885, the post-master-general may contract under a miscellaneous advertisement for the mail service of Alaska, as no newspapers are published in that territory. *U. S. Stat.*, *48th Cong. 1st Sess.*, 157. By act of Aug. 7, 1882, postal routes were established from Willard to Juneau, from Hoonyah to Juneau, from Jackson to Wrangell, from Haines to Juneau, from Boyd to Juneau, and from Jackson via Roberts to Wrangell. *Id.*, *47th Cong. 1st Sess.*, 351. In 1881 there were only three post-offices in Alaska, and those of the fourth class. In 1880 the total number of letters mailed was 6,812, and the total number of pieces of mail matter of all descriptions 7,592. *Postmaster-General's Rept.*, in *House Ex. Doc.*, 1, pt 4, *47th Cong. 1st Sess.*, pp. 80-1, 88.

for the support and education of Indian children of both sexes at industrial schools. In this matter action was at length taken, though of a somewhat negative character. Through Mr Kendall, the presbyterian board of missions at Sitka applied for a portion of the fund. On the recommendation of the commissioner for Indian affairs, the application was granted,[18] and a contract was made with the society to provide for and educate one hundred children at the rate of $120 a year per capita, such contract to be annulled at two months' notice.[19]

Within less than a decade more has been done by this society to advance the cause of education in Alaska than was otherwise accomplished during all the years of American domination.[20] Were it not

[18] In his letter, the commissioner states that in consequence of the total neglect of government to provide for the education of the Alaska Indians, they have been solely indebted for such schools as exist to religious societies, and for most of them to the society represented by Mr Kendall. For the establishment and support of its schools, that society had expended during the past year over $20,000, and for mission work $5,000. It had, therefore, the first claim to assistance from the appropriation. *Scidmore's Alaska*, 234.

[19] *Id.*, 235. It was the original intention to establish a government industrial school after the model of the institution at Carlisle, Pa.

[20] In his letter to the commissioner, dated New York, Dec. 31, 1882, Sheldon Jackson states that there were seven good English schools in the Alexander Archipelago, six of which were maintained at the expense of the board, three of them having boarding and industrial departments. At Haines, in the Chilkat country, near the head of the Lynn canal, a school was established in 1880, a boarding department being added two years later, when the total attendance was about 75. At Willard, 30 miles up the Chilkat River, a branch school was opened with native teachers, and an average attendance of 60. Among the Hoonid tribe, a school was opened in 1881, at a station named Boyd, 100 miles south of Haines. Among the Auks, at the northern portion of Admiralty Island, and at Tseknuksanky, on the mainland near by, schools were opened between 1880 and 1882. At Jackson, in the southern part of Prince of Wales Island, a school was opened in the spring of 1882, with an attendance of 60 to 90. The institution established at Fort Wrangell in 1877, as already mentioned, had in 1882 from 75 to 90 pupils, of whom 50 were young girls provided for at the expense of the mission, and thus rescued from a life of prostitution, into which they would otherwise have been sold by their parents. The Sitka school, opened in 1878, had, in 1880, 130 pupils. In July of this year the school was moved to the old hospital building. In November some of the pupils applied to the teacher for permission to live at the school-house, for at home, they said, there was so much carousing and disturbance that they could not study. The teacher answered that there was neither food, bedding, nor accommodation for them. Still they persisted, and leave being granted, seven Indian boys, about 13 or 14 years of age, bringing each his blanket, took up their quarters in a vacant room provided for them. This was the origin of the boarding-school at Sitka. In February 1881 Capt. Glass established a rule making attendance at the day-

for the efforts of the board of missions, there would probably have been no efficient school, and perhaps no school of any kind, in the territory, apart from those maintained by the Alaska Commercial Company.

It is claimed that the natives are quick to learn and eager to be taught, not from any moral sense, for, excepting perhaps the Chinese, there is no living nation in which the moral idea is so utterly dormant, but because they appreciate the practical benefit of an education. At the school maintained by the Alaska Commercial Company at St Paul Island,[21] one of the pupils displayed such zeal and ability that he was sent at the expense of the company to complete his education at the state normal academy in Massachusetts, and after completing his five years' course with credit, was placed in charge of the schools at the Seal Islands.

In the autumn of 1884 the officials who had been appointed by the president reached their several stations. John H. Kinkead, ex-governor of Nevada, who had formerly resided at Sitka as merchant and postmaster, was chief magistrate;[22] Ward McAllis-

school compulsory. Forcing the natives to cleanse, drain, whitewash, and number the dwellings in their village, he took an accurate census of the inmates. He then caused a tin label to be tied round the neck of each child, on which were two numbers, one of the house where he lived, and the other of the child. If a pupil was found on the streets during school hours, the numbers on his tag were reported to the teacher by a native policeman, appointed for the purpose; and unless his absence was satisfactorily explained, the parent, or chief Indian of that house, was fined. In a few weeks the attendance ran up to 250.

[21] In 1881, 45 pupils were enrolled at this school, with an average attendance of 42. Schools were also maintained by the company at Unalaska and Kadiak. *House Ex. Doc.*, 1, pt 5, *47th Cong. 2d Sess.*, pp. 278, 282.

[22] John Henry Kinkead, a native of Fayette co., Penn., where he was born in 1826, crossed the plains from St Louis to Salt Lake City in 1849, and there engaged in business for several years, proceeding to California in 1854, after which date he had occasion to travel extensively over the Pacific coast. In 1860 we find him in Carson City, on the eve of the admission of Nevada as a territory. Of the part that he played in connection with the political annals of that state mention is made in its place. In 1867 Kinkead was a member of the expedition which sailed for Sitka on board the *John L. Stephens* a few weeks after the purchase. My description of the transfer, after the arrival of the *Ossipee*, though written previous to my interview with Gov. Kinkead, coincides with the account he gave me. In 1871 he returned to Nevada, residing at Unionville, Humboldt co., until 1878, when he was elected governor of the state.

In *Kinkead's Nevada and Alaska*, MS., the author has furnished me with

ter,[23] district judge; E. W. Haskell, district attorney; Andrew T. Lewis, clerk of court; M. C. Hillyer,[24] marshal; and as commissioners, John G. Brady at Sitka, Henry States at Juneau, George P. Ihrie at Wrangell, and Chester Seeber at Unalaska.

On the 1st of October, 1884, some three weeks after his arrival, Governor Kinkead made his report to the president.[25] On the 15th of September the commander of the United States naval forces [26] relin-

a manuscript which, when compared with other sources of information, varies so little that his statements cannot but be accepted as true. Among other topics, he touches on education, mining, agriculture, and the present condition of the native tribes in Alaska. 'The Indians appeared to have a very good idea of business,' he remarks. 'The women were in a better condition and better treated than those of any other tribes of the United States that I have seen, the men generally carrying the children and other burdens, and apparently affectionate to their wives and children, the women mostly doing the trading with the whites.' As to the future of Alaska, he is of opinion that the south-eastern portion of the territory is better adapted to the support of a moderate white population than Norway or Sweden.

During the period of the occupation of Sitka by U. S. troops, all the wood supplied the garrison was cut and delivered by Indian labor.

[23] Formerly assistant U. S. attorney, a resident of San Francisco, and a relative of Hall McAllister, one of the most prominent and highly respected attorneys in that city.

[24] Munson C. Hillyer, a native of Granville, Ohio, was brother of Curtis J. Hillyer and Edgar W. Hillyer, the former an eminent lawyer, and the latter, at the time of his death, U. S. judge in Nevada. Munson came to Cal. in early times and became a flour merchant, and later a mining superintendent—a man of broad experience, warm heart, and having many friends.

[25] The report was presented at Washington on the 17th of Dec. S. F. Bulletin, Dec. 18, 1884.

[26] Lieut H. E. Nichols, commanding the U. S. steamer Pinta, her complement consisting of 7 officers, 40 seamen, and 30 marines for shore duty at Sitka. Nichols had for several years done good service in the southern part of the Alexander Archipelago, while in command of the Hassler, his surveys having been made the basis for several of the new charts published in the Alaska Coast Pilot of 1883, and compiled by William H. Dall. The Pinta is somewhat famous in the annals of the U. S. navy, though her fame is a little unsavory. One of fifteen despatch-boats built during the war, she was stationed for several years at the Brooklyn navy-yard. In 1882, after an unconscionable sum had been spent in repairing her at Norfolk, a board of officers condemned the work, and pronounced the boat unseaworthy. A second survey was then called, and a trial trip being ordered, it was found that she could make but four knots an hour. Soon afterward the Pinta was sent to Boston, where she distinguished herself by running down the brig Tally-Ho, her officers being in consequence brought before a board of inquiry. Finally a man was found daring enough to peril his life by taking her round Cape Horn, her armament being sent ashore until she reached California. Arriving at the Mare Island navy-yard after a six months' voyage, she was again repaired, and her guns being mounted, this much-tinkered vessel was ordered to Sitka. Among the naval officers in command at Sitka before the appointment of Nichols may be mentioned Captain Beardslee, who, in charge of the Jamestown, cruised in all parts of the Alexander Archipelago, kept the Indians

quished to him all civil authority, his duties in that direction being now at an end. The complete organization of the civil government was delayed for a time by the absence of the district judge and the commissioner for Sitka, the former being detained at San Francisco through illness. Meanwhile the board of Indian commissioners assumed judicial authority, settling disputes to the satisfaction of the parties interested.[27] The governor expressed the opinion that mining bade fair to rank foremost among the resources of the territory, and that within the next decade the output of precious metals in Alaska would form no unimportant factor in the finances of the general government. This industry has languished, he says, mainly for the reason that no title to mining lands, other than that of force, has thus far been recognized. For the same reason the grazing and agricultural capabilities of the territory, which he considered full of promise, were yet undeveloped. He urged that timber tracts, building-lots, agricultural areas, and mining lands be made subject to legal titles, for, without such titles, the progress of settlement must be slow and uncertain.

He recommended, also, that mail facilities be increased. There should be at least semi-monthly

in subjection, and afterward made a valuable official report, which has already been quoted in these pages. To him succeeded Captain Glass, an officer of marked ability, who by his firmness and humanity won the respect of the natives, and made several treaties of peace between hostile Indian tribes, maintaining a protectorate over the various settlements until relieved, in 1881, by Commander Lull in the steamer *Wachusett*. In the autumn of 1882 Captain Merriman, in charge of the *Adams*, was detailed for the Alaska station, and discharged his manifold duties as umpire, judge, referee, and preserver of the peace, with considerable tact and discretion. Not infrequently he was called upon to save the lives of persons doomed to death for witchcraft, and to prevent the slaughter of slaves at funerals and potlatches. Merriman was superseded in command of the *Adams* by Capt. J. B. Coghlan, who, finding the Indians peaceable, devoted his leisure to a survey of the most frequented channels of the inside passage, marking off with buoys the channel through Wrangell Narrows and Peril Straits, and designating unknown rocks in Saginaw Channel and Neva Strait. In August 1884 the *Adams* was replaced by the *Pinta. Scidmore's Alaska*, 219-23; *Sacramento Union*, May 20, 1881.

[27] The governor also reinstated the Indian police, discharged by Captain Nichols, after being carried for some years on the pay-rolls of the navy, as he considered them necessary to inspire due respect for the civil authority.

communication with Port Townsend, and a monthly mail-steamer should run between Sitka and Unalaska, touching at several intervening ports. The distance between these ports is twelve hundred miles, but as there is no direct communication, persons wishing to avail themselves of the district court tribunal established at the capital must travel by way of San Francisco, and return by the same route, the entire journey being nearly eight thousand miles. The districts of Kadiak and Kenai, which were altogether ignored in the organic act, should be placed under the protection of the civil authority; for in those districts were several hundred Russians and creoles, who were peaceable, industrious, and eager to share in the benefits of American progress.

The customs service could not be efficiently carried on with the means then at command. For this purpose it was necessary that at least one revenue-cutter should be constantly employed in cruising among the channels and inlets of the coast. At this time illicit traffic prevailed in many portions of the territory. The boundary line between the Portland canal and Mount St Elias should be speedily and definitely settled by a joint survey of the British and American governments, for several of the highways leading into British Columbia lie partly within the limits of Alaska, among them being the one leading to the Stikeen River mines.

On the subject of education the governor remarked that Alaska was entirely without schools for white children, the missionary schools being attended only by natives. The former were growing up in total ignorance, though their parents were most anxious to give them education, and would gladly pay for the services of teachers.

Finally, with regard to traffic in spirituous liquor, he stated that the military commander of the division of the Pacific had the right to grant permits for its introduction into the territory. Whether, or to what extent, the commander exercised that power, he was not aware; but, with or without permission, a very large quantity of liquor found its way into Alaska. The law forbade its introduction, except for certain purposes, but did not forbid its sale after it was introduced, and liquor was openly sold in all the principal settlements; though, on account of the severe penalties enforced by the naval and customs authorities, little of it was disposed of among the natives.[28] The utmost vigilance on the part of officials could not entirely prevent this traffic, for countless devices were practised whereby the law was evaded; but in order to regulate it, the governor suggested the appointment of an executive council, with full power to act in the matter. He also recommended that saloon-keepers, tradesmen, and others should contribute, by a license, tax, or otherwise, to the support of government, paying at least enough to maintain the police and to keep the streets and sidewalks in repair.[29]

It will be observed that, while the governor made some excellent suggestions as to what congress ought to do, he said nothing about what he himself intended to do. As ruler of a country so vast in extent, and containing such varied and conflicting interests, he was necessarily intrusted with discretionary powers. He appears to have fully understood the needs of the country, and had he continued in power, it is not improbable that he might have made some effort to supply them. He did not remain long enough in the territory, however, to frame any important measures, or at least to carry them into effect, although it was provided in the organic act that he should reside within the district during his term of office.

A few weeks after the inauguration of President Cleveland, Kinkead was requested to send in his resig-

[28] The governor stated that, through the efforts of the same authorities, the manufacture of hootchenoo had been almost entirely broken up in the neighborhood of Sitka and other parts of the archipelago.

[29] The text of the governor's report, with some slight omissions, will be found in the *S. F. Bulletin*, Dec. 18, 1884.

nation, A. P. Swineford of Michigan being appointed
in his stead on the 9th of May, 1885.

In the exploration of the interior of Alaska and
the survey of its coasts, bays, and rivers, considerable
progress has been made during recent years, considering the immense area to be explored. Numerous
expeditions have been undertaken in addition to those
mentioned in a previous chapter,[30] and many charts
have been published, some of them valuable, and
others so utterly worthless that the captain who
should follow them would run his vessel at various
points into the mountains of the mainland. Reports
without number have been made by navigators as to
the difficulties encountered among these intricate
channels and dangerous harbors,[31] but no reliable
charts of the entire coast have as yet been made.

In the summer of 1883 Lieutenant Schwatka and
six others[32] traversed the upper Yukon by raft from
its source to Fort Selkirk, a distance of about five
hundred miles, their object being to gather information as to the Indian tribes of that region, and for
geographical exploration. The middle Yukon, as far
as the junction of that river with the Porcupine, and
the lower Yukon, extending from this point to the
delta, had already been explored, as we have seen, by
the servants of the Russian American Company, who
occasionally ascended the stream from the direction
of St Michael sometimes possibly as far as the present
site of Fort Reliance, and thence made their way
partly overland to the Lynn canal. In the summer
of 1883 the lieutenant set forth to explore the river

[30] See pp. 628-9, this vol.
[31] Among others may be mentioned the case of J. C. Glidden, who, in the
summer of 1870, was in command of a vessel voyaging to the gulf of Nushagak, between the parallels of 58° 25' and 59° 2' N. and the meridians of 158°
5 and 158' 43' W. according to Russian surveys. He reports its entrance obstructed by bars and quicksands, which rendered its navigation difficult and
dangerous, though a pilot could usually be obtained at Cape Konstantin.
Trip to Alaska, MS., I. 6-7.
[32] Dr Wilson, Topographical assistant Homan, Sergeant Gloster, Corporal
Shircliff, Private Roth, and a Mr McIntosh. *Century Mag.*, 1885, 739, 819.

from its source to its mouth, the basin of the upper
Yukon being, as he thought, a terra incognita.

Leaving Chilkat on the 7th of June with thirteen
canoes towed by a steam-launch belonging to the
Northwest Trading Company, he passed through the
Lynn canal and the Chilkoot Inlet, arriving at the
mouth of a swift-running stream, some ninety feet
in width, called by the Indians the Dayay. Here he
took leave of the launch, and at this point, as he
claims, his exploration commenced, though in fact he
was on ground perfectly familiar to the Russians, even
in the days of Baranof. Reaching the head of navigation on the 10th, the canoes were unloaded and
their three or four tons of freight packed on the backs
of seventy Indians, the party reaching, the same
night, the head waters of the stream, under banks of
snow, and at the foot of a pass about three thousand
feet in height, which the lieutenant named Perrier
Pass,[33] and where, he says, "long finger-like glaciers
of clear blue ice extended down the granite gulches to
our very level."

The ascent was a difficult one and not unattended
with danger. In places the mountain side appeared
almost perpendicular, and a few stunted juniper roots
protruding through a thin covering of snow afforded
the only support. The footsteps of the guides were
turned inward and planted deep, thus giving a firm
hold, and the remainder followed in their tracks, some
of them using rough alpen-stocks, for the least slip
would have dashed them down the precipitous slope
hundreds of feet into the valley below. Arriving at
the summit without mishap, the party found themselves in a drifting fog, such as many of my readers
may have observed hanging in summer for days at a
time over Snowdon or Ben Nevis, both of which
mountains are but three or four degrees south of the

---

[33] Why he so called it he does not state. I do not find the pass named or
even marked in any of the maps published before 1883, though it is certain
that the lieutenant was not the first white man who made the ascent of the
Dayay River or portage.

point where they now stood. Descending the pass, the lieutenant afterward came in sight of two large lakes connected by a channel about a mile in length, and which he named lakes Lindermann and Bennett.[34]

On the shore of the latter he built his raft, some fifteen by forty feet, with decks fore and aft, space being left for oars at the bow, stern, and sides, so that when laden it could be pulled in still water at a rate of more than half a mile an hour. Behind the forward deck was hoisted a nine-foot mast, a wall-tent serving for a sail, and for a yard its ridge-pole, while the projecting logs that supported the deck were used as belaying-pins. In this strange craft, built in the ice-cold water of the lake, the lieutenant launched forth on the morning of the 19th of June on his exploration of the upper Yukon.

The outset of the voyage was by no means propitious. The wind at first blew gently from the south, and hoisting sail, he made from two to three miles an hour; but the wind freshened into a gale and the gale increased to a cyclone, threatening to carry away the mast, while the waves swept the frail bark fore and aft, deluging all on board, so that rowing became impossible.

On the following afternoon the party reached the northern end of Lake Bennett, and thence, without special adventure, made their way, by the route known as the Indian portage, to a point which Schwatka terms the grand cañon of the Yukon, where are rapids some five miles in length, in places shoal and dangerous even for the navigation of a canoe. At first the waters pour in troubled foam between basaltic pillars, about seventy feet apart, then widen into a basin filled with eddies and whirlpools, and again pass through a second cañon, almost the counterpart of the first. Thus the river flows onward for several miles, after which it narrows almost into a

[34] Both of these lakes, which form a part of the Indian portage, are marked on the U. S. Coast Survey map of 1869.

cascade, less than thirty feet wide, and with waves running five feet high. So swift and turbulent is the stream at this point, that, as the lieutenant relates, its waters dash up the banks on either side, falling back in solid sheets into the seething caldron below.

Stationing a few men below the cascade to render assistance, as the raft shot past them, Schwatka turned its head toward the outlet of the grand cañon of the Yukon, through which he passed.[35]

The party had now overcome their greatest difficulties. Repairing the raft, on the 5th of July they passed the mouth of the Tahkeena River,[36] and thence, without further incident worthy of note, voyaged down the stream to Fort Selkirk, completing the journey mainly by raft down the middle and lower Yukon, and thence proceeded to St Michael, where they were met by the revenue-cutter *Corwin.*[37]

In 1884 and 1885 several expeditions were undertaken by order of General Miles, then in charge of the department of the Columbia, which includes Alaska. In February of the former year Doctor Everette set forth from Vancouver Barracks for the purpose of exploring a portion of the Yukon, and the section of territory near the head of Copper River. Procuring Indian guides at Juneau, he proceeded to Chilkat, and there remained for three months, studying the language of the tribe. Thence, reaching the head waters of the Yukon by way of the Lynn canal and the Dayay River, following about the same route as was taken by Schwatka's party in 1883, he voyaged down the stream, in a boat of his own construction, as far as the first fur-trading station. Here he awaited the arrival of the steamer from the Bering Sea, and being abandoned by his pack Indians, and unable to obtain a supply of provisions for winter use, he had no alternative but to complete his journey on board that vessel, arriving at St Michael during the

[35] The lieut christened his craft the *Resolute.*
[36] Now usually called the Tahk.
[37] *Century Mag.*, Sept. Oct. 1885, 739–51, 819–29; *Scidmore's Alaska*, p. 120.

easy, there being stretches of 100 miles where no
portage was needed, and none of the portages exceeding half a mile.   During their trip they examined
more than a hundred streams, in all of which gold
was discovered, though the ground and even the beds
of streams where was running water were frozen.
Hence, they said, it was impossible to work the
deposits; but the fact that one of the party proceeded
to San Francisco to purchase a schooner and load it
with miners' supplies for that quarter would seem to
indicate that this was not the case.   Between 1880
and 1883 more than two hundred prospectors visited
the Yukon district, the Chilkats keeping control of
the travel, and charging six to ten dollars for each
hundred pounds of baggage conveyed over the portage between the river and the lakes.[40]

The maps of the upper Yukon district made since
the purchase have not changed materially the charts
made by the Russians.   Among them is one prepared
by a native named Kloh-Kutz[41] for Professor Davidson, which has been made the basis for an official
chart.   From the maps and publications of two doc-
tors of the names of Krause, belonging to the geographical society of Bremen, who recently explored
the neighborhood of the Yukon portages, the coast
survey has gathered information of considerable value.

The Takoo mines, and especially those in the neighborhood of Harrisburg, or Juneau,[42] and the quartz

[40] Dr Everette's opinion as to the mining outlook in the Yukon district
was unfavorable.   First, he believed that no mother vein exists in that region,
while the placer diggings contain only fine flour gold which it is very difficult
to save.   One party from Juneau obtained about $2,000 from a bar on the
upper Yukon in 1884, but they exhausted the diggings, and were later prospecting on the White and Stewart Rivers.   Second, the ground only partially
thaws during the brief summer of interior Alaska, the ice opening in May and
closing in again during October.   Third, it is impossible to procure provisions
sufficient for the winter at the fur-trading posts, while freight via Chilkat to
the head of the Yukon is $20 per hundred pounds.   *S. F. Chronicle*, Aug. 30,
1885.   The doctor claims to be versed in mineralogy, and to have had practical experience in the placer mines of the Black Hills and the quartz mines of
New Mexico.

[41] The father of Klohkutz, a chief fur-trader, was among the band of
Chilkats who burned Fort Selkirk in 1851, in consequence of the interference
of the Hudson's Bay Company with their trade.   *Scidmore's Alaska*, 121.

[42] The name Juneau was formally adopted at a meeting of miners held in

veins on Douglas Island, have attracted the most attention within recent years, and are the only districts
that require further mention. The bars and shores
of Takoo River have been searched for miles beyond
the Takoo Inlet, and in most of the adjacent streams
fine gold has been discovered, carried down by the
glaciers that now lie amid the ravines and fiords of
this region.

In 1879 Professor Muir expressed his belief that
valuable quartz leads would be found on the mainland
east of Baranof Island, and that the true mineral belt
would follow the trend of the shore. His prediction
was soon verified. In the following autumn a prospecting party left Sitka in charge of Joseph Juneau
and Richard Harris, and encamping on the present
site of the town of Juneau, followed up a large creek
which discharges into the channel near that point.
Here they found rich placers and several promising
ledges. On their return to Sitka, with sacks full of
specimens, a rush was made for this district, and during the winter a camp was established, which afterward developed into a town, among its inhabitants
being a number of miners from Arizona and British
Columbia. From the placers in this neighborhood it
is estimated that about $300,000 had been obtained
up to the close of 1883.[43] The correct figures, however, cannot be ascertained even approximately, for,
on account of the heavy express charges, many of the
miners, proceeding to Wrangell, Victoria, San Francisco, or wherever they pass the winter, carry with

May 1882, though both are still used. In 1884 the town contained about 50
houses, and there was an Indian village on both sides of it. *Scidmore's Alaska,*
82–3.

[43] As an instance of the little that is known in Washington concerning the
resources of Alaska, it may be mentioned that for the fiscal year ending June
30, 1880, the total bullion product of Alaska was estimated by the director of
the mint at $6,000, and for the ensuing year at $7,000. *House Ex. Doc., 47th
Cong. 1st Sess.,* xiv., p. 269. In *Scidmore's Alaska,* 85, the product of the
placer mines in the Takoo district alone is given for 1881 at $135,000, for 1882
at $250,000, and for 1883 at $400,000. These figures are doubtless too high.
During the seasons of 1881–3 there were probably some 200 miners at work
in this district, and estimating their average earnings at $800 each per season,
we have a total of about $500,000 for the three years.

them their own gold-dust. In 1884 the surface deposits showed signs of exhaustion, and many of the claims were abandoned, though some that were still partially worked yielded fair returns. Meanwhile prospecting was continued, and tunnels, run a short distance into several quartz ledges, disclosed a moderate amount of low-grade gold ore, but nothing that, under existing conditions, would pay for working.

In 1885 the most prominent mine in Alaska, and one of the most prominent on the Pacific coast, was the Treadwell, or as it is now usually termed, the Paris lode, at Douglas Island, discovered[44] and recorded in May 1881, and deeded in November of that year to Mr John Treadwell. The property was afterward transferred to an incorporation styled the Alaska Mill and Mining Company, of which, in 1885, Mr Treadwell was superintendent,[45] and under whose direction $400,000 had been expended on the development of the property.[46] The results, however, fully justified the outlay.[47]

A short time after the company took possession of its property two tunnels were run into the ledge, and thence and from the surface ore was extracted and worked in a five-stamp mill, for the purpose of thoroughly testing the mine. The returns being satisfactory, a third tunnel was run, at a vertical depth of 250 feet. An uprise of 275 feet at the foot-wall, having been made to the surface, is now used for an ore chute. The width of the ledge was found to be 450 feet, the

[44] By Pierre Joseph Ernsara. *Freeborn's Alaska Mill and Mining Co.*, MS.

[45] Receiving this appointment under the first organization, when James Freeborn was chosen president, the directors being J. D. Fry, E. M. Fry, H. L. Hill, and H. H. Shinn. In October 1885 the proprietors were Senator J. P. Jones, Messrs Freeborn, Treadwell, Hill, Shinn, J. D. Fry, and E. M. Fry, all of these gentlemen, with the exception of the first, who held a sixth interest in the property, being still officers of the company. *Id.*

[46] By the company. *Id.* In Kinkead's *Nevada and Alaska*, MS., 15, the total outlay, including what was expended before the transfer of the property by Mr Treadwell, is given at $300,000.

[47] In the *S. F. Chronicle*, Nov. 17, 1884, it is stated that there was at this date $12,000,000 in sight. I give the statement for what it is worth.

ore-body averaging $8.50 per ton in free gold and five per cent of sulphurets, with an assay value of $100 per ton. Thereupon the company decided to erect a 120-stamp mill, with a capacity of 300 tons per day, and with 48 Frue concentrators and 24 Challenge ore-feeders, the mill being completed in the summer of 1885. Between June 19th and September 19th of that year the aggregate yield amounted to $156,000,[48] though for various reasons, the principal one being an unusually dry season, and the fact that during the summer the snow and ice disappeared altogether from the neighboring mountains, the mill stood idle for one third of this period.[49] About the close of 1885, or early in the following year, the superintendent proposed to erect two additional furnaces, and to place electric lights in the mine, mill, and surrounding works.[50]

Adjoining the Paris ledge, and a continuation of the same vein, was the Bear ledge,[51] believed to be

[48] For the month ending July 19th, $55,000, and for the other two months $60,000 and $41,000 respectively, the yield being entirely from free gold and apart from sulphurets. *Freeborn's Alaska Mill and Mining Co.*, MS.

[49] Soon afterward a despatch was received from the superintendent, stating that there was a plentiful supply of water, that the works were all in running order, and that the next bullion shipment would probably be the largest yet made from the mine. *Id.*

[50] The frame-work of the mill was built of lumber cut by the company's saw-mill, which, up to September 1885, had turned out some 2,250,000 feet, the remainder being used for chlorination-works and the usual buildings needed for a mine of this description, among them being boarding-houses for the men, of whom nearly 300 were employed at good wages, the Indians receiving $60 per month, and white men in proportion. A tramway had been constructed for hauling ore from the chute to the mill, and hydraulic machinery has been forwarded for that purpose, which has greatly reduced the cost of transporting the ore. The mine, some 160 miles north-east from Sitka, is 350 yards from the shore of Gastineaux Channel, and the mill 860 feet from the foot of the chute. The president states that during two seasons the company was robbed at least to the amount of $120,000 by surface-miners, who washed off the top of the ledge, and as there were no laws, or none in force, did very much as they pleased.

In *Freeborn's Alaska Mill and Mining Co.*, MS., I have been furnished by the president of the company with a terse and reliable statement as to the condition and working of this mine, from which the above facts and figures are taken.

In this connection may be mentioned recent advices from Kadiak, under date Sept. 22, 1885, according to which this section of Alaska had been totally neglected by the United States and district authorities. From the civil government at Sitka nothing had been heard, and the people were still without official notification of its existence 18 months after the passage of the act creating Alaska a civil and judicial district. *S. F. Bulletin*, Oct. 5, 1885.

[51] Owned in 1884 by Carroll and his partners.

also a valuable property, though as yet the latter
has been but little developed. Elsewhere among
the mountains that ridge Douglas Island from end
to end are quartz lodes innumerable, some of which
seem promising enough to warrant the investment
of capital. That the most permanent mines so far
discovered in Alaska should be found on an island
— the island surveyed by Vancouver more than
ninety years ago—is somewhat of an anomaly in mining annals; but Alaska, with her inland seas, her
glaciers, her midnight suns in midsummer, her phantom
auroras in midwinter, and her phantom government
at all seasons of the year, is the land of anomalies.

At present it may be said that the mining interests
of Alaska are mainly centred in Douglas Island.
Elsewhere there may be large deposits of ore, but none
of them have yet been extensively worked. Those in
northern and central Alaska are too remote to be made
available, and the lodes discovered near Sitka have
proved of little value, the gold-bearing ore being of low
grade and the veins broken in formation. In a country
where travel is difficult and the cost of transportation
excessive, only those mines can be made to pay which
are situated near the coast, unless they be exceptionally rich. Moreover, on account of the forests and
the dense growth of moss which hide the surface,
Alaska is a very difficult country to prospect. As a
rule, outcroppings are rarely found, and leads are
usually discovered by following float ore and tracing it
up stream to the main body. That the territory will,
however, at some future date, contain a not inconsiderable mining population, is almost beyond a peradven-
ture. Provisions are much cheaper than in most of
the mining districts of British Columbia, and fish and
game can be had for nothing. The main drawback
appears to be that in Alaska miners are not content
with such earnings as would elsewhere be considered
a reasonable return for their labor.

Concerning the fisheries of Alaska, a few items remain to be added to those which have been already mentioned. The cannery established by Cutting and Company, at Kasiloff River, on Cook Inlet, in 1882, has been fairly successful, considering the difficulty in establishing a new enterprise of this description, the pack, after the first year, averaging some 20,000 cases. The varieties packed are the king salmon, the silver salmon, and what is known as the red fish, the last being similar to the red salmon of the Fraser River. The Kasiloff is not a navigable stream, its source being a lake about twenty miles from its outlet. Vessels freighted with goods for the cannery, or waiting for the season's pack, are compelled to lie in an open roadstead, where there is a heavy fall and rise of the tide. Notwithstanding this drawback, however, the firm is satisfied with results so far, considering the depressed condition of the market. The Alaska Salmon Packing and Fur Company, at Naha Bay, has also been measurably successful, though in 1885 the pack was only of salt salmon. At that date there were two other canneries in operation, one at Bristol Bay, named the Arctic Packing Company, and the other at Karluk on Kadiak Island, the pack of the latter for 1885 being about 36,000 cases.

The total pack of Alaska salmon was estimated for the year 1885 at about 65,000 cases, and the fact that, in the face of extremely low prices, this industry has not only held its own, but increased considerably, while on the Columbia there has been a considerable decrease in the output, is significant of its future success. Thus far, however, profits have been very light. The amount of capital needed to establish and conduct the business is disproportionately large. Payments for material must be made at least four or five months before the product is laid down in San Francisco or in other markets, and it is found necessary to carry a large surplus stock of stores. The cost of the passage of employés is paid at all the Alaska canneries, together with their wages while journeying to and fro; and the repair of machinery is an unusually expensive item. The prospects of the business depend, of course, mainly on the continuance of heavy runs of fish on the Columbia River, and it is stated that the enormous catch year by year has already begun to tell very seriously on the run.[52] The supply of salmon in the waters of Alaska is practically unlimited, and it is probable that the take is more than offset by the destruction of fur-seals, which devour the food-fish that frequent her shores, as salmon, smelt, and mackerel, each one consuming, it is said, no less than sixty pounds a day.

At Killisnoo, on the island of Kenashoo, originally a whaling-station, the Northwest Trading Company had, in 1885, a large establishment where codfish were dried, and herring and dog-fish oil, and fish guano manufactured. Large warehouses and works were built, near which was a village of Indians employed as fishermen, and receiving two cents apiece for the catch of codfish, boats being provided by the company. About $100,000 was invested in this enterprise, the oil-works alone having cost $70,000. The cod in these waters average about four pounds in weight, and as many as eight thousand are sometimes taken in a single day, producing about fifteen hundred boxes of the dried fish. Of herring, as many as five hundred barrels are occasionally caught at a single haul of the seine, each barrel yielding about three gallons of oil.

Thus it would appear that the fisheries of Alaska alone might furnish the basis of a considerable commerce; but under such conditions as now exist in that district, there is little field for commercial or industrial enterprise, and it may be said that commerce, in its legitimate sense, does not exist. Imports of duty-paying goods, which, as I have said,

[52] *Cutting and Co.'s Alaska Salmon Fisheries*, MS. In this manuscript I have been furnished with a brief and impartial account of the condition and prospects of the Alaska canneries.

for the twelve months ending March 1, 1878, were $3,295, amounted, for the fiscal year ending June 30, 1882, to $8,484; and meanwhile domestic exports showed a slight increase.[53] For the latter year, if we can believe official reports, the entire foreign trade was with British Columbia, though, during that year, fifteen American vessels, with an aggregate measurement of 9,461 tons, and twenty-nine foreign vessels of 8,073 tons, entered Alaskan ports, while the clearances were twelve American vessels of 8,993 tons, and twenty-nine foreign vessels of 8,156 tons.[54] Meanwhile the ship-building industry had fallen somewhat into decadence. In 1882 there was built a single vessel, probably a fishing-smack, with a measurement of 6.43 tons—somewhat of a contrast, compared with the days of the Russian American Company, when, as we have seen, a fleet of sea-going ships was launched in Alaskan waters.

A country where there is no commerce, where there are few industries, where there are no schools except those supported by charity, where no title can be had to land, where there are no representative institutions and no settled administration, and where the rainfall is from five to eight feet a year, does not, of course, hold out any very strong inducements to settlers. Of 690 persons who arrived at Alaskan ports during the year ending June 30, 1880, 583 were merely passengers, the remaining 107 being miners from British Columbia. For the year ending June 30, 1882, matters were still worse, the total arrivals mustering only 27, of whom 17 were miners, while the departures for that year were 387.[55] These, however, are merely the returns forwarded from the customs districts, and I give them for what they are worth.

[53] In the report on commerce and navigation, in *House Ex. Doc.*, 7, *47th Cong. 2d Sess.*, 24, domestic exports for the year ending June 30, 1882, are stated at $38,520; and in *Id.*, 7, *46th Cong. 3d Sess.*, xvi. 24, for the year ending June 30, 1880, at $31,543.

[54] *Id.*, 7, *47th Cong. 2d Sess.*, 736, 739.

[55] Report on commerce and navigation, in *House Ex. Doc.*, 7, *46th Cong. 3d Sess.*, 688, 703; *47th Cong. 2d Sess.*, *Id.*, 7, 678, 696, 730.

While Alaska remains, as it is to-day, little more than a customs district, though in name a civil and judicial district, no better results need be anticipated. If it should happen that in the year 1890, when the lease of the Alaska Commercial Company expires, its privileges be divided, then there would doubtless be a considerable influx of population; but whether such influx would, under present conditions, be of benefit to the territory or to the United States is a somewhat doubtful question. Laying aside, however, the comments of the press, and of disappointed political adventurers, it would seem to an impartial observer that the claims of the company are not altogether unworthy of recognition. Leasing a few leagues of rock, hanging almost midway between the continents, they have, while making larger returns to stockholders year by year than were made by the Russian American Company in a decade, paid over to the United States almost the face of the purchase money, and by their forethought and business tact furnished, though perhaps incidentally, means for wasteful extravagance in other sections of the territory. It is probable that the lessees of the Prybilof Islands were at first no less sorely disappointed with their bargain than were the purchasers of the Treadwell lode, and it is almost certain that in neither instance did the parties foresee the difficulties that lay before them. The fact that they have confronted and overcome those difficulties, and while doing so have laid bare some of the resources of Alaska, is one that needs not be pleaded against them.

What there is to be pleaded against them, save perhaps their success as a business association—the fact that in 1885 they gathered nine tenths of the world's supply of sea-otter skins and three fourths of its supply of fur-seal skins, their chain of posts extending from Kamchatka[56] far inland to the wilderness on the purchase of which the secretary of state

---

[56] Where they collect a few sea-otter skins, a large number of sables, and from 1,500 to 3,000 blue fox skins, the fur of the last, though of a dingy slate color, being considered almost as valuable as that of the white fox.

was accused of wasting $7,200,000; that when they entered upon this business seal-skins were barely salable at a dollar, and have since found a ready market at from twelve to twenty dollars—the reader will judge for himself from the statements that I have laid before him.[57]

Excepting, perhaps, Mr Seward, none whose names are known in Alaskan annals provoked about the year 1870 so much of cheap ridicule as did the firm that now controls the seal islands. "What, Mr Seward," asked a friend, "do you consider the most important measure of your political career?" "The purchase of Alaska," he replied; "but it will take the people a generation to find it out."[58]

[57] Of land peltry the bulk was still gathered in 1885 by the Hudson's Bay Co., which collected 250,000 to 300,000 mink skins, against perhaps 15,000 or 20,000 purchased by the Alaska Commercial Co., the latter also gathering 8,000 or 10,000 beaver, 3,000 or 4,000 marten, 2,000 bear, and 5,000 or 6,000 fox skins.

[58] Presenting to the reader the facts now laid before him and the conclusions at which I have arrived, it remains only to be said that both have been stated not without research and hesitation. Whether these facts and conclusions are such as he will indorse is a matter now submitted to his consideration. Concerning the annals of Alaska after the transfer, there are many conflicting opinions, and even as to the military occupation there is some little conflict of opinion. Says Capt. J. W. White of the revenue service, who was ordered to Alaska in 1867, in command of the cutter *Lincoln*, bearing Professor Davidson, senior coast survey officer, and in charge of the party: 'As I understood at the time from my own observations, and from intercourse with the Russians who could speak English and understood the language, the trouble there was caused by the fact that Prince Maksutof did not happen to be versed in the English language, and there being no trustworthy interpreter present, did not know what he transferred to the United States authorities. His people would go to him and say: "This was my house; the Russian American Company donated it to me. I am informed it belongs to the American government, and am ordered out officially." He would reply: "Go out officially, then." Who the parties were that took possession of the houses I don't know. They might have been government officials, or perhaps mere adventurers; many were renegades from all parts of the world.' *White's Statement*, MS., 5–6.

Captain J. W. White, a native of old Virginia, and by profession a sea-faring man, though first employed as a surveyor on the northern boundary commission, entered the government service in 1855, being then in his 26th year. During the civil war his vessel was stationed at the mouth of the Potomac, and, as he relates, 'would drop inside the enemy's lines at night and pick up the mail-bags.' In command of the U. S. steamer *Lincoln* he voyaged round the Horn in 1865, and returning to California, superintended the building of all the life-boat stations on the Pacific coast, also the construction of nine steamers for the government. Ordered to Alaska in 1867, it remains only to be said of this well-known officer that, arriving at the Prybilof Islands at a somewhat critical juncture, he interfered very reluctantly, though at length decisively, to stop all sealing then and there, only granting the natives the privilege of killing what they needed for food, and recommended that St George and St Paul be made a government reserve, which was accordingly done.

As with the five preceding chapters, I have been compelled to rely mainly on the reports of congress, magazines, newspapers, and in this instance the United States statute relating to Alaska, in presenting to the reader the recent annals of the territory

With the exception of *Alaska, Its Southern Coast and the Sitkan Archipelago, by E. Ruhamah Scidmore*, I am not aware of any work, apart from those of a scientific nature, published within the last two or three years, that contributes anything worthy of note to the small stock of information which the American public now possess concerning their possessions in the far north-west. Most of the above work was first published in serial form in the columns of the *St Louis Globe-Democrat* and the *New York Times*, during the years 1883-4; to which are added the author's notes of a trip made to the Sitkan Archipelago during the summer of the latter year, with brief paragraphs containing information to a later date.

Subjoined I give a more complete list of the authorities consulted in the closing chapter: *H. Ex. Doc.*, 7, *46th Cong. 3d Sess.*, pt 1, 1-25, 86-130, 320-41, 688-90. 703, 740, 743, 834, 842; *Id.*, 1, pt 2, *47th Cong. 1st Sess.*, 190-3, 594, 768-89; *Id.*, 7, pt 4, 80-1, 88; *Id.*, 1, pt 5, 278, 361; *Id.*, 2, 269; *Id.*, 1, pt 5, *47th Cong. 2d Sess.*, 84, 212; *Id.*, pt 5, 278-82; *Id*, 7, pt 4, 4-24, 90-135, 222-77, 680, 691-6, 736, 846, 888; *H. Misc. Doc.*, 42, *47th Cong. 2d Sess.*, 1-80, 93-6, 124-77; *H. Com. Repts*, *47th Cong. 1st Sess.*, 236, 1106; *H. Jour.*, *48th Cong. 1st Sess.*, 1282; *S. Ex. Doc.*, *46th Cong. 3d Sess.*, no. 12, p. 45, 67; *Id.*, *48th Cong. 1st Sess.*, 30; *U. S. Stat. at Large*, 1882-3, 612; *Id.*, 1883-4, 24, 26, 91, 157, 179, 206, 223; *U. S. 10th Census*, i. 695-9; *Circular Bureau Educ.*, no. 2, 1882, 61-75; *Kinkead's Nevada and Alaska*, MS., 5, 15; *Burchard, Report, etc.*, 1881, 169-71; *Id.*, 1882, 184; *Id.*, 1883, 17-35; *Report Direc. of the Mint*, 1881, 19; *Id.*, 1882, 14; *Contemporaneous Biog.*, ii. 333-5; *Scidmore, Alaska*, 81 et seq., 93 et seq., 194-5, 246-7, 260, 307; *The Mines, Miners, etc.*, 507; *Elliott & Co. Hist. Ariz.*, 1, 206; *N. Mex. Revista Cat.*, 1883, 279; *Tucson, Fronterizo*, Jan. 27, 1882; *Salt Lake Tribune*, June 5, 1883; *San Francisco Alta*, Mar. 24, 1881, Sept. 23, Nov. 12, 1882; *Bulletin*, 1881, Mar. 12, 30, May 11, 21, June 2, 13, 17; 1882, Apr. 24; 1884, June 3, July 29, Aug. 19, Dec. 18; *Call*, 1884, May 14, July 30, Oct. 28; *Post*, May 5, 1885; *Chronicle*, 1882, Jan. 17; 1884, June 30, Oct. 28, 29, Nov. 5, 10, 17, 23; 1885, Jan. 22, 26, Feb. 5, May 8, 30; *Sacramento Record-Union*, 1881, May 20, 21, Aug. 26; 1883, Dec. 31; 1884, Feb. 18, June 28.

INDEX.

قصومرى
نم